WAR *and* PEACE

WAR

and

PEACE

FDR'S FINAL ODYSSEY
D-DAY TO YALTA,
1943–1945

Nigel Hamilton

HOUGHTON MIFFLIN HARCOURT

BOSTON · NEW YORK

2019

For information about permission to reproduce selections from this book, write
to trade.permissions@hmhco.com or to Permissions, Houghton Mifflin Harcourt
Publishing Company, 3 Park Avenue, 19th Floor, New York, New York 10016.

hmhco.com

Library of Congress Cataloging-in-Publication Data
Names: Hamilton, Nigel, author.
Title: War and peace : FDR's final odyssey, D-Day to Yalta, 1943–1945 / Nigel Hamilton.
Description: Boston : Houghton Mifflin Harcourt, [2019] | Series: FDR at war; volume 3 |
Includes bibliographical references and index.
Identifiers: LCCN 2018043601 (print) | LCCN 2018051359 (ebook) |
ISBN 9780544868540 (ebook) | ISBN 9780544876804 | ISBN 9780544876804 (hardcover)
Subjects: LCSH: Roosevelt, Franklin D. (Franklin Delano), 1882–1945. |
World War, 1939–1945 — United States. | World War, 1939–1945 — Diplomatic history.
Classification: LCC D753 (ebook) | LCC D753 .H259 2019 (print) | DDC 940.53/2273–dc23
LC record available at https://lccn.loc.gov/2018043601

Printed in the United States of America
DOC 10 9 8 7 6 5 4 3 2 1

Photo credits appear on page 503.

Maps by Mapping Specialists, Ltd.

Contents

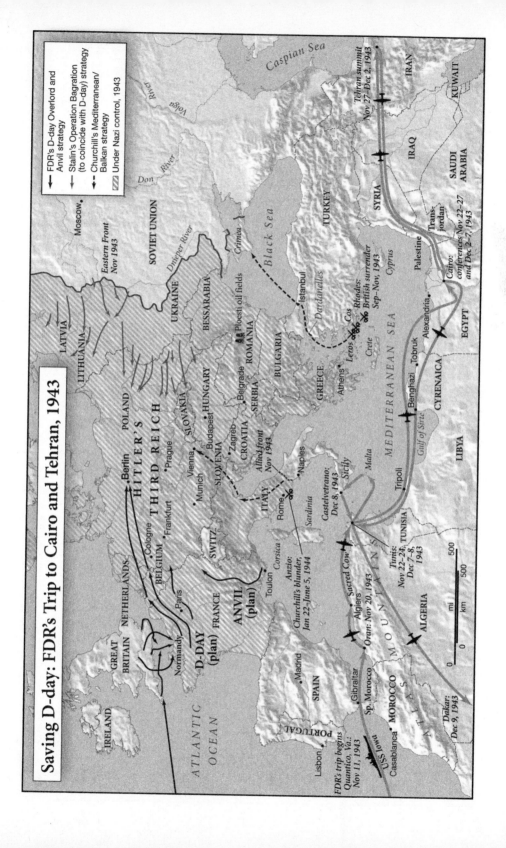

Saving D-day: FDR's Trip to Cairo and Tehran, 1943

Legend:
- → FDR's D-day Overlord and Anvil strategy
- → Stalin's Operation Bagration (to coincide with D-day) strategy
- → Churchill's Mediterranean/Balkan strategy
- ▨ Under Nazi control, 1943

Labels:

Caspian Sea

Moscow

Eastern Front Nov 1943

SOVIET UNION

Volga River

Don River

Dnieper River

IRAN

KUWAIT

SAUDI ARABIA

IRAQ

Tehran summit Nov. 27–Dec 2, 1943

SYRIA

Trans-Jordan

Cairo: conferences Nov 22–27 and Dec 2–7, 1943

Palestine

Cyprus

EGYPT

Alexandria

MEDITERRANEAN SEA

TURKEY

Black Sea

Istanbul

Dardanelles

Rhodes

Cos

Leros

Crete

British surrender Sep–Nov, 1943

Athens

GREECE

Ploesti oil fields

Crimea

UKRAINE

BESSARABIA

ROMANIA

BULGARIA

SERBIA

CROATIA

SLOVENIA

HUNGARY

SLOVAKIA

Belgrade

Zagreb

Budapest

Vienna

Prague

Munich

LATVIA

LITHUANIA

POLAND

Berlin

HITLER'S THIRD REICH

Frankfurt

Cologne

BELGIUM

NETHERLANDS

GREAT BRITAIN

IRELAND

Paris

Normandy

D-DAY (plan)

FRANCE

SWITZ.

Toulon

Corsica

ANVIL (plan)

Anzio: Churchill's blunder, Jan 22–June 5, 1944

Rome

Sardinia

ITALY

Naples

Castelvetrano Dec 8, 1943

Sicily

Malta

Tripoli

LIBYA

Gulf of Sirte

Benghazi

Tobruk

CYRENAICA

ATLANTIC OCEAN

Lisbon

Madrid

SPAIN

PORTUGAL

Gibraltar

Sp. Morocco

Casablanca

USS Iowa

MOROCCO

ATLAS MOUNTAINS

ALGERIA

Oran: Nov 20, 1943

Algiers

Sacred Cow

Tunis: Nov 22–24; Dec 7–8, 1943

TUNISIA

Allied front Nov 1943

FDR's trip begins Quantico, Va.: Nov 11, 1943

Dakar: Dec 9, 1943

0   500   mi

0   500   km

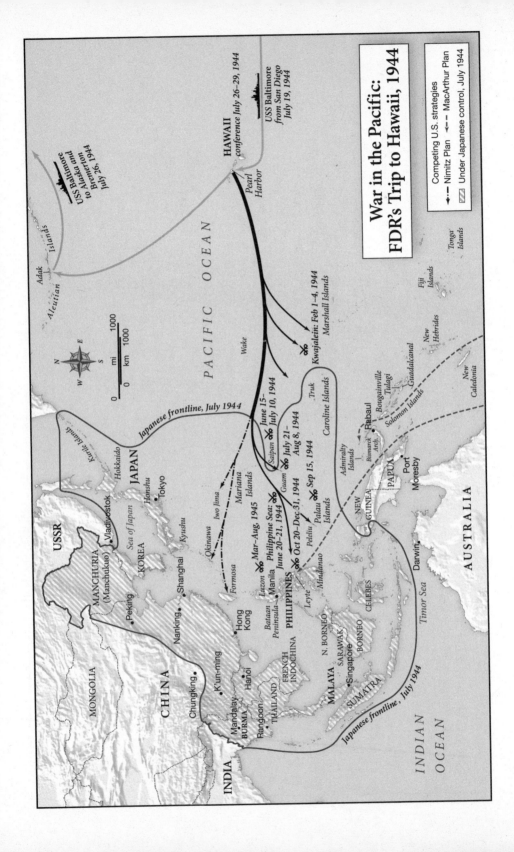

War in the Pacific:
FDR's Trip to Hawaii, 1944

Competing U.S. strategies
· · · · · Nimitz Plan   – · – · Mac Arthur Plan
///// Under Japanese control, July 1944

USS Baltimore to Alaska and
to Bremerton July 26, 1944

HAWAII conference July 26–29, 1944
USS Baltimore from San Diego July 19, 1944
Pearl Harbor

Adak Islands
Aleutian Islands

PACIFIC OCEAN

Wake

Kwajalein: Feb 1–4, 1944
Marshall Islands

Truk
Caroline Islands

Tonga Islands
Fiji Islands

New Hebrides
New Caledonia

Guadalcanal
Tulagi
Bougainville
Solomon Islands
Rabaul
Bismarck Arch.
Admiralty Islands
PAPUA
Port Moresby
NEW GUINEA

Japanese frontline, July 1944

Saipan June 15, 1944   July 10, 1944
Guam July 21–Aug 8, 1944
Palau Islands Peleliu Sep 15, 1944
Oct 20–Dec 31, 1944

Mariana Islands
Iwo Jima
Okinawa
Formosa

KURILE Islands
Hokkaido
Honshu
Tokyo
Kyushu
JAPAN
Sea of Japan
KOREA
Vladivostok

USSR
MANCHURIA (Manchukuo)
Peking
Nanking
Shanghai
Hong Kong
MONGOLIA
CHINA
Chungking
K'un-ming
Mandalay
Hanoi
Rangoon
BURMA
THAILAND
FRENCH INDOCHINA
INDIA

Philippine Sea:
June 20–21, 1944
Mar–Aug, 1945
Luzon
Manila
Bataan Peninsula
PHILIPPINES
Leyte
Mindanao
N. BORNEO
SARAWAK
BORNEO
CELEBES
MALAYA
Singapore
SUMATRA

Timor Sea
Darwin

AUSTRALIA

INDIAN OCEAN

Japanese frontline, July 1944

N
E
W
S

mi 1000
km 1000
0

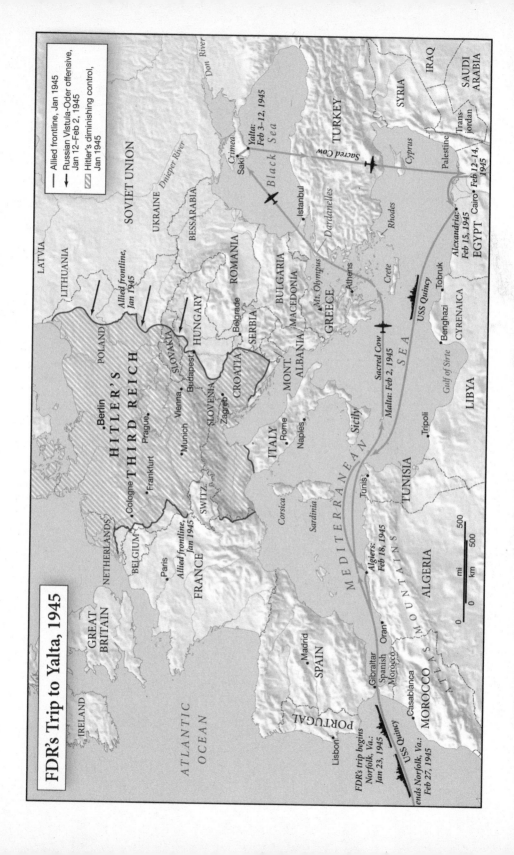

FDR's Trip to Yalta, 1945

Allied frontline, Jan 1945

Russian Vistula-Oder offensive, Jan 12–Feb 2, 1945

Hitler's diminishing control, Jan 1945

IRELAND

GREAT BRITAIN

ATLANTIC OCEAN

Lisbon

PORTUGAL

Madrid

SPAIN

Casablanca

MOROCCO

Spanish Morocco

Gibraltar

Oran

ALGERIA

ATLAS MOUNTAINS

NETHERLANDS

BELGIUM

Paris

FRANCE

Allied frontline, Jan 1945

SWITZ.

Cologne

Frankfurt

Berlin

Munich

HITLER'S THIRD REICH

Prague

Vienna

SLOVAKIA

Budapest

HUNGARY

SLOVENIA

Zagreb

CROATIA

ITALY

Rome

Naples

Corsica

Sardinia

Sicily

Tunis

TUNISIA

Tripoli

LIBYA

Gulf of Sirte

MEDITERRANEAN SEA

Algiers: Feb 18, 1945

Malta: Feb 2, 1945

Sacred Cow

USS Quincy

FDR's trip begins Norfolk, Va.: Jan 23, 1945

ends Norfolk, Va.: Feb 27, 1945

USS Quincy

LATVIA

LITHUANIA

POLAND

Allied frontline, Jan 1945

SOVIET UNION

Don River

Dnieper River

UKRAINE

BESSARABIA

ROMANIA

Belgrade

SERBIA

BULGARIA

MONT.

ALBANIA

MACEDONIA

GREECE

Mt. Olympus

Athens

Crete

Rhodes

Black Sea

Crimea

Saki

Yalta: Feb 3–12, 1945

Istanbul

Dardanelles

TURKEY

Cyprus

SYRIA

IRAQ

SAUDI ARABIA

Trans-jordan

Palestine

EGYPT

Cairo: Feb 12–14, 1945

Alexandria: Feb 15, 1945

Benghazi

Tobruk

CYRENAICA

Sacred Cow

500

500

mi

km

0

Prologue

IN THE SUMMER OF 1940, following evacuation of British and French troops at Dunkirk, the new British prime minister feared an invasion of England by the German Wehrmacht: a prospect that roused him to some of the greatest oratory in history. "We shall fight on the beaches," Mr. Churchill declared before Parliament, "we shall fight on the landing grounds, we shall fight in the fields and in the streets, we shall fight in the hills; we shall never surrender."[1]

It was his greatest speech, and a singular example of leadership of a nation at war.

Three years later, thanks to America's leading contribution to the struggle against Adolf Hitler's Third Reich, the situation was reversed. Hitler was aware the Western Allies were planning an invasion somewhere along the Atlantic Wall, probably on the coast of northwest France, defended by almost a million German troops. "If they attack in the West," he warned his generals in December 1943, "this attack will decide the war." It would come in the spring of 1944, at the end of winter weather, the Führer was certain — though he had the feeling, he said, the British didn't "have their — shall we say — whole heart in this attack."[2]

Hitler was right. Churchill was fearful, and did everything he could as prime minister and quasi commander in chief of the forces of the British Empire to postpone the landings, or sabotage the invasion by embarking on foolish enterprises elsewhere. The story of how President Roosevelt held the feet of the British to the D-day fire is thus a fascinating one. And historic in that Operation Overlord *was* mounted in the spring of 1944. And, as Hitler had warned, it *did* decide the war.

Seventy-five years after the triumphant Allied landings in Normandy it seems a shame, therefore, that FDR's role as commander in chief should largely have been forgotten. For, more than any other single individual, it was Franklin Delano Roosevelt, commanding the Armed Forces of the United States, who *made D-day happen* — moreover who made the fateful decision, in person, in North Africa, over who was to lead the historic landings.

A kind reviewer, Evan Thomas, called *The Mantle of Command,* the first volume of my FDR at War trilogy, "the memoir Roosevelt didn't get to write."[3] While the trilogy is of course a biography rather than a memoir, Thomas's point was that, unlike Winston Churchill, who went on to write his war memoirs, in six grand volumes, FDR did not live to do so. Dying of a cerebral hemorrhage two weeks before Hitler committed suicide, Roosevelt was unable to give his own account of the trials and tribulations he'd faced as U.S. commander in chief since Pearl Harbor, almost three and a half years earlier.

Like Winston Churchill, Franklin Roosevelt had, however, begun to assemble the necessary papers he would need to write his own war story — papers his secretaries had filed in the Oval Office, as well as the secret communications kept under strict security in the White House Map Room. And those, too, that he'd amassed at the presidential library he'd had built beside his home at Hyde Park, and which he proposed to donate to the nation. Four months after the D-day landings, in October 1944, he had even begun to use a young Harvard graduate, Lieutenant George Elsey, the officer in charge of the Map Room team staff, to help him prepare the library to safely house his secret papers from the Oval Office. As Elsey later recalled, "It was remotely possible that [Roosevelt] might lose the [1944 presidential] election to [Thomas] Dewey. He considered it a possibility and he wanted to know what should be done at the library to ensure the safety of his wartime records and papers, which would automatically go with him to Hyde Park. What should be done to protect them" — since, in terms of "the top-secret stuff," the library "was not built with that in mind. So he took me up there, to the library, to make recommendations."

Elsey was later told by the President's naval aide, Admiral Wilson Brown, that there was a reason Elsey had been recommended for the job: that Lieutenant Elsey, "with his background, would be very, very valuable and helpful in doing [FDR's] memoirs." In retrospect, Elsey — who had just prepared his own eyewitness account of the D-day landings and several long reports for the President on U.S. allies such as China — realized "part of the reason why [Roosevelt] spent a good deal of the time with me, talking with me, I think, was that he was just getting better acquainted: sizing me up" for the job of literary assistant.[4]

At the same time, Winston Churchill, too, was contemplating the removal from 10 Downing Street of all the wartime papers he would need to document his leadership in the course of the war — a task in which he would employ a bevy of assistants (military subordinates and the secretary to his wartime cabinet, a group later known as the Syndicate) to help him research and draft his account. Thus when, at the military conference held in Quebec in September 1944, the Canadian prime minister had said he hoped Mr. Churchill would, after war's end, record the saga from his special vantage point as British quasi commander in chief, Churchill had "replied that all of this was practically in his papers already except to give it a certain turn" — assuring Mackenzie King that, in his narrative, he would, in due course, be completely frank, omitting "nothing."[5]

Had Roosevelt survived and published his own account — "He will 'write,'" his cousin Daisy Suckley had noted in September 1944, "and can make a lot of money that way"[6] — the world would have been treated to an interesting postwar literary duel, for FDR's account would have differed markedly from that of Sir Winston (as Churchill became in 1953). The highlight of the tourney would undoubtedly have been their competing accounts of D-day: its inception; the long battle between the two great leaders over its mounting; and its ultimately decisive consequences for the successful prosecution of the war against Hitler.

That literary duel, of course, did not take place. It was the President who died prematurely, at sixty-three, while the aging former prime minister — forced from high office at seventy in the 1945 British general election — devoted himself in his multivolume memoirs to a magisterial if also self-lauding account of how he, rather than Roosevelt, had directed and won World War II.

Given that Sir Winston — whom I deeply admired, and with whom as a college student I proudly stayed for a weekend at Chartwell, his home in Kent, before he died — won the Nobel Prize for Literature in 1953 on the basis of his sextet, and *was* able to "make a lot of money" publishing it, I do not think it unfair to his memory, sixty-five years later, to correct the record regarding his version, and as a historian and biographer to give my own account of the war's military prosecution from President Roosevelt's perspective as U.S. commander in chief.

War and Peace: FDR's Final Odyssey, D-Day to Yalta, 1944–1945, thus commences with the President's voyage abroad to save D-day: averting Churchill's last-ditch efforts to delay and sabotage the landings.

Following that triumphantly successful trip to Tehran, the American Odysseus — a pseudonym FDR had once used at school at Groton — returned to the United States "in the pink": D-day finally and irrevocably set to be mounted in the spring of 1944, under an American general he had personally chosen "on the spot." The invasion, code-named Overlord, would be backed, Stalin had promised him, by a major Russian offensive on the Eastern Front — thus making it impossible for Hitler to reinforce his Wehrmacht armies along the Atlantic Wall. It was the highest point of FDR's career as U.S. commander in chief in World War II.

The Normandy landings, beginning on June 6, 1944, would more than fulfill the President's hopes, and his historic "D-day Prayer," as broadcast to the nation. General Eisenhower's success disproved all Churchill's fears and earlier warnings of disaster; the Allied invasion became, as Hitler had predicted, the "deciding" battle of the war.

Tragically, however, the man who had been ultimately responsible for the Allies' war-winning strategy was unable to take full credit for it. The U.S. commander in chief had fallen gravely ill with flu on his return from the Middle East. And he never got better — a reality his White House doctor, his press secretary, and his staff did their best to hide from snooping reporters and cameramen. For all that he might dream, following the greatest amphibious invasion in history, of setting foot on the shores of liberated Normandy as his U.S. chiefs of staff were able to do, it was not to be. Instead he grew more and more sick with heart disease — more seriously ill, in fact, than any but his closest confidants knew. As Lieutenant Elsey later recalled, the President's health simply plummeted — "he lay in bed, unable to focus or to take an interest, often — just too ill to bother. This was obvious before D-day, and before the fourth election," but it had to be kept from the public lest it affect war morale.[7]

The President never recovered — though he did, miraculously, survive to see at least that the war would be won, and how. As a result, though, his last year as commander in chief was the very opposite of the manner in which he had led the Allies since Pearl Harbor.

Sadly, many historians — too many — have judged Franklin Roosevelt's military role in World War II on the basis of his final year in the Oval Office, thus entirely misconstruing his singular, overarching contribution to victory over the Third Reich and the Empire of Japan. My aim in *War and Peace: FDR's Final Odyssey*, as the culmination of my FDR at War trilogy, therefore, has been not only to chart with fresh clarity how dire was his affliction, but how exactly it affected his decisions and once masterly performance as commander in chief of the Western Allies in World War II after Pearl Harbor. It was a record that Winston Churchill — who had been a great national leader, but a deeply flawed commander in chief of British Empire forces — was only too happy to take from him in literary retrospect.[8]

From triumph to personal tragedy is thus the theme undergirding this volume — for the fact is, from being the victorious captain of the Allied vessel in the momentous struggle against Germany, symbolized in the great D-day landings, the President became thereafter a virtual passenger — with major ramifications not only on the prosecution of the war, but the postwar.

That the President lived long enough to see the approach of unconditional Nazi surrender was, at least, a consolation to those intimates who knew Roosevelt best, and who had seen him *at* his best. As was the sight of him preparing to inaugurate his great contribution to postwar peace: the United Nations. Moreover the fact, too, that he had been able, at least, to die deeply contented in his personal life, despite his cascading ill health. I hope readers of these three volumes will feel the same in coming to the end of this trilogy, seventy-five years after the triumph of his greatest military achievement: D-day.

Book One

PART ONE

Going to See Stalin

1

A Trip to the Mediterranean

THE WEATHER OFF ARGENTIA, Newfoundland, in the fall of 1943 was "bois-terous," Captain John McCrea later remembered, recalling his command of the U.S. Navy's most powerful new battleship, the USS *Iowa*.[1] The huge "battle-wagon" was alternately resting at anchor in the northern Atlantic and carrying out oceangoing exercises for its assigned role: guarding U.S. convoy routes to and from the war in Europe and Russia.[2]

Launched as the first of its class in January that year and drawing some forty feet in depth, the monster vessel had hit a submerged rock in July, while entering Casco Bay, Maine, at low tide. It had been only its second shakedown cruise, and a fifty-foot gash had been torn in its hull, requiring weeks of repair. Not a good omen.[3]

McCrea, as the ship's captain, had been reprimanded but not dismissed. He had, after all, been naval aide to the President and Commander in Chief until taking command of the huge vessel, and the gash was swiftly repaired. In October 1943 the *Iowa* had finally assumed its active role in North Atlantic duties. Manned by more than two and a half thousand sailors and Marines, weighing fifty-five thousand tons when fully loaded, the vessel could make more than thirty-two knots and boasted sixteen-inch guns that could hit targets twenty miles distant. Among the crew there was hope of an imminent naval engage-ment — perhaps even a sea duel with the vessel's equivalent: the Bismarck-class battleship and biggest warship of Hitler's Third Reich, the *Tirpitz*.

Such a sea battle was not improbable. Armed with eight fifteen-inch guns, the *Tirpitz* had constantly threatened U.S. and British convoys to Murmansk in aid of the Russian war effort and menaced the North Atlantic — in fact the *Tir-pitz* had only weeks before slipped its own moorings on the coast of Norway and made a daring, Viking-like raid. Leading a German armada on September 8, 1943, the battleship had carried out an amphibious operation, executed with total surprise: Zitronella, as it was code-named, an attack from the sea that completely destroyed the Allied weather station at Spitsbergen and a refueling base there, and captured many of its defenders.

In bright sunshine and an unusually gentle wind the USS *Iowa* had just weighed anchor, therefore, to undertake further exercises out at sea when the executive officer brought Captain McCrea a message, marked SECRET. It was from Admiral Ernest J. King, commander in chief, U.S. Fleet. The *Iowa* was ordered not to steam toward Norway and possible action, but directly south, back to United States waters.

Captain McCrea had not the faintest idea what was afoot, or afloat. On Mc-Crea's arrival at Hampton Roads naval base, in Virginia, Admiral Royal Ingersoll, commander of the U.S. Atlantic Fleet, greeted him tartly: "I suppose you know why you are here?"[4]

McCrea shook his head.

"You are going to take the President and the Joint Chiefs of Staff in *Iowa* to the Mediterranean."

The entire American high command? To the Mediterranean?

Captain McCrea took a deep breath. He had, to his credit, considerable experience in handling VIPs. As naval aide to the President he'd even accompanied Mr. Roosevelt on the President's historic seaplane journey to North Africa earlier that very year.[5] There, at Casablanca on the shores of Morocco, the military strategy of the Western Allies had been laid down by the President as U.S. commander in chief, overruling the advice of his chiefs of staff.[6] American forces, he had instructed, would first learn *how* to defeat the Wehrmacht in battle, in the Mediterranean, and only then launch a cross-Channel attack, probably in the spring of 1944 — aimed at Berlin.[7]

By October 1943 the year of live-action learning was now almost over. More than a quarter of a million Axis troops had surrendered to General Eisenhower in May 1943, and by July Allied troops were ashore in strength on the island of Sicily — stepping-stone to southern Europe. As Italian troops capitulated or ran away, Wehrmacht units were unable to stem the Allied tide of advance toward Palermo and Reggio, barely three miles from the Italian mainland. The Italian leader, Benito Mussolini, had thereupon been toppled as the Fascist dictator of Italy by his own colleagues; having successfully deposed him, the new Italian government under Marshal Badoglio had surrendered unconditionally.

The war Hitler had declared on America on December 11, 1941, was thus moving toward its climax. What exactly the President had in mind in crossing the Atlantic for a second time that year was unknown to Captain McCrea, as it was to everyone else. But to find out more about the *Iowa*'s role in the President's latest mission, McCrea was ordered to go to the Navy Department in Washington, D.C., and report to Admiral King in person, "tomorrow morning."[8]

Thus began secret preparations for the Commander in Chief of the Armed Forces of the United States to meet, for the first time, the dictator and commander in chief of the Soviet armies, Joseph Stalin.

2

The Meeting Is On

ALL YEAR PRESIDENT ROOSEVELT had pressed Stalin for a meeting — even sending the former ambassador to the Soviet Union, Joseph E. Davies, to Moscow to negotiate a possible rendezvous.[1]

Stalin had several times indicated his willingness to parley. In the end he had always backed out, claiming his responsibilities as commander in chief of all Soviet forces in action against the Wehrmacht were too demanding, and that the bitter battles on the Eastern Front simply precluded him from leaving Russia.

The President had not believed him (Stalin was known to have visited the battlefront only a single time, and only for a day), but had persevered. Hitler's massive invasion of the Soviet Union in 1941 had failed to reach Moscow, and though Wehrmacht troops had neared the Urals in the summer of 1942, that offensive, too, had come to grief. Stalingrad, in February 1943, had marked the end of German advances on the Eastern Front — with Hitler calling off his final massed armored offensive at Kursk in the summer of 1943 when hearing that the Western Allies were ashore in Sicily — threatening to bring down the Pact of Steel and forcing Hitler to divert armored divisions to Italy, not Russia.[2]

The Soviet Union, facing two-thirds of the German army and beginning to defeat the Wehrmacht decisively in battle, would be a major player in the postwar world, the President was well aware. Finding a modus vivendi with Russia would be in America's best interests.[3] It would also be in the interests of the postwar world, too, if a better security system than was set up after World War I could be devised and agreed.[4] Neither Russia nor the United States had been a member of the League of Nations, which Hitler had effectively neutered when announcing Germany's withdrawal in 1933. This time, however, the United States and the Soviet Union could together take a leadership role in guaranteeing postwar peace.

Whether the Soviets would agree to work with the United States and other capitalist nations in the aftermath of the Second World War was another matter. Despite Stalin's radical efforts to industrialize the Soviet Union and mechanize Soviet agriculture, the USSR remained a largely agrarian society, its people ruled by communist dogma, dread of the secret police, fear of forcible resettlement or execution, and paranoia regarding foreign countries. Such paranoia was not only of Stalin's making, however. Hitler's Barbarossa invasion of June 22, 1941, fielding 4 million men drawn from Germany and many other European countries (Austria, Italy, Romania, Hungary, Slovakia, Croatia, Bulgaria, France, and Finland), had resulted in more than 3.5 million casualties by the end of that first year alone. The failure of the United States and Britain to mount a Second Front in 1942, or the year after that, had only increased Russian xenophobia and suspicion. Distrust of those nations bordering the Soviet Union that had aided Hitler in Barbarossa would probably affect relations with Russia for a generation or more, former ambassador Davies had reported to the President on his return from his personal mission to Moscow on behalf of the President in June 1943.[5]

Distrust was one thing. Need, however, was another. Aware the Soviet Union could not continue the war without U.S. Lend-Lease — American exports that were currently supplying more than 10 percent of Russia's war needs — Stalin had closed down the Comintern (the communist, ideological arm of the Soviet Union). In a further, somewhat dubious, demonstration of commitment to the principles of President Roosevelt's Four Freedoms and the Atlantic Charter, the Soviet dictator had even opened Russian churches in the summer of 1943.

But Lend-Lease alone would not be enough to defeat Hitler's legions. Facing no fewer than 260 Axis divisions on the Eastern Front — the majority of them German — the Soviets would never be able to defeat the Third Reich without a Second Front in the west, which would force Hitler to fight major campaigns front and back. Stalin had therefore every interest in Allied military strategy being concerted, which a meeting with President Roosevelt might achieve. At the same time there must be other reasons why it seemed advisable for Stalin *not* to meet with the President, Mr. Roosevelt had mused when discussing the conundrum with his advisers and the people around him. Perhaps his Russian counterpart suffered an "inferiority complex," the President had suggested when talking to his cousin Daisy Suckley.[6] And the Marshal was reported to be deathly afraid of assassination — a fear reflected in his unwillingness to leave the Kremlin. Given his ruthless dictatorship of the USSR since Lenin's death, this was certainly wise. At any rate, whatever the underlying rationale, it had left the coalition of Allies with a sort of vacuum at the very top, in terms of combined military and political strategy — Stalin constantly agreeing to meet and then backing off, offering to send representatives instead.

Finally, in October 1943, Stalin had agreed to a two-week-long international conference of foreign ministers in Moscow. This had produced surprisingly positive results, including provisional agreements between U.S., Soviet, and

British diplomats. Insisting on flying via Africa to Moscow, despite his ill health, Mr. Cordell Hull, the U.S. secretary of state, was even able to get quasi-formal Russian consent to the establishment of an eventual United Nations organization, as well as a private indication from Stalin that the Soviets would join the United States' war against Japan, once Hitler surrendered.

Why, in this case, was it actually *necessary* for Stalin to leave the security of Moscow for a personal meeting with the President of the United States? Why did the President still place so much store by a personal meeting? Why was the President pressing for him to leave Moscow?

Historians, later, tended to see the summit in Tehran — a venue that was ultimately agreed upon only at the last moment, three weeks in advance — as the final compromise in a game of statesmanship, or brinkmanship: the location a matter of competing national honor or pride. To a large extent this was true. In Russian eyes, the U.S. secretary of state had, after all, flown all the way to Moscow — why not, Soviet officials had calculated, the President?

Behind the competing arguments over the venue for this first meeting of the two world leaders, however, there was another reason that would largely elude historians — and certainly eluded the Prime Minister of Britain, the "third wheel" in the proposed conference, at the time.

It did not elude Stalin, though — indeed was, in the end, the reason the Russian premier overcame his reluctance to leave the Soviet Union, or even Moscow: the matter of D-day, as the Second Front landings became known. For without a Second Front the war could not be won.

The Marshal, to be sure, hated the idea of leaving the motherland, where he was secure as an absolute dictator. He was also afraid of flying. But if the British were plotting to back out of D-day, as he'd been given reason to believe, then he had better meet with his two fellow warlords in the struggle to defeat the Third Reich. The Russian premier had thus decided he would go meet the President at a halfway house. The capital of Iran, a "neutral" country across the Caspian Sea, was as far as he would countenance, however. It was currently under Russian and British occupation; it was also a vast American military supply entrepôt — in fact the primary conduit for U.S. Lend-Lease supplies by sea and rail to the Soviet Union.

The three U.S., Russian, and British legations or embassies in Tehran, then, could provide an ideal location for the ultimate high-level, coalition military conference held to decide the Allies' military and political strategy in 1944, in the midst of the most violent war in military history.

The President had accepted Stalin's reasoning. Churchill had reluctantly agreed to the location, too. As prime minister of America's closest military ally he'd insisted, however, that he first meet with President Roosevelt in North Africa or somewhere in the Mediterranean. There, *before* the Tehran summit, he hoped to dissuade the President from following the current plan, agreed at Quebec in August 1943, for the Allied D-day invasion to be mounted in the spring of 1944. Instead Churchill wanted the United States to exploit his latest brainwave: an alternative Mediterranean strategy.

Thus was the stage set for one of the most consequential showdowns in military history — with the President the only man powerful enough to stop Churchill from wrecking Overlord, the agreed battle plan to defeat Nazi Germany.

3

Maximum Secrecy

FOR DAYS SHIPS' CARPENTERS labored on the *Iowa,* as they prepared the huge vessel for its top-secret mission. The crew were given three days' leave.

In the nation's capital McCrea paid a visit to 1600 Pennsylvania Avenue, and saw his old boss at the White House. "I suppose Ernie [Admiral King] has told you about the coming trip?" the President asked McCrea as they sat together in the Oval Office.[1]

Admiral King had — to McCrea's memorable discomfort. At the Navy Department on the Mall (the Navy still refusing to join the Army in the recently completed Pentagon building), the *Iowa*'s captain had innocently remarked that, after delivering the President to the war zone, the battleship would presumably leave North Africa in order to return to combat duties. There was "a moment of silence — ominous silence," McCrea remembered.[2]

Reputed to "shave with a blowtorch," the balding, bullet-headed commander in chief of the U.S. Navy was "strictly business," a man "of few words" — each enunciated with "precision," McCrea later recalled in admiration. There was "never any doubt as to what he said or what he wanted. I can't imagine anyone ever slapping him on the back by way of greeting. He was austere. He was ramrod straight and carried himself with dignity. In my book he was everything a naval officer should have been," McCrea lauded the admiral's memory — discreetly passing over King's well-known penchant for other men's wives.[3] What counted, in McCrea's view, had been the admiral's complete and unequivocal loyalty to the Commander in Chief of the Armed Forces of the United States: the President.

"I shall not subject the President to a Westward, December crossing of the Atlantic in a Heavy Cruiser," King had snapped — which had been the plan McCrea had been informed of earlier. "*Iowa* will remain available for that duty," King ordered, speaking "with a firmness and coldness" that made McCrea regret he'd opened his mouth.[4]

McCrea would thus transport the President to North Africa — and collect him, after he was done.

At the White House the President seemed "in fine fettle," McCrea later recalled. "He looked to be in good health. He had a great zest for living which was contagious," and seemed full of beans. "I am looking forward to it greatly," Mr. Roosevelt remarked — assuring McCrea that in his view there was "nothing so wonderful as a sea voyage by way of relaxation."[5]

A sea voyage in the midst of a world war — in spite of a resurgence of German U-boat attacks on Allied shipping? McCrea was not so sure, but said nothing. As to the departure date, Admiral King had said the President wished first to attend the annual ceremonies of the Unknown Soldier at Arlington Cemetery on Armistice Day, November 11, 1943 — a "must." Immediately afterwards, however, he would take his special armored train, the *Ferdinand Magellan,* to Newport News, and stay on it overnight, in order to board the *Iowa* early the next morning, November 12. Admiral King would travel with the President — as would the other chiefs of staff: Admiral William D. Leahy, the President's White House chief of staff as well as chairman of the U.S. Joint Chiefs of Staff; General George C. Marshall, chief of staff of the U.S. Army; and General Henry H. Arnold, chief of staff of the U.S. Army Air Forces. Also General Brehon Somervell, chief of U.S. Army Service Forces, plus dozens of the chiefs' staffs.

McCrea had taken a deep breath. The entire high command of the United States military, to an active theater of war. On one ship!

Secrecy would thus be of paramount importance.

In Hampton Roads the USS *Iowa* was repainted Atlantic-gray. It was also provisioned for the transatlantic journey. Unusual features were added, too. On Sunday afternoon, November 7, "a derrick lighter came alongside and hoisted two very heavy steel battleship-grey elevators aboard. These were welded at once to the *Iowa*'s starboard main and superstructure decks, almost amidships. One elevator rose from the main to the first superstructure deck and its companion was placed inboard, terminating at the flag and signal bridge level."[6]

As one of the officers remarked, "Anyone with half an eye can guess the nature of our next assignment."[7]

Finally, on November 11, 1943, the *Iowa,* having discharged much of its fuel and drawing significantly less water, anchored a few miles up the Potomac River — for McCrea had persuaded Admiral King and the President to repeat the Potomac ruse of 1941. On that occasion, still in peacetime, the President had pretended to go out fishing on his presidential yacht in order to shake off journalists; once at sea he'd secretly transferred to a warship, to meet with

Churchill at Argentia, where he'd gotten Churchill to sign on to the Atlantic Charter.[8]

The *Iowa* positioned off Cherry Point, Virginia, Captain McCrea now ordered the entire ship's crew to assemble on the main aft deck, and explained what for the most part they had intuited: that they'd been selected "by the President and our Commander in Chief to participate in an important mission." That evening, Admiral King's 258-foot yacht and flagship, the USS *Dauntless* (formerly the privately owned yacht *Delphine*), came alongside, bearing the U.S. chiefs of staff and their staffs — though not the U.S. commander in chief, or Admiral Leahy. One by one the officers were taken to their cabins, and aboard the great battleship they spent the night at anchor.

Roosevelt, aboard the 168-foot USS *Potomac,* meantime sailed all night from the Washington Navy Yard — with no prying journalists following. He'd received Stalin's confirmation, cabled on November 10; the meeting in Tehran was on.[9]

"It was a grey morning and cold" at Cherry Point, the *Iowa* ship's chronicler afterwards recorded. The river looked distinctly uninviting. "A chill wind whipped the surface of the Potomac into fluttering white caps. At fifteen minutes before nine, the tiny, white Presidential Yacht, *Potomac,* hove into distant view. As she drew near the *Iowa*'s starboard side the seal of the Chief Executive could be observed on the bridge. A gangway was rigged between the *Iowa*'s side and the *Potomac*'s main decks aft. The President of the United States boarded the *Iowa* at sixteen minutes past nine to be welcomed by Captain McCrea. Mr. Roosevelt had requested that honors be dispensed with. He wore a soft, brown hat and his famed sea cape over a tan sharkskin suit." Sitting in his wheelchair the President was then taken to the captain's quarters "on the starboard side, forward, of the first superstructure deck."[10]

The President was not alone. This time he was accompanied by both his military aides: Major General Edwin "Pa" Watson and naval aide Rear Admiral Wilson Brown. Also his chief of staff, Admiral William Leahy. His dedicated White House counselor, Harry Hopkins, boarded too. And Admiral Ross McIntire, the President's personal physician. They were all now present — with the President occupying the captain's quarters, and McCrea moving to his seagoing cabin in the conning tower above.

McCrea was fully aware of his responsibility. On the shoulders of the President and his senior military subordinates rested the strategy for the ultimate prosecution of the war in Europe: the endgame. In this sense the journey promised to be more historic even than the President's Atlantic Charter meeting in 1941, or his flight to Casablanca in January 1943. Stringent secrecy remained McCrea's major concern, but there were other worries also. Admiral McIntire was not keen on the onward plane journeys that would necessarily follow, perhaps at high altitudes, once the ship reached North Africa — a concern because of the President's heart. Assuming the *Iowa* even got there! Safety was hardly guaranteed. Neither of the President's military aides had been eager for Mr. Roosevelt to travel by sea, since a transatlantic voyage would be subject to U-boat interception. Once in North Africa air travel would, moreover, be subject to Luftwaffe attack. The latter was no idle threat, either; American pilots had, after all, ambushed and shot down the commander in chief of the Japanese navy in the Pacific, Admiral Yamamoto, *four hundred miles* behind Japanese frontlines earlier in April that very year, killing him.[11]

The President's proposed flight route would be from Oran to Cairo, along the shores of North Africa. From there he would fly to southern Iran, and from there the plan was to travel north to Tehran either by air or by train. "Those of us who had to do with the planning for this expedition were very conscious that the President was running grave personal risk," Admiral Brown later wrote candidly, "because we believed that if the enemy could learn of his whereabouts they would spare no effort to attack by air, submarine or assassin. Even with the strictest censorship, rumors of his activities and whereabouts," he explained, "were almost certain to leak out."[12]

By the early summer of 1943 the U-boat menace had been all but extinguished, thanks to U.S. and British air patrols across the Atlantic. But thanks to new German "snorkels," which permitted U-boats to remain submerged and avoid Allied air reconnaissance, the Atlantic battle had now resurged with wolf-pack vengeance. The undersea menace was not all. Above the waves a "new destructive glider-bomb" had been put into combat, "raising havoc" against Allied shipping in the Mediterranean.[13]

"Havoc" was no exaggeration. Often forgotten after the war, the new German guided missile, the "Fritz X" bomb, had been employed for the first time against Allied naval forces during the U.S. invasion of Italy in September 1943 — the latest example of German engineering. It was the world's first effective remote-controlled combat missile, able to penetrate battleships and heavy cruisers. The powerful projectile was steered by *Funkgerät*, or radio remote-control, operated by a technician aboard a motherplane at eighteen thousand feet behind the flying bomb, aiming it directly toward the target. During the Salerno landings on September 9 two Fritz X bombs had sunk the Italian battleship *Roma* as it attempted to abscond and join the Allies — killing the majority of its 1,850-man crew in the process. Another Fritz X had disabled *Roma*'s sister battleship *Italia*. Hits were also scored on the light cruiser USS *Savannah*, killing two hundred American sailors off Salerno — forcing the cruiser out of action and requiring it to return to the United States for twelve months. The USS *Philadelphia* (on which the President had cruised in 1938) was narrowly missed by a Fritz X the same day, September 11. It was fortunate in being only lightly damaged, but HMS *Uganda*, a British light cruiser, was not so lucky on September 13. It received a direct hit by a Fritz X that penetrated through to its keel—a fate that befell HMS *Warspite,* too, a British battleship that was crippled on September 16 along with a number of Allied supply vessels.

New low-level Henschel Hs 293 guided missiles, also steered from accompanying Luftwaffe motherplanes, were sinking yet more Allied naval vessels in the Mediterranean. With one hit on the USS *Iowa,* once it entered Mediterranean waters through the Gibraltar Straits, the Germans could, theoretically, destroy the entire U.S. high command.

For his part Mr. Roosevelt had refused to listen to such fears. His hands were a trifle shaky, his feet swelled when he was tired, and he was "keyed up and couldn't relax," his cousin and loyal companion Daisy Suckley noted in her diary several days before the President's departure,[14] but nothing would stop him now that Stalin had agreed, definitively, to meet in Iran; there was, after all, simply too much at stake.

4

Setting Sail

DAISY WAS YET another person who hated the idea of a second presidential trip abroad that year. Not only was it dangerous for the partially paralyzed president to travel to an active theater of war, in terms of possible enemy interception, but a flight to Tehran — which was as far as Stalin would agree to travel — involved an ascent "over the mountains of up to 15,000 feet," traversing the Zagros range, and inevitably taxing the President's suspect heart, as she'd noted in her diary on October 30, 1943.[1]

Roosevelt's hands may have developed a noticeable tremor, but mentally the President seemed full of ginger and anticipation — pulling down a map of Africa and the "Bible lands" of the Middle East, in his White House study, and showing Daisy his itinerary for the "Long Trip." From Oran, in Algeria, to Cairo, in Egypt, by air; then again by air over Palestine and Iraq, landing in Iran to take the train. He seemed excited at the thought of being far from Washington, with its endless political backbiting and the further loss of Democratic congressional seats suffered in last year's November elections. Also a possible union coal strike to contend with. His adoring cousin had therefore felt torn — the more so since Eleanor, the President's loyal but exceedingly busy spouse, seemed to pay too little attention, in Daisy's opinion, to his precarious health.

Sitting together, they talked about domestic matters — both private and public. Eleanor had become, in a sense, his eyes and ears with respect to national issues, given her many travels across the country: a pleader of social, economic, and political causes, she would often spend an hour or more making her case for action late at night, when she said goodnight to him. Daisy said nothing, but was concerned. "He is just *too* tired, *too* often. I can't help worrying about him," she confided to her diary. On November 8, for example, he'd had some twenty-three appointments in the Oval Office — even before being subjected to Eleanor's near-midnight entreaties.[2]

Worry or no worry over safety, the Long Trip to Tehran was now beginning.

The USS *Potomac* having cast off, the President greeted his Joint Chiefs of Staff and his White House staff in his comfortably large *Iowa* cabin. Whether the "fishing trip" ruse would really work was anybody's guess, but once the battle-ship weighed anchor no one would know where they were, Admiral Leahy reflected. "Every effort has been made to prevent the leak of any information in regard to the expedition," he noted in his diary that evening; "we will have no communication whatever with the shore, and it is hoped that the President with his staff can succeed in reaching the port of Oran in Africa before the enemy learns of his whereabouts and his intentions."[3]

The *Iowa* thus duly departed from Cherry Point the morning of November 12, 1943. Arriving at Hampton Roads in the evening, it then anchored once more, in darkness, to be refueled in deeper water by two tankers at Berth B, since the ship had pumped out much of its oil in order to have the shallower draft necessary for a Cherry Point rendezvous. Once the tanks were refilled the Commander in Chief asked the ship's captain to wait a few more hours. "You know John," he said to McCrea, "today is Friday. We are about to start on an important mission. Before it is over, many important decisions must be made. I am sailor enough to share the sailors' superstition that Friday is an unlucky day. Do you suppose you could delay getting underway until Saturday — this, of course without interrupting your plans too much?"[4]

Marveling at the Commander in Chief's attention to nautical lore, McCrea therefore ordered the battleship to remain anchored — but with its chains shortened. Its course was designed to take them toward Bermuda, then the Azores, then to continue across the remaining waters of the Atlantic until they reached the narrow Straits of Gibraltar, escorted by successive groups of three destroyers (which carried less fuel), watching for U-boats.

Assuming all went well, the last American destroyer squadron, approach-ing North Africa, would be "beefed up" with additional British destroyers as well as a U.S. aircraft carrier, or flattop. In order to maintain absolute secrecy regarding the *Iowa*'s passengers, however, and the destination of the voyage, "no information" had been given even to the commander of the first destroyer escort, other than the charge to protect the *Iowa*, and then be ready for "distant service."[5]

Copious amounts of presidential china and silverware had been brought along for use on the ship, to be unloaded and taken by air with the presi-dential party, once the passengers were transferred to land. Liquor was also aboard — the President skirting the prohibition against alcohol on U.S. naval vessels by claiming that, as U.S. commander in chief, he could do as he wished. This meant he could have his ritual martini "cocktail hour" at the end of the day. He'd also arranged with Captain McCrea that he would have exclusive use of the outdoor first superstructure deck, port and starboard, where he would spend every afternoon thinking, reading, or napping.

Or making notes in the new journal Daisy had given him for his trip — one of the few diary records Roosevelt would keep during the war. As the *Iowa* thus made its way down the Hampton Roads channel toward the ocean on November 13 — the huge warship piloted by an experienced Coast Guard lieutenant commander — the President inked his first entry in his tall, forward-tilting, emphatic script, with its characteristically high-crossed *t*'s and bold capitals.

"This will be another Odyssey," Franklin Delano Roosevelt penned, thinking of Homer's Odysseus the Cunning — or Ulysses, as the Romans called him. The long journey would take place "much further afield & afloat than the hardy Trojan whose name I used to take at Groton when I was competing for school prizes. But it will be filled with surprises," he predicted — aware that any number of things could go wrong.[6]

The prospect of a week's leisure at sea certainly buoyed the President, however. "Enough motion-picture films for a show every night" had been brought with them, according to the signals lieutenant tasked with drawing up a checklist, plus a "well-stocked library of pocket guides, whodunits, and other reading matter."[7]

"I'm safely on my way," the President wrote Daisy in a last letter he left for her at Hampton Roads. "UJ [Uncle Joe, i.e., Stalin] wired he will meet us, so you know all," he confided — thanking her for her gift of a special chemically induced hot-water maker for the high-altitude flight to Tehran — which now looked like a better option than the train. "It's a lovely day but cold — I am being showered with every security and every comfort — & I am optimistic about results. I much wonder when the cat will get out of the bag!"[8]

Time would tell. He turned in sometime after 10:00 p.m.

They were off.

5

Sheer Madness

THANKS TO LAX British censorship in Cairo, the world was to find out all too soon where the leaders of the Western world were meeting.

In the meantime, however, the President attempted to assure his staff and advisers that all would be well. As he noted in his diary, "We are offshore — escorted by destroyers & planes — very luxurious in the *Iowa,* which with her sister ship the N.J. [USS *New Jersey*] are the largest battleships in the world . . . Capt. McCrea is very proud of the *Iowa* — with its population of 2,700 officers & men." He added, "I have his cabin. In my mess are Ads Leahy, W. Brown, McIntire, Gen. Watson & Harry Hopkins. The Joint Staffs are one deck up — Gens. Marshall, Arnold, Somervell, & Adm. King — And below are 100 members of the Planning Staff."[1] In short, he was proud to be traveling as U.S. commander in chief, taking with him his entire high command to the current theater of battle: the Mediterranean. And absolutely determined that the next battlefield would be — as formally agreed at Quebec — northern France, in the spring of 1944.

"The President has been very straight lately and has stood up to Churchill better than at any time heretofore," the elderly war secretary had recorded after seeing the President on November 4 — though Henry L. Stimson still distrusted the British prime minister. "With all his lip service Churchill is against the Channel operation and instead is determined to push forward new diversions into the Balkans, Turkey, and possibly other places which will inevitably drain off ships and men from the final decisive conflict which we are trying to ensure in France."[2]

Stimson was right to be suspicious of Churchill — who had been acting strangely in recent weeks, according to reports coming back to Washington, as well as long, plaintive cables the Prime Minister had been sending the President.

The initial cause of Churchill's distress had been the disasters that had befallen his unilateral British attempts to seize the Aegean islands of Rhodes,

Kos, Samos, and Leros, near Turkey, in tandem with the Allied landings on the southern coasts of Italy in September. The Aegean landings were fatally misconceived, and execrably executed: launched exclusively by British Empire forces from the Middle East without U.S. help or even knowledge. Instead of accepting their embarrassing defeat by the Wehrmacht as part of the fortunes of war, however, the Prime Minister had in mid-October 1943 begun a new plot to delay and if possible sabotage Overlord, in favor of redoubled efforts in the Mediterranean and Aegean.

Churchill had always been a "meddler," as one of his senior battlefield generals put it[3] — unable to stop himself from trying to influence and if possible direct operations in the field. Had the Prime Minister been a great military commander, this might have made sense. Ever since his tragicomedy when attempting to command the defense of Antwerp in 1914,[4] and masterminding the assault on Gallipoli in 1915,[5] his attempts at generalship had proven fatal for the ill-prepared troops committed by him to combat. His opportunism demonstrated the force of his vivid imagination and sheer courage; it had rarely, if ever, been based on a realistic appreciation of what he could expect his own soldiers to accomplish against a tough or ruthless enemy. This flaw, sadly, was now leading him to the most consequential mistake of his long life, in terms of military strategy and Allied unity: his third and most egregious attempt to subvert the D-day invasion, and instead reinforce failure in the Mediterranean.

Having assembled his chiefs of staff in London the Prime Minister had on the evening of October 19 asked them not to pursue their work on plans for the Overlord invasion — but, instead, to focus all their attention on covert operational plans to invade the Balkans!

"Pray let this enquiry be conducted in a most secret manner," he'd instructed them, "and on the assumption that commitments into which we have already entered [at Quebec] with the Americans, particularly as regards 'Overlord,' could be modified by agreement to meet the exigencies of a changing situation."[6]

By "secret" he meant: *without American knowledge.*

By "modified" he meant: postponement, if possible to 1945.

By "agreement" he meant: using legerdemain with the President, whom he would try to see on his own in Cairo, and convert, before the proposed meeting with Stalin.

General Sir Alan Brooke, as the head of the British Army, was initially mystified by the Prime Minister's new directive. After all, the American president had recently made clear he would tolerate no postponement of Overlord.

Aware from Field Marshal Sir John Dill, the British liaison to the U.S. chiefs of staff, that in London the Prime Minister was plotting further "adventures" in the Mediterranean and Aegean, the President had summarily dismissed Churchill's plea that General Marshall be asked or ordered to attend a conference with Eisenhower and the British air, ground, and naval commanders in North Africa — a conference that Churchill, ominously, wished to chair.[7] Likewise the President had seen no merit in the Prime Minister's cabled recommendation that the United States should provide American support, despite the recent failures in the Aegean,[8] to a new British attempt to recapture Rhodes "as the key" to a new Mediterranean/Aegean/Balkan strategy. In a memo to Admiral Leahy, the President had rejected Churchill's latest petition in three simple words, to be dispatched to Churchill: "OVERLORD is paramount."[9] Later that same day, the President had sent Churchill a more explanatory personal cable, drafted by Leahy, which ran: "I am opposed to any diversion, which will in Eisenhower's opinion jeopardize the security of his current situation in Italy, the buildup of which is extremely slow considering the well known characteristics of his opponent who enjoys a marked superiority in ground troops and panzer divisions."[10] In other words: focus on Italy, not Rhodes, while preparing for Overlord.

To any normal person, the President's response would have closed the matter. Churchill, however, was no ordinary mortal. Unable to let go of his growing obsession with operations in the Mediterranean after the British fiasco in the Aegean, the Prime Minister had brushed aside the President's negative reply. "I am sure that the omission to take Rhodes at this stage and the ignoring of the whole position in the Eastern Mediterranean," he'd cabled back, "would constitute a cardinal error in strategy."[11]

"I am convinced," Churchill continued, in an attempt to explain such strong language, "that if we were round the table together that this operation could be fitted into our plan without detriment either to the advance in Italy of which you know I have always been an advocate, or to the build-up of OVERLORD" — an operation of which he was not an advocate, but which, he assured the President, "I am prepared faithfully to support."[12]

"Faithful" was not a word commonly attributed to Churchill, as a consummate politician who had so often changed parties and allegiances — switching from the Liberal Party to the Conservatives, and from blind fealty to King Edward VIII to King George VI after King Edward, ignoring his advice, had vacated the British throne to marry Mrs. Simpson.

To buttress his argument for immediate Allied operations to retake Rhodes or hang on in the Dodecanese Islands, Churchill had pooh-poohed any idea the Germans would continue to fight for southern Italy. The Allies now had some "15 divisions ashore," with 12 of them already in combat there, he pointed out to the President.[13] Besides, he was convinced from Ultra decrypts of high-grade German signals that German troops were not intending to offer serious resistance south of the Tuscan mountains, in the north of Italy ("the top of the leg of Italy"),[14] to which they were supposedly ordered by the Führer to retreat if pressed.[15]

Churchill's own chiefs of staff had been as puzzled as the President by such obsession with the island of Rhodes. If the Germans withdrew to the north of Italy, all well and good. But what was the advantage in pursuing — in fact re-pursuing — operations in the eastern Mediterranean and Aegean? Why, above all, change the war's higher strategy to a new, unplanned and unhinged campaign in the Balkans when Overlord, the cross-Channel attack, was now barely six months away? How would a small island like Rhodes be critical, when the Wehrmacht still occupied Crete, the largest of the Greek islands, on which the Luftwaffe had good airfields? Nevertheless, the Prime Minister, imagining himself a great strategist, had "worked himself into a frenzy of excitement about the Rhodes attack," Brooke had noted in his diary; in fact Churchill had "magnified its importance so that he can no longer see anything else and has set his heart on capturing this one island even at the expense of endangering his relations with the President, and also the whole future of the Italian campaign."[16] As Brooke had confessed the next day in the diary he kept both for his own sanity and for his wife to read, "I can control him no more."[17] Even Roosevelt's "very cold reply asking him not to influence operations in the Mediterranean" had met with no success, Brooke recorded.[18] Churchill had merely "wired back again asking President to reconsider the matter. The whole thing is sheer madness," Brooke had bemoaned, "and [Churchill] is placing himself quite unnecessarily in a very false position! The Americans are already desperately suspicious of him, and this will make matters far worse."[19]

The realization that such a revision of Allied strategy would lead to yet another transatlantic battle between the British and American high commands had become more and more alarming to General Brooke. Over the next weeks, however, the Prime Minister's obsession had come closer still to insanity, or an inter-Allied parting of the ways. The Prime Minister's note to the British chiefs of staff on the evening of October 19, "wishing to swing round the strategy back to the Mediterranean at the expense of the cross Channel operation," shocked Brooke. "I am in many ways entirely with him," Brooke noted, given his own lack of faith in Overlord's chances of success, and his wish to focus on dealing the Wehrmacht a major blow in Italy, "but God knows where that may lead us to as regards clashes with the Americans."[20]

Yet Churchill was a master of creating great sagas over names he selected, such as Rhodes and Rome, and inflating dangers where it suited him. At the subsequent 10:30 p.m. War Cabinet meeting in London — a conclave to which Prime Minister Jan Smuts, visiting from South Africa, was also invited — Churchill had described a worsening military situation in Italy that he'd not forecast, but which now *necessitated* that the Allies put more of their eggs into the Mediterranean basket. This would, he claimed, mean making a decision not to switch battle-hardened troops to England, in preparation for Overlord, as currently agreed, provisioned, and planned under the Quebec agreement. Instead, by keeping such veteran forces in the Mediterranean, he would be in a position to throw seasoned British and American troops into further operations in the Aegean and the Balkans, with grand consequences, if he could only get the Americans to agree.

Where, though, was this secret new Churchillian strategy supposed to *lead* the Allies? the President and his American chiefs had wondered in Washington. Who in London was subjecting Churchill's opportunism to critical examination? Possessed of amazing bouts of energy, Churchill had seemed determined to make gold out of straw — with no one in London daring or willing to oppose his new strategy. "I shudder at the thought of another meeting with the American Chiefs of Staff," even Brooke noted despairingly after the meeting on the nineteenth, "and wonder if I can face up to the strain of it"[21] — yet he'd not dared contest the issue with his prime minister, instead confining his real thoughts to his diary.

In this way, in the wake of his late-night meetings in London, Churchill had thrust himself into a new strategic campaign, giving rise to new excitement: excitement that would allow him to marshal his considerable talents of persuasion and rhetoric in a renewed, third major bid to switch Allied forces away from Overlord. Once effected, it would make the cross-Channel gamble, shorn of battle-hardened troops, even less credible as an operation of war than before. Undeterred by the President's insistence on maintaining course, the Prime Minister had thus followed his cabinet meeting, several days later, by giving new notice to the President of the United States that he was definitely not happy with the Overlord plan, or timetable, agreed at Quebec.

"Our present plans for 1944 seem open to very grave defects," Churchill had cabled frankly on October 23 — searching for fresh, apocalyptic rhetoric that would awaken Mr. Roosevelt and his military advisers to the supposed disaster lying ahead in the Mediterranean unless Overlord was put on the back burner. Adolf Hitler, "lying in the center of the best communications in the world, can concentrate at least 40 to 50 days" against either Overlord or the Allies in Italy, Churchill had maintained in a long message, "while holding the other" front (the Eastern Front) from interfering.[22]

Churchill's own hopes of a quick advance to Rome, Pisa, and the Tuscan mountains were meanwhile running into tough opposition, the Prime Minister now acknowledged — though he expressed neither responsibility for nor shame at having ignored the difficulties of fighting in the mountainous eastern Mediterranean, where island by island Wehrmacht forces were methodically liquidating the surviving meager British forces that had landed in the Aegean. It was the disastrous Battle of Crete, which the British had ignominiously lost in 1941, all over again — yet the Prime Minister seemed oblivious to the lessons. Instead of questioning his aims and objectives in the Mediterranean theater, Churchill simply used the dashing of his hopes as an argument for reviving them — this time with American arms and blood.

The new situation threatened the Western Allies with "stalemate" in the war's strategy, Churchill now claimed to the President, unless they doubled down on their efforts, not only in Italy but in the Aegean. He himself had coined the term "soft underbelly" for the Mediterranean — but it was a belly that was in fact far from flabby, he now argued — and would require much sharper harpoons. This left Overlord, in Churchill's mind, as a dangerous distraction, not the other way around.

Allied commitment to Overlord, the cross-Channel invasion, was the problem, Churchill argued. Slavish deference to its timetable would hamstring the war in the Mediterranean, he claimed, and deprive the Allies of great prizes. And for this he blamed the President's insistence on Overlord as the Allied number one priority, with its launch date of May 1, 1944 — barely six months away. "The disposition of our forces between the Italian and the Channel theatres has not been settled by strategic needs but by the march of events, by shipping possibilities, and by arbitrary compromises between the British and Americans," the Prime Minister asserted — ignoring the agreed primacy of Overlord as the main plank in Allied strategy, and deliberately failing to acknowledge the fact that it was he himself who had forced "compromises" over the projected timetable. For at Quebec he had personally insisted upon the addition of special lawyer-style escape clauses, in writing, to the agreement, namely to the effect that D-day must be canceled if the Germans brought more Wehrmacht divisions to France to oppose the landings than the current estimated number. Even the projected date, he now claimed, was a phony one. "The date of OVERLORD itself was fixed by splitting the difference between the American and British view," he asserted, ridiculing the military staffs at Quebec — deliberately oblivious of the paramount need, expressed by the Overlord planning team, for a D-day date as early as possible in 1944 to ensure sufficient summer weather for the subsequent land campaign in France.

Overlord, in short, was a theoretical undertaking, in Churchill's eyes, while the Mediterranean was real — a theater that demanded more American and British forces if it was to be kept going or exploited. "It is arguable that neither the forces building up in Italy nor those available for a May OVERLORD are strong enough for the tasks set them," he'd warned the President[23] — urging him to put all Allied eggs in the Italian basket, not the cross-Channel French one.

The frankness, bordering on cheek, of this cable had been amazing to all who saw it on arrival at the Map Room of the White House.[24] Yet Churchill's latest warning hadn't ended there. What he wanted, the Prime Minister pleaded in his cable, was that there be a halt to current D-day preparations for Overlord. In fact he wanted Mr. Roosevelt to order an immediate standstill in the move of all landing craft and American and British troops currently due to be transferred to Britain. Instead, the vessels and men could be put to better use, the Prime Minister urged the President, in combat in southern Italy, lest their absence "cripple Mediterranean operations without the said craft influencing events elsewhere for many months."[25]

Landing craft? The President, for his part, had not been impressed by Churchill's rhetoric; he was even less impressed by the unstated objectives the Prime Minister had in mind for American landing craft. For what, exactly, were they to be used in the Mediterranean? Roosevelt had asked.

Churchill's answer had been revealing. *Rome!*

As a politician Churchill had always been a dealer in symbols — and symbolism in wartime was certainly crucial, as Joseph Goebbels, Hitler's master propagandist, best knew. But why *Rome,* when the Fascist Italian government and Italian forces had already surrendered to General Eisenhower in September?

The little island of Rhodes had seemed to be a typical Churchill bee-in-the-bonnet when the Prime Minister was haranguing his British chiefs of staff. Now, suddenly, it was Rome. All at once, seizing the Eternal City was a matter of highest priority — overriding preparations for D-day and the timetable of Allied strategy settled at Quebec. *Why* exactly? the President wondered. The major port of Naples, after all, had been successfully cleared of German demolitions, and was now safely in Allied hands. As were the great Foggia airfields. Rome itself was irrelevant, from a strictly military point of view — in fact a red herring.

Churchill certainly offered no military argument — yet insisted Italy's capital city now have priority in all Allied planning, operations, and logistics. "We stand by what was agreed" at Quebec, he maintained in his cable of October 23, but "we do not feel that such agreements should be interpreted rigidly and without review in the swiftly changing situations of war."[26]

The accusatory implication — namely that D-day was hampering great opportunities in the Mediterranean — had led Churchill to his direst new prognostication. Unless the President of the United States were to make the Mediterranean and Aegean the immediate new priority of Allied strategic planning, the Prime Minister warned, there would be a disaster: namely, that "if we make serious mistakes in the campaign of 1944, we might give Hitler the chance of a startling come back."[27]

The argument for Churchill's alternative strategy in Italy sounded all too emotional, speculative — and suspicious. Logic had never been the Prime Minister's strongest suit, but there seemed to be a deeper motive behind his warnings of disaster unless he got his way. British invasion forces on Rhodes had fallen to Wehrmacht forces in September, on Kos on October 4, and seemed likely to be captured or flee from Leros and Samos in November. To bolster his argument for focusing on Rome, however, Churchill had added a new plea: that surviving British troops on Leros, in the eastern Aegean, should now be ordered not only to hold out "at all costs," but be immediately reinforced by General Eisenhower's reserve American forces — including those slated for Overlord! There, on Leros, they could form in the Aegean a great stepping-stone to the Balkans, once Turkey was brought into the alliance . . .[28]

Suffering from influenza at the time, the President had been disturbed by the Prime Minister's telegraphic barrage. Churchill remained, in his eyes, a strange and wonderful individual: a creature of moods and passions, blessed with a gift for metaphor that had no equal in the world; a politician personifying great moral leadership, in both the free world and in the occupied countries. Yet what a *calamity* he was as leader of the forces of the British Empire!

Almost every British military operation Churchill had mounted or touched in the war had failed, the President was aware: from Norway in the spring of 1940 to the Aegean in late 1943, where his folly was now approaching its inevitable end.

Churchill had always been prone to switch from extremes of excitement to despair, the President knew: it was part and parcel of his character. His latest cables had been, Roosevelt thus judged, par for Winston's erratic course. Citing his flu the President had thus continued to politely dismiss them, and hold firm to the military strategy formally agreed at Quebec: Overlord, to be launched on or before May 1, 1944.

Until, that is, the President had learned of Churchill's latest mischief in London — and Moscow.

6

Churchill's Improper Act

AT FIRST THE PRESIDENT had been disbelieving. Was it really possible Winston Spencer Churchill would do such a thing? Yet the facts, when presented, were incontrovertible: Churchill had deliberately ordered that Stalin be shown part of a top-secret Allied military cable from General Eisenhower to the Combined Chiefs — without reference or permission from the President. Moreover, the Prime Minister had doctored the message to give the opposite meaning to the one intended!

Of all the machinations Churchill had employed to sabotage Overlord throughout 1943, including his subversive appeals to congressional leaders on his visit to Washington in May that year,[1] this was without question the most deplorable, the President felt. Clearly, having failed to make any headway in his communications with the President, the Prime Minister had decided to work directly on Stalin, behind the President's back!

Roosevelt's supposition was, unfortunately, correct. "Stalin," Churchill confided to his physician, Dr. Charles Wilson, "seems obsessed by this bloody Second Front," and "ought to be told bluntly that OVERLORD might have to be postponed," as the dutiful doctor had noted in his diary in London on October 24. The Prime Minister was digging in — willfully refusing to take into account how his objections to Overlord could upend the whole Allied alliance. "I will not allow the great and fruitful campaign in Italy to be cast away and end in a frightful disaster, for the sake of crossing the Channel in May," he'd given his reasoning to his physician.[2] It was on that obstinate basis, without telling the President, that he'd deliberately cabled to Anthony Eden, the British foreign secretary who was in Moscow at the foreign ministers' conference, the attachment to Eisenhower's top-secret report to the Combined Chiefs. And had instructed Eden to show it personally to Marshal Stalin.

The attachment was a copy of British general Sir Harold Alexander's latest pessimistic battlefield report from Italy, which General Eisenhower had appended to his message to the Combined Chiefs of Staff. Churchill's cable to Eden, however, had deliberately omitted Eisenhower's commentary on the report, as Alexander's superior officer, in which Eisenhower had stated that he saw no reason for pessimism or alarm in Italy.

Eisenhower had expressed himself, in fact, as very *confident* over the Allies' situation in southern Italy, in his cable to the Combined Chiefs. As Allied commander in chief of all forces in the Mediterranean theater he had merely forwarded General Alexander's report as an attachment, for their information, in explaining why he disagreed with his subordinate. Far from believing Overlord should be postponed, Eisenhower felt the current battle in Italy was a perfect way of keeping the Wehrmacht locked in combat in southern Italy — unable to "withdraw divisions from our front in time to oppose OVER-LORD. If we can keep him on his heels until early spring, then the more divisions he uses in a counteroffensive against us, the better it will be for OVER-LORD and it then makes little difference what happens to us if OVERLORD is a success."[3]

In other words, General Eisenhower would *welcome* a German counterattack, with the forces he had. There was no mention of a "frightful disaster" such as Churchill had warned the British cabinet to expect if current Allied strategy was not altered. Nor did Eisenhower see any need to halt the current move of landing craft to England, let alone the now battle-hardened combat troops and commanders being transferred for a successful Overlord in the spring . . .

Que faire? News that the Prime Minister of Great Britain had, without telling the President, forwarded a secret, questionable British combat report to Marshal Stalin — with a message to be given to the Russian commander in chief that Overlord would, in all likelihood, have to be postponed as a result of the dire situation in Italy — was, in the view of the U.S. secretary of war, Henry Stimson, rank treachery. "Jerusalem! this made me angry," Stimson had expostulated in his diary, after hearing of it on October 28.[4]

Stimson had fumed all day at the Pentagon. Thanks to Churchill's duplicity (which the Pentagon had heard about indirectly, via General John R. Deane, head of the U.S. Military Mission in Moscow), "Stalin would not have the counter comment of Eisenhower," Stimson bewailed in his diary, "showing that he was not pessimistic at all."

Fortunately General Marshall had immediately — and on behalf of his fellow Joint Chiefs of Staff — "sent a message to Deane," in Moscow, to make sure that Stalin and the Russian high command were told the *actual* truth: that General Eisenhower, the Allied commander in chief in the Mediterranean, was perfectly happy with the battlefield situation in Italy, and that Eisenhower and the Joint Chiefs of Staff of the United States did not think there was any purpose or reason to delay Overlord. "It was perfectly ridiculous," Stimson noted in his diary. "But this shows how determined Churchill is with all his lip service to stick a knife in the back of Overlord and I feel more bitterly about it than I ever have before."[5]

British soldiers could be magnificent when well led, but their leaders were often — too often — manipulative cowards, Stimson felt. And Churchill the worst of them, he rued. So upset was Stimson, in fact, that the next morning he'd gone to the White House without appointment to see the President's counselor, Harry Hopkins. The President's flu had made Roosevelt "almost inaccessible. He has been sick three or four or five days, and now when he'd come out" of hibernation and was working again in the Oval Office, he had so much work on his desk that "it is as difficult to get at him as it would be to get at Mohammed."[6]

Hopkins had been as concerned as Stimson when hearing of Churchill's new perfidy, however — and had insisted the war secretary see the President in person.

Stimson had thus been ushered into the Oval Office, at 11:40 a.m. on October 29. There he ascertained the President had already gotten word of Churchill's deceitful conduct. Stimson explained how General Marshall, on behalf of the Combined Chiefs, had immediately sent a riposte to be given by General Deane to the Soviet high command in Moscow. To Stimson's relief Roosevelt had been in complete "accord with our views in respect to that," Stimson noted in his diary that night — in fact the President "intervened to tell me what his views were in regard to the Balkans. He said he wouldn't think of touching the Balkans," unless the Russians found themselves struggling in southern central Europe and asked for joint operations — which seemed unlikely. What the Russians needed was a Second Front that would force the Wehrmacht to fight both in the east *and* the west. Overlord in the spring of 1944 was, and would remain, official and paramount American strategy for winning the war against Hitler.

Stimson had been relieved. But if Churchill was willing to go behind the President's back in such a way — "dirty baseball" as Stimson termed it — *what else* might the British prime minister be capable of? Deeply concerned lest Churchill seek to sideline General Marshall once appointed to take command of Overlord in northern Europe — where he would no longer be able to argue against Churchillian idiocies in the Aegean — Secretary Stimson and General Marshall had proposed a cable for the President to send to Churchill, saying he could not "make Marshall available immediately" to take command of Overlord. As their draft cable ran, the President should say to Churchill, "I am none the less anxious that preparations proceed on schedule agreed at Quadrant [code-name of the August 1943 Quebec conference] with target date May 1," 1944. It was the British who should, immediately, appoint a "Deputy Supreme Commander for Overlord" — an officer who would receive the "same measure of support as will eventually be accorded to Marshall," and could "well carry the work forward": namely Field Marshal Dill, Air Marshal Portal, or General Alan Brooke.[7]

Though the President held off sending the signal lest it exacerbate the quarrel, the "unpleasant incident"[8] of Churchill's duplicity continued to rankle in the days after: a harbinger, Stimson worried, of further problems, now that planning for the war's end — the occupation of Germany, the defeat of Japan, and the postwar setup for international security — was gathering pace.

Stimson would never forgive Churchill for his Machiavellian machinations. For President Roosevelt, however, the Prime Minister's latest maneuver was, if anything, even more worrying. It was, after all, not Stimson who would have to deal directly with Stalin's probable reaction — which was not difficult to predict, after two years of Allied failure to mount a promised Second Front. There had already been rumors of serious peace-feelers between Nazi Germany and Russia in August and September, when it became clear to Stalin that the Western Allies might never mount a Second Front. Given that the Soviets were still struggling against three-quarters of the German Wehrmacht, Stalin would inevitably lose respect not only for Britain, but for the United States and its word. How then would Roosevelt be able to negotiate from strength with the Russian dictator over the war's end, and over Soviet participation in the war against Japan? Also over the establishment of a postwar system of security, and a United Nations organization the President wanted Russia to join? Moreover, how would the American public — voters, press, institutions, and Jewish Americans especially, who were hearing more and more about Nazi extermination programs in Poland and eastern Europe — react to the postponement or cancellation of Overlord? Would they not see it as a betrayal of their long, often reluctant support for a "Germany First" policy after Pearl Harbor, when the majority of Americans had wanted the President to focus first on defeating Japan?

The President was as disappointed in Churchill as Stimson was, the war secretary found — the Prime Minister's deceit still rankling a week later, when he saw the President in the Oval Office: Roosevelt describing it as "an improper act"[9] akin to treachery. It posed a threat not only to Allied unity with the Red Army in defeating the Third Reich, but to Anglo-American unity and trust, too, at the very moment when unity among the Allies would be vital in ensuring a peaceful transition to a postwar world. Strategic dissension between the primary Western Allies could only cause Stalin to see how *divided* were the U.S. and British governments — and perhaps take advantage of it, just as the potential defeat of Nazi Germany approached. Would Stalin even agree to meet up with the President, in the circumstances?

Deciding it was best to pretend he did not know of Churchill's deviousness, the President had, in the end, merely continued explaining to the Prime Minister that he had *not* changed his mind over Overlord — and would tolerate no

British backsliding on its timetable, if it was to succeed. Moreover, to make extra sure Stalin had not been taken in by Churchill's recent ruse, the President had gone out of his way, before leaving for North Africa, to check with his trusted new ambassador to Moscow, Averell Harriman — cabling him to find out, preferably by return signal, what were the current strategic views of senior Russian military officials — including Stalin himself, if possible.

Harriman had done so — and the American ambassador had been crystal clear in his direct report to the President from Moscow on November 4, 1943. "It is impossible to over-estimate the importance they place strategically," Harriman had signaled (the cable received and decoded at the White House on November 6), "on the initiation of the so-called 'Second Front' next spring."[10]

7

Torpedo!

SUCH WAS THE SITUATION when the USS *Iowa* had left Hampton Roads. As his own first diary entry demonstrated, the President was hopeful — yet was bracing himself for an odyssey full of surprises. That the first one would come on day two of the voyage was on no one's radar, though.

A lifelong mariner, the President had insisted he be shown each morning the daily navigation charts, marked with positions not only of nearby Allied vessels but also of known or suspected U-boats. In addition to their latest snorkels, German U-boats sported new radar, he'd been told by Captain McCrea, as well as an acoustic homing torpedo: the electric *Zaunkönig*, or Winter Wren, traveling at twenty-five knots, which could hit a target at 5,750 meters, or 3.5 miles.

The *Iowa* was currently traveling at the same speed. By midday on November 14, 1943, the battleship and its escort destroyers were 533 miles across the Atlantic. Wanting his crew to be equally prepared for aerial attack once they approached North Africa and the Mediterranean, Captain McCrea had arranged a demonstration of the battleship's armaments for the President and Joint Chiefs of Staff. As he later recalled, the "weather was good," but there was also "a brisk breeze blowing. The state of the sea was choppy, and a succession of white caps was evident on every hand. It had been arranged to exercise the *Iowa*'s 40-mm anti-aircraft batteries that afternoon at 1400 hours, so that the President and the distinguished passengers might see for themselves the efficacy of this particular segment of the *Iowa*'s anti-aircraft defense."[1]

The special presidential elevator made it easy for Mr. Roosevelt to go from one deck to another in his wheelchair, and be wheeled across "ramps built over the coamings and deck obstructions."[2] Thus, at 2:00 p.m., with the President's wheelchair held fast by Petty Officer Arthur Prettyman, his steward, "the escorting destroyers were informed of *Iowa*'s intentions and the drill got underway as scheduled."[3] Weather balloons were inflated and released as targets — the ship's gunners having been ordered to deliver a veritable "curtain of fire to stop enemy planes."[4]

The guns made such a deafening noise the distinguished passengers had to stuff cotton wool in their ears, and for a while the exercise went well. A number of the balloons were shot down: a creditable performance, General Hap Arnold, the chief of staff of the Army Air Forces, noted in his diary.[5] It would be, Captain McCrea later thought, a nice "surprise to those members of the Army Air Force who probably witnessed for the first time the partial capabilities of a ship's air defenses. The drill had been in progress for, I should say, about twenty minutes when in an urgent tone of voice over the T.B.S. [Talk Between Ships] there was a somewhat panic stricken cry of 'Lion, Lion [*Iowa's* code name]! Torpedo headed your way' — this from the [USS] *Wm D Porter* [destroyer], which at that moment was about 45° on our starboard bow — some 3500 yards distant."[6]

"It should be remarked at this point," McCrea later recalled, "that during the [antiaircraft] firing *Iowa* was on a relatively steady course because the target balloons were going down wind. The *Wm D Porter* was the center ship in the screen. On receipt of the torpedo warning 'Full Speed' was rung up. 'Battle Stations' was immediately sounded. The general alarm gong was clanging — the alarm Boatswains use to prepare the crew to battle stations. Followed by the statement," McCrea recorded, that "'this is not repeat not a drill.'"[7]

"Had there been a leak aboard this trip?" McCrea remembered wondering. "Had we been ambushed?"[8]

"All this took place in seconds. And then a bit late over the T.B.S. from the *Porter* came the statement: 'the torpedo may be ours.'"[9]

Remembering the incident with an embarrassment bordering on shame years later, McCrea allowed that the message had been some "comfort to be sure," in that it meant they were not under enemy attack. This was not much help to the *Iowa,* however; there was still "a torpedo heading our way,"[10] whether German or American.

As ship's captain McCrea now knew, at least, the probable direction from which the torpedo was coming and that there would likely be but one underwater missile. "I immediately altered the course of the ship to the right to head for [USS] *Porter* — this in order to present as narrow a target as possible," he remembered — facing a torpedo, that was, he judged from a professional naval officer's perspective, probably pretty "well aimed."[11]

Would it hit, though? The ship had less than six minutes to respond.

It was just as well McCrea switched course and headed toward the torpedo, for the *Iowa* was 888 feet in length — "12 feet shorter than three football fields laid end to end," as McCrea liked to say.[12]

The captain may have been pedantic in prose, but his swift, instinctive judgment certainly saved the USS *Iowa* from a calamity in the Atlantic Ocean. Below him, down on the first superstructure deck, "President Roosevelt, Admiral Leahy, General Marshall, General Arnold, Harry Hopkins, General Watson,

Admiral Brown and Admiral McIntire had gathered to watch the shooting,"[13] McCrea afterwards recalled.[14] Their admiration soon changed to near-panic.

Harry Hopkins penned his own account that evening. In Hopkins's version, an officer from the bridge two decks above leaned over and yelled, "It's the real thing! It's the real thing!" but the President initially didn't hear. "The president doesn't hear well anyway and with his ears stuffed with cotton he had a hard time getting the officer's words" — words "which I repeated to him several times before he understood. I asked him whether he wanted to go inside — he said, 'No — where is it?'"[15]

Suddenly it seemed as if every gun was trying to hit the racing torpedo, not the barrage balloons — even though, in the choppy ocean water, the torpedo could not clearly be seen, some twenty-five feet below the surface. "More commands from everywhere. Whistles, flags, code signals. The din aboard the ship was terrific," General Arnold later wrote.[16]

Lieutenant William Rigdon, who was part of the President's Map Room signals staff, later described how "President Roosevelt had been watching the gunnery exercise from one of the upper decks when he heard the warning. He called to Arthur Prettyman, his valet: 'Arthur! Arthur! Take me over to the starboard rail! I want to watch the torpedo!'" As Rigdon added, "Prettyman, as he confessed later, was 'shaking all over,'" but he "wheeled the President quickly to a vantage point."[17]

This was scarcely advisable, to say the least, but the President was the President — and Commander in Chief.

Given that the wind "was considerable," and "white caps were everywhere," it was fortunate that at least "the trace" or "wake of the torpedo was visible to us in *Iowa*," McCrea remembered. "Just about the time we had really hit full speed there was a tremendous explosion on our starboard quarter. The ship shuddered mildly but sufficiently to cause me to turn to *Iowa*'s Executive Officer [Cmdr Thos. J. Casey] and remark, 'Tom, do you think we have been hit?'"[18]

Others certainly thought so.[19] Casey thought not, however, or the impact would have caused even more of a shudder — leaving McCrea, in later years, to ponder the reason. "It is my belief that the turbulence caused by *Iowa* at full speed and executing a turn was sufficient to detonate the torpedo's firing mechanism which resulted in its explosion."[20]

General Arnold, for his part, noted in his diary that night what "a grand rest" he'd been enjoying on the voyage, with "not a worry in the world." Then the "whole character of the maneuver and practice changed," once the alarm sounded, and the ship suddenly swung to starboard. "The wake of the torpedo became quite clear," barely six hundred yards away; "a depth charge went off, all the guns started shooting": 40mm, 20mm, and .50–caliber weapons.[21] As Arnold subsequently concluded, however, it was in vain, since "nothing hit the torpedo."[22]

Whatever caused the torpedo to explode, the underwater missile hadn't actually hit the battleship, mercifully. Yet McCrea was not congratulated. "About this time when, of course, my attention was focused ahead there was purred into my ear a low tone, 'Captain McCrea, what is the interlude?'"[23]

It was Admiral King — who had once told McCrea he was not enough of a "sonofabitch" to make a successful senior combat officer. McCrea explained the situation, upon which King, as U.S. Navy fleet commander, rushed down and joined the President's party on the deck below to report.

General Arnold thought the torpedo had missed the stern of the ship by barely twenty yards. As he noted in his diary that night, "No hit, a miss" — which caused "a thousand sighs of relief."[24] They had almost literally dodged a bullet — and a big one.

"In everyone's mind," Arnold later wrote, "was the question: 'Suppose the torpedo had hit, and it had become necessary to take the President and all the high rank off the *Iowa* in those heavy seas'?"[25]

In a letter he intended to send his cousin Daisy once they reached Oran the President thought it best not to mention the near-miss. "I wish I could tell about things each day," he apologized, "but I dare not."[26]

In the new diary his cousin had given him, by contrast, the President *did* record the ominous event, for later reading. "On Monday last at gun drill," he penned, "our escorting destroyer fired a torpedo at us by mistake. We saw it and missed it by less than 1000 feet." This laconic description left, however, a host of questions — and rereading his entry several months later, back in Washington, Roosevelt dictated a note to be attached to the diary, which he intended to use in writing his memoirs, once the war was over:

"The destroyer in the escort was holding torpedo drill, using the *Iowa* as the spotting target. The firing charge was left in the tube, contrary to regulations. The torpedo was fired and the aim was luckily bad. Admiral King was of course much upset and will I fear take rather drastic disciplinary action. We fired the secondary battery to try to divert the torpedo. Finally we saw it explode a mile or two astern."[27]

"Eventually things calmed down and further shooting was called off," McCrea recalled.[28] By visual communication with USS *Porter* — to avoid the use of radio — it became clear it had been a "torpedo all right — but not from a German submarine," as Hopkins put it.[29] As General Arnold noted later that night, "Practice being over, everyone went back to normal duties and pursuits."[30] It had been an accident, thankfully, not an assassination attempt. "It must have come from some damned Republican!" Hopkins quipped at dinner in the President's mess, attempting to make light of it.[31]

The mishap had been serious, though. As Lieutenant Rigdon later wrote, they had been more than fortunate; it had "just missed being a day of tragedy."

8

A Pretty Serious Set-to

THE PRESIDENT WAS NOT the only one heading to Tehran — and by sea. Prime Minister Churchill had left Plymouth on November 12 — the same day as the President — aboard HMS *Renown*, a World War I battle cruiser. Tellingly, the Prime Minister was going without the current plans for Overlord. He was not interested in Overlord. Instead, General Brooke and his colleagues on the British chiefs of staff were taking with them only plans for the Anglo-American forces in Italy to advance to the Pisa-Rimini line in northern Italy, and for other operations in the Aegean if possible. These plans would, Churchill now insisted, necessitate delaying the D-day assault by "some 2 months" at least, as Brooke noted in his diary.[1] He was clear this would entail a "pretty stiff contest!" with his U.S. counterparts, once they met up in Cairo, en route to Tehran, yet in certain ways Brooke had come to welcome the impending clash.[2] It would be a "pretty serious set to," he acknowledged, one that would "strain our relations with the Americans, but I am tired of seeing our strategy warped by their short-sightedness, and their incompetency!"[3] The British chiefs' formal recommendations to the Prime Minister the previous day had thus stated that, in terms of Overlord, "we do not attach vital importance to any particular date or to any particular number of divisions in the assault and follow up" — perhaps the least impressive admission of the entire war. The chiefs seemed to have no idea how important it would be to launch the assault in spring, to give the Allies a full summer to develop their campaign; British strategy should be, instead, to "stretch the German forces to the utmost," in the hope the Wehrmacht would crack somehow or somewhere. They were therefore "firmly opposed to allowing this date to become our master and to prevent us from taking full advantage of all opportunities that occur to us to follow what we believe to be the correct strategy."[4]

It was a lamentable performance.

From his Wolf's Lair headquarters at Rastenburg, in East Prussia, the Führer had also left on a trip. His was by armored train, traveling to southern Germany: a visit designed to buck up German morale now that the Third Reich had lost its primary partner, Italy.

Given the menacing situation on the Eastern Front, where Russian forces had crossed the Dnieper and Wehrmacht forces were being forced to retreat farther and farther toward the Reich, Dr. Joseph Goebbels, the Reichsminister für Propaganda, had thought the Führer wouldn't have time to make such a "political" trip. Hitler, however, had his own ideas. On November 7, 1943, he'd therefore arrived in Munich, in order to address the party faithful at the Löwenbräukeller, where the Nazi Party had been founded twenty years before. His long speech, broadcast on German radio at 8:15 p.m. that night, had awed even Goebbels, who with the Führer's permission had edited it only lightly.[5]

Addressing himself both to his "party comrades" and *Volksgenossen,* or fellow citizens, the Führer had sounded amazingly confident and rational—indulging in his trademark sneering sarcasm, as well as his passionate belief in Germany's historic destiny in fighting Bolshevism and the Jews. What, he asked those present and those listening on their radios, "would have become of Europe and above all, our German Reich and our beloved homeland, had there not been the faith and the willingness of the [party] individual to risk everything for the movement? Germany would still be what it was at the time: the democratic and impotent state of Weimar origin."[6]

The Nazi Party had, the Führer claimed, saved Europe from "world conquest" by the forces of Bolshevism—a political movement he described as a "Bolshevik-Asian colossus" bent upon subjugating Europe until "it is finally broken and defeated." The colossus was one impelled by Jewry, for the "Jewish democracy of the west will sooner or later lead to Bolshevism," he predicted—the "Jewish-plutocratic west" joining the "Jewish-Bolshevik" east, crushing Germany between them . . .

Instead of submitting to such a dark fate, however, the Nazi Party had successfully set about resisting it. "While in the First World War the German Volk went to pieces at home almost without enemy action," the Führer claimed, "it will not lose the power of its resistance even under the most difficult circumstances."[7] And he warned: "let nobody doubt this or delude himself." Only "criminals" could believe anything was to be gained by an Allied victory. Moreover, "we will deal with these criminals!" he snarled. "What happened in 1918 will not repeat itself in Germany a second time . . . If tens of thousands of our best men, our dearest *Volksgenossen,* fall at the front, then we will not shrink from killing a few hundred criminals at home without much ado . . . If we catch one, he will lose his head. Rest assured, it is much more difficult for me to order a small operation at the front in the realization that perhaps hundreds of thousands will fall, than to sign a sentence that will result in the execution of a few dozen rascals, criminals or gangsters."[8] Allied attempts to bomb Germany into submission he ridiculed, for despite the terrible suffering imposed on "women and children," the "damage done to our industry is largely insignificant." Within two or three years of the war's end two to three million apartments would be constructed to house those made homeless by Allied bombing. Thus, while the "Americans and English are right now planning the rebuilding of the world" through a new United Nations agency, he mocked, "I am right now planning the rebuilding of Germany! There will, however, be a difference: while the rebuilding of the world through the Americans and the English will not take place, the rebuilding of Germany through National Socialism will be carried out with precision and according to a plan."[9]

For this grand German reconstruction project the Führer would bring, he explained, not only his vaunted Todt organization, the civil and military construction force headed by Fritz Todt, but "war criminals roped in for the job. For the first time in their lives, the war criminals will do something useful," he stated.[10]

Which thought led Hitler, in turn, to his next great threat: the preparation and use of *Vergeltungswaffen,* or weapons of revenge. The Allies would reap the whirlwind for having bombed German cities. "Whether or not the gentlemen believe it," Hitler warned, "the hour of retribution will come!" And "if we cannot reach America at the moment, there is one state that is within our reach," he declared, "and we shall fasten onto it" — using France as the launchpad for such weapons of mass destruction, aimed at England.[11]

Allied bombing, currently incurring terrible German civilian casualties, could only harden the determination of a typical German civilian or *Volksgenosse* to support the war fought to the bitter end, "since only a victorious war can help him get his belongings back. And so the hundreds of thousands of the bombed-out are the vanguard of revenge," Hitler declared.[12] The enemy "may hope to wear us out by heavy blood sacrifice. This time, however, the blood sacrifice will consist of two, three, or four enemy sacrifices for every German one. No matter how hard it is for us to bear these sacrifices, they simply oblige us to go further. Never again will it come to pass — as in the [First] World War, when we lost two million and this loss was pointless in the end — that we will today pointlessly sacrifice even a single human being," for there would be no capitulation, only victory, he predicted. "Germany will never capitulate. Never will we repeat the mistake of 1918, namely to lay down our arms at a quarter to twelve. You can rest assured of this: the very last party to lay down its arms will be Germany, and this at five minutes after twelve."[13]

"In conclusion," the Führer said, he wanted to add "one more" thing. "Every week I read at least three or four times that I have either suffered a nervous breakdown, or I have dismissed my friend Göring and Göring has gone to Sweden, or again Göring has dismissed me, or the Wehrmacht has dismissed the party, or the party has by contrast dismissed the Wehrmacht, and then again, the generals have revolted against me, and then again, I have arrested the

generals and have had them locked up. You can rest assured: everything is possible," he allowed, "but that I lose my nerve is completely out of the question!"

With this display of black humor, the Führer had signed off. He gave thanks
to the "Almighty," who had blessed Germany and had allowed it to "take this
fight successfully far beyond the borders of the Reich," rather than to have
to fight it "on German soil" — moreover had "helped it to overcome nearly
hopeless positions such as the Italian collapse!"[14] He therefore asked the party
faithful to leave the beer hall "with fanatical confidence and fanatical faith"
that would guarantee Nazi victory, and the domination of Europe. "We fight
for this. Many have already fallen for this, and many will still have to make the
same sacrifice . . . The blood we spill will one day bring rich rewards for our
Volk. Millions of human beings will be granted an existence in new homes,"
to be built by slave labor, supplied by the Todt organization. And war criminals . . . "Sieg Heil!"[15]

Goebbels was delighted, noting in his diary what a propaganda triumph the
speech had been, and what a media defeat for the Allies it would be — especially in the neutral countries. Even the rate of suicide went down in Germany,
he noted afterwards. Hitler had confided to him that in the coming two weeks
he was hoping for "great things" on the Eastern Front, where German counteroffensive moves were being prepared. Despite their own propaganda boasts,
after all, the Russians had been unable to retake the Crimea.

Goebbels was of a mind to believe his supreme leader. After all, German
civilian morale was recovering. The British had been trounced in the Aegean,
and were being held back in southern Italy. In London Churchill was having to warn Parliament of darker, longer days ahead than he'd once predicted.
The recent conference of foreign ministers in Moscow, in which preliminary
discussions had been held as to how Germany should be carved up and its
industry and manpower distributed to the victors, suddenly looked childishly
premature.

"There is only one way for our enemies to win total victory in this war,"
Goebbels summarized in his diary on November 14, 1943 — unaware that President Roosevelt was at sea, halfway across the Atlantic to insist on this very
point — "and that is a successful [Allied] invasion of the West."[16]

9

Marshall: Commander in Chief Against Germany

THREE DAYS OUT AT SEA, at 2:00 p.m. on November 15, 1943, the President summoned his Joint Chiefs of Staff to a formal meeting in his cabin, where they could discuss a paper he'd asked them to draw up to counter the British plea for a new, alternative Allied military strategy in the Mediterranean and Aegean.

At the meeting the U.S. chiefs voiced their adamant opposition to any departure from Overlord and its timetable. "The President said as far as he was concerned — Amen," the minutes of the meeting duly recorded.[1]

How to bring the British back into line, though?

Whitewashed by generations of subsequent historians, this was the great tragedy of the war in late 1943: that at a moment when Hitler and Goebbels had no real idea how they could win the war in Europe beyond stoicism and the use of *Vergeltungswaffen*, and recognized the only way they could lose the war was if the Allies launched a Second Front, the Allied coalition faced the danger of being split apart by Winston Churchill and the British.

Churchill's obsession with the Mediterranean and the Aegean, of course, was nothing new. His Dardanelles operation in World War I had resulted, after all, in a fiasco, entailing terrible loss of life and his own resignation as First Sea Lord, or minister responsible for the Royal Navy. Thereafter he'd insisted upon serving as a battalion commander on the Western Front. This battlefield service had only reinforced his opposition to trench warfare, however, and — ironically — fueled his belief in the use of tanks: the very weapon the Wehrmacht had used in 1940 to smash its way across France, backed by modern tactical air support — yet which Churchill declined to believe the Allies could employ in northern France in 1944, targeting Berlin.

Dreading the inevitable casualties the amphibious invasion would entail, and the subsequent land battle if the Allies even managed to get ashore, Churchill had continued to hope British forces could avoid having to face the main armies of the Wehrmacht in the west. Thus, where the President had seen North Africa and the Mediterranean as a proving ground for U.S. military leadership, interservice cooperation, and combat effectiveness in the run-up to the mounting of a successful cross-Channel invasion, Churchill had drawn the opposite lesson. The complete defeat of the British Expeditionary Force in the retreat to Dunkirk in May 1940, and then the fiasco of the Dieppe raid in August 1942, had sapped his confidence in British Empire troops and their commanders. For him, the Mediterranean was not only a crucial lifeline of colonial empire, but also a means to use traditional British *sea power* to surround German-occupied Europe, not attack it, save with bombers. In this way the Soviets would, if possible, be tasked with defeating Hitler, leaving Britain still intact at the heart of a colonial empire that could be reconstructed after the end of hostilities. The agreement over Overlord, timed to take place on or before May 1, 1944, had in his own mind never been more than a piece of lawyer's paper, as he'd put it: a contract which Britain could simply decline to observe, or could keep asking to defer, each moment the bill came due.

That moment, however, was now coming — and in traveling with his small army of advisers and clerks aboard HMS *Renown* toward the Middle East, the Prime Minister began to recognize the enormity of what he was proposing: namely a complete recasting of Allied war strategy, barely six months before the agreed launch date of Overlord.

Afterwards Churchill would drag his literary coat over the British revolt — his subsequent history of the war completely concealing the way in which he had behaved in London in October 1943, as he plotted with his chiefs of staff to subvert the Quebec agreements made only two months earlier: "one of the most blatant pieces of distortion in his six volumes of memoirs," as the distinguished Cambridge historian David Reynolds would write. Having effective command of all British imperial forces in 1943 as prime minister and minister of defense, Churchill had in September of that year begun a "maverick campaign over the Dodecanese." Then, when this had turned to disaster, he had "come close to throwing Overlord overboard," while subsequently hiding his egregious "strategic machinations" in a "willfully inaccurate account."[2] Composing his war memoirs, Reynolds recounted, Churchill had been persuaded by his writing team to suppress the incriminating "key pieces of evidence" against him: the secret instruction to his chiefs of staff, on October 19, to plan an alternative strategy to the one agreed at Quebec; the duplicitous cable to Eden, to explain the "need" to delay Overlord; and his negative subsequent memo to his chiefs while traveling to Cairo.[3] Moreover, the team had wanted him also to delete his draft explanation for his alternative strategy: namely that his own scheme was "to bring Turkey into the war by dominating the Aegean islands, and thereafter enter the Black Sea with the British Fleet and aid the Russians in all their recovery of its northern coast, the Crimea, etc, as well as debouchements near the mouth of the Danube. No British or American army was to be employed in this. Naval and air forces might have sufficed," as Churchill's draft chapter had it.[4] As Reynolds commented: "Sending a British fleet into the Black Sea was hardly a minor operation. And it sounded a little too close for comfort to Gallipoli in 1915" to be included in the published book. Fortunately, it was removed.[5]

The historical truth remained, however — concealed from the public and later historians, who did not have access to the documents Churchill had purloined from 10 Downing Street when unseated as prime minister in 1945: namely that, in the fall of 1943, Winston Churchill had vowed to do everything in his power in London to sabotage Overlord, at the risk of splitting the Allied alliance. What Reynolds left unexamined was the further question, *why?* What could possibly explain Churchill's willingness to risk the transatlantic partnership — in fact the whole Allied coalition against Hitler? Had he, as the British Army chief of staff, Sir Alan Brooke, put it in his diary, simply gone "mad"?

Scratching their heads, historians would never quite make sense of Churchill's fierce determination to get his own way — even to the point of threatening to resign as prime minister on October 29, 1943, as he did, following the War Cabinet meeting that night.[6]

Certainly, like everyone involved in Overlord, Churchill felt a genuine concern at the casualties the D-day invasion would entail. Yet such an explanation did not really hold water, since operations in the Mediterranean, judging by recent Allied experience in southern Italy and in the Dodecanese Islands, would hardly involve fewer casualties, were they to be mounted as the major Allied campaign of 1944 — opposed, undoubtedly, by do-or-die Wehrmacht forces. And for no strategic purpose, except one, if the aim of the Allies was to defeat Nazi Germany: prolonging the British Empire! Besides, the fear of cross-Channel casualties — as the Prime Minister's doctor noted — had never held back Churchill from undertaking an operation that he himself wished to tackle. Gallipoli alone had caused more than 160,000 British Empire casualties — as well as almost 30,000 French.[7]

What, then, in retrospect, could really explain Churchill's scheming and "machinations," as Professor Reynolds described them,[8] at such a juncture in the war? It was, after all, the *third time* that year he was proposing to ditch the agreed Allied strategy — a Peter-like denial, despite having twice formally signed up for a spring 1944 priority for Overlord. What magic, moreover, had Churchill managed to employ to persuade his entire British chiefs of staff to follow him down this hole, in direct opposition to the President? And how had the Prime Minister gotten the entire British War Cabinet to support him in his latest October crusade, and his dire predictions of "disaster" if they didn't? Was it solely Churchill's fabled way with words, and his stature as prime minister? Or was there some other explanation?

Certainly the U.S. president and his advisers, meeting together aboard the USS *Iowa*, seemed unable to understand Churchill's mounting obstructionism toward Overlord in the run-up to Tehran. What was the Prime Minister *playing* at? Given that the United States had rescued Britain from defeat in 1942, and had deliberately blooded its own forces in the Mediterranean in 1943 in preparation of troops and commanders for Overlord, the latest British rebellion was galling. Why were they *doing* it — and how could they be stopped?

It was this question the President put to his advisers in his cabin on November 15, 1943 — aware that, at the end of the day, there was no actual way to enforce the Quebec agreement, if Churchill resigned or withdrew British commitment to military participation in the May 1944 cross-Channel undertaking. The war against Hitler would, effectively, be lost. As it might equally be lost, too, if the President accepted Churchill's alternative, and the Soviets decided to negotiate with Hitler rather than suffer more casualties in assuming the main burden of combat against the Wehrmacht.

The U.S. military was thus between a rock and a hard place — with no obvious way of breaking the impasse.

By suggesting that a Russian observer might attend the Combined Chiefs of Staff meetings in Cairo, prior to Tehran, the President had first hoped, he told his chiefs, the British could perhaps be shamed in front of Stalin's representative. This tactic had failed, however, the President explained in his cabin — and not only because Prime Minister Churchill was "emphatically against the [Russian observer] proposal."[9] Stalin, too, had wrecked the plan, if inadvertently — for once the Soviet premier heard that Generalissimo Chiang Kaishek would also be present in Cairo, he didn't dare send a senior Soviet official. The Soviet Union was still not at war with Japan — and had no wish to give the Japanese a pretext for declaring war on the Soviet Union, which would in turn force Stalin to withdraw Russian forces from the Eastern Front.

There was therefore probably no alternative, the President felt, but to stonewall once the American team reached Cairo. They would have to try to defer any serious strategic debate over Overlord to "the big conference" in Tehran, where the United States and Russia could together shoot down the British fantasia — even though this would mean facing Stalin, thanks to British intransigence, with a weakened and divided Western Allied hand.

After much discussion, this game plan, then, was decided upon. Regrettably it was the only way for the Americans to proceed, the President made clear. The chiefs would have to ensure, in drawing up an agenda for the preliminary meeting in Cairo, that "the meeting with the [Chinese] Generalissimo and himself and the Joint Chiefs of Staff [was] to be separate from and *precede* any meeting with the British"[10] — i.e., leaving as little time as possible for the British to raise their expected objections to the Quebec agreement before leaving for Tehran.

The only other alternative the chiefs could suggest was a kind of preemptive move: to put on the Cairo Conference agenda a renewed insistence that the yet-to-be-appointed supreme commander of Overlord — an American — should be made supreme commander both of Overlord *and* the Mediterranean — and thus be able to quash any operations in the Mediterranean that might delay Overlord.

It was in the context of this two-part stratagem — namely to stonewall any discussion of changes to Overlord's timetable, while asking the British to agree in Cairo to the merging of both the Second Front *and* Mediterranean operations under one American commander, if necessary, to achieve this objective — that the President finally went on record as stating for the first time, in an official meeting, that the supreme commander of Overlord would be General George Catlett Marshall. As the minutes of the meeting recorded, it was the President's "idea that General Marshall should be the Commander in chief against Germany" — a role in which, in Europe, he would "command all the British, French, Italian and U.S. troops involved in this effort": the defeat of the Third Reich.[11]

10

A Witches' Brew

ABOARD HMS *RENOWN* Winston Churchill was dead set against any such merger of the two theaters, the idea of which he'd learned just before he left England.

The Prime Minister was suffering from a heavy cold, and his mood had darkened aboard the gray British battleship as it made its way south toward the Mediterranean. It didn't help that, on November 15, weather conditions at Gibraltar precluded him from switching to a plane for the onward journey to Malta. Harold Macmillan, the British political adviser to General Eisenhower, thus visited Churchill in his cabin early on November 16, 1943, to witness a "fascinating performance" by the Prime Minister — the "greater part" of which was "a rehearsal of what he is to say at the Military Conference; and he is *terribly* worried and excited about this."[1]

It would be, Churchill explained at Gibraltar, a grand Anglo-American showdown. Far from seeing the Mediterranean as a holding pattern by the Allies while full-scale preparations were made for the spring cross-Channel assault, Churchill was openly caustic about the Allies' failure to be more offensive and flexible in southern Europe — a failure he attributed not only to the "Combined Chiefs of Staff system" but to "our American allies generally." The Americans, he told Macmillan, had all along restrained his military genius, causing the Prime Minister to feel "that all through the war he is fighting like a man with his hands tied behind his back" — and this when he was, ironically, the only man alive who could have "enticed the Americans into the European war at all"[2] — wooing President Roosevelt, as he once put it, "as a man might woo a maid."[3]

The approaching "Sextant" meeting in Cairo, prior to Tehran, was thus, in Churchill's mind, critical to the course of World War II. It would be, Churchill predicted, the war's "'real turning point,'" as the effete, debonair Macmillan recorded Churchill's words in his diary that night, "and the hardest job he [Churchill] has encountered."[4]

The Prime Minister's way with words, of course, was both a mark of his genius and a curse. Macmillan sided with the Prime Minister. Macmillan had been severely wounded on the Western Front, at Loos in 1915, and again in 1916 at the Battle of the Somme — offensive campaigns that had devastated the British Army for no tactical or strategic gain. Like Churchill, Macmillan had been scarred for life by this experience of trench warfare. He'd studied Greek and Latin at Oxford, rather than French or German, and in his role as current British political/diplomatic adviser to General Eisenhower, ever since the Torch invasion of Morocco and Algeria, he'd felt deeply at home in the Mediterranean. He was happy where he was — and hated the very idea of Overlord and a vast Allied campaign in northern France, which might require his transfer to northern Europe. He was, in short, the very last person to point out to the Prime Minister the folly of what he was proposing.

The irony, moreover, was that Macmillan, like Churchill, was half-American — his mother having come from Indiana — and given his daily meetings with General Eisenhower, the seasoned diplomat ought to have foreseen the likely American response to the Prime Minister's obsession with the Mediterranean aimed at Rome. Macmillan found himself too entranced, however, by the brilliance of Churchill's rhetoric to caution him — recording with delight, instead, how Churchill derided his military advisers' pusillanimity: men crushed, Churchill claimed, by the British chiefs of staff system that brought together air, army, and navy strategists. "It leads to weak and faltering decisions — or rather indecisions," the Prime Minister scoffed at their concerns over his Mediterranean plans. "'Why, you may take the most gallant sailor, the most intrepid airman, or the most audacious soldier, put them at a table together — what do you get? *The sum total of their fears!*"[5]

This was a Churchillian bon mot of a very high order — spoken "with frightful sibilant emphasis," as the political adviser noted in his diary, thinking of the hissing/spitting sound the Prime Minister made when delivering such ex cathedra judgments. Yet it was dangerous talk — with potentially dangerous consequences.

Like Churchill, Harold Macmillan was a bon vivant, and something of an English social and intellectual snob, which also played a part in the gathering saga. Despite his New World heritage Macmillan saw American officers as being, for the most part, brash and often ill-educated in comparison with his own classical Eton and Oxford education — and, to be sure, most were. Like other Englishmen he'd thus forgotten the sorry failures of British military forces in Norway, France, Greece, Crete, Libya, and Egypt, and had begun to feel not gratitude for the way the United States had helped save Britain in 1942 by mounting the Torch invasion, but instead a discernible resentment at growing American economic and military might in the Mediterranean. He thus failed to see that, by encouraging Churchill to defy the President and oppose the formally agreed Quebec strategy, the Prime Minister might thereby drive the President of the United States to "make nice" with Stalin in order to put down Churchill's insurrection — with huge potential political as well as military consequences for the Western Allies.

Would it have helped if Macmillan had been instructed to report to Eden, the British foreign minister, rather than directly to Churchill?

It is doubtful. The British foreign secretary was even more culpable than Macmillan in his failure to challenge the Prime Minister's recalcitrance. Anthony Eden knew *in person* how much the Soviets were counting on a spring '44 invasion to help defeat Hitler, yet had not dared to bring the Prime Minister to his senses. Instead, he had simply passed on the Prime Minister's deceitful cable to Stalin, dutifully telling Stalin that "the British 'would do our very best for "Overlord" but it is no use planning for defeat in the field in order to give temporary political satisfaction.'"[6]

The Second Front a "temporary political satisfaction"? Churchill had instructed Eden to tell the Russian premier that all previous assurances given to Stalin "about May 'Overlord'" in 1944 would now be "modified by the exigencies of the battle in Italy." Nothing, the Prime Minister had cabled, would "alter my determination not to throw away the battle in Italy at this juncture. Eisenhower and Alexander must have what they need to win the battle, no matter what effect is produced on subsequent operations. This may certainly affect the date of 'Overlord.'"[7]

Eden had loyally conveyed this warning to the Russian marshal. "I again emphasized," the foreign secretary afterwards reported back to Churchill, "your anxiety that Stalin should have the latest account of the situation in Italy" — unaware Churchill had deliberately deceived both Eden and Stalin by forwarding General Alexander's battlefield report without Eisenhower's accompanying, contrary assessment. As Eden had summarized his audience with the Russian dictator, he'd told Stalin he "should know not only that you were anxious about it but also that you were insistent that battle in Italy had to be nourished and fought out to victory whatever implications on OVERLORD" — his cable sent to Churchill the very night the Prime Minister was threatening his cabinet colleagues he would resign if he did not get his way over the strategic switch to the Mediterranean, Aegean, and Balkans.

It was small wonder Marshal Stalin had been unimpressed. Eden's assertion that, "in view of the vitally important decisions now confronting the Allies," it was "all the more necessary that the three heads of government should meet as soon as possible" had met with Stalin's disbelief, after looking quizzically at Alexander's top-secret negative account of operations in Italy. "Stalin observed with a smile that if there were not sufficient divisions" in Italy, then "a meeting of the heads of government could not create them." Eden had reported Stalin's response word for word to Churchill — as well as Stalin's remark that it was not for the world's leaders to furnish troops, but for the British and American chiefs of staff to do that. "He then asked point blank whether the [Alexander] telegram which he had just read meant a postponement of Overlord."[8]

For his part Anthony Eden had been deeply embarrassed — and could only quote Churchill's message to him that there was "no use planning for defeat" in Italy.

This was the first Stalin had heard of such a possibility, either from General Deane, heading the U.S. Military Mission in Moscow, or Lieutenant General Hastings Ismay, Churchill's military chief of staff, currently in Moscow for the foreign ministers' conference. Nor had Russian observers in the Mediterranean, or Russian military intelligence, reported such a dire military situation necessitating the "postponement" of Overlord, some five months away. Eden had cited the shortage of landing craft. But why were *landing craft* necessary to defend Allied positions from German counterattack in the mountains of southern Italy, rather than being assembled in Britain for the cross-Channel assault in the coming spring? *To evacuate?* Moreover, why was Churchill proposing to halt the planned move of some seven battle-hardened Allied divisions to Britain for Overlord, as agreed at Quebec, and instead to keep them on the battlefield in Italy, if those divisions were considered essential, experienced troops in ensuring the success of Overlord?

Stalin had thereupon given Eden and his companions a brief and revealing master class on military strategy.

"As he saw it there were two courses open to us," Eden afterwards reported to Churchill.

The first was: "To take up a defensive position north of Rome and use the rest of our forces for OVERLORD."

The second was "to push through Italy into Germany."

Which was it to be? Stalin had asked. To which Eden, in all honesty, had only been able to answer, the first. Stalin had agreed — since it would be "very difficult to get through the Alps," he pointed out, "and that it would suit the Germans well to fight us there." Surely, Stalin remarked, the British had sufficient prestige as a military power "to permit us to pass over to the defensive in Italy," rather than pursue red herrings in Italy or the Aegean?

In view of the *two years'* delay by the Allies before they felt ready to mount a Second Front, Anthony Eden had been surprised at how gently he'd been treated, with "no recrimination of the past. It is clear however," Eden had warned his prime minister, "that M. Stalin expects us to make every effort to stage OVERLORD at the earliest possible moment," moreover the "confidence he is placing in our word is to me most striking."[9]

"*Our word.*" Like Eden, Harold Macmillan knew that the story about a possible "disaster" in southern Italy, unless Overlord was postponed or canceled, was a complete fabrication by the Prime Minister.

Opposing Mr. Churchill, however, was not something Harold Macmillan was willing to hazard. Nor was there anyone else on the British side who would confront him. And this, even though the Prime Minister was becoming "more and more dogmatic," as Macmillan himself recorded in his diary.[10]

Macmillan was a diplomat. But why had Britain's military chiefs of staff — General Alan Brooke, Air Marshal Charles Portal, and Admiral Andrew Cunningham — not restrained the Prime Minister from embarking on a divisive, looming confrontation with their American counterparts?

British military standing in the world had, after all, been tarnished once again by Churchill's recent fiasco in the Aegean: disastrous, unilaterally mounted operations, using British forces from the Middle East that were now nearing their final, humiliating end on the island of Leros — to the delight of Goebbels's propaganda machine. Would such British military standing not be still more tainted, in the eyes of the Russians as well as other nations, were it to be found Britain was going back on its "word," as Stalin put it, and was threatening to pull out of its part in the Overlord invasion, in five months' time?

Day after day Churchill lay in bed composing his "indictment" of the current military situation — and his argument that putting *more* forces into battle in the Mediterranean, instead of preparing them to cross the English Channel, would make better war policy. "He was not at his best, and I feel nervous as to the line he may adopt at this conference," Brooke confided in the small leather-bound journal he was keeping for his wife to read, once he returned home. "He is inclined to say to the Americans, all right if you won't play with us in the Mediterranean we won't play with you in the English Channel. And if they say, 'all right well then we shall direct our main effort in the Pacific,' to reply: 'you are welcome to do so if you wish!'"

The prospect of such a scenario "filled me with gloom!" Brooke added later that evening, after dinner with Churchill and the "long military discussions" that had continued till midnight.[11] "There are times when I feel that it is all a horrid nightmare," Brooke confided[12] — a nightmare out of which he knew he must waken, though, since the very outcome of the war against Hitler was now at stake.

Churchill, in Brooke's opinion, was now "floundering about," with no "clear vision" — in fact exhibiting only "lack of vision": a self-styled strategist who saw "war by theatres and without perspective," a man who, moreover, lacked a "clear appreciation of the influence of one theatre on another!"[13] A man who "discusses Command and Commanders," yet who "has never gained a true grasp of Higher Command organization and what it means."[14] For instance,

Churchill's admiration for the Honorable Sir Harold Alexander, Eisenhower's British field deputy, was all too typical: General Alexander a brave but shallow aristocrat, yet a man the Prime Minister now hoped to appoint supreme Allied commander in the Mediterranean and Middle East, combining both theaters for the first time, once Eisenhower was — as Churchill was insisting — removed from the post . . .

The thought made Brooke squirm. Yet no one in Churchill's court had the wit or courage to protest.

In Algiers, at Eisenhower's main Allied headquarters, there was also little doubt as to the magnitude of the looming showdown. Eisenhower's chief of staff, Lieutenant General Bedell Smith, had just returned from Malta. He'd also been invited to a personal conference with the Prime Minister on HMS *Renown,* which had arrived there safely in the harbor, he reported. "The PM and the British are still unconvinced," Smith warned, "as to the wisdom of Overlord." The British were simply "persistent in their desire to pursue our advantages in the Mediterranean, especially through the Balkans" — no matter what had been agreed at Quebec in August.

The approaching pre–Tehran Conference between the American and British military teams would thus be, General Smith predicted, "the hottest one yet."[15]

11

Fullest Guidance

NOT SINCE CAESAR had approached Pompey's forces on the shores of Egypt, close to Cairo, had there been such a threatening confrontation between two hitherto close allies in the midst of war.

Becoming more and more nervous about the seriousness of the feud—especially when receiving a signal on board the *Iowa* on November 17, approaching North Africa, that the British censor in Egypt had permitted a leak of the forthcoming high-level conference, and even its location, at the Mena House Hotel, close to the famed pyramids—the President now convened a second meeting of his Joint Chiefs of Staff in his stateroom.

The *Iowa* was now closing on the Straits of Gibraltar and the Mediterranean. It was time, he felt, to discuss with his military advisers not only the impending clash with the British, but the larger strategy of the war, the postwar—and relations with the Russians.

Given that he'd arranged to meet with Chiang Kai-shek in Cairo before flying to Tehran, the President was displeased by the British leak, to say the least. One of the *Iowa*'s escort vessels had therefore been summoned alongside by the President, to take an important message. When well away from the battleship's true course, the destroyer radioed London in most secret code to communicate the President's displeasure "that meeting place is known to enemy through press and radio." The President wanted more information concerning the "seriousness of the leak," and possible alternative venues for the meetings with Chiang—and also with the Turkish president, should he agree to come. Perhaps Khartoum, in the Sudan, Mr. Roosevelt posited—a thousand miles from Cairo?

Churchill, chastened by the laxity of the British censor in Egypt, had hastily consulted with his British military advisers. Malta would have suited his plans for a showdown with the American team, since he was already there, but it was too close to German airfields for safety. Or comfort. Amenities for hundreds of U.S. and British staff officers, clerks, and diplomats were required, unless they all remained on board their respective battleships — which in turn would present an even bigger target for guided German missiles. As Churchill's secretary noted in a letter home, "It would have meant housing the American staff in a place with a single tap and a single lavatory."[1]

Understandably the Prime Minister attempted to make light of the news. In a new cable to the President he regretted "the fact that it has leaked a few days earlier" than otherwise it would have done, but he did not consider it catastrophic.[2] Khartoum would involve hurried and unsatisfactory preparations, while Malta was simply too dangerous given the number of attendees. In the end the Prime Minister felt that, if security in Egypt was increased by placing more antiaircraft guns around the Mena House Hotel and adjacent Giza pyramids, and if Cairo city itself was made off-limits to all international personnel in order to guard against assassination, the Sino-U.S.-British conference would best be held as per the program.

Leakage of the locale of the impending military conference, however, left something of a sour taste aboard the *Iowa*, which was now joined by an escort carrier, the USS *Santee* — a former oiler bearing a new deck and carrying twenty-five Grumman TBF Avenger aircraft. Distrust of the British had risen several further degrees.

But it was not only the lapse in security that weighed on Roosevelt and his advisers, or the imminent contest with the British. The looming "battle royal" was depressing enough as they approached the Mediterranean, but the widening gap between American and British military officials betokened further, perhaps inevitable, disagreements in the future. For there was no getting away from the fact that, if the Allied coalition managed to hold together and defeat Nazi Germany, followed by Japan, there would be vast postwar problems — economic, social, refugee, diplomatic — to confront. The United States would no longer be able to revert to isolationism, as it had after World War I. It would be the world's richest and most productive economy, besides possessing the most powerful navy and air forces.

It was time, in other words, for the President to hold a sort of conference-within-a-conference with his U.S. chiefs of staff.

The President had already shared with his advisers his vision of a United Nations authority, the postwar peace to be guaranteed by "Four Policemen": the United States, Britain, the Soviet Union, and China. This vision was all very well in theory. But in the real world, recovering from a destructive global war?

The devil would be in the details. How, for example, should Germany be treated, in defeat? How should the European nations, currently occupied by German forces or allies of the Third Reich, be reconstituted? How far would the communist Soviet Union be willing to cooperate with capitalist democracies? What would be the fate of Czechoslovakia, Danzig, and Poland — the tinderboxes Hitler had used to ignite his war of conquest? What about Japan and the European colonies in the Far East that the Japanese had overrun? Should the white European colonial powers — Britain, France, Belgium, the Netherlands — be pressed to grant sovereignty and assist their former colonies rather than exploit them, if postwar revolution and anticolonial wars were to be avoided?

The matter was already becoming urgent. Only days before, the new French governor of two territories mandated to the French after World War I, Syria and the Lebanon, had simply ignored the results of elections there. To worldwide condemnation the French governor had imprisoned the winning candidates, who had dared call for full sovereignty and the end of the French Mandate. In India, there was a full-scale famine in Bengal — with Jawaharlal Nehru and Mahatma Gandhi still under British arrest, and no sign the British would currently discuss Indian self-government, let alone sovereignty, anytime soon. Similarly the French in Indochina, the Dutch in Indonesia . . . Were American sons to fight and die to resurrect such continued European colonial imperialism?

The three-hour meeting the President convened in his captain's quarters with the Joint Chiefs of Staff aboard the *Iowa* in the early afternoon of November 19, 1943, due west of Gibraltar, thus indicated, for the first time, a growing awareness of the *political* as well as military minefields ahead — minefields that in some ways explained the British fear of likely D-day casualties in Overlord. Given the need for occupation troops in order to reinstate their besieged colonial empire and then to police the vital sea lanes from Britain — their traditional pathways to Palestine, the Middle East, India, and Southeast Asia — the imminence of Overlord had caused much soul-searching in the corridors of Westminster, as Field Marshal Dill had already explained in Washington. In this context Mr. Churchill's passionate, unrelenting espousal of major operations in the Mediterranean and Middle East, even at the risk of destroying Allied unity and provoking an American switch to the Pacific, could be understood as issuing from a concern for Britain's colonial and imperial postwar interests, rather than the desire to bring a swift end to Hitler's mastery of all Europe. "In the course of the discussions the President gave the staff a clearer indication of the direction of his thinking and the fullest guidance on politico-military issues he had given them since America's entry into the war," the official historian of U.S. strategy in World War II, Maurice Matloff, would write.[3]

It was certainly high time. These U.S. admirals and generals, after all, would henceforth be commanding the world's most powerful postwar military, for good or ill.

• • •

"Fullest guidance" was something of a misnomer, however. Very few of Roosevelt's conference discussions were ever recorded or transcribed. Understandably the President had a deep-seated concern over leaks to the media, after years of combating the right-wing isolationist agendas of rich American Republican newspaper owners such as William Randolph Hearst, Robert McCormick, and Cissy Patterson — media moguls who not only opposed the President's policies, but had deliberately published top-secret information and made mischievous assertions — such as revealing the President's Victory Plan, two days before Pearl Harbor, or publishing revelations about U.S. intelligence decryption efforts immediately after Midway, military revelations that would have been considered treason in less liberal countries.

Roosevelt himself, of course, had become a master of press and public relations — and manipulation. By the fall of 1943 he'd held more than *nine hundred* presidential press conferences, as well as giving some twenty-six extended "Fireside Chats" on American radio, each averaging thirty minutes. Still and all, he had remained wary of keeping written minutes — knowing the chiefs of staff were often required to testify before Congress, where the political ramifications of transcribed statements could quickly become footballs. Keeping politics out of the purely military direction of the war had therefore been a primary objective for the President — his appointment of two Republicans as his secretary of war and secretary of the navy intended to demonstrate his political evenhandedness as U.S. commander in chief.

With the endgame of the war approaching, however, the President's unwillingness to be pinned down in writing was becoming more difficult to excuse in terms of clear decision-making. It was also potentially counterproductive. For more than a decade he'd masked his intentions with his characteristic charm, humor, intelligence, and patrician goodwill: listening, airing provisional opinions, testing his own and others' prejudices, exploring ideas, before coming to decisions. At cabinet meetings and other formal committee sessions this had often disappointed members and administration officials like Henry Stimson, who preferred clear-cut, lawyerly presentation and then decisions made categorically in front of witnesses, rather than afterwards, *en privé*, in the Oval Office or the President's study upstairs in the mansion. Like others, Stimson felt the President possessed an imperfect sense of intellectual orderliness, which the war secretary thought a distinct failing for a chief executive. Such frustration had considerable merit, but missed, to be sure, the very essence of Roosevelt's style of leadership: namely his wish to remain open-minded and hear from a wide number of people in seeking an eventual consensus of opinion or direction — consensus that would allow him then to proceed with his overall vision or objective with the least resistance.

This approach to leadership had proven amazingly successful, after all, in terms of national unity after Pearl Harbor—as even Joseph Goebbels, constantly seeking a chance to foment or exploit dissension in America, acknowledged in his diary.

In this sense, though never having worn the uniform, the President had proven himself a better military strategist, on a global scale, than either Hitler or the Japanese high command, if grand strategy be understood as the directing of all possible resources of a nation to attain its political objectives. After Pearl Harbor he'd also led his country's military high command with remarkable skill—quietly dropping Admiral Harold Stark from the Joint Chiefs of Staff, promoting Admiral King to run the U.S. Navy, and using the trio of King, Marshall, and Arnold to put his global strategy into action, monitored by Admiral Leahy, whom he'd made his White House chief of staff in the early summer of 1942. By personally conceiving and quietly promoting government-sponsored use of mass production techniques in the manufacturing of modern arms and weaponry, moreover, he had challenged U.S. industry to reach production targets that had flabbergasted both Hitler and Goebbels. Such output had not only provided arms for the nation, but for the forces of America's allies, including Britain and Russia; it had also allowed the President to pursue a patient two-ocean defensive strategy, followed by the offensive in the Pacific after Midway—yet prioritizing the defeat of Nazi Germany, as the linchpin of his "Germany First" strategy. He'd had to overrule his Joint Chiefs of Staff when they attempted to sell him on a premature cross-Channel invasion in 1942, with untested American troops, just as he'd had to overrule them when they called for a Pacific First approach if the British did not cooperate in defeating the Third Reich. And he'd had to do so once again at the start of 1943, when recognizing how important it was for U.S. forces to gain the necessary combat and command skills—involving army, navy, and air force components —before the Wehrmacht could realistically be defeated in a Second Front invasion of France. In his choice of theater commanders, as in his convictions about modern American air power—from bombers to transports, fighters to aircraft carriers—he had, by and large, shown wisdom, resilience, and steel when necessary. And all the time he had, in addition, maintained unity among the United Nations confronting Hitler and Hirohito, becoming their de facto commander in chief. He had kept the public morale in America high, moreover, with a mixture of realism, pride—and positive, forward-looking rhetoric. The fact that he had achieved this in a global war without resorting to dictatorial methods or inciting great or divisive controversy was, given the fractious nature of American politics and individualist society, almost miraculous. But as the war in Europe moved toward its climax, could this last? Would the inevitable political, cultural, and other differences between the coalition partners begin to militate against Allied endgame success—and the peace that was to follow?

The précis of the President's three-and-a-half-hour November 19 meeting with his Joint Chiefs of Staff, as noted in sparse minutes drawn up by Captain F. B. Royal of the U.S. Navy, reads today like selective notes of an overheard conversation on a train. The notes remain, nevertheless, our most intimate glimpse into America's top military conclave in the run-up to the decisive moment in the prosecution of the war against Hitler, as the British prepared to mount in Cairo a final showdown with their own allies: a showdown intended to force the postponement or even abandonment of Overlord, despite D-day (as it universally became known) being the only practical way, as the U.S. team saw it, to achieve unconditional surrender of the Third Reich. Nor was this a matter of mere theoretical discussion. Millions of lives were at stake in extermination camps run by the Third Reich. Yet Churchill was adamant. As Major General John Kennedy, General Brooke's director of military operations at the British War Office, would later confess, "Had we had our way, I think there is little doubt that the invasion of France would not have been done in 1944."[4]

12

On Board the *Iowa*

IRONICALLY THE AMERICAN chiefs of staff aboard the USS *Iowa* were more divided than their British counterparts — not over the paramount need to mount Overlord in the spring of 1944, but how exactly to deal with the looming British insurrection. On this latter point the U.S. chiefs were in frank disagreement with one another.

Admiral Leahy, as chairman of the Joint Chiefs of Staff Committee, favored a complete refusal to countenance the British proposal for a merging of Mediterranean and Middle East theaters under a new British "Supreme Commander South" — at least until Britain got back into line. The best way to force the British to stand by their commitment to Overlord, Leahy thus declared, was "Proposal 'A,'" which he'd drawn up in writing for the President on behalf of the U.S. chiefs: namely the appointment of an Allied supreme commander to direct both north *and* south theaters in Europe. This, he claimed, would be the only sure way to stop Churchill from pushing once again his Aegean nonsense at the expense of a spring 1944 invasion of France.

General Marshall, unfortunately, begged to differ. Marshall was an officer of the highest integrity and principle, but like General Brooke, he could be naive about political warfare. He knew Churchill had cabled Field Marshal Dill in Washington, and that the British would never, ever agree to such a draconian overall command solution. Moreover Marshall agreed with the British, at least to the extent that the current situation in the Mediterranean was unsatisfactory. General Eisenhower currently commanded all Allied forces in the central Mediterranean, but had no authority over the many (mostly British) forces available in the Middle East (Egypt, Palestine, Mesopotamia, Iran). This undoubtedly weakened the potential application of maximum military force where and when it was needed. Speaking as a military man, General Marshall explained he sympathized with the British in their view that their efforts in the Dodecanese had failed not so much because of local German superiority, but because General Eisenhower had refused to help with major forces from his

Mediterranean reserves. As Marshall put it, "The British doubtless feel, and perhaps rightly so," that a supreme commander both of the Mediterranean *and* Middle East forces "would have influenced the attitude of [Air Marshal] Tedder and [General] Spaatz towards additional air support in the Dodecanese," the consequences of which might then "have been different."[1]

Admiral Leahy disagreed with such hypothesizing. He felt air support would not have turned the tide — not only because the Germans were ruthless and professional in defense, but because the Aegean, as he reminded Marshall, was a graveyard, not a stepping-stone. To get distracted by an invasion of the Aegean islands, when the Allies needed every effort to be put into southern Italy after Salerno, had been a grave strategic error by the British. Above all, it would not have been made under an American supreme commander of Allied forces preparing to invade France, while the Wehrmacht was being held fast in southern Italy in a combined North-and-South American command.

General Arnold kept silent, while Admiral King — who had strong political views — said he was unclear whether it was Mr. Churchill on his own who was, in essence, the bull in the china shop. The Prime Minister had always been a maverick rather than a team player. King therefore wondered whether "the British Cabinet" could be prevailed upon to overrule him.

The meeting aboard the *Iowa* was then spent batting the European command question from corner to corner.

For his part the President, as commander in chief, had no illusions. He felt certain the British were pressing their case for a British-led, expanded Allied theater in the south, embracing both Mediterranean and Middle Eastern forces, for a simple reason: namely in order to divert priority of Allied offensive strategy away from Overlord. As Captain Royal noted, the President suggested that the "over-all Mediterranean command proposed by the British might have resulted from an idea in the back of their heads to create a situation in which they could push our troops into Turkey and the Balkans" instead of northern France — where there were too many German divisions, in their view, to avoid a bloodbath.[2]

Admiral King pointed out that, if that proved to be the case, the Combined Chiefs would still have to give "approval" or denial for Balkan operations, whoever was the supposed supreme commander — prompting the President to observe that it was not only the Combined Chiefs committee who had oversight of major Allied operations. In the end he himself was the Commander in Chief of the Armed Forces of the United States — and he was not going near the Aegean. As he put it, "Even if General Alexander" — Churchill's pet nominee — "should become commander in chief" of the enlarged Mediterranean–Middle East theater, and should "desire to use U.S. troops and landing craft against the Dodecanese," then he, the President, "could say no."[3]

The President did not therefore agree with General Marshall — for although Marshall's argument about applying maximum force had merit, it missed the major point. The Aegean fiasco was an illustration not only of poor independent British performance in combat unless backed by American power, but of Churchill's misguided strategic opportunism and avoidance of head-to-head battle with Hitler's Wehrmacht in France. "The President asked, why Leros, why Cos?" Captain Royal recorded. Roosevelt acknowledged that "the Prime Minister had been upset as regards the United States attitude regarding the Dodecanese," but where did those islands *lead,* for heaven's sakes? If they were considered so strategically important to the Allied coalition, why hadn't the British told the United States in advance of the invasions they were launching there? General Marshall said the most he'd been aware of was a "pink dispatch" slip, or cable — and that the "British always regarded the Dodecanese as of greater importance than we in the United States" . . .

Round and round the discussion went.

In the end the President said that, although the notion of pushing Proposal "A" for an all-Europe commander was the better approach in theory, in order to get Overlord mounted on time, it would in practice only lead to the British digging in and refusing to accept it — which they were within their rights as a major ally to do. With regard to "the matter of the Supreme Allied Commander" for "all Europe," as Leahy had called it, the President was thus doubtful. In demanding an all-Europe commander rather than presenting the idea as a negotiating tactic, Marshall was right; the British would refuse, and the American team would be on a hiding to nothing.

As a temporary means to hold the British to the Quebec agreement on Overlord, however, the President's notion of an American "all Europe" — i.e., north and south — was worth pursuing in Cairo. The President himself would therefore aim to stonewall when they all met. They could deliberately decline to reconsider the matter of Overlord and its timetable till they got to Tehran and met with Stalin — where the Russians could help put iron back into the soul of the faltering British. The President said he would like another meeting with the Joint Chiefs before they went into oral battle with the British on the issue in Cairo, though. "He said he would take up the matter [of Proposal "A," an all-Europe supreme commander] with the Prime Minister at the earliest time" in Egypt, but "we may have difficulty," he warned the chiefs.[4] They might well have to agree to a compromise, or quid pro quo — for without British forces, Overlord simply couldn't be mounted. This reality gave the British veto power, which they were quite capable of using. The matter was very delicate, and would require a mix of patience, determination, and dexterity.

To provide himself with ammunition for the Cairo meeting the President had need of a gentle way of reminding the British who was boss. He had therefore asked his chiefs to give him, in writing, a table of the "total forces that the U.S. and United Kingdom would have at home and abroad by the first of January 1944." The figures they now presented at the meeting on the *Iowa* were telling:

TOTAL MILITARY FORCES
U.S. — 11,000,000
U.K. — 4,500,000[5]

Eleven million men versus four and a half million! What better illustration could there be of the tail trying to wag the dog? American armed forces were now contributing more than *twice* the number of troops as the British (by which was understood British Empire and Commonwealth contingents, including those of Canada, Australia, New Zealand, India, and South Africa) were furnishing. Yet even here the outcome of the impending Cairo deliberations was not guaranteed. The vast majority of U.S. troops were still in training, at home, yet to be dispatched to theaters of war. Thus the number of troops on active service abroad was currently about equal between the two powers — the U.S. Army boasting 2.6 million abroad, the U.S. Navy another million, while total British Empire forces amounted to about the same. Churchill would be bound to argue, then, against having an overall supreme Allied commander of "all Europe" — which he would claim was too big a theater for one man to direct. The Prime Minister would undoubtedly insist upon a British supreme commander in the Mediterranean/Middle East, if the supreme commander of the cross-Channel invasion was, as agreed at Quebec, to be an American, once appointed. When that happened, a British commander in the Mediterranean would inevitably be putty in Churchill's wild hands: unable to resist the Prime Minister's pressure for renewed Allied ventures in Italy, in the Aegean, in the Dardanelles and Balkans.

The more the President and his chiefs aboard the *Iowa* surveyed the looming set-to in Cairo, the more ominous the coming conference appeared, in terms of the Western alliance. Thanks to Churchill's latest opposition, the formally drawn-up Quebec agreements were now, effectively, defunct — and there were worse things to come.

Disagreement between the two nations' militaries was brewing over the disposition of U.S. and British military forces in Europe even *after* the war was won. Draft planning proposals, under the code-name Rankin, had been drawn up for the occupation of Germany and its satellite countries, if and when the Germans collapsed prior to Overlord taking place, or immediately after. These posited a division of Germany into three areas: north, south, and east. The President, leading the discussion, thought "Marshal Stalin might 'okay'" such a division," on behalf of the Soviet government: a carve-up in which the Russians would get to occupy all of Prussia, the very seedbed of German militarism. But the British had said they wanted the industrial and Atlantic northern sector of Germany, with the United States having to take the south, below the Moselle River. The President "said he did not like this arrangement. We do not want to be concerned with reconstituting France. France is a British 'baby,'" he told his chiefs. The United States "is not popular in France at the present time," he averred — in part because he had not licensed General de Gaulle to masquerade as an elected French leader before elections could actually take place, once France was liberated. "The British should have France, Luxembourg, Belgium, Baden, Bavaria and Wurtenburg," Mr. Roosevelt therefore argued. "The occupation of these places should be British. The United States should take northwest Germany. We can get our ships into such ports as Bremen and Hamburg, also Norway and Denmark, and we should go as far as Berlin. The Soviets could then take the territory to the east thereof." In his view, the "British plan for the United States to have southern Germany" was anathema, "and he (the President) didn't like it."[6]

The President might have to stomach it, however. As General Marshall pointed out aboard the *Iowa,* if Overlord went ahead — as they all hoped and prayed it would — the plan was for vast numbers of U.S. troops to be fed into France across the Normandy beaches and through floating harbors and French ports, *on the south side of the British.* And this for the simplest reason: namely that the staging areas for U.S. forces were to the southwest or right side of British forces in England. Having subsequently to reverse that communications axis would be a logistical nightmare.

Here was yet another example of the fortunes of war being dependent on geography and supply: the proverbial wagon train.

Military historians would later rue the fact that, in terms of striking across the Rhine into Germany, U.S. forces were located on the right-hand side of the slow and methodical British, rather than on their left. But the effort this redirection would entail, General Marshall pointed out — supported by Admiral King — was just too daunting to consider, however much the President railed against the British plan (even proposing that U.S. occupation forces be sent from the United States via Scotland, in order not to have to cross British lines of communication with the continent).

Such thoughts, in turn, led to the *political* headache the occupation of France would pose — for, as the President predicted, General de Gaulle would "be one mile behind the troops in taking over the government." Mr. Roosevelt therefore "felt that we should get out of France and Italy as soon as possible," once the countries were liberated, "letting the British and French handle their own problem together." There could well be civil war in France, given the ill-feeling between Gaullists and Vichyites, with savage scores to settle. Moreover, with regard to the German capital, if the Third Reich collapsed before, or soon after, the Overlord invasion, there "would definitely be a race for Berlin," Mr. Roosevelt predicted — in competition with the Russians. "We may have to put the United States divisions into Berlin as soon as possible," using Germany's excellent rail system. Ironically, occupying Germany would be a whole lot simpler than France; the "Germans are easier to handle than would be the French under the chaotic conditions that could be expected in France," Admiral Leahy — who had been the President's ambassador to Vichy until the spring of 1942 — opined.[7]

The President thought a million U.S. troops would be needed in Europe "for at least one year, maybe two," to keep order; but as U.S. president he disliked the notion of being "roped in" to any "European sphere of influence." As regards action to be taken on behalf of the United Nations by the "Four Policemen" after the war, there should be no question, he maintained, of using U.S. ground forces to settle "local squabbles in such a place as Yugoslavia. We could use the Army and Navy as an economic blockade and preclude ingress or egress to any area where disorder prevailed." There was even talk of a "buffer state" like Alsace-Lorraine between France and Germany.[8]

There was then talk of China and Korea; of Burma; of Formosa; of bases across the Far East; of the bombing of Japan; of a supreme commander in the Pacific (where currently Admiral Nimitz and General MacArthur commanded separate theaters); of Turkey and the Balkans; and of Churchill's notion of a "European economic federation" — each chief encouraged to voice his opinion.

None of this was of much significance, however, *unless the war against Hitler was won.* And as swiftly as possible. As General Marshall now emphasized, agreeing with the President, the Balkans were a dangerous decoy. Having been asked by the President to reexamine the implications of a Balkan strategy, the U.S. Army chief of staff was clarity itself. "We do not believe that the Balkans are necessary," Captain Royal quoted him saying. "To undertake operations in this region would result in prolonging the war and also lengthening the war in the Pacific. We have now over a million tons of supplies in England for Overlord. It would be going into reverse to undertake the Balkans," and it would "prolong the war materially. It would certainly reduce United States potentialities by two-thirds," he pointed out — adding that "commitments and preparations for Overlord extend as far as the Rocky Mountains in the United States. The British might like to 'ditch' Overlord at this time in order to undertake operations in a country with practically no communications," but for his part he was appalled by such faintheartedness, breach of faith, abrogation of a formal agreement, and deliberate strategic distraction — moreover one that was being pursued purely for British imperial interests. The bottom line was an American no.

"If they insist on any such proposal," Marshall went on, "we could say that if they propose to do that we will pull out and go into the Pacific with all our forces."[9]

A switch to the Pacific? Ironically this was exactly the American response that Churchill was threatening to trigger if he didn't get his way in the Mediterranean, as General Brooke was noting in his diary.[10] This "way" would be accompanied by fantastical Churchillian promises, the President and his chiefs of staff were well aware. The Prime Minister would undoubtedly claim, once in Cairo, that if the Allies moved fast the Danube could be made the key to Berlin. Soviet forces, after all, were now only forty miles from Bessarabia. If in the next two weeks they crossed the Bug River, they'd be "on the point of entering Rumania," the U.S. chiefs envisioned him saying. Churchill's argument would doubtless be that "if someone would now come up from the Adriatic to the Danube, we could readily defeat Germany forthwith."[11] What then?

Dealing with such Churchillian fantasies was, Marshall knew from experience, a constant scourge. For someone who was an experienced, educated soldier in his youth, Churchill had a sense of geography that was often flawed, and it was nothing short of amazing how little account he took of terrain — as well as Wehrmacht opposition, when German forces occupied high ground. Even if the Russians were to ask, at Tehran, for help in striking through Romania toward the Danube — which Marshall doubted — "we will have to be ready to explain to the Soviets the implications of any such move." Air force — i.e., bomber — help, yes; an American army, no. With Overlord only five months away, what was the point, moreover, of dreaming of such wild alternatives? A major Allied campaign in the mountainous Balkans could make projected casualties in Overlord look minuscule! The fact was: the only practical way to force the Germans to surrender unconditionally was to "force the issue from England," shattering the Wehrmacht between Western and Eastern Fronts — Hitler's nightmare. The important thing, in Marshall's view, was that the United States should not even ask the Russians what *they* might like, in terms of military help, whether in Bessarabia or Romania; after all, the war was not being conducted to help the Russians conquer eastern Europe. The U.S. delegation to Tehran should therefore "not bring up the matter of asking the Soviets for their plans until we are committed to our own plans."[12] American plans, pivoting on Overlord . . .

All agreed with General Marshall. But if the British wouldn't commit to Overlord in May?

The chiefs turned to their commander in chief, the President. All now rested upon him.

The task was clear: how to bring an unwilling British bride to the American altar. Only the President, as the bride's brother-in-arms, could get her to the church on time, so to speak, if the war against Hitler was to be won — in fact, if the Western military coalition was to be saved from being sundered by the British.

The next few days, they were all aware, would determine whether Mr. Roosevelt would be successful.

13

In the Footsteps of Scipio and Hannibal

AFTER ITS RACE through the Straits of Gibraltar by night, the USS *Iowa* safely disembarked its top-secret passengers at Mers-el-Kébir, the Mediterranean harbor outside Oran, early the next day, November 20, 1943.

Wearing his familiar cape and sporting his famed cigarette holder, the President was lifted into a motorized whaleboat hanging beneath davits over the deck of the battleship, and was lowered into the translucent waters of the Mediterranean. From there he was taken to the shore — to be greeted "on the dock" by his sons Elliott and Franklin Jr., as the President recorded happily in his new leather-bound diary.[1] And by General Eisenhower, too, in person. "Roosevelt weather!" the President shouted to Ike, as the first sun for several days illuminated the November waterfront.[2] "The sea voyage had done father good," Elliott recalled; "he looked fit; and he was filled with excited anticipation of the days ahead."[3]

From Oran the President was driven with General Eisenhower some fifty miles to La Sénia airport, "where we boarded a big C-54, commanded by my old pilot of Casablanca days, Maj. Otis Bryan," the President noted proudly in his diary. "Then a 3½ (hour) flight past Algiers to Tunis & we saw where much of the fighting took place. A drive took us through the ruins of Carthage (but of a Roman date) to my villa — the Casa Blanca — most apt!"[4]

Carthage was a sort of time capsule of ancient and modern empire. In the distance behind them rose the white-peaked caps of the Atlas Mountains. To the north shimmered the Gulf of Tunis and the blue of the Mediterranean.

Prior to General Eisenhower's tenure, guest villa no. 1 — Maison Blanche, or White House, as it was called — had, to the President's great amusement, formerly housed the Wehrmacht's commander in Tunisia. After lunching with his Joint Chiefs, the President reviewed almost three thousand men of Elliott's six-thousand-strong Northwest African Photographic Reconnaissance Wing at nearby La Marsa airfield. But he was equally curious to see the pre-Roman and Roman remains of Carthage and its surrounding region, if possible. Thus, when Eisenhower dissuaded him from flying the next morning to Cairo, as planned, in broad daylight — a flight which could be visually intercepted by enemy fighter aircraft, as Admiral Yamamoto's had been earlier that year in the Pacific — the President gladly agreed to delay his departure until night-time, on the understanding that Eisenhower would take him "on a personally conducted tour of the battlefields — ancient and modern."[5]

Eisenhower — a student of classical military history — was only too glad to oblige. Sunday afternoon, November 21, 1943, was thus spent in Eisenhower's armored Cadillac, driven by his British female driver, Kay Summersby, and escorted by a phalanx of U.S. Secret Service men in armored vehicles as the President and his Mediterranean theater commander in chief toured a Tunisian battlefield littered with the detritus of recent war, from burned-out tanks to antitank fortifications, and from temporary cemeteries to still-roped-off minefields.

In the presence of his son Franklin Jr., the President "grilled Ike closely, not only on the war that had been fought to a breakthrough by the Allies at Medjez-el-Bab" — where almost three thousand men lay buried, and the famed Hill 609, where American soldiers came of age — but also "on the wars that the Carthaginians had fought in antiquity," as Franklin Jr. related to his brother that night.[6] The President "seemed in good health and was optimistic and confident," Eisenhower himself recalled. "The President's liking for history and his frequent reference to it always gave an added flavor to conversation with him on military subjects."[7] There was, in short, no hint of illness or even fatigue.

As a great maritime empire, the President knew, Phoenicia had dominated the Mediterranean for centuries. The Punic Wars between the Carthaginians and the Greeks, and then the Romans, had led finally to a months-long, historic siege of Carthage — ending in a great naval as well as land assault on the fabled metropolis by Scipio in 146 BC. Thereafter, on the orders of the Roman Senate, Scipio had sacked and demolished the entire city, invoking a curse on anyone who should ever try to rebuild it — or build on it.

In light of the President's discussion of the future of Germany and Berlin with his chiefs of staff, Scipio's actions certainly seemed to have been a salutary example of unconditional enemy surrender. According to the Roman historian Livy, the Carthaginian commander, Hasdrubal, had begged for mercy before Scipio — much to the disgust of Hasdrubal's wife, who threw herself into the flames of a burning building with her children, while her captive husband was taken to Rome in chains to be displayed in Scipio's victory procession, the *triumphus,* along with thousands of chained Carthaginian prisoners, and the spoils of war. And now, several thousand years later, the same proximate city of Tunis had recently been captured from Axis forces in North Africa by the Western Allies, with no escape and after very heavy fighting — yielding on May 12, 1943, more than *a quarter million* Axis prisoners . . .

Berlin, however, was still more than a thousand miles away. Watching a flight of more than fifty U.S. Air Force medium bombers "returning from a tactical mission over the European Continent," the presidential party saw that "some of the 'V's' were not complete, indicating that this particular flight suffered combat losses," the log of the President's trip recorded.[8] There was, clearly, a lot more fighting to be done.

For his part, though, the President seemed visibly moved that, as chief executive and commander in chief of a growing global power, he'd been able to follow in the almost literal footsteps of past conquerors — humbled to be looking at what remained of earlier battlefields. "While traveling through them he speculated upon the possible identity of our battlefields with those of ancient days, particularly with that of Zama," about eighty miles from Tunis, Eisenhower afterwards recalled. There, in October 202 BC, Scipio Africanus, invading from Sicily, had routed the eighty war elephants and forty thousand men of Hannibal's army, using his Roman cavalry and infantry. "So far as either the President or I knew, that battlefield had never been identified by historians, but we were certain, because of the use of elephants by the Carthaginians, that it was located on the level plains rather than in the mountains, where so much of our own fighting," such as Kasserine, took place."[9] Eisenhower therewith recounted for the President the "late battle, the terrain, difficulties encountered, and some of the command personalities"[10] as, in the back of the armored Cadillac, they toured the ground.

Kay Summersby, Eisenhower's driver, found herself starstruck by Mr. Roosevelt, who called her "child," and insisted she dine with him and her boss that evening, before he boarded his plane for the onward journey to Cairo. She was impressed by the President's genuine curiosity — not just about ancient history, but about people. "Child, won't you come here and have lunch with a dull old man?" he'd asked as they sat under a grove of trees, halfway across the battlefield, to enjoy a chicken-sandwich picnic — the sandwiches passed to the President, under the awning, by General Eisenhower. She later wrote she'd "felt as though I had known this vibrant man all my life, as though he were a distant uncle I hadn't seen since babyhood. Mr. Roosevelt had that enviable touch of natural intimacy," she described. He "asked all about my family, about England," as well as posing "keen questions about the role of British women in the war, queries about factory workers, service girls, air raid wardens, and bus 'clippies.'" And "life along the Mediterranean," as she'd experienced it during combat.[11]

How different this was from her meetings with Winston Churchill, who, as his doctor noted, "is not interested in people and cannot follow their thoughts,"

Dr. Wilson reflected in his own diary, as he accompanied the Prime Minister aboard his battleship and ashore at Malta, en route to Cairo. Churchill certainly "likes talking," Dr. Wilson recorded, but was, at best, "an indifferent listener" — one who "has visited nearly all the battlefields and . . . can pick out, in a particular battle, the decisive move that turned the day. But he has never given a thought to what was happening in the soldier's mind, and he has not tried to share his fears. If a soldier does not do his duty, the P.M. says he ought to be shot. It is as simple as that."[12]

14

Two Pieces in a Chess Game

FOR THE PRESIDENT'S military advisers the looming clash with the British was worrying. It also troubled General Eisenhower, for reasons both military and personal.

As Eisenhower explained to the President as they toured the Carthaginian battlefields, he'd been summoned to confer in person with the Prime Minister at Malta on November 18. Before flying there, however, he'd gained some idea of what might be afoot, from Lieutenant General Walter Bedell Smith. Smith had warned his boss that Churchill was spoiling for a fight in Cairo. Eisenhower's strategy of fighting in Italy to tie down German forces so that Overlord would face less opposition was, under Churchill's proposed new plan, to be abandoned in favor of a wild new British strategy in the Mediterranean, Aegean, and Balkans.

Smith's prediction of the impending conference at Cairo being the "hottest one yet" therefore had profound personal implications for General Eisenhower. Ike, as he was known to all, had already been informed by the U.S. Navy secretary, Frank Knox, during Knox's recent visit to the theater, that he would undoubtedly be recalled to Washington to replace General Marshall as U.S. Army chief of staff, once Marshall was appointed to the supreme command of Overlord — for the British would undoubtedly insist on the enlarged Mediterranean command being given to a Brit. This was far from a happy thought for Eisenhower. Not only was he loath to leave an active theater of war, but the top Pentagon post was not one, given his relatively junior status in the U.S. Army hierarchy, that he'd ever coveted or in which he would feel comfortable.

Mr. Churchill had made no bones about the new strategy he was going to fight for in Cairo, Eisenhower now told the President. The Prime Minister had said he was looking "forward with great enthusiasm to his meeting with the President, from whom, he said, he always drew inspiration for tackling the problems of war and of the later peace," Eisenhower later recalled. Such rhetoric was, however, an example of the Prime Minister's manner of first circling his prey — a polite preamble before explaining the reason he'd summoned Eisenhower to Malta: namely to press upon the hapless American theater commander the need to postpone or abandon Overlord. The Prime Minister had thus moved on to address "at length," as Eisenhower remembered several years later, "one of his favorite subjects — the importance of assailing Germany through the 'soft underbelly,' of keeping up the tempo of our Italian attack and extending its scope to include much of the northern shore of the Mediterranean" — the Balkans. "He seemed always to see great and decisive possibilities in the Mediterranean, while the project of invasion across the English Channel left him cold."[1]

The President had listened carefully to Eisenhower's report. A casual visitor might have assumed that the President, a charming and genial conversationalist, was merely putting his subordinate at ease. However, most always the President's conversation had a deeper motive. The time he spent traveling with Eisenhower and inspecting the ruins of Carthage certainly proved no exception. In reviewing Eisenhower's conversation and his bearing the President was surreptitiously measuring how well he thought the general would do in the role of U.S. Army chief of staff back in Washington. Or, alternatively, as Allied supreme commander of Overlord. Or even Overlord *and* the Mediterranean — "all Europe" — if the British would agree to this. And how well Ike could handle Churchill.

Would the British agree to the combination of the two theaters, north and south, in Eisenhower's opinion? the President had asked.

Eisenhower had confirmed they probably wouldn't agree to such an expanded supreme command. In fact at Malta Churchill had stated categorically it wasn't an option. The cross-Channel invasion and the Mediterranean *must*, Churchill had emphasized, remain separate entities, separate theaters. The Prime Minister had loyally accepted, he said — though with great embarrassment, given that he had initially promised the job to General Brooke[2] — the President's recent decision, in mid-August that year, that the supreme command of Overlord go to an American officer. Moreover he'd welcomed, he'd said to Ike, the choice of General Marshall for the post, which would ensure Overlord be backed by "an abundance of American power" — and that Britain would therefore not have to shoulder the majority of casualties in the assault. However as prime minister of Great Britain Mr. Churchill had made equally clear he would not be willing to accept an American as supreme commander of *both* theaters combined. Nor would he even accept Eisenhower remaining as commander in chief in the Mediterranean. "I'm sure you will realize, my dear General, that we are quite happy with you," Churchill had stated, "but it would obviously be unfair to us [British] to be foreclosed from both major commands in Europe."[3]

The President had had cause to wince at this — certain that, once Marshall was appointed to supreme command in Britain, Winston would do everything in his power to downplay or delay Overlord, via a British supreme commander in the Mediterranean: promoting yet more audacious southern schemes. These would involve, it seemed, a new invasion of Rhodes, and even Crete — just when they were about to meet Stalin and ought to be presenting a unified commitment to Overlord and the Second Front to be launched in the coming spring!

It was important, though, President Roosevelt was aware, not to lose sight of the positive side of the equation.

"Ike, if one year ago you had offered to bet that on this day the President of the United States would be having his lunch on a Tunisian roadside, what odds could you have demanded?" the President had said with a typical smile during the picnic near Carthage — and the "thought apparently directed his mind to the extraordinary events of the year just past," Eisenhower vividly recalled. "He told me, first, what a disappointment it had been to him that our African invasion came just after, instead of just before, the 1942 elections" — leaving him with a somewhat contrarian Congress to deal with. "He spoke of Darlan, of Boisson and Giraud. He talked of Italy and Mussolini and of the uneasiness he had felt during the Kasserine affair. He told of instances of disagreement with Mr. Churchill, but earnestly and almost emotionally said: 'No one could have a better or sturdier ally than the old Tory!'"[4]

Compared with French leaders at the time, Winston Churchill had certainly been sturdier. But what would happen if Churchill now gained full control of the Mediterranean and Aegean, via a British supreme commander? If Turkey were to join the United Nations struggle against Hitler, "it would result in drawing away support from other operations," as Admiral King and General Marshall had pointed out on board the *Iowa*[5] — turning Turkish requirements into a veritable sump, draining the Allies of significant military resources. Who could say what schemes Churchill would then seek to perpetrate, via General Alexander as his stooge — schemes that would, inevitably, have to be bailed out by the application of yet more American forces once they met serious resistance, leading inevitably to even *more* delay in mounting Overlord?

Alongside the matter of Churchill's impending insurrection, as the President had been driven around the recent Tunisian battlefield, was also the matter of Eisenhower himself. Would Ike, given his relative youth, be able to prevail in the topmost U.S. Army and Air Force hierarchy, if moved back to Washington? He would have nine million soldiers and airmen under his umbrella. But in the weekly meetings of the Joint Chiefs of Staff, how would he be able to handle his exalted older colleagues — especially "Blowtorch" Admiral King?

Certainly, Eisenhower could bring modern battle–experience and a coalition perspective to the U.S. Army and Navy Departments in Washington, the

President could imagine. Studying the young commander in chief, the President could see, moreover, that Eisenhower was, in his genial, friendly way, not unlike himself. Despite his relative youth Eisenhower stood out as a team leader, at once highly intelligent and energetic, a man whose agreeable personality drew people — especially allies — to serve him, not oppose him. In coalition warfare, as in coalition politics, such a man was indispensable; why, then, incarcerate him with fellow American chiefs of staff in Washington, when he could instead be marshaling the disparate Allied coalition forces on the battlefield, leading to the defeat of Hitler in Europe?

As if to voice such second thoughts the President had proceeded to rehearse with Eisenhower, on the historic battlefield, the reasons George Marshall deserved the Overlord post. A post which he had confirmed would go to Marshall, as recorded aboard the *Iowa*.[6] As Eisenhower recalled, "The President spoke briefly to me about the future Overlord commander and I came to realize, finally, that it was a point of intense official and public interest back home."[7]

Eisenhower might be embarrassed, but he was relieved the matter of Overlord's commander was now at least in the open. Admiral King, the night before, had said he would welcome Ike as a new colleague on the Joint Chiefs of Staff Committee — if that was what the President, as commander in chief, so decided. King had made quite clear, nevertheless, that in his view it would be a mistake.

"We now have a winning combination. Why do we want to make a radical change?" King had asked aloud, in front of both Marshall and Eisenhower. "Each of us knows his own role; each of us has learned how to work with the others. Why doesn't the President send you up to Overlord and keep General Marshall in Washington?" Eisenhower recalled Admiral King's words. "'Marshall is the truly indispensable man of this war; Congress and the public trust him, the President trusts him, his associates in the Combined Chiefs of Staff trust him and the Commanders in the field trust him. Why do we change?' He then said that General Arnold, commanding the United States Army Air Forces, as well as a number of others agreed with him."[8]

General Marshall, although present at the discussion, had declined to comment on such "future command arrangements," however — contenting himself with the prim comment that the "President has to make his own decisions. I shall personally have nothing to do with it."[9]

Marshall's refusal to state either a personal opinion or a military view on the matter bespoke his upright, deeply principled character. He could not bear the idea of being accused of putting ambition before country.

Dwight Eisenhower, who admired General Marshall deeply and owed his promotions of the past several years to the U.S. Army chief of staff, had nevertheless been incredulous the general would not be willing to advise the U.S. Commander in Chief as to the pros and cons of such a vital appointment — despite being one of the President's chief military advisers. As Eisenhower later noted in his unpublished memoir, the President's "problem" in Carthage was not simply the looming insurrection of the British, or the command appointment for Overlord that needed to be made, urgently, if the crucial operation was to succeed. It was also the problem of George Marshall himself! "Marshall's sense of duty," Eisenhower later reflected, "was such that he refused even to hint at a preference concerning a future assignment, either to his friends or his superior."[10]

This was, to be sure, of little help to the President, who felt honor-bound to stand by his commitment to make Marshall the supreme Allied commander, but had no idea where Marshall's own wishes or preference lay. George Marshall was, after all, the principal backer and longtime architect of the operation — which would very likely determine the outcome of the war in Europe, for good or ill: victory or defeat. "I just do not know," the President had thus confided to Eisenhower, "what Marshall would like to do because he will not tell me." As president, Mr. Roosevelt would hate to lose the tall, proud, upright Virginian from the Pentagon, "but of one thing I am sure, in military history it is only the name of Field Commanders that are remembered, not that of a Chief of Staff, even though he be the official superior," Eisenhower quoted him.[11] And to illustrate his point the President had said: "You and I know the name of the Chief of Staff in the Civil War [Henry Halleck], but few Americans outside the professional services do." Despite this, as Eisenhower recalled, the President had added "as if thinking aloud: But it is dangerous to monkey with a winning team."[12]

Clearly the President was of two minds — leaving Eisenhower in something of a bind. "I answered nothing," Eisenhower afterwards recorded, "except to state that I would do my best wherever the government might find use for me."[13]

The President had good reasons, however, for holding off on a decision. So long as General Eisenhower remained Allied commander in chief in the Mediterranean, there was no way Churchill could go ahead with crazy capers, or bend Eisenhower to a different strategy from that which had been agreed and formally confirmed by the Combined Chiefs of Staff at Quebec in August. Moreover, what advantage would there be in the President appointing, at this juncture, General Marshall to be supreme commander of an invasion the British were seeking to delay or abandon? Why lose Marshall's great prestige, authority, and advice in Washington for an operation that, if the British had their way, might never take place? Ergo, as Admiral Leahy had argued on the *Iowa*, General Eisenhower should stay as Allied commander in chief in the Mediter-

ranean for as long as it took to get the primacy of the Overlord invasion reestablished, if necessary through a supreme commander for all Europe.[14]

For Eisenhower the wait would be interminable — indeed in his unpublished memoirs he confessed that he "could not escape the feeling that both
Marshall and I were something like two pieces in a chess game, each compelled to await the pleasure of the Players."[15]

In his diary the President would note how the fields around Carthage con-
tained "many tanks & trucks destroyed by gun-fire & much barbed wire," as
well as "many little cemeteries" — and how different this was to his tour of
battlefields in "France in 1918," when he'd been assistant secretary of the Navy.
Not only the terrain but also the technology and combination of all arms were
reflective, he'd seen, of a new kind of "open warfare," one that was "over in a
very short time in comparison."[16] Overlord, he hoped, would be the same:
applying massive air power in support of the infantry and armored troops of
coalition armies, led by an American, as they relentlessly advanced, and finally
made for Berlin.

Back at the White House in Carthage the President, meantime, bade Eisenhower farewell — thanking the young general for taking the time to look after
him since his arrival in North Africa. "Father was beaming by the time they
got back to the villa," Elliott later recalled — as well as recalling how, according to his brother Franklin Jr., the President, as a seasoned jester, had played
a trick on Ike. The President had put a "restraining hand on his arm," before
Eisenhower departed, telling him he was afraid he was "going to have to do
something to you that you won't like."[17]

Eisenhower had been as mystified as was Franklin Jr. "What was it," the
President's son had wondered to himself. "Calling him [Ike] from his theater
command? Or sarcasm: promoting him on the spot to some new and bigger
command?"[18]

Instead, according to Franklin Jr., it was merely a prelude to the President
telling Eisenhower he might need Ike's naval aide, Lieutenant Commander
Butcher, to help run the government's Office of War Information back in
Washington, when Elmer Davis relinquished the post.

Eisenhower was hugely relieved — assuring the President that would be
fine.

The President then disappeared into Casa Blanca for a last brief supper before flying overnight to Cairo.

Against all blandishments by his father, Franklin Roosevelt Jr. refused to
accompany him to the Egyptian capital. Instead he insisted on returning to his
battle-damaged destroyer, which had to be sailed back to the United States for
repairs. The President therefore ate briefly with just his son Elliott, Admiral

Leahy, and his immediate staff. Then at 10:00 p.m., November 21, 1943, he was driven to El Aouina airport to board, once again, the "Sacred Cow," as the big Douglas C-54 was affectionately termed: Air Transport plane No. 950, piloted by Major Otis Bryan.

As president, Mr. Roosevelt was entitled to one of the two special bunks that had been built at the back of the airplane. White House counselor Harry Hopkins — so gaunt that Eisenhower's driver, Kay Summersby, wondered "just how he remained alive"[19] — occupied the other bunk for the overnight flight. The rest would have to make do in their seats.

Without a bed for the nearly two-thousand-mile journey,[20] Admiral Leahy —"dour and quiet," in Elliott's description[21] — resigned himself to a long and fitful night. In his diary the aging former chief of U.S. naval operations would permit himself only a laconic entry, namely that he was "looking forward to a very busy and to a probably very controversial visit in Cairo."[22]

PART TWO

Stonewall Roosevelt

15

Airy Visions

IN BERLIN THE REICHSMINISTER for Propaganda had been tracking the latest press reports from England.

Since the fall of Mussolini and the surrender of Italy to the Allies it had become increasingly clear the Third Reich's best hope of ultimate survival would be a negotiated peace or armistice — either with the Soviets or with the Western Allies. The latter seemed to Goebbels quite doable, thanks to the fine defensive performance of the Wehrmacht in southern Italy and the brilliance with which German forces had rubbed out British attempts to seize Rhodes, Kos, Samos, and now Leros. Press reports from London, moreover, had suggested growing strains in the once-watertight alliance between the United States and Great Britain.

Churchill's speech at the Mansion House in London, before departing for Cairo, had caused Dr. Goebbels to wonder what exactly might be percolating in the highest echelons of Allied war-making — in fact whether the British were getting cold feet over the long-promised cross-Channel invasion. They seemed more worried, in particular, about their colonies. The British prime minister had extolled Russian successes on the Eastern Front, but with regard to British interests had repeated that, as he'd declared the year before, he "did not consider it any part of my duty to liquidate the British Empire" once the war was won. "I do not conceal from you that I hold the same opinion today," Churchill had stated, openly reaffirming his stance that, in terms of the Atlantic Charter and the postwar "Four-Power Agreement" of the United Nations, just agreed at the conference of foreign ministers in Moscow, his aim would only be to provide "food, work, homes" for the British people. He would not, he'd declared before Parliament, get embroiled in "airy visions" or follow "party doctrines" or "party prejudices" or feed "political appetites" or seek to satisfy "vested interests." The war had still to be won, he'd said — and it wouldn't be easy. Churchill had also sounded worried about Hitler's warning of *Vergeltungswaffen,* or weapons of revenge, that would "certainly call for the utmost efficiency and devotion in our firewatchers and Home Guard," as well as require the "fortitude for which the British nation has won renown." In referring to British efforts in the coming phase of the war he had given nothing away, however, save to say "1944 will see the greatest sacrifice of life by the British armies, and battles far larger and more costly than Waterloo or Gettysburg."[1]

At the end of his speech Churchill had openly appealed for unity between the partners in the Allied coalition, and among their loyal supporters in the press and in ordinary homes. The "good will that now exists throughout the English-speaking world" should be used "to aid our armies in their grim and heavy task. Even if things are said in one country or the other which are untrue, which are provocative, which are clumsy, which are indiscreet, or even malicious, let them be stated without heat or bitterness. We have to give our men in the field the best chance. That is the thought," he'd declared, "which must dominate all speech and action."[2]

In reading the transcript of Churchill's speech, Goebbels had been intrigued. By a huge majority the United States Senate had, on November 5, passed the Connally Resolution, recording Congress's determination to pursue the war "until complete victory is achieved." Congress had, moreover, given full Senate support to "the necessity of there being established at the earliest practicable date a general organization, based on the sovereign equality of all peace-loving states, and open to membership by all such states, large and small, for the maintenance of international peace and security": a United Nations authority.[3]

There seemed, therefore, to be a growing disconnect between British and American attitudes to the war. "In [U.S] government circles the isolationists will clearly be only an insignificant minority in the foreseeable future," Goebbels had reluctantly noted[4] — but in England the opposite appeared to be the case: a rejection of "airy visions." Churchill's latest objection to possible decolonization policies — the "liquidation" of the British Empire — was evidence, perhaps, of a kind of "last-stand" imperial mentality in England. The British military fiasco in the Aegean and the Führer's latest threats to use revenge weapons, in response to the carpet bombing of German cities, were clearly prompting much soul-searching in London, Dr. Goebbels could see.

Here, surely, there was a chance for Germany to exploit the difference between the two English-speaking allies: a split that seemed to be widening, according to newspaper articles in Britain, concerning the conduct and strategy of the war itself. Churchill's appeal for unity in England was surely a sign of this — in fact the wily Goebbels detected a potential propaganda lever he might use, if the Führer agreed. From German intelligence there was as yet no actual evidence of strategic disagreement at the highest levels, behind the scenes, but that did not mean it wasn't happening. It was certainly happening in print. "As far as the Second Front is concerned, the English are doing their best to shift the weight of the war onto the Americans," Goebbels reflected.

The British were getting cold feet. "Their press is full of reports and statistical demonstrations to the effect that the country is simply not able to face the sacrifice in blood of a Second Front. Having got numerous European countries to shed their blood, the English, ruled by the wealthy, would now like to make the Americans take the heat, so that as far as possible the English themselves will end the war with their population intact. But the Americans won't let themselves be taken for such a ride."[5]

In his demonic, endlessly exploitative way, the Reichsminister remained a discerning analyst. The British were, it seemed to him, losing heart. The recent surrender of the last British forces on Leros had only intensified, in Goebbels's account, the recognition in Britain that Germany was by no means beaten — and that a cross-Channel invasion could be suicidal.[6] This would make the English more than ever dependent on Stalin, the communist "mass-murderer," to fight Germany, while the British watched out for themselves and their empire.

News that Churchill and the President were on their way to Cairo — to be joined there by Stalin, it was presumed[7] — thus stunned Goebbels. To his chagrin it suggested that, far from being riven by "malicious" tongues and disagreement, the Allied leaders were, in fact, united in their determination to demand the unconditional surrender of Nazi Germany.

16

The American Sphinx

A LIFELONG, PASSIONATE PHILATELIST, Franklin Roosevelt had always been enamored of geography. As soon as they were airborne over Tunis he'd gone to bed in the rear of the Sacred Cow, but had asked to be wakened early, in order to see the sun rise over Cairo as they came in from the Mediterranean.

Once awake, however, the President had asked Major Bryan whether, as pilot, he could turn the plane first south, over the Egyptian desert, and reach the Nile at a higher point. From there the pilot could bank north, and follow the river's twisting course so that they might see the fabled waterway in the dawn light as it reached the ancient city of Cairo — and the pyramids.

Major Bryan had said yes. A new course had therefore been set. Until then they had followed the long Mediterranean shore, in the dark, but now, reaching the Egyptian border, the pilot banked right, flew south, then east across the arid desert until they reached the famous river, then swung north.

As the day began to break on November 22, 1943, the Sacred Cow followed the snaking course of the Nile — the President treated to a magical approach to the Egyptian capital as the plane swooped low over ancient-looking felucca boats, rigged with lateen sails. For Roosevelt, whose love of sailing went back to his childhood, the picture was breathtaking. "We came in the 'back way,'" the President recorded in his diary, "so as to avoid German planes & from the desert saw the Nile 100 miles So.[uth] of Cairo — an amazing scene — & followed the narrow belt of fertile fields, with many villages, until we came to the great pyramids."[1]

They were in no hurry. "Otis Bryan circled the plane constantly to give the Boss a good view," the White House security chief, Mike Reilly, recalled — recording as well the President's somewhat sad remark, looking down at the pyramids: "Man's desire to be remembered is colossal."[2]

In Egypt, due to strict radio silence, the President's decision to take his own romantic route to the capital had caused something of a "flap," however. "Our unreportable sight-seeing jaunt set the Cairo air headquarters on its ear," Reilly recalled, enjoying in retrospect the idea of the anxiety it had caused the British. It was a good two and a half hours after "plane number two of our party had arrived from Tunis" before the Sacred Cow finally touched down in Egyptian pastures — there to find its late arrival had "caused some concern at the field as to the President's safety. Two different groups of fighter-planes had been at the appointed rendez-vous at the scheduled times but each failed to make contact and eventually had to return to their base for refueling."[3]

The relief of the airfield staff was palpable. From RAF Cairo West the President was driven by limousine straight to the personal residence of the U.S. minister to Egypt, Alexander Kirk, where it had been arranged that Mr. Roosevelt would stay. It was "7 m[iles] from Cairo — very comfortable," the President jotted in his diary — and with regard to the pyramids was wonderfully "close to them," he added, happily.[4]

Prime Minister Churchill had arrived two days before, and was nearby, in a similar villa, as was Generalissimo Chiang Kai-shek, who also arrived that morning. Near the pyramids was the Mena House Hotel, almost a mile away — the whole area reminding participants and visitors of the complex of buildings and villas in which they'd gathered at Casablanca, Morocco, earlier that year. "As at Anfa, the whole area is surrounded by barbed-wire fences, guards, guns, tanks, etc.," Harold Macmillan noted in his diary. "Owing to the leakage in the *Daily Mail* and elsewhere, the security arrangements are fantastic. It is impossible to move anywhere near the 'great' without passing two or three barriers and showing innumerable 'passes.' The military conferences, etc., take place in the hotel (as at Anfa) — the secretariat and the officers (other than the highest who are in villas) are lodged there."[5]

The President's Filipino cooks and stewards had followed from Oran, and at the Kirk villa, as it was called, they prepared all the President's meals. The house was "of medium size and is beautifully furnished," Lieutenant Rigdon recorded in the President's log. "It also has a lovely flower garden in the rear with an overlooking patio," where Mr. Roosevelt could spend his "leisure moments" — assuming there were any.[6] Determined that the President be spared "gippy tummy" — a common stomach complaint in Egypt — large amounts of bottled water, milk, and even a Thanksgiving turkey were unloaded, while other supplies were kept ready for the onward flight to Tehran, if the President opted to fly there, over the northern Iranian mountains.

The President's doctor, Admiral McIntire, was against the idea, in view of the President's cardiac history, his relatively high blood pressure, and the medical dangers of high-altitude flying. There was also the possibility of enemy interception, or mechanical malfunction; Major Bryan was thus asked to fly to Tehran and back ahead of the President's trip, taking Agent Mike Reilly with him to check out security conditions when they reached the Iranian capital.[7]

In the meantime Ambassador Averell Harriman had come straight to see the President on his arrival in Cairo, at 10:30 that morning — bringing the latest news from Moscow. The summit in Tehran would start on November 27, in five days' time.

The President was relieved. Five days, though! Aware that Churchill and his team would be armed with countless arguments for a new military strategy, Roosevelt first lunched, then donned his metaphorical armor to meet the Generalissimo, the bewitching Mrs. Chiang, and Mr. Churchill and Churchill's daughter Sarah, who was accompanying the Prime Minister. A kind of benevolent bonhomie would be the President's approach — similar to the "extreme hospitality" that had worked so well in putting down Churchill's attempted insurrection back in May, that year, when Churchill had arrived in Washington with 160 advisers and staff to argue against the notion of a Second Front.[8] He would simply not allow himself or his team to be provoked or enticed into any major confrontation before meeting the Russian "Tsar" in Tehran. Instead, as agreed aboard the *Iowa,* they would simply stonewall.

Harriman, for his part, confirmed his earlier cables from Moscow: namely that Marshal Stalin was counting on Overlord. Any notion the British were spreading that the Russians would prefer Allied operations in the Mediterranean in order to draw Wehrmacht forces away from the Eastern Front were false. Stalin was, Harriman reported, as suspicious of Allied Aegean and Balkan diversions that would delay a Second Front as was the President — and in Ambassador Harriman's view Stalin would happily act as the President's "enforcer" in Tehran. In a three-person summit where Churchill would be in the minority, the President calculated, the British would *have to* back down.

If this sounded unkind or underhanded toward the British, it was. It was nevertheless better than permitting a breakdown in the Anglo-American military coalition, even before they got to Tehran. The plan had to be carried out, then, whatever taste of deceit it might leave. It meant keeping Generalissimo Chiang Kai-shek and Mrs. Chiang at hand while dealing with Churchill over the next several days. As the President noted almost facetiously in his diary that night, "This p.m. the Prime Minister & his daughter Sara [sic] and the Chiangs came to call. Then we drove out to see the Pyramids & my old friend the Sphinx. We all dined (not the Sphynx) at my villa."[9]

For Churchill, who had spent so many days penning his indictment of American strategy and operations, the President's obvious attempts at diversion were galling. Yet without such a strategy, the President was aware, the war against Hitler might still be lost.

17

Churchill's "Indictment"

CODE-NAMED SEXTANT, the Cairo Conference, prior to Tehran, would now prove for Churchill one of the most frustrating experiences of the entire war — as it would for his entourage, few of whom appeared to understand the President's maneuver.

As Dr. Wilson had observed, Churchill had spent considerable time working on his formal censure of Allied strategy on the journey from England,[1] to be delivered as a grand "indictment of our mismanagement of our operations in the Mediterranean" before a full plenary session of the Chinese, American, and British leaders and their chiefs of staff. "The shadow of 'Overlord,'" as the Prime Minister had written, ominously,[2] haunted them all — and for this shadow he proposed to blame the American chiefs. The military policy laid down at Quebec had been maintained by the Allies "with inflexible rigidity and without regard to the loss and injury to the allied cause thereby," as he'd put it in the latest draft he'd drawn up in Alexandria's harbor, on his arrival there on November 20, before the President reached Egypt. The "fixed date" for Overlord "will continue to wreck and ruin the Mediterranean campaign," he complained, moreover would doom "our affairs" in "the Balkans," and leave the Aegean islands "in German hands." It was "common knowledge in the Armies that the [Mediterranean] theater is to be bled as much as necessary for the sake of an operation elsewhere in the Spring": Overlord.[3] He therefore wanted all further movement of British troops from the Mediterranean to England to be stopped,[4] and told his British chiefs of staff he wanted "the capture of Rome" at the beginning of January and also "the capture of Rhodes at the end" of that month: January 1944.[5]

General Brooke — though he largely agreed with the Prime Minister regarding the chances of Overlord being a potential disaster — found himself deeply worried. "I wish our conference was over," he'd penned in his own diary on arrival in Cairo, before the conference even began. "It will be a most unpleasant one, the most unpleasant one we have had yet, and that is saying a great deal. I despair of ever getting our American friends to have any sort of strategic vision. Their drag on us has seriously affected our Mediterranean strategy and the whole conduct of the war. If they had come wholeheartedly into the Mediterranean with us we should by now have Rome securely, the Balkans would be ablaze, the Dardanelles would be open, and we should be over the high way to getting Rumania and Bulgaria out of the war."[6] He blamed himself for not having resigned his post rather than "compromise," yet he was too sensible not to realize the risks the Prime Minister and the British team were taking in demanding a change of strategy at such a late date, only five months before Overlord — and a few days before the Tehran Conference began. The next day, he noted, the "PM kept us up till after 1 am. He was in a very excitable mood, I am not happy at the line he proposes to take in approaching the conference."[7]

The President, however, seemed to handle Churchill with his customary charm on November 22 — prompting Churchill to tell Brooke he was "very pleased with results of his talks with the President, and thinks we shall not have so very much difficulty. Personally, I doubt this," Brooke added that night.[8]

Neither Churchill nor Brooke seemed to recognize what the President was up to, at the time. Or even afterwards. Writing a decade later, when annotating his diary for partial publication, Brooke would complain that the "whole conference had been thrown out of gear by Chiang Kai-shek arriving here too soon. We should *never* have started our conference with Chiang; by doing so we were putting the cart before the horse. He had nothing to contribute towards the defeat of the Germans . . . Why the Americans attached such importance to Chiang I have never discovered."[9]

Even Churchill's shrewd military chief of staff, General Ismay, was no wiser. For his part he would later lament how, thanks to whole days spent discussing China and the Southeast Asian theater with Chiang Kai-shek, as well as with Admiral Louis Mountbatten, the Allied supreme commander in Southeast Asia, and General Joseph Stilwell, Chiang's American chief of staff, there was little or "no time left to reach agreement as to the exact line which should be taken with the Russians about a Second Front in Europe."[10]

"We should have started this conference by thrashing out thoroughly with the Americans the policy and strategy for the defeat of Germany. We could then have shown a united front to Stalin," Brooke bemoaned in retrospect — ignoring the fact that "the policy and strategy" had already been thrashed out at Quebec.[11] Churchill, though, was of like mind. As he later narrated, what he'd feared on hearing the Chinese generalissimo would arrive in Cairo *before* the Tehran summit, instead of afterwards, "now in fact occurred. The talks of the British and American Staffs were sadly distracted by the Chinese story, which was lengthy, complicated, and minor." The President, to Churchill's chagrin, "was soon closeted in long conferences with the Generalissimo. All hope of persuading Chiang and his wife to go and see the Pyramids and enjoy themselves till we returned from Teheran fell to the ground, with the result that Chinese business occupied first instead of last place at Cairo."[12]

Thus had commenced Franklin Roosevelt's most devious ruse of the war. As the President explained to his son Elliott, who arrived on the afternoon of November 23 — day two of the President's stay in Cairo — "Believe it or not, Elliott, the British are raising questions and doubts again about that western front."[13]

"About OVERLORD?" Elliott responded, amazed. "But I thought that was all settled at Quebec!"[14]

"So did we all," Roosevelt sighed — satisfied, at least, that General Marshall would keep the British at bay in the Combined Chiefs of Staff meetings. These, the President had insisted, must be confined for the moment to the topics of China and Southeast Asia, to prevent the British from tabling a change of Overlord strategy before they all left for Tehran.[15]

To Elliott the President also confided his recognition that Chiang Kai-shek was not fighting the Japanese with much determination, and was not really interested in using Chinese forces to liberate Burma. Why should he, after all, when it was ultimately the British who would then seek to recolonize the country? "Chiang's troops aren't fighting at all — despite the reports that get printed in the papers," the President shared his personal view. "He claims his troops aren't trained, and have no equipment — and that's easy to believe. But it doesn't explain why he's been trying so hard to keep Stilwell from training Chinese troops. And it doesn't explain why he keeps thousands and thousands of his best men up in the northwest — up on the borders of Red China,"[16] where Mao Tse-tung's communist Chinese troops were located.

Political considerations were thus part and parcel of deciding military strategy now, the President accepted. Churchill was seeking to preserve the British Empire and the troops to police it, from Palestine to India and Hong Kong; Chiang was preparing to reopen his civil war with Mao's forces. FDR alone had his eye on the prize. Without Overlord how could the Third Reich be defeated? Only if the Wehrmacht were to be forced to fight hard on two fronts, east and west, could Hitler be crushed.

In an attempt to gain better insight into Churchill's thinking the President had also asked the U.S. ambassador to London, Guy Winant, to come to Cairo. Winant had traveled with Churchill's party. He duly explained to the President how Churchill had gone around London claiming it was Stalin himself who wanted more operations in the Mediterranean, rather than a spring Overlord: the Prime Minister claiming "that Marshal Stalin is chiefly interested at the present moment in stretching German resources and his interest in a second front was not nearly so great as it had been."[17] This simply did not square, however, with what Ambassador Harriman was reporting from his dealings with Stalin in Moscow—another reason for waiting to hear from Stalin's lips, as commander in chief of the Soviet Armies, what was the truth.

In the meantime it was crucial for the Western alliance that there be no meltdown in Cairo. For all that the President had asked his chiefs to keep their cool, tempers in the Combined Chiefs of Staff meetings had quickly become frayed. In discussing Admiral Mountbatten's plans for an amphibious attack on the Andaman Islands as Allied supreme commander in Southeast Asia, for example, the Combined Chiefs of Staff almost came to fisticuffs. General Brooke—skeptical, he claimed, of the project's feasibility—had suddenly suggested that the U.S. landing craft would be better used in a renewed amphibious invasion of Rhodes and the Aegean islands. This suggestion really scattered the pigeons, the President afterwards heard. "Became quite open with all cards on the table, face up at times," General Arnold recorded in his journal.[18] General Stilwell, in his own diary, was blunter. "Brooke got nasty and King got good and sore," he recorded. "King almost climbed over the table at Brooke. God, was he mad. I wished he had socked him."[19]

Churchill's military chief of staff, General Ismay, was of little help in reporting the Combined Chiefs' discussions to his prime minister. Like many staff officers, the affable and rotund Ismay tended to tell his boss what he thought the Prime Minister wanted to hear, rather than the truth. Thus the British team, forced to spend the first days of the conference considering strategy in China and Southeast Asia rather than the Mediterranean, tried desperately to link the two—refusing to back any projected operations in the Far East that might take away from the Prime Minister's intended operations in the Aegean and Mediterranean, despite knowing these had *not* been agreed by the Combined Chiefs of Staff, and that such arguments were infuriating their American counterparts.

By day three of the conference, however, the President's policy of patient stonewalling could be extended no further. At 11:00 on the morning of November 24, the second plenary session began, under the President's chairmanship—and Winston Churchill was finally able to read out his "indictment." It was the Prime Minister's chance to have his threatened showdown, in the President's villa.

18

Showdown

THE PRESIDENT OPENED the session in his most friendly and avuncular way by saying that, having discussed China and the Southeast Asian theater in some detail, they would now have the opportunity to discuss, very briefly, Europe. "Discuss" — but not decide. "Final decisions would depend on the way things went at the conference shortly to be held with Premier Stalin," the President made clear — ruling out, in a few words, British hopes that they could overturn the Quebec strategy *before* going to Tehran. Churchill had blanched.

"There were some reports," the President explained, that Premier Stalin was "only concerned" with Overlord, "to which he attached the highest importance as being the only operation worth considering." Other reports, however, claimed "that Premier Stalin was anxious that, in addition to Overlord in 1944, the Germans should be given no respite throughout the winter, and there should be no idle hands between now and Overlord. The logistic problem was whether we could retain Overlord in all its integrity and, at the same time, keep the Mediterranean ablaze." Lest there be any doubt, the President gave his own view of what they had to expect in Tehran. "Premier Stalin," he predicted, "would be almost certain to demand both the continuation of action in the Mediterranean, and Overlord" — but with Overlord as the primary goal.

The President had asked his ambassador to Moscow to address the U.S. Joint Chiefs of Staff in person earlier that morning, after breakfast, at his villa, in order to put them too in the latest Moscow picture. Harriman had duly warned that, if Overlord "were to be abandoned," then in his opinion the Western Allies had better produce a genuine alternative — i.e., "an operation equally offensive in nature" — if they really expected Russia to go on fighting the Germans. Especially if — as he'd been assured in Moscow was the Soviet "intention" — the Western Allies wanted the Soviets to join "the U.S. and British in the war against Japan as soon as Germany capitulated."[1]

General Deane, for his part, had disagreed, feeling the Soviets wanted more "immediate pressure" to be placed on the Germans in the Mediterranean, to relieve current Wehrmacht pressure on the Eastern Front. In Deane's view the Russians were less concerned about a date for the Overlord invasion than with immediate help.

Once again, the President was open to different views — but chose in this case to reject such supposedly professional military advice. Deane was a good man — former secretary of the Combined Chiefs of Staff — but he was a pen-pusher, not a fighting soldier. As head of the U.S. Military Mission in Moscow he had not even met Stalin — the one individual who decided everything there.

The President's judgment was here at issue, at a critical moment of the war. He trusted Harriman's insight rather than that of General Deane — for in a dictatorship like the Soviet Union, only the dictator's view ultimately counted. As the President explained to the plenary meeting, operations in the eastern Mediterranean would not affect the outcome of the war, in terms of defeating the Third Reich — whereas Overlord manifestly would. To the question where the Germans would go if they were evicted from the Aegean islands, the answer was "nowhere," he pointed out — and this was equally true of the Allies. Unless Turkey agreed to become a belligerent, the eastern Mediterranean was a dead end. Even if Turkey *were* to join the Allies, its inclusion among belligerents would be a logistic drain on Allied resources at best; at worst it would be a quagmire if, as was likely, the Germans persisted in the way they were fighting in Italy and the Balkans.

The President then turned to Mr. Churchill to offer *his* views.

This was Churchill's moment. He had spent the past two weeks dictating, revising, and honing his great "indictment" — and with it on the table before him, he announced his opposition to current Allied policy.

In a long, lawyerly presentation, the Prime Minister ridiculed Allied efforts in the Mediterranean since the invasion at Salerno; criticized the buildup of U.S. air forces in Italy rather than the reinforcement of Allied ground forces there; and insisted upon the capture of the Eternal City of Rome — "for 'whoever holds Rome holds the title deeds of Italy,'" he declared with his characteristic appeal to emotion. The Aegean islands, including Rhodes, should be retaken in the coming weeks and months, he insisted. By sending two divisions, with their landing craft and strong Allied naval forces, the Dardanelles could be used to put pressure on Germany's allies Hungary, Romania, and Bulgaria to change sides, like the Italians . . .[2]

General Brooke, in his diary, thought this a "masterly statement": a brilliant denunciation of the "tyranny" of Overlord, which would "help us in our deliberations" — deliberations to delay and if possible abandon D-day in 1944.[3]

The President and the U.S. chiefs thought the opposite. What on earth, the American participants wondered, was the point of making it a primary Allied objective to "liberate" the rest of Italy, not to mention those nations, like

Austria, Hungary, Romania, and Bulgaria, that were *still* fighting as allies of the Third Reich? Why such a determined British attempt to delay the planned invasion of France, and sabotage the crucial campaign to reach Berlin and end the war in Europe as swiftly as possible, before moving on to Japan?

Perhaps the most unfortunate part of Churchill's peroration, as he read out his long indictment, was not the Prime Minister's obsession with Rhodes, Turkey, and the Dardanelles so much as the growing implication the British were simply afraid of head-to-head confrontation with the Wehrmacht in battle. Behind Churchill's oratory the U.S. chiefs now began to sense a somewhat shameful appeal *not* to fight the Germans in open, major combat, but instead to run away, and fiddle around the periphery of Europe, imagining they would be less costly ventures. And this, even though it was clear to the American team that, to judge by rising casualties in Italy, a Mediterranean strategy might well end up costing *more* lives in the mountainous regions of southern Europe than a straightforward, decisive campaign in the largely flat terrain in northern France, using ever-growing numbers of U.S. tanks, artillery, and armor, and backed by overwhelming Allied air power.

Given that the Germans had already murdered or starved to death some two *million* Russian prisoners, and that Russian losses in battle were worsening on the Eastern Front — where the German Army had recently launched a counteroffensive — it seemed unlikely Marshal Stalin would be impressed by Churchill's alternative Aegean strategy. "Mr. Churchill made a long unconvincing talk," Admiral Leahy noted in his own diary that night, "about the advantage of operations in the Aegean Sea and against the Island of Rhodes" — the admiral contemptuous of what he considered the Prime Minister's disloyalty to the Quebec accords.[4]

In the end President Roosevelt, as chairman of the plenary meeting, had attempted to emphasize the positive — while putting the British team in its place. From his briefcase at the table he thus took out the figures of comparative contributions of the United States and Great Britain to the war effort, and laid them in front of the Prime Minister and the British chiefs of staff.[5] With the Russians putting two *hundred* divisions in the field on the Eastern Front, and an American army of up to ninety divisions to be put into the field in France in the wake of Overlord, the Western and Eastern Fronts could crush the Wehrmacht between them — the same two-front strategy which, after all, had brought slow but absolute victory in North Africa. The Aegean, by contrast, was not only a red herring, but unworthy of great allies.

Sadly, the President's firm yet polite insistence that they stick with the Quebec agenda yielded no change in Churchill's views, or those of his British military advisers. The British team simply stuck to its guns over its appeal for more immediate operations in the eastern Mediterranean. "I put forward our counter proposals for continuing active operations in the Mediterranean at the expense of a postponement of Overlord date," Brooke noted proudly in his private journal — surprised that the American team, looking to the President for guidance, simply declined to discuss the matter further. The showdown had come — but with the President determined still not to permit a revision of Quebec before they met Stalin, or the breakdown of the conference in the meantime.

The next day — with two more days of talks to go — the President attempted to keep U.S.-British "community relations" at least on an even keel. There was a cathedral service in Cairo — with security cast to the four winds, and "everyone present at the service but the cat and the dog," as General Arnold noted humorously in his diary. "Camels and caravans, little ones and big ones, all heading toward the Pyramids or away from them; donkeys and sheep and goats, Arabs and more Arabs."[6] In the evening, at his villa, the President held a Thanksgiving meal, to which he invited the Prime Minister and his entourage — his daughter Sarah, Anthony Eden, Dr. Wilson, the Prime Minister's secretary, and his security officer, Commander Tommy Thompson. The President even made a point of saying, in his toast, that "large families are usually closer united than are small families; and that, this year, with the United Kingdom in our family, we are a large family and more united than ever before."[7]

Not even the President's charm, however, could conceal the fact that relations between the U.S. and British chiefs of staff had become fraught — prompting Admiral Leahy to note in his diary that in the "afternoon session of the Combined Chiefs of Staff held in camera" (so that the secretarial staff and other attendees not be witness to the extent of dissension) "we discussed at length and without any agreement a British proposal to delay cross-channel operations in order to put forth more effort in the Aegean and in Turkey."[8] To disconcert the British, the American chiefs had tabled, for their part, "Proposal A," as a countermemorandum. This asked for the "immediate" appointment of a single supreme commander for all Europe — a commander who would "exercise command over the Allied force commanders in the Mediterranean, in northwest Europe, and the strategic air forces": a commander in chief, Europe, in other words, who would report to the Combined Chiefs of Staff and the national leaders of the U.S. and Great Britain, in order to effect the "common, over-all objective — Defeat of Germany."

It was to no avail.

As the President had feared, the American counterproposal met with a furious rebuttal from Mr. Churchill, who gave his confutation in writing to the President that day.[9]

The standoff was now formalized, ending all hope of the two teams traveling to Tehran other than as still-feuding allies. The British chiefs of staff simply continued to insist that recent "major developments" in the Mediterranean warranted the abandonment of a "fixed date" for Overlord, and claimed "departures" from the Quebec agreements were "not only justified but positively essential." The notion of Overlord "shortening the war" was "entirely illusory," they declared in writing. Overlord would "inevitably paralyze action in other theaters without any guarantee of action across the Channel."[10]

Thus had ended the Allied standoff on Thanksgiving Day, November 25, 1943.

The following day, Friday, November 26, proved even worse — open insults now being traded in the final Combined Chiefs of Staff meeting in the afternoon, called to discuss operations in Burma.

"At 2.30 met Americans," Brooke recorded. "It was not long before Marshall and I had the father and mother of a row!" — this time in front of some forty-four witnesses. Once again all staff officers and stenographers were expelled from the room, leaving just the main service chiefs of the two countries to pursue an "off the record meeting."[11]

Admiral Leahy was beside himself with fury that his British counterparts were willing to back their prime minister to the hilt in canceling amphibious operation plans off Burma — the better to use the landing craft to attack Rhodes, of all places! "The Prime Minister seems determined to remove his landing ships from that effort," Admiral Leahy noted, "and in a discussion that became almost acrimonious at times, I informed our British colleagues that the American staff declined to recede from our present planned operations without orders from the President."[12]

The President, for his part, didn't waver, or change his orders. Overlord as planned and scheduled would go ahead, he insisted; his stonewalling had kept the peace — barely, but effectively. "Today I wound up all that could be accomplished," he noted in his diary for November 26 — "a really successful meeting & a good announcement to be given out in 4 days," when they were no longer there. Overlord was still on track. Meanwhile "we are off to Teheran in the morning" — to meet the Russian dictator and decide the future of the world.[13]

PART THREE

Triumph in Tehran

19

A Vision of the Postwar World

THE TEHRAN SUMMIT would be the most consequential meeting of the war. In the ancient capital of the Persian empire the President hoped at least to nudge his two allies — the one a model of colonial exploitation, the other a model of ruthless communist dictatorship — toward a postwar democratic vision. And this, while maintaining the unity of a United Nations military coalition in struggling to defeat Nazi Germany and the Empire of Japan, and ensuring the majority of people in his own country were willing to back him in a new American role: seeking and guaranteeing postwar peace and economic development on a global stage.

Could such an idealistic vision possibly be made real on the anvil of what was already the most destructive war in human history? In terms of the future, Stalin had never evinced any real interest in the sovereignty or development of noncommunist countries. For his part Churchill had zero interest, as he'd recently said in his speech in London, in decolonizing or dissolving parts of the British Empire. Roosevelt, however, saw himself as a visionary — or practical idealist, as he had once described himself in a letter to the South African premier, Field Marshal Smuts.[1]

Despite the wordy communiqués of the recent Moscow Conference of Foreign Ministers there was as yet no warranty that the summit at Tehran would lead, in reality, to a postwar security system more effective than the League of Nations had been. Yet Roosevelt, as president, while still in office, wanted to give the leader of the Soviet Union and his colleagues an opportunity, at least, to willingly take partial responsibility for the security of the postwar world. Similarly, he hoped Britain could be urged to see its future in a genuine commonwealth of English-speaking nations, rather than continued British exploitation of an oppressive colonial empire that would, he told his son Elliott, only incite resistance and revolution in the coming years. He could not compel either Stalin or Churchill to agree on, let alone work for, such a future — but he could encourage them to give their personal support to his postwar concept of the United Nations authority; a Security Council of the United Nations; and to his notion of the "Four Policemen," who would cauterize and put out fires and flare-ups that threatened world peace: namely the United States, Russia, Great Britain, and China.

Given its burgeoning economic potency and its growing military power, the United States would be able to point the way, the President felt, following defeat of the Axis powers. And the only thing that could hinder that defeat would be if American forces were to become bogged down in the Mediterranean, Aegean, Balkans, and Dardanelles instead of striking across the English Channel in May.

The May 1944 timing of Overlord was crucial, the President was aware. The war would soon be entering its third year in the eyes of American voters. There was still great idealism and hope at home — but would it survive if hostilities, so far from American shores, were prolonged, while the British deliberately postponed Overlord in favor of vague and ill-considered "opportunities" elsewhere?

In Cairo the President had summoned his assistant secretary of war, John McCloy, to his villa. At the President's request McCloy had produced a memorandum on "posthostility policy" in which he noted two "tendencies" that were bound to grow, the closer the Allies came to an end to the war. "Stimulated on the part of our soldiers by their wish to get home," the first tendency, McCloy had reported, was already a growing desire to simply "liquidate the European involvement" — i.e., to win and leave. Or just leave! The other "tendency" was the inevitable hostility to the United States that would increase in Britain and elsewhere, "now that the war is on its way to being won and the invader is no longer at the door." For in McCloy's view the current "dependence on the U.S." — economic and military — would produce an unavoidable adverse reaction.[2] In short, McCloy argued, Americans would want to go home — and Europeans would be glad to get rid of them. As had been the case after World War I.

It was in this context that the assistant secretary of war saw the crucial importance of Winston Churchill — in America. Having helped get the United States to focus its primary efforts on Europe, the Prime Minister now surely needed to help "convince America that she must enter the administration of the peace."[3] Churchill had given a beautiful speech on this subject at Harvard University in September, after the Quebec Conference and agreements.[4] But his latest attempts to sabotage D-day threatened to trigger a tragic American turn *away* from Europe, once again, as after 1918. In McCloy's view it was crucial that the American public should see the liberation of Europe as a great *American* achievement — one that would make the maintaining of postwar peace in Europe a worthwhile *American* objective, after the expenditure of so much American blood and treasure.

Churchill's current antics were, in McCloy's eyes, not simply the airing of an honest disagreement between allies, but a profoundly dangerous twist, threatening American willingness to prosecute the war in Europe — and with potentially tragic consequences. It was vital to convince not only U.S. "leaders, but its citizens, that the United States has a major part in directing the war," McCoy contended[5] — in fact, *the* major part.

In a nutshell, Americans at home should see U.S. forces not simply as auxiliary firemen from a different city, helping European democracies put out the Nazi fire, in the analogy the President had used to promote his Lend-Lease policy before Pearl Harbor, but as the captains of the current war — and also the postwar. "It is vitally necessary to indoctrinate the American people to a recognition of the national responsibility of the country in world affairs," McCloy wrote. "It is essential that the people of America become used to decisions being made in the United States," he continued. "On every cracker barrel in every country store in the U.S.," he'd added, memorably, "there is someone sitting who is convinced that we get hornswoggled every time we attend a European conference."[6]

The President liked the word. Moreover, he agreed to his marrow with McCloy's presentation. Churchill simply could not be allowed to delay or sabotage D-day, nor could he be permitted to use American forces in wild ventures in the Aegean and Balkans that would only convince American voters they were being "hornswoggled." The summit in Tehran was thus a chance to show *Americans* that the U.S. was now in charge: taking full military responsibility for the struggle against the Axis powers, in particular the swiftest possible defeat of Nazi Germany.

McCloy's Cairo memorandum — which closely reflected the views of the secretary of war, Henry Stimson — thus served to stiffen the President's resolve at a critical moment in world conflict.

Churchill should not be permitted, all felt, to ditch his Quebec undertaking. By the same token, however, it was important to avoid causing him to resign as prime minister, as he'd reputedly threatened, or to turn the British cabinet against American postwar policy, as was all too possible. The President would have great need of the Prime Minister, not only as America's junior military ally — his "active and ardent lieutenant," as Churchill had publicly called himself[7] — but as a revered British statesman and leader in the eyes of Americans: encouraging the American people to step up to the postwar plate. Also, if at all possible, to encourage Churchill to see decolonization as a great postwar *ideal* to be embraced, not rejected. Simultaneously, the President must offer the Soviet Union, with its four hundred army divisions under Stalin's direct command, an opportunity also, like America, to grow into a new potential role of international responsibility, in order to help guarantee postwar world peace.

This, in short, was the challenge.

The daytime flight on Saturday, November 27, 1943, at least, allowed the President to look down at the fabled cities of Palestine and the Middle East. At the President's request Major Bryan had circled the plane several times over "Bethlehem & Jerusalem & the Red Sea," Roosevelt recorded in his diary. From the air, however, he wasn't persuaded it was a particularly attractive land: "everything very bare looking—& I don't want Palestine as my homeland," he'd penned with feeling—aware how volatile were the politics of the region, and the competing, often fanatical claims of different religions upon it. "Then hundreds of miles of Arabian desert, then a green ribbon & Bagdad and the Tigris, with another green ribbon, the Euphrates—then bare mountains & we followed the highway over which so much lend lease goes to Russia."

Flying through the mountain passes that Major Bryan had successfully reconnoitered on his exploratory flight, they finally landed at 3:00 p.m., at the Russian air base of Gale Morghe, five miles south of the city. No better symbol of Soviet dependence on American military help to the Soviet Union could there have been than the aircraft they'd seen parked by the runway. "This is a modern airfield," Lieutenant Rigdon wrote in the log, "and on it were noted a large number of [American] lend-lease planes now bearing the Red Star of Russia."[8] From Gale Morghe the President was driven to the U.S. Legation in Tehran—and the historic summit began.

20

In the Russian Compound

ONCE INSTALLED as the guest of Mr. Louis Dreyfus, the American minister to Iran, the President dispatched his naval aide, Admiral Brown, across the city to the Russian Embassy to thank the Soviet government for its invitation to stay there, but to politely turn down the suggestion for the moment. Admiral Brown was tasked, instead, with inviting Marshal Stalin to dinner at the U.S. Legation residence that evening — where, it was assumed, the first of the conference's meetings would take place the next day.

Stalin had left Moscow in a slow, specially camouflaged armored train on November 22 — the same day Roosevelt had arrived in Cairo — and had reached Baku, on the Caspian Sea, on November 26. There — overcoming his mortal fear of flying — the Marshal had boarded an American-manufactured lend-leased C-47 on the morning of November 27 for the three-hundred-mile journey across the Caspian to Tehran — clinging "to his armrests with an expression of utter terror on his face," according to one account.[1] Via his chargé d'affaires, Mr. M. A. Maximov, Stalin duly responded to the President's invitation, saying he was grateful for it, but was fatigued by his long journey. He thus declined.

It was clear that, as in a powwow between two tribal chiefs, honor must first be satisfied before they actually sat down together.

By cable the President had asked Stalin five days earlier where exactly he thought it best he should stay in Tehran — a city located, after all, in the northern, Russian-occupied half of Iran. Stalin, in transit, had not replied. Yet the more the President had thought about the matter, the more he'd recognized the advantages of staying at the Russian or British Embassy — and his arrival at Dreyfus's official U.S. residence, with the time it took to send Admiral Brown through the teeming streets of the city to the Russian Embassy and back, only served to make him more amenable to the idea of a move.

Such an arrangement would spare daily journeys by the Russian and British leaders through the insecure, poorly policed streets of Tehran to and from the U.S. Legation. Which of the two embassies, though? The British Legation was already crowded with personnel, in fact was said to be a somewhat "ramshackle" compound: a former cavalry barracks of the Indian Public Works Department.[2] The Soviet Embassy, by contrast, was reported to be less crowded (its personnel had mostly been moved out, prior to Stalin's arrival) and more comfortable. But also bugged with hidden microphones, in the usual, paranoid Soviet style.

Why not stay at the Russian Embassy, bugged or unbugged, though? Would it not show an American willingness to work with the Russians on both war strategy and postwar security arrangements? Moreover, the very act of choosing a Russian roof over the President's head rather than a British one would symbolize the President's determination not to listen further to Churchill's continuing efforts to press his alternative Mediterranean/Aegean strategy outside the formal plenary meetings. The President had therefore hoped to broach the possibility of a move of living quarters to the Russian Embassy when Stalin came to dinner.

But Stalin's turndown left the President guestless on his first night in Tehran. Belatedly the President had decided he'd better invite Mr. Churchill, who had also arrived in Tehran that morning by plane.

Churchill, however, was not feeling at all well — suffering a heavy cold, again. Flying that morning from the Egyptian capital, his flight had been bumpy and the descent to the ground even bumpier. The Prime Minister, like an irritated headmaster, had whacked his pilot across the ankles with his walking stick when the crew lined up to say goodbye at the airport, complaining of a "bloody bad landing."[3] He'd also lost his voice — yet still hoped he could outmaneuver the President, before the summit-proper began. Banking on Mr. Roosevelt remaining across the city at the U.S. Legation, he'd seen a chance to work on Stalin personally: hoping to convince the Russian dictator in person of his strategy. The Prime Minister thus told his staff he wanted to "start there and then" with a meeting with Stalin, next door, if it could be arranged.

Given his sore throat, his loss of voice, and his aggressive, overwrought mood, however, Dr. Wilson and Churchill's own daughter Sarah dissuaded the Prime Minister. Nor would they allow him to accept the President's tardy invitation to dine that evening at the U.S. Legation, across the city. Instead, on doctor's orders, "he had dinner in bed like a sulky little boy," Sarah recorded.[4]

Day one of the Tehran Summit had thus come to a close with the "Big Three" leaders of the world failing to even sit down with one another. In fact the situation would have been comic, had the summit not been so important in terms of the prosecution of the war — and postwar.

But the real problem was that Joseph Stalin was Russian — and had apparently misunderstood Western protocol: namely the need for him to personally invite the President, if he really wanted Mr. Roosevelt to move quarters to the Russian Embassy, where part of the main building was being converted in great haste into a special guest apartment, complete with a new bathroom. As a result, in typical Soviet fashion, a pedantic subterfuge rather than a simple personal invitation was felt necessary: one in which a German "plot" would suddenly be "discovered," that night, after the President — having dined with Leahy, Hopkins, Brown, Watson, and the two ambassadors he'd brought with him, Winant and Harriman — had gone to bed.

The purpose of the supposed plot was explained late at night by the Russian foreign minister, Vyacheslav Molotov, who'd accompanied Stalin on his train and then plane, to Ambassador Harriman and to the British ambassador to Moscow, A. Clark Kerr. German spies were reported to be plotting an assassination of the President, Molotov asserted with a straight face, having summoned the two diplomats to the Soviet Embassy. The German agents were planning to kill the President at the U.S. Legation, or to attack the great leaders as they moved between the several compounds — the American Legation being over a mile away, through largely unpoliced streets. Marshal Stalin was therefore of the opinion, Mr. Molotov confided to the ambassadors, that the President should move either to the British Legation or to the Russian Embassy, and that the summit meetings should then be held in either the one or other building, to maximize security during the coming days.

Since it was so late the suggestion, based on the fake plot, was only communicated to the President after breakfast at 9:30 a.m. on Sunday, November 28, 1943.

The Russian "discovery" of the plot sounded almost silly, coming after so many weeks of intelligence checks, inspections, and reports. But the Russians were Russians — inscrutable in their inferiority complexes, as FDR had told his cousin Daisy.[5] Churchill once again pressed the President, via his ambassador to Russia, to stay at the British Embassy. However, the Russian offer — in which the President would be housed in a "part of their Embassy that would be under a separate roof and we would have complete independence"[6] — was the more tempting to the President, who, unlike Churchill, had still never met Stalin. Moreover, since Churchill was holding out so adamantly for a change in military strategy, a move to the Russian Embassy would insulate him from the Prime Minister's unending exhortations. Ambassador Harriman was therefore asked to tell Mr. Molotov the President was "delighted with the prospect" of staying with Marshal Stalin[7] — and would move to the Russian compound, he declared, after lunch that very day, at 3:00 p.m., along with his White House staff.

Summoning his U.S. chiefs of staff to the legation residence at 11:30 a.m., the President meanwhile rehearsed with them one last time how to deal with the possibility that Churchill was right, and that the Russians "really need assisting operations" in the Mediterranean to draw off Wehrmacht forces from the Eastern Front.[8]

For ninety minutes the President and his chiefs of staff, together with Harry Hopkins, thus rehearsed the situation. No matter how it was sliced and diced, none of the chiefs could see how Overlord could be mounted in the coming spring, in full measure, if they now allowed Allied forces to be "sucked in" to open-ended Mediterranean and Aegean operations.[9] How, in realistic terms, could Eisenhower or his successor be expected to fight his way to Fiume (annexed by Italy in 1924), on the northeast coast of the Adriatic, in only a matter of weeks, when he had still not got much beyond *Naples*? And when U.S. troops, according to General Mark Clark's reports, were finding the campaign in the mountains of Italy a more and more forbidding challenge, even with Allied air power? Even if the Turks were persuaded to enter the war, they could not be counted on to aid the Allies offensively, the President noted.[10] Could the Allies seriously imagine they could logistically achieve a *working* passage through the Dardanelles in less than "six to eight months"? General Somervell pointed out.[11] And how could the amphibious invasion of Burma, to help free up the transit of supplies to Chiang Kai-shek and provide a U.S. bomber base in the Andaman Islands, proceed, if the necessary landing craft were used in the Mediterranean?

The Germans were "already" aware of the "build-up in the U.K. in preparation for Overlord," and could be expected to toughen their Atlantic Wall still further in the next months — thus *increasing*, not decreasing, the need for the Allies to focus on Overlord, not be distracted elsewhere. Commandos helping guerrillas in the northern Adriatic, or southern France, would be more likely to draw off Wehrmacht divisions — perhaps as many as two — than major, battle-hardened Allied formations getting embroiled in the Dodecanese Islands: islands that would draw away no German forces from the Eastern Front, as the President indicated.[12] "Commando group operations," the President repeated, yes — but "on a small scale."[13] And with regard to Overlord? No major operations elsewhere should be countenanced — especially if they risked losing crucial landing craft needed for the cross-Channel invasion.[14]

It was clear there were simply not enough men or weapons or supplies to do everything simultaneously. In a global conflict logistics ultimately determined what was feasible, and what was not.

Amalgamating the largely British theater of the Middle East with that of the Allied Mediterranean theater might, all agreed, be a sensible idea logistically and in tactical terms, thereby permitting the application of the greatest Allied power at a chosen point. Yet if Marshall thought Churchill would accept the idea of General Eisenhower remaining in supreme command of all Allied forces in the Mediterranean as well as those in the Middle East then Marshall — as presumed commander of Overlord, in the north — was being naive. As the President put it, "We must realize that the British look upon the Mediterranean as an area under British domination" — and the addition of British forces from the Middle East would only make Churchill still *more* determined to exercise his dominion via a British supreme commander — with dire consequences for Overlord. After Rhodes was taken — if it was taken — he would want yet more operations, claiming, "'Now we will have to take Greece.'"[15] This, in turn, would involve yet *more* delay to Overlord — perhaps even its cancellation.[16]

The clock struck one at the American Legation, and the President called an end to the meeting. "The Soviets definitely want something," General Marshall had stated, "and we should find out what it is."[17]

They would find out soon enough — the first plenary session of the summit was due to start at four o'clock that afternoon.

21

The Grand Debate

ENTERING THE GATES of the Russian Embassy the President arrived in front of a "square building of light-brown stone set in a small park," boasting an "imposing portico with white Doric columns," as one historian described it — the park itself "surrounded on all sides by a high stone wall," within which there were fountains, a small lake, villas, and apartments for embassy staff personnel.[1]

The President's assigned quarters were in a house attached to the square main building. "It had three or four large downstairs rooms, as well as quarters for the President's Filipino servants and numerous Secret Service men," the President's interpreter, Charles Bohlen, also recalled — having been asked to join the Commander in Chief there, prior to the expected visit of their host, Marshal Stalin.[2]

A career diplomat, Bohlen had seen the President only a few times in his life — and those at a distance. At thirty-nine, he was understandably nervous to be acting suddenly as personal interpreter to the President, rather than as an attending junior U.S. diplomat. "In the few minutes I had with President Roosevelt before his first meeting with Stalin, I outlined certain considerations regarding interpreting," Bohlen later recounted. "The first and most important was to ask if he would try to remember to break up his comments into short periods." These should best comprise "two or three minutes of conversation," which "would hold their [the Russians'] attention and make my job infinitely easier. Roosevelt understood, and I must say he was an excellent speaker to interpret for, breaking up his statements into short lengths and in a variety of ways showing consideration for my travails. Churchill was much too carried away by his own eloquence to pay much attention to his pleasant and excellent interpreter, short, baldish Major Arthur H. Birse. There were occasions," Bohlen reflected, "when Churchill would speak for five, six, or seven minutes, while poor Major Birse dashed his pencil desperately over the paper, trying to capture enough words to convey the eloquence into Russian."[3]

The President, Bohlen recalled, "seemed to be in excellent health, never showing any signs of fatigue, and holding his magnificent leonine head high. He clearly was the dominating figure at the conference"[4] — the prologue to which now began with Stalin's arrival at the President's quarters at 3:15 p.m.

Dressed in a "simple khaki tunic (he was a Marshal of the Soviet Union) with the Order of Lenin on his chest," and escorted into the President's sitting room by a young American army officer, the five-foot-six-inch Russian dictator entered. The six-foot-three-inch president stretched out his arm from his wheelchair and the two men shook hands.[5] "I am glad to see you," the President — dressed in a blue business suit — said sincerely. "I have tried for a long time to bring this about."[6]

He had — in fact his attempts to arrange a meeting went back more than a year. Stalin, for his part, apologized, citing his "preoccupation with military matters."[7] Then, after that brief introduction, Stalin sat down for forty-five minutes while the two men conversed, seeking to get a measure of each other's personality as they ran through a surprising range of subjects openly and informally.

Bohlen was amazed at how deftly the President put the Russian dictator at ease; likewise, how frank, straightforward, and personal the Marshal was in responding. Warming to his task, Bohlen interpreted for both men as they compared notes on the war and the future.

Stalin flatly admitted that the situation on the Eastern Front was "not too good" — in fact it was "so bad that only in the Ukraine was it possible to take offensive operations," and even there, several important cities such as Zhitomir had recently fallen to German counterattacks.[8] How best to draw off significant numbers of German divisions and reinforcements, the President responded, was in part why he had come to Tehran. Stalin thanked him. The President then switched to postwar reconstruction, offering to share with the Soviet Union some of the Allies' merchant fleet that would become redundant, after hostilities ended — prompting Stalin to say, not only would the Soviet Union be grateful, but how he much hoped "the development of relations between the Soviet Union and the United States" would be "greatly expanded. In return for American equipment, the Soviets, for their part, would like to make available raw materials to the U.S."[9]

Allowing for diplomatic niceties, the sheer optimism about postwar relations was a tremendous relief to Roosevelt — so much so that he launched into a very frank discussion of the Far East, explaining how General Stilwell hoped to supply and train up to sixty Chinese divisions, while Allied forces under Admiral Mountbatten hit Burma from the north, and farther south from the Indian Ocean, to open supply routes to "link up with China."

Burma, however, raised the question of postwar British, French, and Dutch decolonization — a problem already rearing its ugly head in the Lebanon, where the French had refused to grant independence, as promised, despite recent elections — the President blaming de Gaulle and his Free French Committee. "Marshal Stalin said he did not know General De Gaulle personally, but frankly, in his opinion, he was very unreal in his political activities. He explained that General De Gaulle represented the very soul of sympathetic [i.e., anti-Fascist] France, whereas the real physical France" was unfortunately "engaged under Petain in helping our common enemy Germany, by making available French ports, materials, machines, etc., for the German war effort. He said the trouble with De Gaulle was his [Free French] movement had no communication with the physical France, which, in his opinion, should be punished for its attitude during this war. De Gaulle acts as though he were the head of a great state, whereas, in fact, it actually commands very little power."[10]

This was — especially after de Gaulle's personal meeting with Roosevelt at Casablanca in January, earlier that year — music to the President's ears. He "agreed" wholeheartedly — indeed posited, more rhetorically than seriously, that "in the future, no Frenchman over 40, and particularly no Frenchman who had ever taken part in the present French [Vichy] Government should be allowed to return to positions after the war. He said that General Giraud was a good old military type, but with no administrative or political sense, whatsoever." This augured poorly for the eleven French divisions, comprising mostly African soldiers, currently being trained in North Africa. The President's remark in turn prompted Stalin to "expiate" at length "on the French ruling classes," which, the dictator remarked, "should not be entitled to share in any of the benefits of the peace, in view of their past record of collaboration with Germany." Which led the President to declare that he disagreed with Churchill's view that France be "reconstructed as a strong nation," for he felt it ought to be, essentially, punished by hard labor "for many years" before it was reestablished as a worthy nation — not only its government but "the people as well," who should, by honest labor, become "honest citizens."[11]

The President was tiptoeing around the matter of imperialism: the idea that people of color owed the white European nations a living, for which the white colonists were not required to do more than wear smart uniforms, brush their proverbial teeth — and make nice with Hitler. "Marshal Stalin agreed," Bohlen recorded — indeed said he thought it wrong the Allies should be expected by the French to "shed blood to restore Indo-China." Recent "events in the Lebanon" showed how important it would be to train formerly colonized peoples in law and government, ready for "independence." This would be especially important in Southeast Asia and the Pacific, once the Japanese were defeated and removed.

Again Stalin agreed. The "political" challenge of decolonization was, Stalin felt, just as important as the military in "certain colonial areas. He repeated that France should not get back Indochina and that the French must pay for their criminal collaboration with Germany" — views with which the President said he was "100% in agreement with Marshal Stalin." Judging from reports he'd received, the President "remarked that after 100 years of French rule in Indochina, the inhabitants were worse off than they had been before." For his part Chiang Kai-shek had assured him the Chinese had "no designs" on Indochina. With Chiang in Cairo the President had therefore discussed, instead, the idea of a United Nations trusteeship. This would prepare the people of Indochina for complete independence "within a definite period of time, perhaps 20 to 30 years" — and he instanced how this had been the task of U.S. policy in the Philippines, which was due to be given independence immediately after the war with Japan was over. "Marshal Stalin completely agreed with this view" — and with the President's notion of an international fact-finding committee to visit, every year, "the colonies of all nations" and seek to "correct any abuse that they find."[12]

Which led the two world leaders to discuss the largest colonized nation in the world: India. Had millions of Russians and tens of thousands of Americans already died, or been maimed, merely so that Britain could maintain imperial domination over four hundred million people? How could the British keep up a steadfast refusal to grant India self-government, let alone independence? Gandhi and Nehru were still under British arrest, and since August 1943, Churchill had refused to release shipping to send food to Bengal, where by October 1943 serious famine was threatening millions of Indians with starvation and death unless the British acted swiftly.

India, however, was a sacred cow for the Prime Minister, the President warned the Marshal — for Churchill "had no solution to that question, and merely proposed to defer the entire question to the end of the war." Stalin "agreed that this was a sore spot with the British" — to which Roosevelt said he would like to discuss the matter of India again with the Soviet premier "at some future date." Might the answer lie in revolution, as had been the case in Soviet Russia? the President wondered — prompting Stalin, ironically, to caution that India was a "complicated" case, "with different levels of culture," religion, and a caste system that precluded, or would make difficult, an easy transition to sovereign, self-governing nationhood.

For Bohlen the conversation was stunningly informal — each leader seeking to show an openness to the other's personal views and ideas. Given the total suppression of free speech in the Soviet Union, and the complete contrast between their own forms of government — the one proudly capitalistic and democratic, if profoundly racist, the other fiercely communist and a brutal dictatorship — the meeting suggested that the two countries might well find common ground in guiding peaceful development of the world, once the barbaric, expansionist German and Japanese empires were forced to surrender.

All too soon the meeting came to an end, however — for at four o'clock the first plenary session of the summit was due to begin next door, in the conference room of the Soviet Embassy. The Russian dictator exited, the President freshened up, and there now began the long-awaited battle over how best to defeat Hitler.

The President began the meeting, ironically, without his two top military advisers. Owing to a misunderstanding over the time of the first plenary meeting neither General Marshall nor General Arnold was present, having gone instead for a hunting "trip through the mountains," as Arnold noted in embarrassment in his diary.[13] In their absence, at the big circular table at the center of the conference room, the President thus sat with Harriman on his right and Bohlen and Hopkins on his left, while Admiral Leahy, Admiral King, and Major General Deane perched on chairs by the walls of the big room, which was guarded by Soviet secret policemen in plain yet bulky clothes, concealing their pistols.

How would Churchill behave? Warned by the President that there were "storm signals flying in the British legation," the President had sent Ambassador Harriman to see the Prime Minister in the British camp prior to the meeting. Harriman had reported Mr. Churchill happily "waived all claims" to be chairman of the conference, despite being the eldest of the three leaders. He had, however, insisted on "one thing."[14]

The President had asked what it was. To his amusement Harriman explained the Prime Minister wanted to "be allowed to give a dinner party on the 30th," in two days' time, to celebrate his sixty-ninth birthday. Churchill intended to "get thoroughly drunk," as he'd warned the American ambassador, and would "leave the following day."[15]

Clearly Churchill had not lost his sense of humor. Meantime, as the agreed chairman of the conference (the President being the only head of state, not simply a premier or first minister), Mr. Roosevelt opened the proceedings. The British interpreter, Major Birse, later recalled how "Roosevelt sat in his wheeled chair which had been pushed up to the conference table. In that position, with his broad shoulders and fine head, he had the appearance of a tall strong man, and it was only his chair which gave away his infirmity. He beamed on all around the table and looked very much like the kind, rich uncle paying a visit to his poorer relations" — both Stalin and Churchill a foot shorter than the President.[16]

Once again Bohlen was struck by the historic, yet "relaxed" nature of the meeting since "it did not seem possible that the three most powerful men in the world were about to make decisions involving the lives of millions."[17] As the youngest of the leaders the President welcomed his "elders." Although minutes or summaries would be kept for later reference, nothing would be made public for the moment without common consent, so that the leaders could talk with "complete frankness," ensuring their three great nations could work together to prosecute the war, and in the future, when their countries would hopefully continue to enjoy close relations, via similar summits, "for generations to come."[18]

Mr. Churchill seconded the President's introductory remarks.

For his part Stalin welcomed those present to his embassy, saying "history had given to us here a great opportunity," which it was up to them to "use wisely" on behalf of their peoples.[19]

With that the President began his overview of the war — beginning with the Pacific, where American forces were carrying virtually the entire burden of the fight against Japan, together with Australian troops — and in the north, with the Chinese.

"While speaking," Major Birse described the President, "he would frequently take off his pince-nez and use it to emphasize a point."[20] He "summed up the aims" of the operations currently being pursued in the Far East as "(1) to open the road to China and supply that country in order to keep it in the war," and (2) by opening the road to China and through increased use of transport planes to put ourselves in position to bomb Japan proper." In the meantime United States forces would continue to advance in the central and southwest Pacific, moving forward from island to island as they turned back the Japanese rampage. Japan's days of military conquest were numbered, but the "most important theater of the war," he emphasized, was Europe.

For more than eighteen months, the President explained, his high-level conferences with Prime Minister Churchill had been dominated by the challenge of "relieving the German pressure on the Soviet front." Largely because of logistical challenges it hadn't been possible until the Quebec Conference in August that year to "set a date for the cross-channel operations. He pointed out," however, as Bohlen recorded in his dictated notes that evening, "that the English Channel was a disagreeable body of water." As such it "was unsafe for military operations prior to the month of May, and that the plan adopted at Quebec involved an immense expedition and had been set at that time for May 1, 1944."[21]

This was the first time the date of the launching of the Second Front had formally been given to the Russians — for in Moscow, in October, General Ismay, Churchill's chief of staff, had done his best, while he and General Deane shared the Overlord plan with Russian generals, *not* to give a target date to which the British could be held. As if to draw attention away from the date, Churchill now "interceded" to remark how thankful were the British for such a "disagreeable body of water."[22]

Resuming his overview the President explained that, while waiting to mount Overlord, there was the question of how best the American and British forces could help keep or even draw away significant forces of the Wehrmacht from the Russian front. In the spirit of candidness and openness, the President admitted there was currently concern about "what use could be made of allied forces in the Mediterranean in such a way as to bring the maximum aid to the Soviet armies on the Eastern front." Some of these operations, it was warned, might delay the Overlord invasion by "one, two or three months," namely by pursuing schemes "in Italy, the Adriatic and Aegean Seas and Turkey." For his own part, however, the President "emphasized the fact," as he put it, "that in his opinion the large cross-channel operation should not be delayed by secondary operations."[23]

The President's reference to Overlord, his revelation of its target date, and his emphatic declaration that he himself wanted no "delay" or "diversions" left Brooke feeling miserable — a "poor and not very helpful speech," as he sneered in his diary. If so, it was a sign of things to come. "From then on," Brooke added, "the conference went from bad to worse!" — for Stalin *agreed* with the President's preference for Overlord priority, indeed proceeded to advocate "cross Channel operations at the expense of all else"![24]

This was not, in truth, quite what happened — at least as observers other than Brooke saw it. Stalin, in their view, had followed the President's opening resumé by giving a quiet, measured address that impressed everyone. The Marshal began by congratulating the Western Allies on their successes in the Pacific, and assured all those present — American, British, and Russian — that the Soviet Union would definitely join the war against Japan; in fact it would begin sending major forces to Siberia for the task as soon as Nazi Germany was defeated. The Soviet commander in chief then proceeded to give a frank and detailed account of Russian operations since the summer of that year.

As Stalin succinctly put it, the Soviet armies were facing some 260 Wehrmacht divisions, including 10 Hungarian, 20 Finnish, and an estimated 18 Romanian. The Soviets could field 330 divisions, but in offensive warfare this was not enough to guarantee success; moreover, even the "numerical superiority the Soviets possessed" was gradually being "evened out" as Hitler switched more Wehrmacht divisions to the Eastern Front. Winter weather meant that operations had slowed down; the Germans were not only counterattacking but seeking to retake Kiev with 8 panzer divisions — 5 of them fresh — and 23 infantry divisions.

The war, in other words, was by no means won — and if the Allies abandoned their methodical advance and chose half-baked alternatives, it could still be lost. Freeing the Mediterranean for Allied shipping had been a signal success, but to imagine Italy or the northern Adriatic was the proper place to bring down the Third Reich was nonsensical. The Alps, Stalin pointed out, "constituted an almost insuperable barrier" — something "the famous Russian General [Alexander] Suvorov had discovered in his time."[25]

This was a telling admission, since Suvorov had been probably the greatest commander in Russian history: a general who himself had led an Austro-Russian army in Italy; a general who had captured Milan, and who had driven the French out of Italy. He had not subsequently been able to cross the Alps, however, and had been forced to retreat to Russia.

Italy, then, was a futile theater of war, beyond pinning down a limited number of Wehrmacht divisions. The real truth was, it was the Germans who were pinning down significant Allied forces in Italy, rather than the reverse. In the "opinion of the Soviet military leaders," Stalin explained, "Hitler was endeavoring to retain as many allied Divisions as possible where no decision could be reached," in Italy. Whereas, he said, "the best method" — at least in the "Soviet opinion" — "was getting at the heart of Germany with an attack through northern or northwestern France." Even, possibly, an additional attack "through southern France. He admitted that this would be a very difficult operation since the Germans would fight like devils to prevent it" — but better, surely, than wasted efforts in Italy. Or, Stalin added, the Aegean, which was an equally fatuous alternative. For although it would be "helpful" to inveigle Turkey into entering the war on the Allied side, "the Balkans were far from the heart of Germany." As the Marshal concluded, "northern France," or Overlord, "was best."[26]

Churchill, listening to the interpreter's version of Stalin's address, and aware of the twenty other persons in the room, was shocked. Shocked, however, into final reality: the reality that, by seeking to alter the strategy agreed at Quebec, he had taken the British team on a wild goose chase — wasting vital preparatory time for the Overlord invasion, upsetting his most important allies, and pursuing reckless fantasies, the consequences of which had not been thought through and could only shame the British contingent. As cowards, moreover.

All Churchill could do, in the circumstances, was to assure everyone the British "were determined to carry it [Overlord] out in the late spring or early summer of 1944." The Overlord plan envisaged an "initial assault of 16 British [including Canadian] and 19 U.S. Divisions, a total of 35."[27]

Brooke was not impressed by this. "Winston replied and was not at his best," Brooke recorded in his diary. "President chipped in and made matters worse. We finished up with a suggestion partly sponsored by the President that we should close operations in Italy before taking Rome."[28]

Before taking Rome? After all that Brooke and his fellow British chiefs of staff had done over the past two months, on Churchill's instructions, to plot and argue for more offensive action in Italy . . . ? This was the very opposite of music to Brooke's smarting ears. Moreover, the Russian marshal's opinion that Turkey was "beyond hope," as he put it, and his realistic prediction that "nothing could induce her to come into the war on any account," had poured ice-cold water on the Prime Minister's dreams. "Dardanelles were apparently not worth opening," Brooke added. "We sat for 3½ hours and finished up this conference," the British Army head fumed, "by confusing plans more than they ever have before!"[29]

For Churchill the opening meeting had been three and half hours of sheer torture. When, "after the plenary session," Dr. Wilson saw the Prime Minister, he found Churchill "so dispirited" that, as the Prime Minister's personal physician, he "departed from my prudent habit and asked him outright whether anything had gone wrong."

Churchill was nothing if not pithy. "A bloody lot," he declared, "has gone wrong."[30]

So dispirited by the plenary was Churchill, in fact, that Stalin had felt it necessary to assure the Prime Minister he hadn't meant to "belittle" the importance of what had been achieved that year in the Mediterranean, since those operations had been "of very real value." Churchill had "thanked the Marshal for his courtesy," insisting that neither he nor the President had ever considered the Mediterranean "as anything more than a stepping-stone for the main cross-Channel invasion." Britain had a population of only forty-six million, however, and with commitments in "the Middle East, India," et cetera, could not be expected to do too much.[31]

It was a somewhat pathetic confession.

As Stalin had suggested, instead of wasting battle-hardened troops in Italy to take Rome, would it not make more sense, if they really wanted to help guarantee the success of Overlord, to launch a secondary landing in southern France that would draw German divisions away from the English Channel? As a strategist Stalin thus agreed with the President: he would be more "inclined to leave 10 divisions in Italy and postpone the capture of Rome in order to launch the attack in southern France two months in advance of Overlord."[32]

Churchill had been stunned — and had only been able to reply that he hoped "Marshal Stalin would permit him to develop arguments to demonstrate why it was necessary for the allied forces to capture Rome, otherwise it would have the appearance of a great Allied defeat in Italy."[33]

A defeat, when the Italian government had already surrendered?

Stalin had been visibly unimpressed by the value Churchill placed upon such "appearances." Undeterred, Churchill had gone on to make an even more specious argument, claiming that "without the fighter cover which would be possible only from the north Italian fields it would be impossible to invade northern France."

D-day impossible without fighters *operating from northern Italy*?

It was the first the President or any of his chiefs had heard of such a claim. Perhaps the Prime Minister had meant southern France? Whatever he had intended to say, however, it had sounded lame — and the President had put him out of his misery by interceding. The question of "relative timing was very important," Mr. Roosevelt had said — in fact, "nothing should be done to delay the carrying out of Overlord," he'd emphasized. And delay was, clearly, what would happen "if any operations in the eastern Mediterranean were undertaken. He proposed, therefore, that the staffs work out tomorrow morning a plan of operations for striking at southern France," either before, during, or soon after the cross-Channel invasion.[34]

Stalin had concurred, pointing out that "the Russian experience had shown that an attack from one direction was not effective," given the defensive skills of the Wehrmacht. Instead, "the Soviet armies now launched an offensive from two sides at once which forced the enemy to move his reserve back and forth. He added that he thought such a two way operation in France would be very successful."[35]

Still Churchill had resisted, however: loath to surrender his dreams of "victory" in the Mediterranean and Aegean — or to accept a May 1944 launch of an invasion in whose success he had frankly never truly believed. The Prime Minister had therefore countered that "it would be difficult for him to leave idle the British forces in the eastern Mediterranean which numbered some 20 divisions, British controlled, which could not be used outside of that area, merely for the purpose of avoiding any insignificant delay in Overlord."[36]

Even Churchill had realized he wasn't making sense, and that the tide of the plenary meeting was running fiercely against him. He had therefore said that "if such was the decision" to concentrate wholly on Overlord, then the British "would, of course, agree, but they could not wholeheartedly agree to postpone operations in the Mediterranean" on which he'd set his heart — especially an amphibious landing north of Naples that would, he was certain, force the Germans to cede Rome. If Turkey did decline to join the Allies, it would make further Aegean operations pointless, he granted, but "he personally favored some flexibility in the exact date of Overlord. He proposed that the matter be considered overnight and have the staffs examine the various possibilities in the morning."[37]

Stalin could only scoff at such endless obstructionism. As the Russian dictator remarked, he "had not expected to discuss technical military questions" at Tehran, and he had "no military staff" with him. However, if more detailed analysis of the Western powers' own competing plans was required, "Marshal Voroshilov would do his best."[38]

The situation would, in sum, have been risible, had it not been so disheartening. By opposing Overlord's May 1944 date, in defiance of the Quebec agreement, Churchill had not only split the Anglo-American alliance, but had made the British military team look ridiculous — as General Brooke was painfully aware.

Years later, when annotating his diary, Brooke admitted he had had, until then, no idea Stalin was a "strategist." The plenary meeting at the Russian Embassy in Tehran had, however, put this misapprehension to rest. "I rapidly grew to appreciate," he wrote, "the fact that he had a military brain of the very highest calibre. Never once in any of his statements did he make any strategic error, nor did he ever fail to appreciate all the implications of a situation with a quick and unerring eye."[39]

By contrast "Roosevelt never made any great pretence at being a strategist and left Marshall or Leahy to talk for him," Brooke reflected[40] — completely forgetting that General Marshall had not even been present at the meeting. Or that Leahy and King, sitting behind the President, never once spoke. Neither Brooke nor Churchill, in fact, would ever acknowledge their military bungle — or the President's defining role, behind his mask of "country gentleman," in putting down the British revolt.

As for Stalin, he was unequivocal in agreeing with President Roosevelt: a chairman who "filled the part most effectively," as even General Ismay, Churchill's chief of staff, later admitted, recalling that the President was "the picture of health and was at his best throughout the conference — wise conciliatory and paternal," whereas the Prime Minister "was suffering from a feverish cold and loss of voice."[41]

By the evening of November 28, 1943, at Tehran, then, the die was cast, as even General Brooke acknowledged. "This Conference is over when it has only just begun," he complained that night to Churchill's doctor — adding that Stalin "has got the President in his pocket."[42]

Brooke's obtuseness about the President, as about Overlord, was disappointingly representative of the British team supporting the Prime Minister at Tehran, unfortunately: a refusal to face facts prior to Tehran, in Tehran, and after Tehran — indeed even after the war.

Marshal Stalin, however, fascinated them. The Marshal would have made "a fine poker player," General Ismay later recalled. "He did not speak much, but his interventions made in a quiet voice and without any gestures, were direct and decided. Sometimes they were so abrupt as to be rude" to British ears, for he "left no doubt in anyone's mind that he was master in his own house. He saw no point, for example in the proposal that the military experts of the three countries should meet the next morning, at Churchill's request, to examine the implications of Churchill's alternative strategy. 'The decisions are our business,' he said. 'That is what we have come for.'"[43]

Like Brooke, General Ismay would later see Stalin's unwillingness to discuss Churchill's alternative Mediterranean strategy as an example of the dictator's secret plans for postwar Russian hegemony. "It is doubtful if many of those who listened to the discussion grasped the significance of Stalin's determination to keep Anglo-American forces as far as possible away from the Balkans. It was not until later that we realised that his ambitions were just as imperialistic as those of the Czars, whose power and property he now enjoyed," Ismay wrote, "but that he was capable of looking much further ahead than they had ever been."[44]

Such retrospective justifications of British alternative strategy testified to Britain's loyalty to Churchill's political genius and foresight. But in truth they were as silly as Brooke's claim the President was in "Stalin's pocket."

Looking back, Admiral King recalled "the long struggle" it took to get the cross-Channel operation mounted. "You see, the British always shook their heads over what developed as 'Overlord.' They pointed to the highways, the railroads that ran east and west and the ability of the Germans to shift forces up against whatever landing we made before we could get the beachheads established," King later recalled. The "British felt we had posted [connived with] the Russians, so that the Russians and ourselves were of one mind" in relation to Overlord as "the second front" — the Russian front being the first. But such accusations of prior collusion were nonsense, King sniffed. "There was a meeting of our minds," he acknowledged of the Tehran Conference, "but I don't think it was concerted at all. I don't think we prompted the Russians. They had their own ideas" — which simply mirrored those of the United States in terms of clear military strategy: namely how best to defeat Nazi Germany. The British "wanted to recover the Dodecanese," from which they'd been ignominiously expelled in recent weeks; "they wanted to recover Rhodes; they wanted to get into Crete; above all they wanted to go up into Yugoslavia."[45] Stalin had been contemptuous. "Marshal Stalin waved aside all those proposals as side issues. That wasn't what he meant as 'second front.'" Moreover, the Russian marshal was by this time well experienced in the only way to defeat the Wehrmacht in battle. If the Western Allies had so many forces in the Mediterranean, why not use them to reinforce Overlord with landings "in Southern France"? King recalled Stalin's question. The Russian dictator's recommendation of landings in southern France had come as a complete but profoundly welcome surprise to the President and the American team at Tehran, after so much British opposition and backpedaling since Quebec. "I don't think he [Stalin] was prompted by anybody at all in the American side," with regard to southern France. "I don't think Mr. Roosevelt prompted that," King reflected[46] — his memory borne out by the minutes of the meeting.[47]

The Russian marshal, in other words, had spoken as a military strategist who had learned his lesson, after a desperately poor start, in *how to defeat the Wehrmacht* — whereas Churchill and the British chiefs hadn't: forever imagining they could pursue peripheral avenues, from Norway to the Balkans, that took no account of the terrain. Or the enemy.

King had no personal animosity toward the Prime Minister. "King likes

Churchill very much indeed," an American journalist had noted during the summer of 1943, before the Quebec Conference, "although he laughingly said that he always had his hand on his watch when Mr. Churchill was trying to 'sell' a point. Mr. Churchill, said [Admiral] King, is first, last and always for the British Empire and you have to always remember that when dealing with him. This, remarked the Admiral, is as it should be and Churchill is respected for it."[48]

The President, likewise, was fond of Churchill — while holding fast to his pocket watch. Above all Mr. Roosevelt was, as Ismay noted, an experienced chairman: a conciliator who understood that the aging prime minister should if possible be brought down gently. The British could not be bullied into submission — for their full-scale cooperation would be crucial in opening a successful Second Front. Moreover their military presence would be required for years to come in ensuring postwar security, the President reasoned.

Since the U.S. chiefs of staff had already prepared a paper on the pincer-like invasion of southern France ("Anvil") for the Cairo Conference, the President suggested they share it at a Combined Chiefs meeting the next morning, together with Marshal Voroshilov, before the second, afternoon plenary meeting — but should *not* discuss Aegean or other diversions a moment longer.

It was eight o'clock, and Hopkins, for his part, was hungry. "I thought we were going to be late for dinner, when the President suggested an adjournment," Hopkins afterwards told Churchill's doctor.[49]

The President's suggestion had been met with relief all round. The first, three-and-a-half-hour plenary meeting of the world's three most powerful Allied leaders had thus come to an end — Roosevelt retiring to his quarters next door, and as president of the United States inviting Churchill and Stalin to be his guests and dine with him at 8:30 that very evening.

22

A Real Scare

WINSTON CHURCHILL MIGHT be angry, as he admitted to his doctor, but he was too wise not to see he was now outnumbered. He had threatened in front of the British War Cabinet he would resign if he did not get his way with the United States. He had boasted to Harold Macmillan, his political minister at Eisenhower's headquarters, and to his British chiefs of staff, that he was willing to provoke the Americans into switching their forces to the Pacific if he did not get his way over furthering his Mediterranean schemes and delaying Overlord to 1945. It had always been a risky maneuver, however — and the President's stonewalling and refusal to countenance any change in the Quebec agreement in Cairo had effectively disabled the British insurrection.

The fact was, the Prime Minister now recognized, he could not make good on his threats. It was unlikely the deputy prime minister or the British cabinet would support him in walking away from the Tehran Summit, or in deliberately invoking a breakdown in United Nations military strategy, merely to invade Rhodes, a small Greek island. He would have to abide by majority decision-making, lest the "grand alliance" he himself had done so much to create be sundered.

Stalin's open evisceration of Churchill's Mediterranean/Aegean "diversions," however, had cut the Prime Minister to the quick. Tired by the hours-long debate over Overlord, its timetable and its alternatives, the President nevertheless tried to encourage a positive atmosphere in his sitting room, before they sat down to eat. "Roosevelt mixed the pre-dinner cocktails himself, which were unlike anything I have ever tasted," Bohlen remembered. "He put a large quantity of vermouth, both sweet and dry, into a pitcher of ice, added a smaller amount of gin, stirred the concoction rapidly, and poured it out. Stalin accepted the glass and drank but made no comment until Roosevelt asked him how he liked it. 'Well, all right, but it is cold on the stomach,' the dictator said."[1]

It was an "interesting" start to an all-American meal of "steak and baked-potato dinner prepared by his Filipino mess boys," Bohlen recalled.[2] But one that, unfortunately, quickly became as potentially querulous as the plenary; indeed the loose, alcohol-fueled, no-holds-barred discussion at the President's dining table became, in retrospect, shameful: a free-flowing conversation, laced with drink and conducted in front of the leaders' political and diplomatic advisers — Harry Hopkins and Ambassador Harriman, Anthony Eden and Ambassador Kerr, and Russian foreign commissar Vyacheslav Molotov — who, for the most part, listened in horror.

The President's attempts to lighten the tone of the dinner merely led to competitive assertions, claims, and opinions that in hindsight were unworthy of the three leaders, who disparaged not only individuals but whole nations. The French, especially, did not come out well, given that all three leaders detested General de Gaulle, for all that he stood so courageously for French antifascism. Once again, the President and Marshal Stalin voiced an even worse opinion of the French people than of de Gaulle personally. Stalin felt the French deserved no "considerate treatment" once liberated; in his view the "entire French ruling class was rotten to the core." It had "delivered France to the Germans," and was "actively helping our enemies," the Nazis, both in industrial output and manpower supplied to the Third Reich. The dictator "therefore felt that it would be not only unjust but dangerous to leave in French hands any important strategic points after the war."[3]

Roosevelt, who abhorred the idea of the French seeking to reconstitute their colonial empire after the war, agreed about military bases — saying New Caledonia, in the South Pacific, and Dakar, on the west coast of Africa, should not be returned to French rule. Which led Churchill to assure the President and the Premier that for its part, Britain was different from France. Britain was not seeking any territory after victory. Yet "for the future peace of the world" he agreed that the United States, the Soviet Union, Great Britain, and China should definitely have and maintain military bases from which, as the "Four Policemen" of the United Nations, they could nip nascent problems in the bud. Stalin, however, was unwilling to leave it at that. The restoration of Europe's Victorian empires was not, he felt, the purpose in defeating Nazi Germany. "France could not be trusted with any strategic possessions outside her own border," he asserted — claiming that Gaston Bergery, Vichy ambassador to Moscow and then Turkey, was typical: the French more willing to negotiate with their former enemy, the Germans, once the war was over, than with their liberators, the Americans and British.

This was far from an exaggeration — but in its flippant way it offered no constructive idea of how, shorn of its colonial territories, the French were miraculously to be reconditioned as antifascists, let alone anti-Germans. The President's idea of disallowing anyone over the age of forty to stand for election after the war, which he repeated at dinner, was worthless as genuine potential policy. It skirted, moreover, the key to postwar European peace and recon-struction: Germany.

Once again it was the President and Stalin who held court on the moral abomination of Nazism — but with only the vaguest notion, still, of how to deal with it at war's end. "The very word 'Reich,' or 'empire,' should be stricken from the language," the President opined, prompting Stalin not only to agree, wholeheartedly, but to go further, saying that unless the "victorious allies" made sure to "prevent any recrudescence of German militarism, they would have failed in their duty."[4]

Churchill said little, still smarting over the afternoon. Yet the aging prime minister was the only one of the three national leaders who had hands-on knowledge and decades-long experience of dealing with Germany and France. His role in the end-of-war deliberations and decisions yet to be made would be an essential one — especially when considering how the Third Reich should, or should not, be dismembered or reformed.

Fortified by more liquor the conversation then moved on to Poland — an-other matter of huge political significance, since Poland lay between Germany and the Soviet Union. The country was immensely important for Stalin as a buffer state, as all were aware. In the fall of 1939, following Hitler's invasion and military conquest, it had been split between the two signatories to the Hitler-Stalin Pact. Even the Russian occupation of eastern Poland, however, had failed to provide an effective buffer against Nazi dreams of further con-quest. Barbarossa — Hitler's massive, Napoleon-like invasion from German-occupied Poland — had carried the Wehrmacht almost to the brink of the Caspian Sea, and resulted in the death of millions of Russians, as well as the devastating destruction of whole cities such as Stalingrad. Now the boot was on the other foot — and with more than three hundred divisions on the Eastern Front, almost within artillery range of the old Polish border, Stalin proposed — as he had at the Moscow Conference — that the permanent Rus-sian border with Poland be moved west, farther away from Moscow.

With four million Polish American voters in America, the President de-clined to comment. Nor would he discuss the future of the Baltic states of Lithuania, Latvia, and Estonia: traditionally Russian-controlled territories which had become independent after World War I and also had their stalwart supporters in the United States, especially among émigrés. By favoring an in-ternational guarantee of shipping access to and from the Baltic Sea through the Danish-Swedish straits the President hoped to urge the conferees to think positively — to consider open trade and the revival of world commerce rather than defensive positions and possessions. In fact, from this he moved on to float the idea of the future United Nations.[5]

"Roosevelt was about to say something," Bohlen later recalled, "when suddenly, in the flick of an eye, he turned green and great drops of sweat began to bead off his face; he put a shaky hand to his forehead. We were all caught by surprise."[6]

Of the three leaders — despite a long, 7,775-mile journey to Tehran — the President had seemed until that moment the least careworn. Stalin's hair had turned positively gray, according to both Hopkins[7] and the British interpreter,[8] while the Prime Minister, who had very little hair, was still suffering from his bad cold and was tired and out of sorts. The ailing Harry Hopkins, so often looking at death's door himself, now leapt to his feet and wheeled the President to his room, next door. There he was lifted onto the bed and Dr. McIntire examined him.

Poison? Admiral Leahy, in his diary, acknowledged this had been the "immediate assumption" — one so serious in its international implications that for several years there would be no mention of the President's sudden collapse in official minutes, records, memoirs, or histories of the Tehran Summit. Admiral Leahy's diary recorded, however, that "at dinner tonight the President suffered an acute digestive attack which alarmed us because of the possibility that poison had been given to him."[9] Lieutenant Rigdon, in charge of all communications to and from the White House, years later recalled that the "attack threw a real scare into all of us. Our first thought was that his food had been poisoned."[10]

Poison seemed unlikely, if only because the meal had been personally prepared by the President's Filipino staff. Even the cooking range was an unlikely source of the attack, since it had been trucked to the President's quarters that very afternoon, with no advance warning, from General Connolly's Lend-Lease Amirabad compound, when it was realized the Russians had either removed or failed to reinstate all cooking equipment in the President's quarters. A German assassination attempt was, of course, possible — but scarcely a Russian one, given the Soviet Union's dependence upon American supplies, arms, and support in the war.

Was it a *health* scare, then?

The President did not mention the occurrence in his diary. Nor did he in a letter he sent afterwards to Daisy Suckley from Tehran. Neither was it mentioned by Elliott Roosevelt in his detailed postwar memoir covering the conference, published only a year after hostilities ended — perhaps because Elliott hadn't actually been in Tehran that day, or the next (his aircraft having experienced engine trouble in Palestine). Nor did Dr. McIntire mention the incident in his memoirs, also published immediately after the war. The same was the case with Hopkins's biographer, Robert Sherwood, and the White House Secret Service detail commander, Mike Reilly — the President's family and staff by then anxious there be no suggestion, in retrospect, that the President had been ill-advised to have stood for reelection the following year, in 1944.

Rumors of a health scare at Tehran would eventually surface, though. Some would later surmise the President had had a heart attack,[11] or been suffering cancer of the stomach,[12] or gallbladder disease,[13] even a tumor on his liver.[14] Since no further symptoms of a serious medical condition appeared until the following year, however, these would all amount to idle speculation.

In the meantime, assuring himself, his patient, and the President's colleagues that it was merely an attack of acute indigestion, Admiral McIntire insisted the President remain in bed, in his room. For his part Hopkins returned to the dining room, where he reported the doctor's diagnosis to the guests. By this point dinner was over.

Relieved at the news the President's collapse was probably indigestion, the Russian marshal and the Prime Minister retired to a smaller room in the Russian Embassy. There they continued talking into the night — carving up the world, at least in their cups.

For President Roosevelt, Commander in Chief of his nation's armed forces, the historic day was over. There would be at most three more days in Tehran in order to get what he wanted, assuming that he quickly recovered from his gastric attack. Also, that he was able to put down any renewed British attempt to sabotage Overlord.

23

Impasse

MERCIFULLY THE PRESIDENT awoke on Monday, November 29, 1943, feeling much better.

"The President this morning has entirely recovered from his indisposition," Admiral Leahy noted with relief in his diary.[1] "At breakfast in the morning FDR seemed to be completely recovered," Lieutenant Rigdon also recalled,[2] while the President's interpreter, Charles Bohlen, noted the President seemed completely restored to good health and "was alert as ever" when the time came to see Stalin again, privately, at 2:45 p.m., in his quarters.[3]

Mr. Churchill had hoped to have lunch with the President first, but the President had really had enough of Winston's continuing effort to derail Overlord — especially after hearing what had transpired at the special get-together of top American and British chiefs of staff and Russian military officials in the Board Room of the Russian Embassy at 10:30 that morning.

Leahy's report to the President was disturbing. "At a small meeting Marshal Voroshilov, General Brooke, Air Marshal Portal, General Marshall, and I discussed questions to come before the conference," Leahy noted in his diary, but "made little progress toward an agreement because of British desires for postponement of the cross-channel operation that has long been scheduled for next May."[4]

It was really too bad, Leahy sighed. Again and again Marshal Voroshilov had pressed General Brooke to answer why *Turkey*, of all countries, should be allowed to delay or abandon Overlord — for Brooke acknowledged that, by keeping Overlord's essential landing craft in the Mediterranean and Aegean, "the retarding of the date set for Overlord" would definitely be necessary, and that, in pursuance of further Mediterranean "operations he had outlined" — which would involve "the capture of the Dodecanese Islands, beginning with Rhodes" in order to "open sea communications to the Dardanelles," and the establishment of airfields in Turkey — "we should be able to hold and destroy the German forces now in the Mediterranean area while awaiting the date for Overlord."[5]

To Voroshilov — and to the American team — this was pie in the sky, and unworthy of a general who considered himself a great strategist. There were now seven U.S. infantry and two U.S. armored divisions in Britain, training for D-day, with some sixty divisions in the United States to follow them onto the beaches of northern France in 1944. The U.S. chiefs then attempted to discuss Overlord air cover and ports — especially man-made floating ports — but General Brooke's insistence they switch to discussing more operations in the Mediterranean led Voroshilov finally to question whether Brooke really believed in Overlord.

Everything Brooke had hitherto said at the meeting sounded defeatist — from his claim that only three or four divisions could be landed on D-day to his assertion that the May 1, 1944, target date for Overlord could only be met by removing all landing craft "from the Mediterranean now" — a removal that was, in the British view, too perilous to contemplate. It would "bring the Italian operations almost to a standstill," Brooke warned — and to scale down the current fighting in Italy was anathema to the British team. "The British wished, during the preparations for an eventual Overlord, to keep fighting the Germans in the Mediterranean to the maximum degree possible," Brooke had stated. Overlord's landing craft should therefore be kept in the Mediterranean, he insisted. As he argued, "Such operations are necessary not only to hold the Germans in Italy but to create the situation in Northern France which will make Overlord possible."[6]

General Marshall had heard all this before. He emphasized that if further amphibious operations were undertaken in the Mediterranean, "Overlord will inevitably be delayed."[7] Marshal Voroshilov kept pointing out that, from the point of view of coalition warfare — since Soviet forces were anxious to launch a massive simultaneous assault from the east — Overlord *must* have priority, with everything else considered "ancillary": "all the other operations, such as Rome, Rhodes and what not, must be planned to assist Overlord and certainly not hinder it." Brooke's "additional operations" threatened to "hurt Overlord," Voroshilov complained — prompting him to emphasize "that this must not be so. These operations must be planned to secure Overlord, which is the most important operation, and not to hurt it." With Brooke stonewalling, however — the British Army chief predicting that Overlord was "bound to fail" unless his alternatives and provisos were accepted[8] — it became clear to Admiral Leahy that only the three world leaders could break the impasse.

In which case, Leahy reported to the "Big Boss," it would be up to the President of the United States, as chairman of the conference, to engineer a solution that kept the Allies together.

24

Pricking Churchill's Bubble

CHURCHILL WAS NO HELP, the President found when the conferees reassembled. Despite knowing from his British chiefs that their meeting with Marshal Voroshilov and the U.S. Joint Chiefs that morning had gone badly, the Prime Minister simply restated British insistence Overlord be delayed to permit more ventures in the Mediterranean and Aegean.

The President, a paraplegic, had traveled almost eight thousand miles across the world to meet Stalin and rehearse some of the issues their countries would face, once the war was won — prompting Stalin, at dinner the night before, to have his interpreter "tell the President I now understand what it has meant for him to make the effort to come on such a long journey — Tell him that the next time I will go to him."[1] Yet Churchill was relentless. Despite hearing from Stalin's own lips how uninterested were the Russians in any operational plan other than a spring Overlord — if possible with a pincer attack on southern France, together with the planned Russian offensive — to ensure the defeat of Germany in 1944, the British prime minister seemed intent on doing battle *yet again* for his alternative Mediterranean and Aegean strategy.

The President, furious at the British resurrection of their Mediterranean plans that morning, had therefore rejected Churchill's invitation to join him for lunch at the British Legation. Spurned, the Prime Minister was "plainly put out," his doctor noted in his diary, deaf to the reason. "It is not like him," Churchill had murmured, puzzled[2] — and hurt by the excuse Harry Hopkins, as the President's emissary, had attempted to give: that Roosevelt didn't want Stalin to think the Westerners were "ganging up" against him.[3]

For the President, getting a firm decision on the date and absolute priority of Overlord was now more important than Churchill's wounded pride. The Prime Minister's endless efforts to postpone the invasion had begun to sound like a broken, jarring gramophone record. It had taken the President simply too long to effect the encounter with Stalin — a meeting he had always wanted to hold without the Prime Minister, in order that Churchill's attempts to subvert or postpone Overlord should not poison the summit — to now squander the chance of endgame and postwar agreements with the USSR.

It was now day three of the Tehran Summit — and crucial that Churchill's opposition to D-day be put down definitively, so that the leaders could move on to discuss the war's endgame, including the defeat of Japan, as well as the President's postwar plans for a United Nations body. The summit with Stalin had never been intended to be a contentious military confrontation between allies; now, thanks to British intransigence, it was. Instead of Churchill being the President's ardent lieutenant, the Prime Minister had become, at Tehran, the President's most ardent military opponent. He seemed willing not only to risk the Allies losing the war against Hitler, but to vitiate also the possibility of a unified coalition of Western allies, strong and willing to check Soviet communist aspirations, should they proved inimical to Western wishes in the war's endgame — and beyond. It was deplorable — and exactly what, in his heart of hearts, the President had feared when setting off from Hampton Roads with his advisers on November 13.

Aware that Stalin was due to visit him in his quarters at 2:45 p.m., the President meantime thanked Admiral Leahy and General Marshall, who'd come to his rooms at 2:30 to rehearse how best to proceed.

Stalin arrived with Molotov. "Punctual to the minute the Soviet leaders arrived," Elliott Roosevelt, who had arrived almost immediately afterwards, recalled. "I was introduced. We pulled up chairs in front of Father's couch, and I sat back to collect my thoughts."[4] These were largely focused on the face of the small, yet "tremendously dynamic" figure of the dictator, who showed "great reserves of patience and of reassurance" as the President proceeded to sketch out, using a piece of paper, his concept of a postwar peace and security organization that, in contrast to the League of Nations after the Versailles Conference, both of their countries could join this time. It would be, the President outlined, a "large organization composed of some 35 members of the United Nations," which would meet and "make recommendations to a smaller body," or executive committee.

Worldwide or European? Stalin asked.

"World-wide," Roosevelt replied.[5]

Explaining his idea of a UN "executive committee," or security council, the President said it would comprise "the Soviet Union, the United States, United Kingdom and China, together with two additional European states, one South American, one Near East, one Far Eastern country, and one British Dominion." It would deal with "all non-military questions such as agriculture, food, health, and economic questions."[6]

Would it have the power to make binding decisions? Stalin asked. Yes and no, the President responded; it could "make recommendations for settling disputes with the hope that the nations concerned would be guided thereby," but he accepted the U.S. Congress would never agree to be bound, militarily, by "a decision of such a body." Which had led him to his concept of the "Four Policemen," namely the Soviet Union, United States, Great Britain, and China: an ad hoc group that would "have the power to deal immediately with any threat to the peace," as Charles Bohlen noted in his minutes of the conversation, "and any sudden emergency which requires this action."[7]

In later years Bohlen was amazed, as a career diplomat, by Roosevelt's presentation — especially the example the President offered Stalin of a threat "arising out of a revolution or of developments in a small country" that threatened to get out of hand. "This bit of prescience by Roosevelt forecast many of the problems that the United States has had to deal with in the postwar period as a result of communist actions," Bohlen commented in retrospect.

"Stalin did not question Roosevelt's idea on this point," Bohlen recalled — in fact the dictator "never showed any antagonism to the general idea of a world body. It was quite obvious," he reflected, "that Stalin felt it would be much more dangerous to be outside any world organization than to be in it" — providing the Soviet Union could "block actions it did not like."[8] Moreover, when the President argued for a world organization rather than merely a European body — which Churchill favored — and Stalin posited that the United States might, as one of the "Four Policemen," then have to send "American troops to Europe," the President did not demur, though he thought U.S. "planes and ships" rather than land armies would probably be sufficient, especially in enforcing a quarantine rather than embarking on hostilities . . .[9]

The discussion was almost mesmerizing in its visionary nature. It left unexamined, as Stalin pointed out, the question of how to deal with Germany after the Third Reich was defeated. Moreover, Stalin was "dubious about Chinese participation,"[10] despite the President's explanation that this would be an investment in the future, given the sheer size and population of China. For all the myriad details still to be worked out, however, it was at least a blueprint for the postwar world: rough and imprecise, but an ideal all the Allies could *fight* for — if the British would only join with the Overlord program as they had promised at Quebec.

At almost 3:30 p.m. General Watson "looked in the door and announced that everything was ready. We got up and moved into the board room."[11] There the Prime Minister of Great Britain, ever conscious of the magical powers of ceremony, had arranged for a beautiful two-handed sword to be presented as a gift to the citizens of Stalingrad, in recognition of Soviet heroism in defending the crucial city in the winter of 1942–43. The ceremony was accompanied by national anthems played by the Red Army Band.

It was a touching gesture — and Stalin seemed genuinely "moved by this simple act of friendship," Churchill's doctor noted; "he bent over and kissed the sword." His armored train had passed through the ruins of Stalingrad on the way to Tehran, and he planned to visit the city on his way back to Moscow. "Roosevelt said there were tears in his eyes." Ruthless, and unarguably a psychopath in relation to his own people, he appeared, for a moment, actually "human,"[12] Churchill's doctor recorded.[13]

Photographs were duly taken to mark the occasion. Within minutes, however, the second plenary meeting commenced in the conference room — and the fireworks, once more, began.

To open the session the President, as chairman, asked that the British general, Sir Alan Brooke, commence by telling them what had transpired in their military discussions that morning.

Loath to admit the truth — namely, that the military representatives of the three countries had failed utterly to agree on a clear military policy to defeat Nazi Germany — Brooke attempted to paper over the disagreement, hoping that either Churchill would do better in convincing the British and Russians they must postpone the Overlord invasion, or that in yet another meeting of the three nations' generals he could somehow keep badgering the Americans until they, at least, gave in. In which case, he remained confident, the Russians would have to accept the decision, since Overlord was not, in the end, a Russian operation.

If Brooke was really banking on this, however, he was in for a school beating. Which Stalin now administered without turning a hair.

The British were still claiming they believed in Overlord. In that case, he asked: "Who will command Overlord?"[14]

The participants had now come to the critical moment of the Tehran Conference, in Bohlen's later view: "a crisis," as he put it. Moreover one that, sadly, rested entirely on the continued British "objections to fixing a date for Overlord."[15] The Russian dictator's question now cut through to the very core of the deadlock, however. Roosevelt admitted no commander had been appointed.

No commander? For an Allied amphibious assault operation involving perhaps a million men, slated to take place in barely *five months'* time? Could they be serious?

Stalin clearly thought not — for, as Churchill's doctor noted, "he would not believe we meant business until we had decided on the man to command the operation."[16]

For his part the President knew the real reason no commander had been appointed: namely, that he himself had consistently refused to assign his best general, George Catlett Marshall, unless the British agreed to the mounting of the operation on May 1, 1944 — a date which would give it the best chance to succeed. Relishing the embarrassing position in which Stalin's question put the British, the President thus turned to the man responsible for the calamity: Winston Churchill.

Mortified and ashamed, Churchill attempted to explain that a British "chief of staff" to a future commander had been appointed long ago, in March that year: General Frederick Morgan, a staff officer who had served as a headquarters officer in the retreat to Dunkirk. But he was forced to admit that, no. No Allied commander of the war's most critical operation had yet been appointed.

Attempting to disclaim responsibility, Churchill went on to explain the eventual commander would, however, be an American general, with a British commander then taking charge of an enlarged Mediterranean theater. Rather than endure further humiliation in front of so many witnesses Churchill then suggested, blushing, that the question would "best be discussed between the three of them" — the President, Marshal Stalin, and himself — "rather than in the large meeting."[17]

Yet the President was as determined as Marshal Stalin to get the matter of Overlord finally settled — in fact more so. He thus countered that an American supreme commander could only be appointed once the matter of Overlord's priority was resolved right there, at Tehran. This prompted Stalin to assure his allies "the Russians do not expect to have a voice in the selection of the [Overlord] Commander-in-Chief; they merely want to know who he is and to have him appointed as soon as possible" — for "nothing good would come out of the operation unless one man was made responsible not only for the preparation but for the execution of the operation."[18]

Churchill thereupon twisted in the wind — saying, off the top of his head, he "thought the appointment could be announced in a fortnight."[19]

"Winston was not good," Brooke noted frankly in his diary, thinking of the Prime Minister's long, vacillating, and digressive speech. "Bad from beginning to end."[20]

Mr. Roosevelt, in Brooke's eyes, hadn't helped — or rather, had refused to do so. Worse, he'd agreed completely with the Russian dictator's lacerating interrogation of the Prime Minister and his reasons for wanting to delay Overlord. Stalin's clear contempt for Churchill's floundering explanations of British pusillanimity seemed to Brooke, as a professional soldier, to be extremely well-directed. "Stalin meticulous with only two arguments," Brooke scribbled in his diary that night with sneaking admiration. "Cross Channel operation on May 1st, and also offensive in Southern France! Americans supported this view," he lamented.[21]

It was clear to almost everyone, however, that although the President might still be gentle with Churchill, Marshal Stalin, for his part, was losing patience with the Prime Minister. Churchill had wasted *yet another day* of plenary meetings. The Russian commander in chief wanted an end to Winston's ramblings, and to achieve it Stalin proposed they there and then agree to a three-point directive, which all three nations could then adhere to, namely: (1) "a date should be set and the [Overlord] operation should not be postponed," in order that the Soviets could time a simultaneous offensive "from the east"; (2) that a more or less simultaneous invasion of southern France should be mounted by the Western Allies, or immediately after Overlord, to help guarantee its success; and (3) that a commander in chief should be appointed forthwith — if possible at Tehran.[22]

Churchill refused. He pleaded that the Allies hadn't "studied" a South of France invasion; nor had they even contemplated dovetailing Overlord with a simultaneous Russian offensive — both of them untrue statements. The planning for Overlord had been progressing since the beginning of 1943, *eleven months* before. A simultaneous Russian offensive had been considered a sine qua non, and the very reason for General Deane's military mission in Moscow — since it was imperative Hitler not be able to reinforce the west, once Overlord began. Moreover American planners had spent a great deal of time exploring a simultaneous invasion of southern France.

Instead of expressing embarrassment, however, the Prime Minister appealed to his fellow leaders to change the subject, and discuss the possibility of neutral Turkey being enjoined to declare war on Germany. In order to put pressure on the Turks to do so, Churchill maintained, it would be necessary to retain landing craft in the Mediterranean — not for an invasion of southern France, but for operations in Italy or Rhodes. As he put it, using his memorable verbal artistry, "Now is the time to reap the crop if we will pay the small price of this reaping."[23]

As Brooke noted in his diary that night, however, this was familiar Churchillian flimflam: a typical invocation, larded with grand and memorable phrases invented on the spur of the moment, but reeking with sentiment rather than dispassionate military analysis. Redolent, moreover, with wolf cries: such as the claim that, unless landing craft were taken away from operations in the Pacific, there could be "no action" at all in the Mediterranean. In addition, he warned, if there were more than "12 mobile divisions" facing the Western Allies in France, Overlord would not be permitted by the British to take place at all . . .[24]

Given that the Soviet armies were facing *260 German divisions* in the field, this sounded pathetic. But the longer Churchill struggled to make his case for postponing Overlord, the more embarrassed all those present became. "I feel more like entering a lunatic asylum or a nursing home than continuing my present job," Brooke confessed in shame in his diary. "I am absolutely disgusted with the politicians' methods of waging war!! Why will they imagine that they are experts at a job they know nothing about! It is lamentable to listen to them!"[25]

Admiral Leahy, by contrast, was proud of his commander in chief — the

President saying unequivocally as chairman that, having heard out the Prime Minister, he was nevertheless "in favor of adhering to the original date for Overlord set at Quebec, namely, the first part of May."[26]

For his part Stalin, after three hours of Churchill's filibustering, came close to losing his temper. In the aftermath Hopkins related to Dr. Wilson how, when "the P.M. began once more to stress the strategic importance of Turkey and Rhodes, no one was surprised when the President intervened. 'We are all agreed,' he said, 'that Overlord is the dominating operation, and that any operation which might delay it cannot be considered by us.'" As Dr. Wilson quoted Hopkins's account that night, the Soviet dictator had been relieved. "Stalin looked at Winston as much as to say: 'Well, what about that?'"

Stalin, who did not suffer fools gladly, had hitherto shown unusual self-control — but it was clearly running out. He disputed Churchill's estimate of the number of Wehrmacht divisions in the Balkans, and the Prime Minister's claim that "with a minimum effort these divisions might be placed in a position where they could no longer be of any value," i.e., smashed.[27] There was no such thing as "minimum effort" in combat against the Wehrmacht.

The President was of like mind — considering it an attitude that merely led to distressing loss of Allied lives, often to no purpose. Defeating Wehrmacht forces entrenched in terrain suitable for good defense was no simple matter, even with modern Allied air power. The President had said that, in Yugoslavia, "commando raids" should certainly "be undertaken in the Balkans and that we should send all possible supplies to Tito in order to require [Axis forces in] Yugoslavia to keep their divisions there,"[28] but "without making any particular commitment which would interfere with Overlord." With this the Soviet dictator completely agreed. Stalin, moreover, doubted frankly whether Turkey would "enter the war"[29] — and even if it did, *it would not lead to the defeat of Nazi Germany.* Only Overlord, in tandem with a Russian offensive from the Eastern Front, could effect this. The rest were "diversions."[30]

Which led the President to sum up the plenary meeting by saying "we should therefore work out plans to contain" the German divisions in southern Europe, lest they be switched to reinforce those in France, but "only on such a scale as not to divert Overlord at the agreed time."[31]

Whenever the President mentioned the May deadline for Overlord, Churchill's heart sank further — for Stalin was in complete accord with the President, saying: "'You are right' — 'You are right.'"[32]

Still the Prime Minister resisted, though. When the President thus moved to get their formal agreement as to "the timing of Overlord," declaring that "it would be good for Overlord to take place about 1 May, or certainly not later than 15 or 20 May, if possible," to which Stalin agreed, saying "there would be suitable weather in May," Churchill interceded yet again, saying no, "he could not agree to that"![33]

The President had thus far been amazingly diplomatic, but Churchill's refusal to agree to D-day finally brought his legendary patience to an end. The President looked toward Stalin — and acting as the President's quasi-enforcer, Stalin duly took up the cudgel. The Marshal "turned on Churchill," Bohlen's minutes recorded. The Russian dictator "said he would like to ask him a simple question: 'Do the English believe in Overlord, or do they not?'"[34]

Churchill was understandably abashed — unused to being challenged so directly. Once again he asserted he was in support of Overlord, but "did not think that the many great possibilities in the Mediterranean should be ruthlessly cast aside as valueless merely on the question of a month's delay in Overlord."

A month's delay? The assertion sounded jejune, and unworthy of a commander in chief of Britain's military forces since 1940. Stalin clarified that the Russians were not asking them to "do nothing" in the Mediterranean; he simply wanted them to hold fast there, in order to set a real target date for Overlord. Still, however, Churchill objected, continuing to insist upon further "operations in the Eastern Mediterranean" — including a new invasion of Rhodes, and more pressure put on Turkey to enter the war — which would "create conditions indispensable to the success of Overlord."[35]

Rhodes indispensable to Overlord? The more the Prime Minister protested against a firm date in May for Overlord, the more obvious it was to everyone in the committee room that he was deliberately prevaricating. His talk of Turkish air bases, and "operations to drive and starve all German divisions out of the Aegean and open the Dardanelles" — operations that "could not be considered as military commitments of an indefinite character" — and comments that "our future will suffer great misfortune if we do not get Turkey into the war" since it would leave British troops "idle" — were a charade. British idleness in the Mediterranean had nothing to do with a target date for Overlord; it was British idleness in England, and in particular at 10 Downing Street, preparing for D-day, that had everything to do with the success of Overlord — now only months away. When Churchill suggested the subject be thrown back to the "ad hoc" committee of the Russian, British, and American military representatives, requiring yet more days of argument, Stalin pointed out he had only agreed to a summit lasting until December 1, though would extend this to leave on December 2, if necessary.[36]

It was at this point that President Roosevelt, as chairman of the gathering, decided to read out a proposed directive he'd penned on a piece of paper in front of him. It was damning.

"The Committee of the Chiefs of Staff," the President's draft read, "will assume that Overlord is the dominating operation." In considering "subsidiary operations" in the Mediterranean area they must take "into consideration that any delay should not affect Overlord."

Stalin agreed — though pointed out there was no mention of an actual date for D-day. To which the President responded, unequivocally, "that the date for Overlord had been fixed at Quebec," namely May 1, 1944, "and that only some much more important matter could possibly affect that date."[37]

Churchill's long, three-and-a-half-month struggle to delay or ditch Overlord was coming to an end — as Churchill himself at last recognized.

In perhaps the worst display of military leadership of his life he had wasted everyone's time in a vain attempt to avoid the cost of British casualties in mounting a successful Overlord. Yet British and American casualties in his alternative, peripheral strategy would be just as daunting if the Western Allies poured new men into the Mediterranean, Aegean, and Balkans — and to no common purpose. Nazi Germany would not be defeated by such operations. Only by launching Overlord, in tandem with a Russian offensive, could the Third Reich be brought down. Churchill's unending pleas for alternative "cheap" operations in the Mediterranean and Aegean were neither strategically sound, nor realistic in any military sense. As the famous British Eighth Army commander, General Bernard Montgomery, facing stalwart German defense in southern Italy in winter conditions, had written to the director of military operations only a few days before, "Why we start frigging about in the Dodecanese, and dispersing our efforts, beats me."[38]

It beat everyone else. Churchill's "frigging about," however, had finally been exposed at Tehran for what it was, in front of his country's two senior partners in the United Nations coalition. Humiliated, Churchill reluctantly caved in — proposing that the chiefs of staff translate the President's directive into clear tripartite military strategy that the leaders could sign off on, the next day.[39]

It had been a historic meeting. To spare Churchill further shame, the President "observed that within an hour a very good dinner would be awaiting all of them, with Marshal Stalin as their host, and that he for one would have a large appetite for it."

With that, at 7:15 p.m. on Monday, November 29, 1943, the three-hour plenary session broke up.

25

War and Peace

SITTING SILENTLY BEHIND the President during the plenary meeting, Admiral Leahy had found himself somewhat awed. "I am very favorably impressed by the Soviets' direct methods and by their plain speaking," the admiral confessed that night in his journal, writing as a professional naval officer. Though the Russian dictator "appears old and worn," he was "soft-spoken and inflexible in his purpose."

But the hero of the day had been Mr. Roosevelt. The President had ensured Churchill was given a fair chance to have his full say but in the end, they had been able to reach the brave and fateful tripartite decision the President wanted. "The meeting was conducted by the President with skill and a high order of diplomacy," Leahy observed.[1] The three leaders would discuss politics over dinner, without the chiefs of staff — for the strategy and timetable of the war against Hitler was now set. Churchill's strategic insurrection had been defeated, and the Allies could now work together to effect the defeat of Germany, then move on to defeat Japan.

Winston Churchill, however, was deeply distraught — aware he'd failed. Back at the British Legation, before dinner, he asked his doctor to syringe his aching throat — snarling at the humiliation of it all. "Nothing more can be done here," Dr. Wilson heard him muttering. "Bloody," he swore as he "stumped out" to join the President and Marshal Stalin at the Soviet Embassy for dinner.[2]

Left to dine in the British Legation, General Brooke, Air Marshal Portal, and Admiral Cunningham presented the mien of defeated men. "They are always the same, quiet and equable," Dr. Wilson noted in his diary, "but tonight they seemed put out. It had been a bad day for our people."[3]

It had.

"To our unity — war and peace!" the President raised a toast at dinner. To which Stalin had responded, in all seriousness, with the words: "I want to tell you, from the Russian point of view, what the President and the United States have done to win this war. The most important thing in this war are machines.

The United States has proven it can turn out from 8,000 to 10,000 airplanes per month. Russia can only turn out, at most, 3,000 airplanes a month. England turns out 3,000 to 3,500, which are principally heavy bombers. The United States, therefore, is a country of machines. Without the use of these machines, through Lend-Lease, we would lose this war."[4]

It had been an unusual wartime acknowledgment from the Soviet communist dictator, but it was sincere. In fact it had prompted the President to sum up the achievement of Tehran, as he saw it, in his response. "We have differing customs and philosophies and ways of life," he remarked. "Each of us works out our scheme of things according to the desires and ideas of our own peoples. But we have proved here at Tehran that the varying ideals of our nations can come together in a harmonious whole, moving unitedly for the common good of ourselves and of the world." Looking outside, he'd therefore been disposed to see, as he put it metaphorically, "that traditional symbol of hope, the rainbow."[5]

At the end of the long day night had fallen. The decision over Overlord, so endlessly contested, was now a done deal — with only the choice of a supreme commander for D-day to be made by the President, as U.S. commander in chief.

In contrast to the President's sense of achievement, General Sir Alan Brooke felt nothing but despair — unable and unwilling to appreciate the gigantic stride the Allies had made toward winning World War II. All the head of the British Army could see was the British showdown over strategy having failed to ignite. The alternative, evasive British military strategy now seemed in ruins. They would have to get behind Overlord. "May God help us in the future prosecution of this war" were the last words he scribbled in his diary in his slashing green hand before going to sleep, for "we have every hope of making an unholy mess of it."[6]

PART FOUR

---

*Who Will Command
Overlord?*

26

A Commander for Overlord

AT 2:35 P.M. on Thursday, December 2, 1943, the Sacred Cow, piloted by Major Ryan, touched down in Cairo at the end of its thirteen-hundred-mile journey back from Iran.

A "Declaration of the Three Powers" had been jointly signed the night before, and was to be announced to the world once the three leaders had departed. The document, drafted by the President, reaffirmed "our determination that our nations shall work together in war and in the peace that will follow.

"As to war," the declaration had continued, "our military staffs have joined in our round table discussions, and we have concerted our plans for the destruction of the German forces. We have reached complete agreement as to the scope and timing of the operations to be undertaken from the east, west and south."[1]

Three theaters — no longer two! And their "timing" agreed.

Those who'd feared the Allies were bogged down in Italy, or were worried the Soviets were being pushed back in Russia, could now breathe more easily. There could be no rumor or suggestion the Allies were disunited, or no longer working to an agreed inter-Allied plan, or did not mean business in pursuing the unconditional surrender of Nazi Germany and the Empire of Japan. The formal photographs of the three Allied leaders, seated on the front porch of the Russian Embassy in Tehran, said it all: instantly, once published, the most potent image of the war up to that time. (Leahy later likened the scene to that of King Henry VIII meeting François Premier, Roi de France, on the Field of the Cloth of Gold — if only one could ignore, Leahy qualified, the "suffering and squalor" of the golden fields of Tehran.)[2]

"No power on earth can prevent our destroying the German armies by land, their U-boats by sea, and their war planes from the air," the President's text ran. "Our attack will be relentless and increasing. Emerging from these cordial conferences we look with confidence to the day when all peoples of the world may live free lives, untouched by tyranny, and according to their varying desires and their own consciences. We came here with hope and determination. We leave here, friends in fact, in spirit and in purpose."[3]

The document was signed — at Stalin's insistence — in the order "Roosevelt, Stalin, Churchill," reflecting their importance on the world stage. Regarding the postwar world, it recognized "the supreme responsibility resting upon us and all the United Nations to make a peace which will command the good will of the overwhelming mass of the people of the world and banish the scourge and terror of war for many generations. With our diplomatic advisers we have surveyed the problems of the future. We shall seek the cooperation and the active participation of all nations, large and small, whose peoples in heart and mind are dedicated, as our own peoples, to the elimination of tyranny and slavery, oppression and intolerance, into a world family of democratic nations."[4]

Given the non-role the United States had played in international relations in the aftermath of World War I, and then during the Great Depression, the tone and content of such a communiqué struck Dr. Goebbels, in Berlin, as a significant turnaround on the part of the United States. The propaganda minister was frankly puzzled. And alarmed.

The first official announcement that the Allied leaders had met in Cairo had already been made on December 1 — with claims that, joined by Stalin, the Big Three had then met in Tehran, there to prepare a "Propaganda-Manifesto" to be broadcast to the German people. The Reich propaganda minister had duly scorned the idea of such an initiative, thinking it would be a "complete fiasco." The Allied "terror" bombing of German cities had only hardened the determination of the German Volk to resist the "plutocracies," Goebbels recorded in his diary — with some justification. "We're not talking 1918 here," he reflected, "in terms of leadership," since he was confident, thanks to the Führer's political and military stewardship, the German Volk had changed completely in the years since the humiliation of Versailles. Proud of his insight into the German psyche he seemed not to take seriously the three-front warning or timetable, issued by the President and his two allies after the Tehran meeting. Instead, he took heart from the Führer's assurances that with the help of the Reich's growing technical arsenal of new weapons, including *Vergeltungswaffen,* the Allies would be prevented from winning the war, even if Germany could no longer achieve the offensive victory that had seemed so tantalizingly within its grasp in the summer of 1942, the year before.

On the telephone from his military headquarters in East Prussia, Hitler had confided to Goebbels he'd spoken to Goering, the field marshal responsible for the Luftwaffe and aerial warfare. He'd asked the increasingly portly airman to press for "our revenge weapons to be completed as quickly as possible"; in the meantime he himself, as Führer, would hold back the Soviet tide.[5]

For his part, as Gauleiter of Berlin as well as Reich minister for propaganda,

Goebbels assured the Führer the Reich capital would cope with anything the Allies could throw at it from the air. Both men therefore saw the Allied summit in Tehran not as a demonstration of Allied unity, but as part of a "war of nerves" to intimidate the German Volk and break German morale. It wouldn't succeed, both Hitler and Goebbels were confident — and in this respect history would prove them right.

The Allied communiqué was not directed at Germany, though. It was written and released to the Allied press, to be read by soldiers and civilians of the United Nations. Hitler's Third Reich was unlikely to surrender in the same manner as the Italians had done in September, the President felt. Judging by recent combat both on the Eastern Front and in Italy, the Germans had simply become too militarized, too wedded to hard power, and too content with tyranny over other peoples — even fellow German citizens if they were in the least part Jewish, or objected to Nazi doctrine. So effective was Hitler's leadership of the majority of Germans, in fact, Hitler no longer even needed to appear in public; the troops of the vaunted Wehrmacht would take care of the front, and German civilians would take care of the *Vaterland*. Nor was this surprising, in terms of the history of peoples — the record of German prowess and endurance on the field of battle going back thousands of years, to Roman times. The fact was, only military victory on the battlefield, won by Allied soldiers, could now free Europe from the Wehrmacht's iron grip and go on to defeat the Third Reich decisively, followed by Japan. It was a task that would involve significant casualties, the President was well aware, in Europe — and again in the Pacific, if the conquests of the Empire of the Rising Sun in China, Southeast Asia, and the Southwest Pacific were to be rolled back, and a new start to world order be made. In the darkness of a continuing global war such communiqués were thus essential to maintain public faith in the outcome. Moreover, they were an important reminder of what the Allies were fighting *for*, the President insisted. Though the communiqué was signed by all three leaders, the vision of the future was clearly that of the American president, Goebbels recognized. As such it aroused his contempt. He dismissed it as cynical claptrap.

It wasn't, however — even if it smacked of innocent idealism and its goals might not necessarily be realized anytime soon. As the President had recently confided to Walter Lippmann, the syndicated columnist, the Moscow Conference had been a "real success," but the devil would be in the details — and its aims far from easy to achieve. "Sometimes," he'd confided to Lippmann before leaving for Tehran, "I feel that the world will be mighty lucky if it gets 50% of what it seeks out of the war as a permanent success. That might be a high average."[6]

Whatever his inherent skepticism, though, the President understood the power of ideals — and was determined the United States would lead the democratic way, once the war was over. The Soviet Union, which had never known democracy, would have to be encouraged to participate on a global stage, as would the primary colonial empires, which would need to be brought along if wars of independence, such as America's in the eighteenth century, were to be avoided.

In the meantime the British prime minister had shown a welcome "inclination to accept the American point of view on matters that have heretofore been in controversy between the American and British Chiefs of Staff," Leahy had noted with relief in his diary.[7] And in an effort to conciliate the Prime Minister, in return, the President had said he was sending his own plane, the Sacred Cow, to Ankara to bring President Inonu — who'd expressed his willingness through the U.S. ambassador to meet with the President and the Prime Minister — to Cairo, to discuss a possible Turkish entry into the war.

Churchill was touched — though aware, like most members of the delegations, that there was little real hope the Turks would ever fight the Germans, whose ruthlessness was well known to them; they had, after all, been Germany's allies in World War I. Only fools rush in; the Turks would surely wait out the course of the war, and declare their interest only when they saw German defeat in sight.

The more important decision to be made in Cairo before the President and Mr. Churchill went home was thus not the matter of Turkey but of who would command the D-day invasion and subsequent drive to Berlin.

27

A Momentous Decision

LIKE MOST PEOPLE — even Stalin himself — General George Marshall had assumed, before leaving American shores, that he would be made supreme commander of Overlord. So certain had he been, in fact, that his wife, Katherine, had begun sending furniture from the general's official residence, Fort Myer, just outside Washington, into storage, assuming that her husband would be moving to England. A number of Marshall's subordinates in Washington, too, had been notified their services would soon be required abroad.[1] After all, had not the tall, austere, no-nonsense chief of staff of the U.S. Army been assured by the President himself — and on a number of occasions — he would be appointed to the coveted post, most recently during his meeting with the Joint Chiefs aboard the USS *Iowa*?

What, Marshall's colleagues and subordinates later wondered, changed the President's mind? And *when*, exactly, did he change it?

Given the historic importance of the appointment, it would be nothing short of extraordinary that in subsequent years no historian would get even the date right. For the most part historical writers merely glided over it, assigning it little significance — another example, it was generally considered, of the President's easygoing, somewhat hands-off approach to military decision-making compared with Churchill's meddling, sometimes disastrous but always energetic, performance as British commander in chief.

In truth the President took the matter of supreme command of Overlord deeply seriously — perhaps more seriously than any appointment he would make in his entire life. Far from having ignored or underestimated the import of the command, as Stalin assumed, the President had been taking advice for quite some time on the matter, and from many quarters. Back in September 1943, in Washington, he'd written to General John Pershing, for example, to solicit the opinion of the five-star World War I general.

General Pershing knew that the U.S. secretary of war, Henry Stimson, was in favor of Marshall being appointed. As Stimson would put it on November 10, even as the President prepared to leave for Tehran, "Marshall's command of Overlord is imperative for its success."[2] In a tough, uncompromising response in September to the President, however, General Pershing—a professional soldier to his bootstraps, and the legendary commander of U.S. forces in Europe in the previous war—had already warned that, in his opinion, to transfer Marshall to "a tactical command in a limited area, no matter how seemingly important, is to deprive ourselves of the benefit of his outstanding strategical ability and experience. I know of no one at all comparable to replace him as Chief of Staff." In sum, General Pershing had judged it "would be a fundamental and very grave error in our military policy."[3]

The President had been somewhat taken aback by Pershing's vehemence—and surprised, too, given that George Marshall had been director of planning in the First U.S. Division for the Battle of Cantigny, on the Somme, in 1918, and had then served on General Pershing's own headquarters staff in France that year. Marshall was conversant therefore with the battlefields on which the Allies would soon be fighting—battlefields that would be greater even than Pershing's command had been in World War I, for the United States would now be fielding by far the dominant Allied military force in France.

"You are absolutely right about George Marshall," the President had responded with his usual tact, then added, "and yet, I think, you are wrong, too!" General Marshall was by "far and away" the best man to be chief of staff of the U.S. Army at the Pentagon, he agreed. However, the supreme command he was proposing was much more than a "tactical command in a limited area." The "command will include the whole European theater," he'd emphasized.[4]

The whole European theater.

It was this misunderstanding that would confuse later historians—for it was never the President's intention to make Marshall a battlefield commander, when Marshall had never commanded in battle, and when to do so would deprive him of Marshall's superlative talents as the head of the U.S. Army in Washington. His aim, since the spring of 1943, when Churchill came to Washington to plead against the notion of a cross-Channel invasion and beaches that might be littered with British dead, was to hold the feet of the British to the fire: which could be done by ensuring an American commanded "the whole European theater," and could thereby guard against Mediterranean diversions that would imperil Overlord. Marshall was to be, he had thus reaffirmed aboard the USS *Iowa*, in command of "all Europe." Assuming, of course, that the British would agree to such a huge command area (essentially the one commanded by a single NATO supreme commander, beginning in 1952).

They wouldn't, though—and Marshall, aboard the *Iowa*, had ironically agreed with their probable objections, deeming it to be too large a military arena to command effectively. For their part, behind a facade of similar concern over the sheer size of such a fiefdom, the British had no intention of allowing both the Mediterranean and Overlord commands to come under a single supreme commander — unless that commander was British and could be relied upon to do Churchill's bidding. For Winston Churchill was no fool: recognizing that, if the Second Front and Mediterranean theaters were merged under an American commander, his chances of "exploitation" in the Aegean and Balkans would be nullified. The idea of an "all Europe" supreme command had therefore become a bone of Anglo-American contention, rather than a serious command possibility — as Marshall himself had been aware, when sharing with Eisenhower, in Algiers on the way to Tehran, his frustration that the two generals were, as Eisenhower put it, mere "chess pieces" on the President's board.

Churchill had thus claimed, at Cairo, to be perfectly content to accept Marshall in command of British D-day forces — but only on the understanding that Overlord not be permitted to have priority over British schemes in the Mediterranean. Tehran had squelched that possibility, however. The cross-Channel invasion was now cast in stone, as the number one Allied undertaking in the spring of 1944, backed by a simultaneous offensive on the Eastern Front by the Soviets. And with Overlord's primacy and timetable irrevocably established between the three major Allied war powers, the President was now faced with an equally difficult task, from a personal point of view: how to tell Marshall he was not going to go to England, and would not command the historic amphibious invasion.

On the evening of his first full day back in Cairo, Friday, December 3, 1943, Roosevelt thus sent his White House counselor, Harry Hopkins, to Marshall's villa, to sound out how this news would be received.

As the modest, intensely private General Marshall noted in a letter to Harry Hopkins's biographer, Robert Sherwood, after the war, he had not been aware his fellow chiefs of staff had, in previous weeks, "gone to the president opposing my transfer" to the D-day command — nor even that the President had sought General Pershing's opinion on the matter. He was thus astonished when, as he recounted, "Harry Hopkins came to see me Saturday night, before dinner, and told me the President was in some concern of mind over my appointment as Supreme Commander."[5]

Marshall's memory was mistaken, for it was Friday evening, not Saturday, following their return from Tehran. Nevertheless, the general was clear about one thing, in retrospect: namely that the question of his not being appointed supreme commander of Overlord "never came to a head in any way until Hopkins came to see me at Cairo, and told me that the President was very much concerned, because he felt he had to make a decision."[6]

Marshall might have gotten the date wrong, but his recollection as to the

President's urgency was undoubtedly correct. The President had given his assurance to Stalin that he would make the decision on Overlord's command within a couple of days of getting back to Cairo. Moreover, from a purely logistical point of view, the decision on leadership was now critical, since thanks to Churchill the whole Overlord project had been put on virtual hold by the British. If D-day was to be a success, there was not a day to be wasted, Marshall knew. Overlord was the invasion he himself had pressed for, studied carefully, planned for, and had backed for almost two years, even when its chances of success were zero, and the President, as commander in chief, had had to overrule him, and put him in his place.[7] Now, however, the President had gotten Churchill to back off, and D-day to be put on the front burner — with Marshall the clear candidate for the post of supreme commander. Hopkins's visit, in person, therefore threw him. As he himself confessed later, he had no idea how to respond: "I was pulled from many directions and I wouldn't express myself on any of them."[8] For Hopkins's appearance at his villa that evening could in fact mean only one thing: that the President was now having second thoughts.[9]

Embarrassed, Marshall declined to indicate to Hopkins whether he would be disappointed if he was not chosen. He was certainly aware that whoever was selected for the post would go down in history. "I merely endeavored to make it clear that I would go along wholeheartedly with whatever decision the President made. He need have no fears regarding my personal reaction. I declined to state my opinion," he later told Robert Sherwood.[10]

For his part Harry Hopkins was dismayed by Marshall's reaction — for Hopkins had always pressed for Marshall to command the D-day invasion, as had many others — even Churchill,[11] and Stalin. Why didn't Marshall say he was *counting* on getting the historic command; that he *wanted* it; that he felt he was the *right man* to take it?

Marshall, however, was no Patton or MacArthur in terms of putting personal ambition above duty. Besides, at some deeper level he knew it would not help sway or change the President's mind, if the President was not keen to appoint him, for whatever reason.

Hopkins, as go-between, duly brought back the information to Mr. Roosevelt, the Commander in Chief. Marshall would not make "a scene," or be difficult about it, he explained. This was all the President needed to know. Or almost all.

Since so many hundreds of thousands of British and Canadian forces would come under the supreme commander who was appointed, Churchill would have to be consulted — and disarmed, lest he once again attempt to sabotage the Overlord timetable. Before making the appointment official, then, the President made sure he had Churchill's solemn word he would not prejudice Overlord's timing. The next morning at 11:00, on December 4, 1943, in the

President's villa and in front of the assembled Combined Chiefs of Staff, the President thus got Churchill to state formally his "conversion" to Overlord and its timetable: his words to be taken down in minutes of the meeting and typed up by the secretary of the Combined Chiefs of Staff Committee. Churchill, duly but reluctantly, obliged. Overlord was "a task transcending all others," the Prime Minister stated in a characteristic turn of phrase, and it would be launched "during May." He himself would have "preferred the July date," but he was "determined nevertheless to do all in his power to make the May date a complete success."[12]

The President was relieved, and the plenary meeting had subsequently addressed how to support Overlord with the strongest possible pincer landing in southern France — Operation Anvil.

The essential deal, however, was now struck, and in writing. The British would partner with the United States in launching D-day in May 1944, under an American commander. With that cast-iron understanding, the President asked to see Marshall afterwards, on his own. As Marshall recounted, "The President had me call at his Villa, either immediately before or immediately after lunch."

In actuality the President's interview with Marshall was over lunch itself. There, in the comfortable Kirk villa overlooking the pyramids, "in response to his questions, I made virtually the same reply I made to Hopkins," Marshall later explained to Robert Sherwood — namely that "I would not attempt to estimate my capabilities; the President would have to do that. I merely wished to make clear that whatever the decision, I would go along with it wholeheartedly; that the issue was too great for any personal feeling to be considered."[13]

Writing in 1948, Sherwood rightly called the appointment a "momentous decision" — in fact Sherwood considered it "one of the loneliest decisions" the President "ever had to make."[14]

Was it? Sherwood was a playwright in his professional life, but a wartime speechwriter for the President and a man who deeply admired General Marshall. By conveying the loneliness of the decision Sherwood was without doubt trying to soften his account. He wanted to make clear how admired Marshall was by his colleagues, and how much they wanted to see him in the role of supreme commander of the greatest amphibious invasion in military history. As Sherwood wrote, if the President were to choose someone other than Marshall it might even be contested within military and White House circles, for it would not only be against "the impassioned advice of Hopkins," who was not a military man, but against that of the secretary of war, Henry Stimson, who was. It would even go counter to "the known preference of both Stalin and Churchill." In fact it would go against the President's "own proclaimed inclination to give George Marshall the historic opportunity which he so greatly desired and so amply deserved."[15]

While this was true, none of it reflected the real story: namely that the President had never intended to let Marshall leave Washington, unless Marshall himself insisted he wanted and deserved the battlefield command! The President had only spoken of General Marshall as the prospective supreme commander in order to stop Churchill from delaying D-day, without actually making the appointment until Churchill backed down, and the primacy and date of the battle were set in stone — no longer subject to Churchillian sabotage in wild Aegean and Balkan diversions. Once Churchill had formally surrendered over Overlord, there was no need to continue the charade. Unless Marshall insisted on the post — which would complicate matters — the President felt free to appoint the man he now felt certain would be the right individual for the job.

Sherwood's version of the historic decision would become iconic, even being quoted by Churchill in his memoirs,[16] but it was plainly wrong, including the date. The President had never wished to lose Marshall from Washington; he had merely used him as a chess piece in his battle with Churchill, exactly as Marshall had described.

What Sherwood went on to record, however, was certainly true: namely that Roosevelt would never knowingly hurt a friend, or someone who had worked loyally for him. Thus the President's final words, as he lunched with Marshall in Cairo — words that would become famous in the study of command decision-making — were typical of the President's *savoir faire* in complex human relations: "I feel I could not sleep at night with you out of the country."[17]

Of all the President's many tributes and compliments this was perhaps the kindest: a generous recognition of Marshall's extraordinary stature in Washington. Yet even Marshall later recognized there had been much more to it than that: that the decision was not sudden, for the President had in fact been reconsidering the appointment, in the light of General Pershing's advice, for months; that he had also sought the views of Marshall's colleagues on the Joint Chiefs of Staff Committee — and even that of General Eisenhower, on the way to the Egyptian capital.

Marshall had been the President's bishop to Churchill's knight in the long, difficult struggle to get the Prime Minister and the British to conform to a May 1944 invasion date, and fold their Mediterranean/Aegean tents. Now that Churchill had given in, the President had been too much of a gentleman to deny Marshall the command, *if* he said he really wanted it. Sensing the President's underlying intent, however, George Marshall had nobly offered to fall on his sword — denying himself the glory of commanding one of the greatest battles in history. For the fact was, the chess match with Churchill was done. The President wanted someone else for Overlord.

28

A Bad Telegram

WHEN THE SECRETARY OF WAR, Henry Stimson, heard the news at the Pentagon, four days later, he blanched. "I had bad news by telegram today on the United Command of Overlord," Stimson noted in his diary. "Apparently there has been a curious shift there which I just don't understand."[1]

One by one, as the U.S. generals and staff officers flew back from Cairo, Stimson tackled them, urging them to tell him about the "most curious question as to the Commandership."[2] But not even General Somervell, the deputy chief of staff of the U.S. Army, who'd traveled out with the President and had taken part in the Combined Chiefs of Staff meetings in Cairo, could tell him how it had happened, or what was behind the decision.

General Dwight David Eisenhower was also surprised, since he had been under the impression the post was definitely going to Marshall.

The President, however, was the President—and would never regret his decision. Most of his adult life he had had to make choices about subordinates—not least those in the military. Article II, Section 2, of the U.S. Constitution stated that the "President shall be Commander in Chief of the Army and Navy of the United States, and of the Militia of the several States, when called into the actual Service of the United States," and would thereby have the right to appoint all "Officers of the United States." Franklin Roosevelt himself had never served *in* the military; he had, though, served *with* military officers, men and contingents, and for almost a decade, long before he was elected president. Appointed by President Wilson to be assistant secretary of the U.S. Navy in 1913, he'd had almost eight years of daily experience dealing with U.S. naval officers and men—before, during, and in the aftermath of World War I. Becoming U.S. president and commander in chief in 1933, moreover, Roosevelt had amassed a further decade of dealing with army, air, and naval officers and men—and since 1941, the ultimate command of his nation's forces in directing a global war. Unlike the Prime Minister—who *had*, ironically, served in the military—the President was thus for the most part a seasoned, successful chooser of men. Behind his mask of charm and affability, he'd honed over the years an almost unique ability, for a politician, to judge the merits of military officers, according to the context and role in which he wanted them to serve. Admiral Harold Stark, for example, had been a wise counselor to the President as chief of naval operations in peacetime — but not in wartime. The President had quickly but quietly removed him from that role, after Pearl Harbor, sending him as senior U.S. naval liaison to England. Others, too, had had to be retired, sidelined, or transferred.

War, like peace, demanded different talents of different men, he understood. There were those who proved able administrators under stress. There were men who proved efficient and effective planners, but who failed in combat. Officers, too, who proved fine commanders in the field of battle — whether in the air, on ground, or at sea — but poor administrators, or higher commanders. But there were still very few who possessed modern battlefield experience commanding all three services, and international coalition forces. It was a problem the British themselves would fail to resolve in subsequent days, as the Prime Minister and General Brooke argued over who should be appointed supreme commander in the Mediterranean.

Overlord, if successful, would lead to the defeat of the Third Reich, as even Hitler accepted. Its supreme command was therefore a role of vast consequence, both for the individual selected and for the free world. In the American armed forces General MacArthur and Admiral Nimitz were both already in the senior "supreme command" category, directing the army, air, and naval forces of the United States as well as other nations in battle. Douglas MacArthur had, however, declined the President's invitation to fly to Cairo to meet him, sending his chief of staff instead. This was a mistake on MacArthur's part, for in the President's view MacArthur was still a mercurial figure at best: one who might be difficult for the President or Joint Chiefs of Staff to control — a reputation MacArthur could only have countered by a personal appearance, advancing with Mr. Roosevelt the argument that, in battle after battle in the Pacific since his defeat at Bataan, he had proved he was a master of amphibious assault operations, moreover had led Australian commanders and their forces with surprising tact and skill. Equally, Chester Nimitz had shown himself to be a master of amphibious operations and the use of multinational naval, ground, and air combat forces. Of intelligence, too — as at Midway in 1942 and the interception and elimination of his main opponent, Admiral Yamamoto, in 1943. But neither commander had faced the modern Wehrmacht — which they would need to do in the looming do-or-die "face to face" battle with the "remaining masses of the German troops," as Secretary Stimson put it in his weekly survey at the Pentagon: a potentially decisive battle between great armies in northern France.[3] This was a region MacArthur, at least, knew intimately from his heroic World War I experience; Nimitz did not.

By contrast young General Dwight D. Eisenhower was *the man on the spot.* He was a general of now-proven experience in commanding multinational forces of all three services, a commander of high intelligence, popular, and with good political instincts. A man whom other men — whether staff officers or commanders — were proud to serve under. None of the U.S. chiefs of staff had been present when the President spent two days with Eisenhower at Oran and Tunis, before the pre–Tehran Conference in Cairo. Ike had then given his presentation of current strategy and plans in the Mediterranean to the Combined Chiefs before they all left to meet Stalin, which had further impressed the President. In fact the President's mind was by then made up as to whom he would like to appoint — if he could get the British to sign up to D-day, incontrovertibly and definitively, to take place in May 1944. They had, leaving only Marshall's feelings to take into account. Once Hopkins had reported to him that Marshall would naturally be disappointed, but would accept the President's decision with good grace, the President had had no further qualms. This was war. Hundreds of thousands of lives were at stake. He had not hesitated — and, as Hopkins had predicted, Marshall had shown no emotion or disappointment.

General Hap Arnold, chief of staff for the Army Air Forces and Marshall's closest colleague at the Pentagon, thus recorded the historic decision with memorable frankness in his diary that evening, December 4, 1943. "Marshall," the air chief wrote, "had lunch with President; he doesn't get Overlord, Ike does."[4]

Churchill and the British chiefs of staff were informed of the President's decision later that afternoon. That night General Alan Brooke noted in his diary the same as General Arnold. "A difficult day!" Brooke penned as Marshall's mirror figure: chief of staff of his nation's army — and, ironically, the very man who, until the Quebec Conference three months earlier, had not only been promised the supreme command but had counted on it. "Finally asked to dine alone with Winston to discuss questions of command," Brooke recorded, for "the President had today decided that Eisenhower was to command Overlord while Marshall remained as Chief of Staff."[5]

To all intents and purposes the deed, then, was done on December 4, 1943 — not December 5, as Churchill would claim in his memoirs, quoting, as would all historians in the following seven decades, Sherwood's book. By nightfall of December 4, not only were the U.S. and British chiefs of staff aware of the historic decision in the Egyptian capital, but the British prime minister at his own villa near the pyramids, too.[6]

And yet it was not immediately announced, or conveyed to Stalin. Why?

29

Perfidious Albion Redux

SEVEN DECADES LATER it is impossible to know for sure. The personal diaries of those present in Cairo, however, give a clue — for the British contingent, worsted over Overlord at Tehran, appeared determined to have its revenge.

The U.S. chiefs of staff were stunned; in fact could not at first credit what the British were doing. On Friday afternoon, December 3, instead of discussing plans for Anvil, the pincer invasion of southern France to elide with Overlord, the American chiefs had found themselves in "locked horns over Rhodes, Dodecanese, Dardanelles, etc," with the British, General Arnold had noted in his diary.[1]

Rhodes, Dodecanese, *Dardanelles*? Not Anvil?

For almost two hours the U.S. chiefs had afterwards sat with the President and with Hopkins, complaining — hoping, however, it was only a temporary venting of British disappointment. There was clearly "lots to do" in terms of Anvil before they left — but the next day, December 4, had proven even harder. Presiding over the quasi-plenary meeting of the Combined Chiefs of Staff together with the Prime Minister for two hours, the President had wrung out of Churchill his acceptance of Overlord's primacy and timetable — but there were warnings of storms ahead over the logistics necessary to mount Anvil. The British were yet again determined to tie them to operational needs in the Far East. This had entailed a "long involved discussion over war: invasion France," foremost — but also "Burma campaign, Andamans, Aegean Sea, principles to our strategy,"[2] as General Arnold jotted in his diary. For his part Churchill was now insisting on the cancellation of the Andaman Islands invasion, despite the President having promised Generalissimo Chiang Kai-shek it would take place to help the Chinese.

The U.S. chiefs had then gone off to lunch — leaving Marshall alone with the President to be told the President's decision regarding command of Overlord. At 2:30 p.m. the Joint Chiefs had been back again with their opposite numbers, this time at Mena House. There the British declared virtual war on their coalition partners, demanding outright the cancellation of "Buccaneer," the Andaman Islands invasion, while the U.S. chiefs fought to keep it in play. Leahy, King, Marshall, and Arnold were all certain that the British were being deceitful in claiming they needed Buccaneer's landing craft for the Anvil invasion of southern France; they strongly (and correctly) suspected the British were actually aiming at the Aegean islands.

Behind his facade of seemingly endless goodwill, the President, in truth, was becoming more and more disenchanted with the British team. He made clear at the meeting that they only had two days in which to get the Anvil act together. Brooke, who was once again leading the charge, recorded in his diary his fury when he'd "discovered" that morning that his prime minister "had been queering our pitch by suggesting to Leahy that if we did not attack Rhodes we might at any rate starve the place out. We then lunched with the PM and at 2.30 went back for our meeting with the Combined Chiefs of Staff. We were dumbfounded by being informed that the meeting must finish on Sunday at the latest (in 48 hours) as the President was off [to Tunis]! No apologies, nothing. They have completely upset the whole [Cairo and Tehran] meeting by wasting our time with Chiang Kai-shek and Stalin before we had settled any points with them. And now with nothing settled they propose to disappear into the blue and leave all the main points connected with the Mediterranean unsettled. It all looks like some of the worst sharp practice that I have seen for some time," Brooke lamented — insisting yet again that Rhodes be taken by military force *before* Overlord could be tackled.[3]

Why Rhodes? Had it not been agreed at Tehran that the Aegean was not to delay, let alone derail, the Overlord timetable?

In the circumstances, by the end of December 4, 1943, the President had good reason to delay public announcement of his decision to appoint Eisenhower, even to Stalin — for as long as General Eisenhower remained the commander in chief of all Allied forces in the Mediterranean he would be empowered to thwart British plans to invade Rhodes and other diversions. Diversions which, if they met the sort of opposition the Wehrmacht had recently mounted in the Aegean and were still showing in southern Italy, could prejudice the launching of Overlord — the last thing the President wanted Stalin to learn, when Overlord's success depended so much on a massive simultaneous Soviet offensive from the east to preclude reinforcement of their forces in France.

Leahy, for his part, was distraught. By a margin of more than two to one the United States was now the dominant partner in the Western coalition — and would become all the more so in the months ahead. Why did the President have to give in to Churchill?

"Second Cairo," as it became called, would later be whitewashed by Churchill,[4] and be largely overlooked by historians after the war. But as Leahy would note, the U.S. chiefs bravely fought to the very end in the Egyptian capital, on behalf of the President, to avoid having to cancel Buccaneer and risk the whole relationship with the Chinese. It proved a losing battle with the British, however.

At the start of their talks the President "didn't budge" over Buccaneer, Leahy proudly remembered, since Mr. Roosevelt had given Generalissimo Chiang Kai-shek, only the week before — and in person, no less — his solemn promise the operation would take place. He thus had no wish to give the British landing craft for further misadventures in the Mediterranean or Aegean. But as the bitter days of Second Cairo went by, it became obvious the British were not going to give up. "No decision has been made as to the controversy in regard to the Mediterranean versus the Andaman operation," Leahy noted in his diary on the night of December 4, 1943.[5] The next day things were no better. "No progress was made toward a solution of the problem," he recorded[6] — though the President, fearing the worst, began to ask if there were any alternatives, and warned Chiang there might not be enough landing craft for Overlord *and* Buccaneer — though knowing this was not the real reason.[7]

"Neither side would yield," Leahy later recalled. "It was the same story up to 5 p.m. on December 6. At no time in previous or later conferences had the British shown such determined opposition. When the American Chiefs met with Roosevelt at 5 o'clock" that day, it was all over, however. The President was leaving the next morning, and refused to stay to duke it out. He therefore sorrowfully "informed us that in order to bring discussions to an end, he had reluctantly agreed to abandon the Andaman plan and would propose some substitute to Chiang. He was Commander-in-Chief and that ended the argument."[8]

The British had won. Tens of thousands of futile and unnecessary American, British, and Canadian casualties would be the result, at the little Mediterranean town of Anzio, but Churchill was Churchill — and rather than put Overlord in jeopardy, once again, the President had given in.

Admiral Leahy never quite forgave Churchill — not only on behalf of American lives subsequently lost in Italy, but for the effect on Chiang Kai-shek. "It must have been a sad disappointment to Chiang," he reflected later, for the "Chinese leader had every right to feel we had failed to keep a promise." Not only was American honor affected, but the war in Asia. The cancellation of the Andaman plans was bound to affect Chinese willingness to go on fighting the Japanese, rather than turn on their compatriots — Chinese communist troops under Mao Tse-tung. This would leave a huge Japanese army occupying a vast swath of coastal China. Chiang "never had indicated much faith in British intentions, but had relied on the United States. If," therefore, "the Chinese quit, the tasks of MacArthur and Nimitz in the Pacific, already difficult, would be much harder," Leahy lamented. "Japanese man power in great numbers would be released to oppose our advance to the mainland of Japan," he wrote: Chinese territory being the best proposed launching pad for the U.S. air, naval, and army assault.⁹

Admiral King, for his part, was appalled. Marshall had already had a late-night session with Churchill in which the Prime Minister was "red hot" for retaking Rhodes. "All the British were against me," Marshall recalled. "It got hotter and hotter." Finally Churchill had grabbed Marshall's lapels and said, "His Majesty's Government can't have its troops staying idle. Muskets must flame," and "more things like that," Marshall later recounted. "I said, 'God forbid, if I should try to dictate, but' I said, 'not one American soldier is going to die on the goddamned beach.'"¹⁰

The British would not give way, however — insisting that the landing craft released from Buccaneer should be made available for Churchill's immediate plans in the Mediterranean. The final day of the conference had been the worst. "After the matter had been discussed, and Mr. Churchill had pressed his points," King recalled, Leahy and Arnold had both reluctantly surrendered, as did Marshall — "but King remained obdurate, and would not give an inch," he narrated (using the third person for his account), "because he knew that the Chinese, headed by Chiang Kai-shek, would feel they had been sold out — which was the case — and consequently would not do anything to aid Stilwell" in the Far East theater.¹¹

If King was furious, General Stilwell was disbelieving. Summoned to see the President at 4:30 p.m. to hear the bad news, he was the most aggrieved. Understandably incensed, he fumed that night in his diary: "God-awful is no word for it" — Roosevelt "a flighty fool," in his vinegary judgment. "Christ but he's terrible."¹²

King, in retrospect, also blamed the President for going "against the advice of his Joint Chiefs of Staff."¹³ This was certainly justified, if unfair. For the truth was, the President simply had no arrows left in his quiver, if he wanted the British to land alongside American troops on D-day. He could only swallow his disappointment and let Stalin know, at least, the *good* news: a commander of Overlord had been appointed.

It was a bittersweet moment for Marshall. "The appointment of General Eisenhower to command of Overlord operation has been decided on," he wrote in his draft message for the President to sign and send to Stalin, via the White House in Washington. The President added the word "immediate" before "appointment," then appended his signature.¹⁴ It was December 6, 1943 — the eve of the anniversary of Pearl Harbor — with the British determined to sabotage operations in the Far East now in a desperate attempt to slip Rhodes into the agreed D-day timetable, even at the risk of delaying it. As a result,

Marshall decided he would not go back to the United States directly, but would fly to the Pacific, and see for himself how best to deal with the consequences of the latest British pusillanimity.

The President, for his part, tried to look on the bright side. Overlord — the "D-day Invasion," as it would come to be called in world history — was at least, finally, "on," in tandem with a massive Soviet offensive that would bring the Third Reich to its knees. Moreover the President had made the most momentous decision of his life in deciding on Overlord's supreme commander — an appointment to which the British, who would be fielding half the forces for D-day, had at least agreed.

With that the President, taking a deep breath, set off for Tunis, where he intended to inform Eisenhower of the appointment in person. And if possible visit his combat commanders in the field: Patton, Clark, and others.

30

In the Field with Eisenhower

ALL IS WELL and I'm on my way home," the President penned in a note to his cousin Daisy Suckley, to be sent by airmail. "The trip was almost a complete success — especially the Russians," he recorded, proudly.[1]

Almost. In war, as in peace, one had often to accept less than what one would ideally wish. And if the British had proven halfhearted in support of Overlord, even perfidious, the Russians at least had shown they were determined to support the American landings. The President thus chose to look upon the trip, thus far, as successful. When Daisy heard on the radio his plane "'flew over Tunis'" on his way back to the United States, she was beside herself with anticipation. "*I wish he would get home!*" she scribbled anxiously in her diary.[2]

The President had not flown over Tunis, but in fact *to* Tunis. Whatever he had told Churchill about needing to get back to Washington, he was certainly not rushing. In the biographies written after his death, his return to America did not figure as more than a footnote. And in the ledger of Roosevelt's wartime trips, the trip home perhaps did not merit more than that. Yet the journey home would be important to him personally, as he "wound down" in the company of General Eisenhower, the man he'd just appointed to command the D-day invasion. For the President was now able to spend two further days with the young general: intent upon encouraging his new supreme commander in how best to approach his new responsibility. Also, if possible, to fly with Ike to the Allied battlefield in Italy, where American troops were fighting hard to contain Wehrmacht forces. He'd be able to see some of the men who had proved themselves in combat, and who would now be transferred to England for the great Overlord invasion. Also some of those who would remain in the Mediterranean theater and perhaps take part in the southern pincer invasion of France, Operation Anvil, if he could get the British to cease trying to wreck it.

Shortly after breakfast on December 7, 1943, the Sacred Cow thus lifted off the runway at Cairo West airfield for its eight-hour flight to Tunis — by day, this time.

Given that he'd had to undertake several weeks earlier the same leg, in the opposite direction, in total darkness, the President had been determined the reverse trip be done in good light, and should follow if possible "the whole length of the British advance last winter — over El Alamein & Benghasi and Tripoli," as he described in his diary. "Most interesting to see it all from the air — endless desert, but much of it broken country with a good lot of tanks & other equipment not yet picked up," owing to unexploded mines and drifting sands. "In another year or two there will hardly be a trace — for even the shell holes & fox holes will be filled up. What a march that was! Over 1000 miles — with fighting practically all the way. But at the end, with the advance of Montgomery into Tunis from the South," he noted, "we and the British struck from the west — and all of W. Africa was in our hands together with 300,000 prisoners."[3]

How proud he was, as the de facto commander in chief of the Western democracies — and curious to see the scars. Admiral McIntire, the President's doctor, later remembered the enthusiasm with which the President had insisted on the exact route — and the low altitude. "A dangerous business even with a fighter escort, for the Germans still maintained active airfields on Crete," McIntire recalled — airfields that were "no more than two hundred miles from Tobruk." The President, however, "could not be dissuaded. All morning we skimmed over the scenes of Montgomery's stand and Rommel's rout, but while the rest of us scanned the skies for German planes, the President had eyes only for the battlefields. After luncheon, to everybody's relief, he decided on a nap, and we took advantage of it to steer a swift, straight course for Tunis."[4]

In retrospect, at least, the physician was amused. In the President's rapt curiosity the doctor could see what others missed, namely the fascination felt by a paraplegic: a would-be warrior who could not walk. Also just how much the sight of what would become a legendary North African battlefield had meant to the President who, as the United States commander in chief, had made it all possible — not only by sending, on his personal orders, the critical Sherman tanks Montgomery had needed in order to smash Rommel, but the vast U.S. contingent required at the other extremity of North Africa for the simultaneous pincer attack: Operation Torch.

The President's daylight flight across Egypt, Libya, and Tunisia was, in other words, not only giving Mr. Roosevelt a chance to see with his own eyes the magnitude of the Allied achievement, but in terms of terrain, what still lay ahead for the Allies. Which made him doubly anxious, regarding D-day, to see for himself evidence of the great American amphibious assault landings on the island of Sicily, at the very center of the Mediterranean, which had been in many ways a rehearsal for Overlord. And even to see, if it could be arranged, Salerno, south of Naples, as he proposed to discuss with General Eisenhower, who met him at El Aouina airport, Tunis, that afternoon.

"Well, Ike, you are to command Overlord," the President first announced with a confident smile as they sat back in Eisenhower's armored limousine.

Eisenhower later recalled how relieved he was to have the President tell him the news in person — and how grateful he was. "Mr. President," he responded with great tact, "I realize that such an appointment involved difficult decisions. I hope you will not be disappointed."[5]

It was an iconic moment: the Commander in Chief sitting with the man he'd selected to carry out the biggest seaborne assault landing ever undertaken. Amazingly, Eisenhower had never seen the current Overlord plans, or been asked to comment on them, despite having been the commander in chief of the Allied invasion of Sicily, six months before, which had involved 3,000 Allied ships, 4,000 aircraft, and 150,000 ground troops. Overlord would be far more forbidding, however; thanks to Allied deception measures, the Allies had initially faced only two German divisions in Operation Husky, the invasion of Sicily; Overlord would face at least forty.

Driven with the President to the "White House," in Carthage, Eisenhower listened as the Commander in Chief recounted some of what had transpired in Tehran — as well as what had happened in Cairo, on his return from the summit. The wily British prime minister would surely seek to mount more operations in the Mediterranean and Aegean, under Eisenhower's successor — operations that could still affect the Overlord timetable, now that the indefatigable British had gotten their way in canceling Buccaneer. These were the fortunes, or misfortunes, of coalition war. Which Eisenhower, having commanded American, British, French, and other forces, as well as dealing with political representatives of those countries, could appreciate.

The President's desire to fly to the battlefield in Italy the next day, however, put the grateful new Overlord commander on the spot.

Having to tell his Commander in Chief no, so soon after hearing of his new appointment, was tough. But it had to be done, Eisenhower recalled. Three days earlier, Luftwaffe planes had penetrated British air defenses at Bari, in southern Italy, and had sunk no fewer than *seventeen* Allied ships. Among them had been an ammunition vessel, and a fuel tanker that exploded and spread "fiery catastrophe" to other vessels — including one that was carrying World War I nerve gas to be used in retaliation against German forces, if the Wehrmacht resorted to the use of such weapons. The wind had been mercifully offshore, and the "escaping gas caused no casualties," Eisenhower explained to the President.[6] The moral, unfortunately, was that the President was too important a life to risk; the Italian mainland was simply not safe against German air attack.

By contrast the planned visit to Sicily *would* be possible, Eisenhower was able to reassure the President. U.S. air forces would maintain their protection, not British. And he would order General Clark to fly back from the front in

Italy, as well as assembling a contingent of combat medal award-winners, to meet the President at Palermo, on Sicily's north coast, after he and the President had made a quick stop in Malta.

With that assurance the President had gone to bed in the "really lovely villa," as the President had earlier described the house in his letter to Cousin Daisy, "just outside the ruins of ancient Carthage"[7] — thrilled at the prospect of flying at least to the two famed Mediterranean islands the next day.

He nearly didn't make it, however.

31

A Flap at Malta

WHAT A DAY!" Roosevelt noted with relief, pride, and excitement in his diary, late on December 8, 1943 — having survived something of an aerial drama.

At 8:00 a.m. the Sacred Cow, piloted by Major Bryan, had risen in bright sunlight over the Mediterranean. Passing over Cape Bon and Pantelleria it had made for Malta, the fortress-island that had withstood all that the Luftwaffe and Kriegsmarine could throw at it since the spring of 1941. The distance there was only 310 miles — the President's plane duly escorted by a dozen P-38 fighters. But as Major Bryan lowered the landing flaps, it was found there was a problem. The flaps would not go down.

Even with its recent extension, the runway at Valletta was distinctly short for a C-54 plane flying without landing flaps. Parachuting, moreover, was not really an option for the President. There had been a number of air accidents that year, involving transport planes. Wladyslaw Sikorski, prime minister of the Polish government in exile, had drowned when his Liberator had crashed after takeoff at Gibraltar in July — none of the passengers or crew, except for the pilot, having worn life vests. Partly as a result of the Sikorski accident, all those aboard the Sacred Cow, on orders of the pilot, *were* wearing Mae Wests — but the prospects of saving the President in an emergency ocean landing would be slim.

General Eisenhower's heart was understandably in his boots. As the President's host and guide, he had earlier "worried about German fighters still based in Italy." McIntire recalled the general's concern amid the "shaking of heads" that had taken place as to the merits of such a visit by the President to an active war zone. A mechanical malfunction had not, however, figured in such anxieties. McIntire had "stewed over the prospect of another fatiguing day for the President," he related after the war — his concerns, naturally, having been for the President's health. Now, aboard the Sacred Cow, Admiral McIntire found himself anxious for his own health, too — and perhaps life — when "it was discovered that the landing flaps were out of commission."[1]

There was, McIntire narrated later, "great commotion" aboard the aircraft, "but F.D.R. never turned a hair." The situation was almost comic as the plane carrying the President and the new supreme commander of Overlord circled the small island for twenty minutes, losing height, speed, and fuel. "Fine," the President said. "Here's where we see just how good our pilots are."[2]

Luckily the President's faith was not misplaced. "Major Bryan, praise be, lived up to the best traditions of the air service, for he landed us with a skill," McIntire later recorded, "that brought a permanent grin to the face of [U.S. Air Force] General Spaatz."[3]

For his part, Lieutenant Rigdon could scarcely believe how effortlessly Bryan landed the huge four-engined plane. "It was a tense moment — the landing strip we were to use ran right to the water's edge — but we landed with little more than the usual bump and bounce and stopped in plenty of time."[4]

At the foot of the ramp the presidential party was met by the governor, Lord Gort — whose courage and British phlegm were legendary, despite losing an entire army at Dunkirk.[5] "I got into a jeep & reviewed a mixed British Battalion and Navy Marines," the President happily recorded in his diary that night, as well as troops from the Malta defenses regiment.[6] "Photographers in great numbers made pictures of this ceremony," Admiral Leahy recounted in his own diary, "which may sometime in the future be an event in the history studied in our schools of that period": namely a president of the United States inspecting British troops under overall American command, on a historic island that had withstood years of Nazi siege.[7]

"I spoke and presented the illuminated citation I had written before leaving home — Gort received it & made an excellent little speech," the President jotted in his own diary. "We had intended to leave [for Sicily], but the plane had broken the hydraulic pump & it took 2 hours to repair — so with Lord Gort I had a very interesting drive through the harbor part of Valetta, where most of the damage was done to this heavily bombed little island. Nearly all the houses are demolished or bombed but the people stay. The dockyard is running ¾ repaired."[8]

The tour of Valletta was the President's first firsthand witness of the sheer destructiveness of modern urban bombing. Yet it testified also to the deeply questionable results of such a strategy, given the resilience of the civil population. "This is reputed to be the most bombed spot in the world during the present war," Lieutenant Rigdon noted in the log of the President's trip — the area "still generally a mass of shambles."[9] Admiral Leahy, too, noted that the Navy Yard's "buildings and those adjacent thereto were completely destroyed by the enemy."[10] Yet, thanks to "underground workshops," the dockyard itself was "operating at near normal efficiency," Rigdon recounted — and the same seemed true of the inhabitants. Though Churchill continued to put great faith in the bombing of German cities — in fact had given the President a special stereoscopic viewer to look at images of the destruction of the city of Cologne, for example — there was little evidence in Malta that such a tactic achieved much more, in the long run, than the hardening of civilian morale.

On the flight from Tunis to Malta, Hopkins later told his biographer, "Roosevelt talked at great length to Eisenhower about the prodigious difficulties he would confront during the next few months at his new headquarters in London, where he would be surrounded by the majesty of the British Government," Robert Sherwood recorded, recalling Hopkins's mocking account, "and the powerful personality of Winston Churchill, who still believed, in Roosevelt's opinion, that only through failure of a frontal attack across the Channel into France could the United Nations lose the war."[11]

For his part the President believed the opposite: that only by failing to invade France could the Allies lose the war, now they had the men, the means, and the commander to carry out the operation. Ironically Overlord remained a risk that Churchill, for all that he was an inveterate, unashamed gambler, still feared to take, whatever he had agreed to in Tehran. It would be Eisenhower's great task, as supreme commander in England, to restore the Prime Minister's British courage, such as he'd shown in 1940. And if he couldn't, to restrain him from sabotaging the invasion timetable.

Meanwhile, after lunching on board the President's plane, Major Bryan reported at 1:00 p.m. he thought the aircraft was fit to fly to Sicily. Without incident it duly took off at 1:10 p.m. and "Eisenhower listened attentively" to more of the President's advice, Sherwood recounted, while "the 'Sacred Cow' droned over the Mediterranean waters."[12]

At the Tehran Conference, the President related, Marshal Stalin had shown himself to have a sharp, incisive mind, yet also to be surprisingly human. Whether talking of Poland or the Baltic states he had made no bones about Russian "borderland" demands in ending a war that Hitler had waged so mercilessly against the Soviet Union. Beyond that, however, Stalin had appeared to have no territorial or ideological ambitions; client-states, bowing to Russian wishes around the Soviet Union's periphery and probably under Russian military control, seemed far more important to him than the spread of communist ideas. In the aftermath of Tehran Churchill had expressed continuing anxiety about Russian intentions — yet the Prime Minister had evinced no real or practical idea of how to thwart or shrink them. Without consulting any Poles, Churchill had in fact privately suggested to Stalin at Tehran — using three matches to demonstrate — that the Allies "give" the Soviet Union the eastern part of Poland, and compensate the Poles with an equivalent area of eastern Germany.[13] Such shades of Munich had been uncomfortable for the President, who'd not been present, and had declined to "go there," in the absence of actual Poles at this moment in the war, and given likely public and congressional feelings in America.

It wasn't that such things should not be discussed, in closed session, by world statesmen — especially as a sounding board. But it was important to project *power* to the Russians, he felt — *real* power. The Russian dictator had seemed well aware how dependent the Soviet Union was on American largesse, as his toasts on the last night in Tehran had demonstrated. The Soviets, in other words, were still respectful of American economic and industrial power, from which they hoped to benefit after the war. Yet it was vital, Roosevelt explained to Eisenhower, to show the Soviets that the United States could and would use its military power in guaranteeing world peace. He'd deliberately reminded Stalin that the United States, unlike the Soviet Union, was fighting a *global* war, with a vast military commitment in the Pacific. If potential Soviet expansionism was to be discouraged in Europe, it was crucial America strike across the Channel as soon as possible, and defeat the German armies in northern France.

Eisenhower listened, and agreed — reflecting how, in the end, he did not really understand why Churchill, a man of such personal courage and capacity for risk, was so opposed to the cross-Channel assault. "How often I heard him say, in speaking of Overlord's prospects," Eisenhower would later recall, "'We must take care that the tides do not run red with the blood of American and British youth, or the beaches be choked with their bodies.'"[14] Such a fear, though, never quite squared with Churchill's openness to American and British blood being copiously spilled in the Mediterranean or Aegean, Eisenhower noted. Casualties there were mounting inexorably — and might well escalate even more dramatically once a British supreme commander took on Eisenhower's mantle in the Mediterranean at the end of the month . . .

As Eisenhower later recalled, it was difficult to "escape a feeling that Mr. Churchill's views were colored" by considerations "outside the scope of the immediate military problem": that the Prime Minister was all too happy to disregard the military challenges involved when it suited him, preferring to focus on British political, even personal, prizes or "fruits" dangling before him in his capacious mind. When "fired up about a strategic project, logistics did not exist for him," Eisenhower reflected, "the combat troops just floated forward over and around obstacles — nothing was difficult. Once I charged him with this habit, saying, 'Prime Minister, when you want to do something you dismiss logistics with a wave of your hand,'" but when disliking a proposal, he would list so many "'logistic difficulties'" he would "effectively discourage any unwary listener." The Prime Minister "looked at me with a twinkle in his eye," Eisenhower remembered, replying candidly: "'It does make a difference whether your heart is in a project, doesn't it?'"[15]

Overlord was not just a "project," however. Two million men would take part in the invasion and subsequent battle. It would decide the war against Hitler. Everyone's heart *had* to be in it now — especially those of America's best combat commanders. Among them a soldier still under a dark cloud: General George S. Patton.

32

Homeward Bound!

THIRTY MINUTES AFTER TAKEOFF "I saw Mt Aetna, its top white with snow," the President jotted in his diary. "We skirted the So.[uth] West of Sicily, seeing all the American landing places" Patton's Seventh U.S. Army forces had assaulted in July that year, then came down "at a field outside of Palermo."[1]

This was Castelvetrano airfield, where, on descending the special ramp, the President was met by a phalanx of proud American combat officers. Waiting on the tarmac also was General Arnold, his U.S. Army Air Forces chief of staff, who'd followed him in his own plane from Cairo. In pride of place, though, was General Mark Clark, the U.S. Fifth Army commander who'd been summoned from the battlefield in Italy. And George Patton, whose forces had conquered Sicily but whose headquarters were now being disbanded, in preparation for Overlord and Anvil.

Accompanied by photographers, the President "entered a jeep and departed on a tour of the airfield," Lieutenant Rigdon recorded. Infantry, tank, and airfield defense units were "drawn up for inspection by the President," and honors were rendered by the Thirty-Sixth Engineers' Band, after which "the President proceeded to inspect the troops, driving down the ranks in his jeep. He then took a position in the center and at the front of the troops and, while still in the jeep, decorated a number of the officers with the Distinguished Service Cross — including General Clark, whose courage on the beaches at Salerno had tipped the scales during the invasion in September. "General Clark's decoration came as a complete surprise to him, he told us. He had been given no idea of why he had been called down from the front in Italy to Sicily." In bright sun the "assembled troops" then "passed in review before the President," including Company B, 908th Infantry — "a Colored outfit and a unit of the 7th Army," all of whom had taken "an active part in the recent Sicilian campaign."[2] More photographs were taken.

It was at this point that, although General Patton was not being decorated, the President called him over, and had a special word with him.

News that, at the height of the campaign in Sicily, the general had slapped and threatened shell-shocked soldiers in a field hospital had recently swept the press in America. Some members of Congress were demanding the cavalry-man be recalled and demoted for conduct unbecoming of an officer and a gentleman.

Admiral Leahy related later how, in "conversation with the President, General Patton brought up the widely publicized incident of his indiscretion of slapping a soldier whom he believed to be a shirker. Apparently the General still worried about possible repercussions and their effect on his own future." To Patton's huge relief, however, the President "indicated that the matter was a closed incident as far as he was concerned."[3]

He did more, in fact. General Clark later recalled how the President, taking Patton's hand, held it for some time. "General Patton," he murmured from his jeep, "you will have an army command in the great Normandy operation."[4]

Patton — a highly emotional as well as brilliantly aggressive commander — almost fainted. In previous days his mood had swung between despair at the thought of being recalled to the United States and faith in divine intervention. The President's arrival out of the skies above Palermo appeared to be divine. As the President's jeep drove on, according to Mike Reilly of the Secret Service, Patton "burst out sobbing."[5]

For his part the President looked proud and elated. Photographs of President Lincoln visiting his generals on or near the battlefield had become iconic — and here was the thirty-second president, more than a century later, inspecting combat troops and their commanders halfway across the world. Barely two hundred miles from Palermo, American troops were fighting a tough battle against the Wehrmacht on the Rapido River, with American planes supporting them. General Spaatz, whom he'd had a chance to get to know better, would be going with Eisenhower to England for Overlord, he'd decided, after discussing the matter with General Arnold and with Eisenhower. General Eaker, the current U.S. commander of the Eighth Air Force in Britain, would be switched to the Mediterranean, while General Doolittle — whom the President had decorated with the Congressional Medal of Honor on his return to the United States after the bombing of Tokyo the year before — would leave Italy and take Eaker's command in England.

The President, in short, was getting his Overlord ducks in a row, after the seemingly endless, acrimonious "strategical" battle with the British. There were early cocktails and a snack at the Thirty-Second Squadron Officers' Club; then, at 3:30 p.m., the President's party once again reembarked on the Sacred Cow. The lumbering C-54 Skymaster sped down the runway and took off — not to fly to Marrakesh, as had earlier been planned, but now that it was so late, only to Carthage, where the President wanted to spend a final night before the long flight to Dakar, on the west coast of Africa. There, as per Admiral King's instructions, the USS *Iowa* would be waiting. Generals Spaatz and Arnold were meanwhile to fly to Italy.

Ever nervous about assassination — Admiral Darlan, after all, had been assassinated the previous December, in Algiers — the Secret Service had attempted to stop the President from staying another night in Carthage, but they had failed. "The Secret Service men were irritated and fearful," Eisenhower later recalled, "but the President confided to me that he had made up his mind to stay at Carthage an extra night and if a legitimate reason for the delay had not been forthcoming he would have invented one." The delay caused by the wing-flap hydraulics had thus been timely. "I remarked that I assumed the President of the United States would not be questioned in dictating the details of his own travel. He replied with considerable emphasis, 'You haven't had to argue with the Secret Service!'"[6]

An hour before sunrise the next day, December 9, 1943, General Eisenhower, Colonel Elliott Roosevelt, and several other senior officers gathered at El Aouina to say goodbye to the President at the airport. "Mr. Roosevelt was just as friendly and natural as before," Kay Summersby, Ike's chauffeur, later said of his departure. "Mr. Roosevelt complimented me on my driving, thanked me for 'taking care' of him, and then smiled. 'I hope you come to the United States, child. If you do, please be sure to come and see me,'" she remembered him saying. "It was the last time I ever saw him."[7]

Flying across the edge of the Atlas Mountains at eight thousand feet — in thick cloud, but warned by the President's doctor not to go any higher — and then over the Sahara, the Great Desert, the 2,425-mile journey seemed to take forever: Tunisia, Algeria, French Sudan, Mauritania, and finally Senegal.

The port of Dakar had played a menacing role before Operation Torch, given the possibility of German occupation of the Vichy-held navy and air base. But since the Torch invasion, it had been in Allied hands — its U.S.-run airfield, Rufisque, as important as the harbor. "We landed on the field about sunset," the President recorded, greeted there by the general commanding American air units — "a very important point," the President noted, since an "average of 60 planes from the U.S. pass through here every day on their way to the front."[8]

Welcoming the President aboard the USS *Iowa*, Captain McCrea, for his part, was suffering from a scraped leg that had become infected. He'd refused to go to the sick bay, however; instead he showed the Commander in Chief to his captain's quarters, and in great pain climbed to his own cabin on the bridge.

It was as well he did. An incompetent French tugboat pilot almost ran the giant warship aground in the dark,[9] but the President, below, was blissfully content, with cocktails and dinner. "An hour ago," the President noted with relief in his diary, when at last he went to bed, "we weighed anchor & so—homeward bound!"[10]

33

The Odyssey Is Over

ACROSS AMERICA THE TRIUMPH of Tehran had been met with rejoicing —and most of all because the patriarch, by December 17, 1943, was reported in the press to be safely back on American shores.

U.S. TROOPS INVADE NEW BRITAIN, WIN FOOTHOLD; RAF BOMBS BERLIN; "FORTS" ALSO ATTACK REICH; ROOSEVELT IS BACK; CHURCHILL HAS PNEUMONIA ran the *New York Times* banner headline. PRESIDENT ARRIVES. SAFE RETURN DISCLOSED BUT NOT WHEN HE WILL REACH CAPITAL. ABSENT FOR 35 DAYS, the front-page article was headed. "The White House announced today that President Roosevelt had safely returned to this country after his journey to the historic conferences in the Middle East."

The *Times* estimated the President had traveled "over 25,000 miles"—an astonishing figure if it was true. (It wasn't.)

The trip, however, was still shrouded in secrecy. No reporters had accompanied the President to Tehran; the *New York Times* really knew no more than anyone else—and nothing whatever of the historic showdown with Churchill that was to decide the war.

"A completely uneventful voyage," the President meantime summarized the voyage home, writing in his arching, looping hand in the leather-bound diary his cousin had given him. He felt in great form. The USS *Iowa* had been "under escort of destroyers all the way, & of aircraft also for the last 3 days," he penned on December 16, 1943.[1] He'd relaxed, had read books, had sat outside, and had worked on his stamp collection. His White House staff had relaxed, too. They'd passed south of the Cape Verde Islands; Admiral Leahy had had three cavities in his teeth filled, and the ship had made twenty-three knots in "warm trade wind weather," as Leahy noted in his own diary.[2] "Marvellous warm weather & no sea," the President scribbled—"up to yesterday noon when we hit a sudden storm from the coast, & from 60 it dropped last night to 20° Fahrenheit." The crew had changed from khakis into blues, and "this morning early we came in through the Capes. Now we are steaming up Chesapeake Bay. We are all packed up — I am writing in the big room & the boys are having a final game of Gin Rummy."[3]

In truth, while the President was asleep during the storm, and with "visibility zero" outside, the *Iowa* had narrowly missed a merchant vessel standing north of them. "Had it not been for our radar contact, a collision would certainly have occurred," Lieutenant Rigdon subsequently recorded in the President's log.[4]

The President's luck had held, however, and at 4:00 p.m. on December 16 the *Iowa* had anchored off Cherry Point, where its journey had begun. "The little *Potomac* has loomed 6 miles ahead at the mouth of the river and at 4.30 I will transfer to her, after first making a speech to the crew," Roosevelt wrote in high, widely separated words, with *t*'s crossed at the apex. He would stay overnight on his presidential yacht, "and tomorrow morning we should get to the Navy Yard in Washington & soon afterwards I will be at the W.[hite] H.[ouse] & using the telephone. So will end a new Odyssey."[5]

Before disembarking the President made a "short interesting talk to the crew of the U.S.S. *Iowa*" on the ship's quarterdeck, Leahy recorded.[6] In this the President tried to convey something of the import of the conferences in the Middle East. "One of the reasons I went abroad, as you know, was to try by conversations with other nations, to see that this war that we are all engaged in shall not happen again," he explained in his easy, folksy, unmistakable tenor lilt. "We have an idea — all of us, I think — that hereafter we have got to eliminate from the human race nations like Germany and Japan; eliminate them," that was, "from the possibility of ruining the lives of a whole lot of other nations." He'd held "talks in North Africa, Egypt and Persia, with the Chinese, the Russians, Turks and others," and felt "real progress" had been made in looking ahead to an international world order beyond war. "Obviously it will be necessary when we win the war to make the possibility of a future upsetting of our civilization an impossible thing," he'd stated. "I don't say forever," he'd cautioned, however. "None of us can look that far ahead. But I do say as long as any Americans and others who are alive today are still alive. That objective is worth fighting for."[7]

He, Mr. Churchill, and Marshal Stalin had "the same fundamental aims," the President asserted: "stopping what has been going on in these past four years, and that is why I believe from the viewpoint of people — just plain people," the trip had been worthwhile.[8] Despite differing beliefs, they were all "engaged in a common struggle" — a coalition in which the three leaders, as heads of their governments, represented "between two-thirds and three-quarters of the entire population of the world."[9]

Once again Captain McCrea — who was not a natural speaker — was delighted at how the President could deliver such "off-the-cuff talks" that tied the concerns of ordinary men and women to the ideals of a whole nation, in fact all democratic nations.

"After he had embarked on the Yacht *Potomac*," using the special gangway, and once the vessel "pulled away from alongside *Iowa*, with hat in his hand he waved goodbye to us," McCrea recalled.[10]

It would be the last time McCrea saw him, for the *Iowa* was thereafter sent to the Pacific, to take part in many battles and win many battle stars. "The crew," for their part, "responded with a spontaneous cheer."[11]

At 9:15 the next morning, after a final night in the *Potomac* as it made its way upriver, the President was greeted at the Washington Navy Yard by his wife, Eleanor. Following "a month in warmer latitudes," Leahy noted, it was a distinctly bracing return to land.[12] In the bitter cold they were driven to the White House, where at 9:30 a.m. a "large delegation of his friends" were on hand "to welcome him back home," Lieutenant Rigdon recorded.

The cabinet and the quasi cabinet had assembled in the Green Room, before going down, en masse, to the "entrance to the South Door of the White House," Secretary Stimson recorded that night in his own diary — joined by a throng of congressmen who'd come "for the same purpose of greeting him." The President was "wheeled in from his car," Stimson described. "He was in his traveling suit, looked very well, and greeted all of us with very great cheeriness and good humor and kindness. He was at his best. Republicans were mixed with Democrats and they all seemed very glad to have him back safe and sound. We stood around a few minutes." Then the President "went upstairs with Mrs. Roosevelt and the family to their apartment and the rest of us left for our offices."[13]

That afternoon at 2:00, having unpacked and eaten a light lunch, the President then convened the cabinet for the first time since November 5.

The interior secretary, Harold Ickes, had been one of those most deeply worried about the prospect of the trip, and the President's safety. Weeks before, on December 3, Grace Tully, the President's office secretary, had told Ickes that "extraordinary precautions" had been ordered "to protect the parties to the conference," as she reassured him over lunch. His anxiety hadn't, however, been assuaged. "I am more nervous than ever about the President and all of his Army and Navy experts being out of the country where a successful attack might mean the lives of all or at least a large number of them," Ickes had confessed in his diary. It was, in its way, the great weakness of the American constitutional system, he'd reflected. "We would suffer from such an event much more than Great Britain or Russia where the systems of government are so much more flexible, so much so as to permit the strongest leader in each country to be selected" to replace him.[14]

This was debatable — as well as being a slur on his colleague, the vice president, Henry Wallace. It certainly explained, though, why the safe return of the Chief Executive was greeted with almost literal fanfare and jubilation. "He looked very well," Ickes noted after the cabinet meeting. "A lot of us feel easier now that he is back in this country." The "President spoke of his recent conference in Cairo and Tehran. Evidently he was very much taken with Stalin, and this was confirmed later by Ross McIntire," the President's physician. "He likes Stalin because he is open and frank. In discussing Japan, Stalin indicated that he did not care how far the United States and Great Britain went in punishment" — moreover the President "felt the same about Germany, too," after the atrocities the Japanese and Nazis had committed.[15] In Tehran he'd seen the young shah, and had gotten Stalin to sign "an agreement guaranteeing the present and future independence of Iran." The President had suggested to Stalin "that he also sign. Stalin demurred. He said that Russia needed a warm-water port and would like to have one on the Persian Gulf. The President suggested that he believed the government of Iran would be willing to allow Russia to ship in bond through some port and that this would be to the advantage of Iran as well as of Russia. This reservation was made and Stalin signed the agreement."[16]

It was clear that the President saw the Soviet Union as a postwar trading equal — a position that would be far more effective in drawing it out of its repressive, paranoid communist shell than exclusion. "As to Hong Kong, it was suggested that this ought to be given back to China," as part of the inevitable decolonization program the United Nations could oversee, "although Churchill was not very strong for that." He'd advocated "breaking Germany up into five independent states and he also suggested that the industrialized Ruhr," which had fed the Nazi war machine, "and adjacent areas be internationalized."[17]

"He discussed his trip with a very interesting and lithesome touch for the first hour of our meeting," Henry Stimson, the secretary of war, acknowledged. "His narrative, so far as it went, completely confirmed the impressions that I have got from the Minutes concerning Joe Stalin and the part he had taken in it, particularly the scraps that he had had with the Prime Minister. The President said that Joe teased the P.M. like a boy and it was very amusing."[18]

The second hour, however, was devoted to the "terrible mess going on" in America — the MANY MAJOR PROBLEMS [THAT] AWAIT HIM HERE, as the New York Times's headline had noted: rising inflation, a looming countrywide railroad strike, an impending steelworkers strike, and other issues.[19] Nothing had seemed to dampen the President's mood, though, and from the Cabinet Room he was wheeled into the Oval Office shortly after 4:00 p.m. to hold his first press conference since his return — the 927th, almost incredibly, since taking office. He said he planned to give a special radio broadcast to the officers and men of the armed forces, all over the world, in a week's time, on Christmas Eve; then, after the new year, to give his annual State of the Union

address to Congress. In the meantime, he fielded off-the-record questions —
especially ones about Marshal Stalin and the Second Front — which he batted
like flies. When a reporter asked, for example, if "there is anything you can say
at this point about the possibility of General Marshall's going to Europe?" (i.e.,
to command Overlord), the President simply answered "No."[20]

The President confirmed he'd flown by plane to Tehran. Also that he'd recently been "through" Dakar. For security reasons, though, he dodged further
questions regarding his itinerary, save for a few tidbits — such as admitting
he'd stayed in the Russian Embassy in Tehran, where he'd drunk "up to three
hundred and sixty-five toasts."[21] Also that he'd visited with General Eisenhower in the Mediterranean, and been to Sicily, where he'd met General Clark.
And General Patton.

The journalists pricked up their ears. Drew Pearson and other members of
the press were still stirring the Patton scandalpot — SENATORS HOLD UP PAT-
TON PROMOTION: CHANDLER SAYS SUBCOMMITTEE SUSPECTS OTHER
INCIDENTS BESIDES THOSE REVEALED, the *New York Times* headline had
run the day before[22] — but the Commander in Chief squelched any question
regarding his own views on the matter. With a broad, disarming smile, he
quoted the well-worn story of a "former President" — clearly Lincoln — who'd
had "a good deal of trouble in finding a successful commander for the armies
of the United States." And when he finally did find such a commander, Mr.
Roosevelt reminded the assembled correspondents, it was only for the President to be told by "some very good citizens": "You can't keep him. He drinks."

"It must be a good brand of liquor,"[23] the President had memorably responded — and the same held true now, he indicated with a smile.

With that, the journalists were dismissed. The Sun King had seemed as
sunny as ever: jovial, charming, confident — and masking with his customary
savvy the sheer weight of his myriad responsibilities. There was no mention of
his medical drama — his indigestion attack in Tehran — or of the seriousness
of the British insurrection with which he'd had to deal. The way forward for
the Allies was now, at last, clear. *Overlord.* That was the only thing that really
mattered: a matter of sticking to the invasion and its timetable.

On leaving Tunis the President had warned Eisenhower to say nothing yet
about his new appointment, or even the title that he would be given, but to
keep it "strictly secret." The President himself "would do this from Washington," as Eisenhower later recalled the discussion they'd had at Carthage on the
subject. "He toyed with the word 'Supreme' in his conversation but made no
decision at the moment. He merely said that he must devise some designation
that would imply the importance the Allies attached to the new venture."[24]

Miraculously — perhaps as a result of a homily the President gave to
the White House correspondents (and thus their editors) concerning the
often fatal consequences of "leaks," which only served to help the enemy —

Roosevelt was thus able to keep secret his decision regarding Overlord and its new commander for another week — by which time General Marshall would be back from a wide-ranging tour he was making of American commands in the Pacific, including a meeting with General MacArthur.[25]

In the meantime, Secretary Stimson — one of the few who *did* know the President's decision to appoint Eisenhower to command Overlord — burned with anxiety. He yearned to know the reason General Marshall had not been chosen.

Stimson would have to wait, however. The President was looking forward to a good night's sleep in his old bed, on the second floor of the White House mansion: his first night home after the most grueling yet historic trip of his life. And, in terms of his good health, the last.

PART FIVE

In Sickness and in Health

34

Churchill's Resurrection

IN WASHINGTON, D.C., the British ambassador, Lord Halifax, having come down with flu, had been unable to join the throng welcoming the President home at the White House. In his stead his deputy, Ronald Campbell, had attended the gathering. Campbell had reported back that "the President was in good form"[1] — the view of all who saw or spoke to Mr. Roosevelt on his return from Cairo.

Not so the reports that Lord Halifax was receiving from London. "Reports circulated in the afternoon that Winston had died," Halifax noted in his diary — the Prime Minister gravely ill with pneumonia in Carthage, still.[2] "Harry Hopkins rang me up to know if we had any news. I felt pretty sure that this was not likely to be true," he noted of reports of Churchill's death, "but was none the less relieved when the B.B.C. gave a good report in the evening. I imagine the dangerous time though will be after a few days"[3] — for the Prime Minister, staying in the "White House" villa in quick succession to the President, had contracted suspected pleurisy, too, raising fears it could lead (as it did) to heart trouble.

Would Churchill's ill health cause him to resign? many wondered. Churchill's wife, Clemmie, was summoned urgently to Carthage to be at his bedside. For his part King George VI wrote to the Prime Minister, via his royal scribe Sir Alan Lascelles, to say how "cruel" it was that "the P.M.'s triumphant journey should end in this way." As to Churchill's compelled recuperation in North Africa, the monarch hoped that the "comparative rest may be a blessing in disguise." In short, as Lascelles expressed the sovereign's faith, "good may come of evil."[4]

The trip, for Churchill, had been far from triumphant, however, and the "comparative rest" would prove lethal for tens of thousands of unwitting Allied servicemen in Italy, once Churchill emerged from his Lazarus-like bed. Meanwhile, agreeing to see Secretary Stimson privately at the White House on

December 18, 1943, the President confided to Stimson what had actually taken place in Tehran.

"The President and I were alone and he devoted himself to telling of his recent accomplishments at Tehran," Stimson dictated that night. "He said that when he first met Churchill at these meetings he was surprised at the change in him. He seemed unwell, was peevish and had prejudices against people in a way that was quite unusual to him. He came to the first conference [in Cairo] telling the President that he hoped they could now rearrange some of the things that they had taken up before," at Quebec, and "during the discussions he tried to reopen Overlord and the Eastern Mediterranean matters, like the Dodecanese and Rhodes, and finally concentrated on Turkey."[5]

The President had been having none of that, he explained to Stimson, and "said that he himself had fought hard for Overlord and with the aid of Stalin finally won out, and in his charming way he said: 'I have thus brought Overlord back to you safe and sound on the ways for accomplishment.'"[6]

Stimson, having read the top-secret Tehran minutes, was glad to have the President's personal confirmation. "As he put it, the conference had been successful in all military strategic matters except one," namely "the Burma affair" — a typical Churchill maneuver "where as he described it, Churchill had insisted on halting the program which had been approved at the preceding meeting with Chiang Kai-shek by taking away the necessary landing boats for the amphibian Burma operation to use in the Eastern Mediterranean. Roosevelt had opposed this; and had reminded Churchill of the promises made to Chiang, but Churchill had insisted." Running out of time in Cairo they had finally "compromised on the postponement of the Burma operation"[7] — for without British participation, the landings off Burma could not take place. As a result of British objections, the United States would have to try and make things up to Chiang by sending more air supplies over the Himalayan "hump."

"Now I come to the last matter," the President had continued, "and that is the one of Command." As Stimson recorded, "he described his luncheon with Marshall after the conference was over and their return to Cairo. He let drop the fact, which I had supposed to be true, that Churchill wanted Marshall for the Commander and had assumed that it was settled as, in fact, it had been agreed on in Quebec. The President described, however, how he reopened this matter with Marshall at their solitary luncheon together and tried to get Marshall to tell him whether he preferred to hold the Command of Overlord (now that a General Supreme Commander [of all Europe, north and south] was not feasible) or whether he preferred to remain as Chief of Staff."[8]

Having heard McCloy's version the previous evening, Stimson recognized the President was probably telling him the truth — which was not always the case. "He was very explicit in telling me that he urged Marshall to tell him which one of the two he personally preferred, intimating that he would be very glad to give him the one that he did. He said that Marshall stubbornly refused, saying that it was for the President to decide, and that he, Marshall, would do with equal cheerfulness whichever one he was selected for." It had thus been up to Marshall to make his own preference known — and he hadn't. "The President said that he got the impression that Marshall was not only impartial between the two but perhaps really preferred to remain as Chief of Staff. Finally, having been unable to get him to tell his preference, the President said that he decided on a mathematical basis that if Marshall took Overlord it would mean that Eisenhower would become [U.S. Army] Chief of Staff, but, while Eisenhower was a very good soldier and familiar with the European theater, he was unfamiliar with what had been going on in the Pacific and he also would be far less able than Marshall to handle the Congress; that, therefore, he, the President, decided that he would be more comfortable if he kept Marshall at his elbow and turned over Overlord to Eisenhower."[9]

The truth had thus acquired a certain lacquer in the telling — for it was, of course, the President himself who had never really wanted to send Marshall to Europe, unless to command, literally, *all* Europe. The varnish, however, was in a good cause. Stimson's support, as a first-class lawyer and U.S. secretary of war, would be necessary if the army was to take over the railroads across the nation, should the union strike proceed in a few days' time. Moreover Stimson, on behalf of the President, was meeting almost every day with Dr. Vannevar Bush and others about "S-1" — code-name for the atomic bomb project at Los Alamos. There, thanks to Senator Harry S. Truman's investigating committee on government waste and/or corruption in war manufacturing, it was becoming more and more difficult to maintain secrecy — the "installations" getting "so numerous and so big that they are attracting attention in Congress and people are beginning to talk about it," as Stimson had himself recently noted.[10] Above all Stimson was a Republican, and therefore a vital component in the math of the 1944 presidential election — if the President decided to stand for a fourth term.

To the President's delight Stimson — who thought the world of Marshall, and had been unable to understand why the Overlord appointment "seems to have gone to Ike instead of to George" — seemed mollified, though he openly told the President he'd been "staggered when I heard of the change" in the expected appointment of Marshall. As Stimson confided to the President, he'd known "that in the bottom of his heart it was Marshall's secret desire above all things to command this invasion force into Europe." Being the man he was, the general had nobly concealed it, not wishing to put personal ambition before the good of the country, so that Stimson had found it "very hard work to wring out of Marshall that this was so but I had done so finally beyond the possibility of misunderstanding." It was a thousand pities that he, Henry Stimson, had not accompanied Odysseus on his epic journey. "I wish I had been along with you in Cairo. I could have made that point clear," Stimson stated — admitting that he'd warned Marshall, before the trip, not to be diffident when the matter came up for a decision in Cairo, or Tehran.[11] Hearing the President's argument for keeping Marshall in Washington, now that he'd gotten D-day "on the ways," Stimson was relieved, however — for he, too, would benefit from Marshall's steady hand and uncontested authority over the U.S. military.

The President and his war secretary were then joined, after lunch, by Admiral Leahy and General Arnold to discuss the command arrangements for U.S. Army Air Forces in Overlord and Europe. The matter of Marshall's literal dis-appointment was thus left there; it was over. The announcement would be made by the President in his Christmas Eve broadcast, he told them, just as soon as General Marshall returned from the Pacific, where he was meeting with MacArthur, Nimitz, and air force commanders. The President would, he said, make sure in his broadcast that adequate tribute be paid, by name, to General Marshall and his great responsibilities as U.S. Army chief of staff.

With that, the meeting came to an end, and the waiting for D-day — the "deciding" battle of the war, as Hitler put it in a conference with his own generals two days later,[12] began.

35

In the Pink at Hyde Park

ON THE EVENING of December 23, 1943, leaving "behind a day that would have floored many a rugged man,"[1] the President left Washington for Hyde Park. He felt in top form. He'd given orders for the U.S. military to take over striking railroad companies, and was taking with him this time no fewer than nine White House correspondents aboard the *Ferdinand Magellan* — the "first time they have been with us on the homebound train since Pearl Harbor," William Hassett noted in his diary.[2] The next night, Christmas Eve, he would speak to the nation, and to American soldiers, sailors, and airmen across the globe, from his new library building. Even the reporters, Admiral McIntire later wrote, "agreed that he looked 'in the pink.'"[3]

It would be the President's twenty-seventh Fireside Chat. "The Boss, in good humor, joked with photographers, radio men, and newsreel men while waiting to begin," Hassett recorded, and then at 3:00 p.m. on December 24, the broadcast went live.[4] As his family — his wife and thirteen grandchildren — sat on the floor the President began speaking in his characteristically bold but avuncular tone. Sam Rosenman and Robert Sherwood, his speechwriters, had worked night and day to condense his notes, searching for an order in which to best convey his message to American forces.

The result was perhaps the most intimate and human, almost colloquial, account the President had ever given of the war — and the decisions he was making to save humanity. Also America's new role in facing, as he hoped his country would, the great postwar challenge. He did not therefore mention the impending railroad strike, or the threatened steel strike — only the war the United States was fighting abroad, and what would follow on the global stage.

"On this Christmas Eve," he began, "there are over 10 million men in the armed forces of the United States alone. One year ago 1,700,000 were serving overseas. Today, this figure has been more than doubled to 3,800,000 on duty overseas. By next July one that number overseas will rise to over 5,000,000 men and women." Timewise it was midafternoon "here in the United States, and in the Caribbean and on the Northeast Coast of South America," but in "Alaska and in Hawaii and the mid-Pacific, it is still morning," he pointed out — asking listeners and viewers to recognize therein the global nature of the conflict. "In Iceland, in Great Britain, in North Africa, in Italy and the Middle East, it is now evening. In the Southwest Pacific, in Australia, in China and Burma and India, it is already Christmas Day. So we can correctly say that at this moment, in those Far Eastern parts where Americans are fighting, today is tomorrow. But everywhere throughout the world — throughout this war that covers the world — there is a special spirit that has warmed our hearts since our earliest childhood — a spirit that brings us close to our homes, our families, our friends and neighbors: the Christmas spirit of 'peace on earth, good will toward men.' It is an unquenchable spirit.

"During the past years of international gangsterism and brutal aggression in Europe and in Asia, our Christmas celebrations have been darkened with apprehension for the future. We have said, 'Merry Christmas — a Happy New Year,' but we have known in our hearts that the clouds which have hung over our world have prevented us from saying it with full sincerity and conviction. And even this year, we still have much to face in the way of further suffering, and sacrifice, and personal tragedy. Our men, who have been through the fierce battles in the Solomons, and the Gilberts, and Tunisia and Italy know, from their own experience and knowledge of modern war, that many bigger and costlier battles are still to be fought.

"But — on Christmas Eve this year — I can say to you that at last we may look forward into the future with real, substantial confidence that, however great the cost, 'peace on earth, good will toward men' can be and will be realized and ensured . . .

"A great beginning was made in the Moscow conference last October by Mr. Molotov, Mr. Eden, and our own Mr. Hull. There and then the way was paved for the later meetings" — the summit in Iran from which he had just returned.

"At Cairo and Teheran we devoted ourselves not only to military matters; we devoted ourselves also to consideration of the future — to plans for the kind of world which alone can justify all the sacrifices of this war. Of course, as you all know, Mr. Churchill and I have happily met many times before, and we know and understand each other very well. Indeed, Mr. Churchill has become known and beloved by many millions of Americans, and the heartfelt prayers of all of us have been with this great citizen of the world in his recent serious illness.

"The Cairo and Teheran conferences, however, gave me my first opportunity to meet the Generalissimo, Chiang Kai-shek, and Marshal Stalin — and to sit down at the table with these unconquerable men and talk with them face to face. We had planned to talk to each other across the table at Cairo and Teheran; but we soon found that we were all on the same side of the table. We came to the conferences with faith in each other. But we needed the personal contact. And now we have supplemented faith with definite knowledge.

"It was well worth traveling thousands of miles over land and sea to bring about this personal meeting, and to gain the heartening assurance that we are absolutely agreed with one another on all the major objectives — and on the military means of attaining them.

"At Cairo, Prime Minister Churchill and I spent four days with the Generalissimo, Chiang Kai-shek. It was the first time that we had an opportunity to go over the complex situation in the Far East with him personally. We were able not only to settle upon definite military strategy, but also to discuss certain long-range principles which we believe can assure peace in the Far East for many generations to come.

"Those principles are as simple as they are fundamental. They involve the restoration of stolen property to its rightful owners, and the recognition of the rights of millions of people in the Far East to build up their own forms of self-government without molestation. Essential to all peace and security in the Pacific and in the rest of the world is the permanent elimination of the Empire of Japan as a potential force of aggression. Never again must our soldiers and sailors and marines — and other soldiers, sailors, and marines — be compelled to fight from island to island as they are fighting so gallantly and so successfully today.

"Increasingly powerful forces are now hammering at the Japanese at many points over an enormous arc which curves down through the Pacific from the Aleutians to the jungles of Burma. Our own Army and Navy, our Air Forces, the Australians and New Zealanders, the Dutch, and the British land, air, and sea forces are all forming a band of steel which is slowly but surely closing in on Japan.

"On the mainland of Asia, under the Generalissimo's leadership, the Chinese ground and air forces augmented by American air forces are playing a vital part in starting the drive which will push the invaders into the sea.

"Following out the military decisions at Cairo, General Marshall has just flown around the world and has had conferences with General MacArthur and Admiral Nimitz — conferences which will spell plenty of bad news for the Japs in the not too far distant future.

"I met in the Generalissimo a man of great vision, great courage, and a remarkably keen understanding of the problems of today and tomorrow. We discussed all the manifold military plans for striking at Japan with decisive force from many directions, and I believe I can say that he returned to Chungking with the positive assurance of total victory over our common enemy. Today we and the Republic of China are closer together than ever before in deep friendship and in unity of purpose.

"After the Cairo conference, Mr. Churchill and I went by airplane to Teheran. There we met with Marshal Stalin. We talked with complete frankness on every conceivable subject connected with the winning of the war and the establishment of a durable peace after the war. Within three days of intense and consistently amicable discussions, we agreed on every point concerned with the launching of a gigantic attack upon Germany": Overlord.

"The Russian Army will continue its stern offensives on Germany's eastern front, the Allied armies in Italy and Africa will bring relentless pressure on Germany from the south, and now the encirclement will be complete as great American and British forces attack from other points of the compass."

It was at this point in his broadcast that the President at last announced publicly who would command the "gigantic attack." "The Commander selected to lead the combined attack from these other points is General Dwight D. Eisenhower," the President revealed. "His performances in Africa, in Sicily and in Italy have been brilliant. He knows by practical and successful experience the way to coordinate air, sea, and land power. All of these will be under his control. Lieutenant General Carl Spaatz will command the entire American strategic bombing force operating against Germany.

"General Eisenhower gives up his command in the Mediterranean to a British officer whose name is being announced by Mr. Churchill. We now pledge that new Commander that our powerful ground, sea, and air forces in the vital Mediterranean area will stand by his side until every objective in that bitter theater is attained.

"Both of these new Commanders will have American and British subordinate Commanders whose names will be announced in a few days.

"During the last two days [at] Teheran, Marshal Stalin, Mr. Churchill, and I looked ahead, ahead to the days and months and years that will follow Germany's defeat. We were united in determination that Germany must be stripped of her military might and be given no opportunity within the foreseeable future to regain that might.

"The United Nations have no intention to enslave the German people. We wish them to have a normal chance to develop, in peace, as useful and respectable members of the European family. But we most certainly emphasize that word 'respectable' for we intend to rid them once and for all of Nazism and Prussian militarism and the fantastic and disastrous notion that they constitute the 'Master Race.'

"We did discuss international relationships from the point of view of big, broad objectives, rather than details. But on the basis of what we did discuss, I can say even today that I do not think any insoluble differences will arise among Russia, Great Britain, and the United States. In these conferences we were concerned with basic principles—principles which involve the security and the welfare and the standard of living of human beings in countries large and small. To use an American and somewhat ungrammatical colloquialism, I may say that I 'got along fine' with Marshal Stalin. He is a man who combines a tremendous, relentless determination with a stalwart good humor. I believe he is truly representative of the heart and soul of Russia; and I believe that we are going to get along very well with him and the Russian people — very well indeed.

"Britain, Russia, China and the United States and their allies represent more than three-quarters of the total population of the earth. As long as these four nations with great military power stick together in determination to keep the peace there will be no possibility of an aggressor nation arising to start another world war.

"But those four powers must be united with and cooperate with all the freedom-loving peoples of Europe, and Asia, and Africa, and the Americas. The rights of every nation, large or small, must be respected and guarded as jealously as are the rights of every individual within our own republic.

"The doctrine that the strong shall dominate the weak is the doctrine of our enemies — and we reject it. But, at the same time, we are agreed that if force is necessary to keep international peace, international force will be applied for as long as it may be necessary.

"It has been our steady policy — and it is certainly a common sense policy — that the right of each nation to freedom must be measured by the willing-ness of that nation to fight for freedom. And today we salute our unseen allies in occupied countries — the underground resistance groups and the armies of liberation. They will provide potent forces against our enemies, when the day of the counter-invasion comes" — D-day!

D-day led to the theme Roosevelt most wanted to continue seeding: the end of isolationism in America. "Through the development of science the world has become so much smaller," he pointed out, "that we have had to discard the geographical yardsticks of the past. For instance, through our early his-tory the Atlantic and Pacific Oceans were believed to be walls of safety for the United States," he acknowledged. "Until recently very few people, even mili-tary experts, thought that the day would ever come when we might have to de-fend our Pacific coast against Japanese threats of invasion. At the outbreak of the first World War relatively few people thought that our ships and shipping would be menaced by German submarines on the high seas or that the Ger-man militarists would ever attempt to dominate any nation outside of central Europe." Yet that day had come, in World War I, with unrestricted German U-boat warfare — requiring vast resources and determination before Germany pleaded for an armistice.

"After the Armistice in 1918, we thought and hoped that the militaris-tic philosophy of Germany had been crushed; and being full of the milk of human kindness we spent the next twenty years disarming, while the Ger-mans whined so pathetically that the other nations permitted them — and even helped them — to rearm. For too many years we lived on pious hopes that aggressor and warlike nations would learn and understand and carry out the doctrine of purely voluntary peace."

The result had been tragically violent. "The well-intentioned but ill-fated experiments of former years did not work. It is my hope that we will not try them again. No — that is putting it too weakly — it is my intention to do all that I humanly can as President and Commander-in-Chief to see to it that these tragic mistakes shall *not* be made again.

"There have always been cheerful idiots in this country who believed that there would be no more war for us if everybody in America would only return into their homes and lock their front doors behind them. Assuming that their motives were of the highest, events have shown how unwilling they were to face the facts.

"The overwhelming majority of all the people in the world want peace. Most of them are fighting for the attainment of peace — not just a truce, not just an armistice — but peace that is as strongly enforced and as durable as mortal man can make it. If we are willing to fight for peace now, is it not good logic that we should use force if necessary, in the future, to keep the peace?"

He was coming to his deepest conviction: namely that America's destiny in the coming years would have to be the safeguarding of the peace that would follow American victory. "I believe, and I think I can say, that the other three great nations who are fighting so magnificently to gain peace are in complete agreement that we must be prepared to keep the peace by force. If the people of Germany and Japan are made to realize thoroughly that the world is not going to let them break out again, it is possible, and, I hope, probable, that they will abandon the philosophy of aggression — the belief that they can gain the whole world even at the risk of losing their own souls."

Lest there be press speculation over his choice of Eisenhower over Marshall, the President wisely included in his broadcast a further mention of his faithful army chief of staff.

"To the members of our armed forces, to their wives, mothers, and fathers, I want to affirm the great faith and confidence that we have in General Marshall and in Admiral King, who direct all of our armed might throughout the world," he added. "Upon them falls the great responsibility of planning the strategy of determining where and when we shall fight. Both of these men have already gained high places in American history, which will record many evidences of their military genius that cannot be published today."[5]

As FDR ended his broadcast, all were energized by the President's clarity, conviction, and confidence — a commander in chief determined to lead America to victory and beyond. If all went well.

• • •

For a while it did. No sooner had the President returned to the White House after Christmas than he gave another scintillating peroration to correspondents in the Oval Office — a press conference that would become known as the President's "Dr. Win-the-War" talk.

In this the President listed the major progressive accomplishments of his New Deal program that he wanted people to remember, or not take for granted in the hurly-burly of war: saving the banking system, preserving farms from foreclosure, establishing the Securities and Exchange Commission and old-age insurance, creating unemployment insurance, instituting bank deposit insurance, providing federal aid for the blind and the crippled — things he thought no one in their right mind would want to go back on after the war, if Republicans had their way.

It was this liberal agenda which, like so many millions of Americans, he wanted to improve upon rather than repeal "when victory comes" — an agenda that should be seen as international. The "program of the past," he declared, "has got to be carried on, in my judgment, with what is going on in other countries . . . We can't go into an economic isolationism, any more than it would pay to go into a military isolationism. This is not just a question of dollars and cents, although some people think it is. It is a question of the long range, which ties in human beings with dollars, to the benefit of the dollars and the benefit of the human beings as a part of this postwar program, which of course hasn't been settled on at all, except in generalities. But, as I said about the meeting in Teheran and the meeting in Cairo, we are still in the generality stage, not in the detail stage, because we are talking about principles. Later on we will come down to the detail stage, and we can take up anything at all and discuss it then." As he put it, in the meantime "it seems pretty clear that we must plan for, and help to bring about, an expanded economy which will result in more security, in more employment, in more recreation, in more education, in more health, in better housing for all of our citizens, so that the conditions of 1932 and the beginning of 1933 won't come back again."[6]

The newspaper correspondents were, for the most part, agog — amazed by the paraplegic president's vigor and energy. "The public works program, the direction of federal funds to starving people. The principle of a minimum wage and maximum hours. The Civilian Conservation Corps" and its work on "Reforestation. The N.Y.A. [National Youth Administration], for thousands of literally underprivileged young people. Abolishing child labor," which "was not thought to be constitutional in the old days, but . . . turned out to be. Reciprocal trade agreements, which of course do have a tremendous effect on internal [economic] diseases. Stimulation of private home building through the F.H.A [Federal Housing Administration]. The protection of consumers from extortionate rates by utilities. The breaking up of utility monopolies, through Sam Rayburn's law. The resettlement of farmers from marginal lands that ought not to be cultivated; regional physical developments, such as T.V.A. [the Tennessee Valley Authority]; getting electricity out to the farmers through the R.E.A. [Rural Electrification Act]; flood control; and water conservation; drought control — remember the years we went through that! — and drought relief; crop insurance, and the ever normal granary; and assistance to farm cooperatives," plus the "conservation of natural resources." . . .

"Well, my list just totaled up to thirty," the President stated, summarizing the achievements of the New Deal — "and I probably left out half of them." In that context his allegory of Dr. New Deal and Dr. Win-the-War — an orthopedic surgeon called upon to minister to the nation following a "bad accident" (at Pearl Harbor) — was typical Roosevelt: whimsical, but at heart deeply serious, not evasive. The postwar beckoned — and unlike certain unnamed doctors, he was not afraid to discuss or embrace the latest therapy, now "that the patient is back on his feet. He has given up his crutches. He isn't wholly well yet, and he won't be until he wins the war" — victory which was not imminent, but was at last within sight. And the good news was that, although, "at the present time, obviously, the principal emphasis, the overwhelming first emphasis should be on winning the war," the nation nevertheless was able to discuss a forward-looking, progressive agenda. One that was based upon prescriptions that had addressed the "disease" of economic boom and catastrophe in the Great Depression and had, in the New Deal, treated it successfully, without the nation resorting to fascism or dictatorship or aggression. And to which the nation could soon return, and build upon, in a new international environment, or world order.

"In other words, we are suffering from that bad accident," the President ended, "not from an internal disease."

It was the afternoon of December 28, and for the most part the journalists in the Oval Office were struck by how positive, humorous, compassionate, idealistic, and forward-looking was the President, as the eve of the New Year, 1944, approached. As one reporter broke the silence: "Does that all add up to a fourth-term declaration?"[7]

The question caused the room to erupt in laughter.

That night, however, the President admitted he was "feeling a *little* miserably," his cousin Daisy noted in her diary at the White House, where she was staying.[8] She herself had been suffering flu, which seemed to be endemic at that time.

All too soon the President himself seemed to be coming down with the virus. By December 30, he had a fever running almost 101 degrees. He was "a little hectic and flushed," and "at loose ends," Daisy described, after he'd had dinner brought in on a tray, sitting with his daughter Anna, who was visiting from California.[9]

Daisy was not a nurse, but since it seemed there was no one else taking care of the President, she administered aspirin and cough medicine, and called the doctor. He told her "we have to expect the increased temp. for the next 48 hrs. as part of the flu. The P. must not catch cold during the night; he would probably be in a perspiration & should have dry clothes," she recorded in her diary.[10]

He would get over it; he would bounce back; he would be fine, the doctor said.

But he wasn't.

36

Sick

THE PRESIDENT'S COUGH quickly developed into bronchitis; his hands trembled more and more; he suffered more headaches. "So it went on; one day up and one day down," Admiral McIntire, his White House physician, later recalled.[1] Tough domestic problems — strikes on the railroads, threatened strikes in the all-important steel industry — seemed to follow him implacably, "and just to make things worse, he had the bad luck to contract influenza. The attack hung on and finally left behind a nagging inflammation of the bronchial tubes," McIntire chronicled. "Coughing spells racked him by day and broke his rest at night."[2]

The flu — and the bronchitis that accompanied it — left the President feeling like a proverbial wet rag, or worse. He felt constantly tired, but he'd always been a fighter. He'd disliked ever giving way to sickness — concerned lest any sign of ill-health, after fighting his way to be able at least to stand on his steel-braced feet after poliomyelitis, should become ammunition for his Republican enemies. In the aftermath of his long, Odyssean journey to the Middle East, however, he was minded to acknowledge the illness this time publicly, in a sort of Fireside Chat. He'd be able to say, in all honesty, he was too sick to go to Congress to deliver his annual State of the Union address but that, instead, he was broadcasting it live from the White House — even filming a portion of it for newsreel, to be shown in movie houses. For it was now time, as the elected president of the United States in his final year of office, for him to set out a social and economic vision of the future: ideals that Americans could pursue in a world in which they were the new standard-bearers of democracy.

The President's political vision, in the midst of a world war, was an aspect of his leadership that his friend Prime Minister Mackenzie King found perhaps the most extraordinary thing of all, when comparing the President and the Prime Minister of Great Britain after Tehran.

"Churchill has been 'raised up' to meet the need of this day in the realm of war, to fight, with the power of the sword, the brute beasts that would devour their fellow men in their lust for power," the Canadian prime minister noted in his diary, a trifle grandiosely. Roosevelt might not be as great a man as an orator, or military "genius"; nevertheless he was undoubtedly a greater man, the Canadian felt, "in his love for his fellow men and in his very sincere desire to improve their lot."

Churchill's biggest problem, King felt, was drink. "I greatly fear that demon may claim him as its own, before he sees the fruits of victory. I pray it may not be so, and that he may be spared to enjoy some of the fruits of victory, which he more than any other single man deserves. It is clear, however, that already it has him 'down', and however much he may recover, his strength & endurance will be greatly lessened for all time, and at any moment he may suffer an attack which may take him off," King confided in his dictated journal — thoughts that led him to reflect once again on the health, both physical and psychic, of his dearer friend, Franklin Roosevelt.

"The President has overtaxed his strength in other ways. He has had a harder battle in many ways than Churchill. His fight for the people has made him many and bitter enemies" — not least conservatives who worried that Roosevelt was spending too much money, both to win the war and to bind the nation to his social and political vision of the future. "He has done too much, I fear, for purely political reasons — the vast expenditures totally regardless of consequences, & which may leave the United States in an appalling condition some day. He has used public office to ensure continuance of power" and keep it away from Republican special interests. Such government expenses "can scarcely be justified — but I believe he has been sincere in his determination to better the conditions of the masses," King had judged. "He is more human than Churchill; each desire to be at the top: Churchill would like to be the ruler of an Empire (Conservative). Roosevelt the head of a Commonwealth (democrat)."

Mackenzie King wondered which man's vision would prevail — the imperialist's or the postimperialist's? "I wonder if his [Roosevelt's] ambition to figure too largely on a world stage may not be his undoing & the undoing of his strength & of his political power? We shall see," the longtime Canadian prime minister and spiritualist had noted — observing, as he dictated this, that the two hands of the clock were "exactly together at 5 past one."[3]

The two men had thereafter exchanged touching Christmas greetings via telegraph, but once the President was wheeled into the White House Diplomatic Reception Room shortly before 8:00 p.m. on January 11, 1944, to broadcast his New Year's message to Congress, it had become clear Prime Minister King was right about hubris at the highest level: Roosevelt was clearly on a new, domestic warpath, while Churchill remained entirely focused on military glory.

As the President cleared his throat and surveyed the bank of microphones and film cameras in the White House that would take his "message" way beyond the fractured, often regressive Southern Democrats ensuring his control of the Congress, he began by saying he'd wanted to follow his normal custom of appearing in person, but "like a great many other people I have had the flu, and although I am practically recovered, my doctor simply would not let me leave the White House to go up to the Capitol."[4]

Delivered in the midst of a continuing world war, the broadcast would, in terms of domestic public policy, be one of the most significant addresses of the twentieth century in America: containing not only a National Service Act recommendation, but a "Second Bill of Rights," as the President called it — the text shown to no one before transmission, lest anyone attempt to dissuade him from his Luther-like propositions. These he intended to be metaphorically nailed on the door of Congress — a set of theses in which he would articulate his vision of a new, postwar democratic society.

Judge Sam Rosenman and Robert Sherwood, the President's speechwriters, had not even been permitted to go home after helping him with his Christmas broadcast, Rosenman later related. Instead they'd once again been pressed into rhetorical service for a speech so outspoken that its many drafts, on instructions of the President, were typed by Grace Tully alone, and were not mimeographed. "Sherwood and I took all possible precautions to prevent a leak. That is not easy in Washington, as anyone with experience there can testify," Rosenman would recall with amusement[5] — not even Harry Hopkins informed, or any member of the cabinet.

The "Second Bill of Rights" came straight from the President's heart, Rosenman believed. "He had seen our fighting men at close hand, their hardships and danger and sufferings — and those neat but crowded American cemeteries. He came back determined to see that the people back home did their share too," in the form of a national service bill, to help win the war, but also to propose they be assured, once the war was won, of a better economic and social structure than that which had produced the Great Depression after World War I.[6]

"This Republic had its beginning, and grew to its present strength, under the protection of certain inalienable political rights — among them the right of free speech, free press, free worship, trial by jury, freedom from unreasonable searches and seizures," the President introduced his theme on CBS, NBC, and other radio stations that were transmitting his voice, live. "They were our rights to life and liberty," the President went on. "As our Nation has grown in size and stature, however — as our industrial economy expanded — these political rights proved inadequate to assure us *equality* in the pursuit of happiness. We have come to a clear realization of the fact that true individual freedom cannot exist without economic security and independence. 'Necessitous men are not free men.' People who are hungry and out of a job are the stuff of which dictatorships are made," he remarked.

"In our day these economic truths have become accepted as self-evident," he asserted — addressing directly the challenge of inequity. In people's minds, if not yet in law, poorer Americans expected a better deal, thanks to a better economy — an improved economy which had now been achieved. "We have accepted, so to speak, [the need for] a second Bill of Rights under which a new basis of security and prosperity can be established for all regardless of station, race, or creed." Among these were:

> The right to a useful and remunerative job in the industries or shops of farms or mines of the Nation;
>
> The right to earn enough to provide adequate food and clothing and recreation;
>
> The right of every farmer to raise and sell his products at a return which will give him and his family a decent living;
>
> The right of every businessman, large and small, to trade in an atmosphere of freedom from unfair competition and domination by monopolies at home or abroad;
>
> The right of every family to a decent home;
>
> The right to adequate medical care and the opportunity to achieve and enjoy good health;
>
> The right to adequate protection from the economic fears of old age, sickness, accident, and unemployment;
>
> The right to a good education.

"All of these rights spell security," the President insisted. "And after this war is won we must be prepared to move forward, in the implementation of these rights, to new goals of human happiness and well-being."[7]

Inequality — or gross inequality — was the scourge of mankind, the President declared: not only because it was morally wrong, but for practical reasons, because in the end economic inequality, if allowed to grow flagrant, led to economic crises and tyranny when, inevitably, financial bubbles burst. This was self-evident in terms of the rise of fascism in his lifetime. "America's own rightful place in the world depends in large part upon how fully these and similar rights have been carried into practice for our citizens," he maintained. "For unless there is security here at home there cannot be lasting peace in the world. One of the great American industrialists of our day — a man who has rendered yeoman service to his country in this crisis — recently emphasized the grave dangers of 'rightist reaction' in this Nation. All clear-thinking businessmen share his concern. Indeed, if such reaction should develop — if history were to repeat itself and we were to return to the so-called 'normalcy' of the 1920's — then it is certain that even though we shall have conquered our enemies on the battlefields abroad, we shall have yielded to the spirit of Fascism here at home," he warned.[8]

"I ask the Congress to explore the means for implementing this economic bill of rights — for it is definitely the responsibility of the Congress so to do. Many of these problems are already before committees of the Congress in the form of proposed legislation. I shall from time to time communicate with the Congress with respect to these and further proposals. In the event that no adequate program of progress is evolved, I am certain that the Nation will be conscious of the fact."[9]

"The Nation" meant its voters — another reason the President had chosen to broadcast his address over the radio rather than delivering it in Congress in person.

"Our fighting men abroad — and their families at home — expect such a program and have the right to insist upon it. It is to their demands that this Government should pay heed rather than to the whining demands of selfish pressure groups who seek to feather their nests while young Americans are dying.

"The foreign policy that we have been following — the policy that guided us at Moscow, Cairo, and Teheran — is based on the common sense principle which was best expressed by Benjamin Franklin on July 4, 1776: 'We must all hang together, or assuredly we shall all hang separately.'"[10]

"All told, the State of the Union Message was unusually bellicose," Rosenman afterwards admitted, for the President "was in a fighting mood," despite his flu — "and in short order got into some bitter fights with the Congress: one on soldier voting, one on national service, and one on taxes"[11] — the President soon having to veto Congress's budget bill as "relief not for the needy but for the greedy," as he memorably declared (only to have his veto overridden).

Rosenman had been well aware the President would not win all, or indeed any, of his social and economic measures, since he was inevitably facing the rising forces of reaction, following more than a decade of "progressive" Democratic administration. "The fights showed that on domestic, civilian issues the President had lost control of the Congress, and indeed of his own party in Congress" — especially in terms of race, Rosenman would recall. "The small reactionary wing of the Democratic party, principally the Southern members, was working in coalition with the Republican party" — the white supremacists, or "last straws" of slavery and the Civil War: men whose obstructionism convinced Roosevelt there would have to be "a new alignment of political forces in the United States" in the future, in order to head them off.[12]

The President seemed nevertheless determined that, if he undertook to run for a fourth term but didn't win the Democratic Party nomination in the summer of 1944, he would at least go down fighting. Assuming his health recovered.

37

Anzio

IN CARTHAGE, CHURCHILL, too, seemed to have no intention of slowing down, let alone resigning from office, despite pneumonia and atrial fibrillation. "Oh, yes, he's very glad I've come, but in five minutes he'll forget I'm here," his wife, Clemmie — who'd been flown in to be at her possibly dying husband's bedside — had been heard to say.[1]

Mrs. Churchill knew her husband better than anyone. The Prime Minister was frustrated but no longer abashed by his defeat over Overlord. He had, after all, "triumphed" in forcing the cancellation of Buccaneer, the Burmese operation — thus releasing crucial landing craft for his pet schemes in the Mediterranean, once General Eisenhower left to command the cross-Channel invasion. As prime minister and de facto commander in chief of British Empire forces, Churchill had also won out in insisting a British officer replace the departing American. At Sir Alan Brooke's urging, the Prime Minister named General Sir Henry Maitland Wilson as Allied supreme commander in the Mediterranean and Middle East, not General Alexander — persuaded by Harold Macmillan, among others, that General Alexander, if left in situ in Italy, would remain in field command of the armies there — and could thus be browbeaten into seizing Rome by *coup de main,* at the Prime Minister's urging.

Recovering rapidly from his pneumonia, the Prime Minister had a new gleam in his eyes, as everyone who had seen him in Carthage had become aware. With Eisenhower slated to depart the theater, the Prime Minister announced he wished to mount an immediate grand "scoop" in Italy, as he called it, in both senses of the word. It was to be, he said, an amphibious invasion only thirty miles in distance from Rome: one that would be recognized by the whole world as a brilliant military "end-run," as well as a great political coup de théâtre — and carried out under the new British supreme command in the Mediterranean. Overnight Churchill's new brainwave, an "amphibious scoop"[2] or "cat-claw" or "end-run,"[3] would, he declared, force the Germans to retreat from their defensive positions north of Naples, on the Rapido River, and give the Allies the greatest Italian prize of all: possession of the Eternal City.

Like Overlord, Anzio would be a gamble — but a British gamble this time. Gambling, in any case, was Churchill's great love — an addiction of which he was completely unashamed, as of his alcohol intake. Neither the aftereffects of pneumonia, nor the danger of once again splitting the Allies over the issue, had thus seemed to have any effect on Churchill's mood as he recuperated in Eisenhower's guest villa, at Carthage, and plotted his tour de force. Clad in silk pajamas and a florid Japanese dressing gown embroidered with dragons, he had risen from his bed not as Lazarus did but to reign as the god Neptune, warrior lord of the Mediterranean: a trident-wielding leader who began to see himself — not his appointee-to-be, General Wilson — as the ultimate military genius or generalissimo directing the Allied forces in the Mediterranean and Middle East in 1944.

The picture would have been comical had it not been so serious. And tragic, in terms of the largely futile loss of life — especially American life — that ensued as a result. Churchill's recent fiasco in the Aegean islands in October and November had taught him only that he needed American forces to succeed. At Anzio — target of the Prime Minister's gamble — tens of thousands of American lives would be on the line, but with the President and U.S. chiefs of staff unable to stop him under the impending new command arrangements.

Thus the Anzio tragedy had begun to unfold in the wake of Churchill's "resurrection" — while at the same time the President, who had returned to the United States the conquering hero of Tehran, had fallen ill again with influenza, yet more seriously, in fact, than he or anyone around him recognized. Debilitated by this and bronchitis, he had found himself suddenly too exhausted to embark on another struggle with Winston. Obsessed by the lure of the Eternal City, Churchill had proceeded to revive, in a matter of days, an earlier contingency plan for a small-scale, outflanking amphibious assault at Anzio — one that General Clark had long since dropped as too diminutive, too risky — and had inflated the project into a massive amphibious assault landing, dwarfing all other operations in the Mediterranean combined.

Equally tragically Sir Alan Brooke — promoted to the rank of field marshal — supported his prime minister! The normally dour and critical artilleryman had found himself delighted by Churchill's bounce back to good health, after the British defeat at Tehran. Moreover Churchill's focus on Italy, in the first instance, rather than the Aegean, had met with Brooke's strong backing — completely ignoring the likely Wehrmacht response. He had therefore agreed to the Prime Minister's request that he should fly back to London on December 19, 1943, to tell his colleagues at the War Office of the new plan, and if possible win them over — thus leaving Churchill without a minder willing, or able, to challenge him.

In this way one of the war's most unnecessary and unfortunate disasters had gathered pace, just when the Allies seemed on the cusp of unified victory, thanks to the President's patient, tenacious strategy. As Churchill had resurrected the plan for an amphibious assault at Dieppe in the summer of 1942, the Prime Minister now invested the abandoned plans for an end-run at Anzio with fresh energy — but also with the landing craft intended for the President's Anvil operation. The new project, the Prime Minister had assured everyone in Carthage, would be a *coup de foudre,* in fact a *coup de grâce*: a grand operation of war, put together and mounted in the next several weeks with almost no rehearsal — and without first submitting the plan to the President or his U.S. military team in Washington.

Day by day Churchill's blunder had thereafter grown bigger. Convinced of its merits in London — far from the realities of the battlefield — the British chiefs of staff had cabled the Prime Minister on December 22 to say they were "in full agreement" that the "present stagnation" in Italy was one which, as the Prime Minister had correctly declared, "cannot be allowed to continue" — though why, they would not say. In such circumstances, they all concurred, the necessary landing craft — many of them due to be sailed to Britain by mid-January — should therefore now be withheld and be readied in the Mediterranean as swiftly as possible "to strike round the enemy's flank and open up the way for a rapid advance to Rome."[4]

Under the new British supreme commander–designate, General Wilson, shortly to be in overall control of the whole theater, stretching from Gibraltar to the Middle East, the Prime Minister had insisted that General Sir Harold Alexander, Wilson's ground forces commander in Italy, take personal responsibility for planning the amphibious assault landing at Anzio, and command it once launched. For the moment the assault proved successful, it could be trumpeted in the press as a great British victory, causing the Prime Minister — who saw himself as a "sort of super Commander-in-Chief," in the eyes of General Mark Clark — to insist at least half of the invasion troops be British, and be recorded as such in media reports.[5] It would, in essence, be a British-led Mediterranean version of Overlord, *before* Overlord.

It was in this wildly overoptimistic, cavalier mood that both Brooke and Churchill had ignored the warnings even of British combat commanders that "Shingle," the code-name for the Prime Minister's Anzio assault, would not necessarily lead to a "rapid advance to Rome." General Montgomery — who was facing heavy German opposition on the right flank of the Allied forces in Italy, had warned Alan Brooke, when Brooke visited the front in Italy in December, there was no chance of reaching Rome before the spring,[6] and that the Prime Minister's supposed stroke of genius at Anzio was ridiculous. Neither Brooke nor Churchill had proved willing to listen, and Montgomery, in any case, had subsequently been chosen to be Eisenhower's ground forces deputy for Overlord — the British War Cabinet insisting on a more dynamic ground force commander in chief for the cross-Channel invasion, when Churchill had fallen ill with pneumonia.[7]

Summoning Eisenhower, the outgoing American commander in chief of Allied Mediterranean forces, to his villa on December 23, 1943, the recovering Prime Minister had nevertheless made clear to Ike, his host at Carthage, that he himself was taking *personal* charge of the planning of Shingle — and nothing General Eisenhower could say in cautioning him had seemed to have any effect.

The weather in Italy was abysmal, the Allied air forces could not provide much tactical air support, the troops were finding the Italian terrain forbidding in winter, and even Montgomery's Eighth Army, on the supposedly easier Adriatic side of Italy, near Ortona, was making no progress, as Eisenhower noted. Casualties were mounting alarmingly. Bitter experience had shown him that the Wehrmacht, so famed for offensive operations (Blitzkrieg), were even greater masters of defense. As he pointed out to the Prime Minister, the "Nazis had not instantly withdrawn from Africa or Sicily merely because of threats to their rear. On the contrary, they had reinforced and fought the battle out to the end."[8]

It had been no use. Vainly, Eisenhower had warned the necessary landing craft for the operation would probably have to be kept in the Mediterranean "long after the agreed-upon date for their release" for Overlord, or of its pincer-assault, Anvil — thus prejudicing the very operation the President had just appointed him to command.

The Prime Minister had refused to listen to such warnings — Churchill vowing he would work on President Roosevelt to agree to retention of the necessary landing craft in the Mediterranean. More craft could surely be built, or converted before D-day's launch in May, Churchill claimed, as the smoke of his cigar billowed and then dispersed. All would be well, he'd assured Ike: the Allies would win a great military victory. Rome would be theirs! And with that the Prime Minister had assembled, on Christmas Day at Carthage, his British team-to-be, who would take over from Eisenhower on January 1, 1944, or thereabouts: General Sir Maitland Wilson, General Sir Harold Alexander, Admiral Sir John Cunningham, and Air Marshal Sir Arthur Tedder: Knights of the Round Table.

The President had warned Ike, on board the Sacred Cow, that he would be under merciless meddling pressure from the Prime Minister once he got to London as supreme commander of Overlord. That this would happen before Eisenhower even got to London was unfortunate, indeed tragic — Eisenhower finding himself, as the outgoing commander in chief in the Mediterranean, an impotent observer. He could only witness, not chair, the proceedings, which the Prime Minister had conducted in his dressing gown like a Japanese shogun.

"It would be folly to allow the campaign in Italy to drag on," Churchill declared — though without explaining why. Instead, pouring forth a torrent of emotionally larded words to damn the notion of southern Italy being a "mere" holding front, as the President — and Marshal Stalin — had portrayed it, he called for action on a grand scale, in the middle of winter. The Allies should not even think of mounting "the supreme operations 'Overlord' and 'Anvil'" in the coming spring, the Prime Minister had asserted, "with our task in Italy half-finished."[9]

What exactly this strategic military "task" was, beyond the glory of reaching Rome, the Prime Minister did not define. Nor did he explain why it would in any way help, let alone be essential to, the agreed primacy of Overlord in defeating the Third Reich. And why in winter, with no time to prepare or rehearse the formations? What was the hurry?

The amphibious attack, the Prime Minister had insisted, should be launched in three weeks' time: on January 20, 1944. It should land two Allied divisions in the first assault, instead of one. These should then be followed up by yet more Allied divisions in subsequent waves, like breakers rolling onto a beach. Without question it would "decide the battle of Rome, and possibly the destruction of a substantial part of the enemy's army."[10]

The sheer amateurishness of the Prime Minister's concept of modern war would, in retrospect, be mind-boggling — even criminal in its folly. But Churchill was Churchill: a force of nature. With the plan agreed by his British subordinates at Carthage he had thus cabled the President, the day after Christmas, 1943, to appeal for the fifty-six landing craft to be held back in the Mediterranean for the assault landing rather than be assigned to Overlord and Anvil, claiming there could be nothing more dangerous "than to let the Italian battle stagnate and fester on for another three months thus certainly gnawing into all preparation for and thus again affecting Overlord. We cannot afford to go forward" with Overlord and Anvil "leaving a vast half-finished job behind us," he stated categorically. "If this opportunity is not grasped," he claimed, "we must expect the ruin of the Mediterranean campaign of 1944." And if the prospect of "ruin" in Italy was not credible in the President's eyes, he'd added, all the senior generals and admirals present at his special Carthage conference — including General Eisenhower — were agreed "that every effort should be made to bring off 'Shingle' on a two-division basis around January 20th, and orders have been issued to General Alexander to prepare accordingly."[11]

Orders already issued? Before the British were even formally vested with supreme command in the Mediterranean?

It was all, *en bref,* Churchillian bunkum: the same notion, even same language Churchill had used back in October 1943 when once again trying to halt or postpone Overlord. Yet to Churchill's own astonishment, then and later, neither the President, nor Marshall (who had arrived back in Washington on December 20), nor even the U.S. chiefs of staff, tried to stop him.

Apart from insisting that those landing craft released from potential duty in Buccaneer be sailed directly to Britain for Overlord, and that any further plans to invade Rhodes or other Aegean shores "must be sidetracked," the U.S. Joint Chiefs of Staff had, it appeared, decided not to contest the plan for Italy — which they had not seen — either to the President or to Mr. Churchill via the Combined Chiefs of Staff. Instead they had contented themselves with a signal to Churchill, which they drafted for the President on December 26, 1943, to be sent the next day, stating that Overlord "must remain the paramount operation and will be carried out on the date agreed to at Cairo and Tehran."[12]

Only wise Admiral Leahy had smelled a proverbial rat — worried at the White House by Churchill's latest cable. In his diary on December 27 Leahy recorded his skepticism. "Messages from the British Prime Minister bring up for consideration the use of the landing craft and men in the Italian campaign," he had jotted with concern, "with a possible delay in the planned landings in France. This is probably a first attempt by the British to extend operations in the Mediterranean, even at the cost of prolonging the war with Germany."[13]

After the triumph of Tehran, in terms of unified Allied strategy to defeat the Third Reich, the Anzio operation was like shooting oneself in the foot. The support of the British in carrying out Overlord had been considered by the Joint Chiefs of Staff, however, to be so crucial to the successful course of the war — especially after their contentious meetings in Cairo — that they had simply given way, not daring to get into a new fight with the Prime Minister.

Barely able to credit Churchill's new madness, and only beginning to reassemble in Washington, oversee final preparations for Overlord, and also focus their attention on plans for the war's endgame in the Pacific, the American military high command team at the Pentagon and Navy Department had thus simply washed their hands of Shingle — tired of battling with the British after so many months of extended indictments, threats, and showdowns. They had thus fatefully declined to recommend the President — who was entirely focused on the political agenda he wished to put before the nation, and suffering from flu — take issue with Churchill over the new British Mediterranean scheme.

Thus, to his own astonishment, Winston Spencer Churchill got away with his martial coup, almost without American objection.

Even Churchill's official biographer was later astonished. "Churchill was delighted and a little surprised that the Americans had accepted that the Anzio landing was to take place," Sir Martin Gilbert would write — the Prime Minister feeling as if he was living a second life, following his close brush with death. "What better place could I die [in] than here?" he'd asked his police security chief, Inspector Walter Thompson, at Carthage. And to his daughter Sarah he'd confided: "If I die, don't worry — the war is won."[14] But the pneumonia *hadn't* carried him away, mercifully. He hadn't died; he was alive — doubly alive. And on the warpath, once again. Under British supreme command in the Mediterranean theater he would *personally* plan and win a great battle, he was resolved — something he had longed to do, ever since becoming prime minister in 1940.

38

The President's Unpleasant Attitude

DAY AFTER DAY, by contrast, the President attempted to deal with affairs of state in the White House, feeling "rotten," coughing incessantly, and sleeping badly. The morning after his State of the Union broadcast, on January 5, 1944, he saw General Eisenhower, who had been ordered home for a few days' rest, before he took up his post in London.

"Eisenhower is being hailed as the great genius of this war," Goebbels sneered in his diary. "He's being showered with laurels after laurels in advance. In his broadcast Roosevelt explains the U.S. now has 10 million soldiers under arms, of which 3.5 million are already overseas. But he has to admit in his speech that there will be terrible suffering ahead. Fortress Europe will be hit from many sides. The idea is not to enslave Germany — this is said for us — just liquidate the master-race. Which are one and the same," Goebbels pointed out. "But Roosevelt has no chance of making good on such Jewish plans; after all, we are here and in the way."[1]

This was true: the Wehrmacht still the world's most formidable military force in battle. Even when he met with the President in the Oval Office, Ike was under the impression the Anzio operation would not go ahead, since he had not been informed, when he left, it was going operational. Moreover he himself was still, on paper, the Allied commander in chief, Mediterranean — for he had not authorized British general Maitland Wilson to take over from his staff, in Algiers, before January 8. As the new supreme commander of Overlord, Eisenhower wanted all possible landing craft to be "gathered up" and reconditioned for D-day, "so as to produce the maximum number in May. This would mean the abandonment of" the Anzio assault, Operation Shingle, Eisenhower signaled to General Bedell Smith, his chief of staff in Algiers, on January 5. But in any case, he added, "that operation is open to grave objections under present conditions."[2]

Poor Smith had been compelled to notify Eisenhower on January 9, four days later, that none of the British commanders in the Mediterranean had voiced "grave objections" to the Prime Minister's scheme. In fact he'd just attended a meeting, he reported, with General Sir Maitland Wilson, the day before. "It is not, repeat not, pleasant to be the guest where you have been the master," he'd lamented — and informed Eisenhower the British had now made a cast-iron decision, at Prime Minister Churchill's insistence, to undertake Shingle on January 22, in less than two weeks' time.[3]

When Eisenhower thus paid a second visit to the White House on January 12, the day after the President's broadcast to Congress and the nation, it was to tell the flu-ridden President his concerns about the Anzio project and its implications for Overlord. As the general explained to Secretary Stimson twice that same day, he was concerned "about the coming offensive in Italy," and his "fears as to the strain it would make on the number of our landing craft."[4]

Stimson was alarmed, noting that night how Eisenhower had "told me of a talk he had had with the Prime Minister who is dead set on making this offensive for political reasons. He [Churchill] said he would not dare go back before his people with the present offensive stalled and himself not able to tell about the secret plans for Overlord and so forth. So apparently this effort has been decided upon by the British who now have command of the whole Mediterranean."[5]

Churchill's latest reasoning, according to Eisenhower, sounded not only tactically but strategically unsound to Stimson. It was also potentially criminal in terms of the likely American casualties. Stimson was therefore filled with "ill-foreboding because it is almost certain to get a force tied up," he predicted in his diary, "which will be obliged to use a large number of landing craft after it has landed" in order to keep open "its line of communications."[6]

When Stimson had another talk later the same day with Eisenhower, his heart sank still further. "I know too well that there will be delays" in returning the landing craft, he recorded, for the boats would be needed to support the stranded troops at Anzio, if they found themselves ringed by the Germans. Churchill was "banking on pulling off this operation quickly," Stimson noted, but he'd heard such talk before. As things stood, given the likelihood Anzio would either fail or be a prolonged disaster, this "would mean that the loss will have to be taken out of Anvil or Overlord, and Overlord is already down to its lowest limit in landing craft."[7]

Secretary Stimson's fears, expressed ten days before the Anzio landings took place, would prove all too prescient. Given Churchill's personal authorship of the operation, the President was the only person with sufficient authority to stop the offensive.

The President, however, was "ill," Stimson noted — and like the U.S. chiefs of staff simply not up to a new battle with Churchill. Mr. Roosevelt had, as even Goebbels had noted, "further, terrible problems with strikes in his own country. He's being forced to federalize the railways, because he's unable to control [union] calls for a strike." The day the President had seen Eisenhower, on Ike's first visit, he'd also conferred with Frances Perkins, his secretary of labor, despite his fever, and he'd even chaired the Pacific War Council — visibly ailing.

And so it had gone on in early January, 1944 — the President, for all that he felt "rotten," meeting in the Oval Office on Pennsylvania Avenue with the men and women who most counted for governance, administration, economy, legislation, and diplomacy in America, at the ultimate apex of political power. He gave press conference after press conference — and watched documentary films from various theaters of combat that gave a visceral picture of what the airmen, sailors, and ground forces were confronting. General Arnold took him to Washington Airport to see the new B-29 bomber that would change the military face of the skies. He saw emissaries from military headquarters across the world: India, the Pacific, Africa, the Mediterranean.

Yet the President's flu symptoms persisted. The budget director, Harold Smith, saw Roosevelt on January 7, for example, and was surprised the President did not give the matter of finance his usual attention. In his bedroom at the White House, "he seemed worried and worn out. I have never seen him so listless," Smith had noted in his diary. "He is not his acute usual self. In fact I was quite startled, at one stage when he was about two-thirds through the Message" — a document otherwise known as the draft budget to Congress. "As he sat up in bed, I saw his head nod. I could not see into his eyes, but it seemed to me that they were completely shut. Yet, he said something to the effect that 'this paragraph is good.'" Smith was stunned. "I have seen the President before when he was ill in his bedroom," he wrote in his diary that night, "but never so groggy."[8]

The President's attention span simply never improved — thus leading chroniclers, later, to misjudge just how dominant his authority and control over his administration and especially his chiefs of staff had been in years past, prior to his sudden ill health. Appointments now became shorter, the President's energy level grew fainter, his blood pressure higher. He virtually never left the White House, save to take "rests" at Hyde Park — away from prying, or merely watching, journalists.

Meanwhile on January 22, 1944, Shingle — Churchill's much-vaunted amphibious invasion at Anzio — went in over the beaches. It proved, just as Eisenhower and Stimson had feared, a calamity. The *forty-three thousand* Allied casualties suffered on the beaches of Anzio over the following four and a half months — including seven thousand who died there — would be a terrible indictment of Brooke's support for the Prime Minister's "resuscitation," but most of all to Churchill's impetuosity and shallowness.

The fact was, the Prime Minister, when fired up with a fantasy, was almost impossible to control, his energy and conviction illustrating what the philosopher-king Lord Francis Bacon had noted in 1620: namely a mind which, having "once adopted an opinion," was wont to draw "all things else to support and agree with it. And though there be a greater number and weight of instances to be found on the other side, yet these it either neglects and despises, or else by some distinction sets aside and rejects, in order that by this great and pernicious predetermination the authority of its former conclusions may remain inviolate."[9]

In this respect the Prime Minister's autocratic and often wild behavior seemed to Brooke, despite Brooke's own approval of the Shingle plan, to be substantially worse even than in November 1943, when Brooke had despaired of having to work under such an impossible commander in chief. Already the day after Churchill's return from Marrakesh to London on January 18, 1944, Brooke was recording he could not "stand much more of it," after four hours of meetings with him. "In all his plans he lives from hand to mouth. He can never grasp a whole plan, either in its width (ie all fronts) or its depth (long term projects). His method is entirely opportunist, gathering one flower here another there! My God how tired I am of working with him!"[10]

A good "bag" of 172 pheasants he shot with three colleagues at Glemham Hall in the Suffolk countryside, on January 22 — the day the Anzio invasion began — temporarily lightened Brooke's mood, as did the first reports from the War Office in London recording "the landing south of Rome had been a complete surprise" to the Wehrmacht — a "wonderful relief!" as the newly minted field marshal noted in his diary.[11] But the ensuing days proved less and less hopeful. All too soon the Wehrmacht's inevitable reaction put the whole concept of a swift "advance on Rome" in peril. Eventually, a week later, the penny began to drop. Anzio was *not* going to lead to the Eternal City anytime soon — in fact it would take many months, if it could be done at all — and threatened to make Overlord and Anvil impossible to mount successfully.

"Hitler has reacted very strongly and is sending reinforcements fast," Brooke noted in his diary on January 31.[12] As Leahy had forecast, Brooke and his colleagues were soon cabling Washington to "convince them that with the turn operations have taken in the Mediterranean, the only thing to do is to go on fighting the war in Italy," and — more ominously — "give up any idea of a weak landing in Southern France."[13]

The campaign in Italy thereafter went from bad to worse — no less than three consecutive and bloody battles being fought at Cassino to try and link Clark's frontline troops with the stranded Allied forces on the beaches of Anzio, without success.

Italy was, as Admiral Leahy had predicted, a disaster.

In private Winston Churchill himself became worried lest he be publicly denounced, and incriminated for his homicidal meddling. "Anzio was my worst moment in the war," he later confided to his doctor. "I had most to do with it. I didn't want two Suvla Bays [i.e., Gallipolis] in one lifetime,"[14] he confessed — having admitted to Eisenhower, Bedell Smith, and Brooke in late February, 1944, as British and American casualties mounted on the beaches, that he'd hoped "to land a wildcat that would tear out the bowels of the Boche. Instead we have stranded a vast whale with its tail flopping about in the water."[15]

Such clever phrases were memorable enough for Brooke to record them, instantly, in his diary. But they could not save the lives of the men who'd been given an impossible task.

Sick at heart and in body, the President was both distressed and full of sympathy for the troops, since the majority of them — and the casualties — were in fact Americans. Was it all a form of revenge for the British not getting their way in delaying or halting Overlord at Tehran?

Neither the President nor his chiefs of staff were willing to let the fiasco prejudice the launch date of Overlord or its supporting operation, Anvil. They soon had to, though: Churchill and the British chiefs now begging for more Allied forces to be committed in Italy to save Anzio. In the circumstances Overlord would, the U.S. chiefs agreed, probably have to be delayed by a month, to June 1944; the Anvil assault would probably have to be abandoned: the price of Churchill's folly.

Field Marshal Brooke, as coconspirator in resurrecting the Anzio scheme, was meanwhile required not only to bear the brunt of Churchill's frustration, anger, and blame, but the inevitable consequence: the Prime Minister switching his abortive energies to a new campaign, this time the war in the Pacific.

"I am quite exhausted after spending 7½ hours today with Winston, and most of that time engaged in heavy argument," Brooke penned on February 25 — aware that the President and his team in Washington would simply accept no change in overall European strategy, let alone in the Pacific.[16]

Anzio was, in short, a catastrophe. Rome was as far away as ever — causing the despairing prime minister to insist he must have an emergency meeting with the President and the American chiefs of staff, even if it meant his flying to the United States or the Bahamas.

Fortunately the President could, at least, use the lingering effects of his flu and bronchitis as a way of deflecting another Churchill visit — which would undoubtedly involve new British appeals to change agreed Allied plans for Overlord, the Second Front, and the Pacific.

Brooke might complain of the "President's unpleasant attitude lately," as he recorded in his diary on February 25,[17] but in the circumstances it was remarkable the President had continued to maintain a polite tone in his responses to Churchill's ever more strident one, when the Prime Minister was making major difficulties now over the best way to defeat Japan, by once again pressing for an invasion of the northern tip of Sumatra. The President simply but firmly made clear he had no intention of meeting with Churchill, nor would he countenance Churchill's plea to keep Overlord's landing craft in the Mediterranean.[18] There was not to be, he cabled, any change in the Overlord and Anvil plans.

For Churchill the shame, embarrassment, and displaced anger were impossible to swallow. The Prime Minister's residence at 10 Downing Street became a war zone. As Brooke would later reflect, "We were just at the beginning of the most difficult period I had with Winston during the whole of the war" — which was certainly saying something.[19] By March Brooke was recording the entire British chiefs of staff were on the point of resignation, and that he himself was "shattered by the present condition of the PM. He has lost all balance and is in a very dangerous mood" — a mood that had impelled the Prime Minister to ignore the President's cables, and again demand a meeting with Roosevelt and the U.S. chiefs of staff, this time "on the 25th of this month!" as Brooke noted in despair.[20] In Brooke's eyes it would be fatuous to ask for a change to Pacific strategy at such a conference, when the Americans were clearly in complete — and hitherto successful — charge of naval, air, and army operations there. It would also be dangerous in terms of Churchill's fragile health — a trip that could result in yet another bout of pneumonia, followed by heart problems, Lord Moran warned again and again throughout March 1944, as American and British troops fought and died to hang on to their toehold at Anzio.[21]

It was not Churchill's heart that was the problem. It was the President's.

39

Crimes Against Humanity

SINCE ADMIRAL McINTIRE would afterwards remove and destroy (it is believed) all the President's White House medical records, the history of Franklin Roosevelt's health would be, in retrospect, spotty. But in essence the problem at the White House and at Hyde Park in the winter and spring of 1944
was not the severity of the President's influenza or bronchitis. It was their
persistence.

"More disturbing than anything else," McIntire wrote later of the President at this time, "there was the definite loss of his usual ability to come back
quickly" — at least, in the way Churchill had.[1] The burden of the office —
domestic, military, diplomatic — was unrelenting. These three aspects, moreover, were becoming impossible to keep apart: pitting cabinet members, administration officials, and military personnel against one another over a
thousand issues, which only the President, as chief executive and commander
in chief, could decide. For instance, if the U.S. Army was to meet its goal of
ten million servicemen, General Marshall and Secretary Stimson pressed the
President, it was a matter of urgency to end current deferments of young men
working in agriculture and industry. This naturally inflamed cabinet members and officials responsible for agriculture and industry. There was also the
question of whether de Gaulle's Comité Français de la Libération Nationale
should be allowed to pose as the lawful French government and administer
those areas of France that would — hopefully — be liberated by U.S. and Allied
troops in the aftermath of D-day, rather than leaving responsibility to General
Eisenhower as Allied supreme commander. This was a prospect the President
— who had come to despise de Gaulle for his autocratic methods, intense na-
tionalism, and renewed colonialist aspirations — abhorred. As did the secretary of state, Cordell Hull.

There was also the matter of "Manhattan," the development of an atom
bomb, which the President was funding, in secret, via his loyalists in Congress
— and the question of how to keep at bay Senator Harry Truman, chair of an

investigative committee on the national defense program, who had been only vaguely informed of the project, along with senior members of Congress.

In the end Secretary Stimson and General Marshall had gone to see the President in person at the White House on March 13, 1944, arguing for a new executive order to deal with the threat to "our own Army manpower and the danger that it is to Overlord." The President had assured them he would get them the servicemen they needed — but wanted time to work on the Selective Service officials to ensure a consensus that only he, the legendary Magician or Juggler of the White House, could obtain. As for Truman's threat of "dire consequences" if Stimson didn't come clean on the atomic bomb project, the President wholeheartedly backed Stimson's refusal to bow to Truman's pressure. "Truman is a nuisance and a pretty untrustworthy man," the Republican secretary noted in his diary. "He talks smoothly but he acts meanly," he remarked.[2]

By mid-March, however, those closest to the President had become more and more worried about the burdens he was carrying — and the state of his health. Following Secretary Stimson and Marshall's visit on March 13, Admiral McIntire was finally forced to respond to the growing fears.

The Prime Minister's appeal for a "staff meeting on the Teheran scale in Bermuda about the fifth of April" was out of the question. It was all getting too much for a relentlessly sick president. On McIntire's advice Roosevelt cabled Churchill some days later, saying he was not going to be able to oblige. "The old attack of grippe having hung on and on, leaving me with an intermittent temperature, Ross decided a week ago that it is necessary for me to take a complete rest of about two to three weeks in a suitable climate, which I am definitely planning to do at the end of the month," as the President finally explained on March 20. "I see no way out and I am furious."[3]

He wasn't really. True, he was deeply disappointed that the debacle at Anzio had now forced Eisenhower to delay the D-day landings to the end of May or early June, given the paucity of landing craft. But he said nothing of that — indeed his forbearance, in contrast to that of Churchill, was remarkable. He had attended the annual White House Correspondents' Dinner on March 4, and had given no fewer than three press conferences in the week thereafter. His lapses in focus, hearing, and concentration, however, were becoming all too noticeable. By March 14, the President's daughter Anna had finally decided to confront Admiral McIntire. The President's temperature was fluctuating up and down; he had abdominal distress, his hands were trembling almost uncontrollably, he could not sleep at night, was coughing, and was finding it hard to breathe normally.

Responding, McIntire had belatedly insisted on rest and a forthcoming vacation in a warm climate; also that the President immediately go on a diet, both to lose weight (relieving strain on his heart) and improve his digestion.

For the next ten days the President duly followed this prescription. He did not come down to the Oval Office before noon, and was served his dinner on a tray either in his bedroom or his study, upstairs at the White House, with only his cousin Daisy to keep him company, since Eleanor was traveling.

It didn't help. The President was falling asleep sometimes "bolt upright," Daisy noted on March 23.[4] He was in recurrent pain from headaches, fever, and abdominal discomfort. Grace Tully, Roosevelt's loyal office secretary and stenographer, appealed to Anna to *do* something. For three months now the President had been ailing — with no sign of amelioration, in fact the very opposite.

Anna thus insisted Admiral McIntire bring in specialist consultants to examine the President. And with that the final odyssey of the President's life began.

Admiral McIntire — who had no specialist knowledge outside his area of expertise: ear, nose, and throat — duly began making inquiries. Loyalty to his commander in chief trumped all other considerations, however; McIntire insisted no one outside the family circle, and of course no one in the press, should know. An appointment with a navy cardiologist at the Naval Hospital, away from prying eyes, seemed the safest, surely the most secret, way to proceed. A medical exam was thus arranged to take place after the weekend — its scheduling to be kept strictly under wraps.

First, though, the President announced he wished to hold another press conference, in order to make an important statement. He planned to issue a presidential proclamation, he'd decided, on one of the most egregious aspects of the Nazi conquest of Europe: the deliberate extermination of millions of Jews. His proclamation, "promising to help rescue the Jews from Nazi brutality in Europe," his private secretary, Bill Hassett, noted on Friday, March 24, 1944, would make sure no one could claim they were unaware of what was going on behind the Wehrmacht's frontlines. To be certain it got the broadest possible coverage, moreover, he told his secretary, he was going to read it aloud, word by word, at a press conference in the Oval Office, however ill he currently appeared — and felt. He was "not looking so well in his bedroom, nor later when he held a press and radio conference," Hassett recorded in his diary: "voice husky and out of pitch. This latest cold has taken lots out of him. Every morning, in response to inquiry as to how he felt, a characteristic reply has been 'Rotten' or 'Like hell.'"[5] But it had to be done — and was.

One sentence, in particular, he'd thought summed up his own philosophy, and that of most decent people. "The United Nations are fighting to make a world in which tyranny and aggression cannot exist: a world based upon freedom, equality and justice; a world in which all persons regardless of race, color or creed may live in peace, honor and dignity."[6]

A Trip to Tehran

After laying a wreath in Arlington Cemetery on November 11, 1943, FDR sets off with his Joint Chiefs of Staff to Tehran to meet Churchill and Stalin.

Aboard the USS *Iowa,* the latest American battleship, the President works out a plan of how to deal with Churchill's threatened "indictment" of U.S. strategy.

Met at Oran by General Eisenhower, FDR flies with Ike to his Tunis head-quarters. Over two days of talks, FDR weighs whether Marshall or Ike should be the supreme commander of the D-day invasion, Operation Overlord.

Cairo

Arriving in Cairo for a "showdown," Churchill hopes to get D-day postponed in favor of a Balkan strategy. But FDR avoids a battle with the PM by deliberate sightseeing and long talks with Generalissimo Chiang Kai-shek.

Tehran

Flying on to Tehran, FDR is finally able, with Stalin's help, to overcome Churchill's objections to D-day in 1944. He even gets Stalin to promise to launch a massive Russian offensive on the Eastern Front to help Overlord succeed.

The Tehran summit marks FDR's greatest achievement as strategist and U.S. commander in chief in World War II: keeping both Britain and the USSR cooperating as allies.

Who Will Command Overlord?

A triumphant FDR appoints General Eisenhower to be supreme commander of Overlord. He spends further days with Ike in North Africa, taking the general with him to Malta and Sicily to review troops. FDR also decorates General Clark and tells Patton (in background) he will be needed for the cross-Channel invasion.

Triumphant Return

Returning home on the USS *Iowa,* the Commander in Chief is feted at the White House by the cabinet and congressional leaders, including (below) Treasury Secretary Henry Morgenthau (left), Secretary of State Cordell Hull, and Director of War Mobilization Judge Byrnes.

Surrounded by Eleanor and his family at Hyde Park, FDR gives a Christmas Eve broadcast announcing his appointment of General Eisenhower, not General Marshall, to lead the "next blow" against Nazi Germany: D-day. He has never looked or sounded more confident. Even Hitler predicts the Allied invasion of France will "decide the war."

Taking off his pince-nez, the President had turned to the assembled reporters and smiled. "Some of you people who are wandering around asking the bellhop whether we have a foreign policy or not" might think about the statement, the President had reflected aloud, for "I think it's a pretty good paragraph." The words went to the heart of what America now stood for, in a world wracked by violence on a hitherto unimaginable scale. "*We have a foreign policy,*" he'd reminded members of the press. "Some people may not know it, but we have." And with that he'd read out the next paragraph. This, in turn, explained what the United Nations were up against: namely that "in most of Europe and in parts of Asia the systematic torture and murder of civilians — men, women and children — by the Nazis and the Japanese continue unabated."[7]

This was not mere rhetoric, he'd emphasized. "In areas subjugated by the aggressors innocent Poles, Czechs, Norwegians, Dutch, Danes, French, Greeks, Russians, Chinese, Filipinos — many others — are being starved or frozen to death or murdered in cold blood in a campaign of savagery. The slaughters of Warsaw, Lidice, Kharkov and Nanking" — "sometimes people forget about Nanking," he'd paused to comment — "the brutal torture and murder by the Japanese, not only of civilians but of our own gallant American soldiers and fliers — these are startling examples of what goes on day by day, year in and year out, wherever the Nazis and the Japs are in military control — free to follow their barbaric purpose."[8]

Cruelty without conscience: this seemed the mantra of Germany and Japan. The Wehrmacht's military occupation of its ally Hungary on March 19, had alarmed the entire free world — not only because it demonstrated the German intention of fighting to the bitter end, but because it had exposed the sheer evil of Hitler's regime, as news poured in to Washington of Wehrmacht and SS troops rounding up perhaps three-quarters of a million Hungarian Jews for deportation and execution.

Three-quarters of a million! "In one of the blackest crimes of all history — begun by the Nazis in the day of peace and multiplied by them a hundred times in time of war," the President continued, "the wholesale systematic murder of the Jews of Europe goes on unabated every hour. As a result of the events of the last few days, hundreds of thousands of Jews, who while living under persecution have at least found a haven from death in Hungary and the Balkans, are now threatened with annihilation as Hitler's forces descend more heavily upon these lands. That these innocent people, who have already survived a decade of Hitler's fury, should perish on the very eve of triumph over the barbarism which their persecution symbolizes, would be a major tragedy."[9]

In a United States where the press tended to focus on matters of domestic policy or lack of progress in Italy, it was important, he'd emphasized, not to forget what Americans were fighting *for* — apologizing for mentioning "more foreign policy" than the journalists probably wanted to hear. He was not ashamed, however. In the proclamation, which was to be broadcast that night, he'd wished to make clear it was not only Hitler who was guilty of such mass murder, but many thousands of Germans — "functionaries and their subordinates" both in Germany and its satellite countries — who were assisting in the annihilation of completely innocent civilians. "All who knowingly take part in the deportation of Jews to their death in Poland or Norwegians and French to their death in Germany are equally guilty with the executioner himself. All who share the guilt shall share the punishment."[10]

It was at that point the President had read out a phrase in the proclamation that would soon go down in the history of jurisprudence. "Hitler," he pronounced, "is committing these crimes against humanity." And was doing so "in the name of the German people."[11]

Crimes against humanity.

The phrase had once been used, in the late nineteenth century, to protest the Belgian king Leopold II's ravaging of African civilians in the Congo.[12] Now it applied to the fate of millions of innocents in present-day Europe. Such crimes — wholly intentional and deliberate, and trumpeted proudly by Hitler in his recent broadcast — were beyond anything imaginable in a supposedly civilized country. "I am asking," the President had continued, "every German and every person of any other nationality everywhere under Nazi domination to show the world by his action that in his heart he does not share these insane criminal desires." Whether in Hungary or anywhere else in Europe, "let him hide these pursued victims, help them to get over their borders, and do what he can to save them from the Nazi hangman. I am asking him also to keep watch, and to record the evidence that will one day be used to convict the guilty" — for such crimes against humanity would not, he'd warned, go unpunished or ever be forgotten.[13]

"In the meantime," the President stated, coming to the climax of his proclamation, "until the victory that is now assured is won, the United States will persevere in its efforts to rescue the victims of brutality of the Nazis and the Japs." He was speaking therefore not only on his own behalf, but on behalf of his administration. "In so far as the necessity of military operations permit, this Government will use all means at its command to aid the escape of all intended victims of the Nazi and Jap executioner — regardless of race or religion or color. We call upon the free peoples of Europe and Asia temporarily to open their frontiers to all victims of oppression. We shall find havens of refuge for them, and we shall find the means for their maintenance and support until the tyrant is driven from their homelands and they may return. In the name of justice and humanity let all freedom-loving people rally to this righteous undertaking.

"Finis," he'd ended.[14]

The journalists departed to file their stories. Exhausted and unwell, the President was determined to leave the White House for a weekend at Hyde Park. There, despite his condition and before his impending medical exam at Bethesda, he was expecting an important visitor. Her name was Mrs. Lucy Rutherfurd.

40

Late Love

THE VISIT OF ROOSEVELT's former mistress marked, as fate would have it, a critical moment in the President's life. For by the strangest coincidence, as the President's health plummeted, causing his doctor to reluctantly, and in secret, contact a cardiologist, Mrs. Rutherfurd's husband had died, making Lucy a widow. And free to see the President without shame, if that was what he wished.

He did. At a time when the very life force, energy, and joie de vivre had seemed to be visibly sapping from the President, Lucy Mercer Rutherfurd's visit to Hyde Park promised him new vitality, at least.

By this time the affair between Franklin Roosevelt and Lucy Mercer was largely forgotten in the nation's capital — though a quarter century earlier it had caused a veritable scandal in Washington social circles, as everyone who knew the parties was aware.[1]

Some blamed Franklin, some blamed Eleanor, some Lucy.

Elliott Roosevelt — who was himself married five times in the course of his life — later wrote that the affair had begun because of Eleanor's decision to no longer have sex with her husband. After bearing six children over the course of a decade, Eleanor had, in 1916, insisted on separate bedrooms, Elliott claimed. Thereafter, he asserted, "my parents never lived together as husband and wife."[2]

Elliott's older brother James, expressing more sympathy for his mother, later recounted how Eleanor confided to his sister Anna that "sex was an ordeal to be borne" and had never been a pleasure for her. Whatever the case, when Franklin, as assistant secretary of the navy during World War I, had returned from Europe on a stretcher in the midst of a global flu epidemic, suffering double pneumonia, and was admitted to hospital on September 20, 1918, Eleanor accidentally came across her former social secretary's perfumed love letters in her husband's briefcase — and had been mortified.

It was not sexual jealousy that had given rise to the specter of suicide and divorce on Eleanor's part; it had been the sheer depth of Lucy's love for Franklin. Moreover the evidence, in writing, that this love was shared. The realization had devastated Eleanor — an orphan who had grown up rich yet unloved and lonely. The affection, attention, respect, and shared pride in their five surviving children had been everything to her — a blessing that had seemed suddenly worthless in her husband's eyes, she'd felt.

Eleanor had not been mistaken. Franklin's feelings for Miss Mercer had been far more than a temporary infatuation. As Lucy's cousin later recalled, Lucy and Franklin had been "very much in love with each other" — and the affair had been no secret to others, however much the couple had sought to observe decorum in Washington, where Franklin was, after all, assistant secretary of the U.S. Navy. To distract attention from the budding scandal the couple had spawned stories in the gossip press involving other courtiers chasing Lucy. Even if they hadn't convinced their friends, these had served to deceive Eleanor — at least, up to the moment she found the letters.[3] The fact that, after two years of furtive adultery, her tall, dynamic, hugely handsome husband was still passionately in love with a beautiful, quiet, graceful woman, nine years younger than herself, had been for Eleanor a bombshell, in spite of the many rumors she'd heard (and dismissed) all that year and the year before.[4]

"The bottom dropped out of my own particular world and I faced myself, my surroundings, my world, honestly for the first time," Eleanor later admitted, sadly.[5] Overnight the affair had threatened to sunder her privileged domestic and social world, as well as her ever-vulnerable self-confidence in it. Worst of all, her husband's pursuit of Lucy Mercer had clearly not been one of his brief or overnight flirtations, as Eleanor looked back. It was serious. After war was declared in the spring of 1917, Eleanor had told Lucy she intended to economize, and would no longer need her services as social secretary. Franklin, however, had promptly found Lucy a job as a yeoman in his office at the Navy Department. This had been throwing caution to the four winds — with serious potential political consequences for the Wilson administration. Franklin's boss, Navy Secretary Josephus Daniels, had deplored the business; in fact Secretary Daniels had had Miss Mercer summarily fired after six months, owing to mounting "gossip" in the capital. This had not, apparently, dampened the couple's ardor for each other — Franklin and Lucy merely using "safe houses" provided by their friends and relatives, and trying wherever possible to conduct their romance out of town.

A whole network of relatives and friends had necessarily and inevitably become parties to the affair, as well as its duplicity. "I saw you 20 miles out in the country," Alice Longworth Roosevelt, Eleanor's sharp-tongued cousin, for example, had written to taunt — and warn — Franklin. "You didn't see me. Your hands were on the wheel but your eyes were on that perfectly lovely lady," she'd teased him — describing Lucy as a "beautiful, charming, and an absolutely delightful creature."[6] To others Alice Longworth would later snidely remark that Franklin "deserved a good time," given that he "was married to Eleanor" — a less than beautiful woman with a receding chin and big teeth who, in Alice's malicious eyes, lacked any sense of humor or fun.

In short, by the time Eleanor had belatedly learned of the affair, all Washington already knew of it — with no shortage of evidence that could be used in court, including "a register from a motel in Virginia Beach showing that father had checked in as man and wife," James Roosevelt later recorded, and had "spent the night" with Lucy.[7]

Shaken and hurt to her core, Eleanor had favored a divorce. Lucy, for her part, had been convinced that a church annulment of Franklin and Eleanor's marriage could be successfully sought, so that she and Franklin could marry without the necessity of his converting to Catholicism or vice versa. It had been Franklin's mother, Sara, however, who had refused to countenance a social scandal such as the divorce of her beloved and only son would pose. His career would be ruined, she had warned, as well as the family name. Sara had even threatened to disinherit Franklin, it was widely rumored, if he went ahead.

As Alice Longworth later reflected — following her own divorce and those of every single one of Franklin's children (often multiple times) in later years — the Victorian and Edwardian eras were unimaginably different from those that followed. "I don't think one can have any idea how horrendous even the idea of divorce was in those days . . . In those days people just didn't go around divorcing one another. Not done, they said. Emphatically."[8]

In the end it was the beautiful, statuesque Lucy Mercer who'd recognized she couldn't do this to Franklin, whom she adored. She'd therefore backed out, honorably. All had been scarred, though.

Reeling emotionally but determined to do her best, Eleanor had agreed to continue acting as her husband's loyal consort in public, and to remain a devoted fellow parent to their five surviving children. For herself, however, Eleanor had vowed to make, if she could, a new, more independent life — both as a woman and a citizen — whatever anybody thought of her. She thus helped Franklin gain the Democratic nomination for the vice presidency in 1920; she helped nurse him through his poliomyelitis and lower-limb paralysis (sadly without improvement) in 1921; and later, when he'd stood successfully for the governorship of New York in 1928, she had become — and remained — his loyal political advocate, supporting him steadfastly when he stood for the presidency itself, in 1932. But in terms of intimacy, although not mutual respect, the air had gone out of their relationship. "Franklin and Eleanor" had become once more — as, to an extent, they had always been — devoted cousins more than husband and wife. Cousins who not only shared the same name but to a large extent the same compassionate political and social ideals, despite their inherited wealth, however much this caused them to be hated as renegades or "traitors to their class" by conservatives and rich Republicans.

The "Franklin and Eleanor" political combination, at least, had been completely sincere. But in her personal life Eleanor had become determined to be a "new woman" — whatever others might say or sneer. Franklin had had his coterie of male advisers as well as female assistants and supporters, especially his personal assistant, Marguerite "Missy" LeHand, whom Eleanor called his "office wife." For her part, Eleanor sought to broaden her life experience, and to share deeper feelings with her *own* selected colleagues, helpers, and admirers — including a succession of women and younger men she could take under her wing as intimate companions over the years. There were Nancy Cook and Marion Dickerman, a lesbian couple she loved, and with whom she built Val-Kill, a cottage on the grounds of Hyde Park, with Franklin's blessing and even architectural advice; Lorena "Hick" Hickok, a lesbian reporter who became her bosom companion, perhaps even lover, in the White House; Earl Miller, the chauffeur whom her husband insisted she employ as driver and security detail, once she became First Lady; and finally Joseph "Joe" Lash, a young, left-wing student and son of Russian Jewish émigrés, whom she "adopted" in 1939 to the point of obsession, and an FBI investigation — writing almost daily to him and even insisting on being allowed to visit him at Guadalcanal on her Red Cross visit to the Pacific in 1943, where Lash had been posted after being drafted into the U.S. Army.

Eleanor's "infatuations," alongside her tireless work for social and political causes (not least over civil rights, which constantly threatened to alienate Southern Democrats, whose legislative support in Congress was vital to FDR), had been brave, open, even reckless — yet they had rarely caused the President to turn a hair, or even to counsel prudence. His loyal, avuncular-style support of his wife and members of her inner circle had been, in retrospect, amazing. He had granted the ladies a lease-for-life on Val-Kill, next to a stream that the women soon dammed in order to make a summer swimming pool. He had even presented Marion Dickerman with a children's book he'd found, *Little Marion's Pilgrimage,* not only signing it "from her affectionate Uncle Franklin" but writing that the gift was being made on the "occasion of the opening of the Love Nest on the Val-Kill."[9]

The Love Nest.

The President's words had not been sarcastic, nor were they a sign of Louis XIV–like largesse; they simply reflected Franklin's genuine generosity of spirit. Perhaps they betrayed a certain guilt, too: that his love affair with Miss Mercer during World War I had hurt Eleanor's confidence in herself as a woman profoundly. And that, in consequence, he owed it to Eleanor to make amends in kind, by encouraging her friendships, if not in their own romantic hearts — both of which had been broken by the affair and its outcome. For however hard she had tried, Eleanor had never been able to reconcile herself to the "act of being physically unfaithful" that had marked Franklin's relationship with Lucy — an aspect which she attributed to the lesser self-discipline of the "average man."[10]

Certainly the matter was far from simple. Franklin's generosity of feeling toward Eleanor, her friends, devotees, and adoptees, was not out of character — it was something that had first drawn Eleanor to her cousin. It also undoubtedly stemmed from sincere gratitude: his acknowledgment that, less than three years after the bust-up over Lucy, it had been Eleanor who had coped with his devastating polio diagnosis, causing Eleanor — not Lucy — to have to deal thereafter with a grave affliction that could never be cured, despite the seemingly endless treatments, rehabilitation, therapies, and fruitless remedies he'd tried.

Franklin Roosevelt would not have been Franklin Roosevelt, known for his loyalty and goodwill, had he broken off *all* contact with Miss Mercer, though. Or with their mutual friends. When Franklin heard Lucy had married, on the rebound, Mr. Winthrop Rutherfurd, a rich widower twice her age, in February 1920, just as Franklin prepared to embark on his bid to win the Democratic Party's vice presidential nomination, he was said to have "started like a horse in fear of a hornet,"[11] so upset was he at hearing the news. Yet he could scarcely have expected Lucy, single and by then aged twenty-eight, to wait in the wings to see whether Eleanor and Franklin would, despite their renewed vows, fail to mend their marriage. And once Franklin had fallen ill with polio the following year, he was, so to speak, a twice-broken man: an invalid to be pitied, who would need all the care and help his family could give him, not a second upheaval.

For the most part Franklin's letters to Lucy were burned after Franklin's death, to avoid posthumous scandal,[12] while nearly all her own letters to him would vanish after his death, presumably destroyed. The handful of extant letters demonstrate incontrovertibly that Lucy and Franklin maintained at least distant contact over the years of her marriage.

As Franklin's star had risen in the political firmament of the Great Depression and New Deal, the President had continued to correspond with Lucy, even to provide for her stepchildren and her daughter, Barbara — to the point, in fact, where he had become a sort of honorary uncle, even "godfather," as he called himself, to Barbara: his daughter manqué. In moments of special pride, moreover, in his rise to the presidency — unique in history for a paraplegic — he'd wanted Lucy Rutherfurd to be near him, if it could be arranged discreetly. He'd thus made sure that Lucy — whose sister had a house in Georgetown — was fetched by White House limousine to attend his first inauguration as thirty-second president of the United States in March 1933; then his second, in January 1937; and his third in 1941. Thereafter, once her husband, Winty Rutherfurd, had become infirm, housebound, bedbound, and in need of a live-in nurse, the President had begun inviting Lucy to visit him briefly at the White House, when she was in Washington, under an assumed name: "Mrs. Johnson."

The relationship with Lucy had thus always had its special character, at once nostalgic and joyful. When on March 19, 1944, Lucy's husband had finally died at age eighty-two, the President had felt he need not prevaricate or be secretive any longer. He would be free to see Lucy — no longer as Mrs. Johnson, but as Mrs. Rutherfurd, a widow. And at Hyde Park, on March 26, before he was to be examined, secretly, by naval doctors tasked with finding out why he had seemed unable to bounce back to good health after his triumphant trip to Tehran.

For his part the President had told Daisy he was feeling like death warmed over, lying down after his press conference on March 24. But as the *Ferdinand Magellan* had pulled out of the special platform beneath the Bureau of Engraving and Printing near the White House that night, he'd felt almost lightheaded. For Lucy had said she would drive to see him at Springwood, his Hyde Park house, for the first time in her life, on Sunday, March 26. And for the first time in months he'd felt wonderfully alive.

41

In the Last Stages of Consumption

LOVELY MILD WEATHER just made for the P.," Daisy Suckley noted in her diary on the morning of Saturday, March 25, 1944, as the President was taken by car from Highland railway station, across the Hudson River from Pough-keepsie, to his home. "Mrs. Rutherfurd is coming up to see him from New York tomorrow, and he hopes to show her around the place, the library, the cottage etc., so he took things easy—had a good nap before lunch, & after lunch sat in a deck chair in the sun."[1]

"In the afternoon sat out on the terrace in the sun for some time—no visitors," Bill Hassett also noted in his diary—all of them retiring "to bed soon after ten o'clock," to be ready for the big day.[2]

The President on the eve of Lucy's visit had felt both indolent and excited. "I've never done such a thing in my life before," Daisy quoted him saying, as he'd relaxed. He was "Robert Louis Stevenson, in the last stages of consumption," he'd described himself—Daisy leaving him on the veranda reading the *London Daily News,* together with his secretary Grace Tully, who was taking dictation. But he purposely hadn't invited Daisy, or Hassett, or Grace to join him when Lucy arrived the next day for lunch—after which he drove Lucy around the whole estate personally, in his Ford Phaeton convertible, with its special hand controls. He insisted on showing Lucy the library and his cottage. After six hours of reunion he finally said goodbye to her at 6:30 p.m.

He'd overdone it—in fact, no sooner had Lucy left Hyde Park than he "felt fever coming on & went to bed," as he afterwards admitted to Daisy, on the phone. He'd arranged, he'd told her, to take the *Magellan* back to Washington early the next morning. On arrival at the White House he would have dinner served on a bed tray, and a good night's sleep before the medical examination at Bethesda Naval Hospital scheduled for Tuesday. There, hopefully, the cause of his medical misery could be cleared up. It would be a full day in Washington, since Eleanor would be returning from the Caribbean. He would be

"X-rayed etc," Daisy wrote, having remained at her house, Wilderstein, near Hyde Park. "I pray they do the right thing by him."[3]

They did. The result, however, would not be the one either the President or Daisy — who had an obsession with diet, on which she blamed the President's poor condition — was quite expecting.

The medical examination that Admiral McIntire had arranged to take place at 11:30 a.m. on March 28 would change President Roosevelt's life forever. And none too soon.

Three months earlier, the President had invented the cognomen "Dr. Win-the-War." Now, however, it was the President himself who needed a doctor — a better doctor — if he was to win both the war and his battle with the approaching Reaper. This turned out to be Lieutenant Commander Howard Bruenn, a thirty-nine-year-old officer in the U.S. Naval Medical Corps (Reserve), currently stationed at the Bethesda Naval Hospital in Maryland, where he was chief of the electrocardiograph department.

Dr. Bruenn later confessed to being "pretty shocked" when the President was wheeled into his examination room to be lifted onto a so-called Gatch bed, the top end of which could be tilted up. Admiral McIntire had painted for him a wholly fictitious picture of the President, saying merely that Roosevelt "was not himself" and was "thought to have had an upper respiratory infection and had not quite regained his strength," Bruenn later recounted.

An upper respiratory infection?

Bruenn found it hard to conceal his alarm. In newsreels at Christmastime, on his triumphant return from Cairo and Tehran, the President had appeared to Bruenn and millions of others to be fighting fit — in speech, mind, and body — or at least body language. That much had been genuine. What was true three months later, however, was the opposite. Roosevelt's condition, in Bruenn's subsequent account, was "God awful."[4] The President, Bruenn found, was "in acute congestive heart failure," with possibly only weeks to live, at most only months.

The President's aspect, close-up, stunned Bruenn. "He appeared to be very tired, and his face was very gray. Moving caused considerable breathlessness."[5] The President was coughing repeatedly, but could bring up no sputum. "I suspected something was terribly wrong as soon as I looked at him," Bruenn later confessed. "His face was pallid and there was a bluish discoloration of his skin, lips and nail beds."[6] He was clearly not getting enough oxygen.

Bruenn began his formal examination by measuring the President's temperature — slightly high — his pulse and respiration rates, as well as his blood pressure. At 186 over 108 this was not good, but not startling for a man in his sixties carrying huge responsibilities and suddenly in a medical examination room. Readings from earlier visits, after escalating in 1940, showed this number to be consistently high for years now—178/88 in November 1940, 188/105 in 1941. But no readings thereafter. Suspicious, Bruenn asked to see the President's more recent numbers. Admiral McIntire, who took the President's blood pressure twice daily, seemed reluctant to show them, claiming they were back in his office, next to the Map Room at the White House. (Bruenn insisted, and they were eventually fetched. All, when the cardiologist saw them, showed systolic readings above 200.) Yet it was only when Bruenn examined the President's chest more closely that he truly appreciated the implications of what he was discovering. Electrocardiograms and X-rays were taken, as well as blood samples for further analysis.

Dr. Bruenn's main finding was incontrovertible: the President was dying. His heart had ballooned in size; it had also moved position. In fact, according to Bruenn's notes, it was "enormous,"[7] with the consequence that even shifting position on the special examination bed "caused [the President] considerable breathlessness" and puffing. Bruenn was now afraid. "My diagnosis was a bombshell," he later recalled.[8] Speaking as an experienced cardiologist, he told Admiral McIntire that the President was "in left ventricular failure" or "acute congestive heart failure,"[9] a condition in which treatment, even if begun immediately, could not prolong the President's life for very long, since he was suffering fatal "hypertensive heart disease."[10] And that, as Bruenn later recalled, "put a different aspect on the whole situation."[11]

It certainly did. Despite his pretense, Admiral McIntire had known what really lay behind the President's worsening condition, but had not dared confront it. He asked Bruenn to "write out what I thought should be done." When he saw the report, however, the admiral exploded. As Bruenn recalled, "When I gave him my recommendations for bedrest, diet, etc., he said, 'You can't do that. This is the President of the United States!'"[12]

McIntire was rattled. The President's heart had, after all, been his constant, secret concern—especially whenever Roosevelt was required to travel at high altitude, first on the flight to Tehran and subsequently, when flying back around the Atlas Mountains to Dakar. But now the truth could not be evaded. The President's symptoms over the three months since Christmas stemmed not from a case of lingering flu, as McIntire had pretended, or a respiratory infection, as he'd prayed it might be. The excuse that McIntire later gave for not having summoned expert medical advice earlier, since the President's condition was "completely unsuspected up to this time,"[13] would be a complete lie, like the reports he made to the press at the time. It was a lie he'd felt compelled to tell, since he himself would be blamed, as Roosevelt's White House physician, if it was found the President should have been receiving treatment, or medical advice and recommendations, at least, for his worsening heart condition. For if Bruenn was right, the President was suffering from a mortal malady, for which there was no treatment at that time beyond sedation, bed rest, diet — and the administering of digitalis, a potentially toxic extract of purple foxglove, as a palliative.

Unable to accept his mistake, McIntire thus accepted Bruenn's medical findings, but not the severity of the President's condition or his treatment strategy. McIntire's response to the latter was "somewhat unprintable," Bruenn recalled[14] — the cardiologist recommending the "patient" cease all activity, physical or mental, and submit to weeks of absolute bed rest "with nursing care." Also completely refrain from smoking and begin a diet to lose weight. As well as take raw codeine for his other ailment, his "acute bronchitis," and be fully sedated at night so he could actually sleep. Also a digitalis regimen — to begin immediately.

"Summarily rejected," McIntire declared, panicking at the thought of the effect on the nation, in the midst of a global war, if word got out the President was mortally ill.[15] What was Bruenn thinking? "The President can't take time off to go to bed," McIntire snapped, as if Bruenn had gone mad. He was the nation's commander in chief. "You can't simply say to him, 'Do this or do that.'"[16]

As for the administering of toxic digitalis, McIntire was even more contemptuous — the medication was simply too radical a treatment for him to contemplate, especially given Bruenn's suggestion that the President begin treatment immediately, lest he die in the next days or weeks.[17]

Bruenn must have held his ground, however, for McIntire — perhaps to save his own career — thought better of his first reaction. At the end of their discussion McIntire told the young cardiologist he would seek further advice.

Using his authority as an admiral, McIntire duly convened a secret meeting with senior medical staff of the Bethesda hospital. An interim compromise was reached among them, whereby "limitation of daily activity must be emphasized," an hour's rest to be taken "after meals," no more swimming, and laxatives given to avoid "straining" of the bowels.[18]

No straining of the bowels? Bruenn was dismayed — but sworn to silence by Admiral McIntire, and told not to tell the President anything. "Appalled at what I found," Bruenn later noted,[19] he considered the President had not long to live unless digitalis was administered immediately. Nothing was said for the moment to the President himself. "He said they took X-rays & all sorts of tests," but they "found nothing drastically wrong," Daisy innocently recorded in relief in her diary that night, after the President had called her, apart from "one sinus clogged up."[20]

It was clear that the initial medical response to the President's health crisis was risible, indeed culpable — in fact, seldom in the history of medical treatment at that high a level can such willful incompetence have been displayed. However, "they are going to put him on a strict diet," Daisy added, hoping that "lemon juice in hot water before breakfast" might be the answer.[21]

• • •

How much the President truly believed Admiral McIntire or Lieutenant Commander Bruenn, who came up to see him at the White House the next morning, is unclear. He said nothing further to Daisy for five days. Nor did he confide anything to Eleanor, who, back from her Caribbean tour, merely told her children their father was suffering prolonged flu.

Meanwhile Bruenn, for his part, was unwilling to watch his new patient die. "Despite everything else," Bruenn recalled, "the need for digitalization, I thought was overriding. Said so to Admiral McIntire. Told him I literally didn't want to have anything to do with the situation unless" it was administered.[22]

The threat of such a resignation, and possible scandal if the reason got out, certainly won the admiral's attention — and that of Captain John Harper, the Bethesda Naval Hospital's commandant. Harper warned Bruenn that his bleak prognosis — especially his insistence on immediate, aggressive treatment — could end their careers.[23] Digitalis, he reminded him, slows the heart rate and allows the heart muscle to contract more efficiently, but it can have serious side effects — ones that could harm or kill the serving president, beginning with heart palpitations, hallucinations, and blurred vision.

The outcome of *not* giving digitalis, however, could be equally fatal, Bruenn protested: leading inexorably and perhaps imminently to complete "congestive heart failure."[24]

It was in this quandary that McIntire decided he must bring in bigger guns — even if they were not, strictly speaking, naval ones. He therefore called for medical advice from two "honorary consultants" to the U.S. Navy, whose discretion could be trusted: Dr. James Paullin, the former president of the American Medical Association, and Dr. Frank Lahey, founder of the famous Lahey Clinic.

Once Dr. Paullin and Dr. Lahey arrived in the nation's capital two days later, however, the two renowned physicians disagreed with each other on how best to proceed.

Together with Admiral McIntire, Captain Harper, the radiologist Dr. Charles Behrens, and poor Lieutenant Commander Bruenn, the cardiologist, the doctors reviewed the results of the "X rays, electrocardiograms, and the other laboratory data concerning the President" — but did not reexamine the President, lest they alarm him — and give rise to dark rumors.

"There was much discussion," Bruenn later recalled,[25] sitting around the table at the Bethesda Naval Hospital — for Dr. Lahey, as a gastrointestinal expert, thought there could be other problems with the patient's digestive system that might be even worse than his heart, especially in view of the President's abdominal discomfort. The collapse of the President at dinner with Stalin and Churchill in Tehran, an account of which McIntire related, was especially troubling. There was even a question about the President's prostate, which Bruenn insisted should also be examined.[26] Most of all, though, Bruenn pleaded for digitalis to be administered as a matter of urgency. Dr. Paullin felt the opposite — that digitalis might make a critical condition even worse, given how ill the President was said to be. "They thought that was all too drastic and extensive," Bruenn later recalled[27] — Paullin recommending they give no treatment for the moment, and hope for the best.

Without seeing the patient in person, though, they had nothing firm to go on, beyond the exam results in front of them. Paullin and Lahey therefore asked to see the President in person — a request McIntire, with a heavy heart, was compelled to agree to.

It was the "emergency" visit of Paullin and Lahey to the White House in the afternoon of March 31, and then again the next morning, on April 1, which escalated the growing crisis — for with the arrival of such eminent physicians the President could hardly fail to recognize the gravity of the situation. His symptoms had remained "essentially unchanged" since Bruenn's first examination — his heart so "grossly enlarged"[28] that he was still finding it difficult to move or breathe.

The evidence, moreover, could no longer be concealed: namely the President's grim appearance.

One visitor to the White House who saw the President at this time was a top newspaper reporter, Turner Catledge. He later recalled an off-the-record interview with the President he'd been granted by Roosevelt's press secretary, Steve Early. The bearing of the nation's chief executive, once proud and leonine, was diminished, the shadows under his eyes had deepened, his face more lined, the skin slack. "When I entered the President's office," recalled Catledge, "and had my first glimpse of him in several months, I was shocked and horrified — so much so that my impulse was to turn around and leave. I felt that I was seeing something I shouldn't see. He had lost a great deal of weight. His shirt collar hung so loose on his neck that you could have put your hand inside it. He was sitting there with a vague, glassy-eyed expression on his face and his mouth was hanging open. Repeatedly he would lose his train of thought, stop and stare blankly at me. It was an agonizing experience."[29] Grace Tully, taking dictation, had reported the same to the President's daughter Anna: that she had found he had "momentarily lost consciousness while he was signing a document," and that "they were all concerned."[30]

The President's condition seemed to be worsening — "he did not appear as well as he had even before. His color was poor, and he looked tired," moreover suffered "several paroxysms of nonproductive cough," Bruenn recalled. Again, "there was much discussion." The President's blood pressure had now reached 200/106. Lahey was still "particularly interested in the gastrointestinal tract but submitted that no surgical procedure" could or should currently be undertaken — for the President might well not survive it. Together with Bruenn and McIntire there was "much beating around the bush," with Dr. Paullin, the most distinguished doctor present, expressing "much skepticism," as Bruenn recalled, "despite the overwhelming evidence."[31] Lahey, however, felt "that the situation to his mind was serious enough to warrant acquainting the President with the full facts in order to assure his full cooperation"[32] — and it was thus agreed, at long last, the President would take digitalis, to save or end his life.

It was, in the event, a tribute to Dr. Bruenn's strength of character that, despite being the youngest and most junior member of the medical cabal, his insistence on administering digitalis, along with frequent monitoring by electrocardiogram to see if it was working, had finally been accepted.

It was not a moment too soon — the young doctor may well have saved the President's life. Time would tell. Meanwhile, however, McIntire deliberately sought to bamboozle the press — and the nation. The admiral's press conference on March 28, given to tamp down speculation about a president whose own recent press conferences had raised concerns about his health, was a model of what would later be called White House "spin."

How, in fact, Admiral McIntire managed to arrange the series of high-level medical consultations at the White House and at Bethesda Naval Hospital without the press getting to the literal heart of the matter, or recognizing its seriousness, would be a testament to McIntire's effectiveness as a guardian of the truth. As "the country was filled with every variety of wild and reckless lie about his physical condition," it was simply monstrous that anyone should question the need for discretion, McIntire later reflected.[33] After all, "for better or worse, the war was being run by just three men" — Mr. Roosevelt, Marshal Stalin, and Winston Churchill — "and it was not over yet."[34]

This was true — D-day still two months away, thanks to Churchill's machinations in Italy. As Daisy would note in her diary a few weeks later, however, declining to tell the President how sick he was, was futile. The President, "when he found out that they were not telling him the *whole* truth & that he was evidently more sick than they said," was not impressed. It was *his* body — and it was failing. "It is foolish of them to attempt to put anything over on *him!*" Daisy sniffed.[35]

In any event, the President wasn't fooled. Heart disease ran in the Roosevelt family. The President's own father had died of heart disease — in fact "Mr. James," as he was known, had had to resort to a sedentary, no-stress existence for the entire final decade of his life — managing to survive that way to the relatively august age of seventy-two. But in a world war? As U.S. president and commander in chief?

Four weeks after the President's revelatory examination at Bethesda Naval Hospital, Frank Knox, the navy secretary, would die of a heart attack, on April 28. Pa Watson, the President's military attaché and appointments secretary, who'd accompanied him to Tehran, had a serious heart condition; he would die of a cerebral hemorrhage early the following year, at age sixty-one. The President's youngest son, John, would die of a heart attack at age sixty-five, in 1981.

"The greatest criticism we can have," McIntire meantime told the press, "is that we have not been able to provide him with enough exercise and sunshine."[36]

A few weeks in the Caribbean, away from the political stresses and strains of Washington, were duly insisted upon. Preliminary preparations for a Caribbean journey were even made. But it would be demanding, in terms of physical movement when the President's breathing was so labored, and an air flight — the simplest form of travel — was considered a no-no in his current condition, given his failing heart. Thus when the President's friend Bernard Baruch offered the use of Hobcaw, his huge baronial estate in South Carolina, as a place of respite, the President accepted with alacrity.

It was not ideal — a vast estate, but mosquito-ridden and awkward in terms of Secret Service security, let alone military security. In its favor, however, was that it could be reached by train.

And it had another attraction. Hobcaw was a mere hundred miles or so from Widow Rutherfurd's house at Aiken, South Carolina. Given circumstances in which the President might not live very long, it would certainly have been churlish for anyone to oppose Mr. Roosevelt's personal wishes. Hobcaw's very isolation, after all, was a great advantage, in terms of recuperation. As was its distance from prying eyes, and the Washington press corps.

Thus was the President's trip to the Hobcaw Barony arranged. There, in the peace and serenity of South Carolina, he would await Overlord: its target date delayed, Eisenhower had reported to him, till the end of May or early June, owing to the shortage of landing craft.

D-day, as it was now being called: the great invasion plan he, like Hitler, was certain would "decide" the war.

PART SIX

D-day

42

"This Attack Will Decide the War"

HIGH UP IN the Bavarian Alps, at the Berghof, near Berchtesgaden, Hitler was also recuperating — suffering elevated blood pressure, cardiac hypertension, and stomach problems.

The Führer had left the Wolf's Lair, his military headquarters in East Prussia, on February 23, 1944. As the Red Army got closer, the camp had become vulnerable to air attack; it therefore required thicker blastwalls, roofs, and shelters. The reinforcing would take months. In the meantime the Führer would go, he announced, to the peace and tranquility of the mountains he loved.

Back in December 1943, Hitler had predicted "the attack in the West will come in the spring; it is beyond all doubt" — the Allied invasion accompanied by diversionary attacks anywhere between Norway and the Balkans. "There is no doubt about it, they have committed themselves. After mid-February, early March on, the attack will take place in the West. I don't have the feeling," the Führer told his senior staff, "that the British have their — shall we say — whole heart in this attack," since they wanted to keep their "divisions intact" to run their empire after the war. "If you look at India, Africa, the Far East, Australia," the Führer reckoned they must have at least "50% of their armed forces out there," and "they want to maintain that, of course, in order not to lose any territory at the last minute." The empire came first. But the signs were the Americans were insisting on launching the Second Front, however unenthusiastic the British. Assuming the cross-Channel invasion went ahead, then, it would thus be the critical moment of the war: one that Hitler claimed to welcome. "If they attack in the West, then this attack will decide the war. If this attack is driven back, the whole affair will be over. Then we can also take forces out very quickly," from France, he assured his high command staff — switching the Wehrmacht and Luftwaffe to deal with the Soviets on the Eastern Front, as well as holding any remaining Western Allied forces in the southern Mediterranean, even evicting them.[1]

A month later, on January 30, 1944, delighted by the way Churchill's invasion forces at Anzio seemed to have failed even to get off the beachhead, Hitler had given a national radio broadcast from the Wolf's Lair to remind Germans at home and in the occupied countries what they were fighting for. The Jews, he'd claimed, were responsible for the war, and they were behind the Bolsheviks, as he called them. "One thing is certain," he'd declared: "there can be only one victor in this fight, and this will either be Germany or the Soviet Union! A victory by Germany means the preservation of Europe; a victory by the Soviet Union means its destruction."[2]

The Jews, the Führer claimed, were responsible for all the ills of the world, including unemployment and the Great Depression.

The toughest struggle was already over, the Führer said in his broadcast — National Socialism having successfully prevailed in the struggle against internal and international Jewry. "Germany's and Europe's victory over the criminal invaders from the west and the east" was not only "an expression of faith for every National Socialist, but also, at the end of this entire fight, his inner conviction." The *Volkstaat* was expressed by and through the Wehrmacht — and this "front will never lose heart. Even in the hardest days, it will remain strong" — part of a "tremendous, world-shaking process" entailing "suffering and pain," yes, but which was "the eternal law of destiny, which states not only that everything great is gained by fighting, but also that every mortal comes into this world by causing pain."[3]

Hitler's ever-growing obsession with Jewry, even as the thousand-year Third Reich faced destruction after only ten years, was extraordinary. The Jewish ratio of the German population in the 1930s had been less than 1 percent. Moreover the Soviet Union, tyrannous though it might be as a political regime, had not attacked Germany — in fact had signed a nonaggression pact with the nation in 1939 in vain hopes of staving off a German invasion. Historians would therefore be at pains to understand the roots of Hitler's fanatical determination.

Allied soldiers fighting the Wehrmacht in close combat, meantime, were confronted by a conundrum. If the Führer's anti-Semitic claims were so specious and so paranoid, how was it possible that he enjoyed the support of almost eighty million Germans?[4] If he was mad, why were millions of Wehrmacht officers and men still defending their ill-gotten conquests abroad? This enigma baffled not only Allied intelligence officers interrogating German POWs, but would puzzle historians both in Germany and outside for many decades thereafter.[5]

Moving his whole high command headquarters staff with him to Berchtesgaden, the Führer was certain the Allied invasion would come in the spring, as was confirmed by German intelligence as well as Eisenhower's promotion to Allied supreme command in London. Hitler seemed to look forward to the prospect, confident the Wehrmacht in the east would continue to carry out orders from above without question, regardless of the casualties. The German army was, after all, already too deeply implicated in mass murder in Poland and then in Russia during its days of heady, ruthless conquest, along with the SS, to question the radical racial views expressed in his broadcast.

Hitler no longer even needed to appear in public, despite Goebbels's repeated pleas he should do so. He had thus not visited a single one of the cities the Allies had bombed over the past six months — including Berlin. Arriving in Munich on his special armored train with its blinds drawn, on February 24, 1944, he had, however, agreed to address the Nazi Party faithful. In the Festsaal of the sixteenth-century Hofbräuhaus, his personal appearance had been greeted as if he were the messiah.

There had been rumors swirling that he was unwell, explaining his long disappearance from public view. In Munich that evening, however, there had been no sign of ill health. "He looks wonderful," Goebbels noted in his diary, "and both physically and mentally is in great form. He gives an extraordinarily vibrant speech, in fact more so than one has heard him speak for ages." He'd given his comrades a brief overview of the war situation on the Eastern Front and in Italy, and had pointed to ever-improving German defensive success on both fronts. "He stresses that Germany's eventual victory, in which he believes more unshakably than ever, depends on Germany's toughness." If the British claimed they were paying Germany back in kind for the Blitz of 1940 and 1941, they would shortly learn the meaning of *real* revenge: for in April, hopefully, the first V-bombs or missiles would be launched on London, as soon as certain "technical difficulties" had been overcome. Above all, though, it was in northern France that the Führer saw Germany's "great new chance" in the prosecution of the war: the Führer describing to them how the invading forces of the Western Allies would be rubbed out in the same way as at Anzio, in Italy. The years leading up to the Nazi seizure of power in 1933 had been far worse, the Führer claimed, than the present situation: a time when the nation was now so clearly unified behind him. He was going to pursue his aims "remorselessly." As the Jews had been defeated in Germany, they would be defeated in every corner of the world. "The Jews in England and America" would be the next ones to face the music.[6]

Arriving at the Berghof, his once-modest mountain villa, the German messiah had thereafter been greeted by a snowstorm on February 25. And by his blond, younger mistress, Eva Braun, who was shocked by Hitler's appearance: stooped, old, his tremors worse than ever.

Standing in the midst of six square miles of military installations, fences, and checkpoints, the Berghof was shrouded in camouflage netting, but also, often, fog. And smoke from machines employed to conceal the mountain from American bombers — a technique that made Hitler's personal physician, Dr.

Theodor Morell, so sick he had asked to be allowed to stay below, in Berchtes-gaden, driving up to the beleaguered Führer twice a day to administer injections of amphetamines.

To Dr. Goebbels, on March 4, Hitler had confided he was going to have to occupy Hungary, Germany's hitherto loyal ally, with Wehrmacht troops, as a result of Hungary's *Verrat* — treason, in daring to explore surrender negotiations with the enemy — which "must be punished," as Goebbels recorded in his diary. The Hungarian regent, Miklós Horthy, would be taken into custody when he came to visit the Führer, and the Hungarian army would thereupon be disarmed as an unreliable ally. Once that was done, the "question" of the Hungarian aristocracy and "above all the Jews in Budapest" could be addressed — by deportation and liquidation. "For as long as the Jews sit in Budapest," Goebbels noted, one could do nothing with "the city and the country." There were plenty of willing Wehrmacht troops on hand for the task — and the thought that a German officer would question such orders, let alone refuse to carry them out, was unthinkable.

Goebbels's forecast had proven correct. Admiral Horthy had arrived at the Berghof on March 18. He was threatened, placed in "protective custody," and then forced to agree to German occupation and the roundup of more than half a million Jews — with Romania next on Hitler's list.

The Soviets had meantime reopened a huge new offensive in the Ukraine, on an eleven-hundred-kilometer front, as the winter snows melted. But it was in the West the war would be decided, Hitler had rightly predicted — giving rise to a "war of nerves," or propaganda, that tormented Goebbels. What was the Allies' real strategy? They were clinging to the beaches at Anzio, certainly — but why, he wondered, when the campaign had "no clear strategic purpose" in Italy?

As a master propagandist Dr. Goebbels wished to fan the burning embers of anti-Semitism in Britain and America, and thus prepare the way for a negotiated end to the war, leaving Germany in control of most of the continent. For the moment, however, the propaganda minister accepted the Führer's authority and wishes as supreme commander of the Wehrmacht. Germany *had* to continue to go about its deadly business — most importantly by holding fast in the east while preparing to crush the cross-Channel attack when it finally came. Quick defeat of the invasion might even enable Hitler to mount his next offensive on the Eastern Front that very summer, for which "he needs some forty divisions," Goebbels noted in his diary — namely those in France, currently waiting for the expected Allied invasion. Those forces, backed by the Luftwaffe, he'd be able to transfer, just as soon as "we've smashed the invasion" — though where exactly the invasion would come in northern Europe neither he nor the Führer knew for certain.

There was no question but that the Wehrmacht would succeed in its assignment. It was "*absolut sicher*" — absolutely certain. "He describes to me in detail the forces we have at hand to wipe out the invasion — in fact more than enough." There were, to be sure, "a number of new divisions, inexperienced in battle; however they are filled with fantastic human material, so that we need have no concerns on that account. For example, once the SS Hitlerjugend division goes into combat, we can rest assured it'll do its duty. Moreover the Führer intends to put units of his Leibstandarte SS Adolf Hitler into the division, men who'll definitely inspire the Hitlerjugend with their energy. Other forces in France are also first-class: young, educated, well-trained for the task — guaranteeing the outcome for us in their toughness and fortitude. We're even superior to the enemy in our weaponry — especially our tanks. We have the new 'Panther' and 'Tiger' panzers, which are way better than their predecessors; even though we don't have enough of them yet, we can sprinkle them in amongst the others to produce colossal firepower and defensive capability."[7]

Though he was careful not to dictate anything in his diary that might possibly be used against him in the future, Goebbels did add one rider: namely, that he hoped the Führer's optimism would be borne out by the coming battle. "We've been so often disappointed recently that one feels a certain skepticism; but the stakes are so high, I'm sure our soldiers will acquit themselves well."[8]

For Hitler himself, the waiting for D-day at the Berghof seemed to be exhilarating, even if it made him nervous — affecting his digestion and robbing him of sleep.

Only a successful Allied invasion could save the Jews — and as Field Marshal Rommel, commanding all Wehrmacht forces defending the Atlantic Wall from Holland to the Spanish border, told the Führer, his troops would be completely ready by May 1. "The Führer is certain the invasion will fail, in fact that he can give it a drubbing," Goebbels noted proudly when he saw Hitler again in Munich for the funeral of Adolf Wagner, veteran Nazi Gauleiter of Bavaria who had recently died of a stroke. Rommel's optimism had been a blessing to him, the Führer said, for he remained "convinced" the outcome of the war hung on the impending cross-Channel assault. If it failed, President Roosevelt would not get reelected to a fourth term, he assured his propaganda minister (who didn't share this view) — in fact the recent withdrawal of the 1940 contender, Wendell Willkie, from the Republican nomination campaign proved this, in the Führer's view, for Willkie had backed Roosevelt's foreign policy.[9] No, the Americans were simply not enthusiastic about the war in Europe. Failure on D-day would thus empower the eventual Republican winner of the election to negotiate an armistice with the Reich. Meanwhile in England there was so much war-weariness that a massive German V-bomb campaign, launched in tandem with the slaughter of British troops on the beaches of northern France, as at Dieppe in 1942, would surely bring Churchill's downfall. In fact the Führer had decided, he informed Goebbels, not to launch any of the V-1 rockets that were ready that month, but to wait instead for D-day and then fire them in a concentrated attack on London.

It is easy, in the aftermath of war, to ridicule such predictions — but in the context of the time, Hitler's confidence did not seem misplaced. There might be growing resistance to German occupation across western Europe, but there was also anxiety in the Allied camp. If the Western Allies succeeded in defeating the Wehrmacht in northern France and racing to Berlin, Western democracy would be saved. But if D-day did *not* succeed? Stalin's troops could be held at bay on the Eastern Front, or even pushed back; Hitler's forces would then remain masters of Europe — able either to counterattack the Soviets or come to a negotiated nonaggression pact, as in 1939. There were 158,000 German and non-German Todt-organization workers finishing more than twenty thousand fortified posts, planting six million beach mines, and erecting half a million obstacles along the French beaches of the Atlantic Wall. Behind them were some 468,000 Wehrmacht troops in Army Group B area in northern France to immediately repel the invaders as in some medieval siege.

Hitler's military instincts *as a warrior* were thus not flawed. In his battlefield strategy, however, he continually found himself torn between competing advice from his "experts." Field Marshals Rundstedt and Rommel had distinguished themselves in smashing the French and British armies in Belgium and France in 1940. Now the shoe was on the other foot. Led by Americans, the Allied armies were about to assault the Atlantic Wall: the German version of the Maginot Line. Rommel had insisted the invasion must be defeated instantly, on the beaches — pivoting his counterinvasion forces on bombproof strongpoints, lest the Allies advance inland, at which point it might be too late to prevent a buildup of enemy infantry and armored forces, protected by massive Allied air power. But it was still unclear whether the Allies would target the Pas-de-Calais area — as they had done when assaulting Dieppe — or would invade farther southwest, in Normandy or the Cotentin Peninsula around Cherbourg. In this dilemma Hitler was faced by a conundrum: namely where exactly to position his crucial German armored or panzer divisions in order to erase in good time any weakly armed Allied beachheads before the invading forces could expand and break out.

Field Marshal Rundstedt, the commander in chief West, was wisely given control of the Fifth Panzer Army, or Panzer Group West, as well as all reserve divisions. Concerned lest the Allies open their invasion with a diversionary attack designed to draw off his main armored divisions, the Führer insisted on retaining a veto over the Panzer Army's employment, however. As the German official historian, Detlef Vogel, noted, this "panzer controversy" continued right up "until the Allied landing."[10] A compromise was nevertheless reached.

Some armored divisions were allowed to set up camps close to the coasts, but the main body of German armor was held farther inland, near Paris, to be sent into battle once the *Schwerpunkt,* the main impact, of the Allied invasion became certain.

With extensive Allied deception measures being taken (including a dummy army under Patton in eastern England, suggesting to German military intelligence that the Pas-de-Calais was the true target area), no one could be sure, whether at the various German headquarters in the field, or at Berchtesgaden and the Berghof. Only time would tell — Hitler returning by train from Munich on April 18, 1944. Once at the Berghof, he complained to his doctor of stomach pains and headaches, and turned down Goebbels's request that he make a public speech on May 1, saying his nerves were simply not up to it.[11]

Benito Mussolini, who'd been rescued from detention at Gran Sasso in a daring mission carried out by German paratroopers and SS troops, had come to see the Führer at Klessheim Castle in Berchtesgaden on March 22, leaving his mistress Clara Petacci behind while he stayed there for three days of talks.

As head of the new Fascist Republic of Salò (on Lake Garda), the Duce had appealed for better treatment of Italian POWs and forced laborers in Germany, as well as better weapons for the four new Italian Fascist divisions being trained in the Reich. He'd also attempted to interest Hitler in his ideas for the "socialization of businesses" — i.e., to give workers more nationalized power against Italian industry leaders, "the majority of whom were secretly favorable to the British," as the German ambassador to the republic, Rudolf Rahn, noted.[12]

Hitler had listened, but gave short shrift to any hopes of amelioration of Tripartite Pact relations. The Führer "has no interest in the Duce's social-economic measures," Rahn had noted — quoting Hitler saying: "We Germans must get over the habit of thinking we are the doctors of Europe."[13] Rather, they were its executioners — the Führer, with Field Marshal Wilhelm Keitel beside him, assuring Mussolini the Germans were about to launch a new U-boat campaign in the Atlantic; had new jet fighters that would blast Allied bombers and fighters out of the sky; would soon launch "revenge" missiles on London; and would crush the expected cross-Channel landings with a mixture of panzers and concrete. Besides, he'd added, he'd been rereading histories of Frederick the Great and Frederick's father; all coalitions broke apart within five years — and the Allies' time was now up.

How accurate was Hitler's prediction only the next few months would tell.

43

Simplicity of Purpose

WHAT WAS AMAZING to all at the White House, meanwhile, was that the President's spirit or morale seemed unfazed by "the trouble" with his heart, as he described it to Daisy.[1]

Dr. Bruenn's digitalis regimen had served to rescue him miraculously from the brink of heart failure. But he was still liable to lose consciousness at times, and found himself perspiring profusely for no apparent reason. Moreover his digestion, despite his new diet, had been erratic — upset in part by the digitalis, perhaps — giving him chronic abdominal pain.

Strangely, it didn't seem to matter to him. He'd found sudden, unexpected emotional happiness in his life, however fleeting it might prove. Every moment he and Lucy could be together therefore seemed a godsend. If it was not to last more than a few weeks or months, given his condition, then so be it — for this was the elixir that, together with Dr. Bruenn's medical remedy, revived him in the spring of 1944, shortly before D-day.

Churchill had cabled on March 18 saying that, after more than a year of opposition, doubt, and dire predictions if the President's insistence on carrying out D-day was maintained, he was at last "hardening for Overlord as the time gets nearer."[2] This was welcome news. It was not an apology, to be sure, but it was a confession of sorts: enough, at least, that the ailing president had been able to congratulate the Prime Minister on his change of heart — reminding him that Overlord would be not only the greatest Allied amphibious operation of the war but, if all went well, "synchronized with a real Russian breakthrough" on the Eastern Front.[3]

The President's heart remained the problem, though — one that hadn't changed. At certain times of the day he seemed to be a little closer to his normal self, but at others, far, far removed. He was still only sixty-two — the world leader with the lilting voice and jaunty smile who had not only brought the nation through the Great Depression without resort to tyranny, but had guided the country to its current status in the world: the leader of the democracies. Moreover, where Churchill offered no social, economic, or political vision beyond a deeply moral one — freedom and dignity — the President had managed to give his country a positive political and economic *vision* of the future, to be pursued in a postwar peace which the United States, undertaking a new leadership role, would help guarantee. The rights of U.S. servicemen to vote in the forthcoming presidential election would be upheld, too: the necessary "soldier voting bill" having recently been passed by Congress, and a bipartisan War Ballot Commission being currently established to ensure the necessary ballots reached millions of Americans in uniform, serving away from their home constituencies, especially overseas.[4]

The secretary of war, a Republican, had agreed to sit on the commission. The President's enveloping smile, his unfailing confidence in humanity, his humor and bigheartedness were a kind of dynamo that had kept America humming, Stimson felt — even when things had looked dire, or daunting. "The easy-going confidence of a short and quick victory which was so prevalent last autumn and winter has faded out," Stimson had nevertheless acknowledged in his diary on March 22, with the result that people "now realize that they are in for a long war and a very hard fight for the invasion."[5] This would require their president to be even more inspiring than ever. Fixed now for the end of May 1944, Overlord would be a crucial moment in the prosecution of the war, fought under a supreme commander whose appointment Stimson had initially believed was a mistake, but was now beginning to see as a stroke of presidential genius — not least because it left Marshall in Washington, by Stimson's side, and thus able to take a more and more commanding role in the Joint Chiefs of Staff Committee meetings.

D-day remained, as it had always been, the only method of defeating the Wehrmacht and the Third Reich. Italy was a dead end. Moreover, Allied bombing of Germany had resulted in such high losses in aircrew (up to 85 percent not expected to complete their allotted twenty-five missions)[6] that General Arnold worried lest American military morale might break. For all that the Allied air forces targeted military and war-industry installations, their efforts had failed to cripple German output. Instead they seemed to have intensified the enemy's willingness to "stick it out."

However frightening the predictable casualties, then, D-day and the battle for France were the only way to defeat the Nazis. After attending a rehearsal of plans at the headquarters of General Montgomery, Eisenhower's ground forces commander for the invasion, Churchill cabled the President to say for a *second* time he was becoming "very hard set upon Overlord."[7]

So the big question, as the President prepared to take the recuperative vacation his doctors felt was crucial, was this: Should he run again for the presidency, given the party convention that was fast approaching to choose a nominee? Would it be right to do so, when he was so ill? Or should he await the outcome of his R & R in South Carolina, and then of D-day itself?

The President still felt wretched most of the day, but the sedatives he was receiving from Dr. Bruenn were assuring him ten long hours of sleep each night. Even after waking he was not getting up before noon, and was dealing thereafter only with correspondence, not visitors.

Mercifully his brain, the President found, seemed still to be in good shape for part of the day — though he noticed a huge change in himself. Once the most elliptical of thinkers — one who liked to achieve compromise and consensus through friendly discussion by all parties, right up until the moment when momentum seemed to carry his decisions as on a flood tide — he now demanded simplicity of purpose. The details, he felt, would then take care of themselves.

On April 1, 1944, for example, having just seen Dr. Paullin and Dr. Lahey for a second time at the White House, he'd dictated a letter to Cordell Hull telling him he wanted no further State Department attempts to define the meaning of "unconditional surrender" of the Axis powers. "Unconditional surrender" was targeted at America's real "enemies," he said, and should not alarm those lesser actors who, as satellites, had been under the "duress" of Nazi Germany. "Italy surrendered unconditionally but was at the same time given many privileges. This should be so in the event of the surrender of Bulgaria or Rumania or Hungary or Finland," he told Hull. "Lee surrendered unconditionally to Grant but immediately Grant told him that his officers should take their horses home for the Spring plowing. That is the spirit I want to see abroad — but it does not apply to Germany. Germany understands," he cautioned, "only one language."[8]

Four days later the President had stuck to his guns, despite State Department blowback and his own diminishing strength. "From time to time there will have to be exceptions not to the surrender principle but to the application of it in specific cases. That is a very different thing from changing the principle," the President — who had trained as a lawyer — instructed the secretary of state.

Stalin, the President knew, had never been happy with "unconditional surrender." Nevertheless in Moscow the Marshal had subscribed to it, in the name of Allied unity — and he had not opposed it in Tehran. Insofar as the Russian dictator was prepared to back the policy, it was to ensure the Germans made no separate, negotiated settlement with the Western Allies. Unconditional surrender of the Third Reich had thus remained Allied policy since Casablanca — but with a less absolute adherence to the principle in the case of those countries who had allied themselves with the Third Reich, out of fear or special circumstances. The Finns, for example, had taken part in Hitler's Barbarossa offensive solely to get back the territory in Karelia and Saimaa which the Russians had seized in the Winter War of 1939–40. The United States was not even at war with Finland; the President thus welcomed word of Soviet negotiations with the Finnish government — especially since an immediate negotiated settlement would allow Stalin to turn the overwhelming weight of his armies to support the invasion of France — advancing westward, toward Berlin, not north to Helsinki, where there were virtually no Germans. By the same token, however, Roosevelt did not wish to open the door to a World War I–type outcome, which Germans of a subsequent generation might contest. "If we start making exceptions to the general principle [of unconditional surrender] before a specific case arises," he'd therefore argued on April 5, there would be problems once disaffected Germans began secretly seeking a negotiated peace — as had happened in Ankara recently.[9] The same situation as in 1918 would then arise: a future German leader or military claiming the country had never actually been defeated, but had been stabbed in the back by politicians.

Such presidential communication by memos had spoken volumes — the Oval Office becoming less and less inhabited, and less accessible. Moreover the President was currently holding out on his wife in several significant respects. Not only in the matter of his friend, the widow Mrs. Rutherfurd, but the sheer gravity of his medical condition, which Eleanor took to be just an extension of his everlasting flu — or even, possibly, his sadness at the news that their brave but erratic son Elliott was planning to get divorced, once again. "I think the constant tension must tell," Eleanor wrote to her "adoptee," Joe Lash, whom she'd visited in Guadalcanal. She put it down to "the long burden of responsibility" her husband carried, which "has a share in the physical condition I am sure."[10]

The President's "physical condition," was far worse, however, than Eleanor seemed able or willing to confront directly. "FDR is not well," she'd acknowledged, but "I think we can keep him in good health," she'd assured her young friend, who admired Roosevelt immensely. It was just a matter of cutting down his workload — meaning that "he'll have to be more careful" in future.[11] She'd shown no emotion when told by Admiral McIntire about Dr. Bruenn's examination, and the visit of Drs. Paullin and Lahey — the first time in his twelve years as president that outside specialists had entered the White House[12] — but simply accepted McIntire's assurance there was nothing too serious to worry about.

Eleanor, to be sure, was not alone in such willful unconcern. In some ways it was as if, in the first few months of 1944, almost every close aide and subordinate who gathered around the Commander in Chief was pretending to himself or herself that the President's condition was nothing too serious. Thus, even as the President's blood pressure rose steadily into the 200s, and stayed there, reaching 226/118 despite digitalis and Bruenn's ministrations, no alarm bells were rung — the implications of the President's plummeting health simply attributed to flu, bronchitis, walking pneumonia, and the tensions and burdens of the office.

Not all were as lacking in perspicacity, however. Marquis Childs, a well-known columnist, had been allowed to visit with the President at the White House on April 7. In his notes that night the journalist recorded the President speaking "in a firm voice without hesitation. His face was sallow but he appeared in good health," despite "puffiness about the eyes." He was obviously ignoring his doctor's recommendation that he should quit or cut down on his smoking, though, for he smoked "two and perhaps three cigarettes" in the single hour that Childs was with him. On the other hand, in their conversation, the President seemed now "quite deaf," Childs recorded — or perhaps was not listening. "I had the impression of the man's curious aloneness," Childs added — as if Mr. Roosevelt, the father of the nation, had been left to his own devices in the White House.

In a sense, the President had been. In the previous four days he'd accepted only a single formal appointment! When Childs, at their interview, asked about the burden of his office, the President had been stunningly honest. "I wouldn't say burden. You see I don't work so hard any more. I've got this thing simplified . . . I imagine I don't work as many hours as you do."[13]

As a columnist? The President, in other words, was deliberately changing gears. At least for the moment he seemed content to coast along: allowing his trusted administration chiefs to run the country, and only interceding when he felt, or was advised, it was absolutely necessary.

For the President — and for his doctors — this was doubtless the most sensible way forward. But the implications for others were enormous — especially the military. The White House — the powerhouse and apex of American military strategy and command since Pearl Harbor — was going quiet. The Map Room was becoming more and more of an archive, a reference library — not the busy call center of civilization. The President hardly went into the room anymore, recalled the Map Room officer, Lieutenant Elsey[14] — who had asked if, given the relative inactivity, he might join the D-day naval invasion force currently assembling in Britain, and report back on the Allied landings once they took place.

With the D-day invasion now delayed to early June, the President's condition thus left the government of the United States strangely opaque — and vulnerable — at its highest echelon. There were few people who credited the U.S. vice president, Henry Wallace, with the necessary leadership qualities to take over direction of the war, if the President died of a heart attack or was felled by a stroke. And, given current polls showing a major swing of public opinion toward a Republican candidate in the looming presidential election if the President chose not to stand again, there appeared to be little or no chance of a Democrat nominee winning. Inevitably Franklin Delano Roosevelt, the magician of the Western Allies, would be begged to stand for reelection and guide the nation to victory in 1945 or 1946; he would not be permitted to back out. Nor, at the deepest level, was the President really prepared to do so. As Marquis Childs put it in his notes, "The habit of power had grown on him. He wanted to remain as commander [in chief] until the war was won."[15]

The same day as Child's visit, Dr. Paullin and Dr. Lahey had visited the President again. The effect of digitalis had been "spectacular," Bruenn later recalled.[16] Relieved to find the President looking a bit better and sounding better than he had the week before, though still appearing deathly ill, they now agreed — but with no public mention to be made of the decision — that Lieutenant Commander Bruenn should be transferred part-time from his post at Bethesda Naval Hospital to become, in essence, the President's new White House physician: accompanying him wherever he went, and administering the toxic yet effective treatment, while taking great care by daily electrocardiographic monitoring to ensure that it did not kill or incapacitate the President.

Surprisingly, Admiral McIntire did not seem put out by this change of roles. "He knew his shortcomings," Bruenn later reflected; "he wasn't particularly interested in internal medicine or cardiology. This was out of his field. He was perfectly willing to let somebody else take it over."[17]

The President also seemed pleased with the transfer of medical responsibility, for he *did* feel somewhat better, even though he had no illusions. With virtually no visitors allowed at the White House, so few hours spent working, and even meals taken on a tray in bed, it was uncomfortably like quarantine. When speaking with Frank Lahey, after Lahey and Dr. Paullin had both looked at the President's latest medical exam results, he'd greeted the famous surgeon with the words: "You have good news for me, Dr. Lahey?" Lahey had responded that he did indeed have news. But "Mr. President," he'd continued, "you may not care for what I have to say," Lahey later recalled. "That will be all, Dr. Lahey," the President had cut him off, before the eminent surgeon could say another word. The principle was enough; the rest were details.

The President must have talked things over with his widowed friend, however, for twice that week he left the White House secretly in the afternoon with his secretary Grace Tully, to go "motoring" for an hour or more — a euphemism for collecting Lucy from Georgetown in his car, outside her sister's house, and driving incognito in the area.

If Lucy was saddened by the President's dire condition, she was not put off. She'd nursed her husband through his last years of declining health; she was familiar with the approach of death. On the other hand she could see plainly that her very presence in the car, beside him, made the President feel as if he was walking on air — so happy was he to be in her company. And to be, at least for an hour, almost literally careless.

It was thus with Lucy's emotional and moral support — and the understanding they would visit each other in person while in South Carolina — that the ailing president left Washington by train at 9:30 in the evening on April 8, destination Hobcaw Barony, where he would stay, rest, and fish for a period of two weeks at least.

If he died in the interim he would at least die happy. If he survived, he would hopefully see the summation of his war strategy: the invasion he'd nurtured for two long years, parrying everything his own chiefs of staff had done to launch it prematurely, and the British had done to stop it, or delay it to 1945. An invasion he'd gotten the Russians to promise to support with a synchronized offensive on the Eastern Front that would make it impossible for Hitler to transfer German reserves to the west. An invasion whose Supreme allied commander he had personally chosen, despite the disappointment of General Marshall and Secretary Stimson. An invasion to be launched with the might of American air power, armor, artillery, and weapons that would enable Allied forces to fight their way on to Berlin.

44

The Hobcaw Barony

HOBCAW PROMISED WARM WEATHER, but most of all an "oasis of seren-
ity," as Baruch put it: an almost seventeen-thousand-acre former plantation.[1]
Its history had tickled Roosevelt's fancy, moreover. The "Barony" had been
granted by King George II to Lord Carteret, in an area situated alongside the
King's Highway, or main road, between Wilmington, in North Carolina, and
Charleston, South Carolina. It even boasted a British fort from the time of the
Revolutionary War, which Baruch wanted to show the President.

The President was not the first chief executive of the nation to visit Hobcaw.
Grover Cleveland, a governor of New York (like Roosevelt) and twice elected
to the U.S. presidency (like Roosevelt), had twice stayed at the property and
shot waterfowl there. The President was not up to holding a gun, though —
even had he been keen on the sport. He'd been wheeled off the *Magellan* and
driven along back roads by the Secret Service less to ensure his security than to
prevent him from being seen in his debilitated state. But a child by the plantation gate had seemed to recognize the ancient figure in the car. As Baruch later
recalled, the boy had shouted: "Gee! It's George Washington!'"[2]

Accompanying the President and his chief of staff had been only his White
House physician, Admiral McIntire; the masseur of his paralyzed legs, Lieu-
tenant Commander Fox; his naval and army aides, Vice Admiral Brown and
General Pa Watson; his communications officer, Lieutenant Rigdon; his valet,
Arthur Prettyman; and his bodyguard, Agent Fredericks. Also Fala, his little
black terrier. Dr. Bruenn would follow later.

Before leaving Washington the President had called his cousin Daisy, con-
fiding to her he'd changed his plans; he would now stay three or four weeks at
Hobcaw, given the one-month delay the British had caused in the launching
of D-day. He felt as if he had "sleeping-sickness of some sort," he was having
to take so many medications and was so little disposed to work, Daisy had
noted.[3]

· · ·

The whole medical business "depressed and bored" the President; unfortunately things proved no better at Hobcaw, on arrival, than they had been in Washington. The more he lost weight to ease the pressure on his heart, the more "haggard" he looked, as even his doctor admitted.[4] The weather remained cool. It rained. He had breakfast in his room at 9:30, sat in the sun, if conditions were right, at 11:00 a.m. Took lunch and then a nap, followed by some desultory fishing on the dock by the river. Only a single cocktail before dinner with his staff, then early to bed. In a scratchy hand he wrote to Daisy that he was "really feeling no good."[5]

For the commander in chief of more than ten million American soldiers, sailors, and airmen, and at a moment when the Western Allies were making their final preparations for the deciding battle and campaign of the war, it was a strange, almost otherworldly experience: as if he had already died and was now watching from afar. "Every day the bag would come in from the White House with the mail," Dr. Bruenn later described, "and all the papers would be signed. That took about half an hour or so and that was all the business that was done."[6]

Given that the President had, until then, been the energetic, dynamic conductor of an orchestra embracing the entire U.S. administration, as well as its military, the change was momentous, Dr. Bruenn later reflected. "You see, the President *was* the government," he told an interviewer. "He was his own Secretary of the Treasury, his own Secretary of State. He was running the works, including the war."[7]

It was a retrospective exaggeration, of course, yet it did convey a measure of the President's overriding authority as America's "boss," after three terms in office. Whether he could ever recover his magnetic, inspirational skills was doubtful, however — his doctors either forbidden to look into the crystal ball, or say too much about his current condition. In conversation with the President, Dr. Paullin had been more circumspect than Dr. Lahey. Searching for a metaphor, he likened his new patient to the driver of a once-fast car. It was the President's body that was showing "definite signs of wear and tear," after such a long career on the road. The car's engine was knocking. As Paullin had warned, "If you want to finish the journey, traveling the last ten thousand miles without mishap, you can't keep up any seventy-miles-an-hour clip . . . In plain words, you *must live within your reserve*." To this the President had responded, with his trademark laugh: "Well, I'll agree to quit burning up the road."

And he had. He'd reluctantly but dutifully agreed to Dr. McIntire's new regimen, in which he was to see virtually no visitors and do no more than four hours of work a day.[8]

Half an hour, resting at Hobcaw, was not even that.

• • •

It was perhaps a tribute to Roosevelt's choice of administration officials and selection of his military chiefs of staff that the President's absence from Washington did not result in a collapse of government, or a military mishap, other than the failure at Anzio, for which neither the President nor his chiefs of staff bore responsibility. D-day, though delayed as a result, was still on track — and arousing unprecedented hope and determination among the troops who were training to carry out the great operation. Thus, although men like Secretary Stimson had often cursed the managerial weakness of the Roosevelt administration owing to the President's uniquely personal approach to presidential leadership — keeping the ultimate reins of every department in his own hands, but refusing to have clear chains of command — the period before D-day passed off remarkably uneventfully in Washington. It seemed, in fact, as if the administration was running on a kind of autopilot.

With a presidential election looming later that year, however, autopilot was no guarantee of American victory. Could Vice President Henry Wallace take the reins? As the former secretary of agriculture and a former Republican, Wallace had deliberately been put forward (indeed insisted upon) by Roosevelt as his vice presidential nominee in 1940, thus garnering important constituencies in the election. But once world war had commenced for the United States following the attack on Pearl Harbor, Wallace, as chairman of the Board of Economic Warfare as well as the Supply Priorities and Allocation Board, had not prospered. He'd feuded with competing officials. In terms of the anti-Axis alliance, as an outspoken anticolonialist he hadn't been popular with Churchill, either; moreover he'd had the wool pulled over his eyes by the NKVD, Stalin's secret police, on a tour of Russia, it had transpired. And he was certainly not admired by his cabinet colleague Henry Stimson, whose role as secretary of war was critical, not least in bringing development of the atom bomb to combat readiness before the enemy did.

The likely Republican presidential nominee would be New York governor Tom Dewey. If he won the election in November, Dewey, at only forty-two, would become president in January 1945 — a man not regarded as the sort of national leader who, if the war was not over by then, could be trusted to head an international coalition of United Nations fighting the Axis powers. Thanks to the inevitable swing toward a Republican after three full terms of a Democrat in the White House, however, Dewey's chances of winning were growing stronger by the day — assuming, that is, Mr. Roosevelt declined to run. Ergo, Roosevelt, it was argued by many, would simply have to soldier on, despite his health issues.

Should — could — the President stand for a fourth term? This was the abiding, Hamletian question. The President, unfortunately, was still without advice from his loyal White House counselor and companion, Harry Hopkins, who, since Tehran, had been out of action, and out of state, passing the winter mostly in Florida — in and out of hospital with a suspected recurrence of stomach cancer.

As usual, however, the acerbic Hopkins put the conundrum most vividly. When his doctors finally decided by majority vote (5 to 3) to perform abdominal surgery on him once again, in April, Hopkins was heard to say, as he was taken into the Rochester Clinic operating theater: "O.K. boys, move right along. Open me up; maybe you will find the answer to the Fourth Term, or maybe not!"[9]

Maybe not.

Mercifully, after five days in early April the President began to feel somewhat better, even though he still looked a sight — his systolic blood pressure remaining over 200 — and continued to suffer stomach pain. On "the fifth evening he spent a while in the drawing room after dinner" instead of going to bed, Lieutenant Rigdon recorded.[10]

Admiral Leahy, on behalf of the President, stoically continued to deal with what he called in his diary the "unnecessary number of telegraphic messages from Washington and from the dispersed war areas" — messages to which, after discussing the more important ones with the President, "I send replies via the White House." These at least could be dispatched unsigned.[11]

Where the President's genuine signature was required, however, Mr. Roosevelt had to dictate replies to Lieutenant Rigdon, who was a stenographer, "whether he felt like working or not," as Rigdon noted with compassion.[12] It was clearly an unsatisfactory way of running a world war, yet the President was the President; it was up to him to discover how much he could really manage, despite the strain on his heart. Meantime, it was important he should not be seen by anyone in his current state of physical dilapidation. The press — a group of White House correspondents staying at an inn in nearby Georgetown, South Carolina — were therefore kept strictly away, to their disappointment and no little skeptical curiosity about not being permitted anywhere close to Hobcaw. As Admiral McIntire later admitted, though, this deception necessarily came at the price of open democracy. It didn't really work, however — for the President's very absence from Washington, and word of his health issues rippling through the city's press corps, merely gave rise to wild speculation. It was "during the South Carolina stay, when bronchitis was the President's one and only trouble apart from fatigue," Admiral McIntire later wrote, still bluffing, "that the country filled with every variety of wild and reckless lie about his physical condition."[13]

Dr. Bruenn, who'd had to reorganize his department at Bethesda Naval Hospital so that he could join the President, arrived on April 17. The President's "blood pressure remained elevated," he wrote in his clinical notes; in fact it exceeded 230 over 126. His "heart remained enlarged," Bruenn openly admitted.[14] This necessitated giving still-higher doses of digitalis, which in turn affected the President's digestion: a seesaw of ills between his chest and stomach. The President nevertheless forced himself to sit with General Mark Clark on April 18, on a trip home the exhausted general had made at General Marshall's insistence — Marshall wanting both to give moral support to his top American combat commander in the Mediterranean, in the wake of the Anzio fiasco, and for the President to hear, firsthand, "the present military situation in his area," as Leahy recorded in his diary.[15]

Writing after the war, Clark recalled how the President "showed a surprising knowledge of details, and was quick to offer ideas as I explained our plans for reaching Rome"[16] — for Roosevelt well remembered the Anzio stretch of coast south of the capital from his childhood. It was not the same president who'd awarded Clark the DSC in the field in Sicily, only four months earlier. Nor could the President offer any encouragement in terms of an advance north of Rome, once the city was reached — for Roosevelt and Leahy both felt that mounting Anvil in southern France, in order to help support D-day and the march across France, was the only real way to defeat the Third Reich. Italy would essentially be a holding front, to keep Wehrmacht forces away from the main theater.

By April 21, however, the President did feel physically well enough to go on an excursion to the nearby Arcadia Plantation. On the twenty-second the President's little fishing party cast their rods from a patrol boat, some fifteen miles into the Atlantic. The catch of bluefish and bonito was excellent, and the "President thoroughly enjoyed" the afternoon, Leahy recorded, as of an invalid — which, in effect, the President now was.[17] A trip to Myrtle Beach followed, by car, then Belle Isle Gardens, and on April 25[18] Mrs. Roosevelt, her daughter Anna, and Anna's husband, John Boettiger, as well as John Curtin, the Australian prime minister, and his wife, and the president of Costa Rica, all arrived by air from Washington — staying only for the afternoon. It was Eleanor's first and only visit to see her husband in South Carolina — and all the failing president could manage, for he was husbanding his modestly reviving strength for another visitor: Lucy Rutherfurd.

Together with her stepdaughter, stepdaughter-in-law, and her stepgrandson, Mrs. Rutherfurd arrived on April 28 from her own estate at Aiken, 140 miles away — Bernard Baruch having even surrendered his gas ration so they could make the drive. For, as Baruch saw it as the President's friend and financial adviser over many years, it was Lucy Rutherfurd's job to try and cheer up the President at the luncheon. Which, gracefully, Lucy did immediately, seated at his right — Franklin having personally sketched the seating arrangement before the party even arrived.[19]

Baruch, handsome and genial at seventy-three, sat at the other end of the table. Even the President's long-awaited tryst did not last long, for at 1:30, while they were having dessert, news came that the secretary of the U.S. Navy, Frank Knox, had died of a heart attack.

Neither Admiral McIntire nor Lieutenant Commander Bruenn was in favor of the President traveling back to Washington for the funeral. Especially when, that afternoon, the President had another gastric attack, involving "stomach pains, nausea and tremors."[20] Dr. Bruenn was able to give the President an injection of codeine, so that he could at least meet briefly with three of the reporters staying in nearby Georgetown.

In the sitting room at Hobcaw the President was able to give them, in person, a statement they could publish, honoring Knox's service to his country. Moreover he related to the reporters how, when "Mr. Knox came to the White House and announced to him that the Japanese had attacked Pearl Harbor" on December 7, 1941, the navy secretary had said immediately: "With your permission I'm leaving in the morning." The President had asked Knox where on earth he intended to go. When the navy secretary had said Hawaii, the President "asked him what he could do there." Mr. Knox had replied: "At least I can find out a great deal more than here." Within two days the secretary had reached Honolulu, the President told the reporters, and on the third day he'd telephoned "to report to the President, and to suggest to him that he organize an investigating group right away—not experts but common sense people who have the confidence of the country. The President said he followed the suggestion of the secretary in naming [Supreme Court] Justice [Owen] Roberts to head the Pearl Harbor investigating board. The episode, the President related, was typical of Knox."[21]

It was also typical of the President—his story encapsulating one of Knox's finest hours. The President sounded unusually emotional. Had his own altercation with the Reaper, the month before, turned out differently, he might have preceded Colonel Knox—who had suffered a major heart attack—to the grave. "I've been told people of superior breeding never let their emotions come to the surface publicly," one of the journalists, Merriman Smith of United Press, later recalled of the President's closeness to tears as he told the story—his grief unusually visible.[22]

Meantime Dr. Bruenn, alarmed by the severity of the President's abdominal pain, wanted an exam performed to check for gallstones, in Washington, as soon as possible. Even this he recognized was simply out of the question, however, until the President's heart condition improved.

How, then, could the President *think* of running for reelection—something that would require strenuous travel, public appearances, and the whole panoply of a presidential campaign? It seemed inconceivable. And unnecessary, in terms of public sympathy for his plight; his doctors (other than Admiral McIntire) would have happily explained to the world why it was impossible, lest the President keel over like Secretary Knox, and die on the hustings.

Daisy Suckley arrived at Hobcaw on May 4, to help take care of the President and provide feminine company. Under "his tan" he "looks thin & drawn & not a bit well," she noted in her diary — adding he "feels good-for-nothing, had just had some sort of an 'attack 'which seems to be in the upper part of the abdomen. He says they don't know what is the matter with him" — or that they didn't want "to tell him."[23]

But the President already knew.

45

A Dual-Purpose Plan

ROOSEVELT STAYED AT HOBCAW till May 6, 1944. In his final weeks there his health had seemed to improve a little — the President "in a much better physical condition than at the time of his arrival," Admiral Leahy summarized in his diary the day they departed by train back to Washington.[1]

The next morning, May 7, the President was in the White House once again — free to see Lucy. His blood pressure remained high, but his stomach seemed temporarily at peace.

In Washington there was no shortage of people now urging Roosevelt to commit to a fourth term, however — including Robert Hannegan, chair of the Democratic National Committee. In his capacity as the President's physician, Lieutenant Commander Bruenn was appalled, yet fatalistic. He later recalled not only the President's high blood pressure, but the "pressure" that was "put on him to run for the fourth term. All those people around him depended on the President exclusively for their jobs, for their reputations, everything. I'm not only talking about the secretaries but such people as Steve Early, the press secretary, everybody. The President was the center pole, no question about it. He wasn't particularly anxious to run," Bruenn recalled with compassion. Roosevelt felt he'd done his job — that he'd deserved a rest, now that the war was on clear course to victory, hopefully by the end of the year in Europe, at least. Yet the issue of running for reelection remained a moral one for him, rather than medical, and "he never asked any questions" or the advice of his doctor.[2]

To maintain the public fiction of bronchitis, if he did decide to run, Mc-Intire would not permit Bruenn to be photographed with the President, let alone be seen visiting his patient. The lieutenant commander was expected to continue running his electrocardiology department at the Bethesda Naval Hospital, without his colleagues even being aware of his "temporary additional duty."[3] None of the President's advisers Bruenn did meet at the White House, indeed no one there, "asked me whether he should run or not," he recalled. "I was Mr. Anonymous most of the time" — though he was given a car so that he could "drive down in the morning" from Bethesda to the White House "and see him, then go back to work at the hospital."[4]

The President "never asked me a question about the medications I was giving him, what his blood pressure was, nothing. He was not interested," Bruenn recalled — the President seemingly content to leave that aspect of his life in others' hands.[5] And though Bruenn had undoubtedly saved the President's life in March, not all of his efforts had a salutary effect, at least in terms of side effects. Overdigitalization wreaked havoc with the President's sense of taste and digestion, while Bruenn's urging him to lose weight was a double-edged sword — the President's weight being all in his upper body, leaving "nothing" in his paralyzed legs, which resembled sticks more than ever. The treatment had certainly taken stress off the President's heart, but "some of it came off his face" also, Bruenn admitted in retrospect. As a result "he began to look haggard. And then we had a job trying to get him to eat again."[6]

Privately Bruenn was of two minds about whether the President should run. "I must say, in all honesty, if I had been asked what my opinion or judgment was," he later reflected, "I would have been greatly swayed by the circumstances. Here we were in the middle of a great war, which had been conducted fortunately or unfortunately on an almost personal basis between Stalin, Churchill, and Roosevelt."[7] To take Roosevelt out of the equation seemed . . . unwise.

The President, for his part, remained equally unsure. Eleanor was of little help — not for lack of compassion, but because she was herself under constant stress. Her attitude toward his plummeting health thus remained one of distant concern. As First Lady and mother of a large family, she had never had time for sickness in the family. "She had a toughness about physical ailments, always minimizing her own," her friend Joe Lash would later write — quoting a letter she'd written, a few days after her visit to Hobcaw, in which she'd claimed "F. looks well but said he still has no 'Pep.'" Yet Eleanor, uniquely among those close to the President, had seen no cause for alarm — it was more tiredness and stress than anything, she thought. "He ought soon to get well," she predicted, if he would only follow her advice and go to Hyde Park, where he could rest, spending only "two or three days a month" in the White House "during the summer months."[8]

In the midst of a world war?

By constrast Mrs. Rutherfurd, who had nursed her husband through his last years, could read the dark signs in her visits with the President. Yet she, too, saw no way out of his standing again for election. Declining to serve, in war, seemed somehow like cowardice.

The President, in any event, spent as little time as possible in Washington. D-day was scheduled for early June, to take advantage of the tides. He had no wish to interfere — as reports from London indicated Churchill was doing, yet again. The Prime Minister was said to be a bundle of nerves, alternately excited and depressed—in fact the ground forces commander, General Montgomery, threatened to resign unless the Prime Minister stopped trying to meddle in matters over which he not only had no idea, but threatened to break the chain of command.[9]

D-day was now in the hands of the combat commanders and their men. Field Marshal Brooke might express contempt, in his diary, for the President's choice of supreme commander—a post earlier promised to Brooke. General Eisenhower was "a swinger and no real director of thought, plans, energy or direction! Just a coordinator—a good mixer, a champion of inter-allied cooperation," Brooke noted sourly after attending the final rehearsal of D-day plans in London on May 15.[10] It was a monstrously obtuse comment, since with almost electric energy Eisenhower and Montgomery had in four months transformed a plan over which Brooke had backpedaled since its inception, failing to give it the priority and support that he, the head of the British Army, should have provided. By the time Eisenhower and Montgomery had taken charge, even Overlord's own Anglo-American planning staffs were predicting defeat.[11]

Fortunately Ike and Monty, not Brooke—or Churchill—would decide the battle.

In Washington, thousands of miles away, there was meanwhile increasing anticipation and nerves—which the President did his best to ignore. In some respects his heart condition and reduced workload rendered him mercifully immune. He now had the utmost confidence in Eisenhower, in his combat generals, and in his American forces. Ever since the reversal at Kasserine they had been learning what worked, and what didn't, against a formidable enemy. In Normandy there were no mountains or high ground, mercifully, to contend with; American armor would be free, once ashore, to confront the Wehrmacht, backed by huge air power and naval guns. He was sure they would acquit themselves well, and he had no wish to provide anything but encouragement to the supreme commander he had personally appointed.

On May 11, 1944, the President motored to Shangri-la, his retreat in Maryland's Catoctin Mountains, with Anna and Colonel John Boettiger, her husband, and only returned on May 15, full of confidence in the outcome of the invasion—telling Admiral Leahy, in fact, to look into the possibility of his crossing the Atlantic once the D-day landings had, hopefully, secured a firm bridgehead in northern France. He also wanted to go on an "inspection cruise to Alaska and Honolulu leaving Washington July 23 for Seattle, thence by destroyers to Alaska, by Cruiser to Pearl Harbor and return via San Diego, Los Angeles and San Francisco, reaching Washington about 20 August."[12]

France? Hawaii? Alaska?

Admiral Leahy was both puzzled and amazed at the President's new plans. Normandy posed too many dangers for a presidential trip. But with the U.S.

Joint Chiefs in undisguised disagreement over future strategy in the Pacific (currently divided into two theaters: the Central Pacific under Admiral Nimitz, and the Southwest Pacific under General MacArthur), only the President, as commander in chief, could resolve the impasse. And in theory the best way for the President to cut the Gordian knot would be to go out to the Pacific and meet with his two top commanders there. If his health allowed.

The President was never simple to decipher, however, as Leahy knew. The upcoming Democratic convention to choose a presidential candidate would hold its ballot of delegates in Chicago on July 20. Was the proposed trip along the West Coast, before and after the President's return from Honolulu, for military reasons — or *political*? Sitting with the President in the Oval Office, Leahy delicately asked the projected trip's "bearing on the approaching political campaign."

"The President replied with much feeling," Leahy noted in his diary: "'Bill, I just hate to run again for election. Perhaps the war will by that time have progressed to a point that will make it unnecessary for me to be a candidate.'"[13] But if not, he would run for a fourth term.

Leahy, who'd accompanied the President to Hobcaw and back home, was stunned. "While I have long been sure that the President would like to retire from his present office," Roosevelt's chief of staff noted, "this is the first time he has expressed himself to me clearly in regard to his attitude toward renomination."[14]

The next day the President went on to clarify his plans. He dropped all notion of flying or sailing to Britain — unwilling to face Churchill's likely demands that, with the impending breakout of Mark Clark's forces from Cassino toward Rome, the President's Anvil landings should be scrapped and more Allied punch be put into Italy. Not wanting to confront yet another Churchillian machination, the President decided he would stay put in the United States. As soon as the D-day landings had been launched, and were successful, he would go in the opposite direction. He would take the *Magellan* to Chicago with Admiral Leahy, then continue across the country to San Diego. From there he would sail to Pearl Harbor, returning via the Aleutians.

The President had, in other words, an itinerary in mind. A dual-purpose plan of how, in very limited health, he would not only decide Allied strategy in the Pacific "on the spot" — deciding which should be the main axis of advance to ensure the defeat of Japan — but would, if asked, agree to stand for the presidency a fourth time: though only as current U.S. commander in chief in war, without time to commit to campaigning. He would thus be — like Hitler — largely out of public sight.

Assuming, of course, D-day proved a success. And his health held.

46

D-day

D-DAY — DELAYED UNTIL the necessary landing craft were *in situ* — now loomed larger and more fatefully than ever. "How that event hangs over us — has been hanging over us, for months," Daisy Suckley noted in her diary on May 19 at Hyde Park. The President seemed relatively better — but "relative" was a big word. He "seems pretty well but not right yet," she added truthfully,[1] and almost every day she worried about his demeanor. He looked "tired, and his color is not good" on May 22; "very tired at dinner" on May 26; "seems tired" on June 4.[2]

Fewer than eight days in the lead-up to the D-day invasion were spent at the White House of the twenty-two — the President staying either at Hyde Park, or Shangri-la, or at the hundred-acre estate of his longtime military aide, General Pa Watson, at Charlottesville, Virginia. The tan he'd acquired at Hobcaw had long faded. "From my observations of these last 2–3 weeks," Daisy summed up, "it looks to me this way: Two or three or four days in Wash.[ington], when he is rather keyed up," and which "get him over-tired. He gets away, & for the first 2 or 3 days it is a question of getting relaxed. The next day or two he is getting rested, & then the whole process is repeated — Just how long this is to continue only time can tell," she penned. If the good spells were to outweigh the bad, "he will be all right, otherwise he will get sick again."[3]

Why run again for the presidency, then? When Daisy asked whom he would choose as his vice president, Roosevelt was coy. "I haven't even decided if I will run myself," he asserted — suggesting that a gung ho, no-nonsense character like the shipbuilder Henry Kaiser would be a better choice as president, for he'd be tougher and more like "the Churchills, Stalins, etc" of the world.[4]

This was typical Franklin Roosevelt — two steps forward, one back. But when Daisy pressed him and asked what, then, "is going to decide you," given that he was pretty much nominated by common consent of the Democratic Party, he admitted it was his health that would decide the matter. For, as he put it, "it wouldn't be fair to the American people to run for another four years" if he knew he couldn't "carry on" for a full term.[5]

Fair? For a full term?

This, too, was typical FDR — for he knew he had no hope of actually recovering, given his heart condition. In fact it was highly questionable whether he would make it to the end of his *current* term, let alone be well enough to undertake a new one. Two hours of appointments in the morning, and that only when working — which was only a third part of every month? Half an hour's correspondence in the afternoon? Could such a part-time position, by any stretch of the imagination, be considered a valid U.S. presidency — and in wartime? Compared with the responsibilities he'd carried over the past eleven years, the notion was a joke. And yet: as Daisy herself noted, by taking so much time off and limiting his workload to bare essentials, "he is getting slowly but steadily better," she felt (or convinced herself) — something that caused her to "hope and fear, with millions throughout the country, that he will run for a fourth term. The world needs him."[6]

Eleanor felt the same way. She spent only two days with him that month, and at Hyde Park — Daisy noting they were "the first two days they have been alone together for years." But it was Lucy who really counted.

The President had seen Mrs. Rutherfurd again, collecting her from her sister's house in Georgetown and taking her motoring. It was Lucy who persuaded him he must stand. He had become a symbol of hope and purpose, across the world. Referring to the endless burdens of his presidential office in an undated letter (the only letter that would survive posthumous attempts to conceal the relationship, after the war),[7] Lucy had addressed Franklin as "poor darling." She'd ended her missive with a sad reflection. "I know one should be proud — very proud of your greatness instead of wishing for the soft life, with the world shut out," she admitted. "One is proud and thankful for what you have given the world and realizes how much more must still be given this greedy world — which never asks in vain."[8]

This was now a destiny, in the midst of a global struggle, he could simply not walk away from. "You have breathed new life into its spirit — and the fate of all that is good is in your dear & capable hands."[9]

Lucy, in short, expected him to do the right thing by the nation, indeed by the world. And thus, despite all his qualms, the President accepted his fate. In the meantime, D-day grew closer. After meeting with a group of forty congressmen in the Oval Office, and dining quietly with his daughter Anna and her husband, John, as well as Daisy, the President was wheeled into the Diplomatic Reception Room on June 5, 1944, to address the nation.

Not about D-day, however — which was being launched at that very moment, he knew, via the Map Room — but about Italy.

"Yesterday, June 4th, Rome fell to American and Allied troops," the President began in a firm voice — his face, on film, looking lined, the skin beneath his eyes dark, and his neck unusually scrawny as he sat hunched forward at the microphones placed on his desk. Behind him stretched shelves filled with leather-bound tomes.

The Eternal City had been liberated, he announced, "by the armed forces of many Nations" — American and British armies foremost, but "gallant" Canadians, too, as well as "fighting" New Zealanders, "courageous French," and "French Moroccans, South Africans, Poles and East Indians" also — all of them fighting "with us on the bloody approaches to the city of Rome." Rome, the "great symbol" not only of the Roman empire in classical times, but latterly the "seat of Fascism." And of "Christianity, which has reached into almost every part of the world." Italy was, as the President put it, "a great mother nation," one which across the centuries had furnished "leaders in the arts and sciences" — "Gallileo and Marconi, Michelangelo and Dante" — thus "enriching the lives of all mankind." He was convinced the Italian people, following the unconditional surrender of their government the year before, would soon be a "peace-loving nation," and were capable of democratic "self-government" — in fact, some Italian forces, after the surrender of their government to the Allies, were now contributing to the "battles against the German trespassers on their soil." [10]

This brought Roosevelt to military strategy in Europe. "From a military standpoint," the President explained as America's commander in chief, "we had long ago accomplished certain of the main objectives of our Italian campaign": "the control of the sea lanes of the Mediterranean to shorten our combat and supply lines, and the capture of the airports of Foggia from which we have struck telling blows on the continent." Italy, in other words, was not the objective.

Reading the transcript in London, Churchill would, the President knew, be made uncomfortable. The advance on Rome, the "first of the Axis capitals" to fall, was a significant achievement, certainly, in that it had forced Hitler to send more forces south "at great cost of men and materials to their crumbling Eastern line and their Western front." But it "would be unwise," the President cautioned listeners, "to inflate in our own minds the military importance of the capture of Rome."

The fact was, the forces of the United Nations had not, in all candor, inflicted sufficient losses on the Third Reich "to cause collapse" of Hitler's Third Reich. Unlike the Italians, who had folded their hand upon Allied invasion, "Germany has not been driven to surrender. Germany has not yet been driven to the point where she will be unable to recommence world conquest a generation hence. Therefore, the victory still lies some distance ahead," the President warned. "We shall have to push through a long period of greater effort and fiercer fighting before we get to Germany itself. The distance will be covered in due time — have no fear of that. But it will be tough and it will be costly, as I have told you many, many times."[11]

At that very moment tens of thousands of Allied paratroopers were already in the air above the English Channel, and even more troops — almost 150,000 — were embarked in vessels crossing the 120-mile expanse of stormy water. Upon that landing, he was aware, hinged the fate of Europe and the world.

He went to bed shortly after 11:00 p.m., but did not sleep. "No word yet of the invasion," noted his cousin Daisy — who was staying at the White House — "which the P. says is starting tonight."[12]

Forty-five minutes after midnight an announcement came on the radio "from Germany" — monitored in Washington — that the invasion had begun, Daisy began her diary entry for Tuesday, June 6, 1944.

A few minutes later, "German radio says landing forces are battling at Le Havre, that German warships are fighting Allied landing craft. No Allied confirmation." There were reports, too, that Calais and Dunkirk, in the Pas-de-Calais, were being attacked by strong Allied bomber formations — but that no seaborne troops had yet been landed there. "'They say' it might be," Daisy recorded, "an Allied feint."[13]

It was. Around 3:00 a.m. Eastern Time in America, Supreme Allied Headquarters in Portsmouth, England, gave out a statement that was broadcast on radio. "Under the command of General Eisenhower, Allied naval forces, supported by strong air forces, began landing Allied armies this morning on the northern coast of France."[14]

It was now official.

Whether the invasion would succeed — especially in view of the almost gale-strength weather over the English Channel — was uncertain. In his pocket, when walking from his sleeping trailer to Southwick House, his forward headquarters near Portsmouth, General Eisenhower had a folded sheet of paper announcing — if it came to that — the failure of the invasion.

The President, receiving reports sent up by the Map Room and listening to the radio in his bedroom, could do nothing. Eventually he too went to sleep, knowing the coming day would be strenuous — General Marshall and his fellow Joint Chiefs of Staff coming to see him, as arranged, at the White House at 11:30 a.m.

Had he made the right decision in appointing young General Dwight Eisenhower to command the operation?

The President knew from his own sources there had been nasty arguments over the bombing of the bridges, railways, and coastal areas of northern France, given the inevitable French civilian casualties this would entail. The British, for their part, were understandably concerned over the reverse: namely the concrete launch ramps that had appeared in profusion near the French coast, ready to unleash Hitler's dreaded revenge weapons, or V-1 flying bombs. To Eisenhower's frustration the RAF had in fact recently been directed to divert major resources to put them out of action — almost ruining the Allied "Transportation Plan" to interdict Wehrmacht reinforcements that would be sent to meet the landings. The President had turned down Churchill's requests to intervene, however, and had backed Eisenhower to the hilt.[15] Churchill had been compelled to accede — still desperately hoping that, despite his cable to the President only two weeks earlier about his "hardening" to the Overlord project,[16] matters in Italy would crown his months of hope, four and a half months since launching Anzio; and that he could, at the very least, get the Anvil invasion definitively canceled, thereby releasing landing craft for further ventures in the Mediterranean.

All the President could meantime say to newspaper and radio correspondents as they collected in the Oval Office at 4:10 that historic afternoon was: "I think the arrangements seem to be going all right . . . Up to schedule."[17]

The Oval Office was crammed tight with a multitude of reporters, secretaries, and assistants sitting cross-legged around his desk — some 180 of them, "jammed" in, as the White House press secretary remarked.[18] It was the President's 954th such meeting — one he began with the very latest dispatch from General Eisenhower, reporting the loss of just two destroyers and one LST (tank landing ship), and barely 1 percent air losses.

Asked how long he had known the date of the planned invasion, the President confided the approximate date had been settled at Tehran, but the exact date "just within the past few days," owing to the awful weather. He had, however, been informed, even as he made his broadcast the night before on the fall of Rome, "that the troops were actually in the boats — in the vessels — on the way across" to France. Asked why it had required six months since Tehran to mount the landings, he questioned his questioner. Had he ever seen the English Channel?

On hearing he hadn't, the President explained how "roughness" was the simple answer — "considered by passengers one of the greatest trials of life, to have to cross the English Channel." It was therefore "one of the greatly desirable and absolutely essential things" to be sure — like Julius Caesar and later Duke William, the Norman conqueror of Britain, who had abandoned his first attempt — of "relatively small-boat weather, as we call it, to get people actually onto the beach. And such weather doesn't begin much before May."[19] With that he finally confided to them that D-day had actually been postponed by a further day, precisely because of the unpredictable weather.

Gently, the President also explained why "we didn't institute a second front a year ago" when "politicians and others" began "clamoring for it." It was "because their plea for an immediate Second Front last year reminds me a good deal of that famous editor and statesman who said years ago, before most of you were born, during the Wilson administration, 'I am not worried about the defense of America. If we are threatened, a million men will spring to arms overnight.' And of course, somebody said, 'What kind of arms? If you can't arm them, then what's the good of their springing to something that ain't there'?"[20]

He had, in other words, delayed the invasion until the United States was ready — in arms, and in battle-hardened men and commanders. The military strategy of a Second Front, he shared with his audience, went back to December 1941 — in fact to the Victory Plan — a leaked copy of which the isolationist Republican publisher of the *Chicago Tribune*, Robert McCormick, had, in an act of rank treason, deliberately revealed in order to try and embarrass the administration. "But there were so many other things that had to be done, and so little in the way of trained troops and munitions to do it with, we have had to wait to do it," he explained, off the record — the matter coming "to a head — the final determination — in Cairo and Teheran. I think it's safe to say that." Indeed he even proceeded to share with them how, although Stalin had been "yelling for a second front" (as one questioner phrased it), the Russian premier's "mind was entirely cleared up at Teheran, when he understood the problem of going across the Channel; and when this particular time" — originally intended to be May 1, 1944 — "was arrived at and agreed on at Teheran, he was entirely satisfied."[21]

Which brought the President back to what he had warned against in his broadcast the previous evening: overconfidence. D-day had now begun; the "whole country is tremendously thrilled" — "a very reasonable thrill," certainly, but "I hope very much that there will not be again too much over-confidence, because over-confidence destroys the war effort." It was "the thing we have got to avoid in this country. The war isn't over by any means. This operation isn't over by any means. This operation isn't over. You don't just land on a beach and walk through to Berlin. And the quicker this country understands it the better."[22]

The President was asked how he was feeling. Since he had been up most of the night, he said "I'm a little sleepy."[23] Amid laughter this ended the historic press conference.

He wasn't going to be able to rest, however — for there was one more thing he needed to do that night: give his own version of King Henry V's Saint Crispin's Day speech in Shakespeare's famous play, but this time as a prayer.

Wisely, while at the Watson estate at Charlottesville, Virginia, the previous weekend, together with his daughter Anna and her husband, the President had asked the general, his host, to help him draft a radio address.[24] Since General

Eisenhower would probably make a military announcement as soon as the landings took place but before the outcome was clear, the Boettigers had suggested the broadcast take the form of a prayer.

It was an inspired idea — one the President had never tried before. True, he had often pronounced his Christian faith in public, and without inhibition. A proud Episcopalian by birth and upbringing, he saw Catholics very much as fellow Christians. He respected the pope as a spiritual leader, and had been a good friend to the archbishop of New York, Cardinal Spellman, for many years. In February 1940 he'd openly and "heartily deprecated" Nazi and Soviet "banishment" of religion — knowing, though, "that some day Russia would return to religion for the simple reason that four or five thousand years of recorded history have proven that mankind had always believed in God in spite of many abortive attempts to banish God."[25] Later that same year he'd written that, "in teaching this democratic faith to American children, we need the sustaining, buttressing aid of those great ethical religious teachings which are the heritage of our modern civilization. For 'not upon strength nor upon power, but upon the spirit of God' shall our democracy be founded."[26]

"Without any questions, *he* writes his speeches," Daisy had noted in her diary — "Whoever 'helps him' is doing the 'mechanical' part, possibly suggesting a helpful phrase, reminding about a small point, etc. The P. is just as ready to accept a suggestion that sounds right, as he is to reject it if he doesn't agree with the other person. His clarity of mind is amazing, as is his open-mindedness."[27]

Having made his final revisions, and with Anna at his side and Daisy present, the President delivered his latest radio address from the Diplomatic Reception Room at 8:30 p.m. on June 6, 1944, as troops of the United Nations hunkered down for the night ten miles inland from the shores of Normandy. Leaving the dead to be buried behind them, the survivors had battled their way across five main beaches and established a thin but firm series of beachheads between Ouistreham and Grandcamp — noncontiguous beachheads stretching sixty miles along the coast, which needed to be stitched together before the great battle could be fought to victory. Or stalemate; perhaps defeat. Either way, it would decide the war in Europe.

"My fellow Americans," the President began — his voice slow, measured, a trifle sad. "Last night when I spoke with you about the fall of Rome, I knew that at that moment troops of the United States and our Allies were crossing the Channel in another and greater operation."[28] There were long gaps in his delivery, as if the President were not reading but speaking from the very depth of his ailing heart, and as a fellow parent. "In this poignant hour I ask you to join me in a prayer," he asked — a prayer he proceeded to read even more slowly: thoughtfully, compassionately, humbly. Several sentences he'd deleted, some words he'd added at the last moment, and a number of phrases he'd compressed, during the day: "our religion" had been inserted before "our civilization," and "a suffering humanity" had taken the place of "millions of other human beings." "Rent by noise and flames" he'd used to replace "split by fire of many cannon." "Terrible violences" had been cut to just "violences."

The effect was spellbinding in its almost funereal resignation to the prospect, and necessity, of killing on such a vast scale, in order to prevent more killing on an even vaster one:

> Almighty God: Our sons, pride of our Nation, this day have set upon a mighty endeavor, a struggle to preserve our Republic, our religion, and our civilization, and to set free a suffering humanity.
>
> Lead them straight and true; give strength to their arms, stoutness to their hearts, steadfastness in their faith.
>
> They will need Thy blessings. Their road will be long and hard. For the enemy is strong. He may hurl back our forces. Success may not come with rushing speed, but we shall return again and again; and we know that by Thy grace, and by the righteousness of our cause, our sons will triumph.
>
> They will be sore tried, by night and by day, without rest — until the victory is won. The darkness will be rent by noise and flame. Men's souls will be shaken with the violences of war.
>
> For these men are lately drawn from the ways of peace. They fight not for the lust of conquest. They fight to end conquest. They fight to liberate. They fight to let justice arise, and tolerance and good will among all Thy people. They yearn but for the end of battle, for their return to the haven of home.
>
> Some will never return. Embrace these, Father, and receive them, Thy heroic servants, into Thy kingdom.
>
> And for us at home — fathers, mothers, children, wives, sisters, and brothers of brave men overseas — whose thoughts and prayers are ever with them — help us, Almighty God, to rededicate ourselves in renewed faith in Thee in this hour of great sacrifice.

The President's D-day Prayer, as it would become known, ended not with the first-drafted phrase "So be it," but with another. Words this time from the Lord's Prayer: "Thy will be done, Almighty God. Amen."[29]

47

The Deciding Dice of War

AT THE BERGHOF there had been no prayers, no press conferences or radio addresses. Hitler had slept until midday on June 6, after staying up half the night talking to Dr. Goebbels.

Goebbels had arrived at Berchtesgaden the day before. He'd come straight from Nuremberg — the great gathering place of the Nazi Party in the 1930s, as filmed by Leni Riefenstahl in her documentary peon to Hitler, *Triumph of the Will*. There, in the medieval city, Goebbels had given a one-hour speech at the Adolf-Hitler-Platz, before an ecstatic crowd estimated at sixty to seventy thousand. The propaganda minister was now looking forward to seeing the Führer.

Hitler looked "radiant," Goebbels noted in his diary, after arriving, moreover seemed in great good humor — unfazed by the fall of Rome, which he thought completely insignificant in terms of the war, which he believed would be "decided in the West," i.e., in France. "I'm so pleased the Führer sees things so realistically and down-to-earth," Goebbels went on. "Were he to become discouraged, it would have a calamitous effect on his staff, and on the whole nation. Thank God that's not the case. In any case, the [Italian] Fascists have given away their spiritual and political center. People are saying Mussolini's authority has reached bottom with the fall of Rome." Had the Italians fought to defend Sicily, the summer before, none of this would have happened, of course. "We need to be clear," Goebbels concluded: "we Germans alone have the power to defend Europe against the plutocracies and Bolshevism."[1]

As far as the impending Allied invasion of France was concerned, though, the Führer was "full of confidence." Field Marshal Rommel, who had telephoned several days before and was hoping to visit the Führer from his home in Bavaria the next day, had "filled him with high hopes"[2] — such high hopes, in fact, that Goebbels admitted to being a trifle skeptical. For in the mountains of the Obersalzberg on June 5, the Führer seemed eerily remote from conditions in northern France. "Up here one only sees the war in its highest direction; the middle and lower echelons are virtually absent," Dr. Goebbels noted.[3]

Their talk, over lunch that day, had wandered over art and theater, as well as the postwar, "showing the Führer's bigness of mind and extraordinarily deep imagination. He is now convinced it will be impossible to come to an arrangement with Britain. He thinks England is doomed and he has decided, if he has the opportunity, to give it the kiss of death. I'm not clear how, but in the past he's put forward thousands of plans that seemed absurd, but which came to pass." The two men walked down to the Berghof teahouse, alone. Goebbels was driven back to Berchtesgaden, but had returned for dinner in the Berghof, after which he and the Führer had watched the latest official newsreel, and had talked more about movies and theater — Hitler's mistress, Fräulein Braun, impressing Goebbels with her insight and critical judgment. They had sat together till 2:00 a.m. in the lounge, exchanging memories, the Führer asking "about this and that. In short, it was just like the old days."[4]

But these were not the old days. At 10:00 p.m. on June 5 reports had already been received from Wehrmacht headquarters in Berchtesgaden that Allied radio transmissions indicated the great invasion might at last be beginning. "I didn't at first take them seriously," Goebbels noted frankly in his diary. When he'd finally left the Berghof and reached Berchtesgaden — after staying several hours at the home of Martin Bormann, head of the Nazi Party Chancellery and secretary of the Führer, on the way — he found the reports were being confirmed. If so, then "the deciding day of this war has dawned," he recorded in his diary. It was June 6, 1944. "I snatch a couple of hours of sleep — for I expect the coming day will bring plenty of cares and problems."[5]

Goebbels was not wrong in his assessment of Hitler's mood, and improved health. The months of rest and mountain air seemed to have done wonders, both for the Führer's body and for his morale. When Goebbels joined him on the afternoon of June 6 at Klessheim Castle for a visit by the Hungarian prime minister, Döme Sztójay, the Führer seemed delighted the invasion had begun in earnest. The fact that, according to monitoring of BBC radio, Mr. Churchill had already that afternoon in Parliament boasted of a victory was considered a sign of weakness. After all, the Prime Minister had congratulated himself and his armies at the start of the great battle for Crete in the spring of 1941 — and had lived to regret it, when the Wehrmacht had trounced the British within days. Since then he had tended to boast only after a battle was over, not before, Goebbels jeered.

The "great battle that will decide the war is finally at hand," the propaganda minister reflected. "I notice something I've observed many times in the past during big moments of crisis: that the Führer's on edge as the crisis unfolds, but once it reaches its climax, it's as if a huge weight has been lifted from his back."[6] Now that the great day had come, Hitler seemed "utterly exhilarated"[7] — as was Field Marshal Göring, who joined them at Klessheim. The vast armies would now be locked in combat, as the deciding battle was joined: the Wehrmacht having a four-to-one advantage in initial numbers, and a plethora of first-class tanks, including Tigers and Panthers. It was, to be sure, uncertain whether the landings in Normandy were a feint, designed to draw away the German panzer reserves from a possible main assault in the Pas-de-Calais area; the Führer therefore authorized Field Marshal von Rundstedt, headquartered at Saint-Germain, outside Paris, to release only two of his top armored divisions to make for the Normandy beaches that afternoon, holding back the rest.[8]

If the Americans could be stopped from reaching Cherbourg, they'd be cornered in the fields of Normandy, feint or no feint. The Wehrmacht would then have no trouble "rubbing out" the lightly armed paratroopers who'd dropped inland. Low cloud and nasty weather would make RAF bomber sights "unusable" below a hundred meters.

"Göring has almost won the battle already," Goebbels noted of the airman's bravado in his diary; "by contrast I feel we need to be careful, in fact extra careful" with regard to what he called "the politics of news." "We don't want to talk of the scalding soup we're going to serve up to the English, but rather, that this is a serious, historically decisive confrontation, a matter of life or death." The Führer agreed with this more sober approach. "If we defeat the invasion, the whole picture of the war will change," Goebbels predicted, the Führer having "no doubts about the outcome."[9] Rommel had called from his home, and was on his way to his headquarters at La Roche-Guyon, on the Seine; von Rundstedt had never left his own headquarters in Saint-Germain. At the "Little Chancellery" in Berchtesgaden, the chief of operations, General Alfred Jodl, was "convinced" they would crush the invasion. Himmler had great hopes for his SS divisions — one already speeding toward the battle, and more to follow. All would be well.

Suppose President Roosevelt had arranged with Stalin that the Russians mount a similar attack on the Eastern Front, though — stabbing the Wehrmacht in the back? "Will there be an offensive in the East?" Goebbels wondered. "If Stalin wants to coordinate his operations with those of the Americans and British, this would be the time," he remarked.[10]

It was a wise concern. At the castle Hitler bade farewell to Dr. Goebbels, expressing kind words. The propaganda minister was touched. "It's amazing with what certainty," Goebbels noted, "the Führer believes in his mission."[11]

Outside, the valley was covered in thick fog, and there was driving rain. "As I leave Salzburg the situation in the West looks no clearer. Our Panzer forces will soon be in action. But they're not there yet. I'm waiting on tenterhooks for our reserves to be committed. In Salzburg I learn from our propaganda department that the whole of Germany is waiting feverishly. One is aware the deciding dice of the whole war are rolling."[12]

"We've suffered so much bad luck these past two years we surely deserve a bit of good luck," Goebbels mused as he made his way back to Berlin. "To be weighed down by so many cares! A major battle like this grinds at one's nerves."[13] And in a kind of forlorn hope he added: "How nice it would be if, for once, Lady Luck would smile again."

Lady Luck did not oblige. Goebbels meanwhile disdained reports the President of the United States had read a prayer on radio, as night fell over Normandy. "To what depths of shame and sham will this pet poodle of the Jews not sink?" he asked — astonished that the "Jewish press" in America would print, on their leader pages, words from the Lord's Prayer — something inconceivable in Germany. "I find myself shaking with disgust when I read such things."[14]

The President, however, felt the prayers of the American nation were being answered — or could, at a minimum, help citizens in the United States find comfort as American troops poured into Normandy to reinforce those who'd breached the vaunted Atlantic Wall. Places like Pointe du Hoc would become synonymous with heroism. The struggle to get ashore on Omaha Beach had been especially bloody, yet casualties on D-day, it transpired, had not exceeded twenty-five hundred killed — far below what had been projected. All were aware, however, the numbers would go up inexorably in succeeding days, as Wehrmacht forces overcame their surprise at the magnitude and location of the assault.

The numbers of Allied troops debouching across the five beaches also rose — the units striking immediately inland, just as Rommel had feared. Moreover they were backed by massive Allied air support, as well as heavy naval guns firing from vessels offshore, using radio-equipped spotters on land. Bayeux was reached on June 7; Saint-Mère-Église on June 9; and on June 10 the U.S. Second Armored Division came ashore across Omaha Beach. Carentan fell to U.S. forces on June 11, and by June 12, six days into the battle, some 326,000 Allied troops were in Normandy, with four of the Allied beachheads joined — the day Generals Marshall and Arnold and Admiral King came ashore with General Eisenhower to assess, with pride and gratitude, American progress.

To the President, Marshall radioed a brief report — and his own view of what was to come. "Morale of all our troops and particularly higher commanders, is high. Replacements of men and materiel are being promptly executed throughout the US beachhead. I was very much impressed by the calm competence of 1st Army Commander Bradley, and by the aggressive tactics of his corps commanders," especially General "Lightning Joe" Lawton Collins. "Our new divisions, as well as those which have been battle tested, are doing splendidly and the Airborne Divisions have been magnificent" — as were beach personnel, and the Navy's temporary, portable floating Mulberry harbor. About the man the President had chosen to be supreme commander, he had nothing but praise. "Eisenhower and his Staff," he radioed, "are cool and confident, carrying out an affair of incredible magnitude and complication with superlative efficiency. I think we have these Huns at the top of the toboggan slide, and the full crash of the Russian offensive should put the skids under them. There will be hard fighting and the enemy will seize every opportunity for a skillful counter stroke," he predicted, "but I think he faces a grim prospect. Releases and estimates from General Eisenhower's Headquarters have been and should continue to be conservative in tone. The foregoing is my personal and confidential estimate."[15]

This was exactly what the President was hoping to hear—aware that the Wehrmacht could well become even more fanatical when facing defeat than in victory. In Oradour-sur-Glane, for example, a detachment of Hitler's SS Das Reich Division, ordered north to take part in the battle of Normandy, had already massacred and burned alive some 642 of the village's inhabitants—200 women and children deliberately locked and incinerated in the local church on June 10: a bitter warning to the people of France of atrocities to follow, as Waffen-SS units sought retribution among the weakest and most defenseless civilians for the gathering Allied success on the battlefield.

Even Stalin was impressed by accounts of the Allied assault. On June 13, at his weekly press conference, the President was able to read to reporters in the Oval Office a personal signal from the Russian marshal, via the U.S. ambassador in Moscow: "The history of war has never witnessed such a grandiose operation, an operation Napoleon himself had never even attempted."[16]

The President was also able to share with them a cable from General Eisenhower, which "came in yesterday." In it Eisenhower paid tribute to the courage and training of American, British, and Canadian troops, many of whom had been "committed to battle for the first time," and who had "conducted themselves in a manner worthy of their more experienced comrades" in the invasion—men who had learned how to "conquer the German in Africa, Sicily, Italy."[17]

The President's dogged strategy for engaging and defeating the Third Reich was working: seasoned troops alongside virgin soldiers, fighting in Normandy under a young supreme commander Mr. Roosevelt had personally appointed, and who was proving himself to be almost Rooseveltian in his ability to harness individuals of different talents, nationalities, and personalities under his leadership.

48

Architect of Victory

OVER THE ENSUING DAYS the Battle of Normandy now became, as had been predicted, a trial by fire. It was a battle General Montgomery, commanding the Allied armies, was well equipped to fight, with his British and Canadian troops holding back Hitler's massed Panzer Army forces on the left flank of the bridgehead, while General Bradley's U.S. First Army pressed farther inland, orchard by orchard, as well as striking westward to cut off the Cotentin Peninsula, in order to gain possession of the crucial port of Cherbourg — with General Patton held in readiness, as the President had promised, to be unleashed with American armor, once the Allies were ready.

By June 22, 1944, Cherbourg was ready to fall to the Allies — which, despite orders from the Führer to fight to the last man and put up suicidal resistance, it finally did, four days later. Reading the battlefield reports, Secretary Stimson finally confided to his diary that he'd been wrong: that keeping Marshall in Washington in the "position of Chief of Staff rather than to take command in the invasion" had been the right decision by the President, after all. "Now that Eisenhower, who was appointed to the commandership, is doing so well," Stimson recognized, belatedly, "we can afford to have Marshall in supreme command at home where he can see the whole field and throw his influence in every part of the global warfare."[1]

With the Normandy beachhead secure and the Allied armies advancing inland, backed by armor, artillery, and close air support, Stimson excoriated Churchill for having been so "strongly against" Overlord.[2] In doing so, however, the war secretary conveniently erased from his memory how hard he himself had pressed the President for the assault to be mounted in 1942,[3] when it would have been crushed, and how, yet again in early 1943, he had pleaded that an invasion of France be mounted that year, before U.S. forces had scarcely fired a shot against the Germans, only against Vichy French.[4] Nor did he mention how he had bet the President that Torch, the President's "great pet scheme" to invade Vichy-held Morocco and Algeria to crush the Germans in Northwest

Africa, while the British advanced from Egypt in November 1942, would fail.[5] In the flush of victory on June 22, Stimson was thus of a mind to see himself, not the President — who had "wobbled over the lot at different times"[6] — as the great architect of Allied victory.[7]

More than any individual alive President Roosevelt had in truth been responsible for ensuring that Overlord would be mounted successfully in the spring of 1944 — an achievement, sadly, that would not be recognized in the President's lifetime. Or indeed afterwards, as others claimed the glory.

Recognition, however, was not something the President sought, nor was he in a state to think about it a great deal in June 1944. It was the soldiers, the airmen, and the brave naval forces who deserved the greatest credit, the President felt — for they had proven they could defeat the vaunted Wehrmacht in combat, on the level playing field of Normandy — laying down their lives to end the Nazi nightmare in Europe for all time.

In a moment of concern lest his "unconditional surrender" policy be an obstacle to German capitulation, the President had suggested before D-day a possible message to the German people, to be broadcast by the leaders of the United States, the Soviet Union, and the United Kingdom, once the battle in Normandy and in Russia was joined. Such a message could point out the futility of further bloodshed, when Germans were opposed by the majority of the world's population of nearly two billion people. "Every German knows in his heart, Germany and Japan have made a terrible mistake," he'd suggested as its logic; they should be warned to "abandon the teachings of evil," since the "more quickly the end in the fighting and the slaughter the more quickly shall we come to a decent civilization in the whole world."[8]

Churchill, often sleepless at the prospect of a Dieppe-style fiasco in Normandy, had rightly been unimpressed. Evoking noble intentions on the one hand while wielding the sword of Damocles with the other? Despite his vaunted rhetorical skills the Prime Minister was reluctant to turn such a suggestion into an Allied appeal anytime soon. It would look like a "peace feeler," he warned the President, rather than an attempt to convince ordinary Germans of the folly of fighting to the last man in defense of tyranny. Moreover it raised weighty questions, such as what was to become of Germany after such a surrender — questions that had only been cursorily addressed at Tehran, in terms of reparations, borders, and the integrity or division of Germany itself. Besides, as Churchill had added in one of his characteristically tart turns of phrase, "nothing of this document would get down to the German pillboxes and front line to affect the fighting troops."[9]

Time and again Churchill had been infamously wrong on strategy. But in this case, the President had concluded, the Prime Minister was probably right:

no good would be served by being "nice" in advance of complete victory. Every yard would be contested by a Wehrmacht not only guilty of evil, but wedded to evil in the many countries it had so ruthlessly conquered or occupied, such as Hungary earlier that spring, and even in Germany itself—especially with regard to Jews, gypsies, Russian prisoners, and political opponents. Appeals to "ordinary Germans" to convince them of Allied moral sincerity, shortly after launching a massive, historic invasion, would do no good, and seemed some-what strange, given the President's implacable insistence upon unconditional surrender. A mark, possibly, of the President's declining health, about which Churchill had been warned by John Curtin, the visiting Australian prime min-ister. And the absence of trusted political advisers close to the President, like Harry Hopkins, who was still convalescing.

In any event the idea of such an appeal to save further bloodshed had been quietly dropped. The killing would have to go on in Normandy, mano a mano, until the battle was won. In terms of higher strategy, what was important in the President's mind, in any case, was to ensure that victory in France, when it came, did not result in the Allies becoming mired in new ventures that the im-petuous prime minister was once again pressing to advance, behind the scenes —especially in the Mediterranean.

At the end of May, as the liberation of Rome had finally approached, Churchill had admitted to the President that his Anzio operation to seize the city had finally paid a "dividend six months later than I hoped."[10]

It was probably the nearest Churchill would ever get to a confession of error, the President considered. Moreover the belated dividend was something of a Pyrrhic victory, as the President gently pointed out in his Rome broadcast, for Field Marshal Kesselring's forces had merely retreated to a new defensive Trasimene Line along the Orcia River north of Rome—leaving the question of how best to use Allied strength in the Mediterranean. It was a new battle the U.S. chiefs of staff would be facing with their opposite numbers in Lon-don: landings in the Bay of Biscay or the south coast of France to support the Overlord battle (Anvil), or further offensives in Italy and Yugoslavia, even the eastern Mediterranean.

For the moment, the President simply withdrew from decision-making. The truth was, he was hors de combat—physically and mentally. He felt he'd done his part in ensuring D-day was launched, together with Stalin's impend-ing offensive in the East. Whether he could undertake more than an hour or two's work a day, let alone accept Churchill's invitation to come to Britain, rather than Normandy, was doubtful. "How I wish I could be with you to see our war machine in operation!" the President had cabled Churchill on June 6[11]—knowing Winston himself was desperate to cross the Channel and witness at least some of the action in a battle he had done so much, for so long, to prevent, but which was now real. Yet the President knew he couldn't manage it. The American "war machine" would have to work on its own. Allowing Roosevelt, in the meantime, to focus his own limited energies on the next "deciding battle" of the world war: Allied strategy in the Pacific.

And whether, in fact, to run for a fourth term.

49

To Be, or Not to Be

LIKE THE PRIME MINISTER, the Führer had for his part become determined to get closer to the battle, given how much hinged upon its outcome. On June 13, 1944, he had given orders, as he'd promised Goebbels he would, for the first massive barrage of *Vergeltungswaffen,* or revenge weapons, to be loosed: targeted indiscriminately on London. Either they would force the Allies to attempt a second, perhaps larger, invasion, which he could with ease "rub out" this time in the Pas-de-Calais with the panzer forces he'd held back, or the bombs would discourage the Allies from attempting such a direct Channel crossing.

The weapons proved frightening and bloody — but inconsequential in military terms. No such actual landings in the Pas-de-Calais had been contemplated by the Allies, in any case, beyond deception measures — Operation Fortitude — which had made the threat of an assault on that coast seem real, and had mercifully kept Hitler's reserve of armored and infantry divisions away from Normandy. The Wehrmacht had thus wasted vital days waiting for landings that never came. Furious, four days later the Führer flew to Wolf's Glen, his heavily protected advance headquarters at Neuville-sur-Margival, near Soissons. In an angry meeting with Field Marshals Rommel and Rundstedt on June 17 he'd called for urgent counterattacks to be launched — just as General Marshall had predicted. These, too, failed — as Marshall had also predicted.

Then, on June 22, came the blow that Stalin had formally promised the President and the Prime Minister at Tehran, if the Western Allies would only commit to a spring Overlord: Operation Bagration, the Belorussian Strategic Offensive Operation, employing more than half a million Russian troops, five thousand tanks, and five thousand aircraft. The nightmare Hitler and Goebbels had always feared — major offensive war against the Wehrmacht on two converging fronts — had finally come to pass.

Now, unable to draw reinforcements from Germany or the Eastern Front, the Wehrmacht armies in France were doomed. By the end of June, the German line in Normandy was "stretched almost to breaking point," the deputy chief of the operations staff, General Walter Warlimont, later described. The Allied "invasion had succeeded," he chronicled. "The 'second front' — or rather the third — was established. Hitler might now have thought back to his statement that an Allied success in the West would decide the war and have drawn the necessary conclusions from it; but instead he was to be seen in front of the assembled company at a briefing conference, using ruler and compass to work out the small number of square miles occupied by the enemy in Normandy and compare them to the great area of France still in German hands."[1]

It was an extraordinary image — the Führer trying to convince himself and his military staff that Germany still occupied more territory in France than the Allies. "Was this really all he was capable of as a military leader? Or did he think that this elementary method" — a ruler and compass — "would have some propaganda effect on his audience? It was a sight," Warlimont wrote with bitterness, "I shall not readily forget."[2]

The President, by contrast, declined to interfere in the battle — which Eisenhower and Montgomery were conducting with steely skill. Montgomery's three battle phases — "the Break-in," "the Dogfight," and "the Break-out" — were now backed by tactical air support on a scale never seen before: an Allied version of Blitzkrieg. But for his part, the President's primary attention had now switched to the Pacific — where the first major bombing raid on the Japanese islands had been carried out on June 15 by B-29 Superfortress planes. On June 19, in waters east of the Philippine Islands, the Japanese navy had, moreover, lost three of its aircraft carriers (the *Taiho*, *Shokaku*, and *Hiyo*) and more than *six hundred* planes, in a new, large-scale naval battle: a spectacular example of modern naval combat by air and submarine forces that became known as the Battle of the Philippine Sea — and was soon nicknamed "the Great Marianas Turkey Shoot."[3]

· Looking back over recent months, Churchill, in a cable to the President on June 23, admitted he could not "think of any moment when the burden of the war has laid more heavily upon me or when I have felt so unequal to its ever-more entangled problems" — problems that now caused him to "greatly admire the strength and courage with which you face your difficulties, especially in a year when you have, what I may venture to call, other preoccupations" — namely the looming party conventions to choose presidential candidates.[4]

But the President's "strength and courage" — as well as his relative silence — masked a much simpler, direr truth: that his days were numbered.

Aboard the *Ferdinand Magellan* the President had gone to Hyde Park on June 15, 1944. There he had stayed at his home for a week, accepting no appointments or undertaking any work, beyond minimal correspondence.

None of the President's close advisers were with him, not even Admiral Leahy. It was as if the President was, not to put too fine a point on it, in a funk. On June 20 he openly confessed to his cousin Daisy he did not know what to do — or rather, what he would choose to do, in terms of reelection. He knew he was dying, but not how long he might have — and this the doctors would not say. Visiting Daisy and members of her family and friends for tea, Daisy's friend Renee Chrisment found the President, at Daisy's baronial house, Wilderstein, "looking much older than last year, but otherwise pretty well," if without "his usual energy & vitality & effervescence." Daisy was more observant, however. "I notice," she confided in her diary, that for all his show of normality and his still-blue eyes, he looked lonely in a corner of the Wilderstein porch where "he sits rather tiredly on his chair, and you can see his heart thumping beneath his shirt."[5]

There was party trouble in Texas, the President confided to Daisy — the Democratic Party tearing itself apart over civil rights in a nasty sign of their chances in the November elections, unless they could pull together behind the President's vision of the future. If the Democratic Party were to split, thanks to the threatened walkout of the Dixiecrats, the President said to her, he simply "will not run." "There would be no justification for a fourth term if he wasn't unanimously demanded," the President's cousin noted. Which brought her thoughts back to an earlier president of the United States, before a similarly important election, in 1920.

"I pray the P. does not have to go through a period of illness and disappointment like Mr. [Woodrow] Wilson," she noted, thinking of the twenty-ninth president, who had suffered a massive, paralyzing stroke. The prospect, for her beloved thirty-second president, seemed ominously similar. "Here we are, only a month away from the De.[mocratic] Convention & the P. doesn't know if he will run, or not."[6]

Book Two

PART SEVEN

The July Plot

50

A Soldier of Mankind

FROM SAN DIEGO to Pearl Harbor is a distance of 3,022 nautical miles — longer, of course, on a ship zigzagging to avoid detection by Japanese submarines.

The President had not visited Hawaii since 1934, when he'd made the voyage also by heavy cruiser. This time his task was to decide, as commander in chief, between two competing strategies for attacking and defeating Japan: that of Admiral Nimitz and that of General MacArthur.

On July 8, 1944 — the day the Allies began carpet bombing German forces in Normandy in order to break the cordon of Wehrmacht and SS divisions defending Caen and the direct route to Paris — the President had made a reluctant but momentous decision as to whether he should run for a fourth term. But not about whom he should take as his running mate.

The matter was far from straightforward. On July 5 he'd shared with Daisy the reports he was getting from Democratic Party stalwarts that Vice President Henry Wallace did not have enough national support to stand successfully either as the presidential or vice presidential nominee. "The opposition to Wallace has become very strong & active in the last 6 weeks," Daisy had noted of his remarks, "and something has to be done about it."[1]

Was the President himself moving toward an irrevocable decision? Daisy had wondered. He remained, she thought, "rather uncertain in his mind about himself: whether he is strong enough to take on another term — whether he ought to try it when the future is so difficult — On the other hand, whether it is not his *duty* to carry on, as long as he is able . . . Terrible decisions to have to make . . . for he *has* to make them, himself. Sometimes, he looks fine, other times he looks thin, & pale and old. If one could only *do* something to help him. The doctors are so *half*-efficient with their modern methods."[2]

It was one of the President's doctors, in the end, who had the courage to speak up — though not to the President himself.

Dr. Frank Lahey saw Roosevelt at the White House for a "private consultation" on the afternoon of July 5 — and told Admiral McIntire, afterwards, that he felt strongly the President should *not* run for a fourth term.

Lahey was well aware of the gravity of what he was recommending — in fact he would draw up a formal memorandum several days later, written in the first person, to document what had transpired. Lahey was one of the most distinguished medical professionals in America. He'd not only personally examined the President but had reviewed his medical files, his X-rays, and lab results going back several years. To Admiral McIntire, a fellow doctor, he'd therefore stated frankly "that I did not believe . . . if Mr. Roosevelt was elected again, he had the physical capacity to complete a term." As he recapped in the memorandum he dictated for the record, ever since Roosevelt's return from Tehran, the President had been "in a state which was, if not in heart failure, at least on the verge of it." The President's high blood pressure, and the undoubted coronary damage he had suffered, now made it certain he would soon be felled — in fact "he would again have heart failure," like the episode in March, and would therefore "be unable to complete" another term as president.[3]

"Admiral McIntire was in agreement with this," Dr. Lahey's memorandum recorded, and the admiral assured Lahey he'd conveyed his negative counsel to the President, as well as Lahey's warning that "if he does accept another term, he had a very serious responsibility concerning who is the Vice President."[4]

The President, then, had been officially — or professionally, at least — warned *not* to run. And the President, according to McIntire, fully understood the advice and the implications of not heeding it.

Dr. Lahey's warning was significant, Admiral McIntire had been aware, not only because it confirmed what he and the President already knew, but because it would be increasingly hard, if not impossible, to keep the matter of Roosevelt's health status quiet if he did choose to run — especially with Governor Dewey openly campaigning on the issue of "the age of the members of the cabinet" and "F.D.R.'s health, etc.,"[5] as Daisy noted, having listened with the President and his daughter Anna to candidate Dewey speak in a radio broadcast. A final decision, therefore, must clearly be made.

At 6:20 p.m. on July 8, 1944, after a rare swim in the White House pool, the President was thus driven to 2238 Q Street in Georgetown, where Lucy Rutherfurd was staying with her sister Violetta. Collecting Lucy in person, he brought her back in his car to dinner at the White House — his daughter Anna and her husband, John, joining them there for the first time.

Watching her father as "he talked" with Lucy, Anna "realized this woman had all the qualities of giving a man her undivided attention. She certainly had innate dignity."[6] After dinner they'd all watched a movie, then Anna and John had retired, leaving the President and his former lover alone together until Lucy left, shortly after midnight.

This was not what the doctor had ordered — but may well have continued to preserve, if not save, the President's life. He was now phoning Lucy, according to the chronicler of Roosevelt's last year in office, every day to talk. Despite his veritable death sentence he seemed happy[7] — which was not something his daughter Anna could object to. Or even felt she wished to. He was changing before her eyes: not only in how he looked, but in how he acted. General de Gaulle had visited the President on July 6, at FDR's reluctant invitation, and been given a formal state dinner on July 7 at the White House — where, overcoming his long animosity, the President had treated the proud, arrogant French leader with extraordinary politeness and charm, so that de Gaulle had departed in good spirits.

Some profound shift, then, had taken place in the President's mind, or spirit. Fate had dealt the harshest of blows, at age sixty-two, to his physical heart — but in other ways he currently seemed the happiest man alive. He was up early (for him), the next day, July 9, collecting Lucy once again from Q Street, and with her passed the entire day at Shangri-la, his beloved mountain retreat, returning only at 10:30 p.m.

Thus was the fateful decision discussed and reached, with Lucy's blessing — and against Dr. Lacey's firm advice, for good or ill.

Two days later, at eleven o'clock on the morning of July 11, the President told Steve Early to lock the doors of the Oval Office just as soon as the White House correspondents and other journalists were safely in. It was to be his 961st press and radio conference — and one of the most consequential.

To reporters the President seemed in a surprisingly jovial mood compared with earlier conferences, at the time of D-day. Given that there were close to a hundred people present, he said he himself had asked for the doors to be secured in order to avoid a stampede to the exit once he made his announcement. For he had, he'd stated with a smile, some important news to share with them.

As the President explained to reporters, he'd recently spoken with Robert Hannegan, the chairman of the Democratic Party, at the White House. From Mr. Hannegan he'd received an official request to stand for reelection as president of the United States, since the "clear majority of the delegates to the National Convention" were, "by certified numbers in primaries," now requesting him to run for a fourth term as the Democratic nominee.

Reporters' pens raced across their notepads as they took down the President's words. "This action," he said, reading aloud Hannegan's written request, "is a reflection of the vast majority of the American people that you continue as President in this crucial period in the nation's history." The chairman was therefore tendering "to you the nomination of the Party," the President continued, using his pince-nez, "as it is the solemn belief of the rank and file of Democrats, as well as many other Americans, that the nation and the world need the continuation of your leadership." In an oblique reference to rumors of ill health, Hannegan had expressed his confidence "that the people recognize the tremendous burdens of your office, but I am equally confident that you must continue until the war is won and a firm basis for an abiding peace among men is established."[8]

The President then read out to reporters the reply he'd sent Hannegan the previous night — a message that, he admitted, was "hurried." He'd felt he owed Mr. Hannegan, as he put it, "a simple statement of my position. If the Convention should carry this out" and vote to nominate him for reelection, "I shall accept," he'd written. "If the people elect me, I will serve. Every one of our sons serving in this war has officers from whom he takes his orders. The President is the Commander-in-Chief and he, too, has his superior officer — the people of the United States."[9]

The President added one qualification, however — namely that, "for myself, I do not want to run. By next spring I shall have been President and Commander-in-Chief of the Armed Forces for twelve years." He paused there. "All that is within me cries out to go back to my home on the Hudson River, to avoid public responsibilities, and to avoid also the publicity which in our democracy follows every step of the Nation's Chief Executive."

He paused again. "Such would be my choice. But we of this generation chance to live in a day and hour when our Nation has been attacked, and when its future existence and the future existence of our chosen method of government are at stake.

"To win this war wholeheartedly, unequivocally and as quickly as we can is our task of the first importance. To win this war in such a way that there will be — that there will be no further world wars in the foreseeable future is our second objective. To provide occupations, and to provide a decent standard of living for our men in the Armed Forces after the war, and for all Americans, are the final objectives. Therefore, reluctantly, but as a good soldier, I repeat that I will accept and serve in this office, if I am so ordered by the Commander-in-Chief of us all — the sovereign people of the United States."[10]

In her diary, at Wilderstein, Daisy Suckley penned her disappointment — not at the decision itself, which she'd felt was inevitable in the circumstances, but that the President had not had time to call her personally beforehand. Or afterwards. "He announced to his press conference this morning, that he will run for the presidency if he is wanted — that settles that, at least, & his wondering & pondering is over."

Further, Daisy knew just "how mixed his feelings are on the subject." She could therefore "commiserate & congratulate with equal truthfulness." What was clear, however, was that, in contrast to his mood all spring, the President had now decided. He was going to do his best, as a soldier of mankind.

"He evidently feels well enough," she jotted thoughtfully, "to carry on" — knowing it would kill him.[11]

51

Missouri Compromise

LATE ON JULY 13, 1944, the President set off—destination Hawaii, but via Hyde Park and Chicago, where the *Ferdinand Magellan* was serviced and became a maelstrom of visits, phone calls, and political meetings in the run-up to the Democratic National Convention.

With the prospect of a deeply contested ballot splitting Southern and Northern Democrats, the party chairman, Robert Hannegan, came aboard in person to have the President sign and postdate a secret letter of support for two compromise vice presidential candidates, should no clear winner emerge between Wallace and James F. Byrnes. For Wallace, in two meetings with the President at the White House, had refused to withdraw his candidacy for vice president, and Judge Byrnes, the director of the War Mobilization Office and former Supreme Court justice, was intent on running for the position.

"The P. says Wallace is much nearer to the President's thoughts & view of things" in terms of the postwar peace—an anticolonialist and genuine supporter of the New Deal and civil rights—"but [he] is a poor administrator," despite being the rich owner and CEO of an expanding agricultural feed company, Daisy Suckley recorded in her diary.[1] Owing to Wallace's internecine squabbles with Jesse Jones, the commerce secretary, the President had in fact been compelled to remove Wallace from his chairmanship of the boards of Economic Warfare and Supply Priorities and Allocation, and to send him overseas, to Russia and China—a trip that would add to Wallace's global perspective and reputation. In the bare-bones business of election campaigning across America, however, the vice president was known to have erratic religious beliefs, having begun life as a Presbyterian, become a Theosophist, and then an Episcopalian. This would make him vulnerable to Republican attack if, as expected, the election campaign became bitter.

For his part Jim Byrnes, the diminutive former congressman, former senator, and former U.S. Supreme Court justice, was an extremely effective, if widely disliked, administrator: a Southerner who had loyally backed Roosevelt's New Deal in South Carolina. But Byrnes had also attacked the proposed antilynching law in Congress, as well as the Fair Standards Act — thus making him an enemy both of Northerners *and* labor. In an open, national vote Byrnes stood little chance of winning the Democratic Party nomination for vice president — at least, not without a tremendous and potentially divisive fight that might well sink the party's chances, especially when contrasted with the first-ballot choice of the Republican contender, the young New York governor Thomas Dewey and *his* vice presidential nominee, Ohio governor John Bricker. Byrnes, too, could be vulnerable to religious scrutiny, for he had been baptized a Catholic and had only switched to Protestantism on his marriage. "Well, by next Friday, that question will have been decided," Daisy had ended her diary entry on July 14, after the President had left Washington for Hawaii, "& the P. can relax on the high seas, with no newspapers and no telephones."[2]

The drama in Chicago, however, suggested it would not be so simple. Hannegan favored a dark horse candidate, his former political boss in Missouri: Senator Harry S. Truman, chairman of the Senate subcommittee investigating U.S. war production, and senior member of several other Senate committees. Yet another alternative was an outlier: the still-young (age forty-six) associate justice of the Supreme Court, William O. Douglas, who had worked for the Securities and Exchange Commission from its inception during the Depression to clean up Wall Street.

None of these were inspiring choices, given the somewhat dire situation: namely that anyone in politics with half a brain was aware, by this time, that the rumors of the President's ill health were correct. The President was hardly ever to be seen in Washington, and when he was, he seemed a ghost of his former self. He would, widespread speculation now ran, be unlikely to live out a fourth term. He might not even reach the beginning of such a term next January, 1945. Certainly every delegate who pressed Truman, the reluctant senator from Missouri, to run for the vice presidential nomination in Chicago had made clear to the senator it would inevitably mean the burden of the presidency itself, ere long. Thus when a reporter pointed out that, if he threw his hat into the ring, he might well soon "succeed to the throne," Truman had shown no surprise. In fact he had shaken his broad bespectacled head, saying, "Hell, I don't want to be President"[3] — at least not that way, via "the back door."

Truman had not counted, however, on the President's byzantine way of coming to a firm, ultimate decision. The President's pre-Hawaii trip itinerary would allow him to remain absent for the further backroom shenanigans of the nominating process in Chicago once the train left the city on July 15; making a leisurely cross-country rail journey to California that very afternoon would allow him to let the Democratic Party bigwigs and delegates duke it out in the Windy City, so that he could not be accused of interfering. And his heart condition was a boon, for it caused him to not really care at a certain level: to be, in short, uncharacteristically fatalistic.

Had the President put his presidential weight behind Henry Wallace's candidacy, Truman biographer David McCullough later noted, the vice president would undoubtedly have been nominated by the convention, as in 1940 — indeed, Wallace very nearly was, once the 1944 convention unfolded. But the convention was not the American electorate; moreover the President was strangely unwilling to intercede — absolved by his medical condition, which made stress potentially fatal.

In Missouri, Senator Truman's elderly mother had told reporters she knew the rumors about the President. "They keep predicting that Roosevelt will die in office if he's elected," Mary Ellen Truman was quoted. "The Republicans hope he will," she'd said disparagingly. "They keep saying that I'll die, too, and I'm almost 92. I hope Roosevelt fools 'em."[4]

With Harry Hopkins still convalescing, the President had meantime asked Judge Sam Rosenman to travel with him aboard the *Ferdinand Magellan* as speechwriter and political adviser — first across America, then across the Pacific Ocean to Honolulu. As Rosenman afterwards recalled, the President simply did not have the energy to fight for Wallace, as he had in 1940. Nor did he have the conviction that Wallace would make a strong "national" president, if and when required to take the reins. In Rosenman's words the President "saw as the big task for his fourth term the creation and successful functioning of the United Nations Organization. This would require the complete co-operation of his own party, but the co-operation of the Republican party as well. He was determined not to repeat the mistake of Woodrow Wilson by framing the future peace of the world by himself or with his own party alone." It would therefore have to be a collaborative, "bipartisan approach."[5]

By the time the *Ferdinand Magellan* reached California on July 19 — mobbed by crowds at railway halts throughout Iowa, Missouri, Kansas, Oklahoma, Texas, New Mexico, and Arizona, despite attempts to keep the President's train trip secret — the bartering and excitement among the twenty thousand delegates and party stalwarts back in Chicago had reached fever pitch. Byrnes had by then decided he couldn't win, and had withdrawn his candidacy for the vice presidential spot. Wallace had not, however: leaving him, for a while, the sole surviving contender. His supporters thus planned to stampede the convention into voting for him as the party's vice presidential nominee, once the President had accepted the presidential nomination.

But Wallace's backers had not reckoned with Roosevelt's legendary legerdemain, even when a shell of his former self. At a conference of party bigwigs upstairs at the White House on July 11, the consensus had been unequivocal. "When all the names had been fully canvassed," the President had announced "with an air of finality," if without particular enthusiasm, "'It's Truman,'" Rosenman later wrote[6] — and the President had duly told Wallace this was the consensus. In fact the President had also told Wallace that political experts were warning him the vice president, if renominated, could be responsible for losing up to *three million votes* across the country, given the rising Republican tide. Wallace, however, had produced his own statistics, showing he had 65 percent support in the Democratic Party. In vain the President had noted that this was not the point: such delegates could guarantee him the VP nomination, but lose the party the whole election.

Wallace's obstinacy had made the matter distinctly unpleasant for the ailing president. Truman was, in the end, "the only one with no enemies," the President had explained to Wallace; moreover the Missouri senator would "add a little independent" — i.e., bipartisan — "strength"[7] to the ticket. But Wallace had dug in his heels. He wasn't listening. And the President had been too ill — and by nature too nonconfrontational — to insist.

How the President eventually managed to persuade Truman to overcome his diffidence — as well as his puzzlement as to why the President had not discussed the matter directly with him, before the decision became acute — was to become one of the legendary stories of American political history, with numerous versions. That the President did, however, intercede was never contested. Truman, unwilling to potentially enter the White House by the back door, and having backed Judge Byrnes for the vice presidential nomination, initially declared he would not allow his name to go forward, and he refused to back down even when Hannegan assured him he was the choice not only of the Democratic Committee's board, but also of the President — showing him Mr. Roosevelt's postdated letter regarding two compromise candidates he would be pleased to run with, if the convention became locked: Harry Truman or Bill Douglas.

Mr. Roosevelt's wishes, as President and thus the senior Democrat in the nation, were obviously paramount, Truman conceded. But what in all truth, he countered, were these wishes, when the President was thousands of miles away, en route to more distant climes?

Only when the President's train reached the Marine Corps base siding at San Diego was a telephone call from Hannegan put through to the President from the Blackstone Hotel in Chicago on July 19, 1944. A clear, unmistakable presidential preference, expressed in his actual voice, was now essential in order to avoid bedlam in Chicago, Hannegan explained.

The President's train had arrived in the middle of the night. He was not well. In addition to his heart condition the President had almost been suffocated by the heat in Yuma, Arizona, the previous afternoon, where "the temperature on the station platform was 125 F. at 4 p.m.," Admiral Leahy had noted in his diary.[8] Nevertheless the President agreed to take Hannegan's call. Whether he was aware Truman was also in Hannegan's room is unclear, but the metaphorical temperature in Chicago, it seemed, was now higher than in Yuma. It was the eleventh hour. "I was sitting on one twin bed, and Bob was on the other," Truman himself later recalled. The first convention ballots would be cast that night. "Roosevelt said, 'Bob, have you got that guy lined up yet on that Vice Presidency?'"[9]

Given the seesawing arguments that had colored deliberations in Chicago since the President's brief presence in the city, four days before, as well as the President's failure to provide firm leadership over the matter — a matter of potentially world-historical consequence — this was both a shambles and shameless. Hannegan, who had asked Truman to listen in on the call, and if necessary speak with the President directly, took a deep breath. "'No,'" Hannegan responded. "'He's the contrariest goddamn mule from Missouri I ever saw.'

"'Well,' Roosevelt said, 'you tell him if he wants to break up the Democratic Party in the middle of the war and maybe lose that war that's up to him.'"[10]

If these were the President's words, they were well chosen. Hannegan promised the President, on the phone, he would make it happen.

Truman was completely flummoxed. Why had the President not discussed the matter with him in the run-up to the nomination? "He never said a word to me about the situation. And I said to Bob, 'Why in hell didn't he tell me that when he was here [in Chicago] or before I left Washington?'"

Hannegan shrugged. If Truman was the contrariest mule, the President was the most enigmatic.

Reluctantly, Truman had then agreed to stand for the vice presidency: the vote slated to take place at the convention the next evening, July 20.[11]

52

The July Plot

ELEANOR ROOSEVELT HAD TRAVELED to the West Coast on the *Ferdinand Magellan* with the President. She wanted to have the chance to see two of her sons there: Elliott, the airman, and Jimmy, the Marine — both of them combat colonels — and their families.

Once the Chicago decision was made on July 19, the President had felt well enough to visit patients at the San Diego Naval Hospital, and after that to have a family dinner, hosted by Jimmy Roosevelt in nearby Coronado, by the bay. It was also arranged that Jimmy, who was on the staff of the Fifth Marine Division stationed at San Diego, would collect his father from the train the next morning and take him to observe a live-fire Marine beach assault training exercise, prior to the President shipping out to the Pacific.

Jimmy arrived early. "Before the exercise began, I was alone with Father in his private railroad car," he later recalled. "We talked of many things — the war, family, and politics . . . I was struck by Father's irritability over what was happening in Chicago and by his apparent indifference as to whom the convention selected as his fourth-term running mate. He made it clear that he was resigned to the dumping of Vice-President Henry A. Wallace" if the Democrats were to have any real chance of winning, for "he felt that Wallace had become a political liability" in the country, not only in the party. The nomination voting was due to take place later that day. The President had "professed not to 'give a damn'" about whom the delegates came up with once the process came to its climax. "His mind was on the war; the fourth-term race was simply a job that had to be accomplished, and his attitude toward the coming political campaign was one of 'let's get on with it,'" if it had to be done.[1]

At this juncture, just before "we were to leave for the exercise, Father suddenly turned white, his face took an agonized look, and he said to me: 'Jimmy, I don't know if I can make it — I have horrible pains!' It was a struggle for him to get the words out."

"I was so scared," the Marine colonel candidly recalled, "I did not know what to think or do."[2]

At his father's insistence they did not call Dr. Bruenn. Canceling the President's presence at the ten-thousand-man exercise, some forty miles away, was not the major issue. It was the intended radio broadcast that evening that was the problem, for it had been set up with all national radio networks, as well as a swarm of reporters, film cameramen, and photographers. Broadcasting from a special additional railway car, the President would that night deliver his formal acceptance of the 1944 Democratic nomination on national live radio. He would make it in the form of a speech — one on which he'd worked with Rosenman and Elmer Davis, the head of the Office of War Information, for several days. It would be historic, too: the first such nomination acceptance address made during hostilities since the Civil War. And an opportunity to lay out, once again, the President's vision of the future.

But if the acceptance speech had to be canceled?

Given the rumors surrounding the President's health, not being well enough to speak would probably end his father's reelection chances, Colonel James Roosevelt was aware. Convinced, however, that the stomach pain mirrored the one he'd suffered in Tehran while dining with Stalin and Churchill, the President asked only that his son help him out of his chair "and let me stretch out flat on the deck for a while — that may help."[3]

Eleanor was not informed, nor Anna. For "perhaps ten minutes, while I kept as quiet as possible, Father lay on the floor of the railroad car, his eyes closed, his face drawn, his powerful torso occasionally convulsed as the waves of pain stabbed him. Never in all my life," Jimmy later wrote, "had I felt so alone with him — and so helpless."[4]

By the strangest of coincidences, an even bigger crisis was taking place in the Third Reich that same day.

Hitler had left his home in the Obersalzberg at the same time the President had left Hyde Park. He was now at his headquarters in Rastenburg, in East Prussia — having flown there in his Condor — the last journey he would ever make by plane. He'd had another stormy meeting on June 29 with Field Marshals Rundstedt and Rommel at the Berghof. The battle in Normandy was going badly — in fact German defeat was, frankly, now inevitable, given Stalin's simultaneous offensive on the Eastern Front. Cherbourg had fallen, despite the Führer's injunction against surrender. Negotiation was the only option "regarding Germany," in order to save the nation further futile bloodshed, Rommel had begun to argue, when Hitler, in cold fury, had interrupted him and in a rage commanded Rommel to leave the room for his insolence in attempting to speak on "political" matters, about which he knew nothing.[5]

The Führer had been beside himself with anger — unable to accept that a

German general, particularly a popular and decorated general, should dare make such a suggestion. To negotiate except from a strong position was anathema to Hitler. He had seen no future in the proposition — not, at least, until and unless the Wehrmacht turned the tables on the Western Allies. In his own mind this was still achievable. A tremendous storm in the English Channel had destroyed the Mulberry artificial harbor in Normandy's American sector, putting back the Allied reinforcement timetable by five days. The first of Hitler's *Vergeltungswaffen*, the Fieseler Fi.103 (known to the Allies as the buzz bomb), was causing considerable alarm, even panic, in southern England. In addition to the V-1, the Führer still had a second *Vergeltungswaffe* up his sleeve, namely ballistic missiles that could not be shot down by antiaircraft fire or fast fighters; also the new Messerschmitt 262 fighters, powered by jet engines — another miracle of German engineering. It was crucial to hold back the Allies in Normandy and stabilize the Eastern Front, following the massive Russian offensive. Only then could one think of negotiation — especially if the Allies could be split apart politically. These were matters that generals were utterly incompetent to recognize, let alone handle.

Having arrived at the now reinforced Wolf's Lair near the Eastern Front, Hitler had moved into the guest bunker, since his own main accommodation was still in the process of renovation. He'd then summoned Field Marshal Kesselring from Italy on July 19 and awarded him the Knight's Cross of the Iron Cross with Oak Leaves, Swords, and Diamonds, for his sterling performance on the Mediterranean front.

The Eastern Front was still of great concern, though, and at midday on July 20 the Führer was just chairing an operations conference of his senior military staff — some twenty-four officers — in an outdoor hut used as a meeting room, when at 12:42 p.m. there was a terrific explosion. The blast blew the air and debris through the open windows, just as the Führer leaned over the map-covered table on his elbows, poring over air-reconnaissance charts of Russian positions. There was mayhem inside — blood, splinters, dust, and rubble.

"Linge, someone has tried to kill me," the Führer cried to his valet,[6] having been flung against a doorpost and having then made his way from the smoking havoc to the guest bunker — his gray jacket torn and his white underwear showing under his shredded black trousers, like a medieval court jester.

Someone had: Colonel Claus von Stauffenberg, chief of staff to General Fromm, commander of the Reserve, or Replacement, Army. After three failed attempts to set up an assassination at the Berghof, Stauffenberg had managed to prime one of two explosive devices in the Wolf's Lair toilet, which he intended to put in his briefcase and place on the floor near the Führer. He had not quite had time to prime the second one, however, before being called back into the conference hut. Had he been able to put both devices in his briefcase, even with one unprimed, they would have detonated together, killing Hitler.

Alternatively, had the meeting been held in the normal concrete bunker, the ricochet of the blast would have been enough to erase the Führer and obliterate his entire senior staff, including Field Marshal Wilhelm Keitel, head of the Wehrmacht Armed Forces high command, and General Alfred Jodl, chief of staff to Keitel (both later executed at Nuremberg). Instead it merely grazed the Führer and ruptured his eardrums — though it did also puncture the flesh of his right forearm, causing nerve damage.

His hair singed, the bandaged Führer was thus able to change clothes and greet the visiting Benito Mussolini around 3:30 p.m. — though, with his right arm in a sling, he was unable to return Mussolini's Sieg Heil salute.

Amazed that so many had survived the blast, considering the utterly devastated interior of the hut to which Hitler took him, and impressed by the Führer's sangfroid, Mussolini declared: "After all I have seen here, I agree with you completely. This is a sign from Heaven!"[7]

A number of the staff officers had been gravely wounded, however; four of them died over subsequent days. Thinking it was the work of impressed laborers still reinforcing the bunker, Hitler was initially unaware that the attempt had been part of a putsch, or coup d'état, to be mounted in Berlin, Paris, and other cities, just as soon as word of Hitler's death was communicated by Stauffenberg to his fellow conspirators. Ironically, Stauffenberg, who had left the hut after placing his briefcase under Hitler's table, assumed from the huge blast the Führer had been killed; from the nearby airfield he thus telephoned Berlin with the secret code word "Valkyrie," indicating success.

This was another fateful error, for it led inevitably to the plotters emerging, being swiftly rounded up, and then executed, once Hitler's survival was affirmed. From Berlin Dr. Goebbels was soon able to assure the Führer by phone that the capital of the Reich was under full Nazi control. Moreover he was able to persuade the reluctant Führer to give a major radio broadcast that very night. In this the Führer would be able to make clear both to the world and to any others who were still conspiring against him that, contrary to rumor, he had survived the assassination attempt. And that the Third Reich was still under his command.

"I speak to you today for two reasons," Hitler began his broadcast, in an unusually somber, sober, almost listless tone — first "so that you can hear my voice and know that I was not injured and am in good health." Second, "so that you learn about the details of this crime, which is without equal in German history."[8]

For decades, night and day, he had worked, Hitler claimed, "only for my Volk!" Any claims he was dead, or that the Wehrmacht was involved, were specious, he lied — his Austrian accent enough to persuade listeners the broadcast was authentic. No civilian was to take instructions from any department that had been "appropriated by the usurpers," he ordered, announcing that Heinrich Himmler would take command of the Replacement Army from General Fromm, while General Guderian would replace General Schmundt, the operations chief of the general staff, who had been severely wounded—perhaps mortally.

"I am convinced that by crushing this very small clique of traitors and conspirators," the Führer assured listeners, an atmosphere could be reestablished at home to reflect that of the many courageous German soldiers fighting at the front. "After all, it is not right that hundreds of thousands and millions of brave men give everything, while a very small coterie of ambitious, pitiful creatures at home constantly tries to undermine this attitude. This time we will settle accounts in the way we are used to as National Socialists," Hitler warned. (Almost five thousand political opponents were ultimately executed.) There were several mentions of gratitude to "Providence and my Creator" for having saved his life—not on his account, but so that he could "persevere in my work." Orders, moreover, had already gone out to "all troops. They will execute them in blind faith and in accordance with the type of obedience which the German army knows."[9]

Fortuitously the Führer was not alone in Rastenburg. Field Marshal Goering, Foreign Minister Ribbentrop, Martin Bormann, and other dignitaries had also gathered that afternoon, having been invited to be present for the Duce's visit. Following the Führer's broadcast they now listened as Hitler that night gave way to a rage more venomous, if such were possible, than they had ever heard before.

In September 1943 it had been the Italians who'd betrayed their noble allies; this time, however—particularly with Mussolini present—Hitler needed new scapegoats, and he found them in the senior German officer class he had always suspected of despising him as a mere corporal with a low-class Austrian accent. There would have to be an immediate investigation—a military court of honor, set up and charged with executing the guilty. Not by firing squad, either, as befitting commissioned officers. "They must hang immediately," the Führer raved, "without mercy," and in their prison clothes, as common criminals. "He is absolutely determined to set a bloody example and to eradicate a freemasons' lodge which has been opposed to us all the time," Goebbels recorded in his diary, one that "has only awaited the moment to stab us in the back in the most critical hour. The punishment which must now be meted out must have historic dimensions."[10]

Six thousand miles away the President of the United States meantime faced the task of his own radio address that same evening.

Jimmy Roosevelt was unsure whether his father could pull it off. Lifting him from the floor of the *Ferdinand Magellan,* he had that morning "helped him get ready, and the Commander in Chief went to review the exercises," Jimmy recalled — the two of them being driven at 9:10 a.m. to the bluffs to watch the "colossal" mock invasion by Marines.

The day before, the President had listened as senior Marine and naval officers, visiting him on his train, had filled him in on the scope and purpose of the training exercise, which would be on the same lines as the current invasion of the Marianas. How much the President was really able to take in of the exercise was unclear. "In the many photographs taken of him that day, Pa looked tired," Jimmy remembered. "In most of them, however, he wore a big smile; no one would have guessed what he had just been through."[11]

The President had claimed he was feeling better, but in actuality he'd asked to go back to the train less than an hour later. "I had a grand view of the landing operation at Camp Pendleton," he wrote afterwards to Eleanor — who had meantime departed for Los Angeles — but he'd unfortunately "got the collywobbles," he recounted, making light of the episode.[12] In truth he'd had to cancel lunch at the home of his daughter-in-law, John's wife, in Coronado, instead spending "the afternoon in his private car resting and listening to the Democratic Convention news as it was broadcast over the radio" — culminating in his official renomination request.[13] Jimmy and his wife then had a quiet dinner with him on board the *Ferdinand Magellan* before his broadcast.

The whole saga — the President having another health emergency at the very moment when twenty thousand delegates and supporters were assembling in Chicago to hear Senator Samuel Jackson, the convention chair, declare FDR to be in good health, and as the delegates prepared to listen to him accept his nomination by radio from San Diego — was almost surreal.

The President was determined to fulfill his commitment, however — the more so since word had come through that there had been a putsch in Germany, with an attempted assassination of the Führer. With Hitler dead, the war might well be over soon. If the attempt had been successful.

At 8:30 p.m. the President was finally wheeled to the extra car to give his speech.

The broadcast took fifteen long minutes to read on air — something the President did in such a firm, authoritative voice that no one listening could have imagined his cardiologist, Dr. Bruenn, was all the time sitting close by in the crowded car, concerned about the President's astronomic blood pressure — or that his son Jimmy, next to him, had only hours earlier wondered if his father were dying at his feet.

What had caused the sudden pains and collapse?

The real reason would never be identified, given the President's recovery that very evening. He had clearly been a near-wreck, though, the rest of that day, July 20 — somewhat surprised, like Hitler, to be alive.

• • •

The President's broadcast from San Diego was the very opposite of the one Hitler had given from Rastenburg.

Where Hitler had delivered his broadcast in dry, punitive, snarling diction, Roosevelt's easy tenor voice sought to embrace his listeners in a serious yet inspiring personal conversation: at once intimate and rational. Sam Rosenman had traveled with him, working each day on the script; this the President managed to deliver with his trademark cadences: his voice soaring and then resuming its proud, determined rhetoric as he bade listeners understand, once again, that he would prefer not to have to serve another term, but would rather "retire to the quiet of private life." He was being called to duty by the Democratic Party convention — and by another convention, namely the "sense of obligation to serve if called upon to do so by the people of the United States" in November that year.

"I shall not campaign, in the usual sense, for the office. In these days of tragic sorrow, I do not consider it fitting. And besides," he added — economizing with the truth — "in these days of global warfare, I shall not be able to find the time." He'd just traversed, he explained, "the whole width of the continent," and was now at "a naval base where I am speaking to you. As I was crossing the fertile lands and the wide plains and the Great Divide, I could not fail to think of the relationship between the people of our farms and cities and villages and the people of the rest of the world overseas — on the islands in the Pacific, in the Far East, and in other Americas, in Britain and Normandy and Germany and Poland and Russia itself." For the states through which he'd traveled "are becoming a part of all these distant spots."

Current battles being fought "in Normandy and on Saipan" affected the "security and well-being of every human being in Oklahoma and California," the President pointed out. A new world beckoned Americans, rousing the country from its long sleep. "Mankind changes the scope and breadth of its thought and vision slowly indeed," he reflected — but change was coming, indeed had already taken place.

America's mission — its bipartisan government's mission — was thus: "First, to win the war — to win the war fast, to win it overpoweringly. Second to form worldwide international organizations, and to arrange the armed forces of the sovereign Nations of the world to make another war impossible within the foreseeable future. And third to build an economy for our returning veterans and for all Americans — which will provide employment and provide decent standards of living." This was not a mission that could be handed to "inexperienced or immature hands" — men "who opposed lend-lease and international cooperation against the forces of tyranny," and who would return the country to "breadlines and apple-selling." With this in mind, he quoted, as the climax of his oration, "the greatest wartime President in our history," Abraham Lincoln, who in 1865 had set the goals of the nation — "as God gives us the right" — to "strive on to finish the work we are in; to bind up the nation's wounds; to care for him who shall have borne the battle, and for his widow, and his orphan — to do all which may achieve a just and lasting peace among ourselves, and with all Nations."[14]

It was an exemplary radio performance — one of the President's best ever.

It was not quite enough, however. The President was then asked to reread passages from the speech for the newsreel film cameras, to be shown around the world, and to pose for photographs.

This proved a big mistake. The President's speech had exhausted him, as much mentally as physically. It had capped an extraordinary day, in terms of his health — but the medical crisis had been kept quiet. "One of the pictures was a most unfortunate one," recalled Judge Rosenman later. "It was snapped while the President, with his head bowed over the printed page, was pronouncing a broad vowel, so that his mouth was wide open at the click of the camera." Taken by an Associated Press pool photographer, the photo told the true story, which even a thousand words could not, of "a tragic-looking figure," Rosenman candidly admitted. His "face appeared to be very emaciated because of the downward angle and open mouth; it looked weary, sick, discouraged, and exhausted."[15]

In Washington, the secretary of the interior, Harold Ickes, was appalled. "It was a terrible picture," Ickes recorded in his diary. "The President looked like a sitting ghost and the picture has created a bad impression" — one that might have serious consequences on the November election.[16]

Since the White House press secretary, Steve Early, was not aboard the *Magellan,* there had been no media supervision; the photograph, late that night, was carelessly transmitted to the wire services for general distribution — giving a dreadful yet accurate portrayal of the President's ill health. After more than six months in which the President had avoided the glare of publicity, with only carefully monitored coverage that deliberately disguised the true seriousness of his condition, the photo was like a bombshell.

Panic ensued in the Democratic Party. The picture gave the impression, as one distinguished newspaper editor later wrote, "of a failing elder, a candidate for a nursing home, gasping out his last words, the opposite of the impression his confident, sonorous voice left with the party faithful in distant Chicago," or even those who saw the newsreel film.[17] As Rosenman recorded, the photo "was later published with great glee by enemies of the President, who urged it as proof of their charge that he was no longer physically or mentally competent to manage his office."[18]

Rightly or wrongly, it was the first real indication to the public, behind the many rumors, that the President *was* seriously ill — no longer the same man who had addressed Congress after Japan's attack on Pearl Harbor, or in the many speeches and Fireside Chats he'd given over the years since then.

In the controversy that followed, the hapless photographer was banned from the train and the White House. Meanwhile the FBI, under its director, J. Edgar Hoover, was asked to track down rumors about the President's plummeting health: stories that the President was receiving secret treatment for a fatal illness, and would not survive a fourth term, if elected.

Ironically, the same was the case in Germany. Hitler had survived the *attentat*, miraculously. However, rumors the Führer was now only a shell of his former self soon abounded — and in certain respects were true. He was by now sleeping uninterruptedly for only two hours a night.

Close-up, the Nazi leader often looked a shuffling wreck. Summoned to diagnose the damage to Hitler's ears, Major Erwin Giesing, an ENT specialist at the nearby Lötzen field hospital in East Prussia, found the once-strutting Führer a sorry sight. "He looked to me like an ageing man — almost burned out and exhausted," Giesing would afterwards recall, "like somebody husbanding every last ounce of his strength."[19]

Because of the damage to his eardrums, Hitler was no longer able to fly. "I would so much have liked," he told Dr. Giesing, "to get over to the west," where the Allied armies now numbered more than a million men ashore, and a breakout could happen any day. He would still do so, he claimed, even "as gunner in a single-engined plane" if "the dams burst" in Normandy and the Allies broke out of the bridgehead.[20] Field Marshal Rommel had already reported to him, moreover, what was inevitable. "The troops are everywhere fighting heroically, but the unequal struggle is approaching its end" — the same language the so-called Desert Fox had used at the climax of the Battle of Alamein.

Alamein had been near Cairo — more than seventeen hundred miles from Berlin. Now the "deciding" battle of the war was being fought in northern France, with the Allied frontline barely a hundred miles from Paris: gateway to the borders of the Reich. "It is urgently necessary," Rommel had pleaded, "for the proper conclusion to be drawn from this situation."[21]

The Führer had ignored him. Rommel, in any case, had been gravely wounded on July 17 — the day General Bradley's First U.S. Army forces captured Saint-Lô. The Brittany ports and the Loire Valley now beckoned as the general massed his infantry and armor for a concentrated, massive American attack with heavy U.S. Air Force support, while the British and Canadians tied down four-fifths of German panzers around Caen.

Recuperating at his headquarters, Hitler not only never spoke again in public, but would rarely allow photographs to be taken, save when posed. More than ever he was convinced he was the only person left alive with the iron will and experience of World War I to fight the war to a satisfactory German conclusion, whatever that might be. Retreat, let alone negotiating the surrender of the Third Reich, was not an option.

In San Diego, receiving via the White House Map Room confirmation that Hitler had survived the assassination attempt, the ailing president felt likewise. There would be military reverses to come, in all likelihood, and further attempts to split the Allies. There would be disagreements about the best way to end the war, and about the global structure of the postwar. But, in the struggle with Adolf Hitler, commanding the relentlessly disciplined and blinkered forces of the Third Reich, only he, Franklin Delano Roosevelt, had the necessary experience, strategic vision, as well as leadership ability to direct the United States and its allies to victory. And lay the foundations for successful postwar peace — no matter how sick he was.

It would be, in effect, Roosevelt versus Hitler. A struggle to the bitter end.

PART EIGHT

Hawaii

53

War in the Pacific

ONCE AGAIN OBSERVING the sailors' superstition about Friday departures, the USS *Baltimore* — a heavy cruiser weighing more than fourteen thousand tons — slipped out of San Diego harbor in the early minutes of Saturday, July 22, 1944, escorted by four destroyers. Destination: Pearl Harbor. Passenger: Mr. Franklin Roosevelt, President of the United States.

Bristling with big eight-inch guns — nine in total, as well as twelve five-inch thirty-eight-caliber dual-purpose cannons, some seventy-two antiaircraft guns, and two floatplanes — the giant warship was only a year old but already heavily battle-scarred, having participated in attacks on Eniwetok, Kwajalein, Tinian, Palau, Hollandia, Truk, Satawan, Marcus Island, Wake Island, Guam, and Rota. It had just returned, in fact, from the invasion of Saipan in the Marianas, as well as participating in a carrier task force raid on Iwo Jima — 760 miles short of Tokyo. As such the *Baltimore* was a symbol of the U.S. Navy's revolution in conducting modern offensive war: heavy cruisers being used as offshore artillery or bombardment platforms, and antiaircraft screening vessels; U.S. submarines decimating enemy supply vessels; U.S. aircraft carriers supporting assault landings — while also tempting the enemy into major fleet action.

What a contrast this made with the disaster at Pearl Harbor, in barely two and a half years! The ailing President, as a lifelong "navy man," could take personal pride in such a military renaissance — a transformation that reflected on the one hand the miracle of American war production, for which he could take the ultimate credit, and on the other his consistent military strategy since 1941 of a two-ocean war, for the most part under American supreme command.

Installed in the captain's quarters on the starboard side, the President did not, however, appear on deck for several days. Nor did he hold any meetings on board with his Joint Chiefs of Staff — for he was traveling without them, other than his White House chief of staff, Admiral Leahy.

It was the first time in the war, in fact, that the President was traveling outside the United States without his top military advisers — and this for a very good reason, namely that they themselves were at war with one another over strategy in the Pacific. Not only strategy, moreover, but with the problem of how to manage the personal dispute between the two supreme commanders there: General Douglas MacArthur, in the Southwest Pacific, and Admiral Chester Nimitz, in the Central Pacific.

Not one of his Joint Chiefs of Staff—General Marshall, Admiral King, and General Arnold—knew how to handle MacArthur, who had his own views on how best to defeat Japan. Dealing with MacArthur, whom the President had summoned by cable to meet with him in person in Hawaii, where Admiral Nimitz had his Central Pacific command headquarters, would be a trial for the President in his current state of health. But it had to be done. And besides, as U.S. commander in chief it would take the President away from the glare of American media, following his acceptance of the Democratic mantle for the coming presidential election. The six-day, three-thousand-mile voyage across the Pacific would hopefully assure the President enough rest to grapple with MacArthur, and then Governor Dewey. And besides: he would have a chance to inspect his army, navy, and air force contingents on Oahu—thereby debunking, by his very presence, General MacArthur's constant cry that the Pacific was the forgotten theater of the war.

Though he had not been invited to accompany the President, Admiral King was responsible for arranging the naval details of the voyage. He was, moreover, all too well acquainted with what was at stake—in fact had decided to go out to Honolulu for a week to prepare the ground, so to speak. He had stayed in Hawaii for ten days, in the end—anxious to ensure that Admiral Nimitz, who he thought too complaisant in army-navy relations, did not allow MacArthur to bend the President's ear when the general arrived there. MacArthur, King knew, would continue to argue for an immediate and unnecessary invasion of the Philippines, as he had been doing all spring and summer.

King himself was utterly opposed to another Philippines campaign, other than perhaps to establish a military base in Mindanao. The admiral figured that U.S. air and naval forces from the Central Pacific could be better used to target Formosa and the Chinese mainland directly and leave the Japanese-occupied Philippine Islands to wither on the vine. During his ten-day mission King had thus reviewed current and future strategic plans with Nimitz, whom he treated as his avatar at the forthcoming meeting with the President. They had even sailed together to the Marianas to see, in person, some of the islands and atolls that U.S. Marines, playing the dominant part, had recently assaulted with extraordinary heroism. King had still been in Honolulu on July 22, the day the President began his own journey to Hawaii aboard the USS *Baltimore*, though the naval operations chief had left Hickam Field that night—having fully prepped Admiral Nimitz.

Above all, King had urged Nimitz, no effort or expense should be spared in hosting the President, whose role as U.S. commander in chief was to be emphasized during the trip, to avoid accusations at home of the Navy aiding his election campaign in the immediate aftermath of the Democratic convention. This would also play to the President's vanity as commander in chief — King having heard from Admiral Leahy that FDR wasn't keen on the rather lax way King referred to himself as "Commander in Chief, U.S. Fleet," and his constant pressure to create a new five-star title, such as "Grand Admiral," for himself.

Impressed by the U.S. naval and military installations and suitably entertained — perhaps with a fishing expedition arranged, and an evening of Hawaiian music — the President would, King thought, be more partial to Nimitz's Central Pacific strategy for defeating Japan directly, over General MacArthur's laborious, costly, and circuitous route around the Western Pacific perimeter and the Philippines.

Would Admiral Nimitz be *assertive* enough, though? King had wondered as he'd left. The fair-haired admiral was a wonderful navy officer, and popular with his subordinates in Hawaii. But he was not a showman like MacArthur. This worried King.

For himself the President was well aware what was brewing. Ever since U.S. forces proved successful in stemming the Japanese rampage in the Pacific and assumed the offensive at Guadalcanal and Midway, the great strategic question had haunted military planners: What was the best way to advance on Tokyo?

At the high-level summit and Combined Chiefs conference at Quebec in August 1943, it had been agreed that a multipronged advance was best: including an offensive war against Japan waged by the British in northern India and Burma, and in China itself by Chiang Kai-shek, whose forces were based at Chungking, in the Chinese interior. In the Pacific, meanwhile, the war against Japan would go on as before, on two axes.

In the Central Pacific Admiral Nimitz would continue to contain the still-powerful Japanese fleet, while pushing amphibious forces across the ocean toward the Marshalls, Marianas, and Guam. This would put the Army Air Force's new B-29 long-range high-altitude bombers within striking distance of the Japanese islands. Meanwhile MacArthur, backed by smaller naval forces but more ground troops and army air support, would continue his series of "leapfrogging" assaults along the northern coast of New Guinea — bypassing heavily defended Japanese bases to avoid heavy casualties, and putting himself within striking distance of Mindanao and the Philippines.

By following this dual strategy, the United States would have two possible pincers with which to approach and cauterize the main Japanese islands — in fact three pincers, if British forces could open an overland supply route to

China, and U.S. air and naval bases could be built up on the southern Chinese mainland or Formosa.

Since the Quebec Conference, however, this overall Allied strategy had proven a disappointment in India and Burma, where British commanders, in the view of General Stilwell, had indulged in "endless walla-walla and very little fighting."[1] Stilwell himself had been unable to do much better in China, since Chiang Kai-shek seemed at permanent personal loggerheads with "Vinegar Joe" — an ardent warrior who wanted Chinese nationalist forces to fight the Japanese, not be held back to deal with communist troops under Mao.

In the Pacific, by contrast, the U.S. double-axis strategy had worked faster and more successfully than had been anticipated at Quebec — so much so that with the Marshalls falling early to American forces and MacArthur's forces establishing control of the northern coast of New Guinea, it had become imperative to decide which axis was the better one to focus on next. And it was over this conundrum, unfortunately, that the U.S. Joint Chiefs of Staff had become irremediably divided.

All spring and early summer General Arnold had favored the seizure of atolls and air bases in the Central Pacific. General Marshall, however, had wanted a more cautious advance around the Pacific Rim, under MacArthur. Admiral King had opposed this idea, since Nimitz's ships and carriers would, he pointed out, be unable to support MacArthur's army troops ashore when under threat from Japanese land-based bombers in the Philippines. It was a reality the British had learned to their cost when the *Prince of Wales* and HMS *Repulse* had been sunk by Japanese land-based aircraft in December 1941, off the coast of Malaya. King did not intend the U.S. Navy to make the same mistake.

But General MacArthur, the man on the spot, was gung ho to invade the Philippines — in fact had long seen himself as the obvious man to command the entire Pacific theater. Pressing his cause via every visitor to Australia, as well as via correspondence with senators and congressmen, MacArthur had been delighted by a growing movement in Congress and in the anti-Roosevelt press in the late fall of 1943 to have him made the single supreme commander in the Pacific, similar to pressure at that time to make General Marshall the single supreme commander for "all Europe."

The "Navy fails to understand the strategy of the Pacific," MacArthur had complained in writing to the secretary of war in January 1944, pointing out that all operations against Japanese land forces in the Pacific *had* to be backed by land-based American air power, otherwise the "attacks by the [U.S.] Navy, as at Tarawa," would lead to casualties the people of the United States would never tolerate. He hoped Stimson would make this clear to the President.[2]

Statistics had certainly been on MacArthur's side. Tarawa — an atoll in the Gilbert Islands that had been attacked by Nimitz's forces in November 1943

—had resulted in almost four thousand U.S. casualties: 1,696 killed. Similar attacks would meet the same result, MacArthur had prophesied: "tragic and unnecessary massacres of American lives." Ergo, the President must appoint him supremo in the Pacific, with all the backing the U.S. Navy could bring to bear to support his efforts. "Mr. Roosevelt is Navy minded," he'd argued, and Mr. Stimson "must persuade him. Give me central direction of the war in the Pacific," he'd begged, "and I will be in the Philippines in ten months . . . Don't let the Navy's pride of position and ignorance continue this great tragedy to our country."[3]

The President, however, had heard such wild claims from MacArthur before — in fact repeatedly, ever since MacArthur's forces had been attacked in the Philippines in 1941. He was thus unwilling to give the general carte blanche, when Admiral Nimitz had been directing the war in the Central Pacific with even greater naval success. Wisely the President had therefore declined to interfere — the more so since General Arnold had promised him, at the White House, that increasing numbers of the new B-29 Superfortress bombers would be available in the spring of 1944. They would be able, once airfields were established, to bomb Japan from China *and* the Central Pacific, if the Navy managed to seize the islands of the Marianas: Saipan, Tinian, and Guam.

The question of casualties in invading the Marianas, however, had aroused fierce arguments similar to those over Overlord — MacArthur continuing to disparage the idea of seizing the islands, and pressing for a more methodical, leapfrogging peripheral advance.

For a while MacArthur's strategic view, supported by Marshall, had prevailed. The Japanese were clearly going to defend to the last man the territories they had conquered in their 1941–42 rampage — in fact the closer the Allied forces advanced toward the home islands, the more suicidal the Japanese would become, as a matter of martial honor. A mere seventeen men out of almost five thousand soldiers had surrendered at Tarawa. As one historian later wrote, "collective death" seemed to be the preference of the Japanese military rather than "the ignominy of surrender."[4] Even Admiral Nimitz had been of a mind to favor MacArthur's plan of advancing via the Philippines and merely blockading the Japanese islands, until overruled by Admiral King in Washington.

King had been appalled. As he'd pointed out, the Japanese were going to defend *all* their conquests, bar none — like the Germans — whether in the Philippines or other Pacific islands. Retreat was dishonorable in their eyes. It was therefore important to strike before the Japanese had time to reinforce their positions — especially those positions that would be strategically helpful to the Allies. Establishing bases in the Marianas for U.S. strategic bomber forces would be important not only for the bombing of Japan's war industries, but also for protecting U.S. naval forces by providing airfields for land-based

U.S. planes — thus allowing the United States to dominate both the Western and Central Pacific. Occupying the Mariana Islands promised to provide not only airfields, but harbors and submarine facilities. Such a direct, D-day-like assault on the Marianas might even lure the Japanese Combined Fleet into leaving the security of the Sulu Sea, north of Borneo, and accepting large-scale naval battle. Proving his point, successful seizure of the Marshalls had been achieved at relatively little cost, and had been followed by the destruction of the crucial Japanese air and naval base at Truk, which was hammered from the air and largely left by the U.S. Navy to die a slow death. Nimitz's success had thus transformed the war and the balance of power between himself and MacArthur, in King's eyes. In fact King had taken Nimitz to see the ailing president in person at the White House — two weeks before the President's diagnosis of heart failure — to recognize his achievement.

Nimitz had found the President "obviously not well," the admiral's biographer later described, using interviews and Nimitz's own papers. "His face was ashen and his hands trembled. Yet he smiled and turned on the Roosevelt charm for his visitors." He'd also seemed satisfied with the emergency Joint Chiefs' recommendations that morning for "immediate operations in the Pacific Area," after listening to MacArthur's surly deputy, Richard Sutherland, as well as Nimitz himself: namely that Nimitz should help MacArthur vault his way along the New Guinea coast to Hollandia, in April 1944, but that Nimitz should thereafter go ahead and invade the Marianas, in the Central Pacific, on June 15 — to be followed by the Palaus in September, from which the bombing of Japan proper could begin. In November MacArthur would then invade Mindanao, the second largest of the Philippine Islands — leaving open the question of whether to then move on to Luzon, the largest and northernmost island, in February 1945, or to ignore the Philippines and assault directly Japanese-held positions in southern China or Formosa. The President had "listened with attention to the briefing and approved the strategy" — glad, he'd said, "to see that the drives were directed toward the China coast, for he was determined to keep China in the war."[5]

The strategic plans hadn't addressed, however, how Japan was actually to be *defeated* — which was, in the end, "his objective." Japan's actual defeat and surrender, the President had emphasized, was a project he wanted undertaken just "as soon as the Allies had enough forces" for the task, for it was only then that his United Nations vision could be implemented. After that cautionary remark, the President's concentration had appeared to fail. "He began asking irrelevant questions and making random comments," Nimitz's biographer recorded.

It had been clear to Nimitz that Roosevelt was "getting tired," and when the President had asked the admiral why, after neutralizing Truk in recent weeks, he'd sent his carriers to "raid the Marianas" in advance of the assault landings

— thus giving the Japanese advance warning of future invasion — Nimitz had taken a deep breath. He'd told the President the story of a famous surgeon who'd added an extra procedure to an appendectomy "as an encore" for his colleagues who'd come to witness the operation. "So you see Mr. President, that was the way it was. We just hit Tinian and Saipan for an encore."[6]

The President had thrown back his head and laughed — but hadn't had the energy or focus to belabor the point. Or his lingering concern.

Nimitz or MacArthur? MacArthur's brief foray into the 1944 presidential nomination campaign had certainly not helped his cause. Asking MacArthur simply to sit still in Australia, Senator Vandenberg — the President's fiercest isolationist foe in the Senate — had plotted to get a silent MacArthur drafted by the Republican Party by acclamation at its convention.[7]

Asking MacArthur to be patient, however, had been naive of Vandenberg. MacArthur would not have been MacArthur had he been willing to hold his tongue, let alone allow others to shepherd his ascent to the presidential throne on the assumption — or presumption — that they would then have control over his actions. MacArthur had thus taken time out from his military duties to respond to an insignificant Nebraska congressman's letter — praising, in a written response of his own, the congressman's recent diatribe against the President's New Deal.

Once published by Congressman Arthur L. Miller, MacArthur's letter had overnight ruined Vandenberg's plan — "crucifying the whole MacArthur movement in one inane moment," as Vandenberg noted in his diary.[8] "MacArthur would have been incomparably the greatest Commander in Chief we could have had in this war," Vandenberg had afterwards rued, and "our most eligible President" at the ultimate "peace table"[9] — completely unaware how unbalanced MacArthur could be at times, how incapable he was of working with any but subordinates, and how often loopy was his military judgment.

Publication of the general's correspondence had, in any event, forced MacArthur to declare he would not accept the Republican nomination even if it were offered to him, acknowledging the "widespread public opinion that it is detrimental to our war effort to have an officer in high position on active service at the front considered for President." As Vandenberg had noted in the privacy of his diary, however, "That is not the *real* reason."[10]

MacArthur's lack of political judgment, in Vandenberg's eyes, had been compounded by hearing stories of "veterans returning from the South Pacific" who were not "enthusiastic about our friend," as the senator had earlier confided to retired general Robert Wood, founder of the America First movement and chairman of Sears, Roebuck and Company. A "frank canvass of the men out there" in the Pacific, from a soldier he trusted, had revealed MacArthur's "growing unpopularity. What does this mean?" Vandenberg had asked Wood, deeply "disturbed."[11] Governor Dewey, meantime, had swept the Republican primaries and ended MacArthur's dream.

As he now sailed to Pearl Harbor, the President was aware, after summoning MacArthur to meet him there, that the very failure of his political aspirations would only make the general more difficult to handle — MacArthur determined to have his way at least over military strategy in the Pacific.

Certainly none of the U.S. chiefs of staff dared to do battle with "Dug-out Doug," as MacArthur was widely known by his army troops. For his part Admiral King deeply — and rightly — resented MacArthur's repeated claim that the U.S. Navy could have "saved" the Philippines after Pearl Harbor, if only Admiral King had been more offensive-minded. Yet King, for all his reputation as a "blowtorch" admiral toward his subordinates in the Navy, had never met MacArthur in person — and remained disinclined to do so. A lamentable public speaker — fearful of giving a talk in front of others unless he had a script before him — King was often so nasty toward army and air colleagues in small meetings that General Marshall, on one occasion, had "finally said to him, thumping the table, 'I will not have the meetings of the Joint Chiefs of Staff dominated by a policy of hatred. I will not have any meetings carried on with this hatred'"[12] — an eruption that had, apparently, "shut up King."[13]

King might be a difficult colleague, but MacArthur was in a league of his own — a veritable nightmare to deal with. Once rescued from Corregidor on the President's orders in March 1942, MacArthur had behaved in an almost megalomaniacal manner in Brisbane — yet had also become irreplaceable as an American leader when restoring Australian self-confidence, following the fall of the Philippines. Moreover as a combat general, MacArthur was no man of straw. Provided he had effective, selfless, and subordinate army, air, and navy combat commanders to do his bidding, he was highly professional, paternalistic, and supportive — as long as they did not detract from "his" limelight.

Irrespective of MacArthur's deplorable vanity, then, the achievements of the general's Southwest Pacific forces had, in short, been commendable. It was in the realm *beyond* his own command orbit that the real problems arose — especially with the U.S. Navy.

As General Marshall would confide later, behind the scenes, the war in the Pacific was a disaster area: "a war of personalities — a very vicious war." The "feeling was so bitter, the prejudice so great," in terms of interservice, intercommand hostility, that "the main thing was to get [them] in agreement."[14]

In the end only one person could achieve it: Mr. Roosevelt, the man who'd appointed both men to their current posts.

Hawaii, in short, would reveal whether the dying commander in chief could still command.

54

Deus ex Machina

THE CLOSER the USS *Baltimore* drew to the Hawaiian Islands on the morning of July 26, 1944, the more obvious it became that the President's arrival would be nothing like his entry into the harbor at Oran, in the Mediterranean, eight months before. This time the warship found itself escorted by some eighteen patrol planes from Oahu, then a further two *hundred* aircraft "operating from carriers at sea off Oahu."[1]

The President was in fact steaming toward a huge Hawaiian welcome.

"I was up on the bridge," Lieutenant Commander Bruenn later recalled. "The President and a couple admirals were there too. We were all very casually dressed in khakis and no neckties. As we came into Pearl Harbor a little boat came out":[2] an admiral's launch bearing the naval district commander, Admiral Robert Ghormley, and the supreme commander in the Central Pacific, Admiral Nimitz, coming to greet the President in person, together with General Robert Richardson, the army officer commanding U.S. Army troops in the Central Pacific. Also Territorial Governor Ingram Stainback (Hawaii was still a U.S. territory, not a state), and other notables. The sun was shining, the temperature was still in the midseventies with only a light wind.

"We assumed, as we neared our destination, that our expected arrival had been kept a secret. Imagine our surprise, therefore, when we steamed into the harbor and up toward the docks, to see all the Navy ships with the men at attention at the rails," recalled Judge Rosenman.[3] "The President's flag," Lieutenant Rigdon recorded in his "Log of the President's Inspection Trip to the Pacific," was "hoisted at the main in the *Baltimore* in recognition of honors rendered" — a "violation of sound security measures in time of war," he noted, "but it was found that the news of the President's visit," in disregard of censorship, "had become common knowledge in Honolulu two days before."[4] "As we entered the harbor there must have been a hundred ships there with sailors manning the rails in whites,"[5] Bruenn described.

A hundred ships? It was a deeply satisfying moment for the President — if not for Mike Reilly and the Secret Service detail, who had flown ahead to Hawaii. In a matter of two and a half years the United States had become the most powerful global military power in the world, bar none — and for the third time in sixteen months the U.S. Commander in Chief was inspecting his forces abroad in an active theater of war.

As the USS *Baltimore* docked at Pier 22-B in the Navy Yard, immediately behind the USS *Enterprise* carrier, the mood on shore was one of understandable excitement. "We finally docked and at least 20 or 24 flag officers came aboard to pay their respects," Dr. Bruenn recalled — "Navy, Army, Marines, Air Corps, the works." As well as the USS *Enterprise* there were no fewer than six more U.S. aircraft carriers moored in the harbor, and three huge battleships, nineteen submarines, more than thirty destroyers, and almost two hundred landing craft and auxiliary vessels.

This was Pearl Harbor, 1944: epicenter of modern American military might in the Pacific, and a reason for all to celebrate. All, to be sure, save General MacArthur, whose plane had reportedly landed from Brisbane, but who was conspicuous by his absence at the pier.

Afterwards, in serious military historiography, it would be FDR's arbitration in the great strategy debate that would be considered the primary feature of the President's trip to Pearl Harbor. And to a large extent this was so — Mr. Roosevelt's personal mediation between Nimitz and MacArthur proving crucial to the conduct of the war in the Pacific. Yet the Commander in Chief was going out to the Pacific as president, too — and Judge Rosenman, his speechwriter and White House counselor, was with him throughout, judging the temper of the times in terms of the President's reelection chances.

Rosenman, in particular, was interested to see the people of Hawaii, not only dignitaries, gathering in the tens of thousands to celebrate the President's arrival. No stone was to be left unturned in hosting the President, Admiral King had instructed — and it was clear Nimitz had followed his orders to the letter, as the huge crowds of civilians and military personnel at the quayside showed.

Though he still often felt desperately ill, the President was touched. As always he was energized by public support, but he nevertheless had his own agenda. By winding MacArthur into his official inspection of the island, he hoped to *educate* the wayward general. Hawaii remained the primary Pacific military headquarters — one that MacArthur had still not visited a single time in all the years he'd been in Australia! Somehow the President must show the prickly egoist there were no hard feelings about his brief foray into presidential politics that spring, and no bias toward one service or command over another. They were all now part of one team and must therefore work to defeat Japan together, not apart — this would be his mantra.

MacArthur's absence from the quayside thus came as something of an insult, for there was no sign of the general, or word from him. "Everybody sat around for maybe half an hour. All of a sudden over the loud speaker: 'General MacArthur is coming aboard,'" Dr. Bruenn remembered. "And here he came wearing a leather jacket and his soft hat, making his appearance. He was that kind of guy."[6]

The general's late appearance certainly stole the show. As Rosenman put it, MacArthur "could be dramatic — at dramatic moments."[7]

Whether it was the President or Admiral Leahy who remarked to MacArthur that wearing a heavy red leather flying jacket was perhaps de trop in summer weather would be disputed later. Either way, MacArthur was, all concurred, completely unembarrassed. He'd failed to get Republican acclamation as presidential nominee, but had now made a spectacular entrance, in front of a vast audience on the quayside, and had no reason to feel shame at his tardiness — or his attire. "Well, you haven't been where I came from, and it's cold up there in the sky"[8] was his rejoinder — deliberately reminding the President how far he'd had to fly to get to the meeting.

There were photographs taken on deck, after which the President asked Nimitz, MacArthur, Ghormley, and Richardson to come to his cabin. There it was agreed they'd all meet the next morning at the residence in Waikiki where the President was going to stay. Together they would tour the island's installations — thus ensuring MacArthur would gain a better idea of the Central Pacific theater's main base. After this they would dine at Waikiki as the President's guests. Only the following day, Friday, July 28, would the President, Nimitz, and MacArthur get together, with Admiral Leahy, at the Waikiki house, to discuss future strategy.

In other words, the President was hoping to "soften up" his two supreme commanders before, like gladiators, they faced off against each other in front of him.

With that agreed, they went briefly back on deck for more photographs and newsreel filming and then went their separate ways.

MacArthur was furious.

55

Slow Torture

THE HOLMES ESTATE on Kalakaua Avenue, Waikiki Beach, was palatial. "Since Mr. Holmes' death a short while ago," wrote Lieutenant Rigdon, "his home has been used by our naval aviators attached to carriers of the Pacific Fleet as a rest home between missions. It is an ideal spot for this purpose as we found it very comfortable and quiet there"[1] — the fliers less happy at having to rest elsewhere, however, during the President's stay.

The grand home fronted the famous beach, with rolling white breakers rippling toward the shore. Behind high walls it possessed grounds "studded with shrubs and tall Royal Hawaiian palm trees," and spouting water fountains. The President occupied a large suite on the third floor, accessible via an outside elevator. Dr. Bruenn was lodged there, too, to be on hand if there was any sign of new heart problems.

General MacArthur was surprised by the President's unmistakable physical decline, despite the restorative effects of the sea voyage to Hawaii. Indeed he would tell his own doctor, on returning to Brisbane: "Doc, the mark of death is upon him! In six months he'll be in his grave."[2]

In his memoirs, two decades later, MacArthur remembered how "shocked" he'd been by the President's "appearance. I had not seen him for a number of years, and physically he was just a shell of the man I had known. It was clearly evident that his days were numbered."[3] Yet, as MacArthur noted, it was more a physical change than a mental deterioration: the President still as focused and determined, in the few hours a day that he was able to work, as ever. Even physically the President's cascading health was not evident save close-up. In photographs and newsreels, taken at a distance, he still looked the leonine figure who'd steered his country in peace and war for a record twelve years: his demeanor as authoritative as ever.

That the President had a shrewd agenda was immediately apparent to Mac-Arthur, who was no fool. There had been no meeting of minds or even social gathering the first evening, following the President's arrival, leaving MacArthur to dine alone with General Richardson and contemplate the next day's "political junket," as MacArthur had disparaged it on the flight from Brisbane. His friend Frazier Hunt, a toadying print and radio journalist who was taking care of MacArthur's correspondence at his headquarters in Australia, later re-created MacArthur's mood at General Richardson's house. "As he walked the floor of his bedroom here in Richardson's quarters this late July night of 1944, he talked without restraint to a trusted member of his staff [probably his press officer and former journalist, Lloyd Lehrbas, who had traveled with him] regarding his long years of struggle and his many defeats and frustrations: and he spoke of his country's inadequate leadership, the terrible mistakes made in the war and America's uncertain future. He seemed to unburden himself in a way he had seldom if ever done before in all his life."[4]

The general had every reason to feel he'd been snookered. He had brought with him his press officer — who censored on MacArthur's behalf all communiqués in and out of the Southwest Pacific until they became, as one biographer wrote, "as lush as the New Guinea jungle" — but the President had also brought his *own* contingent of press officers and journalists: the Office of War Information director, Elmer Davis, and three White House press agency correspondents, Merriman Smith, Howard Fleiger, and Robert Nixon, as well as three radio pool correspondents. Further war reporters and photographers, moreover, were on tap in Hawaii — none of whom would be subject to MacArthur's publicity edicts and manipulation. The general would thus have to travel the breadth of Oahu the next day in the company and shadow of the President of the United States ahead of the following day's strategic duel with Nimitz before the Commander in Chief, at the Holmes estate.

MacArthur was understandably frustrated. He had not even brought his deputy, General Sutherland, only Lehrbas and Bonner Fellers, his military secretary — without maps, even. As MacArthur later wrote, he'd planned to fly straight back to Australia after the military discussion — and had had no interest in touring military camps containing ordinary soldiers, sailors, and airmen. It was no small wonder he felt "as depressed and frustrated" as he had on Corregidor.[5]

The President, however, saw matters very differently.

Admiral Ghormley had come to his suite at Waikiki after dinner on Wednesday to "arrange the schedule of the three-day visit" in detail.[6] MacArthur's showy appearance at the quayside had not unduly upset the President; rather, it had spurred his competitive spirit. He had therefore asked Ghormley for a comfortable open limousine to be sequestered. A famous red one belonging to a local madam was turned down for obvious reasons, but the big black one belonging to the local fire chief, when suggested, had been considered perfect — for the President wanted, he said, to sit three abreast with his two supreme commanders in the theater, literally, of war. The photos and news-reels would play extremely well at home, once he'd departed: the equivalent of those memorable photos of himself with Joseph Stalin and Winston Churchill in Tehran. In this case, though, instead of showing him at the Russian Embassy in Iran, he would be at the heart of the war in the Pacific, together with his two top commanders. Moreover, seen live by servicemen and the people of Oahu, they would present a vivid picture that, contrary to reports of intertheater jeal-ousies, there was a Nimitz-MacArthur unity of strategic and tactical direction of the war in the Pacific, under the aegis of the nation's commander in chief. The President would sit in his usual place on the curb side (for ease of egress in emergency) of the vehicle, with Nimitz on the offside — and MacArthur squashed between them, unable to escape!

The only question was: would the President be able to manage *six hours* of inspection in different venues, when he had barely survived one hour in San Diego? His doctors were ambivalent, but the President insisted. He had rested for almost a week on the USS *Baltimore*; it was time to see whether, standing for reelection in the fall, he could possibly manage one half day.

With two big Stars and Stripes mounted over the limo's front wheels, the flags fluttering in the breeze, they rode past "Base Hospital Number 8 (at Mc-Grew Point, Pearl Harbor), past the many activities at Aiea; past the sugar mill at Waipahu; and on to our first stop — the Marine Corps Air Station." The "Naval Air Station at nearby Barbers Point" followed, and the Naval Ammuni-tion Depot at Lualualei, as they drove through the "many scattered magazines and ammunition stowage facilities," and on to the Navy's "main radio trans-mitting station for Hawaii," which was "high atop the Waianai Mountains," Lieutenant Rigdon recorded.[7]

As supreme commander, MacArthur had earned an unfortunate reputation for ignoring modern naval warfare techniques — in fact he was known to have set foot aboard a navy vessel only once since being rescued by PT boat from the Philippines. The tour of the island's naval facilities was thus an education. At the Schofield Barracks, forty thousand airmen and army troops had the chance to see the President as he was driven past "long lines of tanks" and "the hangars and plane-covered aprons of Wheeler Field," where wounded men from the battles on Saipan and Guam were being lifted down on stretchers to be taken to the post hospital. With the President's car driven up onto a special raised stand, the troops marched past — even Japanese American troops, since the President had emphatically overridden his Secret Service advice against exposing himself to "any Japanese fanatic in the ranks" who might "shoot the President at point blank range."[8]

After lunch at the officers' mess, the President explained he had not come to make speeches, but to see "with my own eyes" the change since his last visit in 1934, "ten years to the day today," as he said in brief remarks. Of twelve tanks at the review in 1934, "seven broke down before they could get past," and the air review was similarly deficient. He was thus delighted by the transformation. "It is being felt all through this area. All the way down to General MacArthur's area, which, thank the Lord, is coming a little closer towards us, and automatically closer to the enemy than it was two years ago. It is good to see the three services together, because I think this morning I have seen not only the Marine Corps Air working together, but the Navy Air and the Army Air working together in all their component parts. I wish everybody back home could see and understand a little more of what's going on out here."[9]

For MacArthur this was a form of slow torture: a testament to modern amphibious warfare under Admiral Nimitz, but one that left MacArthur looking somewhat tortoise-like. General Richardson marched his entire Seventh Division before the President after lunch, but MacArthur could see his old army friend now only as a sort of prisoner of the Navy: "an unhappy man. He lives like a prince with fine cars and a fine home," MacArthur described, "but he has no authority." There had been an unholy row after the commanding officer of the U.S. Twenty-Seventh Division, fighting alongside U.S. Marines, had had to be relieved by a Marine general during the battle on Saipan as insufficiently aggressive, and Richardson was still smarting. "He is a fine, courteous gentleman, so the Navy have him licked," MacArthur railed at what he considered an insult to the Army. But, as MacArthur put it, "they have beaten him so many times there is nothing more he can do."[10]

The afternoon was no less exhausting than the morning: inspection of the Naval Construction Battalions camp at Moanalua Ridge (the "Seabees," as the President said in his remarks there, "now known on every ocean and every continent" — in fact a part of the armed forces that had "come forward as an institution more quickly than any one I know of in the whole of our history"); then Camp Catlin, home of a unit of the Fleet Marine Force, Pacific; and finally the Royal Hawaiian Hotel, which was partly used "as a rest center for U.S. submarine crews" — and where the President himself had stayed in 1934.[11]

Poor MacArthur had been forced not only to eat camp fare all day, but humble pie, in his own opinion — making only small talk as the presidential party toured the military installations and the President spoke to his Marines, soldiers, sailors, submariners, and airmen. And after six hours of that, there was still dinner to come — for MacArthur was expected to return and dine two hours later, at the Holmes mansion, along with Admiral Nimitz, Admiral Leahy, and Admiral Halsey, commander of the Third Fleet, who was flying in to Honolulu from the United States that afternoon.

General MacArthur could later remember nothing of the meal, only that he was completely without support staff — and at the next morning's strategy conference would have to "go it alone," as he put it.[12]

He would certainly never forget what happened after the meal. The President, who had undertaken more that day in Hawaii than on any single day since his trip to see Stalin eight months earlier, seemed to have accessed some hidden reservoir of energy. As the staff removed the dessert plates, he announced that the commanders were to follow him into the conference room next door, where military and naval maps covered the tables. From one wall hung a ten-foot-high map of the Pacific — and settling into bamboo chairs before it, the two supreme commanders in the Pacific were each asked, without preparation, to make a presentation.

Taking a long bamboo pointer, the President pointed at the Marianas and New Guinea. "Well, Doug," he shot at MacArthur, turning to face the general. "Where do we go from here?"[13]

56

In the Examination Room

As ONE MACARTHUR BIOGRAPHER NOTED, "Even a dying FDR was formidable."[1]

MacArthur was first up. "'Mindaneo,' Mr. President, then Leyte,'" the general answered, using the bamboo pole to locate the islands, "and then Luzon.'"

Luzon was the northernmost of the Philippine Islands. Was it really necessary, in a war to defeat Japan? The parallel with Italy, in terms of the defeat of Hitler's Third Reich, was unavoidable. MacArthur's argument, however, was that possession of the islands would allow American forces to cut Japan off from its vital sources of oil and other necessities of war. It would have major political implications, he added. The liberation of the islands, and the granting of immediate independence to the Philippines — as mandated under the Tydings-McDuffie Act, which the President himself had signed in 1934 — would demonstrate to the world the United States was *not* pursuing an imperialist agenda.

Admiral Nimitz then presented his alternative strategy: bypassing the Philippines, where there were more than three hundred thousand Japanese troops defending the islands, and advancing instead straight across the Pacific to Formosa by the summer of 1945, from which the main Japanese islands could either be blockaded or invaded.

MacArthur, in private, was "sure" Nimitz's argument was Admiral King's "and not his own." In front of the President, though, MacArthur did not see, as he later described his performance, how Nimitz could leave hundreds of thousands of Japanese troops "in his rear in the Philippines," where there were substantial numbers of POWs and civilians. Who knew what the Japanese were capable of, in terms of atrocities? And the casualties involved in a direct line of attack across the Pacific would be, he claimed, daunting.

MacArthur had come to the meeting without staff, but he had done his homework. He was convinced that the President already knew from his Joint

Chiefs of Staff in Washington "the general concept of the [King/Nimitz] plan" but was "doubtful of it." He supposed it was the President's very doubts that had led him to Hawaii to make a decision that he could otherwise have communicated from Washington. The President was nevertheless "entirely neutral in handling the discussion," MacArthur remembered gratefully.[2]

Although no minutes were kept of the meeting, Admiral Leahy's diary entry that night confirmed MacArthur's memory. Having witnessed how the President had run the Tehran meetings, Leahy was no stranger to his skills as a chairman who allowed both sides to present their case, before coming to a decision. In his journal Leahy noted: "General MacArthur is convinced that an occupation of the Philippines is essential before any serious attack on Japanese-held territory north of Luzon. He stated that he now has in his command sufficient ground and air forces to take the Philippine Islands, and his additional needs are only landing craft and naval support."[3]

Nimitz contested MacArthur's claim. The Japanese possessed substantial, well-embedded military forces in the Philippines, but they also had significant naval and air strength in the shallow and contorted island waters, meaning that an American assault landing could not be backed by U.S. naval forces, vulnerable to land-based air attack, but only by U.S. submarines. MacArthur's preferred Philippine strategy would thus not allow for the use of the very weapon Nimitz's forces had so brilliantly developed over previous months: their ability to mount D-day-like amphibious assaults on any chosen island or atoll, while bypassing and neutralizing those that were too heavily defended.

Backwards and forwards the arguments were batted — with the President alive to the strengths and weaknesses of each position.

Formosa was close to the Chinese mainland, yes — and certainly closer to Japan than Luzon — but there were still a million Japanese troops in China, and powerful Japanese defense forces on Formosa itself. Above all, Formosa was nearly two thousand miles from the Marianas. Eisenhower's D-day assault on the beaches of Normandy had been mounted across eighty miles of the English Channel, already an immense undertaking that Churchill had feared would fail. This proposal was of an entirely different order, even with U.S. carrier support.

Under questioning Nimitz agreed, however, that some, at least, of the Philippine Islands would have to be seized by MacArthur, if only to protect Nimitz's left flank, and in order to interdict Japanese reinforcement elsewhere. MacArthur, for his part, was made to face up to the enormity of what he was proposing: namely attacking a huge Japanese army, in well-established defensive positions, in the difficult jungle terrain of the Philippines — islands the Japanese were already reinforcing. Military intelligence was estimating almost ninety thousand Japanese troops on Luzon, with a further twenty-four thousand on the island of Leyte, and perhaps sixty thousand on Mindanao. How did he propose to defeat those forces with only the forces he currently had, as he claimed? And what of U.S. casualties? "But Douglas," the President said, "to take Luzon would demand heavier losses than we can stand. It seems to me we *must* bypass it."[4]

Challenged by the President, MacArthur said that his "losses would not be heavy, any more than they have been in the past. The days of frontal assault are over. Modern infantry weapons are too deadly, and direct assault is no longer feasible. Only mediocre commanders still use it. Your good commanders do not turn in heavy losses." Filipinos, too, would probably assist the U.S. liberators, like the Maquis in France, whereas on Formosa, which had been under Japanese control for half a century, there was no promise of aid.

As Leahy saw it, this was one of the President's finest hours as U.S. commander in chief: questioning and maintaining focus so that, in a calmly professional manner, the two supreme commanders each had their say — and took account of each other's positions. Certainly in the history of the war on the Allied side there had never been anything like it. "Roosevelt was at his best as he tactfully steered the discussion from one point to another and narrowed down the area of disagreement between MacArthur and Nimitz," Leahy later recalled. "The discussion remained on a friendly basis the entire time."[5]

Decades of military historians would later underplay the significance of the parley. Yet to Leahy it was a landmark in the prosecution of the war, a "much more peaceful" argument "than I had been hearing in Washington. Here in Honolulu we were working with facts, not with emotional reactions of politicians." The reported antipathy between the commanders was not evident, either, despite MacArthur's reputation even in his own service. "It was no secret that in the Pentagon Building in Washington there were men who disliked him, to state the matter mildly," Leahy noted with his customary understatement.[6] Before the President in Hawaii, however, the two supreme commanders had exemplified as nowhere else the vast changes in modern warfare — technological, tactical, and logistical — while they pushed their pointers across the great wall map of the Pacific.

For all their military savvy in fighting the Japanese, both MacArthur and Nimitz knew the war was gradually moving into a new phase in the Pacific: one where politics could no longer be excluded. Just as had been the case in Cairo and Tehran, the closer the Allies moved to victory over the once-omnipotent military empires of the Third Reich and Japan, the more did the endgame pose political questions. Admiral King had left a memo with Nimitz to give to MacArthur, detailing British aspirations in the Pacific: namely British occupation of the Dutch East Indies, Admiral Mountbatten to assume responsibility for Australia also, while MacArthur's forces moved into the Philippines, and the transfer of Royal Navy vessels, currently in the Indian Ocean, to the Pacific. Clearly the British, having had to be rescued by the United States military, now wished to reestablish their colonial empire and territories in the Far East, from India to Hong Kong, on the coast of China — and possibly garner more.

The future in Asia — given the war-within-a-war between Chiang Kai-shek's forces and those of Mao Tse-tung in China — was equally uncertain. Even the military challenge would have political consequences, not least at home. Evicting the Japanese from the territories they had overrun promised to be immensely costly, in blood and treasure, before U.S. forces even got to Japan proper. If the Japanese continued to fight to the last man standing, could the war possibly be won without incurring casualties unacceptable to the people of America? Would not Russian help be required, not only in providing air bases for U.S. bombers and harbors for U.S. military supplies, but troops as well, in Manchuria, where a three-quarters-of-a-million-strong Japanese army was stationed?

It was testament to the President's acumen that, listening to his two supreme commanders, he recognized their two unique merits both as commanders and strategists. Nimitz, quiet and determined, had proven MacArthur utterly wrong in the general's adamant opposition to Operation Forager, the recent seizure of the Marianas. Nimitz's brilliant amphibious invasions of Saipan, Tinian, and now Guam had not only permitted the United States to acquire inviolable bases from which to bomb Japan and dominate the Central Pacific with naval forces, including submarines, but would now allow it to establish and maintain such naval bases across the Pacific *after the war was won,* without needing to become a colonial empire like the British — or the Dutch or French.

By the same token, however, MacArthur's operations along the northern coast of New Guinea had been exemplary, confounding Nimitz's predictions. By advancing in leaps and bounds — "leapfrogging" — and by bypassing Japanese strongholds, MacArthur had minimized casualties while pushing his forces within striking distance of the southern Philippines.

Yet for all that, it was MacArthur's political vision that most impressed the President. The general had, it seemed, learned his lesson. In February 1942 the President had had to spur MacArthur into refusing to allow the president of the Philippines to negotiate with the Japanese, arguing that the United States must show the world its commitment to democratic principles, not Japanese militarism.[7] Now, two and a half years later, here was Douglas MacArthur arguing that, in addition to the importance of defeating the Japanese, he and the United States had a "sacred" obligation to the people of the Philippines to liberate them — and demonstrate to the world the genuineness of American principles by returning sovereignty to the islands, as per the Tydings-McDuffie Act of 1934. Fulfilling that goal, MacArthur reasoned, would probably do more to persuade postwar Asia of America's good intentions, and at less ultimate cost, than anything else the United States could do.

The President was of the same strategic mind. If, of course, it could be done successfully, without too great a slaughter.

The specter of slaughter also hung over Admiral Nimitz's proposals to invade Iwo Jima, the Bonin Islands, and Formosa.

Iwo Jima and Formosa, under Nimitz's outline plan, could be used as launchpads for an invasion of Okinawa, the Japanese island halfway between Formosa and the Japanese home islands. The President acknowledged such a strategy to be by far the most direct route to Tokyo. But at what cost in blood, if the Japanese continued to contest, suicidally, every inch and every atoll they had conquered?

The President certainly did not buy MacArthur's claim that the Philippines could have been "relieved" by counteraggressive naval action in early 1942. Nor did he agree that failing to "relieve" the islands as a matter of priority in 1944–45 would not be forgiven by the people of America, let alone the Philippines. War was war. But so was postwar!

MacArthur was surely right in seeing the liberation of the Philippines as a symbolic and political duty of the United States, for it was in the Philippines where the difference between Japanese militarism and American democracy could best be seen by the world. Defeating the Japanese military as swiftly as possible was one thing, but showing that difference in the Philippines — where Japanese occupying forces were committing atrocities on a frightening scale — was arguably more important. Who knew what the Japanese would do to American POWs and civilians in captivity if the Japanese soldiers in the Philippines saw their own homeland being bombed and invaded?

It was a sickening thought for all of them. At midnight the President called it a day, and sent the supreme commanders back to their quarters, "with the President making no final decision," as MacArthur related.[8] They were asked, though, to return at 10:15 a.m. to continue the discussion. That the President had conducted such an intense strategy session at the end of a long day inspecting troops was nothing less than a miracle, given his state of health. Or ill health.

By the next morning both supreme commanders seemed to better understand and respect each other's views, at least. MacArthur argued that, once in possession of the Philippines, he could "sweep down" on the Japanese forces in the Dutch East Indies "from the rear." Moreover, bypassing the Philippines, and thereby forfeiting logistical backup to Nimitz's plans for direct assault, would not make military sense, he claimed, given the gamble Nimitz would be taking in mounting invasions of Formosa and Okinawa, which MacArthur accepted as the most direct way of defeating Japan. However tough the task, the northernmost Philippine island, Luzon, would simply have to be taken. And with this view Admiral Nimitz, departing from King's script, felt compelled to agree.

Thus the consensus emerged — beginning with the decision that the British would be denied a role in the Pacific lest they cause the same kind of problems they had caused in the Mediterranean. With the British considered irrelevant, the two supreme commanders in the Pacific should pursue a biaxial strategy: MacArthur would be responsible for liberating the Philippines and doubling back on the Dutch East Indies, with as much naval and carrier support as Nimitz could give, while Nimitz, for his part, would continue to deal with the Japanese fleet, and establish major strategic bomber airfields on Guam and the Marianas. He would set up naval bases and a new Central Pacific forward headquarters there also, and plan the invasions of Iwo Jima, Formosa, and Okinawa for the next year. Whatever happened in China, this strategy would hopefully be enough to force the Japanese to sue for surrender, unconditionally.

The President had achieved his aim: the two theater commanders were now allies, not rivals. MacArthur would completely rethink his plan of starting his assault on the Philippines by an invasion of Mindanao, where there were more than sixty thousand Japanese troops; Nimitz would rethink his idea of invading Formosa. "I personally am convinced that they are together the best qualified officers in our service for this tremendous task," Leahy considered, "and that they will work together in full agreement toward the common end of defeating Japan."[9]

Could any other commander in chief have managed this? In newsreel film shot that morning, the President looked well — certainly no worse than bald Admiral Leahy, or even MacArthur, whose thin dark hair was pasted across his balding head and who looked pinched and reserved, while Nimitz looked grandfatherly under his thick white hair. Unfortunately this was, of course, an optical illusion — as Admiral Charles Lockwood, commanding the submarine base whose mariners the President had addressed at the Royal Hawaiian Hotel the day before, recalled. The "President's appearance was distressing," he later related, noting that his "skin had that grayish tinge one often sees in the very ill."[10]

Nonetheless the President had seemed masterful in mind and spirit — nursing his limited energy for when it counted, and then pulling out all the stops. There was a brief lunch with MacArthur and Nimitz, both of whom then took their leave of the President: Nimitz to return to his headquarters, MacArthur to fly back from Hickam Field to Brisbane.[11]

The President, however, carried on with a full afternoon of inspections, beginning with the Army Jungle Training Center in Kahana Bay, conducted from the fire chief's open limousine. There he was witness to every aspect of jungle warfare, from enfilading to pillbox assault, bridging to hand-to-hand fighting, with live ammunition; thence to the Naval Air Station at Kaneohe Bay, to inspect Fleet Air Wing Two's carrier pilot-and-aircrew training station. And from there to Kailua, to the amphibious warfare station at Wailupe, followed by the Coast Guard base at Diamond Head. Finally, back at the Holmes estate, there was a "small" dinner party for the President, with music provided by the famous Hawaiian composer and bandleader Bill Akamuhou.

Admiral Leahy was impressed, as he confided to his diary — the performance given "between the house and the sea and under the palm trees, the leaves of which were alternately black and silver in the bright light of a half moon, a very lovely setting and a beautiful sight."[12]

In the midst of the most violent war in human history, it was an idyllic end to an extraordinary day — the last such night the President would experience in his dwindling life.

An even more exhausting schedule of inspections had been set for the next day before the President was to board the USS *Baltimore* in the evening for the voyage home via the Aleutian Islands. Whether this was wise or not, it was a schedule the President declared he was going to keep — and did.

Above all, by continuing his grueling itinerary Roosevelt wanted to prove he could still manage not only the tough business of being president and commander in chief in war, but the physical and mental challenges of standing for reelection a fourth time, with all that would involve — including facing the press.

And so, at 4:45 p.m. on July 29, 1944, two hours before leaving Waikiki, the President addressed a gathering of reporters and radio journalists — telling them, with some emotion, what a "pipe dream" his visit to Hawaii had been. He'd seen America's former "outpost" in the Pacific become its centerpiece — the "main distributing point" for America's prosecution of the war against Japan, which would be pursued relentlessly until the "unconditional surrender" of that empire, just as that of the Third Reich. A willingness to discuss terms in advance might theoretically lead to swifter surrender, he acknowledged — but would only produce the same result as after World War I. "Practically every German denies the fact they surrendered in the last war, but this time they are going to know it. And so are the Japs," he declared. His meetings with Admiral Nimitz and MacArthur over the past two days had been "very successful," and though he obviously could not reveal what had been agreed, the discussions had "involved new offensives against Japan." No meeting with Winston Churchill was planned, since the war in the Pacific was being conducted under American supreme commanders — and would, yes, include the liberation of the Philippines. He did not wish "to possibly give the enemy an inkling as to which way we are going," he said, but "we are going to get the

Philippines back, and without question General MacArthur will take part in it. Whether he goes direct or not, I can't say." As to whether he had merely confirmed existing strategy, or set a new one, the President was typically coy. As he put it, "You review or re-establish strategy about once a week as you go along, it's just normal procedure. But it was very useful, this particular conference. I think it was one of the most important we have held in some time."[13]

It was. But at a greater cost to the President's remaining strength than he would acknowledge. Sam Rosenman and Elmer Davis had been especially concerned lest the sheer intensity of his program of military talks and inspections result in an exhaustion, even physical breakdown, of the President that could not be concealed from public view. Miraculously the opposite had been the case. At Hickam Field the President had spoken to wounded men on stretchers, airlifted from Guam. "What surprise and cheer those boys showed on unexpectedly facing their President!" Lieutenant Rigdon noted.[14]

In the new Naval Hospital at Aiea, above Pearl Harbor, the President had left his car and without self-consciousness toured some of the wards in his wheelchair, wheeled by one of his Secret Service detail.

Many of the patients who had lost arms or legs had had no idea their President was himself disabled. As Rosenman, who accompanied Mr. Roosevelt, later recalled, the President had "insisted on going past each individual bed. He had known for twenty-three years what it was to be deprived of the use of both legs. He wanted to display himself and his useless legs to those boys who would have to face the same bitterness. This crippled man on the little wheel chair wanted to show them that it was possible to rise above such physical handicaps. With a cheery smile to each of them, and a pleasant word at the bedside of a score or more, this man who had risen from a bed of helplessness ultimately to become President of the United States and leader of the free world was living proof of what the human spirit could do to conquer the incapacities of the human body . . . The expressions on the faces on the pillows, as he slowly passed by and smiled, showed how effective was this self-display of crippled helplessness. I never saw Roosevelt with tears in his eyes," Rosenman added; but "that day as he was wheeled out of the hospital he was close to them."[15]

When asked by a reporter, several weeks later, what he made of Republicans' criticism that "the whole trip is political," the President could only smile, and say — to laughter — "Well, they must know better than I do."[16]

Rosenman, for his part, had left the President's group to fly home and work on the coming political campaign. He was also taking a note with him for Eleanor.

"Dearest Babs," the President had scribbled. "Just off — hectic 3 days — very good results. All is well. Ever so much love. Devotedly, F."[17]

57

A Terrible Mistake

LEAVING PEARL HARBOR, the President had every reason to be proud of his trip — the results as good and as historic, he thought, as those he'd gotten at Tehran.

Meantime the press were excited by the President's royal reception in Hawaii — and evidence of his good health. Though their reports would have to be held up until the President was safely back on American soil, their delayed stories from Honolulu carried photos of the President with his supreme commanders and of a host of inspection tours he had made, too — a powerful visual demonstration of America's growing war effort in the Pacific. "New and crushing blows to bring the enemy to his knees and unconditional surrender were planned at a conference by the President," the *Boston Globe*'s war correspondent, Martin Sheridan, reported,[1] together with accounts of Roosevelt's breakneck visit to military installations across Oahu, while the *New York Times* carried the texts of his speeches and talks to troops, Seabees, and wounded soldiers at Aiea.

Elmer Davis, directing the Office of War Information, and Steve Early, the President's press secretary, were both delighted. Moreover when a newspaper in Texas printed a letter from a soldier in Hawaii saying the President of the United States had been there and was going to the Aleutians, the decision was made to release on August 11 all delayed war correspondents' reports from Honolulu.

Davis's and Early's jubilation turned to horror the next day, however.

The President, having reached the Aleutians, had made his two-day tour of the islands, aboard a U.S. destroyer, in miserable weather. At Bremerton he was then scheduled to make a speech to several thousand navy yard workers gathered at the dock, which would also be carried as a radio broadcast to the nation. For reasons no one could ever quite explain, the President was expected to give his address — thirty-five minutes long — standing. Not only standing, but alone, at a lectern, before a crowd that had, by the time the moment arrived, swollen to an estimated ten thousand — and millions more, listening on radio, with further tens of thousands watching newsreel of him that would subsequently be shown in theaters.

The President had not actually stood upright, using his steel leg braces, for more than eight months, however. He had lost so much weight — some twenty pounds — that the braces no longer fit around his waist, it was found, and the steel dug into his skin, beneath his dark suit. Clearly Steve Early's political intent was to show the nation and the world a president returning from the sort of military inspection tour abroad that bespoke his role as U.S. commander in chief, standing on the deck of a U.S. Navy warship returning from Pearl Harbor. But if so, Early had no idea what he was asking of the ailing president.

Whether Roosevelt realized it was not going to work would never be clear. At 5:00 p.m. the President did manage to reach the lectern — holding on to it for dear life, while also having to turn the pages of his script.

Crouching behind the gun turret on the USS *Cummings*, his daughter watched with desperation as her father, in obvious physical distress, did his best. A searing pain, as at San Diego three weeks earlier, ripped his chest, but higher this time: symptoms of the heart attack his doctors had always dreaded.

"He began his address at 5 pm and spoke for 35 min.," Dr. Bruenn chronicled a quarter century after the President's death, when he could no longer be accused of unpatriotic revelation. "During the early part of the speech the President for the first time experienced substernal oppression with radiation to both shoulders. The discomfort lasted about 15 min, gradually subsiding at the end of the period."[2]

A further twenty years later Bruenn disclosed that the heart attack was almost inevitable, following the "heart failure" the President had suffered in the spring. The miracle was that, giving his speech, standing alone at the lectern, Roosevelt hadn't flinched. "He kept on with the speech," Bruenn told an interviewer, recalling the President's sheer determination, then "came below and said, 'I had a helluva pain.' We stripped him down in the cabin of the ship, took a cardiogram" — using equipment transferred from the *Baltimore* — "some blood and so forth." And collectively held their breath.

"Fortunately it was a transient episode, a so-called angina, not a myocardial infarction," which could well have led to death. "But that was really a very disturbing situation," Bruenn reflected — "the first time under my observation that he had something like this. He had denied any pain before" — the President concealing from Bruenn his attack aboard the *Magellan* on July 20. "It was, nevertheless proof positive that he had coronary disease, no question about it."[3]

Roosevelt's courage, unfortunately, was for naught. It certainly went unappreciated by the crowd attending the speech, who were deeply disappointed. With General Patton's breakout toward Paris hitting the headlines, shipyard workers on the West Coast wanted an upbeat speech about the war in the Pacific, the likely defeat of Japan, the kind of peace to come. What they got instead was a dying man's halting account of what he had seen on his trip, as if he'd been a tourist, not the U.S. commander in chief — the President not even mentioning Pearl Harbor until halfway through his peroration.

"No very great enthusiasm was shown by the thousands gathered about the Bremerton dock," Admiral Leahy recalled later.[4]

It was small wonder. As Judge Rosenman noted, having listened in Washington, D.C., to the President's account on the radio, the "report of his trip" was execrable. "Whilst this was not an important speech, it was a major one," Rosenman acknowledged, "and deserved much more attention"[5] than the few afternoon hours the President had spent dictating the draft to Lieutenant Rigdon on board the USS *Cummings* — dictation without input from another soul, or a sounding board to measure how it would come across to a local audience in Washington State. Or, more importantly, to its national audience, which was said to have exceeded forty million listeners.

"The people had not heard the President since the acceptance speech of July 20; he had in the meantime journeyed out to Hawaii and Alaska; Dewey had been out strenuously campaigning" — and accusing the Roosevelt administration of being led by tired old men. "The American people expected that the President had something to say and would say it," Rosenman chronicled, adding, "but the speech had nothing to say, and said it poorly." At best, it was a "rambling account of his journeys and experiences during the past month, and he adlibbed a great deal in a very ineffective manner. It was a dismal failure. That speech, together with the unfortunate photograph of the President in San Diego a few weeks earlier, started tongues wagging — friendly and unfriendly tongues — all through the United States. His enemies concluded that 'the old man is through, finished.' His friends and supporters of many years shook their heads sorrowfully and said, 'It looks like the old master had lost his touch. His campaigning days must be over. It's going to look mighty sad when he begins to trade punches with young Dewey.'"[6]

The fact was, the trip to Hawaii (eventually totaling 13,912 miles) had done the President in; he would, as it transpired, never be the same again.

PART NINE

Quebec

58

A Redundant Conference

A MONTH LATER, at 9:00 a.m. on September 11, 1944, the *Ferdinand Magellan* pulled into Wolfe's Cove, Quebec, on the banks of the St. Lawrence River — the very spot where, during the French and Indian War, General James Wolfe had landed and, after scaling the cliffs and storming the Plains of Abraham on September 13, 1759, been mortally wounded in hand-to-hand combat, as was the defending general Louis-Joseph de Montcalm. In the subsequent Treaty of Paris, the French colonies of North America had been formally ceded to Great Britain, and had become Canada.

Under the Statute of Westminster in 1931, after a century and a half of British rule, the colony or Dominion of Canada had finally become coequal with Britain. Now, in anticipation of the arrival of the President of the United States and the Prime Minister of Great Britain, the Canadian prime minister had made his way by train from Ottawa to Quebec, where he had spent the night at the Citadel, the residence of the governor-general, the Earl of Athlone. There Mr. Roosevelt would also stay, as would Mr. Churchill. For Quebec was once again the site for a major Allied war conference or summit — the second time in barely two years.

Why it was being held at all was a mystery.

The venue, at least, had been the idea of Canadian prime minister Mackenzie King. A Liberal politician now in his ninth consecutive year in office, King had offered to host the conference, following the great triumph in Normandy. The arrival of visitors as august as FDR and Churchill, for a second year in succession, would improve his own chances of reelection, the prime minister felt — knowing he would probably have to go to the polls as the end of the war in Europe approached. With an entire First Canadian Army fighting in France and still more Canadian divisions fighting in Italy, in addition to massive aid being given to Britain, Canada was now a major military coalition ally. Representatives of some forty nations were already preparing to assemble in Montreal for a United Nations Relief and Rehabilitation Administration (UNRRA) conference; the city of Quebec, though, was the more imposing, and would be available for the warrior caste and their film crews. "Canada has emerged in every sense of the word into a world power," King congratulated himself. It was a remarkable improvement over the dark days of 1940, only four years earlier, when he might well, as Canadian prime minister, have found himself hosting refugees and exiles from a defeated England.[1] Now, however, he would be hosting two of the three primary military powers that still counted in Allied military decision-making: the United States, Russia, and Britain, with the end of the war in Europe believed to be at hand.

But not by Mr. Roosevelt. The closer to Germany the Allies advanced, the harder the Germans, like the Japanese, would fight, the President felt — especially after the survival of their beloved Führer on July 20. Roosevelt nonetheless had complete confidence in General Eisenhower as supreme commander in northern Europe. The Allies, after all, had vaulted the Seine by August 20. Paris had fallen to Allied forces on August 24. Despite their precipitate retreat, there seemed no sign of Wehrmacht collapse. German garrisons in the Channel ports were resisting to the death, and few Germans were surrendering unless surrounded; they could be expected to fight even more tenaciously on German soil, the President lamented. The end, in other words, could be bloodier even than the beginning.

Churchill had for months added to the President's strategic concerns: the U.S. Joint Chiefs of Staff telling him that, according to their London liaison staff, the Prime Minister had been an ogre more than an ally in arguing to be allowed to open new Allied fronts in the Mediterranean at the expense of Anvil — the invasion of France from the south that Churchill claimed was now irrelevant. Instead the Prime Minister, it appeared, had again become infatuated with the wacky notion of Blitzkrieg in the forbidding mountains of northern Italy and Yugoslavia — fixating on the so-called Ljubljana Gap, or gateway to Vienna. It was a notion the U.S. chiefs and the President considered ludicrously naive — indeed reminiscent of the British Charge of the Light Brigade at Balaclava in the Crimean War. When Churchill's seemingly unending entreaties had failed, and the Anvil (renamed "Dragoon") assault was launched on August 15, 1944, it had proved, contrary to all Churchill's predictions of ghastly failure, an American triumph.

Once more Churchill had been proven completely wrong as a strategist and tactician. The great port of Marseilles was overrun and liberated in a week, providing major new logistical backup to the Allies in northern France. Within ten days of landing, General Jacob Devers's Sixth Army had joined forces with Eisenhower's troops. Churchill had, in short, egg on his face.

In such circumstances Churchill's urgent pleas for yet another military conference, moreover one to be held to recast Allied military strategy, had seemed fatuous. Marshal Stalin, whose forces were now capitalizing on their great success in Operation Bagration, had certainly shown zero interest in the idea. The war was simply moving too fast; his Russian armies were approaching Warsaw in the north, and in the south Soviet forces were advancing on Bucharest — followed by Soviet troops threatening to overrun Bulgaria in the days after that. Given such progress on the battlefield, what was there to discuss, militarily? Stalin had therefore declined an invitation to meet with his American and British allies in Scotland, the first suggested venue.

The President had not been surprised. In terms of influence in the eventual end-of-war arrangements, as in all property disputes, *possession,* not Map Room charts, would be nine-tenths of the law — and Eisenhower's forces were advancing as fast as possible across northern Europe. It was thus vital not to be distracted by extraneous Churchillian schemes in Italy, the Mediterranean, and the Aegean, which the Germans would in any case inevitably vacate, once the Allies breached the Siegfried Line, protecting their homeland. Instead Eisenhower should be given every conceivable military assistance — including the First Allied Airborne Army — in driving his forces to Berlin, not Florence, Rhodes, or Yugoslavia. This airborne army, the President was assured by General Marshall, would help Eisenhower and Montgomery leapfrog German resistance — and vault, if possible, the Rhine, not the Arno. The paratroopers, tankers, and infantrymen would have to win this battle on the ground: a challenge that a new international conference over military strategy could only distract from.

A summit addressing political or diplomatic issues was equally premature at that moment. A major high-level conference had, after all, already been convened; it was meeting in earnest at Dumbarton Oaks in Washington, D.C. It would prepare the way for a postwar international organization and security setup, with its first meeting to be attended by senior representatives of the Soviet Union, Great Britain, China, and the United States.

Quebec, then, was simply not necessary in the summer of 1944. Moreover it promised a hiding to nothing if Churchill, as was rumored, intended to come to North America with new schemes for the Mediterranean or even the Far East.

Despite this, the more the ailing president had pondered the matter, the more he had begun to warm to Churchill's idea of a military conference. Assembling the U.S. Chiefs of Staff together with senior officers of Great Britain would give him an authentic reason to leave Washington. With only weeks to go before the November election, it would, if held in September, permit him to continue his charade: namely that he was too busy with his duties as U.S. commander in chief to take time to campaign against Governor Dewey.

It was in this less than virtuous way the President had found the notion of a second military conference in Quebec to be a worthwhile project, even without

Stalin's participation. It would placate the ever-argumentative Mr. Churchill. In their meetings with their British opposite numbers, the U.S. chiefs of staff would help the President keep the Prime Minister's wild schemes in check. There would be photographs and film taken — though always from a distance — of the President in his commanding role, as in 1943. In the meantime, back in the United States, his new vice presidential nominee, Senator Harry Truman, could barnstorm the country addressing domestic issues on behalf of the Democratic Party.

Thus had the dubious plot been concocted for the President to go to Quebec, rather than to Scotland, "where he will have a meeting with a distinguished Englishman," Vice President Wallace had noted in his diary after lunching with the President at the White House.[2]

59

The Complete Setting for a Novel

THE NEED FOR THE PRESIDENT not to be seen up close or in public, it was felt by the President's political advisers such as Steve Early, was critical, given the state of the President's health — and morale. Eleven days earlier, immediately on his return from San Diego, the President had asked his new running mate, Harry Truman, to lunch with him at the White House. Truman had come — and been appalled.

It had been a hot day, and the two men had eaten outside, under the famous magnolia tree planted by President Jackson. The President's daughter Anna, who was now acting as his personal assistant, was also there. Photographers had taken pictures of the two men, sitting in shirtsleeves on the South Lawn — pictures the White House press secretary policed lest there be any repetition of Bremerton or San Diego. "The President looked fine and ate a bigger lunch than I did," Truman claimed to reporters afterwards.

Unhappily, this wasn't true. The President was *not* fine.

At his weekly press conference in the Oval Office that morning the President's initial answers to questions from journalists had been almost incoherent — so quiet, also, that reporters had had to ask him to speak louder. He'd seemed distracted, becoming energized only when talking of the possibility of a national work service program for young people after the war, rather than military training.

In the West Wing, before lunch, he'd shown Truman silent movies of his Hawaii trip to meet with MacArthur and Nimitz. Over lunch itself, however, they'd spoken only of the election campaign, with no mention of military matters. Truman had been shocked by the President's appearance — and by the fact that his hand shook so much he was unable to pour cream into his coffee.

"I want you to do some campaigning," Truman later recalled the President saying.

"I'll make some plane reservations to go around over the country," the senator had assured "the Boss" — in fact, "anywhere you want me to go."[1] Truman would never forget the President's response. "Don't fly. Ride the trains," Roosevelt had ordered. "Can't both of us afford to take chances."[2]

The President, it was clear, was running against the clock of life. On August 22, as they'd had tea at Top Cottage on his Hyde Park estate, Roosevelt had confided to Daisy Suckley that he might soon be meeting Churchill in Quebec, where he would stay a week, followed by a day or two together with the Prime Minister at Springwood.[3] He hadn't sounded confident about winning the election, though — or even caring too much if he didn't, to Daisy's astonishment.

This was precisely what worried those who felt the anti-Axis alliance would fall apart, thanks to inter-Allied squabbles, if the President didn't win. Even Vice President Wallace was frank in his diary about the reports he'd been hearing of Roosevelt's health.

"It is curious how many people think the President is completely washed up physically," the vice president had noted on August 16. "In most cases the judgment seems to be based on his appearance at the time of his broadcast at San Diego and the manner of his broadcast from Seattle." But there were others, too, who'd met with the President, or furnished similar reports of other appearances by him. Men such as Captain Maurice Sheehy, a navy chaplain and loyal Roosevelt supporter, who had just returned from Hawaii. Sheehy had reported to Wallace the President "was in terrible shape" there, and "that his hands shook so he could scarcely lift his food to his mouth. He thinks the President will be unable to campaign and that he will have to resign from the nomination" — causing Wallace to reflect: "In that case Dewey will win easily."[4]

Dewey win?

A sort of fatalism seemed to overwhelm the President. As Robert Sherwood, Roosevelt's speechwriter, recalled, "It was not what Dewey was doing or saying that provided the present cause for worry to Hopkins and the others in the White House" in August 1944; "it was the indifferent attitude of Roosevelt himself. He seemed to feel that he had done his duty by allowing his name to be placed before the American people, and if they did not want to re-elect him, that would be perfectly all right with him." As his military aide and appointments secretary General Pa Watson put it to Sherwood, "He just doesn't seem to give a damn."[5]

As Sherwood recalled, "the main problem" in Washington had therefore become how "to persuade the President to descend from his position of dignified eminence as Commander-in-Chief and get into the dusty political arena where he was still undisputed champion."[6] Eleanor, the President's wife, was no help in this regard; she seemed just as fatalistic, perhaps even more so than the President — having long ago renounced her right to persuade him one way

Anzio

Both FDR and Churchill fall ill after Tehran. FDR never recovers, but Churchill does. With FDR too sick to stop him, the PM ignores Ike's warnings. Under new British command in the Mediterranean, Churchill demands an instant Allied invasion at Anzio to reach Rome. It is a disaster, incurring 43,000 casualties over four months, to no purpose.

The Triumph of D-day

PRAYER READ BY THE PRESIDENT ON THE RADIO
THE WHITE HOUSE
JUNE 6, 1944

MY FELLOW AMERICANS: *Last night when I spoke with you about the fall of Rome, I knew that within At that moment Troops of the US or* In this poignant hour, I ask you to join me in *our allies* prayer:

Almighty God: Our sons, pride of our nation, this day have set upon a mighty endeavor, a struggle to preserve our Republic, our religion, and our civilization, and to set free a suffering humanity.

Lead them straight and true; give strength to their arms, stoutness to their hearts, steadfastness to their faith.

They will need Thy blessings. Their road will be long and hard. The enemy is strong. He may hurl back our forces. Success may not come with rushing speed, but we shall return again and again; and we know that by Thy grace,

In contrast to Anzio, FDR's Overlord strategy works brilliantly. His appointee, Eisenhower, performs splendidly, with Montgomery as Allied ground forces commander. The triumphant landings answer FDR's famous D-day Prayer, and the subsequent campaign does decide the war, as Hitler feared.

The Bomb Plot

July 20, 1944, is a fateful day. In San Diego FDR watches a Marine Corps rehearsal for Pacific landings, while in East Prussia Hitler welcomes the deposed Mussolini to his head-quarters. But FDR has suffered a medical crisis, and Hitler is almost assassinated. Both men broadcast that night: FDR to accept the Democratic nomina-tion for President, Hitler to prove he has survived as Führer.

The 1944 Democratic convention in Chicago is a confidence trick; Dr. Frank Lahey warned FDR he could never survive a fourth term. But with no other Democrat able to beat the Republican nominee, Governor Thomas Dewey, FDR is forced to run. He belatedly backs Senator Harry Truman as his running mate, then sails to Pearl Harbor aboard the USS *Baltimore*.

Hawaii

General MacArthur had hoped, vainly, to be the 1944 Republican presidential nominee. Instead, summoned to Pearl Harbor by FDR, he is forced to meet with Admiral Nimitz and Admiral Leahy to tour the navy, air, and army installations there for the first time. Also to debate, before the Commander in Chief, the best way to defeat Japan.

Returning from Pearl Harbor, FDR tries to insulate himself from election campaigning—and the cameras recording his plummeting health—but fails. His speech aboard the USS *Cummings* at Bremerton shipyard is a disaster. Backed by Senator Truman, though, he wins a fourth term and is inaugurated on the White House portico on January 20, 1945.

Aboard the USS *Quincy*, FDR is hailed as a hero at Malta (above), but Yalta is torture for him, given his failing health. Yet no one else can keep the Allied coalition together to defeat the Third Reich and Japan. The summit at least fulfills FDR's dream of a UN organization backed by the Russians and ensures Soviet help in defeating Japan.

Reporting to Congress, the President can no longer stand. The war is almost won; still, Hitler attempts to divide the Allies. Withdrawing to the Little White House, Warm Springs, FDR appeals for common purpose: the defeat of Nazi Germany, then Japan. On April 12, 1945, he dies beside the love of his life, the widowed Lucy Rutherfurd.

or another in his decisions, while she proceeded independently with her own life and causes.

The President had seen Ambassador Halifax on August 19 — causing Halifax to note in his diary he was "not sure how well I thought the President looked. He seemed rather fine drawn, and looked older. He also seemed to be snuffling a bit, with a handkerchief on the table!" He'd said he was delighted with Eisenhower's progress in France, but had sounded dubious about the Germans suing for surrender, even with the Soviets pressing from the east. It was, he thought, "unlikely that any German official would sign unconditional surrender," and the war would continue "rather longer than some optimists" — such as Halifax, who was betting it would all be over in November — "thought." The President had also told Halifax that not only the war but "the election was going to be tough, and that he would suffer from the non-recording of much of the Army vote" — despite the latest decision to let soldiers from some states, at least, vote — "and also of the labour vote"[7] given how many workers were employed in factories away from their home constituencies . . .

Thereafter the President had set off from Hyde Park — Eleanor remaining there, at her Val-Kill cottage, while the President returned to Washington to see the secretary of war, Henry Stimson, after which he was slated to greet the dozens of national representatives participating in the Dumbarton Oaks Conference.

Would relying on his role as U.S. commander in chief be enough, however, to win a presidential election — especially if the President didn't really *want* to win? No one knew.

In the event, only one person could, arguably, inspire the President to fight for the presidency, given how deathly ill he often felt: Lucy Rutherfurd. Without her intercession it seemed doubtful he could make the effort, *or even possessed the will to do so.*

It is unclear if anyone spoke to Lucy about the problem, but perhaps no one needed to — for Mrs. Rutherfurd could see it clearly for herself. Immediately after the Dumbarton Oaks delegates had left the White House on August 23, at any rate, she'd come for tea with him on the lawn by the South Portico, together with her daughter Barbara — whom the President called his "goddaughter" — and Lucy's stepson John Rutherfurd, a U.S. Navy officer. There they'd hatched a plot for the President to spend a day with them at Lucy's Allamuchy estate in New Jersey, on his way back to Hyde Park for Labor Day weekend.

With this lure the President's spirits had seemed miraculously to rekindle: for Lucy, more than any person alive, knew not only how to flatter Franklin by her deep affection, but how to play on his pride as a man: as a father and, in many ways, the father of the nation in war. It was a knack the president's cousin Daisy, who had no children, indeed had never married, simply did not possess.

Military service, moreover, was part and parcel of Lucy Rutherfurd's life. The President had arranged for all three of her stepsons to obtain sea duty in the U.S. Navy at their (and her) insistent request. The Rutherfurd boys were all determined to serve—and there was simply no way, as the idol of the Rutherfurd family, that the President, for his part, would fail to do his part as their commander in chief, however debilitated he felt.

As Lucy later confided to his Russian-language interpreter, Charles Bohlen, who was a friend of the Rutherfurds, the President "kept no wartime secrets or burdens from her."[8] He would have preferred, in his condition, to retire gracefully, at the end of his third term as president. But he had met Stalin in person, now—and had Stalin's respect and cooperation in more ways than anyone could have imagined earlier in the war. Why abandon that personal, highest-level relationship?

True, the Russians were still an enigma, as allies. At Dumbarton Oaks the Russian representative was still insisting on having no fewer than *sixteen* other delegates in the nascent United Nations: one for each Soviet republic, plus the Union. This was a distinct political stumbling block. Moreover despite a personal appeal, the President had completely failed thus far to persuade Stalin to intercede in the struggle for Warsaw, where the Soviets were refusing to lift a finger to help the Polish national uprising that had begun on August 1, only forty miles from the Russian front. The Soviets would thus be a continuing nightmare to deal with: culturally, politically, militarily. Yet without them the war against Hitler might still not be won—and without them the war against Japan might take years to win, as well as incur terrible American bloodshed, given Japanese determination not to surrender an inch of their conquests, let alone their home islands.

In spite of his ill health the President had therefore remained confident he could probably keep Stalin to his promise, at Tehran, to enter the war against Japan, and could eventually persuade Stalin to drop Soviet demands for exaggerated representation at the UN, without wrecking the UN's chances of success. Likewise, he'd shared with Lucy, he could probably handle Winston Churchill, whom he now knew so well, in Quebec. And seeing in her eyes such admiration, any notion of defeatism in terms of the looming election had simply evaporated.

It was in this context the President had hatched his secret plot to visit Lucy—a very risky idea.

In the end, as things developed, it was decided to make Mr. Roosevelt's visit to Mrs. Rutherfurd "above board." It would require, in any case, considerable preparation.

First off, Mike Reilly of the White House Secret Service detail would have to be suborned, since until now the Secret Service had objected to the President taking the train across the bowstring-truss "Hell Gate" bridge in New York, which had been the target of German agents, landed by U-boat, back in 1942. Though the would-be saboteurs had been captured and executed,[9] the Secret Service veto on the President's train using the bridge had been observed ever since.

Reilly was soon dealt with. German sabotage, in September 1944, seemed pretty ridiculous. At the President's insistence, the *Ferdinand Magellan's* route was therefore reconfigured to follow the Pennsylvania-LeHigh line to Allamuchy, New Jersey, and from there to Hyde Park. The trip to Lucy was on.

Soon after 10:00 p.m. on August 31, 1944, *Magellan* had steamed out of the Bureau of Engraving in darkness, bearing the President, the President's private secretary Bill Hassett, his office secretaries Grace Tully and Dorothy Brady, and Daisy Suckley, too.

Daisy had already found the President "looking awfully tired" at the White House, and having lost yet more weight since his trip to the Pacific, despite daily extra eggnogs.[10] Hassett recorded the same in his own diary, describing the President as still "tense and nervous — not yet rested from his five weeks' trip into the Pacific area via land and sea." The stress of being president was simply too much for him: "Too many visitors at mealtimes — all ages, sexes, and previous conditions of servitude — hardly relaxing for a tired man."[11] However once the train pulled up to a railway crossing on the Rutherfurd estate at 8:30 a.m. on September 1, the next morning, the President had seemed transformed — met there by Mrs. Rutherfurd and her stepson John, John's wife, and their children.

"She is a lovely person," Daisy noted in her diary that morning, "full of charm and with beauty of character shining in her face; no wonder the Pres. has cherished her friendship all these years —. She came on the train hatless & stockingless, in a black figured dress, & black gloves — She is tall & good-looking rather than beautiful or even pretty — Though I remember her as tall & calm & pretty & sad, when her daughter was 6 mos. old, at Aiken," more than twenty years before. Lucy was older now — and by no means triste, Daisy noted, in fact the reverse was the case. "She does not look sad now," the President's cousin described Lucy's happy face — acknowledging "how little one knows about the inner life of others" — especially their love lives.[12]

Rutherfurd Hall was vastly bigger than the President's own house at Hyde Park — an eighteen-thousand-square-foot Elizabethan-style mansion built in 1902, with thirty-eight rooms, a thousand-acre deer park, and farms stretching over five thousand acres. Daisy was asked to play with the children and Fala, while the President — whose car had been driven off the train by its special ramp — "is going to look over" what were known as the Tranquility Estate farms, Daisy recorded—"woods, etc."—and "advise them what to do" in his self-described profession as forester.[13]

Sitting by Allamuchy Pond, "on a cushion on the grass at the water's edge" while Fala and the children played, Daisy had found herself almost in disbelief. "Another adventure!" she'd jotted. It had not ended there, however. Back at the Allamuchy house Lucy "had a lovely room all ready for the P. to take his rest, even to turning down the best linen sheets." But the President had demurred; "he wasn't going to miss any of his visit," Daisy noted.[14]

Lunch for a dozen guests was to have been lobster, but since the President had dined on lobster the night before, and was slated to have it again with Eleanor at Val-Kill that evening, Lucy had arranged for squab or young pigeon to be served with vegetables and salad, and afterwards ice cream. The President "did not rest until we got back on the train." Finally at 3:35 they all "dashed off" to the railway halt, "& got started on schedule," Daisy noted that night. "It was a really lovely day, centering around Mrs. Rutherfurd, who becomes more lovely as one thinks about her — The whole thing was out of a book — a complete setting for a novel, with all the characters at that lunch," including Winty Rutherfurd's former sister-in-law, who'd married a prince, and other Rutherfurds and their wives and husbands, as well as "absent husbands and wives etc."[15]

One of those absent wives, of course, was Eleanor, who would be at Highland station, waiting to take the President and his traveling companions to Val-Kill, "for supper" — a special meal to feature not only lobster, Daisy recorded, but Eleanor's friend Mrs. Pratt's "speciality": German "'appelkuchen.'"[16]

60

Two Sick Men

IF THE PRESIDENT'S ENTOURAGE had become more and more concerned in recent weeks about Roosevelt's declining health, the same could be said of Churchill's courtiers. The Prime Minister's transatlantic voyage aboard the *Queen Mary* had begun at Greenock, Scotland, on September 5, 1944. His doctor, Lord Moran, was taking no chances, and had insisted on taking with him an eminent bacteriologist and nurse, as there were shadows on the Prime Minister's lung X-rays that suggested a possible recurrence of pneumonia.

The intent of the conference, the President had made clear via his ambassador in London, John Winant, was to address military matters only. For Churchill this had been frustrating, given his desire to map out a political future in terms of British imperial interests in the postwar world, but it was a restriction the Prime Minister was forced to accept. The President, now in the midst of an election campaign, naturally wished to avoid accusations of secret political discussions or agreements being made. Such a limitation, Churchill felt, was inherently silly, however. Military strategy at this stage of the war was bound to carry major political implications; he had wisely, therefore, invited both Lord Leathers, his minister in charge of shipping and transport (and an expert on Lend-Lease), and Lord Cherwell, paymaster-general and scientific adviser to the Prime Minister.

Suffering suspected pneumonia, Churchill was neither well nor well-disposed. As far as military strategy was concerned, his agenda for Quebec was at odds with even that of his chiefs of staff, who would be sitting down with their American colleagues on the Combined Chiefs of Staff Committee in the Château de Frontenac. Throughout the voyage the Prime Minister was, his chiefs complained, "quite impossible" to "argue with," as Field Marshal Brooke would later recall. "It was a ghastly time from which I have carried away the bitterest of memories."[1]

• • •

Churchill, for his part, felt the same about Brooke, and even Andrew B. Cunningham, Admiral "ABC," head of the Royal Navy — officers who were collectively "framing up against him," he growled.[2] It "takes little to rouse his vengeful temper," Cunningham noted in his own diary. The admiral was concerned lest this lead to a further souring of relations with their U.S. counterparts, for "he will do anything then to get the better of our allies."[3]

Brooke, who did not tolerate fools gladly, was the most despairing among the Prime Minister's cohort. He found Churchill "old. Unwell, and depressed" during the journey. "He gave me the feeling of a man who is finished, can no longer keep a grip of things, and is beginning to realize it," Brooke confided. "Here we are within 72 hours of meeting the Americans and there is not a single point that we are in agreement with!" he noted with near-despair in his diary. Contradicting the views of his military chiefs, Brooke observed, the Prime Minister was adamant the looming conference should have but a single purpose: namely to get approval for a new Allied bid to reach Vienna from the Adriatic, and that "we were coming to Quebec solely to obtain 20 landing ships out of the Americans to carry out an operation against Istria to seize Trieste."

Vienna?

Even if the idea were feasible militarily — which it was not — Brooke recorded on September 8, "with the rate at which events were moving, Istria might be of no value."[4] At a moment when the Wehrmacht was fighting even harder in the mountains of Italy, an attempt to land a whole army at Istria and strike through the Alps to Vienna was asking for trouble — Anzio all over again. And wholly pointless, given Russian advances in Romania. The terrain beyond Trieste — the so-called Ljubljana Gap — was hazardous in the extreme. The gap was simply impassable if contested in winter, and thus risked more casualties even than the mountains of Italy. Yet the Prime Minister was insistent. Was Churchill then mad, Brooke wondered — or perhaps ill? When the Prime Minister ran a temperature again that evening, Brooke decided he was "very definitely ill," physically and mentally, and it was "doubtful how much longer he will last. The tragedy is that in his present condition he may well do untold harm!"[5]

The next day proved even worse — the Prime Minister determined to speed up planning without any thought to the enemy's likely response. "He knows no details, has only half the picture in his mind, talks absurdities and makes my blood boil to listen to his nonsense," Brooke railed in his diary.[6]

"I find it hard to remain civil," he continued. "And the wonderful thing is that ¾ of the population of the world imagine that Winston Churchill is one of the Strategists of History, a second Marlborough, and the other ¼ have no conception what a public menace he is and has been throughout this war!"[7]

In terms of public support, it was, of course, "far better" the public should remain unaware of this, Brooke judged, "and never suspect the feet of clay of that otherwise superhuman being" — for without the Prime Minister's brave stand in 1940, "England was lost for a certainty" — yet "with him," as Brooke knew best, "England has been on the verge of disaster time and time again."[8]

It was quite an indictment: "Never have I admired and despised a man simultaneously to the same extent," the field marshal concluded.[9]

The truth, as would become clear, was that the two major leaders of the democracies were traveling to a meeting that was unnecessary — moreover was one that neither man was well enough to direct.

Even their arrival was a botched affair.

Mackenzie King, the President's host, was confounded. At the Château de Frontenac, where he spent the night, he'd received a message "from the President that he would like me to go to his [rail] car if there were a few minutes before Mr. Churchill's train arrived," King recorded in his diary on September 11.

Before Mr. Churchill's train?

When King got to the station, he found it was true — "one of the President's staff came to me and said the President was waiting to see me," without even the governor-general having arrived yet!

A British prime minister, on British Empire soil, being deliberately relegated to second place by an American president? Brushing away King's concerns about diplomatic protocol, the President's staff officer "explained that the car was there and the President was anxious to see" him. Swallowing his surprise, Mackenzie King "went in. [President Roosevelt] was seated," the Canadian prime minister recorded in his diary, and to the President's right was "Mrs. Roosevelt" — who had joined the presidential train at Hyde Park — "standing in front of the sofa."[10]

Roosevelt was quite candid. "The President said at once: I wanted to see you first; also to be ahead of Winston, so I gave orders to have the car moved in."[11]

A sort of schoolboy prank?

The President's behavior was most unlike him. As King commented in his diary, "It seemed to me that the President was rather assuming that he was in his own country." More worrying, however, was the sight of the Commander in Chief — for it was clear this was not the man King had welcomed to Quebec the previous year, in August 1943. "It seemed to me, looking at the President, that he had failed very much since I last saw him. He is very much thinner in body and also is much thinner in his face. He looks distinctly older and worn. I confess I was just a little bit shocked by his appearance."[12]

The President asked Mr. King to accompany him in his open automobile, which was being unloaded, to the Citadel — prompting the embarrassed prime minister to protest that the governor-general, as the representative of Canada's monarch, King George VI, was not there yet. He, Earl Athlone, should be the one to accompany the President, King pointed out, and therefore left the *Magellan* to bring in the governor-general for an audience with the President, when he arrived. After that, like a vizier to the President of the United States, King went out again and fetched Prime Minister Churchill, who by then had arrived in his own train, and was completely nonplussed by the strange procedure. All were being brought aboard the *Ferdinand Magellan,* on Canadian soil, just as if Mr. Roosevelt were the Sun King.

Inasmuch as the United States — as Churchill would admit that day in conversation with the President — was by now far and away the "strongest military power today, speaking of air, sea and land"[13] — the scene at Wolfe's Cove was symbolic. Yet it revealed an equally significant development, one far more important than the reversal of diplomatic protocol: namely the stunning change in the President' health since the officers had last seen him in Cairo, following Tehran.

Churchill's military assistant, for example, would later write how "shocked" he was to see "the great change that had taken place in the President's appearance since the Cairo Conference. He seemed to have shrunk: his coat sagged over his broad shoulders, and his collar looked several sizes too big. What a difference from the first time that I had set eyes on him less than two and a half years ago!" General Ismay reflected. It had been in Washington, at the White House. "Seated at the desk of his study, on what I shall always remember as 'Tobruk morning'" — receiving news of the abject British surrender in North Africa to General Rommel — "he had looked the picture of health and vitality. His instinctive and instantaneous reaction to the shattering telegram had won my heart forever. No formal expression of sympathy, no useless regrets: only transparent friendship and an unshakeable determination to stand by his allies. 'Winston, what can we do to help?'"[14]

Now a different Franklin Delano Roosevelt was before the British contingent: a ghost of his former self.

61

Churchill's Imperial Wars

THE COMBINED CHIEFS OF STAFF soon began their military sessions at the Château de Frontenac. But since the first plenary session of Octagon, as the conference was code-named, was not scheduled to take place until September 13, on the third day of the Combined Chiefs of Staff meetings, the President and Prime Minister were, in effect, free to do whatever they wished in the meantime — Mr. Roosevelt and Mr. Churchill staying in the nearby Citadel.

Unlike the year before, in Quebec, there was now an underlying sense of fraud about the conference, beyond obligatory group photographs, newsreels, and dinners. In some respects it promised to be like a bad play in which the players, for the most part, did not believe in the script — the Prime Minister at odds with his own chiefs of staff, while the President seemed strangely distant, even disconnected from his.

To Churchill's surprise the President had brought with him neither Harry Hopkins (who had largely recovered since his major surgery) nor any senior member of his White House team, beyond Admiral Leahy. And his U.S. Joint Chiefs of Staff and their staffs, who would look good in photographs and newsreels. Quebec was, in effect, literal as well as metaphorical window dressing — Churchill afterwards snorting, in disgust: "What is this conference? Two talks with the Chiefs of Staff; the rest was waiting to put in a word with the President."[1]

At lunch on September 11 the Canadian prime minister discussed with the President, in confidence, the forthcoming election — one that King did not propose calling in Canada until the war was over, himself, lest it put in question French Canadian support for the war — and postwar. Mr. Roosevelt, however, had no such electoral leeway — and seemed anxious about those states in America, he said, that were still unwilling to permit soldiers to vote — especially soldiers "favorable to the President." "I can see that he is really concerned; also that he is genuinely tired and weary," King noted again. "He has lost much weight — 30 pounds."

Thirty pounds? The result was alarming; "he looks much thinner in the face and is quite drawn. His eyes," King confided in his diary, seeking to be more specific, were "quite weary," like those of a dying dog.[2] Prime Minister Churchill confided the same to his young assistant private secretary, John Colville, saying the President was now "very frail"[3] — and his eyes "glazed," as Colville himself later noticed when he met him.[4]

Churchill, relishing the chance to "take some Scotch as well as a couple of brandies," seemed physically, by comparison, "as fresh as a baby," King commented, ironically: waxing loquaciously, and in "a distinguished way" that was "not affected," he felt, "but genuine."[5]

As a dutiful diarist, King could not but record the difference between the two men's states of health, even if nothing could be said in public. At dinner on the first night, for example, Mr. Roosevelt responded to the governor-general's extended toast with a charming reference to the presence of the First Lady, Eleanor, his own wife, and of Mr. Churchill and *his* wife, Clementine, as well as mentioning his long friendship with Mackenzie King, who was unmarried. King, who paid the closest attention to people's language as also to the ever-significant hands of the clock at special moments, had listened carefully — noting, with alarm, not only what the President had said, but also what he had not said. Roosevelt "made one reference which makes a good deal of how he is feeling," King afterwards reflected. "He referred to the abuse and attacks on himself as 'a senile old man,'" which clearly pained him. Yet in the course of his speech he had admitted that, if he lost the election, he would not mind. It would offer him the "freedom" to "enjoy friendships."[6] And with that the President had simply ended his toast.

Churchill, recognizing instantly the President's faux pas, had leaned straight across Princess Alice, the governor-general's wife, who was between them, "and reminded him about proposing the King."[7]

King George VI was, after all, not only king of England but of Canada, too. It was an error, King was aware, the President would never have made in earlier days. Attempting to make up for his mistake, the President had then given a long, belabored account of King George VI's visit to Hyde Park in 1939, and how "close their friendship would always be. He then proposed the health of the King. It seemed to me," King reflected, "that [his] language was very loosely used. There was the oldest friendship with everyone — the same for the King, the same for the Athlones, the same for Churchill, etc. Rather a lack of discrimination," the Canadian prime minister thought.[8]

Mackenzie King's observation was all too penetrating. The once-enchanting tenor of the President's voice, and the nuanced, playful, humorous way in which he had always expressed himself, were gone. "I felt as the President spoke," King lamented, "that more than ever he had lost his old hearty self and his laugh." As a devout Christian, however, King allowed as how the President "has suffered a good deal" in the many trials he'd faced in life, and most obviously, his paralysis. Yet the fact remained that he "really is a man who is losing his strength."[9]

From this point, September 11, 1944, King's diary account of the conference was filled with sadness and disappointment, given that the President was still only sixty-two — seven years younger than King himself.

It was Mrs. Churchill, however, who would pen the most perspicacious account of what was happening, behind the public facade. It came in a letter she sent her daughter Mary, who was back in England, but who had stayed with the President at Hyde Park the previous September, after the first Quebec Conference. Clemmie was amazed how Harry Hopkins had "quite dropped out of the picture." Moreover she could not "quite make out whether Harry's old place in the President's confidence is vacant, or whether Admiral Leahy is gradually moulding into it. One must hope that this is so, because the President, with all his genius does not — indeed cannot (partly because of his health and partly because of his make-up) — function round the clock, like your Father. I should not think that his mind was pinpointed on the war," she described the President, "for more than four hours a day, which is not really enough when one is a supreme war lord."[10]

Despite this, the strange, almost surreal, gathering of Western Allies got under its anointed way in the French Canadian city above the St. Lawrence River — Mackenzie King noticing, as Eleanor pushed her husband's wheelchair while he looked at little models Churchill had proudly brought with him of the D-day Mulberry harbors, constructed in Britain, "that out of sheer weakness there was perspiration on his [the President's] forehead. While he looked better today" — September 12 — "than yesterday, he still looks very weak," King confided that night. "I feel great concern for him," he added — touched by the way Eleanor, normally somewhat indifferent to the President's daily agenda, at last seemed to recognize his distress, indeed seemed unusually protective, saying that she was "anxious to get him off to bed for an afternoon rest."[11]

Churchill meantime stayed behind — and without further ado led Mackenzie King off to his portable map room in the Citadel, to rehearse his plenary speech to the meeting of the Combined Chiefs of Staff the next day.

This was something Churchill liked to do, as King knew, before any speech or parliamentary declamation he was to give, spending not only hours but sometimes whole days practicing to get the words and his diction right. In this case the burden of his great speech, however, would be to appeal for presidential approval of his scheme for a new military thrust from the Adriatic to Vienna — which would require not only American but Canadian soldiers.

Instead of welcoming Churchill's latest brainwave, Mackenzie King felt deeply worried.

Like all Canadians, King was immensely proud of what Canadian forces had achieved on D-day and in the titanic battle that had followed in Normandy, as the Canadian Corps expanded into an entire Canadian Army. This had led to the crescendo of the Normandy battle, at Falaise, where the Wehrmacht's Army Group B was eviscerated, and to Patton's extraordinary race with armored divisions around the German southern flank to seize Paris. King was proud, too, of Canadian divisions fighting in the British Eighth Army in Italy — thereby holding a number of Wehrmacht divisions as far south as possible in Europe, while the great battle for France was fought out between armies numbering in the millions. Churchill's alternative schemes, both political and military, had always made King uncomfortable, however. Now, once again, they did so as Churchill envisioned, in his suite at the Canadian Citadel, *yet another* major front in central Europe — and one using Canadian forces!

King, as prime minister of a "lesser" power than Britain, would not be invited to hear the actual speech at the forthcoming plenary session, but listening to Churchill, he recognized with a sinking heart the Vienna scheme would almost certainly require mandatory conscription in Canada — for Canadian casualties in Normandy and Italy had already been severe, and were still mounting. Nor was this the only new theater in which Churchill wished to commit Canadian troops, on behalf of the British Empire. He was, he said, adamant that British Empire naval and air forces should participate with American forces in the fighting in the Southwest and Central Pacific — this on the assumption that Canada would contribute men (who were all volunteers, beyond the regular Canadian military), munitions, and money. In this way, Churchill argued, the British Empire would not be deprived of credit in defeating the Japanese.

For Mackenzie King the very phrase "the British Empire" raised certain hackles, since it was clear that Churchill's vision — his determination to reassert British colonial and imperial authority in Asia and the Far East, as before the war — was inimical to the liberal vision of the postwar world that King had repeatedly discussed and shared with President Roosevelt ever since the war began. There was, in short, too much Churchillian talk of British "honor and glory" from a prime minister who had not himself set foot in India since 1899, had never visited China, had never ventured to the Pacific, moreover who seemed to have too little concern with the military realities — and casualties — of the battlefield when fighting implacable foes such as the Germans and Japanese.

"I held very strongly the view that no government in Canada would send its men to India, Burma and Singapore to fight with any [U.K.] forces and hope to get through a general election successfully," once the European war was over, King warned Churchill. About this he had been completely forthright, not only to Churchill but to members of his own Canadian War Committee. Patriotism was one thing; imperial refurbishing, at the end of another world war, another. "That to permit this," King would maintain the next day, "would be to raise at a general election, a nation-wide cry of Imperial wars versus Canada as a nation."[12]

So worried was King, in fact, that he warned Louis St. Laurent, the deputy for Quebec and a member of his cabinet, that he would resign as prime minister of Canada if pressed by Churchill, or by members of his own government, to send Canadians to fight "what would certainly be construed as Imperial wars."[13]

Churchill, however, was Churchill — listening neither to his own chiefs of staff, nor to the Canadian prime minister. Only the President had ever been able to control him — leaving the question: would the President be well enough to do so at the first plenary meeting on September 13, 1944?

62

A Stab in the Armpit

ON THE DAY of the first plenary meeting at 11:45 a.m. the President began by welcoming the participants. He then invited Mr. Churchill to open the discussion.

The Prime Minister's peroration was pure Churchill: a mix of glittering phrases, fine flattery — and bravado. "I would have given a great deal to tell him what I thought of him," Brooke confessed in his diary, having dreaded what was to come.[1]

The Prime Minister might have been speaking to several hundred members of Parliament, instead of the fourteen members of his audience, for all that it mattered. In a quite masterly way he first lauded the "revolutionary turn for the good" that had recently taken place. "Everything we had touched had turned to gold," the minutes of the meeting recorded, "and during the last seven weeks there had been an unbroken run of military successes. The manner in which the situation had developed since the Teheran Conference," he averred, in praise of the officers present, conveyed "the impression of remarkable design and precision of execution" — overlooking his Anzio debacle. He "wished to congratulate the United States Chiefs of Staff," he added, not only on D-day but on Operation Dragoon (Anvil), "which had produced the most gratifying results," he now admitted — omitting his titanic efforts to sink it. General Eisenhower was managing the campaign in France and the Low Countries, he said, "brilliantly." Moreover the British were, he claimed, playing a significant role in the fighting, especially in Italy . . .

As the U.S. chiefs suspected, the Prime Minister's preamble was clearly intended to soften them up for what was to come — for it was in Italy, the Prime Minister declared, that he now saw a great strategic opportunity arising. General Alexander was poised to smash Kesselring's forces, and "if the Germans were run out of Italy we should have to look for fresh fields and pastures new. It would never do for our armies to remain idle. He had always been attracted by a right-handed movement, with the purpose of giving Germany a stab in the armpit. Our objective should be Vienna."[2]

A *"stab in the armpit"*?

The phrase sounded much less inspiring than the Prime Minister's earlier notion of attacking Germany's "soft underbelly" — an underbelly, which had proved far from soft, as all were aware, and was still proving so. The British Eighth Army, comprising two Canadian, one New Zealand, one South African, four Indian, and eight U.K. divisions, had suffered some *eight thousand* casualties in the past month alone. A strike across the Adriatic to Trieste and from there across the mountains to Vienna, if the Wehrmacht forces miraculously collapsed and fled from Italy and Yugoslavia? It might certainly be worth preparing for, in terms of "contingency" planning. Yet there was no sign whatever of such an imminent German withdrawal, nor could mountain conditions — ones that were ideal for the Wehrmacht to defend, especially in autumn or winter weather — ever be seriously likened to an armpit. "Pit" seemed a more appropriate word.

Brooke, at a meeting of the Combined Chiefs of Staff the previous morning, had acknowledged "great advantages" for the Allies if the Wehrmacht miraculously retreated to Berlin, and General Wilson sent forces north to advance via the Ljubljana Gap to Vienna. "However," Brooke had cautioned, "if German resistance was strong, he did not visualize the possibility of our forces getting through to Vienna during the winter."[3] As if completely deaf to his own chiefs of staff, here was the Prime Minister, now advancing the scheme as something to be undertaken *immediately*, in order to take advantage of the grand military victory Churchill was certain General Alexander was about to win in Italy . . .

Considering that, as the British military historian Sir Michael Howard would later acknowledge, the "distance from Rome to Vienna is some six hundred miles — about three times the distance from Naples to Rome which it had taken the Allies six months to cover," and that German forces would be "falling back along their own lines of communication,"[4] Brooke had, in the Combined Chiefs of Staff meeting, shown great loyalty to his boss, the Prime Minister, when tabling the idea, though indicating his own skepticism of it. The Ljubljana Gap was, after all, only thirty miles wide, and two thousand feet high in elevation, flanked by higher ground. It led to a range of mountains six thousand feet high. As Brooke later noted in an annotation to his diary, "We had no plans for Vienna, nor did I ever look at this operation as becoming possible."[5] All Brooke had proposed as a possible contingency plan was for Allied staff officers to look into the implications of a limited Allied occupation of the Istrian Peninsula, using landing craft no longer needed for Dragoon, now that Marseilles was in Allied hands. This could, if thought worthwhile, give the Allies a base from which to launch a 1945 campaign, he'd pointed out, or at the very least one through which to funnel Allied occupation forces "in the event of Germany crumbling" — a worthwhile political consideration "in view of the [recent] Russian advances in the Balkans."[6]

The plan certainly had merit in hypothetical terms. As such it was worthy of discussion by the Combined Chiefs, even if not ultimately favored as worth the effort or the inevitable casualties if the operation foundered, as at Anzio. Unfortunately this was *not* what the Prime Minister had traveled all the way across the Atlantic to North America to secure as a new Allied military commitment. As he had once become fixated on capturing Rome, Churchill now seemed fixated on Vienna and Singapore — with no thought to the obstacles and casualties such commitments would entail; nor to their effect on Eisenhower's drive to Berlin; or Nimitz and MacArthur's operations against Japan.

Brooke, on the voyage across the Atlantic, had feared provoking another Anglo-American dispute, threatening the alliance. Yet to his immense relief he had, on arrival in Quebec, found the U.S. chiefs had almost fallen over themselves to be polite, even friendly, and they had politely moved on to other matters.

Unfortunately the Prime Minister was not interested in "contingency" plans, the plenary participants were now told. Mr. Churchill wanted, as he'd famously attached to the papers that landed on his desk as prime minister, "Action This Day." With his trademark afflatus the Prime Minister thus formally repeated his *grande ideé*. "Our object," he declared, "should be Vienna."[7]

Before the assembled officers could react, Churchill then continued his speech. He had, he informed the meeting, given "considerable thought" to such a drive. The landing craft were available, and an "added reason for this right-handed movement was the rapid encroachment of the Russians into the Balkans and the consequent dangerous spread of Russian influence in the area. He preferred to get into Vienna before the Russians," the minutes ran, "as he did not know what Russia's policy would be after she took it."[8]

Brooke cringed — recording that night "a long statement by the PM giving his views as to how the war should be run. According to him we had two main objectives, first an advance on Vienna," for which they had apparently come to Quebec, and "secondly, the capture of Singapore!"[9]

Brooke was ashamed. For a prime minister who had trained at Sandhurst Military College and had studied not only his ancestor's famous campaigns in Europe but even the battles of the American Civil War, Churchill's utter disregard of terrain, of the cost in men's lives, and of the strategic primacy of first defeating the Wehrmacht in northwest Europe was a grave indictment. Anyone could — and should — voice concern about long-term communist Russian ambitions in eastern and central Europe given the four hundred divisions they had at their disposal. A serious military strategist, however, had to consider what was realistic, or feasible, in terms of potential accomplishment — and the costs, especially in human life. Also the matter of priorities — of what should, in the final analysis, be the most important goal of the Western Allies: *defeating Hitler.*

The following day, mortified and disgusted, Churchill's military chief of staff, General Ismay, showed Brooke his letter of resignation as military assistant to the Prime Minister as minister of defense, or de facto British commander in chief. Ismay had had enough. As Brooke later noted, the "fact that dear old patient Pug had at last reached the end of his tether and could stand Winston's moods no longer is some indication of what we had been through."[10]

For the President, however, Churchill's insistent espousal of fresh schemes and strategic plans were merely part and parcel of Churchill's extraordinary personality and imagination. So too was his sheer obstinacy, which had helped save his country after the debacle of Dunkirk in the summer of 1940, when all had seemed over for the Western democracies. Like Brooke, the President had been less impressed by the Prime Minister's performance since then. Churchill's most recent cable, on August 29, 1944, calling for an amphibious landing at Istria "in four or five weeks," had given ample warning of his new Viennese tack.[11]

The President had been unconvinced. He had remained so in September, as Churchill's forecast of a smashing victory by Alexander in Italy to "converge" with two armies "on Bologna" had proven another empty promise by the Meddler. Summoning his dwindling energies at the Citadel on September 13, he thanked "the Prime Minister for his lucid and comprehensive review of the situation." He remarked, too, that with each conference the level of inter-Allied amity had increased — "an ever increasing solidarity of outlook and identity of basic thought," as well as "an atmosphere of cordiality and friendship. Our fortunes had prospered," he agreed with Churchill. Nevertheless, he cautioned, "it was still not quite possible to forecast the date of the end of the war with Germany."[12]

At a moment when so many were predicting the imminent collapse of the Third Reich — two million Allied troops ashore since D-day, fifty thousand Wehrmacht troops having surrendered in France, and ten thousand killed in the Falaise pocket alone — this was a sober warning. Romania had surrendered to Russian forces, and Wehrmacht forces were now pulling out of Greece, yes — but they had done so to shorten their lines, not because they were ready to give up their fight for the Führer. The Germans were thus, the President pointed out, certainly "withdrawing from the Balkans," and it "appeared likely that in Italy they would retire to the line of the Alps," eventually, with the Russians already on the "edge of Hungary" — but this didn't mean they would magically surrender, any more than would the Japanese. "The Germans have shown themselves good at staging withdrawals," he reminded his audience, and had "been able to save large numbers of personnel," despite their losses in "material." Clarity was essential. While he was all for General Alexander maintaining "maximum intensity" of operations in Italy to keep Hitler from reinforcing his other fronts at a critical juncture, the President foresaw that in the north "the Germans would retire behind the Rhine" now. It was a huge river, the President emphasized, that "would present a formidable obstacle." How to vault it would be tough — and "for this purpose our plans must be flexible. The Germans could not yet be counted out and one more big battle would have to be fought."[13]

The Battle of the Bulge, nine weeks later, would demonstrate the President's quiet realism as U.S. commander in chief. At Quebec, however, it was like cold water poured over the long, overoptimistic discourse the Prime Minister had given. Cold, to be sure, but without reminding the Prime Minister of his almost unending failures as a commander in chief and strategist. The President, once again, thus appeared at his very best, despite his frailty: using his natural charm, his spurning of theatrics, his maintaining of Allied unity, his invoking of common purpose. Moreover, what he said was expressed in such a kind, avuncular manner that it did not resemble in any way the put-down he and Stalin had been compelled to administer to the Prime Minister at Tehran.

Quietly the President then went on to address the ramifications of a longer war in Europe than the Prime Minister was assuming: namely, its effect on the eventual defeat of Japan. He did not think it worth spending too much time on Burma, beyond its avenue to China. The current "American plan was to regain the Philippines or Formosa and [attack] from bridgeheads which would be seized in China" — but the burden of American experience in the vast Pacific theater was that it was unwise to get bogged down in major confrontational battles, when Japanese forces could be bypassed — a "bypassing technique which had been employed with considerable success at small cost of life" by General MacArthur, as in the case of Rabaul. "Would it not be equally possible to by-pass Singapore by seizing an area to the north or east of it, for example Bangkok?" he asked. After all, "Singapore," the President reflected sagely, "may be very strong," and for his part he was "opposed to going up against strong positions," unless part of an overarching strategy, as at D-day — and now the Rhine.[14]

Disappointed, the Prime Minister had attempted to defend his dream. "As far as Singapore was concerned he did not favor the by-passing method," he'd responded. Ignoring the President's point about unnecessary casualties he'd declared there "would undoubtedly be a large force of Japanese in the Malay Peninsula and it would help the American operations in the Pacific if we could bring these forces to action and destroy them in addition to the great prize of the recapture of Singapore."[15]

Brooke could only groan at his prime minister's display of casualness in the face of casualties, his repeated talk of "destroying" the enemy, his indifference to geography, and his rank ignorance of modern military combat — for they reflected, as so often, a sort of jejune approach to modern warfare. Or the realities of Hitler's and Hirohito's mind-set. If "Hitler was beaten, say, by January [1945], and Japan was confronted with the three most powerful nations in the world" — given Stalin's promise the Russians would join the war against Japan just as soon as Hitler "was beaten" — then the Japanese, Churchill had airily claimed, "would undoubtedly have cause for reflection as to whether they could continue the fight."[16]

The President had shaken his head at such naiveté. Responding, the President "referred to the almost fanatical Japanese tenacity" in defending their conquests and islands. To prove his point he gave as a recent example that of Saipan, where, he pointed out, some ten thousand Japanese had leaped off the cliffs at Marpi Point on July 12, 1944, to their deaths — "not only the soldiers but also the civilians had committed suicide," he emphasized, "rather than be taken."[17]

The war, in other words, would take longer, and take a much more realistic direction, than the Prime Minister was blandly assuming. The Combined Chiefs should be left to do this, their job; this was the President's gentle but firm opinion, as U.S. commander in chief.

The chiefs, for their part, were delighted — Admiral Leahy, the senior member of the Combined Chiefs of Staff, wrapping up the plenary meeting on the President's behalf by stating that he did not "foresee any insuperable difficulties in reaching agreement on all points at issue."[18]

With that the chiefs had all gone back to the Château de Frontenac for lunch and further meetings.

Field Marshal Brooke was also relieved. "My mind is now much more at rest," Brooke confided to his diary. With the exception of a brief temper tantrum by Admiral King over the possible use of a Royal Navy fleet entering the Pacific, things "have gone well on the whole," the field marshal considered the next day, in spite of Winston's "unbearable moods."[19] He hadn't been able to stop Churchill sending a cable to Field Marshal Wilson, with a copy to General Alexander, claiming that the "Americans talk without any hesitation of our pushing on to Vienna, if the war lasts long enough," and calling on Wilson to prepare operational plans in a "spirit of audacious enterprise."[20] This was, Brooke knew, a bald-faced lie, yet Brooke was sure he could, at least, put the kibosh on any such nonsense the Prime Minister might try to order without American authorization. For the simple fact was, the Americans were now finally in charge of global strategy, and the best the British chiefs could do, he recognized belatedly, was to help them as far as they were able.

"On the whole we have been very successful in getting the agreement which we have achieved, and the Americans have shown a wonderful spirit of co-operation," Brooke thus recorded on September 15 — a mood spoiled only by the Prime Minister, who had been "in one of his worst tempers. Now Heaven only knows what will happen tomorrow at our final Plenary meeting . . . The tragedy is that the Americans whilst admiring him as a man have little opinion of him as a strategist."[21]

The war, in other words, was being left to the professionals, now that its strategic direction had been set by the President — and all British diversions had successfully been squashed.

Behind the scenes, unfortunately, a new monster had appeared in the Citadel: one that would overshadow Allied amity and the clear military strategy achieved and displayed by the generals at Quebec in 1944. One presented, moreover, by an American, who had no connection with the military conference, and had not even been invited to it, when it began: Henry Morgenthau Jr., the secretary of the U.S. Treasury.

63

The Morgenthau Plan

THE TREASURY SECRETARY'S PLAN was an extraordinary document; a vision of how to deal with Germany after the war.

The proposal was radically dystopian, namely to eviscerate German heavy industry and mines, and force Germany back to the agricultural economy of the eighteenth century — forgetting the merciless wars of central Europe that predated even the eighteenth century. Once the existence of the plan was leaked in the United States and became known, it would prove manna to Joseph Goebbels in Berlin. It would offer his Propaganda Ministry the very proof needed for asking Germans to continue waging total war. With documented Allied intentions to destroy not only Nazism but the entire country, the Mephisto of Nazi propaganda would be able to persuade German soldiers and civilians they must be prepared to fight to the very death to protect their homeland from deliberate, outright Allied devastation if ever they surrendered.

In every aspect the Morgenthau Plan thus became a crisis that should never have taken place. Nor would it have happened, in all probability, had the President been well, or if Churchill had not brought with him Lord Leathers. After all, there was no pressing need at Quebec to address an issue that was already being examined by the European Advisory Commission in London, set up in conformity with the Moscow Agreements of November 1943, and also in Washington. At the White House, the President had approved on August 25, 1944, a new cabinet-level committee comprising the secretaries of war, state, and Treasury, with Harry Hopkins acting as the President's committee counselor. It was tasked with addressing the question of Germany's future, from an American perspective. Concerned by reports that Eisenhower, the Allied supreme commander, was already being urged to be "soft" on the Germans in a supposedly official U.S. War Department handbook — in fact was being urged to undertake measures similar to the New Deal, such as the Works Progress Administration and Civilian Conservation Corps — the President had been incensed. Such magnanimity, he'd felt, was premature. "The German nation as a whole," he'd complained to Secretary Stimson, "must have it driven home to them that the whole nation" — not just the Gestapo, or SS — "had been engaged in a lawless conspiracy against the decencies of civilization."[1] The Cabinet Committee on Germany had thus been tasked with advising the President on how best to drive this home, once unconditional German surrender was obtained.

For Secretary Stimson, the "treatment of Germany and the Germans" was clearly a military concern, since guidance would have to be given to General Eisenhower in advance of final victory. For Secretary Hull, it was a matter of international relations, since the major Allied powers would be occupying Germany and must decide what kind of postwar country Germany should be — constitutionally, geographically, and politically. For Secretary Morgenthau, however, it was a matter of economics — which he saw as his preserve. Should the German economy be reconstituted as part of a new postwar Europe, or was it vital to smash the German war-making machine for all conceivable time, Germany having provoked two world wars in thirty years?

At the meetings of the Committee on Germany in late August it had become clear the three U.S. cabinet secretaries were at loggerheads — with Hopkins tending to side with the Treasury secretary's simple-sounding solution: namely to remove all heavy industry from the Ruhr, flood the Saar mines, and make Germany a peasant economy once again. This sounded awfully like biblical punishment. Yet to Stimson's horror, Morgenthau's plan had caught the ailing president's attention — and all practical sense had flown out the window.

There was, to be sure, consensus on demilitarizing Germany upon its surrender; dissolving all Nazi institutions; establishing Allied control over the press and education; deferring discussion of partition for a later date; deciding against reparations to be made to the United States; and on prosecuting and — where found guilty — executing all war criminals. Nevertheless Secretary Stimson had objected to Morgenthau's specific, punitive recommendation that the "great industrialized regions of Germany known as the Saar and the Ruhr with their very important deposits of coal and ore should be totally transformed into a non-industrialized area of agricultural land. I cannot conceive of such a proposition being either possible or effective," Stimson had warned in a memo to the President on September 6, "and I can see enormous general evils coming from an attempt to so treat it."[2] Such a destructive program, for one thing, defied the whole economic march of history in Europe. The result — beyond leading millions of Germans to starve, since there was not enough agricultural land to feed seventy million people — would not only slow Europe's postwar economic recovery, but morally it would place the Allies in the invidious position of being as ruthless as the Nazis — and certainly no better than the Russians, who were expected to dismantle and remove all German industrial machinery they could, taking the materials to the Soviet Union as war reparations.

Aware the matter was becoming deeply contentious the President had therefore summoned committee members to the White House on Saturday morning, September 9, for a two-hour meeting before he left for Quebec. Once in the Oval Office Stimson had realized how ill was the President: no longer able to process their arguments, and unable to manage more than a forty-five-minute discussion, even as he prepared to go meet the British.

Forty-five minutes to resolve the destiny of the main enemy of the United States in World War II?

"I have been much troubled by the President's physical condition," Stimson confided in the privacy of his diary. "He was distinctly not himself on Saturday. He had a cold and seemed tired out. I rather fear for the effects of this hard conference upon him. I am particularly troubled," the war secretary had added, "that he is going up there [to Quebec] without any real preparation for the solution of the underlying and fundamental problem of how to treat Germany. So far as he has evidenced it in his talks with us, he has had absolutely no study or training in the very difficult problem which we have to decide, namely of how far we can introduce preventive measures to protect the world from Germany running amuck again and how far we must refrain from measures which will simply provoke the wrong reaction." If the subject was addressed at Quebec, Stimson commented, "I hope the British have brought better trained men with them than we are likely to have to meet them."[3]

Currently aboard the *Queen Mary* the British hadn't even thought to address the matter! Nor, once they arrived in Quebec, was the subject ever once raised in the daily Combined Chiefs of Staff meetings, or mentioned in the minutes or diaries of their deliberations in Quebec. So why, historians wondered afterwards, had Mr. Roosevelt felt it necessary to raise it with Mr. Churchill — especially when he was not taking anyone with him to advise him on the matter, not even Harry Hopkins?

Certainly no historian could later explain the President's sudden focus on the plan of "pastoralizing" postwar Germany, save in terms of growing dementia. In the weeks before Quebec he had been heard objecting to those arguing for generosity in treating the Germans after the war, given the terrible deeds enacted not only by Nazis but many German soldiers and civilians — and which were ongoing. The systematic arrest, deportation, and presumed "liquidation" of hundreds of thousands of Jews in Hungary sickened him. That they were continuing the deliberate extermination of vast numbers of Jews and other defenseless citizens in Nazi concentration camps across Europe without the least concern among "ordinary" Germans was horrifying — and reports that the Wehrmacht was defending every yard of territory it had conquered to the last man standing did not make the President feel magnanimous, understandably, in terms of bringing the people of Germany back into the fold when they were finally forced to surrender. But deliberately and forever laying waste to the Ruhr and the Saar, the very kernel of the European economy, as a punishment?

Stimson's several memoranda on the subject, copied to the President, were among the most articulate the aging lawyer had ever composed, assembled with the help of his large staff at the Pentagon — including General Marshall; Harvey Bundy, special assistant to Stimson; and John McCloy, assistant secretary of war. Such a "draconian" punishment of Germany would amount, Stimson had argued, to cutting off the Western Allies' nose to spite their face — and, if they were seriously to contemplate such a radical measure, would it not require far more serious discussion than Secretary Morgenthau's seemingly vengeful, half-baked proposal?

In this respect the President was undone not only by his own ill health, but by the very concept of a military conference, away from Washington, in which his only role was to take part in two plenary sessions, several days apart. This left Roosevelt more or less alone with Churchill, without agenda or purpose. In short, the President and the Prime Minister were virtually unemployed in the Citadel, with no political discussions supposedly permitted, lest controversy be cast on the President's election campaign. Thus it was — with Churchill seeming "very glum" when shorn of his Viennese and Singapore "diversions" at the first plenary — that on a whim, it seemed, the President had summoned Morgenthau, the Treasury secretary, to Quebec. On his own — that is, without his fellow committee members, namely Stimson and Hull. Or Harry Hopkins.

Such a unilateral invitation by the President completely ruined whatever chance there was for further considered debate or discussion of the issue by experts from different departments. True, the secretary of war had managed to get the President to promise to take "the papers we have written on the subject with him," but he "has not invited any further discussion on the matter with us," or with his longtime White House counselor, Harry Hopkins, Stimson noted in his diary on September 13. "Instead apparently today he has invited Morgenthau up there," Stimson rued, "or Morgenthau has got himself invited." Either way, "I cannot believe that he will follow Morgenthau's views. If he does," he predicted, "it will certainly be a disaster."[4]

It was: Morgenthau triggering a far worse scandal than the mere deindustrialization plan for the Ruhr. For no sooner had he arrived in Quebec than he set about converting Churchill to his cause — by bribing the Prime Minister.

This was, in retrospect, perhaps the most egregious aspect of the crisis. For his part Mackenzie King was neither consulted nor invited to participate.

After escorting Mrs. Roosevelt and Mrs. Churchill to the Château Frontenac for a dinner on September 13 — the meal serenaded by the Royal Canadian Mounted Police Band — King had returned to the Citadel. There he had found "Churchill and the President and a small party still at the table" where he'd left them. "They had been seated there when I left at 9, and were still seated at half past eleven," King noted. Churchill was sitting immediately opposite the President, and "both of them seemed to be speaking to the numbers assembled which included Morgenthau, Lord Cherwell, Lord Leathers, Lord Moran, and two or three others. Morgenthau," the U.S. Treasury secretary, had "arrived this afternoon. Anthony Eden is to arrive in the morning."[5]

Looking at her husband's pale, drawn face, Eleanor was alarmed. Telling Mackenzie King the President had not "had any rest this afternoon as he was talking to different persons through the day," she "got the President to come off immediately to bed."[6]

It was too late, however — in both senses. The President had gently but firmly put down Churchill's military dreams concerning Vienna and Singapore that morning, but he was obviously debilitated — and what he had concocted with Winston Churchill, while King escorted their two wives to dinner, would do neither man much historical credit. For when the President had brought up the matter of postwar Germany, the subject had become as contentious as it had been in Washington: the very last thing the President needed with his systolic blood pressure already registering 230, as Dr. Bruenn later noted.

Admiral Leahy, in his diary, recorded that night that the "subjects discussed at dinner were generally international politics, economics and shipping; and the peace terms and punishment that should be imposed upon Germany when that country surrenders to the Allies."[7]

Told by his British table companions that this subject was something that would be addressed in London by his government and civil service colleagues on the tripartite European Advisory Commission, Churchill had sounded furious it was being tabled in London without him. "What are my Cabinet members doing discussing plans for Germany without first discussing them with me?" he'd demanded — prompting the President to suggest that Morgenthau and Lord Cherwell, Churchill's scientific adviser, could talk about the matter the next day. Churchill, however, had always hated to put off to the morrow what could be dealt with today. "Why don't we discuss Germany now?" the Prime Minister had asked the President[8] — and with that, and with the President's approval, Henry Morgenthau had presented his controversial draft plan.

Churchill, facing the President, could not at first believe his ears — in fact the Prime Minister initially "reacted violently against it, even disagreeably so," Morgenthau himself admitted to Stimson when he got back to Washington several days later.[9] He "blew up against it and said he could never accept such a paper" — in fact demanded of the President at one point: "Is this what you asked me to come all the way over here to discuss?"[10]

The plan, as Morgenthau described it, was in Churchill's view "unnatural, unchristian and unnecessary" — words that bespoke the best in Churchill's character. His gift for metaphor was memorably on display, moreover, when he gave vent to "the full flood of his rhetoric, sarcasm and violence" — adding that, far from helping Britain in the postwar years, Morgenthau's deindustrialization of the Ruhr and the flooding of its mines would leave England "chained to a dead body."[11]

"The President said very little in reply to Churchill's views," Harry Dexter White, Morgenthau's deputy, recorded of the "men's dinner" discussion.[12] This had not, however, inhibited others at the table. Churchill's doctor, Lord Moran (as Dr. Wilson now was), recorded in his diary that the Prime Minister "did not seem happy about all this toughness. 'I'm all for disarming Germany,' he said, 'but we ought not to prevent her living decently. There are bonds between the working classes of all countries, and the English people will not stand for the policy you are advocating . . . I agree with Burke. You cannot indict a whole nation.'" In terms of punishment, the Prime Minister "kept saying, 'At any rate, what is to be done should be done quickly. Kill the criminals, but don't carry on the business for years.'"[13]

Moran noted how little the President spoke. "The President mostly listened" — save to say, at one point, that Stalin, at Tehran, had mentioned how even a German factory that "made steel furniture could be turned overnight to war production"[14] — a way of reminding those present that, unless the Western Allies imposed tough terms, the Russians would suspect them of permitting, even financing, the future remilitarization of Germany, as in the 1930s under Hitler.

The discussion might have been considered mere dinner conversation, and of no lasting import. But Morgenthau had not come up to Quebec to converse. He was bearing gifts he thought might interest Mr. Churchill — even persuade him to change his mind on the matter. It was in this way that the next day, September 14, the President and the Prime Minister drew up, literally overnight, a formal plan to punish Germany by reducing its economy to its eighteenth-century agricultural origins. Why?

64

Beyond the Dreams of Avarice

WORKING FIRST THROUGH LORD CHERWELL, Secretary Morgenthau offered the British $6.5 billion in Lend-Lease credit, if his plan for pastoralizing Germany was accepted.

The Prime Minister, who had become alarmed at reports Britain would soon be bankrupt, was electrified — and in a matter of minutes his opposition to Morgenthau's plan evaporated. Moreover, when the President, that afternoon, seemed to be delaying the drawing up of a memorandum of Lend-Lease agreement on such huge financial numbers, Churchill became so "nervous and eager to have the memorandum agreed, he finally burst out: 'What do you want me to do? Get on my hind legs and beg like Fala?'"[1]

This was not a remark the President liked, and indicated how volatile the subject could become. Morgenthau's offer was thus confirmed.

Going to bed that night the Prime Minister seemed over the moon. Britain would be saved from penury; the empire would flourish once more. Boasting to his assistant private secretary of "the financial advantages the Americans had promised us," he seemed almost to levitate as he undressed. "Beyond the dreams of avarice," his secretary commented, as impressed as his boss. It was a phrase that pricked the Prime Minister's sleepy conscience, though. "Beyond," he corrected the young man, "the dreams of justice."

To ensure it was not a mere verbal understanding, the following day, September 15, 1944, the Morgenthau Plan was formally dictated by Churchill himself to a stenographer, to be written up in the manner of a contract between the United States and Britain — to be initialed both by the President and the Prime Minister.[2]

Though the President was too ill to help in drafting the text of the document, he certainly did nothing to question the terms of the plan — in fact he suggested, upon reading the stenographer's first draft, that they widen the scope of the plan to cover *all* potential war-making industries — metallurgical, chemical, and electrical, across the whole of postwar Germany, not simply the Ruhr and the Saar. According to Morgenthau, Churchill became "quite emotional" about the Lend-Lease agreement, and when "the thing was finally signed, he told the President how grateful he was, thanked him most effusively, and said that this was something they were doing for both countries." Britain would not go bankrupt — indeed, with the output of the Ruhr and the Saar mines extinguished, Britain's postwar prosperity would be guaranteed, for Germany would be removed as a postwar economic competitor.[3]

Anthony Eden, arriving posthaste from England, was appalled, hating the very mention of such a deal. "Eden seemed quite shocked at what he heard," Morgenthau later admitted, "and he turned to Churchill and said, 'You can't do this. After all, you and I have said quite the opposite.'"

Churchill had merely batted away his objections.

The President, for his part, had remained silent; he "took no part in it," leaving it to Morgenthau to emphasize the advantages to Britain "in the way of trade," for they would then "get the export trade of Germany."

"How do you know what it is or where it is?" Eden had countered, fully aware of the Prime Minister's ignorance of economics. "Well, we will get it wherever it is," Churchill had responded, "testily" — and had forbidden Eden to return to Britain and inflame the War Cabinet against the plan, before he himself could get back. "After all, the future of my people is at stake," Churchill had declared, "and when I have to choose between my people and the German people, I am going to choose my people."[4]

Secretary Stimson, hearing what the President had done from John McCloy on the long-distance scrambler-phone from Quebec, was aghast. "Apparently he has gone over completely to the Morgenthau proposition," Stimson recorded; moreover had "gotten Churchill and Lord Cherwell" — an individual Stimson considered "an old fool" — "with them."[5] It was essentially, he would later write in hand on his copy of the Morgenthau Plan, a "Bribe to the U.K."[6]

As Stimson lamented in his diary on September 15, "It is a terrible thing to think that the total power of the United States and the United Kingdom in such a critical matter as this is in the hands of two men, both of whom are similar in their impulsiveness and their lack of systematic study." The deindustrializing plan was "Carthaginian" — one that could only shame the United States, and which horrified everyone Stimson spoke to about it.

Unable to live with his conscience if he did not protest, Stimson had penned a rebuke he cabled to the President that night. As he pointed out, he felt he had already objected to the Treasury secretary's proposal, in writing, several times. Nothing he'd learned since then had changed his conviction that the plan "would in the long run certainly defeat what we hope to attain by a complete military victory — that is, the peace of the world, and the assurance of social, economic and political stability in the world."[7]

It was not a matter of "whether we should be soft or tough on the German people, but rather whether the course proposed will in fact best attain our agreed objective, continued peace. If I thought that the Treasury proposals would accomplish that objective, I would not persist in my objections. But I cannot believe that they will make for a lasting peace. In spirit and emphasis they are punitive, not in my judgment, corrective or constructive. They will tend through bitterness and suffering to breed another war, not to make another war undesired by the Germans nor impossible in fact. It is not within the realm of possibility that a whole nation of seventy million people, who have been outstanding for many years in the arts and sciences and who through their efficiency and energy have attained one of the highest industrial levels in Europe, can by force be required to abandon all their previous methods of life, be reduced to a peasant level with virtually complete control of industry and science left to other people.

"The question is not whether we want Germans to suffer for their sins. Many of us would like to see them suffer the tortures they have inflicted on others. The only question is whether over the years a group of seventy million educated, efficient and imaginative people can be kept within bounds on such a low level of subsistence as the Treasury proposals contemplate." It would be "a crime as the Germans themselves hoped to perpetrate on their victims — it would be a crime against civilization itself." It went against the President's own Atlantic Charter, and his Four Freedoms — which sought "freedom of all from want and from fear."[8]

Paragraph after paragraph Stimson panned Morgenthau's plan, not because he thought it unmerited, but because it wouldn't work — and could only rebound on America — and Britain. "The benefit to England by the suppression of German competition is greatly stressed in the Treasury memorandum," he noted. "But this is an argument addressed to a shortsighted cupidity of the victors and the negation of all that Secretary Hull has been trying to accomplish since 1933. I am aware of England's need, but I do not and cannot believe that she wishes this kind of remedy." For, as Stimson remarked, "the total elimination of a competitor (who is also a potential purchaser) is rarely a satisfactory solution of a commercial problem."[9]

Harry Hopkins, reading Stimson's plea to the President, undertook to get it to the President himself. Neither of them, however, was aware Franklin Roosevelt had passed a point of no return: that he was not merely dying of heart disease, but that his once-capacious, genial, and elastic mind was now in severe decline.

65

The President Is Gaga

THE AFTERMATH OF QUEBEC would prove embarrassing. The President rested in Hyde Park, but showed no improvement, in body or spirit. By September 20 the President was predicting Governor Dewey would win the election, as suggested by the latest polls — and seemed actually to welcome the prospect, to Daisy's astonishment. "The Pres. is planning his life after he leaves the W.H. It will be so different, without the many 'services' supplied by the govt. He will 'write'; and can make a lot of money that way — also his corr. [espondence] will be tremendous," necessitating Daisy's assistance, as Grace Tully would want to move closer to her family.[1]

It was at this point that the President's mistake over the Morgenthau Plan caught up with him — for on September 21, 1944, Drew Pearson revealed in the *Washington Post* that trouble was brewing at the War Department. There, senior personnel were "quaking in their boots" after issuing a Handbook on Germany that was ridiculously mild — whereas the President wanted the Germans to receive, Pearson wrote, no more than "three bowls of soup a day."[2]

Three bowls of soup?

Convinced that Morgenthau himself had planted the leak, Stimson's War Department counterleaked: the *New York Times* running an article the next day, written by Arthur Krock, about the Cabinet Committee on Germany: revealing, moreover, that Secretary Morgenthau, but not Stimson or Hull, had traveled to Quebec. The proverbial fat was in the fire — with the President left looking, as even Morgenthau recognized, at the very least, like a "bad administrator."[3]

For a chief executive barely able to function as president or commander in chief, the fiasco was the very disaster Stimson had foretold. Governor Dewey's campaign workers were overjoyed. "After a reporter at the Quebec Conference told Dewey he was convinced that Roosevelt was a dying man, and that the Republican contender had 'an absolute duty' to reveal the true state of the President's health," his biographer recorded, "Dewey and his advisers sweated blood over the issue. 'There wasn't a single night went by we didn't argue that one out,'" Dewey's campaign manager later recalled — with some wanting "'to go all out, stating that he was on his death bed, and getting all the evidence that we could.'"[4] In the meantime, revelation of the Morgenthau Plan would do nicely.

Morgenthau, for his part, was embarrassed and ashamed — especially when Nazi newspapers began quoting the American press about the affair, and General Marshall complained to him in person, over a luncheon, how the publicity could affect the war effort on the Western Front. "We have got loudspeakers on the German lines telling them to surrender," Marshall remonstrated, and "this doesn't help one bit"[5] — Wehrmacht troops being inspired to resist to the bitter end, as even the *Washington Post* warned. Should the Germans believe "nothing but complete destruction" of their country awaited them after surrender, "then they will fight on," the *Post* lectured. "Let's stop helping Dr. Goebbels."[6]

With German radio claiming the Allies would "exterminate forty-three million Germans," and the *Völkischer Beobachter* running a headline, ROOSEVELT AND CHURCHILL AGREE TO JEWISH MURDER PLAN!, Morgenthau was doubly embarrassed — the German press silent on the mass murder, thus far, of over five million Jews in Europe, yet more than willing to quote supposed American intentions to starve many more millions of Germans.

The President did his best to console Morgenthau, whom he'd known as a Dutchess County farming neighbor since 1913. He'd appointed him to the Treasury in 1933, and considered he had done a remarkably successful job — especially in selling war bonds — given that Morgenthau had no training or experience in finance. Knowledge of the ruthless German extermination program had only made the President more compassionate toward Morgenthau — for despite calls for bombing of the concentration camps or the railtracks leading to them, there was nothing the Allies could realistically do to stop the Nazis, save issue warnings of arrest for crimes against humanity and defeat the Wehrmacht as soon as humanly possible.[7]

Secretary Hull was just as disappointed by the scandal as the staff of the *Washington Post* — indeed, he felt particularly sore that Morgenthau, without consultation with the State Department, had gone ahead and promised the British a $6.5 billion get-out-of-debtors-jail card without recompense of any kind, such as imperial trade concessions or even possible military bases. By September 24, 1944, newspapers were widely reporting a "split in the Cabinet"[8] — and the President finally asked to talk with him.

"Now the pack is in full cry," Stimson noted in his diary on September 25.

At a moment when Field Marshal Montgomery's great airborne operation to bounce the Rhine in northern Holland had met with fierce Wehrmacht resistance — an entire British airborne division being rubbed out at Arnhem (the "Bridge Too Far"), and two magnificent American airborne divisions, having secured crossings over the Maas and Waal Rivers, suffering serious casualties — the Quebec fiasco, or "hell of a hubbub," as John McCloy called it, was becoming deeply damaging not only to the President's reelection chances, but to the Allied cause. "The papers have taken it up violently and almost unanimously against Morgenthau and the President himself," the war secretary noted. Morgenthau might cry foul, given leaks to the press, but the President himself "had already evidently reached the conclusion that he had made a false step and was trying to work out of it." As long as the memorandum itself was kept secret, the President would meantime deny all newspaper accounts of his supposed policy. A phone call from the President on September 27 confirmed this — as well as a meeting in person arranged at the White House on October 3.[9]

It was in this way that, behind the scenes, the biggest change in the military direction of World War II since Pearl Harbor was implicitly acknowledged by Secretary Stimson. The President of the United States was no longer really fit to carry out his constitutional role as commander in chief. Word had come from China that the Japanese were attacking Chiang Kai-shek's forces and pushing them back — with huge implications for the course of the war against Japan. Stimson had prepared himself to discuss the situation as a matter of urgency with the President over lunch. "When I got to the White House and saw him," Stimson noted, however, "I saw that it would be impossible. He was ill again with a cold and looked tired and worn" — so much so, in fact, that Stimson was asked to lunch with him "in the main building [mansion] because the mere lunch with me was a violation of his doctor's routine that he should not waste strength at lunches at his office."[10] He even had his daughter Anna there, to see he didn't get stressed or too tired.

Discussing China was clearly beyond the President, so no "business" was conducted during the meal — and then only in the gentlest fashion. When the President denied having signed a paper with Churchill about turning Germany back into an agrarian, preindustrial state, Stimson pulled out his copy of the Morgenthau Plan, with its final sentence calling for "eliminating the war-making industries in the Ruhr and the Saar" and "converting Germany into a country primarily agricultural and pastoral in its character." The intent was plain as a pikestaff. As Stimson recorded that night, the President "was frankly staggered by this and said he had no idea how he could have initialed this; that he had evidently done it without much thought"[11] — openly confessing, "Henry, I have not the faintest recollection of this at all."[12]

No recollection?

The frank admission allowed Stimson to remind the President of the true import of the matter.

"I told him that in my opinion the most serious danger of the situation was the getting abroad of the idea of vengeance instead of preventive punishment and that it was the language of the Treasury paper which had alarmed me on the subject. I told him that, knowing his likeness [*sic*] for brevity and slogans, I had tried to think of a brief crystallization of the way I looked at it. I said I thought that our problem was analogous to the problem of an operation for cancer where it is necessary to cut deeply to get out the malignant tissue even at the expense of much sound tissue in the process, but not to the extent of cutting out any vital organs which by killing the patient would frustrate the benefit of the operation. I said in the same way that what we were after was preventive punishment, even educative punishment, but not vengeance. I told him that I had throughout had in mind his postwar leadership in which he would represent America. I said throughout the war his leadership had been on a high moral plane and he had fought for the highest moral objectives. Now during the postwar readjustment 'You must not poison this position' which he and our country held with anything like mere hatred or vengeance." Stimson was at pains to emphasize the friendship he, Stimson, felt for Morgenthau, and how concerned he'd been by how "misrepresented," in pursuing such a plan, a "man of his race" — i.e., Jewish — would be.[13]

The President was chastened. His excuses that he'd wanted to be nice to the British, who were facing bankruptcy, were lame. Moreover, though it had shown deep and genuine compassion for his friend, and outrage at what the Nazis had done — and were still doing — the plan would not, in the long run, do any good. Nor would it even work, since it would only make seventy million Germans susceptible to a future Hitler. In short, America's moral agenda had to rise above such understandably punitive feelings in order to embrace the future: a future in which the United States would be the new leader of the democracies, whatever the Russians might do.

With that the luncheon visit ended.

Anna, the President's daughter, was clearly grateful for Stimson's kind, even tender manner — Stimson recording in his diary that he'd spoken in front of the two of them "with all the friendliness and tact possible — and after all," he added, "I feel a very real and deep friendship for him."[14]

Their relationship had now changed, though. As King George VI was told in London, the President had "sadly aged. He never ventures to wear his [leg] 'braces,' now — i.e. never walks at all; and in a long sitting" at Quebec, "his jaw would drop, and his thoughts obviously wander"[15] — the king's counselor, Alan Lascelles, being privately told by General Ismay that the President was, effectively and ominously, "gaga."

Secretary Stimson and General Marshall, in other words, would now be running the war — as well as addressing the military aspects of the postwar. On behalf of a president who was now, essentially, a figurehead, with Admiral Leahy caretaker of the White House and linchpin of the chiefs.

With that, Stimson had left the White House — and the unfortunate business of Quebec.

PART TEN

Yalta

66

Outward Bound

ALMOST FOUR MONTHS LATER, at 8:31 a.m. on January 23, 1945, the USS *Quincy*, an American heavy cruiser, cast off from Pier 6 at Newport News, Virginia, bearing the President of the United States.

Sister vessel to the USS *Baltimore*, which had taken the President to Hawaii the previous summer, the two Baltimore-class battle cruisers were almost identical in firepower. The President was not the same man, however, who had sailed to Pearl Harbor in August 1944 — let alone the commander in chief who had journeyed to Oran and back home in late 1943 aboard the USS *Iowa*. Able only to harness his mental faculties for an hour or two a day, and often exhausted by that effort, he was by January 1945 another heart attack, or major stroke, waiting to happen. How, two months before, on November 7, 1944, he had won a fourth term in the White House was something of a miracle — or a monstrous act of deception, depending on how one viewed the presidential election.

From somewhere in his ailing body and spirit the President had drawn upon his final reserves of energy. He had made several campaign speeches, and been driven in an open car through the often rain-swept streets of Philadelphia, Chicago, New York, and Boston to prove he was not only still alive, but kicking. His notorious address to members of the Teamsters union at a dinner in Washington, in which he remarked that he was not bothered by attacks his Republican opponents made on him, but that they did upset Fala, his dog, demonstrated the President still had a sense of humor — a quality his opponent, Governor Dewey, sadly lacked. But with polls showing a swing away from the current sclerotic administration, after twelve years in power, even the President had thought Dewey would win.

And Dewey came close to doing so — in fact, more than was comfortable to the Democrats behind the numbers. In the early hours of November 8, Dewey's campaign cohort was still urging him not to concede, for it had proved the closest election since 1916. With the tide of the country's voters running to the right, the younger Dewey-Bricker ticket had seemed not only menacing to Democrats but almost invincible in the eyes even of their strategists, given the mood of a nation seemingly tired of the same old faces and twelve years of Democratic rule. Only the President's personal popularity could reliably stave off a Republican victory, they had figured — and reports of his worsening health had therefore threatened to make defeat probable, if not certain.

Dewey was done in by his own party, however, which failed to understand the need for idealism. By standing for reelection on the domestic and international platform that he'd chosen — a New Deal for veterans after the war, and an end to isolationism abroad — the President had forced the nation to choose whether, under younger personnel, to go back to Hoover's Great Crash, Depression, and an "America First" retreat from international involvement that had characterized Republican politicking in the 1930s, or to move forward — albeit under increasingly doddery old men.

Compelled by the President to take either the high road in terms of domestic and international policy or the low road of Republican self-interest, Dewey had waffled — Republican voters at his rallies across the country so bored by his initial attempts to articulate a course change that they booed him. What they'd wanted was a fight: an old-fashioned political bar fight. Changing his tune, the young New York governor — a neophyte in terms of international politics — had finally delivered it: railing at the President's New Deal results; at big government; at high taxes; at Jews and communists running the nation's unions. And the sheer senility of the Roosevelt administration.

Roosevelt's stature as the nation's commander in chief in war, and his highminded appeal to American idealism in terms of postwar security, had thus outweighed the rumors of his ill health — enough, at any rate, to keep the majority of the nation's voters resolute in prosecuting the war and in bracing themselves for high, global responsibilities once the war was won.

This was, in the circumstances, no mean achievement. So irresponsible did Dewey become, in fact, that he was prevented from revealing Magic, the breaking of Japanese codes at the time of Pearl Harbor, only by way of a personal meeting sought by General Marshall. The chief of staff of the U.S. Army had told the young governor that such a disclosure would amount to an act of treason, given that U.S. cryptographers were still using Magic to great effect — moreover that it would be committed solely to embarrass the Roosevelt administration for its failure to warn Hawaii more effectively in December 1941, without concern as to how many American lives would be put in jeopardy at present, should the breaking of the United States' most secret diplomatic and military codes become known to the Japanese.

Tom Dewey had duly backed off — though he subsequently blamed his defeat, in private, on General Marshall, who he claimed had been personally responsible for failing to issue a more emphatic warning to U.S. bases in the Pacific to prepare for a Japanese sneak attack. Other Republicans were less sure, however; a political campaign based on past mistakes, at a time of world war, and without a vision of America's future in the world had probably been a mistake. The ailing president had shown himself to be the more courageous candidate — unafraid, in particular, to address the matter of global security and the need to move beyond isolationism in a postwar world. Thanks to the antiquated electoral college system, a switch of less than three hundred thousand votes in certain states could, in theory, have put Dewey in the White House; instead, the President's ultimate margin of victory had proved to be close to a landslide: 432 college delegates to 99.

In ballots cast across the country, too, the President had trounced his rival, garnering almost three and a half million more votes than his opponent. In a presidential election the Republicans ought on paper to have won, had they been less focused on domestic issues with an eye to their own wealth, the writing was on the wall. No sooner was the election over, therefore, than more thoughtful Republican leaders had begun to rethink their prewar isolationist positions.

How far should the U.S. government go in working with, or appeasing, the Soviets in terms of postwar policy? The question was certainly debatable, but whatever the answer, the Russians could not, as current allies, be ignored. They had provided the essential manpower to defeat the Nazis — and would be a major world power after the war's conclusion: victory, moreover, that was still to be won, whatever casualties it took.

Isolationism would simply not be an option, the former America First senator Arthur Vandenberg had finally acknowledged in the wake of the election. Other Republican stalwarts had begun to follow suit. Even Governor Dewey, following his failed campaign, had spurned his advisers — urging the New York State Legislature to embrace progressive principles in its political and economic programs, from rent control to massive electricity infrastructure projects, antidiscrimination laws, and public education programs, while supporting a new internationalism — earning the sobriquet "a Liberal without blinkers."[1] After the last hurrahs of a bitter general election campaign, idealism was returning, finally, to the Republican agenda.

It was Senator Vandenberg himself who led the new charge. On January 10, 1945, in a dramatic address in the U.S. Senate — one that became known as the "speech heard round the world" — the senator had finally and formally announced his conversion from prewar reclusion to postwar internationalism. Worried that, as victory neared, greed and self-interest would disunite the Allies, Vandenberg — "a big, loud, vain, and self-important man, who could strut sitting down," in the words of one reporter[2] — had appealed for a collective, collaborative international approach to postwar peace — and peacekeeping. Again and again the President's former enemy number one — the very senator who had tried to get MacArthur nominated as the Republican candidate for the presidency in the spring of 1944 — had openly admitted he'd been wrong. To the consternation of his peers in the chamber he had repeatedly quoted President Roosevelt's January 6 message to Congress — verbatim.

The President's message had certainly been forceful: delivered, on camera and on radio, in a firm, lilting voice that completely belied his plummeting health. It had been, in truth, an 8,253-word oration crafted by the President's speech-writers, Sam Rosenman and Robert Sherwood, and had addressed, head-on, "the status of the war, the international situation during and after the war, the formation of the peace," as Rosenman later recalled — as well as "the United Nations Organization, and the future of America."[3]

Broadcast in the very midst of the Battle of the Bulge — the massive, initially successful German surprise counterattack by three Wehrmacht armies in the Ardennes — the President had taken pains to declare, as U.S. commander in chief, his "complete confidence" in General Eisenhower. The young general was the nation's "supreme commander in complete control of all the allied armies in France" — a commander who "has faced this period of trial with admirable calm and resolution and with steadily increasing success." Unity among allies in war was, the President had been at pains to emphasize, the ultimate reason no German military counterattack, no matter how lethal (American casualties in the Ardennes and Alsace would amount to more than one hundred thousand killed, wounded, captured, or missing, including nineteen thousand dead), would in the end succeed. Yet it was Roosevelt's appeal for unity and common purpose in creating a United Nations organization *after* the war that had most impressed Senator Vandenberg.

"Again I agree wholeheartedly with President Roosevelt when he says, 'We must not let such differences [between allies] divide us and blind us to our more important common and continuing interests in winning the war and building the peace,'" Vandenberg had declared in Congress, quoting the President. By all accounts Russia was contemplating "a surrounding circle of buffer states, contrary to what we thought we were fighting for in respect to the rights of small nations and a just peace" — including states such as Poland. In terms of Russian national self-interest this was "a perfectly understandable reason," Vandenberg had allowed — but hardly a recipe for postwar peace on a larger, global scale. Isolationism and regional balance-of-power politics would never be enough, he declared, to guard against a third world war — as the rise of Hitler and Japanese militarists had shown, with literally devastating consequences. "The alternative is collective security," Vandenberg had emphasized on the Senate floor, citing again the President's January 6 message to Congress — in fact Vandenberg had gone further: urging, on behalf of his colleagues in the Senate, that the President should enjoy "full power to join our military force with others in a new peace league," or United Nations, in order to keep "Germany and Japan demilitarized." In this way Germany would pose no threat to the Soviet Union after the war. Moreover such "full power" should be accorded the President without his having to "refer any such action back to Congress," to be hobbled once again by isolationists, such as himself in the run-up to Pearl Harbor.

Delighted to read this, the President had ordered fifty copies of Vandenberg's speech to be printed immediately, which he could take with him when he left the Bureau of Engraving station on the *Ferdinand Magellan* two days later, bound for the USS *Quincy.* There were myriad domestic problems to face in Washington — most urgently the fury being unleashed in Congress by the replacement of Commerce Secretary Jesse Jones by the now-former vice president, Henry Wallace — but the President could take satisfaction in having almost single-handedly won the constitutional backing of the American people for his internationalist postwar program, in spite of his debilitated state of health. Not only the support of the voting public, moreover: Republicans and Democrats in Congress, too, pace Senator Vandenberg.

The President's public backing for General Eisenhower was not window dressing.

The British commander of the northern Allied armies, Field Marshal Montgomery, had caused an uproar in the press on January 6, 1945, by posing as the savior of the Allied forces in stopping German panzer armies from reaching the Meuse and splitting the Allies apart, as they'd done in 1940. Like General Patton, who had swiveled his U.S. Third Army to attack the southern flank of the German bulge, in order to smash the side door of the German breakthrough and relieve Bastogne, Montgomery was certainly a field commander of rare distinction in modern warfare. Like Patton, also, he had been endowed, both by nature and his growing fame as a warrior, with a big mouth. Not content with "saving" the American army in the Ardennes, the field marshal had revived his calls to be given back permanently the field command of the main Allied armies he'd held during the Normandy campaign, and which he'd regained once the magnitude of the German offensive in the Ardennes was appreciated. Field Marshal Alan Brooke, moreover, had backed Montgomery in this effort — one in which General Eisenhower's hand would be removed from the Allies' operational tiller.

Though he admired Montgomery's achievements in combat, the President was impressed by General Eisenhower's performance as a coalition supreme commander even more. He had therefore welcomed the chance to state in public, before the nation and the world, his support for the officer he had personally chosen to be supreme commander not only of D-day, but the consequent campaign to defeat the Wehrmacht.

The Germans, Eisenhower had memorably told him at the Villa Dar es Saada in Casablanca before the Battle of Kasserine, were tough, ideologically ruthless, and well trained; they made amazingly good combat soldiers, from senior officers down to corporals and GIs.[4] Where the Italians had become less and less effective soldiers since the time of Caesar's legions, the Germans — who had already been fearsome tribal warriors, north of the Rhine, in Caesar's day — had become steadily more accomplished in military terms. The great technological advances of modern industrialized warfare, from panzers to jet fighters, ballistic missiles to U-boats, suited them: their century-long investment in higher education and science had been rewarded in spades. Moreover the complete separation of technology from morality had permitted the Wehrmacht to conquer democratic Europe in a matter of months — its officers ignoring any consideration outside loyal service to the Führer and the Reich. The secretly executed counteroffensive in the Ardennes — the Battle of the Bulge, as it became known — had shown the Wehrmacht at its most proficient, and morally ruthless — epitomized by the massacre of American prisoners by firing squad at Malmedy, Belgium, on December 17, 1944, committed by units of the First SS Panzer Division.

The President, in disclaiming responsibility for the Morgenthau Plan, had wanted to rise above vengeance as a national policy. The heavy casualties U.S. forces were suffering in the Ardennes, however, had appalled him, and had certainly not inclined him to become more generous in addressing the question of what to do with Germany, once unconditional surrender was achieved: a matter that was now coming to a head. For the question of how to deal with Germany would be a major issue in his second proposed summit with Marshal Stalin and Prime Minister Churchill: a sort of Tehran 2.

Where, exactly, would it take place, though — and when?

67

Light of the President's Fading Life

AFTER MUCH BEATING AROUND the proverbial bush (with possible venues ranging from Scotland, Athens, Piraeus, Salonika, Jerusalem, Istanbul, Rome, Alexandria, Cyprus, Malta, and the French Riviera)[1] it had been the President himself who had settled on Yalta, in the Crimea: a kind of Russian Riviera on the Black Sea and erstwhile summer resort of the czars. Also the favorite winter resort of the playwright and short story writer Anton Chekhov.

Stalin had insisted the summit be on Russian soil, if it was really urgent — which he doubted. His Russian forces were currently overstretched; some were, however, within striking distance of Berlin, if the Wehrmacht did not launch another Battle of the Bulge on his own front. He needed, he'd therefore claimed, to be in constant supervision of his armies as they fought their way through Poland and across the Oder River to the German border. Why was it necessary that the national leaders meet now?

The urgency was, in the end, the President's health. Roosevelt had already lived longer than many observers, from his doctors in Washington to the *New York Times,* had thought likely or possible the previous summer. In his diary Lord Halifax had noted he'd been told by James Reston, a young reporter, "that before the President went away on his holiday" to Hobcaw, "the *New York Times,* on their information, had made up their mind that it was quite likely he was going to die, and had accordingly prepared a full obituary front page, with all the right photographs."[2]

The President hadn't died, however, and his personal relationship with Stalin, based on their years of correspondence and their meeting in Tehran, still held out strong hope the United Nations authority could at least be set up before war's end, avoiding the likely divisions that would arise between different countries' postwar self-interests, as Senator Vandenberg had also warned. The Dumbarton Oaks Conference had ended with considerable Allied agreement — but without resolving continuing Russian demands for multiple Soviet delegates to the embryonic UN. A personal summit with Stalin could hopefully cut that Gordian knot, before the Russians became too powerful, as well as tying down military-political agreements, such as zones of occupation in a defeated Germany, and Russian entry into the war against Japan. If the President's health held out.

In short, there was not a moment to lose. Russian ground forces were growing stronger by the day, not weaker. Soviet troops were already occupying most of Poland, Romania, and Bulgaria; they would soon be in Hungary — in fact they were close to the Slovakian border in the Carpathian Mountains. By early February they would be only forty miles from Berlin.

Thanks to Hitler's counteroffensive in the Ardennes, the prospects for a major crossing of the Rhine by the Western Allies and a drive on Berlin had been downgraded to somewhere between unlikely and nil, with Eisenhower's broad-front offensive plans, north and south of the Ruhr, put back by months. If the President wished to keep the Allied military and political coalition together and get the United Nations established on a sound preliminary basis, it would have to be done *now*, he was aware — before the sheer tide of national self-interest disunited the prospective member states — before Japan could be defeated.

That the President's medical condition spoke against the strain of such a long trip — especially the air journey from Malta to Yalta — was a serious negative. Using new metal-and-leather braces, and holding on to firm handlebars attached to the lectern on the South Portico of the White House — aided as well by his son James, at his side to assist him if he lost balance — he had managed to give his brief, fifteen-minute fourth inaugural address on January 20, 1945, standing. His cousin Daisy had even persuaded him to try out, in secret, the services of Harry Setaro, a prizefighter turned religious healer who employed massage to revive ailing organs. Setaro had worked on the President's spleen and legs, and the massage had led the President to claim he sensed a tingling in one toe that he hadn't felt since being diagnosed with poliomyelitis in 1921.[3] But in truth it was an illusion: the triumph of hope over experience. The President's doctors had turned a blind eye to it, though, since Setaro's ministrations could do no harm, they reckoned, even if they did no good.

Such obvious quackery, however, had had no relevance, in the doctors' eyes, to the President's ever-worsening congestive heart disease — one that would lead inexorably to failure: a valiant heart still pumping, aided by digitalis, but with no earthly prospect of improvement, let alone recovery. A stroke or heart failure could come at any moment — and in response to any prolonged mental effort or stress, it was noted by both the President's doctors. The President's systolic blood pressure would constantly leap from the 190s to the 230s and 240s. Attending a summit in the Crimea, five thousand miles away, was thus a grave gamble.

Hubris, though, played its part. Rightly or wrongly Roosevelt remained convinced—and was encouraged by all around him to believe—that he was the only national leader who could, by means of his world stature, get the foundation stone of postwar security laid, before the inevitable discords of postwar factionalism. Certainly this was what Lucy Rutherfurd, the light of the President's life at this point, recommended—overcoming not only her concern for his cascading health but any hope of an alternative ending to his life: namely retirement and an arrangement, possibly separation or divorce, with Eleanor, so that she and Franklin could be together in his final months.

Lucy had been among the seven thousand people admitted to the snow-covered South Lawn of the mansion, by special invitation, for the inauguration. What she didn't know was that the President had suffered another attack of abdominal pain, shortly before the event, similar to the one he'd experienced on July 20, 1944, before giving his party-nomination acceptance speech. Ordered by his father to fly from the Philippines to attend the inauguration and assist him, as he stood to give his speech from the flag-draped, pillared portico, Colonel Roosevelt had found himself once again shocked.

"The first moment I saw Father I realized something was wrong. He looked awful, and regardless of what the doctors said, I knew his days were numbered."[4]

Though his father had managed the fifteen-minute speech to the end, he was riven by abdominal pain afterwards, if "somewhat less acute" than in San Diego, James later recalled—shocked as much by his father's reaction to the attack as by its suddenness. "Jimmy, I can't take this unless you get me a stiff drink," he'd said. And had added: "You'd better make it straight." As James later reflected, "In all my years, I had never seen Father take a drink in that manner"—like life-saving medicine. "I was deeply disturbed."[5]

There were other signs to the Marine colonel, moreover, that his father was not going to make it—and was more and more resigned to his "death warrant."[6] He'd already given his secretaries and his cousin Daisy items chosen from his study, which, when he'd pressed them, they'd said they would like to remember him by. To James he said he was going to give him his gold family ring—and discussed his will, since James was to be his executor.

His father's whole demeanor was that of a dying man, James later described, sadly—his days "surely numbered. It showed in the way he talked, the way he looked. There was a drawn, almost ethereal look about him. At times the old zestfulness was there, but often—particularly when he let down his guard —he seemed thousands of miles away."[7] At the reception, indoors, others were similarly shocked, including the new secretary of state, Edward Stettinius— who was to meet up with the President, for the journey to Yalta, once Mr. Roosevelt reached Malta by sea.

"He had seemed to tremble all over" as he gave his inaugural address, Stettinius later recorded the President's condition. "It was not just that his hands shook, but his whole body, as well . . . It seemed to me that some kind of deterioration in the President's health had taken place between the middle of December and the inauguration."[8]

The widow of President Wilson, Edith Bolling Wilson, was also at the reception. She was more fatalistic. "He looks exactly as my husband did when he went into his decline," she told the labor secretary, Frances Perkins. "Don't say that to another soul," she begged, however. "He has a great and terrible job to do, and he's got to do it, even if it kills him."[9]

Given that Mrs. Rutherfurd could hardly be invited to join Eleanor and the VIPs in the White House without a scandal, Daisy Suckley had gone afterwards to Q Street, where Lucy was staying with her sister, to report on the reception — and she did so again, the next day. Thanking Daisy in a letter several weeks later, Lucy referred to "great sorrows and shock" that tended to leave one "with a tremendous incapacity or fear of thinking" — and therefore unable to "think anything through."[10]

Was this a reference to the President's mortal illness, and imminent death? Should the President therefore resign on grounds of ill health? Senator Truman had been sworn in as vice president; he had looked, in contrast to the President, the embodiment of energy and determination behind his broad chest and thick spectacles. Lucy was unsure. "There seems so much to be decided — What is right and what is wrong for so many people & and I feel myself incapable of judging anything. Yes," Lucy had added to her letter to Daisy — "it is difficult when we must speak in riddles but we have spoken to one another very frankly — and it must rest there — One cannot *discuss* something that is sacred — and even simple relationships of friendship and affection are sacred & personal."[11]

Lucy's friendship with the President had certainly become more and more intimate over the preceding months, as his health continued its downward slide. She had joined Franklin at the Little White House, his personal retreat in Warm Springs, Georgia, soon after he'd gone there after Thanksgiving — the President having "lost 10lbs" during the election campaign, which left him looking "very thin," as Daisy herself had noted. Even in Warm Springs, doing almost nothing, the President had "looked pale & thin & tired," she'd described. "I try so hard to make myself think he looks well," she'd mourned, "but he doesn't." He looked positively "grey when tired" — a sign of lack of oxygen in the blood — in fact he "looks ten years older than last year, to me. — Of course I wouldn't confess that to anyone, least of all to him, but he knows it himself."[12]

What had seemed to bring the President back to life had been Lucy's arrival in Warm Springs on December 1, with her daughter Barbara — the President asking both Daisy and Polly Delano, his bosom companions, to move from the Little White House to one of the guesthouses on the property, in order to make way for his former lover. "Mrs. Rutherfurd is perfectly lovely, tall, stately, & with the sweetest expression," Daisy had penned in her diary that night. "She is much worried by the Pres.'[s] looks," in fact she "finds him thin and tired looking," as she'd confessed to Daisy — but the evening had turned quite romantic when "all the lights went out!" and candles were lit. The "Pres. jokes, cocktails are brought, the Pres. mixes them by the light of one candle." He had even compelled Lucy — who didn't really drink — to have "an old fashioned, made half-strength, but is given two, I notice, against her wishes!" Daisy had noted, amused — and touched. "She says she never took one until she was fifty."

The four of them had had dinner together when the lights came back on, as well as "delightful conversation & at a quarter to eleven the Pres. decided to send us all to bed — Polly & I to the guest house,"[13] while Lucy stayed with the President.

The next day they had all gotten into the "big car" and gone for a noonday drive, with the top down and glass windshields on the sides up. "Mrs. Rutherfurd climbs in & sits next to him," Daisy — squeezed in the corner — had described, and together they'd been driven in cold but clear sunshine to "the Knob" — Dowdell's Knob, the highest point in the Pine Mountain range, with its incomparable views. By this point Daisy was wholly won over by the visitor, who "is a perfectly lovely person in every way one can think of," Daisy had felt compelled to admit, "and is a wonderful friend to him."[14]

Lucy had stayed with the President a second night, but had not been deceived by the President's light mood. Before leaving by car on December 3 she'd confided to Daisy she was "worried & does worry terribly, about him, & has felt for years that he has been terribly lonely." Harry Hopkins had been a wonderful companion as well as White House counselor, much like a roommate, but Hopkins's marriage and eventual departure to live in Georgetown with his new wife, Louise, had left the President "entirely alone" after work in the Oval Office, since Eleanor lived pretty much her own life, was constantly traveling, had her own bosom companions, and thus was seldom to be found even in the same house as her husband.

Daisy's occasional companionship, coming over from Wilderstein to the President's home and library, as well as to the White House at times, had been a boon, as had Anna Roosevelt's move to the White House with her husband, John Boettiger. But still . . . "We got to the point of literally weeping on each other's shoulder & we kissed each other, I think just because we each feel thankful that the other understood," Daisy had recorded of her growing bond with Lucy.[15]

After lunch the President had insisted on taking Lucy in the big car all the way to Augusta, almost two hundred miles away, sitting alone with him. There,

Lucy's own chauffeur had caught up with them and had driven Lucy and her daughter on to Aiken, while the President had been brought back to Warm Springs. "We miss them," Daisy had described — adding that "Franklin was 'let down' after the visitors had gone, and I was glad when he went off to bed."[16]

Though the President had resided for three long weeks in Warm Springs, doing almost no work and without even Admiral Leahy, his chief of staff, with him, the stay had done little to help his condition other than to ensure he was spared a medical emergency. Moreover, Roosevelt had continued to miss Mrs. Rutherfurd. On the way back to Washington on December 17 the *Ferdinand Magellan* had stopped in Atlanta, where Lucy met the train. "Lucy has just come on board and I have left her with the Pres.," Daisy had noted in her diary, "so they can have a little talk without an audience."[17]

Christmas had been spent by the President with his family — Eleanor, their children, and their thirteen grandchildren — at Hyde Park, by family custom, and with all the trappings of tradition, from the exchange of gifts to the President's reading of Dickens's *A Christmas Carol* — or part of it, when the grandchildren became too restless and the President's voice too strained. Then, after returning to the White House and giving his State of the Union broadcast in Washington on January 6, 1945, the President had boarded the *Ferdinand Magellan* to travel to Hyde Park on the evening of January 11 — and had taken Mrs. Rutherfurd with him, *alone*. Lucy had even spent the night with him aboard the train, and had remained the following day closeted with him at the Springwood house.

In the afternoon of January 12 the President had then shown Lucy the library, where Daisy worked. "My new cousin," Daisy called Lucy, noting that they had "one very big thing in common: our unselfish devotion to F." "I took myself off as soon as I had finished my coffee," Daisy had added, "so they could talk."[18]

In short, all subterfuge had been dropped. From the President's daughter to his doctors, from the Secret Service to the staff at the White House, Warm Springs, and the Springwood mansion, scores of people had become aware the President had a special friend — and though looking at death's door, seemed to be strangely reconciled to his fate. He had made, his private secretary had noted, practical and legal "preparations" for the end. Yet there had been no sign of sadness, despite the probability that his life would be cut short. And what seemed to best explain his calm acceptance of his approaching death but also the way he was hanging on to life, despite his exhaustion and discomfort, was the strange, late-life romance he'd discovered with the woman he'd loved so passionately at the height of physical well-being, before his poliomyelitis: a still-youthful-looking yet very private, modest woman who had come back to him as a widow, in the evening of his life — and who clearly still loved him as deeply as he loved her.

It was with that special emotional comfort — having prematurely celebrated his sixty-third birthday at the White House on January 21 with his family and the crown prince and princess of Norway as well as the Morgenthaus and others — the four-time elected president of the United States had set forth on what would surely be his last foreign trip: dreading it, as he'd confided to Daisy, since it would undoubtedly be, he forecast, "very wearing." Yet conscious, too, how crucial it would be to the successful ending of the war, and cementing the foundations of postwar international security.

He himself would have to be particularly careful, the President had told Daisy, to be "on the alert, in his conversations with Uncle Joe and W.S.C." His counterparts would assuredly have their own agendas, from Soviet expansion to British reoccupation of lost colonies and revived imperialism. "The conversations will last interminably & involve very complicated questions."[19]

There had been no alternative to going to Yalta, however. No one else possessed his prestige, or stood a chance of getting the three most powerful men in the world to agree and sign off on the establishment and structure of the United Nations, as well as laying the foundations of a new world order.

If all went well.

68

Aboard the USS *Quincy*

WITH HIM, on the journey to Malta and Yalta, the President was taking his daughter Mrs. Anna Roosevelt Boettiger.

Afterwards, the First Lady had expressed disappointment he hadn't taken her. He had, after all, promised to take Eleanor to England in the aftermath of a successful Allied D-day invasion in 1944 — yet hadn't done so. In the context of his fourth-term election campaign, the English trip, he'd explained, had become a plan too politically controversial, and would offer an easy target for right-wing attack by Republicans at home. The journey to Yalta, however, was different. The election was over. Eleanor was his spouse. Not, unfortunately, the sort of spouse he could count on to keep down his blood pressure, since she herself felt so strongly about the political issues to be discussed!

Though Eleanor meant well — indeed was memorably said to be her husband's social and political "conscience" — her advocacy frequently exhausted the ailing president. Brittle, opinionated, and energetic, Eleanor seemed to take all too little cognizance of his now-plunging health. Even her young confidant and subsequent biographer, Joseph Lash, would later quote a tart letter Eleanor had posted to Franklin while the President was recuperating in Warm Springs after the election.

Lash had been a sort of idealized son to whom Eleanor was still loyally writing every few days in letters that expressed deep maternal tenderness, thoughtfulness, and sensitivity. Eleanor's correspondence with her own husband, by contrast, had been nowhere near as tender, Lash later observed — especially in the period before the President's trip to Yalta. So hectoring was one letter that Lash felt, as her conscientious biographer, he would have to quote it in full, he explained, "for it shows how tough, relentless, and perhaps unfair, she could be."[1]

The letter had indeed been harsh — in part because Eleanor could see Franklin was not the man he'd once been, even a year before, and thus needed to stand up more aggressively to those she saw as the worst elements in the

Democratic Party and administration: officials who were pro-fascist, ruthlessly capitalist, deeply racist, and often anti-Semitic. "I realize very well," she'd begun her diatribe, "that I do not know the reasons why things may be necessary, nor whether you intend to do them or do not intend to do them." Such reasons would not, nor should not, she wrote, prevent her from speaking her mind. In the State Department, she said, she saw demons who would drastically alter American foreign policy now that Secretary Hull had retired as secretary of state the previous November for health reasons — unlike the President.

Franklin had always maintained that he himself, if truth be told, was the nation's secretary of state — but in his current state of health this no longer held good, Eleanor had pointed out. Men like James Dunn, a senior State Department officer on the U.S. Dumbarton Oaks team, was a man committed to helping restore the British and French colonial empires after the war — and would run rings round him, she warned, if Franklin was not careful. It was, Eleanor chided, "pretty poor administration to have a man in whom you know you cannot put any trust, to carry out the things which you tell him to do. The reason I feel we cannot trust Dunne [*sic*] is that we know he backed Franco and his regime in Spain," she pointed out — using the royal "we." To her horror Dunn was now pressing the U.S. ambassador in London, Guy Winant — "and the War Department," she added — "in favor of using German industrialists to rehabilitate Germany" — and this because, she maintained, "he belongs to the same group" as Will Clayton, the Surplus War Property Administrator under Jimmy Byrnes, and "others, who believe we must have business going in Germany for the sake of business here."[2]

Greedy American capitalism was now in danger of triumphing over higher American morality and idealism, in Eleanor's view — and given her special access to the President, she had felt it her duty to protest. She'd gone on, then, to explain why she'd sent Franklin a long memo on Yugoslavia, since she'd wished to defend Tito's actions there. She had already written Franklin of suspected American skulduggery in Spain, where she saw "the fine Catholic hand" becoming all too "visible in Europe and in our State Department." As she'd summarized, with "Dunne, Clayton and Acheson under Secretary Stettinius," Mr. Hull's successor, "I can hardly see that the set-up will be very much different from what it might have been under Dewey." The fact that Harry Hopkins had supported Clayton made her "even more worried. I hate to irritate you and I won't speak of any of this again but I wouldn't feel honest if I didn't tell you now."[3]

The letter had come with "Much love."

Reading it the President, still feeling "let down" after Lucy Rutherfurd's departure from Warm Springs, had sensed little affection in it. He could only groan — for Eleanor's underlying criticism had been quite fair: he was not showing his former presidential mettle. He simply no longer possessed the energy to direct or appoint, let alone fight, his own new administration. He had, in short, become a virtual passenger aboard the USS *Commander in Chief* after Quebec — and was now becoming a passenger aboard the USS *State Department,* as well as other administration vessels captained by former subordinates. Even his promise to make his outgoing vice president, Henry Wallace, the new secretary of commerce was leading to humiliatingly open opposition from Democrats in Congress: Senate and House of Representatives members who no longer bowed to his authority, despite his brave victory at the polls on behalf of their party on November 7.

To another soldier, who was stationed in China, Eleanor had written that, with regard to race and a raft of other issues, "either we are going to give in to our diehard Southern Congressmen or we are going to be the liberal party." With that prospect in mind Eleanor had felt she could not simply sit idly by and watch the former happen.[4] Chiding Franklin could not make him better, however, when he was clearly dying.

Franklin respected Eleanor's views — especially in relation to racism in America. But taking her to the Crimea, in his ever-deteriorating health, would have been a hiding to hell, the President had felt. She had correctly criticized him for no longer being the steward of his own administration — a sort of fellow traveler in it. But what could he do in the circumstances — i.e., his state of health? He was taking to Yalta his new secretary of state, Edward Stettinius, to be at his side; all he himself could undertake — and was determined to achieve — was the sealing of a formal, signed agreement with Stalin and Churchill to create the United Nations, and an effective UN Security Council. And button down a Russian declaration of war on Japan. Beyond that, the chips would fall where they would in a world in which the interplay of forces, domestically and internationally, he himself could do almost nothing to control.

The President's handsome blond daughter Anna, therefore, not his wife, would accompany him to the Crimea — just as Churchill, the President had learned, was once again taking his daughter, the porcelain-pretty Sarah Oliver.

And so it had been settled. Anna would have her own quarters (and bathroom) on the all-male USS *Quincy,* while the President himself would have two special elevators to take him to different decks. In Malta he would meet up with U.S. chiefs of staff after their deliberations with the British chiefs there, as also with Harry Hopkins and Secretary Stettinius, who would have meantime shared their thoughts and ideas about the coming summit with their opposite British numbers, Alex Cadogan and Anthony Eden.

The long sea voyage, if the January seas weren't too rough, would theoretically allow the President time to read the many documents and reports that had been drawn up for him in preparation for the conference. Yet, as the huge vessel steamed beyond Virginia and American waters (the President telling Anna, on deck, about "the bird life of these shores," then "suddenly and casually" remarking, with an outstretched arm, that "over there is where Lucy grew up"),[5] it was obvious to his small entourage — Admiral Leahy, Justice Byrnes, Steve Early, Democratic political adviser Ed Flynn, his naval and military aides, his two doctors, and three officers from his Map Room — that the President of the United States was not even up to that amount of reading. He tended, they observed, to lose concentration after only a few minutes. He had another cold — with runny nose and cough, which Admiral McIntire treated with "coryza tablets."[6] He seemed desperately, desperately weary.

Day by day the huge American warship zigzagged at speed across the Atlantic to avoid lurking U-boats ("the sea running too high for a sub to keep up with us," Anna noted),[7] protected by a U.S. destroyer escort as well as daylight U.S. air cover. There were movies in Anna's flag cabin in the evening, and after six days at sea, on Sunday, January 28, 1945, the USS *Quincy* entered "the European-African-Middle East Theatre of War" by crossing the 35th meridian — some twenty-five hundred miles from Newport News.

By January 31 — the day after the President's birthday had been celebrated with gifts on the ship's deck, and five candlelit cakes shared with his staff in his cabin — the USS *Quincy* passed through the Straits of Gibraltar in predawn hours, under waning moonlight. The President had explained to his daughter, as she noted in the diary she'd decided to keep, that "the last time he went thru (last year returning from Cairo-Teheran Conf)" three searchlights had illuminated his ship, directed "from somewhere on the Spanish shore. He says no one knows if they were friendly or otherwise. Nothing like that this time."[8]

Conserving his energy, the President hadn't actually risen to see the Rock — in fact he rarely rose before midday. He wasn't feeling at all well, he admitted, though his cold had cleared up. Eleanor's cables wearied him — her signal on February 1, begging him to intercede in a new fight in the Senate over Wallace's nomination, being particularly hard, not least because he'd warned her he would be unable to send radio messages while at sea, lest they thereby give away their location en route to Malta. "A message came this morning from Mrs. Roosevelt urging the President to make some kind of statement in favor of the confirmation of Mr. Wallace as Secretary of Commerce," Admiral Leahy recorded in his diary. "The idealistic attitudes of Mrs. Roosevelt and Mr. Wallace are not very different," the admiral added, amazed that Wallace could have thought, the previous summer, he could win his party's nomination for vice president a second time, when he had great difficulty even getting confirmed in Congress as commerce secretary. The two individuals were "about equally impracticable."[9]

For her part Anna, who was belatedly told their ultimate and still-secret destination, became anxious as to whether her father was really going to be able to manage the subsequent journey by air to the Crimea from Malta, then a long drive to the promised accommodations at Yalta, and after that, tortuous negotiations with Churchill and Stalin. Not to speak of the many people, from aides and advisers to honor guards, whom he would have to meet, inspect, impress.

Time would tell — and soon did, once they passed the snow-covered coast of Spanish Morocco, Oran, Tunis, Cape Bon, and Pantelleria to sail, finally, through the submarine net at 9:30 a.m. on February 2, 1945, and enter the Grand Harbor at Valletta, Malta. The "entrance to the harbor is so small that it seemed impossible for our big ship to get thru, and it looked like a touch and go proposition as we successfully swung our way past the breakwater, then past the USS Memphis, the HMS Cyrius and the HMS Orion."[10]

Anna stood on the flag bridge. "FDR sat by the railing on the deck immediately below," she noted in her diary — able to see, through her binoculars, the British and U.S. chiefs of staff, Ambassador Harriman, Harry Hopkins, Anthony Eden, and other "dignitaries going to the Conf. all lined [by] the rail of the HMS Orion, with the P.M. standing stiffly and trimly at attention."[11]

With ships' crews in dress whites, it was an almost royal welcome to the U.S. president and commander in chief — just as Churchill had specially arranged. From "the very large crowd evident, it appeared that all Malta was out to greet him," the keeper of the President's log, Lieutenant Rigdon, recorded.[12] "Both sides of the channel were lined with people" out to welcome him.[13]

Rigdon, as the President's designated chronicler on the voyage, was not exaggerating. Ed Flynn, accompanying the President, wrote his wife it was "quite an emotional moment," with dignitaries and crowds all seeming to feel the same sense of history being made, after patiently waiting for four days. Finally the President of the United States had arrived — the band on HMS *Orion* playing "The Star-Spangled Banner," while the USS *Quincy*'s musicians played "God Save the King."[14]

Recalling the scene many years later, Eden wrote how "the great warship sailed into the battered harbor" — a harbor in which "every vessel was manned, every roof and vantage point crammed with spectators. While the bands played and amid so much that reeked of war, on the bridge, just discernible to the naked eye, sat one civilian figure" — the President of the United States. "In his sensitive hands lay much of the world's fate. All heads were turned his way and a sudden quietness fell. It was one of those moments when all seems to stand still, and one is conscious of a mark in history."[15]

69

Hardly in This World

THE FIRST TO COME ABOARD the USS *Quincy* were the new U.S. secretary of state, Mr. Stettinius; the U.S. ambassador to Moscow, Averell Harriman; and Harry Hopkins, following his two-week fact-finding mission across Europe.

In cables to the President from London, while the President was *en voyage,* Hopkins had warned how much Mr. Churchill was dreading Yalta. Not for its difficult diplomatic challenges, which he relished, but as a locale. The Prime Minister "says that if we had spent ten years on research we could not have found a worse place in the world than Yalta," Hopkins had signaled — somewhat embarrassed, since holding the conference in the Crimea had been his own inspiration. Once renowned as a holiday resort in the time of the czars, and known for its mild winter climate, it was now only "good for typhus," the Prime Minister had memorably sniffed after reading a bad report, "and deadly lice which thrive in those parts." Lice, moreover, that could only be survived "by bringing an adequate supply of whiskey."[1] A drive over mountain roads — roads that were extremely narrow, steep, winding, and, thanks to snow, often impassable — would be necessary to reach the meeting venue. The decision having been made, however, Churchill — who had already flown to Moscow to see Stalin on his own in October 1944, after the Quebec Conference — had no wish to be left out.

In view of the Prime Minister's misgivings, and at the President's request, Ambassador Harriman had personally checked out the Yalta situation with his daughter Kathleen. Coming aboard the USS *Quincy* he was able to report to the President the good news: the Russians had performed a virtual miracle in recent weeks. The town of Yalta had apparently been razed during the bitter fighting there, but the former czarist homes that would house the conference delegates had mercifully been spared. All were a five- or six-hour drive from the airfield at Saki, where they would land following their overnight flight from Malta.

The Livadia Palace, where the American president and his team would be quartered, had been Czar Nicholas II's summer retreat, looted by the Wehrmacht down to its plumbing pipes before the Germans evacuated the Crimea, Harriman reported. It had been entirely refurbished in recent weeks, however, by a veritable army of Russian workers, prisoners of war, and craftsmen using materials brought from the top former czarist hotels in Moscow. The Livadia Palace, in other words, now offered an excellent setting for the conference. Moreover an American medical team from the USS *Catoctin,* the U.S. Navy's communications vessel for the conference, had thoroughly cleansed and deloused the Livadia's rooms. There were telephones aplenty, and the drive there "would not be too tiring if completed by daylight," Harriman thus assured the President.[2]

Relieved, the President greeted his next visitors to come aboard: the British governor-general, Sir Edmond Schreiber, followed by General Marshall and Admiral King—who in the course of ten minutes told him they had completed three days of meetings with their British opposite numbers, which had gone surprisingly well.

Seeing how frail was the President—"in fact I was quite shocked by his looks," Marshall later confided[3]—the U.S. chiefs had not gone into detail about their discussions with Field Marshal Brooke and his colleagues. In a veritable admission of the futility of Churchill's obsession with Italy the British chiefs had, mercifully, agreed to all the proposals of the American chiefs, including the belated shifting of another six British and Canadian divisions from Italy to reinforce Eisenhower's forces on the German frontier. Later that afternoon, on February 2, they would tell the President that the only point of contention had been whether Eisenhower should be encouraged to cross the Rhine north and south of the Ruhr, i.e., on a broad front. Or, they later explained to the President, to put all Allied efforts into the northern thrust under Field Marshal Montgomery. The field marshal had masterfully blunted Rundstedt's offensive, but his recent January 6 press conference had rubbed salt in General Bradley's wounds (Bradley had been compelled to give up command of his First and Ninth U.S. Armies to Montgomery), as well as managing to infuriate the American reporters and senior officers alike. The U.S. chiefs thus favored General Eisenhower's strategy—as did the President.

In the meantime, for his part, Secretary Stettinius reported to the President that he'd gotten on extremely well with Mr. Eden, and that they were both agreed as to the voting—and vetoing—procedure for the United Nations, which they hoped the Russians would agree to at Yalta. Thus, when Prime Minister Churchill finally arrived on board the USS *Quincy* at 11:48 a.m. for lunch with the President, everything had seemed straightforward. A lighted candle and a cigar had been placed near Churchill's lunch plate, which the Prime Minister took as a touching sign of presidential amity. Throughout the lunch Churchill then "monopolized" the conversation, Leahy noted in his diary, discoursing on "English problems in war time, the high-purpose of the so-called Atlantic Charter, and his complete devotion to the principles enunciated in America's Declaration of Independence."[4]

According to the cabled letter the Prime Minister sent his wife in London that night, the President had arrived "in best of health and spirits." But the Prime Minister had not been paying attention. "No one else who saw the President that day" described Mr. Roosevelt in such positive terms, Churchill's most devoted biographer, Martin Gilbert, later noted — in fact there was consternation over the deterioration in the President's health.[5]

Anthony Eden, present at the luncheon, certainly found himself disturbed. As the British foreign minister confided in his diary, the President "gives the impression of failing powers."[6]

On the American side Harry Hopkins — himself a ghost of his former self[7] — was equally concerned. Charles Bohlen had been asked by the State Department to accompany Hopkins to Europe on his pre-Malta mission, meeting with de Gaulle and the British, so that he could add further memoranda to the President's bulging State Department "briefing books." Like Hopkins, Bohlen was dismayed by the further decline in the President's condition. The young diplomat had watched the USS *Quincy* make its stately entrance into Valletta harbor, had seen the President "acknowledging the salutes from the British men-of-war and the rolling cheers of spectators crowding the quays," like a modern czar. The President had become a global icon, he felt: the embodiment of Allied military success in defeating the Nazis — "very much a historical figure," as he put it. But "when I boarded the *Quincy*," he recalled, "I was shocked by Roosevelt's physical appearance. His condition had deteriorated markedly in the less than two weeks since I had seen him. He was not only frail and desperately tired, he looked ill." Despite "a week's leisurely voyage at sea, where he could rest," Bohlen later recorded, "I never saw Roosevelt look as bad as he did then."[8]

As the President's chosen personal assistant for the trip, Anna knew there was no way her father could manage a whole afternoon session with his British visitors; they were therefore encouraged to leave Mr. Roosevelt's sitting room immediately after luncheon. Instead she took her father for a two-hour drive around the island with Sir Edmond Schreiber — a drive during which he would not have to make more than gentle, polite conversation with the governor-general in the car, while Anna got her "first glimpse of mass destruction in this war," as she scribbled in notes for her diary.[9]

On the President's return, however, the official visits resumed. At 4:30 p.m. Marshall, King, and Major General Laurence Kuter (stand-in for General Arnold, whose heart problems had returned; he would be unable to attend the summit) explained in greater detail the agreements they'd come to with the British. ("President supported the Joint Chiefs of Staff completely," Leahy recorded in his diary that night.[10]) Then at 6:00 p.m. the President received the Prime Minister and his British chiefs of staff — "a plenary meeting on board, at which the Combined Chiefs of Staff were able to report that they had reached agreement on all the points at issue," as General Ismay recorded — though "Roosevelt looked a very sick man."[11]

Churchill finally took note: how much the President was able to comprehend, beyond small talk, seemed unclear. Yet there was still an informal dinner for twelve in the President's cabin to follow, given for the Prime Minister and his daughter Sarah, as well as for Mr. Eden, Harry Hopkins, and Anna Boettiger.

Eden found himself increasingly worried. To the British foreign secretary, at least, it was quite clear that, among the Western Allies, the United States was now the dominant partner. American military and political strategy would henceforth prevail, for good or ill. What was also apparent, however, was that the American team would now be going in to bat with a seriously ill team leader — a president who had deliberately turned down Churchill's request he spend a few days in Malta before continuing to Yalta. And for the simple reason that he was not well enough to spend more time with his coalition partners!

Any hope of flying to Yalta with an agreed Anglo-American approach was rapidly flying out of the cabin window. To Hopkins the foreign secretary thus confided, at the table, his concern they were "going into a decisive conference" with nothing in the bank — having "so far neither agreed what we would discuss nor how to handle matters with a Bear who would certainly know his own mind."[12]

It was too late, however. There was no opportunity to talk after the dinner, either. No sooner was the meal over and the guests departed than the President left the warship and was taken by car to Luqa airfield, where some seven hundred members of the two national Yalta-bound delegations were assembling. The President's new C-54 plane — the latest, custom-equipped Sacred Cow — would be one of the last to take off from Malta. A special elevator had been installed so that the President could board without needing a separate ramp. Aboard the aircraft he was greeted by his old pilot, Major Otis Bryan, but then went straight to his special compartment at the rear, where he tried to rest.

"It is certainly luxurious," wrote Anna, who had not seen the new plane before. "FDR has his own cabin with a nice wide bed. Ross, Leahy, Brown, Watson and I have comfy bunks, and Bruenn and Mike and Arthur Prettyman have to sit up." Unable to rest she "wandered over to Churchill's plane" — a gift from the President — "and someone was nice enough to offer to show me thru it. It's also a C-54 — I gather it was presented to the P.M. by this government. Both planes cruise at about 200 miles per hour, which is faster than most C-54s. It is differently appointed than Father's, but very comfortable."[13]

One by one, beginning at 11:30 p.m., the flight of twenty C-54s took off into the night, bound for the Crimea. "We took off at 3.30 and the P.M. at 3.35 a.m.," Anna recorded — both of them accompanied by six fighter-plane escorts, since "there are still some Germans in the Dodecanese Islands" and the Nazis "might have got wind of the trip and have imported some of their own fighters" to the area.[14]

The President seemed unworried about enemy fighters, being more concerned about the looming conference — and his own ability to steer it in the right direction in his dire state of health. Once finally airborne, according to Dr. Bruenn, he "slept rather poorly, because of the noise and vibration."[15]

The omens for success did not look particularly good.

70

"A Pretty Extraordinary Achievement"

THE PRESIDENT WAS NOT the only one having difficulty sleeping. Adolf Hitler had also been on the move. As the President sailed across the Atlantic, the Führer had boarded his special armored train on January 15, 1945, and had moved back to Berlin from the Wolfsschlucht (Wolf Canyon II), from which he'd directed his grand counteroffensive through the Ardennes.

Even to Hitler it had become clear that his surprise attack, though inflicting a major initial defeat on Eisenhower's armies, had failed to reach the Channel and slice Allied forces in two. Moreover that the Soviets, meantime, were massing for a renewed offensive on the Eastern Front. To prevent a complete Soviet breakthrough he would therefore have to transfer troops from the west to the east. To try and keep the Allies on the defensive he had ordered an armored counteroffensive in Alsace on January 16, using Panzer Mark V Panthers, which produced a tactical victory for the Wehrmacht and inflicted a further fourteen thousand casualties on the U.S. Sixth Corps in ten days' heavy fighting.[1] It had not changed the tide of war, however.

As Dr. Goebbels and others noted, victory on anything more than a local scale was now a chimera. The Führer's only hope his Thousand-Year Reich could survive was that the Allies would become un-Allied. Eisenhower had an estimated two million troops assembling in the Netherlands, Belgium, and France to cross the Rhine from the west, and a similar number of Soviet troops were advancing toward the Oder in the east. But if the inherent differences between the Allies' national objectives, as well as their political and social systems, were to erupt, finally, in a clash of goals, then the amazing unity the Führer had sought to inculcate in the *Vaterland* might yet prevail, as Hitler had assured Goebbels on January 22.[2] The structures he had established as Nazi overlord — with himself at the center, as Führer — were proving extraordinarily robust, despite seemingly overwhelming enemy military superiority.[3]

Aware that a Big Three Allied summit was about to take place — though not knowing where — Hitler feared that Stalin would come to genuine agreements

with Roosevelt and Churchill. By contrast, Dr. Goebbels clung to the conviction the Western Allies would inevitably break with the Soviets. Faced with
daunting Russian successes on the battlefield, surely the peoples of the West
would recognize, he argued, how noble had been Nazi intentions in conquering all Europe by military force. "We Germans have never wanted to do anything save to offer Europe peace and social happiness," Goebbels maintained
in his diary — "good intentions" that "the Jews with their infernal propaganda"
had managed to subvert.[4] But if Roosevelt, with his vision of a "so-called
United Nations" based on the "principles of the Atlantic Charter," succeeded in
harnessing Stalin to the cause, then the Führer was right: the whole Nazi edi-
fice, ethos, and extermination programs would come down and be obliterated,
together with Hitler's attempt to present himself as a great "European." Goebbels thus agreed with Hitler that a Big Three summit, if it succeeded, would
be very bad for Germany, permitting Stalin to "integrate Anglo-American war
aims with his own." Goebbels could not bring himself to believe this would
happen, though; Stalin was "not that kind of character. He's not one of those
people who is easily won over." Bolshevism marched to an "inner law," which
not "even Stalin, with his huge dictatorial powers," would be able to thwart.
"Bolshevism will undoubtedly follow its world-imperialist and revolutionary
aims — and it's here we have a great political opportunity. Hopefully the Big
Three conference will shortly take place soon, at a moment when Stalin is
at the pinnacle of his military triumph. He'll be bound to argue and fall out
with Churchill and Roosevelt, which may develop into a real break behind the
scenes. If that happens, that would present us with a favorable political situation" — the Allies divided, and Hitler able to parlay his way out of imminent
German defeat by negotiating with the Western Allies. "Either way, these will
be the most fateful weeks of the war," Goebbels noted in his diary. "The crisis
on the Eastern Front is potentially fatal. But the Führer" — who seemed to
Goebbels once again "reinvigorated" by the crisis, one that was not tiring him
but making him wonderfully mentally "elastic," so that he "radiated an unbe-
lievable confidence and faith"[5] — "is convinced we'll be able to deal with it. He
believes in his destiny. There's no doubt, nonetheless, we have to overcome the
military crisis, and that we can leave no stone unturned to do so."[6]

In pursuit of "total war," Goebbels had successfully culled, he claimed, a million more German civilians and had put them into combat-ready uniform in
German barracks. For his part the Führer was delighted by newsreel footage
of his V-1 and also his V-2 weapons, which, if a "thousand of them" could be
launched against England over the coming month, might lead to a "fundamental change" in the British political and diplomatic approach to negotiations to
end the war, Hitler mused.[7] Fickle press and public opinion in the democratic
West could be manipulated to German advantage — Western journalists and

commentators having no idea how contemptuous Hitler remained with regard to the "antiquated" bourgeoisie of Europe, which he proposed to "liquidate" in due course.[8] The very idea of smaller countries like Norway or Denmark being given any say in the future of the continent, as recently advanced by Norway's puppet leader, Vidkun Quisling, in a visit to the Führer, was equally foreign to Hitler's thinking—a notion Goebbels dismissed as utter *Quatsch*, or nonsense.[9]

Splitting the Allies by playing on their inherent political contradictions, and the risible innocence of their commentators regarding the nature and intentions of the Nazi leadership, was, in short, the Führer's "elastic" vision: holding the Russians at bay in the east and hammering England and even Paris, now, with V-bomb weapons, Messerschmitt jet fighter-bombers, and Wehrmacht counterattacks that were—according to Allied POWs—disheartening American troops, who had no business being in Europe.

In this respect Dr. Goebbels was amazed at how astutely Roosevelt had managed to lead American public opinion. In terms of Normandy and then the Ardennes he had asked a "sacrifice in blood" that Goebbels had imagined would be unacceptable to most Americans, who had scant interest in Europe or its fate. "Yet he's managed to bring the U.S. right behind him," Goebbels acknowledged in his diary. "That's a pretty extraordinary achievement, for one has to remember Americans only have a secondary interest in the war in Europe and are only inspired by the war against Japan."[10]

Day after day Goebbels had visited the Führer in the Reich Chancellery, and its warren-like bunker downstairs—the two men on tenterhooks about the forthcoming Allied summit. Surely Stalin would cancel or defer it, given that he was now the military master of eastern Europe, able to dictate the postwar setup by simple virtue of Russian bayonets. But to both Hitler's and Goebbels's consternation there seemed to be no sign of a split, yet, in the Allied coalition. Nor—as Hitler hoped—did it look as if Stalin was going to decline Roosevelt's request that the Russians join the war against Japan, Germany's war-partner, once Germany was defeated. *The Allies were holding together—* leaving the Nazis no hope of survival unless the Germans could defeat the Allies on the battlefield. And this—despite their V-bombs, their phenomenal counteroffensive in the Ardennes, and even their recent efforts around Strasbourg—they were unlikely to accomplish, if truth be told. In which case, Goebbels recognized, his and Hitler's lives would be over.

By January 28, when Goebbels again visited Hitler at the Chancellery, the Führer looked "tired and stressed."[11] He was working sixteen- to eighteen-hour days, he told Goebbels, but was still hoping to withdraw forces from Norway, Italy, Hungary, and other fronts to mount a new counteroffensive. "The enemy coalition—and the Führer is quite right in this—is bound to break apart,"

Goebbels recorded, noting that the Führer's radio broadcast the next night, January 30, would be one of huge significance, not only within the Reich but in its likely impact across the world.[12]

The broadcast — Hitler's first since the July bomb plot — duly impressed listeners by its relatively philosophical, reflective tone, surprising even those who despised Hitler, such as Churchill's private secretary John Colville, who thought it "gloomy but more eloquent than of late," as he recorded in his diary.[13]

Certainly the Führer's tone was less belligerent and more philosophical. The "era of unbridled economic liberalism has outlived itself," Hitler insisted, a liberalism that "can only lead to its self-destruction," resulting in world disorder: a world in which "the tasks of our time can be mastered only under an authoritarian co-ordination of national strength," he argued, as well as "duties" — such as the extermination of Jews and others, which went unsaid. After all, the Führer claimed, the "fight against this Jewish Asiatic bolshevism had been raging long before National Socialism came to power." Bolshevism had begun "systematically to undermine our nation from within," with help from a "narrow-minded" German bourgeoisie who refused to recognize that "the era of a bourgeois world is ended and will never again return."[14] Dictatorship was the only way forward.

Continuing to resist the Allied onslaught was, in this case, "the safest guarantor of final victory" for the Third Reich. "God the Almighty," the Führer asserted in unusually religious terms, "has made our nation. By defending its existence we are defending His work. The fact that this defense is fraught with incalculable misery, suffering and hardships makes us even more attached to this nation. But it also gives us the hard will needed to fulfill our duty even in the most critical struggle; that is, not only to fulfill our duty toward the decent, noble Germans," he declared, "but also our duty toward those few infamous ones who turn their backs on their people."[15]

Were there any "decent, noble Germans" left after the barbarism the Nazis had inculcated and demonstrated across Europe, from Poland to Hungary, the Ukraine to the Urals? some listeners in the still-occupied territories wondered. Even Hitler acknowledged the outlook was less promising than when he had attacked Russia in 1941. Mass German civilian and refugee flight was gathering pace in the east, amounting to a veritable "hurricane from Central Asia,"[16] yet the Führer denied he was responsible for starting such a cataclysm, arguing it was the outcome of simple "envy" on the part of Germany's "democratic, impotent neighbors" and a "plutocratic-Bolshevistic conspiracy" — one which must be resisted "until final victory crowns our efforts."[17]

Behind the Führer's sober-sounding assertions, however, Wehrmacht desertions were increasing,[18] leading to kangaroo-court execution of those accused of cowardice or disobedience.[19] The gas chambers at Auschwitz had been ordered shut down by Himmler in November 1944, once word of the Morgenthau Plan and punitive Allied retribution had become public in Germany, yet the concentration camps themselves had continued to be run by the SS. Some seven hundred thousand inmates were forcibly marched, or taken in cattle trucks, to other concentration camps as Soviet forces overran still more death camps in January 1945. An estimated one-third of the defenseless prisoners died in the process.[20]

Goebbels's heart went out to German refugees, he claimed in his diary, but not to German Jews and other concentration camp inmates, whose fate was common knowledge. "The Führer won't let us fall into Russian hands. He'll gas us instead," one German refugee quipped darkly, in East Prussia.[21] As Hitler's biographer Ian Kershaw would later summarize, the "terror which had earlier been 'exported' to the subjugated peoples under the Nazi jackboot was now being directed by the regime, in its death throes, at the German people themselves."[22] The war in Europe was coming to a climax.

In his radio broadcast Hitler repeatedly blamed the Jews, while thanking "Providence" for not having "snuffed" him out on July 20, 1944, with a "bomb that exploded only one and a half meters from me" and could easily have terminated "my life's work. That the Almighty protected me on that day I consider a renewed affirmation of the task entrusted to me," he claimed: namely to fight for National Socialism "with utmost fanaticism" to final German victory.[23]

The Führer's once-omnipotent life was collapsing around him, though, like the Nazi nation. The Reich Chancellery in Berlin had already been destroyed by Allied bombing, and much of the New Chancellery, including his private apartments, was also hit. This now forced him to live two stories below, in the deep Führerbunker: a labyrinthine network resembling "a maze of trenches," Goebbels described. "The enemy coalition would break, and *must* break," the Führer had told Goebbels. The Nazi Party must simply bide its time until the right occasion, before taking the "political initiative" — i.e., negotiations.[24] It was, as Kershaw put it, "a matter of holding out until the moment arrived."[25]

The question was, could Hitler himself hold out? "He was more haggard, aged, and bent than ever," Hitler's biographer later described, "shuffling in an unsteady gait as if dragging his legs. His left hand and arm trembled uncontrollably. His face was drained of colour; his eyes bloodshot, with bags underneath them; occasionally a drop of saliva trickled from the corner of his mouth."[26] He could hardly lift a glass to his mouth without spilling its contents.

Hitler's speech was not considered by his own acolytes to be as inspirational as his earlier broadcasts.[27] It did remind Germans, however, that the Führer was still alive, was still in command — and was still determined that the German nation, collectively, should fight to the bitter end: "that everybody who can fight, fights, and that everybody who can work, works, and that they all sacrifice in common, filled with but one thought: to safeguard freedom and national honor and thus the future of life."[28] It would be a test of national, Nazi-led will, with the underlying hope that the forthcoming Big Three conference — whether in Moscow, Tehran, or Odessa, German intelligence had been unable to decide[29] — would be a disaster for the Allies, forcing them to split apart.[30]

That possibility was something President Roosevelt, however ill he felt en route to the Crimea, was equally determined would not happen.

71

One Ultimate Goal

IN BELIEVING THE ALLIED COALITION was now in danger of dissolution, the Führer and Dr. Goebbels were not entirely wrong. The British contingent, for example, had spent four days in Malta waiting for the President. They were both angry and disappointed "by Roosevelt's refusal to discuss either tactical or substantive questions regarding Yalta" when he arrived, which concerned the diplomat Charles Bohlen as much as it did Harry Hopkins.

The matter continued to puzzle Bohlen in later years, and the distinguished diplomat wondered if the President's health at the time "might" explain it.[1] "Everyone noticed the President's condition," Bohlen acknowledged, "and we in the American delegation began to talk among ourselves about the basic state of his health," which was perplexing. "Our leader was ill," he recalled the feeling, and just at the moment when the American team was making its way to "the most important of the wartime conferences." Yet the President himself seemed almost unconcerned — in fact, almost removed from reality. Perhaps the ailing president wanted to "save his energy for Yalta," Bohlen later posited, rather than get immersed in black books and negotiating tactics. But if so, would this not put the U.S. team at a disadvantage vis-à-vis the well-prepared Soviets?[2]

The President had said little at Malta, in part because he felt so ill, but in part deliberately. For what concerned him was not what his diplomatic team was anxious about. Where they had assembled a small library of black books to back their negotiating positions in the impending conference, the President was neither mentally fit enough to argue on their behalf in the looming meetings, nor did he feel it would be the best use of his fading but still-world-renowned skills as a statesman. He was thus determined, simply, to make sure the Big Three conference would *not* result in a breakdown of the Allied coalition at the very brink of Allied military victory in Europe. Eisenhower's delayed offensive aimed at closing up to, and then crossing, the northern Rhine would kick off the next week, on February 8, 1945, General Marshall had informed him (Operation Veritable, to be followed by Operation Plunder), but those forces were still three hundred miles from Berlin. The Wehrmacht was fighting fanatically, on all fronts. The Nazis must therefore be given no chance of evading their fate by Allied dissension. The establishment of a United Nations organization should be agreed and announced, *jointly*, along with a signed, formal, though necessarily secret undertaking by the Soviets that they would declare war on Japan once Hitler surrendered, and would then aid the United States in completing the swift defeat of Japanese forces in the Pacific — and in China.

Simplistic or not, the Allies, the President felt, must present to the world — and especially to the Germans and Japanese — an inviolable unity. Hitler's latest statement of Nazi resolve in his broadcast to the people of Germany — which had included mention of the Morgenthau Plan, unfortunately — *must* be countered by an even *greater* demonstration of common, higher Allied purpose: one that would inspire the men and women of the many United Nations fighting the Axis powers enough to attain complete surrender of the Third Reich. The symbolism of unity between the Big Three Allies at Yalta, in other words, was as important — perhaps more important — than the details of the negotiated agreements that would be hammered out by the national teams.

Winston Churchill, normally so aware of the symbolism of events and names, seemed initially slow to appreciate this larger aspect of the approaching summit. He had been heard, in particular, to question the notion of unconditional German surrender. He wanted Britain to be given an extra seat in the proposed United Nations organization for India — still a British colony, not a self-governing dominion. In fact the Prime Minister had had, he wrote his wife, Clemmie, from Malta, "for some time a feeling of despair about the British connection with India, and still more about what will happen if it is suddenly broken." He was determined "to go fighting on as long as possible" for the British colonial empire and to "make sure the Flag" was "not let down while I am at the wheel."[3]

Stalin, too, would fight for the resumption of *his* empire, now that his forces had shown such military resilience in facing Hitler's legions, and had demonstrated their growing effectiveness on the battlefield, not simply in policing their communist realm. This was something the President understood — and worried about. If the world was to have confidence in an international postwar order modeled not on Hitler's social Darwinism but on the United Nations organization and its Security Council, then the Yalta summit must inspire faith in the unity and higher purpose of the Allied coalition.

A demonstration to the world of the willingness to differ over political systems of government but agree on confronting aggression and the occupation of other countries by military conquest would at least present a defining contrast to the rampant militarism and inhumanity symbolized by the gas chambers of the Third Reich, as well as the atrocities still being committed by the Japanese across Asia. Winning national benefits in Allied negotiations over details, as evinced in the State Department black books, was thus perfectly understandable in terms of American self-interest, but something the President would best leave to Stettinius, Justice Byrnes, and the U.S. chiefs of staff teams. For himself, with so little strength left in his failing body and mind, he could only focus, ultimately, on one goal — ensuring the Big Three summit did not lead to a breakdown of Allied unity, but enhanced it; ensuring the imminent defeat of the Third Reich, the swift defeat of Japan, and the establishment of a postwar world order that would be more effective than the League of Nations had been in the aftermath of World War I.

Whether, in these circumstances and within his failing powers, the President would be able to hitch his wagon to his star remained to be seen. There would be casualties: issues, from Polish independence to French recolonization, that would doubtless constitute major obstacles to the outcome he hoped to achieve. Yet he was all the more determined, tossing and turning on the Sacred Cow, that he could at least achieve a significant symbolic demonstration of joint Allied purpose.

Admiral Leahy did not sleep much, either. "Air travel in the President's special four-motored transport plane is luxurious in comparison within my previous experience," the admiral noted in his ponderous, somewhat antiquated style in his diary, "but I continue to prefer travel by ship, by railroad, or even on foot if time is available."[4]

Time wasn't. "The President's bed was perpendicular to the plane's axis," the President's cardiologist recalled forty-five years later. "It was a big, wide bed. But he refused to have a safety belt" — raising fears that, if they encountered bad weather or were fired upon, "he would be tossed right out." Mike Reilly, heading the White House Secret Service detail, "and the rest of us" had talked it over "before we took off." They had "decided that when all the lights were out, I would creep in and position myself on one side of the bed so that if he fell out of bed he'd fall on me. We took off without any problems."[5]

Bruenn crept in.

"The next morning, the President said, 'It's lucky I recognized you as you came in.'"[6]

72

In the Land of the Czars

AT 12:10 P.M. on February 3, 1945, the Sacred Cow landed at Saki airfield, near Sevastopol. Stalin had not yet arrived in the Crimea, the President was told, so on his behalf the plane was met by Vyacheslav Molotov, the Soviet foreign minister, and Averell Harriman, the U.S. ambassador to the USSR.

The President waited aboard his plane with Molotov and Harriman until Prime Minister Churchill's own C-54 touched down: "Quite a sight to watch," Anna noted in her diary, "with its six accompanying fighters (American P38's)." This was at 12:30. "Molotov left Father to go to Churchill's plane, and soon they were gathered around our plane. FDR came out," she described, "via the neat little elevator, got into a jeep and with Molotov and Churchill walking beside him, the procession proceeded to an open roadway where a Russian guard of honor and band were most smartly drawn up. There were Russian still and movie camera men by the peck" — something that concerned Anna, who was "a bit worried because FDR did look tired after his hard day yesterday and a short night's sleep on the plane."[1]

Formalities, however, had to be observed. The Russian band "played the Star Spangled Banner first, then God Save the King, then the new Russian anthem — which seems to me a bit sad for this type of song. Then the guard snapped to attention, marched away from us and came back, in review, before us — marching in goose-step, though I'm sure the Russians don't call it that! The soldiers' faces were most interesting to me because they represented so many different races," Anna added. "They were all a fine, strong and healthy looking bunch."[2]

Lord Moran, the Prime Minister's physician, was not so impressed. The seven-hour flight, covering fourteen hundred miles, had finished with a bumpy landing on the snow-swept runway. The commander of the guard had "held his sword straight in front of him like a great icicle," Moran recorded sniffily in his diary. "They were preceded by a crowd of camera-men, walking backwards as they took shots."[3]

Clearly, Moran was unaware of the need for visual symbolism: the President having brought Steve Early all the way to the Crimea with him to ensure the tripartite nature of the historic conference was stressed — without mishap this time. In black and white, and even in color, photographs of the Big Three would subsequently be published in newspapers across the world, and shown on cinema screens. Early's job, too, was to ensure that these images mask, as far as possible, the President's gray, ashen countenance beneath his winter hat.

In truth, close-up, the President "looked old and thin and drawn," Moran noted in his later-revised, heavily edited diary; "he had a cape or shawl over his shoulders and appeared shrunken; he sat looking straight ahead with his mouth open, as if he were not taking things in. Everyone was shocked by his appearance and gabbled about it afterwards."[4]

Moran's most upsetting memory, as a proud Briton, was watching as the "P.M. walked by the side of the President," who sat in his jeep, just as "in her old age an Indian attendant accompanied Queen Victoria's phaeton."[5]

Moran's description of the President might be honest, but his sneer was unfair. Churchill had often expressed hostile feelings about the President and the increasing difference in power they represented, to be sure, but Winston was not without affection for his soi-disant American cousin. Whatever he might write to Clemmie in a cable that other eyes might well see, he was becoming belatedly aware the President was not simply unwell, but failing dramatically. In fact Churchill, having recently turned seventy, felt almost guilty at his own ability to bounce back after bouts of fever, pneumonia, or angina, whereas the President, having only just turned sixty-three, was not so blessed. The Prime Minister thus felt like a protective, still-energetic older brother to the desperately frail-looking president. Walking beside Mr. Roosevelt as he sat in his jeep was, if anything, an act of compassion and unity, however Moran might worry about the implied deference — the Prime Minister ready to march forward and go into battle beside his ailing warrior chieftain.

An hour later, at the inspection's end, "we all got into autos and made our way toward Yalta," Anna noted that night[6] — Churchill driven to the British compound at the Vorontsov Palace, twelve miles from the town, while the President was taken in a Lend-Lease armored Packard to the Livadia Palace, two miles from the city.

The President had survived the ordeal, but Anna was taking no chances. She was now sufficiently anxious over her father's condition that she'd insisted she "ride with FDR" in the Russian-chauffeured limousine, "so that he could sleep as much as he wanted and would not have to 'make' conversation," with staff or advisers who might exhaust him on the five-hour, eighty-mile journey, before the summit even began.

At the Livadia Palace the President's systolic blood pressure was found, thankfully, to be back below 230, despite the flight and the tortuous, twenty-mile-per-hour car journey up the winding mountain roads, and then down. The accommodations seemed duly palatial—with the mâitre d' addressing the President as "Your Excellency." "I can't understand Winston's concern," the President was heard to remark, relieved. "This place has all the comforts of home."[7]

For herself Anna didn't like the architecture (built in 1910, in Renaissance Italianate style), but admired the setting, overlooking the ocean. Also the surprising warmth inside—certainly warmer than Hyde Park. "You go in the front door to a huge reception hall. To the right of the hall is a ball room—to be used as the Conference room. Straight ahead to the left is a door to the study off the room which FDR is to occupy," she noted, "—and which must have been the Tsar's main bedroom suite. Straight ahead to the right is a corridor leading to the dining room, study, Father's bedroom," and other rooms, which "all have big, handsome fireplaces. When we arrived, fires were blazing merrily in all the downstairs rooms—and were most welcome as we were pretty frozen after our five hour drive."[8] The President thus felt up to having supper in his dining room with Stettinius, Harriman, Leahy, Watson, Brown, and several others, including Anna and Harriman's daughter, Kathleen. As at Tehran, he told Harriman, he'd like a short personal talk with Stalin the next afternoon, before the first plenary meeting, and asked Harriman to extend an invitation to dinner, too, to Stalin, along with Churchill, to be held immediately after the plenary finished.

Harry Hopkins, who had been too ill to come from his first-floor room to the dinner—a five-course affair, with five glasses at each setting—had been ordered straight to bed by Admiral McIntire. Alone in his room he was limited to a diet of cereal and cabbage soup; but he himself was in a "stew," Anna found when visiting him after her own meal—especially when hearing the President would not be seeing Churchill *before* the plenary the next day. "He gave me a long song and dance," saying "that FDR must see Churchill in the morning for a longer meeting." When Anna protested her father would simply not be able to manage such a meeting, then the one with Stalin, and then the long plenary in the afternoon, Hopkins "made a few insulting remarks to the effect that after all FDR had asked for this job, and that now whether he liked it or not, he had to do the work, and that it was imperative that FDR and Churchill have some prearrangements before the Big Conference started," as Anna jotted in her diary. "I had never quite realized how pro-British Harry is."[9]

Anna, in her caregiver role, calmed "the Hop" down. She trusted her father knew what he was doing, she assured Hopkins—and with good reason. Her father had not the energy or the wherewithal now to "do the work," in terms of conducting complex international negotiations. That, however, was not the reason why her father was not communing privately with Churchill; nor did her father feel that an Anglo-British "front" would achieve what he wanted from the Yalta summit. All he hoped to obtain, beyond military cooperation between the U.S., British, and Russian military chiefs of staff, was a signed agreement he could announce to the world: one that would put an end to any speculation in the press, in diplomatic circles, or in governments spanning the globe, including Berlin, about whether the Allies were allied — and relentless in their insistence upon the unconditional surrender of the Third Reich.

Unity of *military* purpose was thus goal number one.

Second, he hoped to get formal agreement as to the Allied military occupation and treatment of Germany.

Third, establishing the United Nations organization.

Fourth, the problem of Poland.

And finally fifth: Russian entry into the war against Japan.

Beyond that, for good or ill, he had neither the strength nor the will; it would be, he figured, up to others, later, to negotiate the details — as well as other issues, such as what would, or should, happen to former colonized territories such as Indochina, currently occupied by the Japanese. In other words, another, later conference would have to be arranged. In the meantime, though, the Yalta summit would show the Germans and the world that the Allied coalition was still watertight, and would proceed, inexorably, not only to defeat Hitler but to defeat Japan — even though, since the Soviets were not at war with Japan and could not marshal the forces to conduct a successful war on both fronts, Stalin would not be able to announce this publicly. A preconference huddle with Churchill would not help in this. In fact the likelihood was that he, the President, would have to act the arbiter, or mediator, in the arguments that promised to arise between the Prime Minister and the Russian dictator, given their conflicting imperialisms.

If this was disappointing to Hopkins and others like General Deane in Moscow,[10] who felt the United States should use more muscle and bang the table, given its global military power — in the air and at sea, especially — as well as its increasing economic predominance, then so be it. With Eisenhower's forces still west of the Rhine, and Soviet forces having crossed the Oder at Frankfurt and battling their way toward Berlin, it was the best he felt he could do. The two northern Soviet fronts under Marshals Konev and Zhukov alone amounted to two and a quarter million men, backed by thirty-three thousand guns, seven thousand tanks, and forty-seven hundred aircraft.[11] Possession would be nine-tenths of the law — and the United States still needed Soviet help to defeat Japan, even after the surrender of the Third Reich.

General Deane had protested that by being so generous towards the Russians, in terms of Lend-Lease, and asking so little of them in return, the picture was "neither dignified nor healthy for U.S. prestige."[12] But the President didn't feel that way, nor did Harriman, for all that he deplored Russian xenophobia. The Soviets had borne the brunt of the casualties and destruction in the war Hitler had declared and waged against the Allies. They had engaged some three-quarters of the Wehrmacht, in contrast to the Western Allies — thus giving the United States time to build up its military forces, and to learn how to conduct modern war successfully on two fronts after a disastrous start. Moreover, the President did not in any way feel he had sacrificed American dignity or prestige. In fact he felt the opposite: that the world now looked towards the United States with a greater respect than ever in its history. He himself had conducted an amazingly effective war strategy since the initial U.S. defeat at Pearl Harbor. He could take justified pride in now having U.S. forces assembling for their own big offensive across the Rhine, as well as the extraordinary advances U.S. forces had already made in the Pacific, and with more to come. Given the intrinsic and inevitable weaknesses of a democracy compared with military dictatorships, it had been a miraculous American recovery, in barely two years. In short, he saw no reason to "refuse assistance," as Deane recommended, unless the Russians ceased being Russians. And besides, he had an American secret weapon.

After Admiral McIntire had given the President some nose drops and Dr. Bruenn had taken his blood pressure, Arthur Prettyman had withdrawn and Roosevelt had turned out his light. He would need a good sleep, for the next day, February 4, 1945, the historic Yalta Conference would begin.

73

The Atom Bomb

THE ENTIRE EIGHTY-MILE ROUTE from Saki to Yalta had been lined by Russian soldiers, many of them female, and civilians. Anna was fascinated by people's "drab" clothing and felt boots. "Others wore what looked like down-at-heel, low or ankle high leather shoes with thick soles. Men's trousers were as drab and unshapely as the women's skirts. Children wore all kinds of clothes — but equally drab. Most were warmly dressed, but fairly often you would see a child with long, heavy cotton stockings held up by garters, then bare skin before coming to a too short skirt or pair of pants"[1] — much like Astrid Lindgren's Pippi Longstocking, whose first appearance would be made that year.

Hitler had described such people as Asiatic *Untermenschen,* but to the President and his daughter they simply looked like Menschen — with the President, commenting on the scrubby land beyond Simferopol, "saying that he was going to tell Marshal Stalin how this part of the country should be reforested," especially with evergreens.[2]

The President was ill, but he was neither intimidated by the challenges of the trip, nor the burgeoning military power of the Soviets. The Western Allies had, it was true, suffered a major reverse in the Ardennes, and had endured heavy fighting in Alsace. But he had no real anxiety about the ultimate outcome, or the subsequent dominance on land of the Soviets. And this for a simple reason most American officers, such as General Deane, and State Department officials knew nothing about. An atom bomb, that would shortly be combat-ready.

Despite the fact that the Soviets were known to be bugging all rooms with listening devices, as well as eavesdropping on all telecommunications, the President thus had good reason to be confident about America's future. The Soviet Union was a main ally in the struggle against Hitler, but he had zero illusions about the Russians or about Soviet communism, as he'd confided to Cardinal Spellman in the fall of 1943.[3] Communism was a godless ideology: an idealized system of human government that could only be maintained by operating a ruthless police state — one that was not substantially different from Nazism. All who spoke against either system became traitors — as did those who were merely suspect: "othered" and arrested for mass deportation, incarceration, and execution — such as Tatars who were being secretly evicted en masse from the Crimea on Stalin's orders, even as the Yalta Conference took place.

But Hitler was the more dangerous and egregious of the two, in terms of his military conquests and "liquidations," and was thus the first enemy of the democracies. As Churchill had said, the self-appointed Führer was worse than the Devil, indeed "if Hitler invaded Hell," Churchill, as prime minister of Great Britain, would "at least make a favourable reference to the Devil!"[4] In short, inasmuch as Stalin was the Devil and the lesser of two evils, the British and the American governments had had to work with him, not against him, in order to defeat Hitler. Moreover, given the Führer's astonishing and enduring hold on the people of the Third Reich and its ruthlessly obedient military forces, Hitler *could* only be brought down with Russian military might — a Red Army that was a double-edged sword.

However much the Russian saber hung heavy over eastern and central Europe, the President — thanks to what he understood of the latest reports of his atom bomb — thus showed no sign whatever of being daunted. Out of almost nothing the United States had built its own military might, with more than nine million men now in uniform and able to operate on a global scale, unlike the Soviet Union. Moreover, its secret weapon was one that not even Hitler's V-2 ballistic missiles could match.

The Manhattan Project to develop an atomic bomb, or "S-1" as it was code-named, was now nearing critical mass. From the start, when Albert Einstein had convinced him of its feasibility in 1939, the President had seen its development as a race, namely to "see that the Nazis don't blow us up" first, as he'd put it to Alexander Sachs, his young, Harvard-educated, Russian-born Jewish adviser, at a White House meeting on October 11, 1939.[5] It had been a prescient decision. The President had thereafter authorized, arranged secret funding for, and watched over five years of development at Oak Ridge, Los Alamos, and elsewhere; he had also shared development of the bomb with the British, once Japan and Germany had declared war on the United States. The outcome would be potentially war-winning — or war-losing if the experiments failed in the United States but proved successful in German and Japanese weapons laboratories.

They didn't. As the project had grown — employing 130,000 people and costing $2 billion — and the weapon had approached completion, the President had even invited to the White House the distinguished scientist Niels Bohr. On July 5, 1944, Bohr — who had left Copenhagen on word he would soon be arrested as half-Jewish, making his way then via Sweden and Britain to Los Alamos — had spoken to Roosevelt privately. This was before the

President accepted the Democratic nomination for a fourth term, and left on his journey to the Pacific — where, if Emperor Hirohito and his government still declined to surrender following the defeat of the Third Reich, an eventual atomic bomb could be used to save further American and Japanese lives.

Bohr had argued for sharing the knowledge and know-how with scientists in other United Nations, so that there would develop no arms race, since no one could "win" such a war. The nuclear fallout could well destroy the planet.[6]

The President had agreed, both in theory and in practice. But the weapon itself was *not* yet ready, and the war was *not* yet won. The Allied landings in Normandy, four weeks before the President's meeting with Dr. Bohr, had proved a triumph, but fighting in Normandy in July 1944 was still hand-to-hand in places, with almost eight hundred miles more to go to reach Berlin. Operation Bagration had begun, as Stalin had promised at Tehran, but even with the Allies attacking on three fronts — including Italy — there had been no guarantee the war would be over in Europe by Christmas, given the way the Wehrmacht was continuing to fight. War in the Pacific would take much longer, with even more loss of life. Indeed, the current prediction by U.S. planning staffs was that it would require Soviet assistance and another *year and a half's* fighting, after German surrender, to defeat Japan militarily. All manner of things in the meantime could go wrong in U.S.-Soviet relations, given their contrasting ideologies. It had therefore seemed to Secretary Stimson and most of those involved on the American military team unwise to give the S-1 secret to Russian scientists, yet.

Churchill, for his part, had argued even more fiercely for continued secrecy — i.e., maintaining exclusive Anglo-American development of, and information about, the weapon. At Hyde Park, in September 1944, together with Harry Hopkins, the Prime Minister had persuaded the President to sign a secret aide-mémoire, which Churchill himself had written out. "The suggestion that the world should be informed regarding tube alloys [British code word for S-1], with a view to an international agreement regarding its control and use, is not accepted," Churchill had declared on behalf of the President and himself. "The matter should continue to be regarded as of the utmost secrecy; but when a 'bomb' is finally available it might perhaps, after mature consideration, be used against the Japanese, who should be warned that this bombardment will be repeated until they surrender." As for Niels Bohr the idealist, he should now be considered a prime liberal suspect, Churchill had added, and put under American surveillance to ensure there was "no leakage of information to the Russians."[7]

The President, in other words, was far closer to Churchill than anyone — save those at the highest echelons of atomic research — could know. In his role as commander in chief the President had seen to it that, in just five years and in total secrecy, the United States would be the first combatant nation in the war to produce an atomic weapon — thus successfully beating both the Germans and the Japanese. Axis attempts, mercifully, were still way behind that of the United States, General Leslie Groves, the commanding officer of the Los Alamos program, had then been able to confirm to the President in September 1944, after the fall of Paris.[8]

And the Russians? For their part the Soviets, having heard from Soviet spies in America something of the Manhattan Project,[9] had independently set up their *own* covert institute to work on nuclear fission in 1943, without informing the United States. Known as Laboratory No. 2, it was supposed to produce the necessary purity of uranium and graphite for an atomic bomb, as well as separating uranium isotopes,[10] all in the strictest secrecy, but Stalin had not given it priority or much in the way of financing, as the President had. As a result Laboratory No. 2 had numbered only twenty scientists and thirty technicians.

In the race to make a usable atomic bomb the United States was thus still leagues ahead of its enemies — and its Russian ally. As one veteran scientist would put it, the "formidable array of factories and laboratories" comprising the Manhattan Project was "as large as the entire automobile industry of the United States at that date."[11] Even Bohr himself was impressed, later telling Edward Teller of the U.S. Manhattan team: "You see, I told you it couldn't be done without turning the whole country into a factory. You have done just that."[12]

The United States, the President was aware in Yalta, now possessed an important advantage over the Soviets, not simply the Germans and the Japanese. Indeed Mr. Roosevelt had been told by Secretary Stimson, before he left Washington, that "we would not gain anything at the present time by further easy concessions to Russia." Spurred by General Deane's memorandum from Moscow, Stimson had recommended to the President that "we should be more vigorous on insisting upon a quid pro quo. And in this connection I told him of my thoughts as to the future of S-1 in connection with Russia; that I knew they were spying on our work but that they had not yet gotten any real knowledge of it and that, while I was troubled about the possible effect of keeping from them even now that work, I believed that it was essential not to take them into our confidence until we were sure to get a real quid pro quo from our frankness. I said I had no illusions as to the possibility of keeping permanently such a secret but that I did not think it was yet time to share it with Russia. He said he thought he agreed with me."[13]

The Russians, then, would not be informed about the weapon's progress for the moment. Knowing of it, however, would give the new secretary of state, Edward Stettinius, extra, if hidden, leverage, and on Stimson's advice the President had authorized his war secretary to take Stettinius into his confidence about the atomic program. This had been done four days later, on January 3, before Stettinius left for Malta. Thus, before the President and his team left the United States on January 22, 1945, for the Crimea, the President, Admiral Leahy, General Marshall, the U.S. chiefs of staff, and Mr. Stettinius had all been told via General Groves that the first atomic bomb "should probably be ready about 1 August 1945." Moreover, a second one ought to be "ready by the end of the year."[14] If it worked.

At Malta the President and Mr. Stettinius, as well as the chiefs of staff, had agreed to say nothing aloud. Or between themselves — even in the privacy of their rooms at the Livadia Palace. Nevertheless, General Groves's news had been a welcome new arrow in their quiver: something that helped explain why, despite the recent American reverses in the Ardennes, Secretary Stettinius had appeared to all in Malta to be in "tremendous form," as Sir Alexander Cadogan noted.[15]

However ill their President might appear, and however little prior discussion there had been as to an Anglo-American approach to the conference at Yalta, the leaders of the American delegation, in short, gave the impression of being amazingly assured. And with good reason — for the American team had not come four thousand miles to be pushed around, or treated as anything but top global wardog. Even their Russian hosts seemed unusually deferential. It was as if in Yalta, a thousand miles from their common objective, Berlin, an extraordinary international amity, prevailed, rather than the suspicion, tension, and awkwardness that had been present in Tehran — almost as if Stalin were aware of the ace up the American sleeve.

74

Riviera of Hades

STALIN HAD IN REALITY arrived in Yalta the day before the President and Mr. Churchill — installing himself, with his entourage, at the old Yusupov Palace outside Yalta, two miles from the Livadia Palace. He'd got in on the evening of February 2, 1945, following a three-day armored-train journey from Moscow,[1] concerned to have everything ready for his visitors, and that they should feel safe on Russian soil. Four entire NKVD regiments guarded the Soviet, American, and British enclaves, with batteries of antiaircraft guns and 160 fighter aircraft patrolling the skies: a deliberate demonstration of Russian efficiency and power. Looking down at the Black Sea, Churchill would call it the "Riviera of Hades" — ruler of the Greek underworld.[2]

Marshal Stalin seemed on his best behavior. Before driving to greet the President, as arranged, at 4:00 p.m. on February 4, the dictator paid a call on the Prime Minister at the Vorontsov Palace. He even suggested to the Prime Minister and Field Marshal Alexander, when they proudly showed the Marshal their wall maps of the military situation in Churchill's portable map room, that although the primary Soviet and Anglo-American forces should continue to crush the Wehrmacht between them in northern Germany, there was now no real danger of a German counteroffensive in Italy. The bulk of the British-led forces in Italy might therefore safely be transferred to Yugoslavia, if the British wished, and fight their way north to meet up with Red Army forces in Vienna.

Whether Stalin was testing or teasing Churchill by offering *un petit cadeau*, a consolation prize, neither Churchill nor Field Marshal Alexander could be sure (nor were historians later). Given Stalin's ice-cold response at Tehran to any British alternatives to, or diversions from, the mounting of the long-promised Second Front in the spring of 1944, the idea of such an amphibious new invasion and subsidiary campaign through Slovenia seemed positively open-minded. Now that Churchill's Mediterranean obsession was no longer an obstacle to defeating Hitler, Stalin seemed relaxed, even genial. The Wehrmacht was at last truly close to defeat, and Stalin, some officers conjectured, was perhaps more of an opportunist than depicted.

Clearly, though, *Yalta was not Tehran* — the dictator's irritation with Churchill's endless reasons for not mounting D-day in the spring of 1944 a thing of the past. Overlord had proved a phenomenal success: the deciding battle of the war. Blazoned across Churchill's wall maps at the Vorontsov Palace, the results could be seen in stark contrast to the Western Allies' positions in December 1943, when their armies were stuck north of Naples, in southern Italy. Though Alexander's forces were still not much farther north than Pisa, Hitler's control of western Europe was crumbling — just as the President and Stalin had predicted at Tehran. Paris had been liberated in seven weeks, with the Wehrmacht streaming back from Normandy in tatters and Soviet forces smashing all German attempts to hold a defensive line in the Ukraine.

Churchill, aware he'd blundered over D-day's decisive importance, shook his head. Given the huge logistical and organizational requirements of such a seaborne switch of British, American, French, and other forces from Italy to Yugoslavia for a Ljubljana campaign, he thanked the Marshal, but said it was now unnecessary: thanks to its current rate of progress, "the Red Army might not give us time to complete it."[3] Left unsaid was the fact that, following their reverses in the Ardennes, the U.S. military had expressed even greater opposition to yet another Churchillian diversion from their main effort, just at the moment when Eisenhower's forces, stretching all the way from Antwerp to Switzerland, were now seriously short of infantry.

Politeness, in sum, was a more probable reason for Stalin's suggestion — and surprising. The dictator, after all, was not known for his politeness — indicating, possibly, a major change had taken place in the Russians' attitude to their coalition Allies. If true, it presaged the very thing which neither Hitler nor Goebbels, in their conversations at the Reich Chancellery in Berlin, had considered possible: *increasing*, not decreasing Allied unity.

As Stalin departed the Vorontsov Palace to meet the President, the British team was left mulling over the signs. Had the leopard changed its spots?

Even at a local, practical level the omens seemed better than anticipated. For years — certainly since the German invasion of the USSR in 1941 — the Russians had displayed an almost paranoid fear of personal contact with Western officials, even when accepting crucial Lend-Lease help. Suddenly things seemed different. At Saki, for example, Soviet, American, and British air force personnel shared control of the large airfield, the Russians responsible for the two big runways, fuel, provisioning, and security; the U.S. team for transport; the British for meteorology, communications, the control tower, and briefing and clearance of aircraft. The airfield had thus received twenty Allied four-engine planes in five hours, escorted by fighters, without mishap and within seconds of their estimated time of arrival, following their fourteen-hundred-mile flights.[4] Similarly, in the three designated palaces and at Allied personnel quarters in Sevastopol, there was found to be a level of hospitality and determination to make the conference a success that could only bode badly for Hitler and Hirohito.

In any event, at 4:15 p.m., with a bevy of armed guards and accompanied by Foreign Minister Molotov, Stalin arrived at the Livadia Palace for a half-hour pre-plenary private session with the President.

To Bohlen, who was to act as the President's sole personal interpreter for the length of the conference, the President, waiting in his palatial, gilded study, did not look good, physically. He was, however, "much better than at Malta."[5]

75

Russian Military Cooperation

THE PRESIDENT HAD BEEN at the height of his physical and mental powers during his last meeting with the Russians at Tehran, fourteen months earlier. Now, they recognized immediately, a terrible change had taken place. They were stunned to see him so shrunk. Yet Mr. Roosevelt acted as if nothing were amiss, displaying something of his old charm as he bade Marshal Stalin sit beside him on the sofa, next to the wooden table in his study with its delicate diamond-design inlay and ashtray, beneath a huge painting from czarist times (one of only two that had not been looted by the Germans).

Stalin certainly allowed no shock to show on his face, which "cracked in one of his rare, if slight, smiles," Bohlen recalled, as he "expressed pleasure at seeing the President again."[1] The small but stocky Georgian wore his new, high-collared military tunic bearing the epaulettes of a marshal of the Soviet Union; the President sat beside him in a light-gray suit, with a flowery silk tie and his trademark pince-nez — his face thinner, and his hair, too, in fact grayer than before, but his blue eyes still alert and friendly.

With sincerity the President thanked Mr. Stalin for Soviet hospitality — especially the decision to hold all plenary meetings at the Livadia Palace, thus saving him from having to travel to other buildings. They both expressed satisfaction with the military situation — the Western Allies massing on the Rhine, the Russians on the Oder. It was clear the Russians were poised to reach Berlin — though whether the Soviets would take the city before the Americans took Manila, in the Philippines, was a moot point. It had been the subject of bets taken aboard the USS *Quincy,* the President explained, but Stalin rightly doubted how straightforward the capture of Berlin would prove, given the intensity with which the Germans were resisting the Russians on the Eastern Front. There was, he confessed in all honesty, "very hard fighting going on for the Oder line."[2] (It was small wonder; Dr. Goebbels noted in his diary how *Volksturm* units were fighting to defend German-occupied Poland, or Posen, with more fanaticism even than Wehrmacht units.[3])

There was very hard fighting going on in the Philippines, too, following MacArthur's invasions of Leyte and Luzon — the Japanese fighting no less hard than Germans to hang on to their conquests, or obliterate them if they could not. Beginning the previous day, the battle for the city of Manila would alone take four weeks for U.S. forces to win. The result was not only almost seventeen thousand Japanese dead and almost six thousand wounded, but the destruction of virtually the entire walled city. (In what became known later as the Manila Massacre, the Japanese local commander had deliberately disobeyed General Yamashita's order to evacuate the city. Instead he led a suicidal campaign, using Filipinos as human shields, before eventually committing ritual seppuku on February 26, 1945.[4])

The war was becoming a deliberate *Götterdämmerung*, or twilight of the gods — both the Japanese and the Germans aware they had committed evil on a scale so vast they would never be forgiven, and would be held accountable once they surrendered, with many (including Yamashita) facing execution for their atrocities.

The sheer destruction the President had seen on his five-hour car journey from Saki to Yalta, however, was nothing, Stalin corrected him, compared to what the Germans had done in the Ukraine, with "method and calculation," as Bohlen's record ran of their conversation. "He said the Germans were savages and seemed to hate with a sadistic hatred" the monuments and buildings their opponents had built over the centuries — while complaining bitterly at Allied bombing of their own cities. The President agreed; the same was the case in western Europe, where German garrisons were still holding out in bypassed French ports on the Atlantic and the English Channel, such as Lorient and Saint-Nazaire, Boulogne, Calais, and Dunkirk, as well as threatening to destroy the Dutch dikes rather than retreat before the Canadian Army as it advanced into the western and northern Netherlands.[5]

What emerged, then, in the first hour in the President's study in the Livadia Palace was that the two most powerful commanders in chief in the world were beginning their historic conference on the same military page: namely their determination the Third Reich should be brought to unconditional surrender by their combined armies. The President raised the matter of the three proposed occupation zones, to follow German surrender, and the possibility of adding a fourth which the French could police. And given German culpability in the recent extermination of more than half a million Hungarian Jews, in addition to Hitler's liquidation program since 1942, the President even suggested that Stalin repeat, at the dinner to follow the plenary later that evening, his Tehran toast regarding the execution of fifty thousand SS officers responsible for running the Nazi concentration camps, summary executions, mass murder without trial or indictment, and other war atrocities.

Some later historians would consider the President's suggestion to be in bad taste. He didn't, in all truth, mean it, given his respect for law, which he'd studied after college. But would law bring the culprits to justice? He had cause to wonder — a concern that would prove, in the event, well founded. The majority of atrocities committed by SS officers and men would, in the war's aftermath, simply go unpunished. In the meantime, though, he had at least made clear as president of the United States that, due to the enormity of German war crimes, he was no advocate of carte blanche forgiveness.

Above all, the President was keen, in his brief preconference meeting with his Russian counterpart, to carry out the promise he'd given his Joint Chiefs of Staff that morning, when they'd held a short meeting in the study. The military teams of the three primary combatant nations would be meeting to hammer out their combined plans to defeat both the Third Reich and — though in secrecy at this stage — the Empire of Japan. General Marshall had therefore asked if the President could help them. There had been commendable communication between Washington and Moscow regarding military operations in Europe, but not much in the way of action. It was not that the Russians were uncooperative so much as they seemed stuck in a kind of bureaucratic pyramid, General Deane had reported from Moscow. No serious decision could be made without authorization from above — that is, Marshal Stalin, as Soviet commander in chief. Could not the President tackle Stalin on the issue?

The President had said he would — and did. Assured the three Allies were sincere in their approach to the surrender of their common enemies, Stalin immediately promised greater Russian military cooperation and decisiveness.

As the President was wheeled into the Grand Ballroom at 5:15 p.m. and took his seat at the huge Arthurian table for the first plenary session of the Yalta Conference, then, he and Stalin seemed remarkably collegial. As did Churchill, who had meantime arrived from the Vorontsov Palace.

76

Making History

ONCE ALL WERE PRESENT in the Livadia Palace ballroom, the three main leaders of the United Nations got down to business, aided by their interpreters and advisers, at the sixteen place settings, and further back, additional advisers seated around the hall. Stalin had brought "General Antonov, deputy chief of staff of the Red Army, Fleet Admiral Kuznetsov, and Air Marshal Khudikov" with him, as Admiral Leahy noted in his diary,[1] as well as Ivan Maisky and Andrei Gromyko, his former Russian ambassador to Britain and his current ambassador to the United States.

Some thirty Soviet and more than a dozen Western photographers had gathered to record the arrival of the participants, but they were only briefly allowed into the chamber, where the proceedings themselves would be secret until official communiqués were drawn up and given out. All, however, were aware that the imagery of that day — and the days to come — would be as important in what the conference represented to the world as the actual decisions made there.

For Steve Early this would become a challenge, for although the President still looked relatively good as he was wheeled into the ballroom after the tête-à-tête with Stalin across the front hall, the deliberations at the big table would, he knew, soon exhaust his boss and the result appear all too visible on camera, unless careful supervision was made of photos before release. He therefore urged the American contingent to agree that Robert Hopkins, a young U.S. Army photographer and son of the presidential counselor Harry Hopkins, should be the sole designated photographer at the palace. He could be relied upon not to abuse his privileged status.[2]

Once the photographers had been barred from the ballroom, Marshal Stalin, as conference host, asked if the President would open the proceedings and act as chairman of this and subsequent plenary sessions, all of which would take place in the Livadia ballroom.

Accepting the task, the President duly thanked Marshal Stalin, for the record. As he'd just shared with the Marshal, they would be tackling further aspects of military strategy across the globe during the coming week. However, he wanted this first session to address only the situation on the Eastern and Western Fronts, together with questions arising, so that the senior military staffs of the three countries could thereafter address them together in military discussions, on their own.

Stalin nodded. On the Marshal's instruction General Antonov gave a detailed report of Soviet operations on the Eastern Front, including the recent capture of the Silesian coal and oil fields — Stalin pointing out not only the Red Army's two-to-one superiority in numbers across the whole front, but its huge preponderance in heavy artillery support. This had led to "300,000 Germans killed, and 1,000,000 prisoners taken" — a fearsome example of the kill-to-mere-casualty ratio. Antonov's account finally climaxed with a main concern he expressed on behalf of the Soviets: that the Western Allies should do everything possible to block more attempts by Hitler to withdraw Wehrmacht divisions from Norway, the Western Front, Italy, and the interior of Germany to reinforce the Eastern Front, where the Wehrmacht was fighting to the literal death.

Understandably impressed by the professionalism, scale, and candor of the Russian account, the Western Allies' military team responded. At Churchill's request and with the President's approval, General Marshall was asked to give the latest picture: namely General Eisenhower's recent regrouping of his forces to close up to and cross the Maas and Lower Rhine in the next few days. Thereupon major American and British armored forces, under command of Field Marshal Montgomery, would be funneled into Germany north of the Ruhr, to be matched by U.S. divisions south of the Ruhr, tasked with completely enveloping Germany's industrial heartland. Significantly, there was no mention now of distant Berlin, which had been their goal in the heady days following the fall of Paris — and which the major German counteroffensive had successfully parried.

Even the diplomats present at Yalta were awed by this first plenary hour of the summit. Although the conference would later become famous — or infamous — for the political discussions held necessarily in secret, it was the military deliberations of the "triumvirate" that would make Yalta unique in the annals of warfare. Never before in this, the most destructive war in history, had the most senior military representatives of the anti-Axis coalition partners all met together. In November 1943 Stalin had taken only one major military adviser to Tehran, on the mistaken assumption the get-together would be a political meeting. But now the situation was very different. The Russian military delegation was in full force, with specific requests to make of its Western partners, and vice versa — from bomb lines to ultimate occupation lines, Schwerpunkts to interdictions, as their teams began trading details of what worked in fighting Hitler's Wehrmacht, and what didn't.

The level of shared Allied military discourse was especially stunning, given Russian paranoia and fear of execution for imparting "secrets" to a coalition ally without higher NKVD authorization. At least and at last, however, it was *happening,* with Stalin's approval.

The Big Three listened in the Livadia ballroom as their generals held forth, and commented as the reports were delivered. Stalin's military acumen, in this respect, astonished even his own team as the dictator, after discussing the ratio of heavy artillery to kilometers in Russian offensive operations, openly debated the difference between Russian and Allied infantry and tank superiority over Wehrmacht forces in battle. Stalin found himself astonished, for example, to learn that where the Russians needed at least a four-to-one ratio to break through at chosen points in German defenses, the Western Allies often had no more than an equivalence in infantry, relying instead largely on their tactical and heavy-bomber air power to penetrate.

Such talk had led Stalin to wax (for him) lyrical on the nature of military cooperation that, as allies, they were now reaching. He instanced, rightly, how in Moscow he had received Air Marshal Tedder, General Eisenhower's deputy supreme commander, during the Battle of the Bulge, and as a result had brought forward the timing of the next Soviet offensive, despite terrible weather.[3] His aim, he claimed, was "to emphasize the spirit of Soviet leaders who not only fulfilled formal obligations but went farther and acted on what they conceived to be their moral duty to their Allies."[4]

Bohlen, as interpreter, would specifically recall the words three decades later, since they had represented, for a brief moment in history, what promised to be a genuine tripartite military alliance, on similar lines to that which existed between the United States and Britain — a first real indication the three nations *could* work together, not only to ensure the unconditional surrender of Nazi Germany and Japan, but to develop a global security system in a United Nations to be set up thereafter.[5]

The President, for his part, was tired but moved — applauding this indication of genuine military cooperation, rather than fighting separately for the same goal. However, it was Churchill himself — ever the historian — who best articulated this new turning point in the war: namely the "highest importance" they were now attaching to the business of cooperation. The "three [military] staffs which were assembling here for the first time" were making history, he declared, as if speaking before Parliament, and were about to "really work out together detailed plans for the coordination of joint blows against Germany." In this way, "if the current Soviet offensive were to come to a halt because of the weather or road conditions," the Western "Allied armies" would still attack. Indeed, the Allies would attack the shrinking German Reich "simultaneously" if at all possible.[6]

Given that Churchill had refused to countenance a meeting of the Combined Chiefs of Staff with their Russian opposite numbers in Cairo, before Tehran, or to include them as observers in Combined Chiefs of Staff meetings, this was a historic turnabout for Churchill — and certainly one that dashed any hope that, by appealing to the Prime Minister, the Führer and his government might still remain in power. Stalin even asked that the meeting instruct the three Allied military teams to prepare, together, joint U.S.-British Soviet plans for a contingency Allied summer 1945 offensive, "because he was not so sure that the war would be over before summer." Churchill agreed to this, saying they should "take full advantage of this gathering."[7]

The plenary had now been going on for almost two hours. The President was clearly wilting; moreover dinner was ready for the summit leaders, who were invited to attend a small banquet with their foreign ministers in his dining room. Before they did so, however, it was agreed the three military staffs would meet the next morning at Stalin's residence, the Yusupov Palace — former property of the wealthy Oxford-educated prince who had assassinated Rasputin before the Russian revolution — and continue their joint military deliberations there.

The President, in other words, had done exactly as General Marshall had requested: he had broken the proverbial ice, and gotten Stalin to sanction the kind of inter-Allied military discussions, even decisions, that would increasingly be needed as their forces converged — or collided — on German soil. He'd also gotten agreement that the issue of zones of military occupation would be formally addressed the next afternoon, at the Livadia Palace, when there would be a second plenary of the three leaders, this time with their foreign ministers at hand. They would discuss, he said, the "political treatment of Germany" — a euphemism for occupation zones; dismemberment of the Third Reich; reparations Germany would be required to pay for the destruction the Wehrmacht had caused; and the punishment of war criminals.

With that the military teams were dismissed. The President retired to his private quarters with Stalin, the two men "talking together in the study," as Anna Roosevelt noted in her diary, while Churchill "freshened up" in Stettinius's room.

It was at this point that poor Anna was approached by Dr. Bruenn, warning her of an impending disaster. Judge Byrnes was apparently refusing to attend the first formal summit dinner on the grounds that, although he was director of war mobilization, he had not been permitted to attend the plenary dinner for security reasons. "A tantrum was putting it mildly! Fire was shooting from his eyes!" Anna described in her diary — managing, mercifully, to put out the fire with the help of Averell Harriman, who warned that they could not expose the ailing president to such childishness, when the conference had kicked off to such a hopeful start.

77

A Silent President

THE DINNER IN THE PRESIDENT'S DINING ROOM consisted of vodka, five different wines, fresh caviar, bread and butter, consommé, sturgeon with tomatoes, beef and macaroni, sweet cake, tea, coffee, and fruit. It lasted three hours.

The President made a brave effort to keep awake and alert, but the day's meetings had clearly drained him. Apart from friendly chitchat and a multitude of toasts, there was in fact no political discussion, despite the presence of the foreign ministers of the Big Three — the President, as dinner host, simply too weary to discuss anything. Only in the last half hour did the matter of the United Nations organization come up — and without enthusiasm on the part of Stalin, who ridiculed the notion that "small" countries should have the same postwar representation as the Three Great Powers, as he put it. Those small countries were, after all, not the nations who, at great cost in blood and treasure, had "won the war," and whose representatives "were present at this dinner," as Bohlen noted in his minutes.[1] Churchill, from his capacious mind, tried to nip the developing argument in the bud by quoting an old saying, to wit: "the eagle should permit the small birds to sing and care not whereof they sang."[2]

It was clearly a struggle for the President to stay awake, let alone direct or follow the conversation. Word of his condition was already causing concern, indeed dismay, especially at the British team's residence. There, dining with the British chiefs of staff on their return from the plenary session, Churchill's physician listened as the generals told him how pleased they were with the plenary's outcome, yet how worried they were by what they'd seen of the President. "Everyone seemed to agree," Moran wrote in his diary, "that the President had gone to bits physically," and had "intervened very little in the discussions, sitting with his mouth open; they kept asking me what might be the cause."[3]

Moran, despite being a fine doctor, was unsure, having been lied to by Admiral McIntire at the Quebec Conference, six months earlier. There, too, the

President had been largely and unusually silent during discussions, the chiefs said. His deteriorating health hadn't been so apparent in Quebec, since "what he did say was always shrewd," covering up his relative detachment from the details of the proceedings. "Now, they say, the shrewdness has gone, and there is nothing left," Moran recorded. "I doubt, from what I have seen, whether he is fit for his job here."[4]

Moran's comment sounded cruel, yet was all too close to the mark. Brooke, delighted with the day's work, did not remark on the President's performance in his own diary, but Admiral Cunningham complained in his that the "President, who is undoubtedly in bad shape & finding difficulty, did not rise to the occasion." Fortunately, "Stalin was good & clear in his point, the PM also very good but the President does not appear to know what he is talking about and clings to one idea."[5]

That idea would be the making of the conference, however.

It was not only among the British contingent that there was anxiety expressed at the decline in the President's health. Everyone on the American delegation, most of all Admiral McIntire, was aware of it, yet there was nothing that could be done medically. Or politically. There was no one else on the America team, perhaps even on the planet, who could take the President's place at that moment. In fact, there was no one who could really take the place of any of the three Allied commanders in chief at Yalta. They had become the three icons of the Allied coalition — not only symbols of the Grand Alliance, as Churchill called it, but the only leaders whose command of their military forces was incontestable, and irreplaceable if they collapsed or died. As Alexander Cadogan, the permanent undersecretary to the British foreign secretary, would write privately to his wife from Yalta, the "President in particular is very woolly and wobbly. Lord Moran says there's no doubt which of the three will go first."[6]

Somehow, however, with the conference currently slated to last only a further four or five days, the President would have to get through it, or be brought through.

"The dinner broke up early — about midnight," Anna recorded. As the opening act of the summit, despite the President's condition, all had gone amazingly well. "FDR seemed happy about both the Conf. and the dinner," Anna noted — in fact her father told her, before turning in, that "Byrnes had made a fine toast," rescuing him from a faux pas when he'd revealed in his meandering toast that he and Mr. Churchill were wont to call Stalin, between themselves, "Uncle Joe."[7]

The President had meant it as a sign of friendship, not disrespect. Stalin, who had by then drunk a great deal, took it as a slight, however. The Marshal had even made as if to leave the dinner, in pique. Byrnes, who was considered smart as a whippet, had stepped in. Proposing a new toast, he had pointed out that the President's term was one of affection, similar to the way Russians would refer to "Uncle Sam."

The day had thus come to a friendly close, leaving only Churchill and Eden to have a first-class row over voting rights in any putative UN organization, in the ballroom, while Stalin went back to the Yusupov Palace.[8]

78

Kennan's Warning

BOTH STALIN AND CHURCHILL were opposed to a United Nations organization that might tie their communist or colonialist hands. But it was not only Stalin and Churchill who did not care for the idea. A number of American officials, too, opposed the President's proposal. An urgent letter from Moscow had been given to the President's interpreter immediately upon Bohlen's arrival at Yalta. It had come from George Kennan, the top political counselor to Ambassador Harriman at the U.S. Embassy in Moscow: a long, preconference warning in which Kennan confided how much he disagreed with the President's war and postwar policy. The President's idea of a United Nations organization, Kennan advised, should, despite the preliminary Dumbarton Oaks accords, be dumped "as quickly and quietly as possible" at Yalta.[1]

This came as something of a shock to the President's interpreter and rising star in the State Department. As Bohlen understood things, the whole purpose of holding the Yalta summit, from the American point of view, was to show the Nazis and the world that a new postwar world order was being created, under the aegis of a United Nations authority, as discussed at Dumbarton Oaks: one that would authorize military power to be applied via a small Security Council if any nation ever attempted again to do what Hitler or Hirohito had done. Ambassador Harriman had discussed this and the President's vision at length with Stalin, and with Molotov, in the weeks and months since the Dumbarton Oaks Conference — the preliminary agreements of which were only held up by differences of opinion over voting numbers and rights. Kennan now argued, however, that Germany should be broken up and partitioned into separate states, and Europe divided "frankly into spheres of influence." Americans should keep "ourselves out of the Russian sphere," and the Russians stay "out of ours."[2] And no UN created, lest it hamstring future American use of "armed force."[3]

Roosevelt disagreed with this free-for-all — which looked suspiciously like the world before the First World War. The President hoped to announce agreement on the UN to an anxious world in February 1945. Without some kind of international body the future looked dark, and would offer little practical hope or ideals to mankind, after a devastating world war. Whereas, if a UN organization could be established "with teeth" this time, as the President had put it, the prospect of renewed wars of conquest could hopefully be averted — and much positive, constructive postwar work be done meanwhile, in a collective spirit of improvement, from global health initiatives to economic development and education.

Moreover, there was the matter of timing: something which Kennan, as a diplomat, should have been the first to understand. "First things first" had been the President's mantra, reflected in his methodical military strategy since Pearl Harbor: "Germany First," then Japan. How could Germany be broken up and partitioned, as Kennan claimed he wanted it to be, unless its unconditional surrender was first obtained? From all reports of the fighting, as from diplomatic efforts, this would not be possible without military victory by the Allies. And for this to happen, the cooperation of the Soviets was still crucial — cooperation that could be used to promote a more responsible approach to world peace and development, since refusing to join such a United Nations organization would make the Soviet Union into a pariah state.

The Allies were now within a few months of defeating the Wehrmacht, if all went well. How would it possibly help attain the unconditional surrender of the Third Reich if, at a conference with Marshal Stalin and Mr. Churchill in Yalta, the United States President and his secretary of state, Mr. Stettinius, should now announce they were *burying* the Dumbarton Oaks plans, largely agreed with the Russians, for a United Nations organization — and "as quickly as possible," as Kennan suggested?

In an all-out world war that had not yet been won this seemed daft to Bohlen. Those nations next to, or close to, Russia's borders which had contributed military forces to help Hitler attack the Soviet Union — Romania, Finland, Hungary, Slovakia, Romania, and Croatia — faced a future that was hardly rosy. Yet the United States had not entered the war to take responsibility for the democratic future of such enemies — which they had effectively become as German allies, following Hitler's declaration of war on America on December 11, 1941. There was in reality little that the United States could actually do to "save" them from communism; this did not mean, however, abandoning the notion of a United Nations organization. Or that the United States should not do everything in its power to liberate, via its military, as much of western Europe as it currently could. By setting out the principles and ideals of a United Nations organization at this moment, when the Big Three were fighting as allies, the President might yet get the Soviets to back the concept, if Roosevelt could persuade Stalin, upon whom all Russian decisions depended.

Kennan's suggestion the United States should either announce at Yalta it would defend the integrity and independence of democratic eastern and southeastern European states — even to the point of going to war with the Soviets — or simply and openly "write off" the region for Soviet domination and retreat into its own "spheres of influence," thus seemed to Bohlen not only morally wrong at this moment in the war; it did not even reflect what Americans were fighting *for*. Would American voters really subscribe to such a new strategy of open abandonment of international leadership and ideals, before the war against Hitler was even won? In the aftermath of nearly a hundred thousand American casualties suffered in the Ardennes and Alsace — combatting ruthlessly indoctrinated Nazis, who had openly massacred American prisoners taken on the battlefield? Equally, would U.S. troops or voters want their leaders to announce in public, in advance of the end of the war, they were going to "write off" Poland and all those central European Russian borderland states, which had been Hitler's war-partners, and simply withdraw to "spheres of interest"? If so, who then would enforce the breakup of Germany which Kennan supposedly wanted, after the war? Would the U.S. not retreat into isolationism — as had happened, after Versailles?

Bohlen certainly admitted that the prospects of "saving" Poland and Hitler's allies in eastern and central Europe from Soviet communism — i.e., political and social suppression and oppression — were currently slim, as things stood. The vision of a United Nations organization, and a Security Council acting on its behalf, was nonetheless worth supporting, dedicated to principles of democracy and self-determination, surely, even if those principles proved in the short term difficult, if not impossible, to fulfill, given Russian forces in control of eastern and central Europe. The United States would at least have *tried* — which it had *not* done after World War I. As Bohlen later wrote, "I recall feeling quite strongly that to abandon the United Nations would be an error of the first magnitude" — not because he thought the UN would necessarily or automatically "prevent big-power aggression," but because, as a trained diplomat, he felt it would "keep the United States involved in world affairs" — and without necessarily "committing us to use force when we did not want to," assuming the U.S. would have the right of veto against military action in the Security Council. Moreover to openly subscribe, at this point, to a "formal, or even an informal, attempt to give the Soviet Union a sphere of influence in Eastern Europe" would, if it became known in February 1945, be akin to Chamberlain's Munich agreement: indeed would be playing into Hitler's hands, rather than asserting the *principle* of democracy, at least, for post-fascist central and east European territories — especially those who had assisted Hitler in Operation Barbarossa. As Bohlen wrote back in "a hasty reply" to Kennan: "Quarreling" with the Soviets at Yalta "would be so easy," given the contrasting democratic-communist ideological beliefs held by the two military allies, "but we can always come to that."[4]

In his reply to Kennan, Bohlen had confessed that his personal views were "tempered" by his association with the President, who believed in idealistic realism, and by the recent weeks he'd spent with Harry Hopkins, meeting leaders in Europe. The existence of tyrant-led communism, whether in Russia or in other countries, was "a political fact of life" that Americans had every right to deplore, in terms of individual citizens' rights and freedoms. But, after fighting a "long, hard war," the United States surely "deserved at least an attempt" to "get along with the Soviets," whatever it felt about their political system. As the diplomat later put it, the President had but two "major goals" at the impending conference: namely "to pin down Stalin on the timing and extent of entering the war in Asia," once Germany surrendered; and to create a United Nations organization to stop the United States from "slipping back into isolationism," as the Kennans of the world wanted, or were willing to risk.[5]

The fact was, Bohlen felt, the United States had ultimately failed in its recent attempt to remain an isolationist, "America First" nation — forced to watch as the Axis powers overran country after country with impunity. Now, having become the world's most powerful nation economically and militarily, in a bare three years of war, the United States had a duty to itself and to the world to become a world *leader* of partner nations, not simply an isolationist, or limited "sphere of interest," power, Bohlen was convinced. For if not the United States, who else would step up to the challenge, as the United States had done in leading the Western Allies after Pearl Harbor? The British Empire? The French Empire?

Britain, at the end of the day, was close to bankruptcy, economically. Politically, too — more concerned with clasping its far-flung colonial territories (when recovered with American help) than creating a world organization based on the Atlantic Alliance. Which left the problem of possible future German revanchism, à la Hitler, if Germany was broken up and partitioned, pace Kennan. Who, then, in the years to come, would act?

But if neither Russian nationalists nor British imperialists had a genuine interest in establishing a United Nations organization — one in which the Soviet Union would, in the proposed UN Assembly and in its Security Council, be outnumbered by other countries, as would Britain — what chance had the President of persuading them to support his vision? Were "spheres of interest" the inevitable face of the postwar future — British, Russian, French, Chinese — as it had been in the 1930s? Had the President undertaken an impossible challenge at Yalta?

· · ·

Looking at the President in his study that morning, greeting Stalin with a warm smile and an outstretched hand from his sofa, Bohlen had been fully aware not only of what the President was up against, but also how slim was the chance that his ailing boss could make it happen — at least in his current state of health. Yet there was, in reality, no one else on the American team who could get the Soviets and the British to back the establishment of a United Nations! Edward Stettinius, the new secretary of state? Justice Byrnes, the director of war mobilization? Harry Hopkins, the White House counselor, or political adviser, to the President? Averell Harriman, the U.S. ambassador to Moscow? Not one of these men had been elected to his present position. And the vice president, Harry Truman, was not even there: unable to leave the country while the President was abroad, and in any case a neophyte with regard to international issues.

Only the President could achieve it, at that moment, Bohlen recognized. Nothing would be lost that would not have been lost anyhow, if he failed. It was, therefore, worth trying, in Bohlen's view. The President, after all, now appeared to have the backing not only of most Democrats but of most Senate Republicans in Congress, swayed by the recent 180-degree turn by Senator Vandenberg. Moreover, unlike Churchill — and certainly unlike Stalin — the President had just won a popular mandate from American voters for such an attempt: one he had laid squarely before the entire American electorate in the November '44 election. With 25.6 million ballots cast and 432 electoral college votes he had won a resounding fourth term as president and commander in chief. It was worth an attempt, surely — unless the effort killed the President, at the very moment Hitler and his regime were on the ropes.

This, sadly, was far from unlikely. Plagued by a "paroxysmal cough" that had kept waking him the previous night (though he "denied dyspnea, orthopnea, or cardiac pain," as Bruenn recalled),[6] the President had dreaded the long, unavoidable dinners, with their endless toasts — just as he'd shuddered at the prospect of the disagreements that would inevitably arise over political issues, especially Poland. But as Hopkins had said, he had signed up for this, however reluctantly. And if his ill health precluded him from following all the arguments in detail: in some ways this was also a blessing. He would stick, he was determined, to his simple, single-minded agenda: close military cooperation; a signed agreement by the Big Three to establish a United Nations organization; and a necessarily undisclosed, but formal Russian agreement to join the United States in the war against Japan once the Third Reich surrendered.

Whether the President would leave Yalta on a plane or in a casket remained to be seen, but he was determined to do his best. For the rest, he could not answer.

79

A World Security Organization

THUS THE SAGA of Yalta began to unfold on February 5, 1945. Over the next several days the generals, admirals, and airmen of the three nations, aided by their staffs, conferred not only about the endgame in Germany — bombing targets and airfield arrangements, in particular — but over detailed plans for American air bases to be secretly set up in the Soviet Union, ready for the day when Russia would declare war on Japan — which Stalin would formally agree to do in secret.

This left, for the President, the final setup and establishment of a United Nations organization to be agreed and announced. Behind the scenes tempers flared, dissension arose, and arguments threatened at times to derail the main proceedings. As Bohlen later put it, the "conference was organized in such a way that there was no orderly discussion and resolution of each problem by the leaders. Instead, issues were brought up, discussed, then shunted off to the Foreign Ministers or military chiefs or just dropped for a few hours."[1] As Sir Alexander Cadogan reported to his wife, the place became, initially, "a madhouse," and took — like all conferences — "days to get on the rails."[2]

Gradually it became clear to all participants, however, that it was too early to make hard and fast agreements about the future political map of the world when the war itself was still not won, and the United Nations organization had not been set up.

Territorial discussions among the various political and diplomatic advisers were the most contentious matters, resembling shooting stars before dawn — leaving Churchill, in the plenary sessions, to display his rhetorical virtuosity and Stalin his more focused acerbity, in equal measure. This left the ailing American chairman often reeling. "The President has certainly aged,"[3] Cadogan noted on February 7 — Roosevelt trying, as chairman, to keep the place, the pace, the peace, and the purpose of the deliberations advancing each day.

Whether the President realized he only had weeks to live no one would ever know, since Lucy Rutherfurd subsequently burned all his letters, and Anna — charged with the daily care of her father — discontinued her diary after the first two days. For their part, though, the President's doctors monitored his condition with increasing concern as the conference reached the fifth plenary session in the Livadia ballroom at 4 p.m. on Thursday, February 8, 1945.

For the President this was to be the climax of the Yalta Conference: getting agreement on what was termed the "World Security Organization": namely those who had signed the "United Nations Declaration" on January 1, 1942, and who would now be "summoned for Wednesday, 25th April, 1945," before the war ended, for an inaugural meeting to "be held in the United States of America."

Stalin expressed concern that some of these states had no diplomatic relations with the Soviet Union, but the President deftly dealt with this by saying the Soviet Union had already "sat down with these states at Bretton Woods and the UNRRA conferences." Moreover Stalin's next grumble that there was a difference between those "nations who had really waged war and had suffered," in the struggle against the Nazis, and "others who had wavered and speculated on being on the winning side" was equally deftly dealt with by the President. It was time not to look back, but for the world to move on — and by inviting to the UN, he proposed, all those nations who now "declared war" on Germany by "the first of March," 1945, they would have the corpus of an organization they could be proud of creating.[4]

Stalin and Churchill had thus reluctantly given their assent — Stalin even agreeing to drop his suggestion that White Russia (Belarus) and the Ukraine qualify separately for invitation by signing retrospectively the 1942 United Nations Declaration, though pressing for this; it would be left up to the nascent UN, Stalin agreed, however, to decide on whether White Russia and the Ukraine should have separate seats, distinct from the USSR.

The President had thus good reason to be proud of what he'd accomplished by February 8. But with the military side of the conference done (the generals slated to hold a final tripartite military meeting the next day and report to the President), and the UN/World Security Organization settled by the early evening, the plenary would have to return to the knotty issue of Poland: its future frontiers and its provisional government. A much more difficult proposition.

80

Poland

AT THE FULCRUM of central Europe, Poland had endured a long, often savage, often contested history. The country had recovered its independence in 1918—one that was ratified in the Treaty of Versailles, and which Poles had successfully defended against Russian forces in 1919–21 in what was called the "miracle of the Vistula." That independence had been lost yet again when it was invaded and overrun by Hitler's Wehrmacht forces on September 1, 1939. Two weeks later the Soviets had invaded Poland from the east, via the Ukraine, and had annexed eastern Poland in accordance with secret protocols in the Molotov-Ribbentrop Pact regarding "spheres of influence"—the term for occupation or control of puppet regimes.

The spheres had not lasted long, however, thanks to Hitler's agenda, backed by the Wehrmacht. The Soviet-controlled Polish territories east of the Curzon Line had been steamrollered in Operation Barbarossa on June 22, 1941, in which almost four million troops from Germany, Romania, Finland, Italy, Hungary, Slovakia, and Croatia were thrust into full-scale war against the Soviet Union. Of the five million Russians captured during the Barbarossa invasion, almost none returned to Russia alive.

Now, in 1945, Poland had been triumphantly "liberated"—but by Russians, not Poles themselves or the Western Allies. Stalin had been pressing both Churchill and Roosevelt since before the Tehran Summit in 1943 to acknowledge a permanent new eastern Polish frontier in the event of German defeat, which could be done by formally shifting the future border between Poland and the Ukraine. This would follow the so-called Curzon Line—a frontier that had been suggested, the Russians had pointed out, as the ethnic boundary between Poland and Russia by Lord Curzon and the Supreme Allied War Council during World War I. It had also been the line which the Russians had already established in the 1939 partition of the country in the Molotov-Ribbentrop Pact.

What, then, Stalin had kept asking, had changed the minds of the Western Allies about this border since then?

Communism, for one thing. Although Churchill and the British government actually favored such a new, or renewed, Polish border, with a sidestep of the country's western boundary into Prussia to compensate for the territory "lost," the President had cited potential political repercussions in the U.S., where there was a significant Polish-American population (sometimes estimated at six million). He had therefore declined to agree such a new frontier line at Tehran, in spite of Churchill's urging. Now that he had been successfully reelected, Stalin could not see why the President should fear a Polish-American political backlash. In the area east of the Curzon Line, as this became liberated by the Red Army, the Soviets had installed a provisional Polish government, drawn from "Lublin" Poles in exile in Moscow — just as the Allies, liberating France, had permitted one in Paris, under de Gaulle. These "Moscow Poles" accepted both the Curzon Line and Churchill's suggestion of compensation to be given them in East Prussia, once Germany surrendered.

To Churchill's chagrin, however, the Polish government in exile in London, under Stanislaw Mikolajczyk, had adamantly refused to agree either to the Curzon Line boundary or to sidestepping the nation's western frontiers into German East Prussia. Nothing Churchill had done, or could do, seemed sufficient to change their minds. This had set the stage for an international dispute as potentially volatile as that of September 1939.

For the ailing president this was the last problem he wished to deal with at Yalta — yet Stalin, obsessed with his notion of a cordon sanitaire against future German attack, was determined it should be addressed forthwith, *before* the United Nations organization was established. The UN, he figured, might well rule against the boundary change. Since Stalin was willing to accept de Gaulle's French Committee of National Liberation as the provisional government of France, legitimated by the Allies, why should the Polish Committee of National Liberation, legitimated by the Soviet Union, not be accepted by the Allies?

This was a truly Gordian knot.

Principles of self-determination and self-government through popular election, as well as common agreement on borders, were easy enough to urge on paper, in the midst of a world war, the President was aware; enforcing such an outcome against the wishes and security concerns of the nation that had actually liberated Poland (which the Western Allies had been unable to do) was a very different proposition. Moreover even on paper, Western diplomats were on uncertain ground; the Monroe Doctrine as cordon sanitaire had, after all, characterized American policy in the Americas since the early nineteenth century. It remained still the underlying strategic principle of U.S. diplomacy and military power in early 1945 — a reality that made it difficult for Americans, whose continent had never been invaded since the British in 1812, to object to the wishes of Russians, who had twice been invaded via Poland by huge armies in the past thirty years alone.

Que faire?

The principle of self-determination mattered to the President, indeed was the bedrock of his pride as an American, whose country had cast off its oppressive British straitjacket in 1776. He had made it the kernel of his Atlantic Charter, and had then made that charter the core principle of the United Nations Declaration, which he'd gotten all the anti-Axis nations to sign in Washington immediately after Pearl Harbor, on January 1, 1942.

At the same time, however, the ailing president was too much a realist to imagine the United States could now *compel* the Soviets to cut their own communist throats by encouraging the creation of a democratic state on their own borders, on the very cusp of their costly victory over the Axis powers. And how, in any case, could such an insistence be safeguarded after the war when there was currently almost zero support in the United States for a continuing American military presence in Europe beyond the unconditional surrender of the Third Reich?

Poland's fate thus hung in the paper balance at Yalta. Certainly no one could have spoken more eloquently than had Churchill on behalf of Poland in the plenary on February 6. The Prime Minister did so once again on February 8: Mr. Churchill citing Poland's long, distressing history, its brief but courageous resistance against Hitler in 1939, and its Polish army in exile that had fought the Nazis with such distinction under British command in Italy, Normandy, and Holland. Yet for all the Prime Minister's grandiloquence, the simple fact had remained: British forces were no more able to defend Poland in 1945 than they were when Hitler invaded the country on September 1, 1939 — whereas Italy, ironically, which had been Hitler's main ally, and still had Italian units in the north of the country training and fighting with the Wehrmacht, was set to become a free democratic nation again, protected by the Western Allies and with the pope still on his throne.

The situation was, in short, unjust, even tragic — yet in the circumstances unavoidable. Poland, the central European nation which had *not* been a partner to Hitler but a victim of German aggression, and whose military forces had fought so bravely for the Western Allies, now faced Soviet postwar rule, while perfidious Italy got away scot free . . .

To add to this dark prognosis was the manner in which Poland had already suffered at the hands of Russian communists. Not only had the Russian NKVD deliberately murdered more than fifteen thousand Polish officers in cold blood in the Katyn forest in 1940, but on Stalin's orders the Stavka, or high command of the Red Army, had deliberately decided *not* to provide military assistance during the Warsaw Uprising in the summer of 1944 — the heartbreaking, forlorn attempt by Polish resistance fighters to liberate their capital from German occupation that had resulted in a further fifteen thousand Poles being ruthlessly slaughtered by the Wehrmacht.

Churchill portrayed the issue of Poland's postwar political independence, morally speaking, as the "crucial point of this great conference." Failure to agree on this matter would, he warned, represent a "cleavage" between the Allies — and at the very moment when the entire free world so fervently wanted the representatives at "this conference to separate on a note of agreement."[1]

In reality Churchill knew it was futile. As a lifelong parliamentarian, the Prime Minister was fully aware his appeal was *pour l'histoire*, rather than practical: a valiant *cri de coeur* on behalf of brave Poles. In the melting pot that would comprise central and southern Europe at the end of hostilities, Soviet possession would inevitably be nine-tenths of the law, wherever Russian security strategy was concerned. It was a bitter truth Churchill not only knew but secretly accepted, as per the confidential agreement he'd made in Moscow, closeted alone with Stalin, the previous October, with regard to the fates of Greece, the Balkans, and Yugoslavia. There, in the Russian capital, he had somewhat callously drawn up his famous (some would say infamous) "percentages" agreement on "spheres of influence" in Europe that he'd written on a piece of paper he'd passed across the table to Stalin — and which Stalin had ticked, approvingly.

Greece, however, was not Poland. The Greeks were not located on the Soviet Union's western border; Poland was.

Over the issue of Poland, then, Stalin simply remained intractable and implacable — and the plenary on February 8, 1945, which the President had intended to represent the climax of his efforts at Yalta, in terms of war with Japan and the creation of the United Nations, now turned sour as Churchill proclaimed he could not reconcile himself to accepting Stalin's position on Poland.

As tensions rose in the discussion, so did hypocrisy — especially Russian. The Prime Minister could only roll his eyes when Stalin claimed the Poles, who the Marshal openly admitted had every reason to hate the Soviets after their country had in the past been partitioned three times by Russians, were now filled with "good will" for the Red Army, whose liberation of their country from the Nazis had "completely changed their psychology."[2] But Stalin's point that the Western Allies were opposing the provisional Lublin government whereas he had not objected to de Gaulle forming a provisional French government, ahead of elections to be held at the end of the war — indeed had agreed that France should have an occupation zone when Germany surrendered — put Churchill in a serious bind. It was one the President could only do his best to paper over when wisely suggesting they defer further discussion, and leave it to their foreign ministers.

In the meantime, the President summarized, they were all at least in agreement over the recognition of Poland's borders as the Curzon Line in the east, and to be sidestepped somewhere yet to be determined in German East Prussia in the west.[3] Under pressure from both the President and Mr. Churchill, Marshal Stalin even agreed that "free elections" should be held in Poland, as soon as the war was over, as in France — though how "free" they would be remained open to doubt.

It was a most imperfect, somewhat Munich-like deferment of the issue, but it would have to do. It was all the President could manage at the moment, without the conference being derailed. And with that, at his suggestion, the fifth plenary was thus adjourned to the next day.

81

Pulsus Alternans

CHURCHILL, BOTH AS A HISTORIAN and as a prime witness to events in Europe in the 1930s, had been genuinely tormented, and his passionate plea for Poland's democratic future had been sincere — something Stalin, for his part, respected.

As if to reassure the President he harbored no ill feelings towards the Prime Minister, the Russian dictator was the soul of goodwill at the dinner that night at the Yusupov Palace, or Villa. He toasted the Prime Minister with unmistakable sincerity: lauding Churchill's stand in 1940 as "the bravest governmental figure in the world," according to the minutes which Charles Bohlen wrote up that night.

As Stalin put it, "Due in large measure to Mr. Churchill's courage and staunchness, England, when she stood alone, had divided the might of Hitlerite Germany when the rest of Europe was falling flat on its face before Hitler. He said that Great Britain, under Mr. Churchill's leadership, had carried on the fight alone irrespective of existing or potential allies. He concluded that he knew of few examples in history where the courage of one man had been so important to the future history of the world" — and he'd raised his champagne glass with this accolade to his "fighting friend and a brave man."[1]

After Churchill had responded, Stalin had gone on to propose the health of the President, in similar vein: pointing out that where he and Churchill had been "fighting for their very existence against Hitlerite Germany," the President had had "a broader conception of national interest." Even though his "country had not been seriously threatened with invasion," the President had become "the chief forger of the instruments which had led to the mobilization of the world against Hitler. He mentioned in this connection Lend-Lease as one of the President's most remarkable and vital achievements in the formation of the Anti-Hitler combination and in keeping the Allies in the field against Hitler."[2]

Nothing in such toasts had suggested Stalin was being disingenuous. He seemed genuinely to admire Churchill's character. Moreover he respected the

Prime Minister's rhetorical skills, even when finding them long-winded, or directed against himself. By the same token he genuinely admired the capitalist president of the United States for his global perspective, and was profoundly grateful for American military and economic help — without which, he acknowledged, the Soviet Union could not have held out against the Wehrmacht, or have driven it back. He accepted that what lay ahead of their three countries would not necessarily be easier than what lay behind. As he remarked, it was "not so difficult to keep unity in time of war" when there was "a common enemy." The "difficult task came after the war when diverse interests tended to divide the allies" — Bohlen recording his exact words in another toast the Marshal had made that evening. "He said he was confident that the present alliance would meet this test also and that it was our duty to see that it would, and that our relations in peacetime should be as strong as they had been in war."[3]

Time would tell. Admiral Leahy thought it had been an extraordinary day. "The dinner, starting at nine o'clock, lasted until 1:00 a.m.," he wrote in his diary, "with great quantities of food, 38 standing toasts, and mosquitoes under the tables that worked very successfully on my ankles." Glasses had to be physically clinked, Russian-style, with "the person toasted" — Leahy approached by Molotov, Stalin, and Churchill, no less.

Leahy was not entirely won over, however. "With the amount of important work we have each day," the admiral added, "such dinner celebrations are in my opinion an unwarranted waste of time. We did not succeed in returning to our quarters in Livadia Palace until after one o'clock a.m."[4]

It was at this point that Lieutenant Commander Bruenn was finally able to check how the President was faring, medically. He and Admiral McIntire were shocked. The President's color "looked very poor (gray)," Bruenn revealed twenty-five years later.

Alarmed, Bruenn asked if he might examine the President's lungs and his heart rate before Mr. Roosevelt went to bed. These appeared to be OK. However, "for the first time," Bruenn chronicled in his clinical notes, the President's blood pressure "showed *pulsus alternans*." Strong, then weak, heartbeats.

It was the classic indication of the onset of serious left-sided heart failure.

82

The Prime Minister Goes Ballistic

IN HIS FAMOUS, deeply autobiographical working-class novel *Sons and Lovers,* D. H. Lawrence describes the last hours of his hero's mother, Mrs. Morel. Looking out the window Paul Morel sees the Nottinghamshire countryside "bleak and pallid under the snow," Lawrence had written. "Then he felt her pulse. There was a strong stroke and a weak one, like a sound and its echo. That was supposed to betoken the end," which came soon after — accelerated by the extra morphine Paul and his sister give their mother in filial compassion, without the doctor's knowledge, since "he says Mrs. Morel cannot last more than a few more days."

Lawrence was recording very much what he himself had witnessed. No such candor was shown by Admiral McIntire, the President's doctor who afterwards maintained that the President was fine at Yalta, merely tired. "As a result of malicious and persistent propaganda," McIntire would write the year after the Crimea Conference, "it has come to be accepted as a fact that the President was not himself at Yalta, either physically or mentally." Retiring as surgeon general of the U.S. Navy in 1946, the admiral declared "these charges" to be "every whit as false and baseless as the whisper about his breakdown in Teheran." The President had reached Yalta "in fine fettle," McIntire lied. And though the Livadia Palace sessions were "long and exhausting, and there were evenings when he confessed to being 'pretty well fagged,'" there was "never" any "loss of vigor and clarity."[1]

By 1946, of course, McIntire was trying to contest growing right-wing Republican claims that the President had been deathly sick and had more or less given away the capitalist store, as McIntire summarized their critique of the dead commander in chief — the President acting merely "as a rubber stamp for Marshal Stalin," and "weakly yielding to his demands at every point."[2]

In this respect, at least, McIntire was right to protest, for the President's performance at Yalta had been no rubber stamp, as McIntire was aware. In his last weeks of life, the President had in fact been able to achieve all his chosen objectives. The USSR being what it was — a police state, under the absolute rule of an often psychopathic dictator — the President had never seriously imagined he could make postwar *political* decisions acceptable to all, especially Polish patriots. What he could do, though, was at least rehearse the issues there, in the open, while the Big Three and their advisers were gathered together, in advance of the establishment of the United Nations organization and Security Council: a UN organization that neither the Soviet Union nor Britain favored, but which the President had been determined to establish — and which, however reluctantly, Stalin and Churchill now declared they were willing to support.

Shocked as his physicians were by the President's heartbeat variations at Yalta on the fourth night of the Yalta Conference, meantime, Bruenn administered more digitalis in the early hours of February 9, 1945, and a sleeping draft. To Anna the doctors were both adamant, however: no one, but no one, should henceforth be allowed to see the President before noonday. Also the President must have at least an hour's sleep or rest before each subsequent plenary began, or he would die in the Crimea, not in the aftermath.

The physicians, of course, could do nothing to lessen the rising tensions over the Polish issue — and on the afternoon of February 9, the oral ructions began all over again.

Fortunately the President had slept well — and thanks to the digitalis his *pulsus alternans* had seemed miraculously to vanish. His Joint Chiefs of Staff arrived to report they'd reached complete agreement with their Soviet counterparts on all matters relating to the war in Europe, and that they had begun detailed planning for the combined defeat of Japan. The President was delighted — and congratulated them as commander in chief.

This left just the Declaration on Liberated Europe, which the President had asked his secretary of state, Ed Stettinius, to draft — and which, he was told, seemed to have found favor with all three foreign ministers of the Big Three. As chairman at the 4:00 p.m. sixth plenary session, the President would only have to get Stalin and Churchill to approve the declaration draft, which they could do just as soon as they ended the previous day's unfinished discussion of Poland.

The sixth plenary began politely enough. On behalf of the three foreign ministers Secretary Stettinius gave his account to date on how they viewed the Polish conundrum — saying they'd decided it was best to defer discussion of "this question to a later date and to report that the three Foreign Ministers thus far had not reached an agreement on this matter."[3]

Had the foreign ministers had their way, the issue of Poland would therefore have been postponed, and dropped from the Yalta agreements. For Churchill, however, this was unacceptable. His motto, in heading the British government since 1940, had been "Action This Day" — and on February 9, 1945, he was determined to live up to it. "It was decided, at Mr. Churchill's request, that the Polish question would be discussed before Mr. Stettinius proceeded with the balance of his report," Charles Bohlen recorded in his minutes.[4]

"The Polish question." This was not, at Yalta, the matter of Poland's proposed new frontiers, but the business of "free" elections. The foreign ministers had agreed, between them, that the provisional government of Poland should be broadened "on a wider democratic basis with the inclusion of democratic leaders from Poland itself and from those living abroad" — i.e., London — "to be called the National Provisional Government." To this American proposal Mr. Molotov had formally assented. Yet Molotov wanted to "eliminate" his colleagues' proposal for a special commission of their nations' future three ambassadors to Warsaw — one that would be asked to "observe and report" to their three governments "on the carrying out of the free elections." And this because, as Molotov put it, it would "be offensive to the Poles and needlessly complicate discussions."[5]

What Molotov meant, of course, was that it would be offensive to Stalin and the Soviets — implying the Russians would otherwise manipulate the results.

The President could only groan — for although "free elections" were the very bedrock of democracy, the Soviet Union was not, by any stretch of the imagination, a democracy. Moreover it was unlikely ever to permit such a state to flower on its very doorstep. Once Churchill had the floor, though, it was too late; the plenary now became a sort of verbal food fight — one that quickly threatened to get out of hand and wreck the summit.

Churchill began by declaring he was glad "an advance had been made" by the foreign secretaries, and to hear Mr. Molotov's report regarding the "urgent, immediate and painful problem of Poland. He said he wished to make some general suggestions that he hoped would not affect" the President's game plan for the conference, but "here, in this general atmosphere of agreement, we should not put our feet in the stirrups and ride off. He said that he felt it would be a great mistake to take hurried decisions on these grave matters. He felt we must study the Polish proposals before giving any opinion."

To this the President could only agree — suggesting that, once Stettinius had finished his report, which would include the Declaration on Liberated Europe, they could adjourn for half an hour to discuss Molotov's proposed amendment. Stettinius thus resumed giving his foreign minister's report regarding reparations and, following this, the "machinery in the World Organization [i.e., UN] for dealing with territorial trusteeships and dependent areas."[6]

At the mention of "trusteeships," however, Churchill went ballistic. "The Prime Minister interrupted with great vigor to say that he did not agree with one single word of this report on trusteeships. He said that he had not been consulted nor had he heard of this subject up to now. He said that under no circumstances would he ever consent to forty or fifty nations thrusting inter-fering fingers into the life's existence of the British Empire. As long as he was [Prime] Minister, he would never yield one scrap of their heritage. He contin-ued in this vein for some minutes," Bohlen minuted.[7] For his part, Admiral Leahy recorded that night how Churchill had "refused to consider permitting any agency to deal with any territory under the British flag, saying, 'While there is life in my body no transfer of British sovereignty will be permitted.'"[8]

Alger Hiss, on behalf of the U.S. State Department team, also noted Churchill's vehemence: "I will not have 1 scrap of the Brit Empire [lost], after all we have done in the war," the Prime Minister had declared. "I will not con-sent to a repres[entative] of Brit Em[pire] going to any conference where we will be placed in the dock & asked to defend ourselves. Never, Never, Never . . . Every scrap of terr.[itory] over which Brit flag flies is immune." Churchill's interpreter, Major Birse, wisely omitted the Prime Minister's outburst from his plenary minutes that night, but the damage, in a sense, had been done. Churchill had demonstrated, to Eden's chagrin, that the British were, in a sense, frauds: demanding observation rights in Poland, a country the Soviets had, at great cost, cleared of Nazis, yet denouncing in fury any idea that once liberated, British colonial or mandated possessions should be subjected to any kind of "observation." "I must be able to tell Parliament that elections will be free and fair," in Poland, Churchill had insisted — but not in the British Em-pire, it appeared.[9]

The Prime Minister's position was now tainted, in front of the entire plenary entourage — Stalin, with a trace of mockery, asking about elections to be held in Greece, where British troops were being used to guard against a communist insurgency. Churchill was compelled to assure him Russian observers would be welcome there, as well as in Italy. He even extolled Egypt as a model of free elections — causing the Russian dictator to say he'd heard "that the very great-est politicians spent their time buying each other" in Egypt, "but this could not be compared with Poland since there was a high degree of literacy in Poland. He inquired as to the literacy in Egypt, and neither the Prime Minister or Mr. Eden had this information at hand."[10]

This was not the direction the ailing president wanted for the summit. The election in Poland, he said — trying to pour oil on roiling waters — was "the crux of the whole matter, and since it was true, as Marshal Stalin had said, that the Poles were quarrelsome people not only at home but also abroad, he would like to have some assurance for the six million Poles in the United States that these elections would be freely held." If such an assurance were given "that elections would be held by the Poles," then "there would be no doubt as to the sincerity of the agreement reached here."[11] In other words, the conference was not being held to lay down specific rules or systems in any one country, only to define at least the principles of future democratic government, which rested upon elections. Agreement over this was not only important to quarrelsome Poles, he urged. Just as important, it would give hope to people in occupied or now liberated countries that the age of tyranny by military conquest was coming to an end. The President hoped therefore that Stalin would accept his proposed Declaration on Liberated Europe.

The Declaration was long — and directed as much to Germans as to those in occupied countries. "The establishment of order in Europe and the rebuilding of national economic life," it ran, "must be achieved by processes which will enable the liberated peoples to destroy the last vestiges of Nazism and Fascism and to create democratic institutions of their own choice. This is the promise of the Atlantic Charter — the right of all peoples to choose the government under which they will live — the restoration of sovereign rights and self-government to those people who have been forcibly deprived of them." And it ended with the summons to a new world order. "By this declaration," it stated on behalf of its signatories, "we reaffirm our faith in the principles of the Atlantic Charter, our pledge in the Declaration by United Nations, and our determination to build in cooperation with other peace-loving nations a world order under law, dedicated to peace, security, freedom, and general well-being of all mankind."[12]

To the President's relief Stalin assented, suggesting (though not insisting) only that they add a sentence about helping especially those nations that had actually "taken an active part in the struggle against the German invaders."[13]

The Prime Minister, however, was appalled. For his part he "said he did not dissent from the President's proposed Declaration as long as it was clearly understood that the reference to the Atlantic Charter did not apply to the British Empire."

Did not apply to the British Empire?

Since Churchill had drawn up the Atlantic Charter with the President in 1941, this sounded ominous. So much so that Churchill, embarrassed, felt obliged to explain that "on my return from Newfoundland" in 1941, he had "read to the H[ouse] of C[ommons] that we were pursuing these aims in Brit Em[pire]. That is part of our [British] interpretation"[14] of the Atlantic Charter. Moreover that he had "given Mr. [Wendell] Willkie a copy of his statement on the subject,"[15] when Willkie was in London on his world tour, back in 1942: to wit, that although the Atlantic Charter might be appropriate for countries to be liberated in Europe, it did not pertain to those countries Britain ruled — that "every scrap of terr.[itory] over which Brit flag flies is immune."[16]

Considering the way Churchill had telegraphed the British viceroy in India to ask "why Gandhi hadn't died yet" in 1944,[17] had only approved Gandhi's release from prison on medical grounds that the Mahatma might otherwise die in British custody,[18] and that Wendell Willkie had been deeply disappointed by Churchill's refusal to countenance Indian self-government, the President could only smile — "inquiring if that was what had killed Mr. Willkie"?[19]

Clearly, a conference in which the deeds and misdeeds of the Big Three were hung out like washing would be a recipe for failure. Sensing the President's attempt at levity, Stalin assured Churchill "he had complete confidence in British policy in Greece,"[20] and would not think of sending a Soviet observer to Athens. By the same token, he did not favor British monitors in Warsaw.

With that — and brief discussion of the treatment of war criminals — the contentious plenary came to a quieter close. The various advisers went their ways: the foreign ministers tasked with drawing up a suitable, face-saving pledge regarding Poland, while the "Big Three" retired to their respective palaces to rest, and have dinner on their own.

The President was once more exhausted, but still alive, at least. If he could manage one more day, he reckoned, they could issue a communiqué before his health gave out completely. He'd gotten all he'd really hoped for from the summit; the rest was only the final wording and signatures. Thus after the seventh plenary the next afternoon, February 10, and a private, confidential meeting with Stalin and Harriman regarding Russian entry into the war against Japan, followed by dinner at Churchill's quarters in the Vorontsov Palace in the evening, the way was open to agree and sign the crucial announcement to the world.

The final dinner held at the Vorontsov Palace was a relatively small and short affair, with just the three heads of government, their foreign secretaries, and their interpreters present. Stalin claimed to be disappointed he had not gotten Mr. Churchill to agree an actual figure for war reparations that he could take back to Moscow — that he "feared to have to go back to the Soviet Union and tell the Soviet people they were not going to get any reparations because the British were opposed to it."

Since Stalin had seldom referred to the Soviet people, the fear sounded somewhat unlikely. Churchill assured him the Russians would get "large quantities" of reparation, to be assessed by the War Reparations Committee they'd agreed to be set up — but, recalling his own bitter experience at Versailles after World War I, he cautioned Stalin that the sum should not be a "figure at more than the capacity of Germany to pay."[21]

With his vast experience of war and politics since the 1890s, Churchill was clearly a match for anything Stalin — or anyone else — could throw at the elderly but combative and astute Prime Minister. But Stalin did insist that a clause about reparations be inserted in the communiqué, in order that the Germans know what lay ahead, even if this made them fight the harder to the bitter end.

The mention of "the people," however, led to discussion of the Prime Minister's chances of success in the general election which would soon have to be held in Britain, once the Labor Party left the current National Government. Marshal Stalin — not an expert on free elections — assured Mr. Churchill he would be a shoo-in, after all he had done for his country in the war.

The President, for his part, said he also hoped so. But he warned "that in his opinion any leader of a people must take care of their primary needs. He said he remembered when he first became President" the United States "was close to revolution because the people lacked food, clothing and shelter," thanks to the Great Depression. He had campaigned on the platform that, "If you elect me President I will give you these things" — and his New Deal intervention, using the powers of the federal government, had worked. Since then, he stated with pride, "there was little problem in regard to social disorder in the United States."[22]

It was a simplistic reflection, but a salutary one. Churchill, sparring with Stalin, consuming glass after glass of wine and Georgian champagne, gave the President's warning no more than cursory note — something he would soon have cause to regret.

For his part, the President had no election to face, only Congress.

And his maker.

83

The Yalta Communiqué

THE YALTA SUMMIT was now over, save for signing the requisite documents. Before leaving the Vorontsov dinner on February 10, the President had proposed that the final plenary at the Livadia Palace begin earlier, at noon the next day, to be followed by a working lunch during which they could all put their signatures to the Yalta communiqué, as well as to the secret protocol on Soviet entry into the war against Japan. After that they would be free to go home.

Every participant in the conference would have his or her memory of the summit — and personal verdict. For his part Charles Bohlen felt it historic that the President had changed position in the seventh plenary on February 10 by supporting Churchill's recommendation that France should have a place on the Allied Control Commission in Germany. "I had translated at his [Stalin's] private meeting with the President on the first day of the conference when Stalin expressed an unfavorable view of de Gaulle and the French. We had been opposed to giving France a seat on the Control Council for Germany when the subject first came up at the conference. When Roosevelt switched to Churchill's position, there was little Stalin could do without engendering French hostility."[1] On the negative side, Poland's democratic future would probably not be secured beyond window-dressing — but democracy across western Europe would at least be bolstered by a stronger France than the President had originally envisaged.

Together with the Russian protocol on war against Japan, and the agreed setup for the creation of the United Nations organization (with the Soviet Union dropping its claim on initial seats to just one by the end of the conference, with two more to be discussed in San Francisco), Bohlen felt the President had done astonishingly well for a leader so direly ill. Even the decision not to inform Chiang Kai-shek with regard to a continued Russian presence in Mongolia, once Russia joined the war against Japan, was, in the context of Mr. Roosevelt's insistence on China being one of the five permanent members of the proposed UN Security Council, along with France, a wise one, given the notorious lack of security in Chungking, and the likelihood the Japanese would otherwise learn of the Soviet commitment to enter the war. Moreover the agreement reached on voting procedure in the UN Security Council — giving its members the right to veto action, but not the right to veto discussion of a major security issue or threat, even where its own country was under scrutiny — was a major American achievement at the conference. As was, in Bohlen's view, persuading Stalin to at least sign the Declaration on Liberated Europe, which gave dignity, objectives, and moral idealism to the Yalta summit — however much Churchill had railed against it, and Stalin first hesitated to commit the Soviet Union to such a formal document.

All in all, then, Bohlen was proud of the President's performance. "Our leader was ill at Yalta, the most important of the wartime conferences, but he was effective. I so believed at the time and still so believe," the interpreter-diplomat wrote almost thirty years later.[2]

Not all were so impressed, however — including Admiral Leahy, the President's chief of staff. The signing of the official communiqué at lunch on February 11, and in particular the secret, formal agreement with Stalin on Soviet entry into the war against Japan, were undoubtedly historic, Leahy granted. With regard to the war against Hitler and the Third Reich, he found himself "deeply impressed by the unanimous and amicable agreement of the President, the Prime Minister of Great Britain and Marshal Stalin of Russia on the action that shall be taken to destroy Germany as a military power," he wrote that night in his diary. But he admitted to being far more worried by the leaders' agreement to "dismember" postwar Germany than their questionable agreement regarding Polish elections. "These three men, who together control the most powerful military force ever assembled, sitting about a round table in the Crimea with their military and political staffs, have agreed to disarm and dismember Germany, to destroy its industry that is capable of manufacturing war material, to transfer territory from Germany to Poland that will necessitate the deportation of the survivors of between seven and ten million [German] inhabitants thereof, and to exact reparations in kind and in forced labor that will practically reduce the present highly industrialized Germany to the status of two or more agricultural states," he noted of what he took away from the conference's decision.[3] In the long term this, though a gross exaggeration of the Declaration, did not bode well, in Leahy's conservative view, despite the welcome cooperation between the triumvirate's militaries.

"While the German nation had in this barbarous war of conquest deserved all the punishment that can be administered," Leahy allowed, "the proposed peace," nevertheless, "seems to me a frightening 'sowing of dragon's teeth' that carries germs of an appalling war of revenge at some time in the distant future," under another Hitler-like tyrant. "I do not know of any other way to punish this nation of highly intelligent, highly reproductive, and basically military minded people for their war crimes, but the prospect of their reaction in desperation at some time in the more or less distant future is frightening," the admiral confessed. And while the prospect of a second, future Hitler worried him, the Soviets did also. "One result of enforcing the peace terms accepted at this conference will be to make Russia the dominant power in Europe, which in itself carries a certainty of future international disagreements and prospects of another war."[4] By actively encouraging Russia to become a responsible global superpower, the civilized nations of the West were taking a huge gamble.

Like Kennan, Leahy had grave concerns about the United Nations organization—the "United Nations Association to Preserve Peace," as he mockingly called the President's nascent body. Far from applauding the President's late-conference switch to supporting France on the forthcoming UN Security Council, Admiral Leahy deplored, moreover, the "fiction that France is a great nation." Though Stalin had agreed to the President's recommendation, it would lead, in Leahy's opinion, to the UN's inevitable "disintegration," since France would then have veto power in its Security Council. And France, under de Gaulle, could be counted upon to be irritating, if not impossible to deal with. It would simply destroy the effectiveness of the UN that Leahy had, in "great hope," initially relied upon.[5]

In short, Admiral Leahy was not sanguine—though Field Marshal Brooke, on the British bench, was surprisingly contented by the conference's results. "A satisfactory feeling that the conference is finished and has on the whole been as satisfactory as could be hoped for, and certainly a most friendly one," Brooke had already jotted in his diary in his slashing, emphatic green pen as chief of the Imperial General Staff on February 9, 1945, before leaving Yalta and the Crimea the next morning, together with all the military chiefs of staff.[6] Photographs and film, including color film, had duly been taken outside; their work was done.

And the President? His *pulsus alternans* had miraculously "subsided," Dr. Bruenn later recalled. His blood pressure was passable (for him), and his facial coloration had gotten somewhat better.[7] He didn't look well in the photographs, in fact looked ten years older than either Stalin or Churchill, but in some respects he looked the most seigneurial of the three, with a commanding presence—his hair having turned white, but his demeanor almost monumental, his eyebrows pronounced and his jaw firm as, with an arm resting on the side of his chair in the Livadia courtyard, he held a cigarette between his elegant fingers, and his other hand, placed upon his thigh, drew attention to his long, though long-paralyzed, legs.

He had gotten pretty much all he'd counted on. When, at the final dinner at the Vorontsov Palace, the Prime Minister had begged for more time—a further day for debate over Poland—the President had simply said no, he could stay no longer, since he had "three Kings" to meet in the Middle East on his way back home — Ibn Saud, king of Saudi Arabia; Haile Selassie, the emperor of Ethiopia; and King Farouk of Egypt.

This was true; but it was not the real reason. The fact was, he did not think he would get more from Stalin over Poland, especially after Stalin's concession regarding France, and Greece; nor did he think, in all honesty, he could summon the energy and concentration necessary to try.

In some ways it had been a marvel the President had survived nine long days of discussion and argument. Thanks to digitalis and his no-visitor regime, he had kept going somehow. "We certainly put the clamps on him by cutting down on his activities for the next 24 hours," Bruenn recalled of the crisis on the night of February 8 — and it had succeeded.[8]

Churchill's doctor later referred in his diary (much doctored before publication) to the President's "decrepitude" at Yalta — but Moran had not been present himself during a single one of the plenary meetings, or the dinners. Bohlen's minutes, by contrast, testified to the way the President had steered the plenaries toward his preferred ends, and the extent to which Stalin had deferred to him — the Soviet dictator determined to deny Hitler the chance of splitting the Allies, and therefore willing to sign the Declaration on Liberated Europe and accommodate the President's idea of a postwar United Nations system. For these concessions the Soviet Union would, the President assured him, continue to get American Lend-Lease assistance in rebuilding its country and economy.

"I'm in the last stretch of the conference," the President had written on the last day at Livadia to his loyal cousin Daisy, "& though the P.M. meetings are long and tiring I'm *really all right*," he'd claimed, "& it has been I think a real success. I either work or sleep! I am in the palace of the Czar!" he'd added — tickled pink by the unlikeliness of such regal accommodations, in a communist country.[9]

Thus the Yalta Conference duly wrapped up — the President handing to Stalin the version of the joint communiqué which his staff had typed up, and the dictator approving and ticking each of its nine paragraphs.[10] With that done, the three world leaders bade each other goodbye. The President thanked Stalin once again for his Crimean hospitality, and gifts (vodka, caviar, etc.) were exchanged, as well as decorations for the military commanders. Then "Stalin, like some genie, just disappeared," Churchill's daughter Sarah noted in astonishment in a letter home.[11]

The President likewise disappeared — leaving the Livadia Palace by car at 4:00 p.m., bound for Sevastopol, where it had been arranged he would board the USS *Catoctin*, dine, and get a good night's rest before his onward flight aboard the Sacred Cow to Egypt, where the USS *Quincy* was moored in the

Great Bitter Lake. "Three hours after the last handshake," Churchill's daughter noted, "Yalta was deserted."[12]

"I am a bit exhausted but really all right," the President wrote home to Eleanor that night, before turning in.[13] It wasn't true. He was very far from "all right." With the help of Harry Hopkins — who was convinced the conference had been a triumph for the Western Allies — he now intended to sail home very slowly from the Great Bitter Lake. This would give him time to recover from the stress of the meetings, and to prepare with Hopkins, aboard the USS *Quincy*, the presentation he'd have to give to Congress on his return, in hope of securing backing for the April 25 inaugural meeting of the United Nations organization in San Francisco.

Hopkins was by then more ill than President Roosevelt. Unable to withstand the car journey to Sevastopol owing to his dysentery, he was driven to Simferopol, and from there he was conveyed by wooden Pullman train to Saki, more dead than alive, to meet the President at the airfield.[14] General Watson, the President's army aide, became desperately sick during the drive, and though there was grilled steak for all on the *Catoctin*, he suffered a heart attack that, along with a "serious prostate problem," rendered him comatose. He was only kept alive, in fact, Dr. Bruenn recalled, with oxygen.[15]

For Roosevelt things were not much better. "The President had a ghastly night and I think it affected his health," Harriman would later recall, owing to the fact that his cabin was overheated, although Dr. Bruenn recollected no specific medical crisis aboard the *Catoctin*, apart from that of General Watson. In any event it was an exhausted and debilitated American presidential team, despite its summit achievement, that assembled at Saki airfield at 10:30 the next morning, February 12, 1945, to board the Sacred Cow. The President appeared to most people to be completely spent. One army planner who'd seen him during the conference later noted how "gaunt" he'd looked — "his eyes sunken deep in his lined face; he looked very tired and ill, as though he were existing on pure iron determination to see the war to the end."[16]

It was an apt description. "He looked ghastly, sort of dead and dug up," another U.S. diplomat, Carmel Opie, would note.[17] Even the comforts of the USS *Quincy*, which the President boarded after being driven the seventeen miles from RAF Deversoir airfield, northeast of Cairo, on the afternoon of February 12, didn't help — his days now filled with the meetings he'd arranged with King Ibn Saud, Emperor Haile Selassie, King Farouk — and Winston Churchill, who insisted they meet once again, in Alexandria harbor, on February 15.

The President had asked General Eisenhower to join them, but with the final Allied offensive having started in inauspiciously wet weather in Holland on February 8, Ike had had to decline — not only a sign of the supreme commander's anxious focus on the imminent Allied crossing of the Rhine, but an indication that the war, in its final stages, would now be the province of the generals, no longer the Commander in Chief. In a cable drafted by Admiral Leahy, the President thus responded that he was "following your grand offensive with the greatest attention," and "shall always welcome a statement from you of what we can do to help and how you plan the future."[18]

With General Watson belowdecks on life support, and Harry Hopkins resembling death only slightly warmed up, the cruiser had the air of a hospital ship rather than a war vessel. Churchill brought Lord Cherwell with him, for he was anxious to talk about possible use of the atom bomb, as well as Britain's right to develop its own atomic program after the war. The President "made no objection of any kind," Churchill later recalled.[19]

The President had, in truth, now become simply too weak to do more than follow the gist of conversation much of the time. As Admiral Alan Kirk, commander of U.S. naval forces in the Mediterranean, who met the President when the *Quincy* put in at Algiers several days later, remarked to a colleague: it was "really a ship of death and everyone responsible in encouraging that man to go to Yalta has done a disservice to the United States and ought to be shot."[20]

Churchill later described their final meeting more elegiacally. "I felt that he had a slender contact with life. I was not to see him again. We bade affectionate farewells."[21]

84

The End of Hitler's Dreams

IN BERLIN, as the Yalta Conference had continued, there had been only gloom. Day after day the mood had become steadily more anxious — indeed the longer the summit had gone on, the more concerned Dr. Goebbels had become. The conference had not collapsed, as he and the Führer had assumed it would; on the contrary, its very duration spelled doom for the Third Reich.

The Führer at first refused to believe it. "Coalition wars never survive the coalitions with which they start," Hitler airily informed Goebbels; "it's possible that overnight the whole war picture could change completely, according to the political and military situation."[1] He was confident, he assured Goebbels, that with the Wehrmacht forces he was withdrawing from other conquests such as Norway, he would in a matter of "days" be in a position to launch counteroffensives against the Russians on the Eastern Front. On the Western Front, meanwhile, the miserable winter weather had inundated the ground, so that the Allies were effectively stalemated; the Wehrmacht merely had to stand firm there. Shorter lines to defend, he now claimed (in contrast to his military strategy for the past several years), meant the Wehrmacht held the advantage.

Goebbels attempted, as always, to be encouraging. Tentatively he suggested that Mr. Churchill might now be open to negotiation, given growing concerns in certain quarters in England over the future domination of Europe by the Soviets. Hitler, however, shook his head; it was too soon for this, he said. The military situation must first favor Germany, then would be the time to talk. One must be patient; the British, in frustration, might even resort to nerve gas, to hasten Germany's end, he speculated. In that case he was determined that the quarter-million British and American POWs currently in German captivity were, in reprisal, to be slaughtered, "en masse."

Gas?

The world war that the Führer had launched, along with the mass murder of Jewish, political, partisan, and other *Untermenschen*, had now come full circle: "gas warfare" an almost inevitable extension in Hitler's eyes. For him hostilities had now "reached a level of national German suffering," thanks to Allied bombing, the Führer claimed, "where one would be forced" to turn to means such as the execution of POWs — "the only thing left that can impress the British and the Americans."[2]

Much the same was being discussed in Tokyo, where biological warfare had already been tested in China; also, in the Philippines, where General MacArthur had felt he must liberate Allied prisoners in Manila by U.S. paratroop forces before Admiral Iwabuchi could use them as human shields, and perhaps slaughter them.

"The Fuhrer is still convinced that the enemy coalition will fall apart this year," Goebbels had nevertheless noted. "We just have to hold on, defend ourselves and stand." The Führer "believes unwaveringly in our coming victory, albeit without knowing exactly where and how it can be wrought," he recorded on February 11, 1945 — the very moment when the President was leaving the Livadia Palace with the nine signed Allied agreements, plus the still-secret Soviet undertaking to assist the United States in defeating Japan, as soon as the Third Reich surrendered.

Trying not to sound defeatist, Goebbels had suggested to the Führer it might be time at least for Germany to put out a "clear statement of its war aims" — *ein klares Kriegsziel vor Augen stellen* — if the Führer wanted to rally fascist Europe.[3] It was too late, however. The announcement of the Yalta communiqué on February 12, the next day, took the wind out of the propaganda minister's prospective sails — in fact the Allied document left Goebbels utterly deflated, as much by its length and detail as by its unity and firmness. The nine separate sections of the joint agreement covered not only how the Allies proposed to end the war, with specified zones of occupation and the treatment of a defeated Third Reich, but also how they would establish a new security system for the postwar. Having brought such chaos and suffering to the world, Germany would not be allowed to take part in this, at least in the form Hitler had intended; it was to be completely demilitarized as a menace to mankind.

One by one Goebbels listed the communiqué's themes pertaining to Germany, beginning with the Third Reich's unconditional surrender. Four zones of Allied military occupation: Soviet, American, British, and French; total German disarmament and the destruction of its warmaking potential; an Allied commission in control in Berlin; the dissolution of the German high command; the arrest of German war criminals and their punishment; the complete denazification of the country (the Nazi Party weeded out "root and branch"); massive reparations to be paid; "provisional" governments in the liberated countries to be followed by free elections and the wholesale shifting of Poland's new borders westward, taking a part of German East Prussia . . .

Hitler's dream of an inevitable breakdown in the Allied coalition had thus turned to dust. If Germany was defeated in the next months, as seemed likely, his great war to expand the nation's frontiers and establish control of all Europe would result not only in ruin, but in a smaller, defeated, and disarmed Germany. It was a prognosis Hitler could not bear to think about. He instructed Goebbels never to speak of reaching out to either the Russians or the Western Allies again. It could only demoralize German troops and civilians at home, he warned, in their hour of suffering.

The two princes of darkness continued to speak together for a while in the bunker. "He looks to me rather tired and sick," Goebbels admitted frankly in his diary. "He tells me he didn't sleep much last night. It's because he is working so hard. The last fortnight he's carried huge responsibilities that would have felled any ordinary mortal."[4]

Could a German counteroffensive possibly succeed in staving off the inevitable, as the Führer promised?

The Ardennes offensive had initially stunned the Allies — but the massive armored assault by three Wehrmacht armies had required *months* of secret preparation, had involved almost half a million troops, and had been launched in weather that precluded Allied air defense.

As Reich propaganda minister, nevertheless, Goebbels had no option but to maintain his faith in the leader for whom he'd sacrificed his first hopes as a novelist, and for whom he'd dedicated his whole career of unmitigated evil. In four or five days, the Führer had reassured him, German armored attacks would be ready to be launched on the Eastern Front. Meantime there was to be no letup on the Western Front. If the Wehrmacht could just succeed in striking a significant blow on the enemy "on one front or the other," Goebbels summarized, "then we'll be able to talk."[5]

There would be no talk, however. The Thousand-Year Reich, begun with such military fanfare, was almost finished. Yalta had betokened its end. And with it, Goebbels's and Hitler's lives.

PART ELEVEN

Warm Springs

85

King Odysseus

SIX WEEKS LATER, at 4:00 p.m. on March 29, 1945, the President boarded the *Ferdinand Magellan* for what would be his final journey. Destination: the Little White House, Warm Springs, Georgia.

Once again the President was exhausted — indeed by rights he ought to have put down his burden and resigned, now that he had gotten the endgame of the war agreed with his British and Russian allies. On March 7 enterprising U.S. troops had seized the Ludendorff railroad bridge across the Rhine River at Remagen, and had held it against repeated counterattack; then on March 23 three vast Allied armies under Field Marshal Montgomery — First Allied Airborne Army, Ninth U.S. Army, and Second British Army — launched a series of coordinated assault crossings north and south of Wesel, threatening the Ruhr, the industrial engine of the Third Reich. In the Pacific, the crucial island of Iwo Jima had been invaded and cleared of Japanese troops in hand-to-hand combat by March 16, providing fighter air cover for B-29 bombers over Japan. A second, major assault landing on Okinawa was scheduled to take place on April 1, aimed at putting ashore a quarter of a million men.

As U.S. commander in chief the President had done his work; like King Odysseus, he had returned from Yalta and deserved, surely, a peaceful life after his travails. His enemies were reeling and close to defeat — Manila, capital of the Philippines, liberated on March 3, Tokyo firebombed on March 9.

Like Odysseus, however, the President seemed driven to complete his victory by ensuring peace in the aftermath — telling Polly Delano and Daisy Suckley, his two companion-carers, on April 6 he aimed now to retire "by next year," as Daisy noted in her diary, "after he gets the peace organization started."[1]

Daisy was skeptical. Not even the President really believed this, she acknowledged. "I don't believe he thinks he will be *able* to carry on," she recorded, for it seemed a miracle he was still alive. Polly Delano did not believe it, either. On February 28, when Polly had first seen the President again, after his return from Yalta, "she didn't think," in all frankness, "he would live to go to the San Francisco conference," scheduled for April 25.[2] Nor had there been much improvement thereafter. To Daisy herself the President had looked "terribly badly — so tired that every word seems an effort," she'd noted while they were still in Hyde Park on March 25.[3] The slow train journey and his first days spent in Georgia without visitors, away from the stress of Washington, had seen him recover a little; in fact, what had seemed like a deathwatch gradually looked slightly less forbidding.

Not enough, however, to convince Daisy, his loyal and devoted friend. "On thinking further, one realizes that if he cannot, physically, carry on, he will *have* to resign. There is no possible sense in his killing himself by slow degrees, the while not filling his job," she confessed. "Far better," she reflected on April 6, to hand over the reins of office while he could, and avoid the specter of a stroke, like President Wilson, when he wouldn't even "be *able* to function."[4] He was, after all, still managing to sign congressional bills as they were sent from the White House. He could initial cables that Admiral Leahy, remaining at his post in the White House, drafted, on the President's behalf, to be sent from the Map Room — messages to Churchill, Stalin, MacArthur, Eisenhower, and others. Even, in fact, to dictate a few letters, at the Little White House, to his private secretary, Bill Hassett, or his office secretaries, Grace Tully and Dorothy Brady.

Essentially, though, it was a sham — as everyone close to the President knew. He had no military aides or political advisers with him now, only doctors — one of whom later admitted that the President "began to look bad. His color was poor, and he appeared to be very tired," with questions being asked about possible dementia, in the wake of small strokes. It was, however, a tribute to his long and kingly leadership that no one dared tell the President he simply must prepare to step down, and should immediately begin helping his vice president, former senator Harry Truman, to assume the mantle of command.

"He is slipping away from us and no earthly power can keep him here," Bill Hassett confessed to Dr. Bruenn on March 30 when they arrived in Warm Springs.[5] Bruenn had asked what made Hassett so sure, given the President's survival since his fatal diagnosis twelve months before.

Normally so discreet and proper, the stalwart private secretary said he understood Bruenn's Hippocratic oath to keep a patient alive to the bitter end. For himself, he could no longer maintain the fiction. He'd wondered already if it would happen the previous November, after the President's election victory; now, however, he was certain. "To all the staff, to the family, and with the Boss himself I have maintained the bluff; but I am convinced that there is no help for him."[6]

The two men — doctor and secretary — were close to tears. For a year, since the spring of 1944, Hassett had known the President was in trouble —

especially the previous July when Roosevelt hadn't acted "like a man who cared a damn about the election." Only Governor Dewey's campaign barbs had roused him — getting "his Dutch up," as Hassett explained to Bruenn. "That did the trick. That was the turning point to my mind" — the President determined to fight, especially in contesting Dewey's wild lies, such as his claim the President opposed demobilization. Yet "I could not but notice his increasing weariness as I handled his papers with him, particularly at Hyde Park, trip after trip. He was always willing to go through the day's routine, but there was less and less talk about all manner of things — fewer Hyde Park stories, politics, books, pictures. The old zest was going." In his opinion, Hassett told Bruenn on the evening of March 30, 1945, "the Boss" was now "beyond all human resources" — even those of Dr. Bruenn.[7]

The President wasn't quite willing to depart the world yet, Hassett now found. He seemed absolutely determined to attend the inaugural meeting of the United Nations organization in San Francisco on April 25, to which he would take the train, he said, spending a day in the Golden Gate City. The UN was, after all, his creation, which he had envisioned and nurtured since 1942; and, with the Soviet Union now a promised member, irrespective of whether the two extra Soviet republics were granted seats, the organization and its proposed Security Council were crucial to the President's concept of a new world order.

Roosevelt had another reason to keep on living, one which the bookworm Hassett — aware that his diary, kept since shortly after Pearl Harbor, might one day be worth publishing — hesitated to set down in ink: namely that the dying president, despite having lost "twenty-five pounds" in the past few weeks and looking now "worn, weary, exhausted,"[8] was surprisingly happy.

86

In the Well of Congress

THE PRESIDENT'S ENTOURAGE at Warm Springs were not the only ones on deathwatch — or dying. Harry Hopkins had felt so ill he'd refused to return to the United States by ship, insisting on flying instead to Marrakesh — forcing the President to cable for Judge Rosenman to fly out from Washington, if possible, and join him on the USS *Quincy* in Algiers on February 18.

The President had been more than disappointed; Eisenhower too busy to meet him,[1] de Gaulle refusing his invitation (incensed he had not been invited to Yalta), and General Pa Watson in a coma, belowdecks. "All in all it was a sorry ship," Rosenman described.[2]

Interviewing both Hopkins and Bohlen in Hopkins's cabin, the judge — who was charged with helping to draft the President's forthcoming speech to Congress — had done his best to piece together an idea of what had happened at the Yalta summit, using Bohlen's minutes and a special memorandum Bohlen had drawn up for him, too. Thinking he could draft the speech in twenty-four hours, go over it with the President, get it typed, and then disembark at Gibraltar and fly back to Washington directly, the President's loyal speechwriter "soon saw that was going to be impossible, and after the first few hours I gave up the idea and resigned myself to the long trip home."[3]

To Rosenman the situation was worse than sad. "I had never seen him look so tired. He had lost a great deal more weight; he was listless and apparently uninterested in conversation — he was all burnt out."[4] When the ailing Hopkins had come to the President's quarters to say farewell at Algiers, the President had merely muttered "Goodbye," and turned away, as if he did not know who Hopkins was. "All the buoyancy of the campaign, all the excitement of arranging and preparing for the conference, had disappeared," wrote Rosenman; "in their place was gray fatigue — sheer exhaustion." Yalta had been the "climactic project of his life — to arrange for a permanent peace." Yet despite spending the subsequent week with the President aboard the USS *Quincy* —

lunching and dining with Roosevelt every day — Rosenman had been unable to get the President to speak an intelligible word on Yalta — the President either reading, sleeping, or sitting on deck with Anna, his daughter, if weather permitted, "or just smoking and staring at the horizon."[5]

Two days out from Algiers, General Watson died of a cerebral hemorrhage. Even that event did not appear to greatly impact the President, who seemed either vacant or in depression. Asked later if the President had shown any grief, Dr. Bruenn said, frankly, "No. He showed what you would if a good friend of yours passed on. He felt very sorry and reminisced a bit about their past and so forth," but nothing more.[6] In fact, as Rosenman recalled, Pa Watson's death had merely "increased the President's reluctance to go to work."[7] He had simply left Rosenman, Leahy, and Anna to work together on the proposed speech, slated to be delivered the day after he reached the White House, on March 1.

In Rosenman's opinion the result had been a near-catastrophe in terms of presidential leadership. The occasion was to report to Congress and the world the most important achievement of the President's life to date: the creation of the UN and the inevitability of the defeat of Nazi Germany and Japan — his confidence about the latter resting upon the secret agreement with the Russians for their part in the endgame of the war. In the event, the triumphal moment had been reduced, in the well of the House of Representatives at midday on March 1, 1945, to a long, desultory, rambling, often incoherent talk from his wheelchair: the President openly admitting that he had felt too weak to stand upright in his heavy metal braces for the occasion — the first time he'd failed to stand when giving an address to Congress in the Capitol since he became the nation's chief executive, and a shock to many who had never known he was paralyzed from the waist down.

Worse still was the President's mental deterioration. "I was dismayed at the halting, ineffective manner of delivery," Rosenman later recalled. "He ad-libbed a great deal — as frequently as I had ever heard him. Some of his extemporaneous remarks were wholly irrelevant, and some of them almost bordered on the ridiculous," the judge noted, sadly.[8] Many of those who'd listened to the President's address to Congress on radio, Dr. Bruenn admitted, noticed "that his speech was hesitant and that he occasionally appeared to be at a loss for words."[9] He claimed afterwards that he'd "spoken at intervals from memory and 'off the record' and then had slight difficulty in finding the proper place when returning to read the printed words of his address,"[10] but few were convinced. In a speech that was broadcast on national radio, "off the record" was a dubious description.

For his part the British ambassador, Lord Halifax, had found it "rather difficult to hear." What he did hear, however, the one-armed ambassador "did not think" was very good, as he noted in his diary. "There were no fireworks and no surprises in it"; the details had long since been printed in the national press, and there were "no philosophical reflections, such as add quality to a factual narrative," only inconsequential memories.[11]

Mercifully Halifax had learned from Senator Vandenberg that the senator was still enthused with the United Nations idea. The upcoming San Francisco Conference was now attracting much excitement in the press and public. The UN would be established, supported wholeheartedly by Congress — a tribute to the President's great statesmanship. Yet the clear signs of dementia were frightening — deeply distressing those who had witnessed him in his prime, a bare year before.

87

Appeasers Become Warmongers

HAD FRANKLIN ROOSEVELT, like General Pa Watson, died of a cerebral hemorrhage aboard the USS *Quincy*, his stature and reputation might not have suffered as they now did, darkened by his last weeks of life: the sight and sound of the once-lyrical but now wandering, incoherent president of the United States, seated in a wheelchair, finally admitting, on radio and film camera, to being disabled by polio and dependent on heavy metal stilts to stand (a fact hitherto known only to a tiny percentage of the electorate) — leaving people stunned and confused.

Was this the six-foot-three-inch giant of a man — a politician who had successfully stood for reelection a fourth time, as recently as three months ago — they had admired, even when disagreeing with his liberal political agenda? As rumors of still-secret Yalta protocols began to leak out in the days of early March, 1945, there had been no commanding president to shoot down critics — only a dying head of state whom his cabinet and colleagues looked to despairingly for leadership.

Churchill had addressed his own parliament on February 27, two days before the President's speech. The Prime Minister had spoken almost nonstop for two long hours, in sparklingly restored health — and parliamentary authority. He was confident the Yalta summit was a harbinger of peace, he'd declared, for the "impression I brought back from the Crimea, and from all my other contacts, is that Marshal Stalin and the Soviet leaders wish to live in honourable friendship and equality with the western democracies. I feel also that their word is their bond."[1] Using his unsurpassed rhetorical skills he had gotten the House of Commons to approve — or agree not to contest — the "declaration of joint policy agreed to by the three Great Powers at the Crimea Conference," as well as the "new world structure" of the United Nations.

Some of Churchill's own Conservative Party colleagues had hated both ideas — in fact they had forced a vote over an amendment which they'd tabled, regretting "the decision to transfer the territory of an ally [Poland]" to Russia.

The vote itself they duly lost, 396 to 25 — but Churchill, not only a lifelong student of history, but a witness to and maker of it, had been conscious of the irony. As he noted afterwards, drinking with colleagues in the Smoking Room, "The warmongers of the Munich period have now become the appeasers" — such as himself — "while the appeasers have become the warmongers."[2]

It was an apt aperçu. All too soon the Prime Minister would come under increasing attack for his failure to "save" Poland — indeed for this, and his tone-deaf "failures" of government on the domestic front, he and his Conservative Party colleagues would be voted out of office in the British general election four months later.

Though Churchill would be deposed as prime minister, he would at least survive — and "repackaged himself," as the British historian David Reynolds later put it, "as a fierce Cold Warrior with his 'Iron Curtain' speech in March 1946, whereas Roosevelt, being dead, could not retrieve his reputation."[3]

Professor Reynolds was right, in retrospect. The President would not live to "repackage" himself. By March 1945 night had closed in on the President's career — his press secretary, Steve Early, doing everything possible to keep photographers away from the White House, and the press from reporting that the President of the United States was becoming, to all intents and purposes, a passenger aboard the USS *America* — with the War and Navy Departments pretty much taking responsibility for the war's finale.

Perhaps the best insights into the President's condition in his final weeks of life in Washington were noted in diaries that were only made public decades later — namely those of Daisy Suckley and William Lyon Mackenzie King, the prime minister of Canada.

The President had arrived at Hyde Park on Sunday, March 4, 1945, looking "very tired and sleepy," Daisy Suckley had noted. She herself was unsurprised, since he "has had, & is having, an exhausting time seeing people — 'fixing' things which have gotten out of hand during his absence," according to the description he had given her of his nonstop stint at the White House since his return.[4] Daisy's only answer had been to bring back Harry Setaro, the quack doctor or masseur — though both of them knew only real rest could now keep his heart from simply stopping.

The three days at home in Hyde Park had certainly helped. The President returned to Washington on March 8 in good spirits. In the Oval Office he'd seen his vice president, Harry Truman, along with the Senate majority leader, Alben Barkley; Sam Rayburn, the Speaker of the House; and John McCormack, the second-ranking House Democrat: trusting they would finally get the contentious national service bill passed (ensuring enough infantry to continue the war), and Congress lined up to support his United Nations project. He'd also lunched with Admiral Bill Halsey, whom he'd decorated with the

Congressional Medal of Honor. The next day he had felt well enough to give a brief press conference, then had lunch with Admiral Nimitz in the mansion and in the late afternoon, in the Oval Office, discussed with the admiral the latest plans for the eventual seaborne invasion of Japan. And then greeted Mackenzie King, the Canadian prime minister, who had arrived from Ottawa and was going to stay the night.

Mackenzie King was by then already sitting with Eleanor in the mansion — and had been warned by her that he might be shocked by the change in the President's state of health. The President, she said, had been "pretty tired after his journey" to Yalta, and had lost a lot of weight and was looking "pretty thin." Also, she said, there was "the unpleasant side of politics; how ungrateful people were, terrible pressure, etc," on him. "She herself looks a bit older and more worn," King observed in his diary.[5]

Nothing, however, had quite prepared the gentle Canadian premier, who'd known Roosevelt for over forty years, for the man who had now appeared at 5:30 that evening, March 9, 1945.

88

Mackenzie King's Last Visit

WILLIAM LYON MACKENZIE KING had recently turned seventy; Franklin Delano Roosevelt was only sixty-three. As Eleanor's secretary, Malvina Thompson, had left the room, "the President came in in his chair," King described. "When I saw him, I felt deep compassion for him," he admitted, for he was shocked — the face of death upon his longtime liberal friend. "He looked much older; face very much thinner, particularly the lower part. Quite thin. When I went over and shook hands with him, I bent over and kissed him on the cheek. He turned it toward me for the purpose."[1]

It was an affecting moment, almost in the vein of Admiral Nelson and Captain Hardy.

Over the next several days King would talk with Mr. Roosevelt about the President's life; about the Crimea; about recent events; current problems; future hopes. King's nightly dictation to his secretary, Edouard Handy, remains probably the last intimate record of conversations with Franklin Roosevelt by a contemporary of the same political standing.

Mackenzie King had many times been with the President at moments of high decision. It was to King, after all, the President had confided, in December 1943, his decision to pursue the "unconditional surrender" of the Axis powers, a month before he flew to Casablanca — as well as, in confidence, his military strategy, in opposition to his own headstrong Joint Chiefs of Staff, of ensuring American troops and commanders learn how to defeat the Wehrmacht in combat in the Mediterranean *before* launching a cross-Channel invasion in 1944.[2] Also his battles to guard against the threat from Churchill's incessant plans to lose the war or cause it to end in stalemate in 1943, when Churchill had done everything possible to subvert, sabotage, and postpone D-day. King had witnessed in person how, with extraordinary patience and steely consistency, the President had nevertheless prevailed — allowing the United States to take the lead in prosecuting the war against Hitler, and the approach of victory.

For this reason it was all the more galling, in fact tragic, to witness his good friend's spiraling state of health.

The President "got from his chair on to the sofa and asked me to sit beside him," King recorded — with Eleanor on the other side. Roosevelt related the story of Yalta, and of his meeting with Ibn Saud — who had rebuffed all attempts by the President to use his influence to rehouse the million or more Jewish survivors of the Nazi mass-murder program. Rather than put pressure on the people of Palestine, Saud had responded to the President, the Allies should instead give to Jewish survivors land taken from the Germans responsible for the bloodshed in Europe — not from Arabs who had done nothing to deserve more Jewish immigration: millions of refugees whose ancestors had had no connection with Palestine for the past two thousand years. As Harry Hopkins later recalled, the President had been utterly naive to assume he could charm the "born soldier" Ibn Saud to leave Jidda, meet with him on the USS *Quincy*, and change the old warrior's mind. Inevitably, despite all blandishments, including the offer of a private plane and pilot, when the President had pressed the Saudi Arabian king, saying the number of proposed immigrants/ survivors of Nazi death camps was "such a small percentage of the total population of the Arab world," he had gotten the bluntest of answers. Ibn Saud had merely stared at him and "without a smile, said, 'No.'"[3]

It was Ibn Saud's repeated no, and with zero indication he would ever change his mind — in fact would happily go to war with the Jews rather than permit another immigrant influx, especially when the United States itself had curtailed further Jewish immigration at thirty thousand — that had caused the President, in an aside during his subsequent address to Congress, to confess that, "on the problem of Arabia, I learned more about that problem — the Muslim problem, the Jewish problem — by talking with Ibn Saud for five minutes than I could have learned in the exchange of two or three dozen letters."[4]

"I asked him about Stalin," Mackenzie King also recorded that night. "He mentioned that Churchill had done about 90% of the talking at the Conference," but that "Stalin had quite a sense of humor. That once when Churchill was making a long speech, Stalin put up his hand to the side of his face, turned to the President and winked one of his eyes as much as to say: there he is talking again." The humor, however, had been a good sign, in the President's view — "Stalin's relations and Churchill's are much friendlier in every way than they were," Roosevelt had reflected. Stalin's humor, in a man known to be merciless in the way he ruled Russia, was beguiling, the President admitted, saying he "liked him. Found him very direct. Later told me he did not think there was anything to fear particularly from Stalin in the future," outside of the Soviet Union and its cordon sanitaire. "He had a big programme himself to deal with": rebuilding the country and its economy following the devastation wreaked by the German invasion and Hitler's *Untermenschen* program. "He also told me privately at night that Stalin would likely break off with the Japanese but wished to be sure to be able to have his divisions up to the front near Manchuria before taking that formal step," and that in the meantime he would authorize preparations to be made, in secret, to "give the Allies bases to operate from."[5]

In terms of his military strategy, then, the President was confident the war against Germany was almost won — and Japan's fate also sealed. "News of the American First Army having crossed the Rhine" at Remagen, released that day, had caused King to think it "the greatest day since the war began." The President clearly had no anxieties on that account. "I asked him about what he thought about the duration of the war. He said he has not ventured to make any statement," in public, "but he, himself, felt that before the end of April, as far as Europe was concerned, it should be over." Japan "would collapse very soon thereafter. Spoke of possibly 3 months."[6]

Such accurate predictions, almost to the week, showed that however ill he was, the President had been *au fait* with the military situation, despite the death of General Watson, his army aide, who'd been replaced by Colonel Park, Watson's assistant; moreover that he was completely realistic. Still, the gentle Canadian hadn't been fooled as to the President's deteriorating condition — not only physically, but mentally.

Upstairs, after dinner, Anna and Eleanor had left the two leaders to talk together in the President's study — Eleanor having begged King to stay for two or three days, since she was leaving the next day for Philadelphia with her companion, Lorena Hickok. The President, she'd admitted, would be alone — implying he would be without company thereafter. King, who had planned on going to Williamsburg to work on the major speech he was slated to give to the Canadian parliament, was torn.

"The President and I then went into the circular room. He asked me to sit beside him on the sofa. I suggested it might be easier for him if I sat opposite so I pulled up a chair. We talked steadily from 8.30 until 20 past 11 when I looked at the clock." Roosevelt, however, "said he was not tired; was enjoying the talk. We talked then until a quarter of an hour of midnight."[7]

The subjects had included S-1. "When I asked about certain weapons that might be used," King dictated coyly to his secretary before finally going to bed, the President "said he thought that would be in shape by August; that the difficulty was knowing just how to have the material used over the country itself" — Japan.[8]

Having been the father of the atom bomb, the President, in other words, was willing, if necessary, to use it.

• • •

Given that the atom bomb, outside of the Los Alamos complex, was a secret known only to a handful of people other than the President and Prime Minister Mackenzie King, and given that the secret had not been shared thus far with the Soviets, King had asked Roosevelt directly about his view on that matter.

In answer, the President "said he thought the Russians had been experimenting and knew something about what was being done."[9] Henry Stimson, the war secretary, thought the time had not come to share progress, though . . .

The President had thought this the wrong way to proceed. *Informing* the Russians privately about advances being made on the bomb would demonstrate coalition solidarity — and ensure the Soviets not underestimate American resolve to stand by the Yalta agreements on the zones of occupation of Germany. It would, in short, exemplify his fifth cousin's famous maxim: "Speak softly and carry a big stick." The President thus "thought the time had come to tell them how far developments had gone. Churchill was opposed to doing this" — for economic reasons. "Churchill is considering the possible commercial use later," the President explained[10] — on the grounds that the development could, if the Soviets were excluded, be kept as an Anglo-American monopoly.

King had found himself disappointed by Winston's cupidity. "I said it seemed to me that if the Russians discovered later that some things had been held back from them, it would be unfortunate" in terms of future international relations. Moreover, withholding the information might even threaten Russia's preparations to fight the major Japanese army and air forces in Manchuria.

Whatever might be decided on the information side, however, Roosevelt was pleased by the latest reports he had from Los Alamos, where "great progress was being made at present" in bringing the bomb to readiness, the President confided to King.[11] With the Russians threatening to engage the Japanese army in Manchuria, the Japanese government might eventually see the light and surrender without the need to drop it.

Which left the United Nations.

If the atom bomb was America's defining contribution to modern warfare — thwarting Nazi Germany (and the Japanese) in the race to develop such a weapon of mass destruction — the United Nations organization was to be the President's greatest potential contribution to postwar world peace, Mackenzie King noted.

"Speaking of the San Francisco Conference, he thought it might last a month. That it would be a mistake if it lasted longer. Work would be done by half a dozen main committees. Some things might be left over" for subsequent decision. "He himself would go to the conference to open it but would not stay. I asked if Churchill was likely to come over. He thought not" — the Prime Minister never having been much of a supporter of the UN idea, as opposed to "spheres of influence."[12]

Cordell Hull, who had worked so hard to promote the concept of the new organization, had been in hospital at Bethesda for almost five months, an invalid; it was unlikely he would be well enough to go to San Francisco. Edward Stettinius, Hull's successor, would therefore take charge — he should probably go to Ottawa now, the President had suggested, to discuss possible subsequent, post–San Francisco UN locations — perhaps the Azores to address European affairs, Canada for North American, Hawaii for Pacific matters.

"I pointed out that there might be considerable difficulty" in using multiple locations, King recorded. The permanent staff would be larger than the current number of officials involved in the Dumbarton Oaks talks and committees, and they would need accommodation, making diverse locales difficult, "particularly in relation to the Assembly." Whatever location was chosen, the President had remarked, "Geneva had not a good name" — seat of the ill-fated League of Nations. Perhaps naming one location subsequent to San Francisco would, for the moment, be worth considering, King had suggested.[13]

It was clear that the two politicians, who'd done so much to infuse the Allies with ideals beyond patriotism — ideals that men and women could fight for, not simply against — were extraordinarily close. Not even King had credited, though, how much the President trusted him as a personal friend — as the next few days would show.

The next morning King had once again spent time with the President at lunch in the mansion and then, privately, in his study — Roosevelt telling him more about his plans to visit not only England, but Holland and France, probably in June 1945. He intended to go "from the ship to Buckingham Palace and stay there, and then drive with the King through the streets of London and at the week-end, spend time with Churchill at Chequers. Also giving an address before the Houses of Parliament and get the freedom of the city of London." Then, he'd said, he would inspect American troops "on the battlefields," followed by "a visit to Queen Wilhelmina in Holland," where he would "stay at the Hague. From there, he would perhaps pay a visit to Paris" — though in view of General de Gaulle's prickly nature he "would not say more about that till the moment came."[14]

The Canadian prime minister was amazed by such ambitious plans for such a clearly sick, in fact dying, president. "It is clear to me from this that he and Churchill have worked out plans quite clearly contemplating that the war will be over before June," King noted — something that would have important political implications both for King himself and for Winston Churchill, in terms of new elections. Meantime the President's trip to Europe would be a "sort of triumphal close to the war itself."

"This in some ways is the most important information he has given me thus far," King dictated to his diary, with respect to his own career.

And with respect to the President's? How much longer could Franklin possibly go on? The President had spoken of a time "three years from now when I am through with here" — for he was, he said, thinking of starting a "newspaper which will be the size of four pages of foolscap." It would be "something like what is used for daily news on board ship. Have no editorials; just give the main news truthfully" — an aim he saw as crucial to the survival of democracy. "By means of radio photography, have it distributed in every city and town of America and sold for one cent."[15]

King had scarcely been able to believe his ears. Three *years* hence? To combat right-wing political agendas, and promote reliable information? Was he dreaming?

Charles Bohlen, now acting as liaison between the President and the State Department, observed that the President's health was becoming dire — Roosevelt's hands "shook so that he had difficulty holding a telegram. His weariness and general lassitude were apparent to all," yet even for Bohlen loss of the President was unthinkable. Thus "the thought did not occur to me that he was near death," Bohlen later recalled. "Although I was in the White House daily, I did not become sufficiently intimate with anyone there to talk to him about the President's health."[16] Admiral Leahy was too remote a figure; Hopkins was in hospital; the engine of U.S. government was working, fitfully but nevertheless working, in Bohlen's view — and that of many others.

In King's eyes, it was a conundrum. For all that the President seemed to have such a tenuous, precarious hold on life, he had, after all, traveled fourteen thousand miles to the Crimea and back in just the last month. This made King's journey by railcar from Ottawa, and need for quiet in which to prepare his report to Parliament in Ottawa, look pretty tame. "I confess he seemed to be in better shape physically than I had thought when I saw him yesterday," King allowed in his diary on March 10 — though he had to admit that much of what the President shared with him was given in broad brushstrokes, the President lacking the mental energy or even the capacity, now, to go into sharp detail, or complexity.

"I find he repeats himself a great deal," King had added. The President had, for example, shared with King his reflections on Jimmy Byrnes, his top civil administrator, currently guiding the national service bill through Congress. In the President's telling, the "renegade" Catholic possessed a brilliant mind, but had married a Presbyterian lady, which in the 1944 election would have lost one or two million votes on that score alone, had he won the Democratic Party vice presidential nomination. The next day the President had repeated the same account. Another repetition was the story he'd heard tell of Winston Churchill bathing naked at Miami, and "defying the waves for rolling him over" — determined nevertheless to go on and swim, before admitting defeat: a paradigm, he felt, of the Prime Minister's obstinacy. "Tonight he repeated the same story without apparently recollecting that he had told it last night," King noted — the President's wife, Eleanor, his daughter Anna, and even his son-in-law John Boettiger, too "embarrassed" to say "anything" to stop him. "There have been several of these occurrences. Indeed some of the stories he is telling he has told me on previous occasions. This of course is a sign of failing memory. I noticed in looking at his eyes very closely, that one eye has a clear, direct look — that is the left eye as he faces one. The right one is not quite on the square with the left one but has a little sort of stigmata appearance in the centre."

The President had seemed to be losing connection with reality, too, at times — claiming personal or sole credit for things in a way he'd never done before — such as the design of the Navy Hospital in Bethesda, and the United Nations.[17]

After dinner, to which Ambassador Robert Murphy was invited together with one of de Gaulle's young Free French officers, Jean Woirin, they had watched newsreel film of the President's trip to Yalta; his address to Congress; discovery of "German massacres in Poland," such as the concentration camps at Auschwitz and Chelmno; and "the landing of marines at Iwo Jima" — the pictures amazingly realistic, "being photographs actually taken during the battle. They surpassed anything I had seen," King recorded — the Japanese determined to kill ten Americans for every Japanese soldier who died, either in combat or by suicide, rather than live with the dishonor of defeat after failing their emperor's orders to conquer all Asia.

The incendiary bombing of Tokyo, the Japanese capital, the night before had shocked even the President, who "told me tonight that the destruction had been terrible, a big part of the city had been burnt out."[18]

King — by nature and religion a pacifist, and thus a reluctant wartime prime minister — had been unsurprised by the news, or its necessity. Earlier that day he'd been warned by the acting secretary of state, Joseph Grew, visiting the President, that "there will be very hard fighting still" to defeat the Japanese: the toughest enemy the United States had ever faced. Grew, who had been ambassador to Japan at the time of Pearl Harbor, had said, however, "he thought it was best not to destroy the Emperor at present, as he was the only person who could issue a rescript which would lead to a conclusion of the war," King noted — a recommendation the President had taken seriously. More U.S. Marines were being killed than Japanese defenders in the ongoing battle for Iwo Jima; "each island would be more difficult to take than the last," Grew had warned[19] — just as, in Europe, fanatical elements of the Wehrmacht seemed still willing to fight to the death rather than admit defeat in Holland, where they were threatening to breach the seawalls and dikes that would ruin the land for generations if the Allies dared come a step closer.

Would the war thus *really* be finished in Europe by the end of April, and in the Pacific by August? King had wondered. The President assured King it would be. He had faith in the supreme commander he'd appointed, and in Eisenhower's plans. Yet he himself had seemed almost disconnected from events — as if watching them unfold rather than directing them, now. And nowhere had this been more evident than in the brouhaha over Operation Sunrise.

89

Operation Sunrise

FOR SOME HISTORIANS the military fracas that arose between the Allies in March 1945 presaged the Cold War. If so, there was little the President, as commander in chief, could do, in his condition, other than watch — and try not to despair. Secretary Stimson and General Marshall, together with Admiral King, were, to all intents and purposes, now running the war — from the culmination of the S-1 Manhattan Project to final efforts, on land, at sea, and in the air, to obtain the unconditional surrender of Germany and Japan by conventional means.

Inevitably, perhaps, the first intimations that the Germans were getting closer to surrendering had come from an SS general in benighted Italy — the country that had for so long been the source of strategic strife, misunderstanding, and contested Allied plans in conducting the war.

General Joe McNarney, commanding U.S. Army Forces in the Mediterranean, had sent a series of messages to the Pentagon regarding secret German offers to surrender, in defiance of Hitler's orders. On March 11, Secretary Stimson had been informed — General Marshall being away from the office, moving house. And when Stimson learned that Winston Churchill had deliberately become involved, in fact had informed the Russians of the offers, the "McNarney Affair" had turned into more than a military surrender offer in Italy. It became a deeply divisive, explosive issue: causing Stimson at 12:30 p.m. on March 11 to go see the President in person.

Unknown to Stimson, sadly, was the fact that the Nazis were playing the Western Allies, including Allen Dulles, the head of the OSS office in Switzerland, for fools — claiming the surrender offer was coming from Field Marshal Kesselring, the Wehrmacht commander of Army Group C in Italy (and Kesselring's replacement, General Vietinghoff, once Kesselring was ordered to take command of the Wehrmacht on the Western Front). In reality the "feeler" was coming from a particularly odious Waffen-SS general, Karl Wolff: a die-hard Nazi seeking (and succeeding) to save his own skin by "offering" to get his former boss, Heinrich Himmler, commander in chief of the SS, to parley with the Allies.[1] With Hitler's secret consent, Himmler was working to sow discord between the Allies, and get the Western nations to join with the Nazis in fighting the Soviets. His operation was called, appropriately, Operation Wool.

It had been agreed since Casablanca that, in pursuing the President's unconditional-surrender policy, commanders of Allied armies — whether Soviet, British, or American — would only negotiate with direct emissaries of an enemy seeking to surrender, under a flag of truce. Field Marshal Alexander, unfortunately, had informed Prime Minister Churchill that an offer had come from General Wolff, commanding Waffen-SS forces in Italy, *though not the Wehrmacht*. And Churchill, overruling his own chiefs of staff, had insisted not only on becoming involved, but on involving Stalin, instead of simply refusing to parley unless the offer was under a white flag from Kesselring or Vietinghoff, the Wehrmacht commanders.

Realizing the matter could easily "backfire," as Stimson noted in his diary, the U.S. war secretary had thereupon decided that, if Prime Minister Churchill was getting involved, so too should the President. "So at about half past twelve" on March 11, "I motored over to the White House and found the President in his study and told him what we were doing. He had heard of the matter through Admiral Leahy but had not heard of the action of the British with Churchill so he was very glad that I told him. He approved the course that we were taking over at the Pentagon so I felt easy in going ahead"[2] — without Stimson realizing it was a Nazi ruse.

Thus the minor tragedy had unfolded. Aware from Russian intelligence the Germans were trying to get the Western Allies to turn against the USSR, the Soviets had protested against such negotiations being conducted by the OSS in Switzerland. What should have been nipped in the bud — as Molotov demanded[3] — became an Allied mess, involving Himmler, Wolff, the OSS, British intelligence, the State Department, Russian intelligence, the British Foreign Office, the Russian Foreign Office, Ambassador Harriman, Ambassador Kerr, General Deane, half the Pentagon, Stalin, Churchill — and the ailing president. As they neared straightforward military victory, in the wake of the triumphantly successful Yalta Conference, the matter had then escalated into a first-class row between the Allies.

By March 13 the Wolff negotiations were spinning out of control.[4] Stettinius had told Stimson that, already at Yalta, Churchill had been "very erratic," as well as unpredictable.[5] Stimson, hearing what Churchill was up to over the Wolff affair, had felt this to be yet another example of "Churchill's erraticness" — moreover one that he himself would have "to settle in regard to what I have called the McNarney negotiations," on behalf of the President. As Stimson summarized in his diary, the "British and American [military] staffs both wanted those negotiations to be on a strictly military level without going into political affairs at all and not being therefore handled by politicians. It was to be purely the surrender of an army. We felt however that we must notify the Russians simply of the existence of the negotiations so that they would not feel they were being intentionally kept in ignorance. Somehow or other the English papers [documents] fell into the hands of Churchill and he overruled his staff and sent a note inviting the Russians to come and did this after our people sent off their letter which simply notified the Russians." Churchill's involvement had aroused immediate suspicion in the Russian camp — "a difficult place to wriggle out of," Stimson noted. With Ambassador Harriman — frustrated by Russian intransigence over Poland and backtracking over repatriation of U.S. POWs — firing off telegrams to the State Department and War Department from Moscow, advising his colleagues to stand firm and not allow Russian interference in military matters on a front (Italy) where Russian forces were not engaged, Stimson had taken advice from his War Department staff, and then "hurried over to the White House" with the cables, "and explained it to the President before the Joint Chiefs of Staff had yet acted." The President "backed me up and the Joint Chiefs of Staff took their position in the afternoon and passed the papers in the way which I had recommended."[6]

It proved a terrible mistake. By the time Prime Minister Mackenzie King had returned to the White House from Williamsburg at 3:30 p.m., to see or stay with the President on his way back to Canada, Stimson had inadvertently locked the U.S. government into a corner, struggling vainly to undo Churchill's unwitting mischief, and unaware the Western Allies were being fooled by the Nazis. As the President said to Mackenzie King, before asking him to sit with him for his weekly press conference, he was "afraid Winston had acted too suddenly and they [the British] had made the situation very difficult. He had cabled Churchill this morning, pointing out there was no objection to the Russian Generals coming as observors [sic], but that this should be between the British and the Americans and the Germans in Italy," not the Russians. "He says he is actually waiting further word from Churchill, but feels quite anxious about the situation lest this chance [i.e., army-to-army surrender] may have been lost. Alexander, he said, was agreeable to it, but it was a matter entirely for the military and should be kept as such. This is interesting indeed," King commented.[7]

It was. The negotiations — which Dulles called Operation Sunrise — were disastrous to Allied unity, just as Himmler and Wolff had hoped. They poured poison into the relationship between the Western Allies and the Soviets in the worst possible way — and over a nefarious SS general, who not only had no power to negotiate military surrender of a Wehrmacht army group in Italy, but who was allegedly responsible for the murder of three hundred thousand Jews and Russians. In truth Operation Wool — as recorded in SS Lieutenant

Guido Zimmer's diary—had been approved by Hitler himself in a meeting with Wolff in Berlin on February 4, 1945, the very day the Yalta Conference began. By mid-March its goal of splitting the Allies had proven extraordinarily successful, with Harriman in Moscow completely taken in, even as Russian intelligence learned it was a scam.[8]

The affair was enough to break the President's heart, after all he'd done to improve trust and relations between the Big Three, and to prepare for a clear, decisive, and *united* Allied victory over the Third Reich. Time and again over the following three weeks poor Admiral Leahy was to be tasked with having to draft explanatory, apologetic, and sadly untruthful cables to Stalin, who became incensed at what he saw as Anglo-American double-dealing with the Nazis.

For the President, too ill to find out himself what was the real truth behind the "McNarney negotiations," the subject became a nightmare, as he tried, amid the flurry of accusatory cables from Stalin—cables that vainly warned the Western Allies had been duped by Wolff—to try and rescue their plummeting relationship: hoping against hope it would not affect Stalin's commitment to declare war on Japan, and that he would continue with preparations to send major Russian forces to defeat the Japanese army in Manchuria. Moreover, that it would not compromise Soviet commitment to join the United Nations organization — especially when, in pique, Stalin announced that Mr. Molotov, furious that the Western Allies would not break off negotiations with the nefarious Wolff, would not be going to San Francisco, as he'd initially planned.

It was in the midst of this depressing military finale to the war against Hitler that the President had asked Mackenzie King to dine with him on March 13 — and meet the light of his life, who was probably doing more to keep him alive than his doctors: Mrs. Rutherfurd.

90

No More Barbarossas!

THE PRESIDENT HAD YEARNED to get away to Warm Springs, where he'd be able, he thought, to work in peace and quiet on his United Nations opening address in San Francisco. In the meantime he had left Henry Stimson, James Forrestal, Admiral Leahy, and the Joint Chiefs of Staff — as well as Eisenhower, Nimitz, and MacArthur on the battlefields — to run the military side of the war. And had turned to Lucy Rutherfurd for emotional support.

In later years there would be inevitable speculation about the President's relationship with Eleanor in the final period of his life, fueled by assertions that Mrs. Roosevelt tormented her husband with her demands, her lack of patience — and her failure to understand he was at death's door. Moreover that it was Eleanor's remoteness that caused Franklin to turn to Lucy.

This was not the case. By March 1945 Eleanor knew Franklin's days were numbered — just not how much time he had left. She had ceded to her daughter Anna the responsibility for day-to-day care of her husband, and the need to keep down the number of visitors to the White House. It was true, however, that after the election a long phone call she'd made to him while he was at Warm Springs had caused his blood pressure, according to Dr. Bruenn, to rise fifty points — the "veins in his forehead standing out."[1]

Having earlier tested Mrs. Roosevelt for a possible medical condition, Bruenn had discovered Eleanor's metabolism was low. "Just imagine what she would have been like if she had been up to par!" the doctor later remarked, mockingly.[2] Yet Franklin had spent a lifetime with Eleanor; he knew, accepted, and respected her for the woman she was: mother of their five children, as well as a devotee of humanitarian and social causes — not least those of civil rights, refugees, women's inequality, and poverty. "It is very hard to live with someone who is almost a saint," Roosevelt's labor adviser, Anna Rosenberg, later commented[3] — yet Franklin had managed to do so for almost a quarter of a century since they made their pact to stay married. And though both were under great strain in March 1945, there was every indication they were as devoted to each other as they had ever been, indeed possibly more so: writing each other and telephoning whenever apart, sharing news and concern about their four sons in uniform — three in the Pacific — and making preparations for the end of the war and Franklin's resignation on grounds of ill health, whichever came first. "I say a prayer daily that he may be able to carry on till we are at peace & we are set in the right direction," Eleanor wrote her aunt Maude Gray.[4] For it was clear, once Hitler's Germany was defeated — to be followed by the swift surrender of Japan — the President would not continue in the Oval Office. "I am all ready to hand over to others now in all that I do and go home to live in retirement," Eleanor would tell her friend Margaret Fayerweather on March 28 — adding how Franklin (who had for the first time in their marriage asked her to drive him in his beloved Ford Phaeton car, with its special hand controls) had spoken to her of their moving to the Middle East, after his run-in with Ibn Saud; "I believe I'd like to go and live there," he'd said a few days before. Now that he'd met with representatives of both sides in the dispute over a larger Jewish home in Palestine, "I feel quite an expert," he'd said to her. Eleanor had been appalled. "Can't you think of something harder to do?" she'd asked him. At which point he'd suggested India, China, Thailand, and Indochina.[5]

Eleanor had admired his spunk. "*I'm* all ready to sit back. *He's* still looking forward to more work," she'd reported to Margaret.[6]

Franklin was joking, of course — as she knew. The very business of staying alive was about as much as he could manage. Why, then, in the circumstances, did he not summon Harry Truman, his chosen vice president, to come and discuss, in private, the challenges the former senator would soon enough have to face? This was something no biographer or historian would ever be able to comprehend. Exhaustion? A psychological block in taking such a step? Denial? Delusion that he still had enough time to do so?

The President had told Truman on March 1, the day he'd addressed Congress, that he was tired and intended to go down to Warm Springs before addressing the United Nations conference. Yet in the subsequent four weeks before he left the capital he met with Truman only once, for ninety minutes: and that was in the company again of Speaker Rayburn, Rayburn's deputy McCormack, and the Senate majority leader, Barkley, to discuss the domestic political agenda. Moreover Truman had not complained. Highly intelligent, a quick study, and a *bon viveur* when it came to whiskey and cards, Truman had not thought to request a private meeting, contenting himself with the weekly cabinet meeting at the White House.

Thus the President — having decided to leave Washington for Warm Springs on March 28 — had sought to keep going. And to see Lucy as much as he decently could, if she was agreeable. Which she was.

In other circumstances this would qualify as one of the great love stories of the century: of lost love that had been refound, and remained as powerful and romantic for both parties as it had ever been, even if physical love was no longer possible — or perhaps even wanted by the parties. What the President wanted, it seemed, was just to be near Lucy. Whether or not Eleanor facilitated this consciously or unconsciously would never be known; it seems hard to believe that with the President's personal staff, secretaries, White House staff, Warm Springs staff, Hyde Park staff, Secret Service officers, doctors, drivers, and others all "in the know," Eleanor — whose own longtime lover, Lorena Hickok, still lived in the White House, on the top floor — could have remained ignorant of the resumed relationship.

There was certainly very little attempt to hide it. Almost every day the President had arranged to see Lucy. He'd collected her for a drive in his big seven-seat Lincoln V-12 "Sunshine Special" armored convertible on March 12 — avoiding the need to be lifted out of the car and into Lucy's sister Violetta's house at 2238 Q Street, Georgetown — and had then brought Lucy back to the White House to have dinner with him and his daughter, as well as Anna's husband, John Boettiger. Anna and John had then left them together to talk for several hours in the President's study after dinner, when the car duly took her home. The following evening he'd asked her back to dine with him and his closest political friend, Mackenzie King.

"I noticed in talking with the President that he seemed very tired," King had noted in his diary, after the press conference he'd just given with King in the Oval Office, attended by many reporters. But "he seemed to enjoy talking on with me — seemed in no hurry about sending for his letters to be signed or other things. I spoke a couple of times about letting him rest, or not waiting for dinner" — since King was to spend the night back on his train, en route to New York — "but he said to me he would like me to stay. He said for dinner he was having just his daughter and her husband and another relative, Mrs. Rutherfurd. It would be just a quiet family meal which we would have early if I wished, so as to get off to the train early. I felt the President has pretty well lost his spring," King recorded, sadly. "He is a very tired man. He is kindly, gentle and humorous, but I can see is hardly in shape to cope with problems. He wisely lets himself be guided by others and has everything brought carefully before him."[7]

This was probably the most succinct and accurate description of the President of the United States in mid-March, 1945, four weeks before his death. Returning to his room, King had dictated the entry, taken a twenty-minute nap, and then rejoined the President, Anna, and John. And also "Mrs. Rutherfurd of Carolina a relative of the President, a very lovely woman and of great charm."[8]

King — who had dined with Eleanor only two nights before — was evidently dazzled by Lucy, as many men were. A lifelong bachelor who knew and accepted his own limitations in terms of personality, King was always curious about people — their self-importance, reliability, agendas. Mrs. Rutherfurd stunned him, not having heard about her before. "I should think she has an exceptionally fine character," he reflected later that night, aboard his special train — so taken with her, in fact, that "I made an exception in my rule and took a cocktail which the President himself mixed before going into dinner. We dined upstairs in the little hall and the five of us had a very happy talk together."[9]

It was the last time King would see the President. Roosevelt had said they would "soon meet again at San Francisco." By then, King had remarked, the war in Europe would be hopefully over, to which the President had said "there is a very good chance" it might be. And King, who had not quite dared believe the long, dark years of hostilities would soon be done, had been relieved by that at least. "I do not know," King confessed to his stenographer, "that I would have felt sure enough to say so with such assurance until today."[10]

The President might be wrong about meeting King in San Francisco, but he was certainly correct about the war's approaching end. With the Ruhr swiftly surrounded by American forces, and the Ninth U.S. Army advancing to the Elbe River, within striking distance of Berlin, the military situation once again tilted back in favor of the Western armies rather than the Eastern allies. Taking his cue from the Yalta agreements, including the agreed zones of Allied occupation, as well as the predicted casualties that would be suffered in attacking Berlin from the west, Eisenhower decided unilaterally not to authorize an assault on the capital, but to leave it to the Russians to take, house by house — with Hitler refusing to leave the city and remaining in the bunker below the Chancellery, now that the Chancellery itself had been more or less erased by Allied bombing.

Churchill had thought Eisenhower's decision not to attack Berlin from the west a terrible mistake — indeed he found himself aghast at what he saw as a naive deference to the Yalta map. All too soon, in fact, he would order plans to be drawn up for an Anglo-American Barbarossa: an attack from the Dresden area "so as to impose upon Russia the will of the United States and the British Empire" — in part to attain "a square deal" for Poland, though this aim would "not necessarily limit the commitment." It would involve almost fifty — mostly American — divisions, and up to a hundred thousand Wehrmacht troops! It was to be launched, moreover, four days before the British general election: Operation Unthinkable.

The Prime Minister's secret plan, mercifully, was not put into effect, and would never have been authorized by an American commander in chief. It was duly dropped when Churchill lost the election in 1945, though only shelved. Concealed for the next forty years, it was considered by later historians to be appropriately titled, save in defense against a Soviet invasion of western Europe.

The very preparation of plans for Operation Unthinkable would, however, indicate how views on the future of Europe were shifting at senior levels in the spring of 1945 — men like Ambassador Harriman, General Deane, and others indignant that too much was being "given away" to the Russians simply because they had furnished — and were continuing to provide — the essential warrior-manpower for the war. When Eisenhower refused pleas by Field Marshal Montgomery to be allowed to press on with American forces under his command to Berlin — the supreme commander removing the Ninth U.S. Army from Montgomery's Twenty-First Army Group, lest the often insubordinate general turn a Nelson-like telescope to his blind eye and ignore the signal — there had been an outcry at 10 Downing Street, with Churchill sending more exhorting cables to the President to protest the loss of such an opportunity.[11]

The President ignored Churchill. He had ceded his role as U.S. commander in chief to Stimson and Marshall, and for their part they were tired of Churchill's repeated warnings of missed opportunities or even doom if his proposals were not accepted. Mr. Churchill was not president of the United States. Without American forces — and inevitable casualties — his British Empire forces were now junior allies in Europe and even more so in the Pacific; it was a case of the tail perpetually trying to wag the dog — moreover a tail that had, in all truth, a deeply suspect record in terms of strategic or tactical military success. Stimson and Marshall had therefore had no hesitation in backing General Eisenhower, however much the Prime Minister might complain. Besides, Eisenhower had on March 28 already sent his signal to Stalin, explaining his decision.[12] Without starting another McNarney-like arousal of Soviet suspicion that the Western powers were about to switch tack, and combine with German forces to strike at the Soviets, it was too late to revoke.

In subsequent years General Marshall, especially, would be accused of political naiveté by the smear-artist senator Joseph McCarthy. Yet the fact was, there had been remarkable unanimity of American thinking among U.S. military minds at this time — Roosevelt approving every decision about which, via Admiral Leahy, they informed him.

Germany first. Then Japan.

For better or for worse the President had come to see his role as that of underwriter: endorsing the generals who were bringing the war to a successful military end against ongoing, fanatical German and Japanese opposition. And declining to plot a new war, which few if any serving American soldiers at that time would have been prepared to fight. There would be problems enough in getting western Europe back on its feet, once the Nazis surrendered unconditionally. With German officers already plotting to raise a Freikorps if and when defeat came, the President was determined to ensure they would never be able to claim later that German forces had been winning the war but were "stabbed in the back" by their own politicians. Moreover, peaceful postwar coexistence with the Soviets was worth *trying* to achieve, at least — and as history would have it, would prove more or less effective, despite a number of "hot" incidents.

In short: no more Barbarossas!

Thus, as planned, the President of the United States had briefly appeared in the Oval Office on the morning of March 28, 1945, and left the White House that same afternoon for Warm Springs.

At breakfast with Eleanor — the last he would ever take with her — he told her friend Margaret Fayerweather he'd now chosen the spot in the Hyde Park rose garden where he wished to be interred — a spot where "to his certain knowledge, have been buried an old mule, two horses, and a dozen or so of the family dogs," as he joked.[13]

The President clearly still had a vestige of his old sense of humor, but he was "far from well," the British ambassador noted that day[14] — markedly sicker than three weeks before, when Halifax had last seen him. By 3:00 p.m. even his longtime office secretary, Grace Tully, felt the President had "failed dangerously" just in the hours since lunchtime. "His face was ashen, highlighted by the darkening shadows under his eyes, and with his cheeks drawn gauntly," Tully later recalled.[15] His new press secretary, Jonathan Daniels, agreed — as did others.

Alben Barkley, the Senate majority leader, who saw the President shortly after midday in the Oval Office, said to a colleague: "I'm afraid he'll never return alive."[16]

However exhausted he felt, the President was intent upon hanging on to life for a few more days. He'd seen Lucy Rutherfurd every day from March 18 to March 21. As one biographer put it, "A romance which endures for thirty years is not an affair"[17] — and perhaps at some deeper level, the President was simply not willing to go into the dark without seeing Lucy one more time in Warm Springs. They'd discussed Lucy driving down to stay with him, perhaps bringing her friend Elizabeth Shoumatoff, who'd painted a small portrait of FDR in 1943. Once back at Aiken, Lucy asked Elizabeth to paint another portrait of the President; the artist was at first dubious, the photographs of the President at Yalta being, in Elizabeth's word, "ghastly."[18]

Lucy hadn't denied this to Elizabeth. "He is thin and frail," she'd acknowledged, "but there is something about his face that shows more the way he looked when he was young," she'd said. Clearly reminiscing, she'd added: "Having lost so much weight, his features, always handsome, are more definitely chiseled, I think." And then, "in an even lower tone, 'if this portrait is painted, it should not be postponed.'"[19]

Thus was the arrangement made. Lucy would come with Mme Shoumatoff and stay with the President at Warm Springs, after Easter — in approximately a week's time.

Having seen Franklin so often in the previous two weeks, Lucy herself cannot have been under any illusions; she had, after all, watched her husband, Winty Rutherfurd, die the year before, after a long illness.

And the new, life-size portrait, in watercolor? It might well be a last such portrait, Lucy was aware — Douglas Chandler having finished a fine one at the White House on March 16, 1945. Not a death mask, per se, but a farewell-to-life portrayal — painted by a Russian Orthodox Christian whose brother, an expert, had met with the President at Hyde Park and become an unofficial adviser to him on icons of the saints. Beginning in the Late Middle Ages it had been traditional in Europe to take death masks in wax or plaster; in the United States, however, there had been no such tradition. Elizabeth's portrait, then, would have to suffice — accompanied by photographs, which had come to perform a similar role. And since it was Elizabeth Shoumatoff's practice to have a photographer aid her in achieving accuracy in her compositions, she would bring one with her — to which the President had, in principle, agreed.

Whether he would last until they came, however, was another matter.

91

The End

PULLED BY TWO LOCOMOTIVES, the nine-car *Ferdinand Magellan* arrived at the Warm Springs halt at 1:30 p.m. on March 30, 1945, bearing the President of the United States; a handful of his office and personal staff; his communications team; his law partner, Basil O'Connor; and the Canadian ambassador, Leighton McCarthy — but no senior military staff, or even his White House doctor, Admiral McIntire.

In her diary Daisy Suckley — who with Polly Delano was also traveling with the President to provide him with care and company — had noted how both O'Connor and McCarthy, after boarding the train with the President, were "alarmed at his looks." These did not improve.

He "looks really ill — thin & worn — but joking & laughing & carrying the conversation on as usual," Daisy recorded.[1] He even asked the Catholics in his entourage whether they wished to disembark and celebrate Easter Mass in Atlanta, then follow on later. If so they should feel free to do so, he insisted.[2] By the time he himself was transferred to the waiting car at Warm Springs, however, the President looked almost comatose — unable to lift even an arm to help Mike Reilly carry him from his wheelchair. "Just like setting up a dead man," a railwayman commented. Once he'd been wheeled off to bed, his valet, Arthur Prettyman, overheard Leighton McCarthy saying to Basil O'Connor, "Our friend is dying."[3]

It was no wonder. The President's blood pressure was 240 over 130, though dropping at times to 170 over 88. Calling Admiral McIntire in Washington to tell him how worried he was, Bruenn was advised to continue as normal, and not under any circumstances to call on outside medical assistance or advice, which might make the three accompanying press agency reporters suspect it was a final, fatal journey.

Buoyed perhaps by knowing Lucy would be coming to stay on April 9, the President thus clung to life a little longer. In Washington, Stimson, Marshall, and Leahy dealt with the increasingly admonitory (and all too justified) cables from Stalin, culminating in that of April 3, in which Stalin gently commented the President had "not been fully informed" about the true negotiations by General Wolff in Bern, and claiming, rightly, that "my colleagues are close to the truth." If such negotiations were designed to ease the path of the Western Allies into the "heart of Germany," then "why was it necessary to conceal this from the Russians?" he asked. It might give a "momentary advantage" to the Western Allies, but not one of which they could be proud, if they were concerned about "the preservation and strengthening of trust among the Allies."[4]

Leahy was understandably alarmed. "The president today received a disturbing telegram from Marshal Stalin which stated that the Soviet Army had information that the Anglo-American Command had entered into an agreement with the German Command, which arranged for the Allied break-through of the western front in exchange for softer surrender terms than would be accepted by the Soviet Government," he noted in his diary. "This message clearly shows Soviet suspicion and distrust of our motives, and of our promises, a sad prospect of any successful cooperative agreement at the approaching Political conference in San Francisco."[5]

It was too bad — and would probably never have arisen had the President been well, for he had resolutely refused to countenance negotiations other than unconditional surrender, under army-to-army aegis. But he was now not even well enough to draft a reply, Leahy recording with complete frankness in his diary how "I prepared for the President, and sent to Marshal Stalin, a sharp reply to his message that approaches as closely to a rebuke as is permitted in diplomatic exchanges between states."[6]

Leahy was not exaggerating. Sent back to his chief of staff via the radio railway car and then in original by daily pouch, the reply was simply marked AP-PROVED — the President's message denying the Soviet assertion, saying he had "complete confidence in General Eisenhower and know he would certainly inform me before entering into any agreement with the Germans"; moreover that, as supreme commander on the Western Front, Eisenhower was as determined as ever "to bring about together with you an unconditional surrender of the Nazis." Leahy had then added, "It would be one of the great tragedies of history if at the very moment of victory now within our grasp, such distrust, such lack of faith should prejudice the entire undertaking after the colossal losses of life, materiel and treasure involved. Frankly I cannot avoid a feeling of bitter resentment toward your informers, whoever they are, for such vile misrepresentation of my actions or those of my trusted subordinates."[7]

Crafted in Washington by Leahy, with the support of his colleagues, the message did the trick — causing Stalin, who remained certain the President was being either deliberately or inadvertently misinformed by his subordinates, to back down. The Marshal cabled back that he had "never doubted your honesty and dependability, as well as the honesty and dependability of Mr. Churchill" — though he quietly insisted his informants were telling the truth, and "have no intention of insulting anyone."[8] Accepting the President's assurance there would be no eleventh-hour deal with Hitler or his henchmen such as Himmler and Wolff, he made clear he would stand by the Yalta agreement he'd made with Mr. Roosevelt. And he did.

The Japanese ambassador was summoned by Foreign Minister Molotov to the Kremlin. There Mr. Sato was told that, in view of Japanese hostilities "against the United States and Britain, which are allies of the Soviet Union," the Soviet-Japanese nonaggression pact was finished — the prelude to war.[9] As Leahy noted, this could mean an attack by Japan on the Soviet Union, but "the Soviet Government is well informed in regard to Japanese history in the past century and should be adequately prepared. Hostilities between Japan and the Soviets would be definitely advantageous to our present war effort in the Pacific," he concluded gratefully.[10] His tough language had been effective; Stalin was holding to the secret Yalta agreement.

The President, informed of this in Warm Springs, breathed a sigh of relief. Dulles's misbegotten Operation Sunrise had threatened, but mercifully had not wrecked, the military finale to the war against Hitler's Third Reich — nor the defeat, thereafter, of the Empire of Japan. This, together with the prospect of seeing Lucy again, had heartened him. He'd already stopped Churchill, on March 11, from sending "any message to Uncle Joe at this juncture — especially as I feel that certain parts of your proposed text might produce a reaction quite contrary to your intent"[11] — and Stalin had now borne out the President's trust in the Russian commitment regarding Japan.

Reluctantly, Churchill cabled on April 5 to say that he finally accepted the President's decision not to order Eisenhower to send American forces to take Berlin from the west — particularly in view of the suspicions the Wolff imbroglio had raised of an Anglo-American plot — and regarded "the matter as closed." Moreover to "prove my sincerity, I will use one of my very few Latin quotations, '*Ammantium irae amoris integration est*'" — meaning "Lovers' quarrels always go with true love."[12]

Lucy, the President's actual lover, certainly looked forward to seeing Franklin as much as the President longed to see her. On April 5 she'd written to Warm Springs to thank Grace Tully for making the necessary preparations for her visit. Mindful of how weak the President was, however, she'd added: "If you should change your mind & think it would be better for me not to come — call me up. I really am terribly worried — as I imagine you all are."[13]

For his part Franklin could hardly wait, however — his excitement worrying Daisy Suckley lest it raise his blood pressure still higher. Granted, it would be a "pleasure," Daisy noted in her diary, after confirmation that Lucy would arrive on April 9, but it would be "another interruption in the routine we are trying to keep."[14]

That interruption was precisely what the President yearned for. On the morning of Friday, April 6, he was working on his stamp collection when he hit upon the idea of a new three-cent stamp to be issued on the opening day of the San Francisco Conference, bearing the words "April 25, 1945; Towards United Nations."[15]

Could the stamp be issued in time? He called the postmaster general, Frank Walker, who said it could. Moreover, Walker assured the President designs for his approval could be with him by April 10 or 11. "So," Daisy commented in her diary, it was still possible that "people in high places sometimes get things done in a few minutes!" Later, before going to sleep, the President smoked a cigarette and "talked seriously about the S. Francisco Conference, & his part in World Peace, etc. He says again that he can probably resign some time next year, when the peace organization — the United Nations — is well started."[16]

Some time *next year?*

It seemed risible. Yet each day, as April 9 approached, the President looked better and better — and sunnier. "He sits a little straighter in his chair, his voice is a little clearer and stronger, his face less drawn & he is happier!" Daisy noted on April 8. "We are now looking forward to Lucy Rutherfurd's visit. She comes tomorrow, bringing Madame Shoumatoff, for another portrait of F.D.R., and a photographer." To her relief "Lucy and Mme S. go into the guest house," Daisy penned with a certain satisfaction, for the last time Lucy had come, after the '44 election, Daisy and Polly had been asked to move out of the Little White House to make way for her. On the President's instructions, however, "Polly & I are going to get flowers" for the guesthouse, "to make it look attractive. Lizzie the maid had been cleaning for two days — and it will be very nice," she assured the President — since, given his poor health, "F. has never gone in there to see it."[17]

Unable to wait until Lucy arrived at Warm Springs in Madame Shoumatoff's car, though, the President had told Lucy by phone he would meet her in person at 4:00 p.m., in Macon, Georgia, some eighty miles away, so that she could transfer and travel with him the last part of her journey. After a good afternoon's sleep the President thus set off for Macon on April 9, taking Daisy with him and leaving Polly to arrange the flowers.

"It was a beautiful evening for a drive & we enjoyed it tremendously — on & on," Daisy jotted that night, "away from the sun" and wondering whether, if Lucy was early, she might motor on and they would pass each other — a prospect that left the anxious president "scanning every car that headed towards us, imagining it was slowing up."[18]

If the President was aware how strange this might seem to others — the

Commander in Chief of the United States being driven in his trusty Ford Phaeton, with one Secret Service vehicle in front and one behind, to meet his former lover — he was completely indifferent. They made their way along "old Route 41 and down the old narrow road between the low-slung clay cliffs and fields of wildflowers to level ground, the road full of sudden turns between hummocks of tall trees," Jim Bishop later wrote, reconstructing the drive.[19]

To the President's chagrin, however, there was no sign of Lucy's car in Macon, at 4:00 p.m.

"Finally, after driving 85 miles," Daisy recorded, "we turned around & started toward the setting sun." The President was disappointed. "It got quite chilly" in the open-topped car, "& F put on his cape & I my rain coat which, though not warm, is a good windbreaker. We stopped in front of the drugstore in Manchester, for a 'Coke' & at that moment Lucy & her party also drove up on the curb!"[20]

As it turned out, the map-reading skills of the Russian photographer Nicholas Robbins, né Kotzubinsky, had been insufficient for them to arrive in Macon on time. As Elizabeth later wrote, Robbins had been in love with Mrs. Rutherfurd since meeting her in 1943 and, sitting in the back with the maps, had spent more time gazing at Lucy than at the signposts. "As a result we reached Macon way after four o'clock. The beauty of that town, with its enchanting old houses and Civil War atmosphere, turned us away for a while from the rather annoying feeling that we were late. Lucy powdered her nose and seemed very nervous. Driving out of Macon we began carefully looking for the presidential car. Nothing in sight. We drove for quite a while. 'Nobody loves us, nobody cares for us,' sighed Lucy in a joking fashion, but I felt she was really disappointed. It was a beautiful evening and the sun was beginning to set. As we entered Greenville, a village near Warm Springs, we suddenly noticed, by a corner drugstore, several cars and quite a crowd gathered around them. We drove up and there in an open car was FDR himself, in his Navy cape, drinking Coca-Cola! We pulled to the curb. Lucy and I got out of the car."[21]

It was thus, on this somehow quintessential American 1940s stage, that the two former lovers were reunited. "The expression of joy on FDR's face upon seeing Lucy," Elizabeth Shoumatoff later recorded, was something she would never forget — in part because she found herself, as intended portraitist, so shocked by the change in the President "since I painted him in 1943." He had been so vibrant, then: so humorous, so filled with life and curiosity, both in the White House and at Hyde Park. "My first thought," now, "was how I could make a portrait of such a sick man? His face was gray and he looked to me like President Wilson in his last years."[22]

The President was over the moon, however. "Lucy and Shoumie got into the car, I on the little [jump] seat, & we drove home to this 'Little White House,'"

Daisy recorded contentedly before she went to sleep — the President's blood pressure up, and looking "awfully tired all evening," but, in the dying day, almost deliriously happy.[23]

It is there we shall leave the President. His private secretary, Bill Hassett, was aware "the Boss's" hours were now numbered. The President knew it, too — whatever he might say to Daisy about planning to retire the following year. He'd told his office secretary, Dorothy Brady, that she'd soon enough be able to visit her farm, outside Washington, "more often." Every day, in the meantime, he would go for a drive with Lucy — and Fala, his beloved terrier — to Dowdell's Knob.

Watching the President and Lucy together, Daisy was filled with concern. Eleanor was tough, and very much in control of her own life and emotions. Without Franklin, Daisy asked herself, where would Lucy be, once he died? A "very different future, rather alone," Daisy reflected — especially as "she isn't very well and that makes it more difficult to face life & make decisions." The President, Daisy recorded, was worried about her, and how she would manage — which Daisy rather resented, feeling "that she should face her own life & not put too much of its difficulties on *his* shoulders."[24]

The President didn't mind, though — indeed it was a mark of his generous character that he was always "helping others & making others happy," Daisy acknowledged — excited that, if the President survived the next few weeks, she and Polly could travel with him, he'd told them, to San Francisco on the *Ferdinand Magellan*.[25]

Concern, hope, and sadness thus mixed together. The President was only sixty-three, Lucy fifty-three. Yet there was no way, in all candor, his death could be far off. Admiral Leahy had told him how senior French officials, on behalf of de Gaulle, were pressing for U.S. transport to be arranged for their forces to be shipped to India, ready to move into Indochina, while Dutch officials were pressing for the same, to reestablish colonial rule in the Dutch East Indies,[26] while the British were putting pressure on Admiral King to permit British naval forces into the Pacific for the same reason. In his current condition, all the President felt up to saying was: discuss this with the Joint Chiefs of Staff, as well as Secretaries Henry Stimson and James Forrestal.

During the drive to the Knob on April 11 he had asked Daisy to come with them, and Daisy had watched the couple closely. "Lucy is so sweet with F — No wonder he loves to have her around — Toward the end of the [2-hour] drive, it began to be chilly and she put her sweater over his knees," Daisy noted in her diary. This was still a very private romance, but something beautiful to witness, in terms of Lucy's caring. "I can imagine just how she took care of her husband — She would think of little things which make so much difference to a semi-invalid, or even a person who is just tired, like F."[27]

Henry Morgenthau, the Treasury secretary, who happened to be in the area, had asked to come dine with them, and that night he and the President had shared stories about events and people they both knew, especially Winston Churchill. Morgenthau — who was anxious over his wife, who'd recently had a stroke and heart attack — asked to speak privately with Dr. Bruenn. But his question was not about his spouse. The President was slipping far faster than his own wife — the President's hands "shook so that he started to knock the glasses over," as he'd offered Henry one of his famous cocktails.[28]

The climax came quicker even than expected, the following day, shortly before lunch was served.

To pose for his portrait, at Mme Shoumatoff's suggestion, the President was wearing his double-breasted gray suit with his Harvard Crimson tie, "looking very fine," Daisy noted.[29] Elizabeth even complimented him on his good color that day — to be told later that this might well have presaged what now happened.

Bill Hassett had dried the fifty-odd papers the President had signed, in ink. Once gathered, like laundry, the private secretary had put them neatly into a folder on the card table which the President used as his desk. Lucy and Daisy were sitting on the sofa, watching Mme Shoumatoff at work on the life-size watercolor. She was painting as fast as she could, filling in the sitter's eyes, but became aware suddenly that "his gaze had a faraway look and was completely solemn." He'd just told her about the stamp he'd asked for, to celebrate the upcoming conference — "Wait 'til you see the San Francisco stamps, with the United Nations"[30] — but seemed then to have moved somewhere else in his mind, staring at Lucy, next to him. It was about 1:15 p.m.

To the Filipino butler, Joe Esperancilla, the President had said they needed "fifteen more minutes to work" before taking lunch, which he was looking forward to. "Suddenly," Elizabeth recalled, "he raised his right hand and passed it over his forehead several times in a strange jerky way, without emitting a sound" — at least as far as she could hear.[31]

Daisy Suckley, crocheting on the sofa, recalled the President "looking for something: his head forward, his hands fumbling." Immediately she rose. "I went forward & looked into his face. 'Have you dropped your cigarette?'" she asked him, alarmed. "He looked at me with his forehead furrowed in pain and tried to smile. He put his left hand up to the back of his head & said: 'I have a terrific pain in the back of my head.'"[32]

These would be the President's last words — Daisy quite certain of them, afterwards. "He said it distinctly, but so low that I don't think anyone else heard it — My head was not a foot from his — I told him to [put] his head back on his chair." "The President is sick, call the doctor," Mme Shoumatoff meanwhile yelled.[33]

Dr. Bruenn was at the bottom of the hill, in the big rehabilitation pool with other polio patients. By the time he'd dressed and arrived up at the Little White House, fifteen minutes had passed. Arthur Prettyman and Joe Esperancilla had carried the "dead weight" of the President, with Polly holding his feet, to his bedroom, and there they'd laid him on his bed, where he'd lost all consciousness — loud snoring sounds coming from his throat.

Injections of papaverine, nitroglycerine, and amyl nitrite were administered by Dr. Bruenn — for the President's heart, paradoxically, was still pumping. He had, however, suffered a "massive cerebral hemorrhage," or catastrophic stroke; his blood pressure was 300 over 190, and there was nothing — despite attempted artificial respiration by the President's masseur, Lieutenant Commander Fox — that could be done, except to wait for the end.

Bruenn telephoned Admiral McIntire, the President's White House doctor, who was still in Washington, and warned him that "a long siege" was ahead. Bruenn was forcing himself to show no emotion — having told Daisy only a few days before that he had come to love the President so much that he would "jump out of the window" for him, "without hesitation."[34]

In the event, the siege did not last long. Lucy Rutherfurd, recognizing immediately the end was approaching, told Elizabeth Shoumatoff to pack her easel and bags and summon Nicholas Robbins. In the white Cadillac they set off from the estate before the press could arrive. They would only hear whether or not the President had actually passed away when they stopped to telephone the Little White House, on their journey home. The flag at Macon was already at half-mast. The operator, before putting the call through, asked if they knew what had already become national — in fact global — news at 3:35 p.m., local time, April 12, 1945.

The Commander in Chief was dead.

Acknowledgments

I began FDR at War thinking it would be a single, stand-alone volume, not a trilogy. It was to be about 350 pages: a modest attempt by an Anglo-American author to fill a strange gap in World War II historiography. Over the decades since the war ended we have as readers been the beneficiaries of a cornucopia of books about wartime leaders, generals, and "ordinary" servicemen and women, but no real account of Franklin D. Roosevelt's role as commander in chief of the Armed Forces of the United States in what was the most violent and destructive war in human history. This had seemed to me, when writing *American Caesars,* my history of postwar American presidents, to be quite wrong — a gap that had puzzled me both as a military historian and as a biographer.

Thus I proposed to my agent such a work, and began my quest, beginning to research it ten years ago. My editor, Bruce Nichols, of Houghton Mifflin Harcourt, welcomed and helped prefinance the project, but neither he nor I initially had any idea it would stretch across a decade — or that my British publisher, Random House, would balk at the multivolume size. I therefore wish here to thank Bruce for his faith and loyalty to the project — a project which has, I hoped, made a valuable contribution both to our understanding of World War II and the singular, hitherto unacknowledged role of Franklin Roosevelt in achieving Allied military victory. Without FDR's extraordinary military leadership after Pearl Harbor, the course of World War II might well have turned out differently — and I would probably not be here, writing about it. Or at such length. I will always remember Bruce's pained email to me, on reading the first draft of FDR at War. "I've reached page 800 in the manuscript, Nigel, and have enjoyed it immensely. But we're only in November 1942 — where's the rest of the war?"

The "rest," thanks to Bruce's patience and goodwill, took a bit longer. I wanted not only to document FDR's performance in the role of commander in chief in World War II, but to help put the reader in the room with him as he made the decisions which, for good or ill, would determine the war's outcome. Marrying history and biography, in other words, I attempted to reconstruct the saga of World War II at the very highest level of decision-making — and on both sides of the drama, once Hitler declared war on the United States on December 11, 1941.

On the Allied side, FDR's primary partner in the great conflict was, of course, Winston Churchill, Prime Minister of Great Britain, and quasi commander in chief of British Empire forces in World War II. Churchill duly recounted his own role in six masterly volumes of memoir and history, *The Second World War*, between 1948 and 1953, which certainly helped him win the Nobel Prize for Literature. To some extent my task therefore became that of countering Winston's version, especially in relation to the dominating role of President Roosevelt as U.S. commander in chief. For behind the scenes Churchill's military leadership, after his valiant stand in 1940, had been deplorable. As the head of the British Army under Churchill, Field Marshal Brooke would confide in his famous diary, after D-day, three quarters of the world imagined the Prime Minister to be a great strategist, whereas in truth he had been a constant "menace," responsible for unending disasters.

Such was the power of Winston's postwar prose, however, and the veneration in which he was held in the United States, especially, that Brooke's candid view (omitted from Arthur Bryant's 1959 version of Brooke's diaries, and only published in 2001) was considered hard cheese by a general who had been passed over for command of D-day.

Addressing that misperception and rechronicling the war from FDR's perspective as, ultimately, the military mastermind of World War II has thus been for me a challenging yet deeply rewarding task as a historian who believes in the power of biography to revise and correct history. The FDR who emerges from this decade-long tapestry is both human and fallible. His greatest virtues are his patience and his inner resolve, on behalf of his country and the free world. How he masterminded a two-ocean war, how he overruled his own Joint Chiefs of Staff, how he "delivered" D-day despite everything Churchill did to sabotage the Allied invasion, from 1943 to the very eve of its mounting, is the core thread of my trilogy — and one of which I have a measure of special, personal connection and pride, inasmuch as my father took part in the triumphant landings as a twenty-five-year-old British infantry battalion commander, later winning the DSO in battle. The landings did not fail; and as Hitler had warned his own generals in December 1943, they did decide the outcome of the war in Europe.

The saddest part of my long, earlier years as official biographer of Field Marshal Montgomery, commander in chief of the D-day invasion armies, had been my father's illness and his death, soon after I finished the Monty trilogy in 1987. This time, reaching the end of the FDR at War trilogy thirty years later, I was beset by similar sadness: recounting the way in which FDR's fatal heart disease was secretly diagnosed before the D-day landings, and—hidden from the public—transformed his role as U.S. commander in chief thereafter. The triumph of his D-day project was subsumed in the tragedy of his ill health, and though the final book became a story of great personal courage and determination, it was strangely hard for me, as author, to narrate. Only when a member of my writers group in New Orleans pointed out that I myself had reached *un certain âge,* namely when death seems so much nearer than in earlier decades, did I realize how deeply invested I was in surviving to set the record of this man's contribution to the history of humanity straight—and how much, in the course of researching and writing the trilogy, I had come to respect, understand, and admire him for it. At a moment when the new world order he created seemed to be fraying, perhaps collapsing, the sheer magnitude of FDR's accomplishment—an accomplishment that had framed my life since birth in 1944—appeared monumental.

Now that the trilogy—though only half the size of Churchill's!—is complete, I'd like to thank some, at least, of the many people who, over the years, encouraged and assisted its making.

First and foremost, for her patience and faith in the outcome, my wife, Raynel Shepard, who simultaneously launched her new career as a jazz vocalist as I sought to complete mine as a military historian. Also my fellow author-historians Carlo D'Este, Roger Cirillo, James Scott, Mark Schneider, David Kaiser, Douglas Brinkley, David Reynolds, Ron Spector, Fredrik Logevall, Kai Bird, Mark Stoler, Niall Barr, Rick Atkinson, Hans Renders, Doeko Bosscher, Robert Citino, Susan Butler, Lynne Olson, and the many other scholars, friends, and readers who, over the years, have contributed to our better understanding and knowledge of World War II, and of FDR.

At the Franklin Roosevelt Presidential Library Archives I'd like to thank, for their help in preparing this book, archivists Virginia Lewick and Matt Hansen; at the Eisenhower Presidential Library, deputy director Timothy Reeves, and audiovisual archivist Kathy Struss; at the Library of Congress the head of Reference and Reader Services, the indispensable Jeffrey Flannery; at the Marshall Foundation, Director Rob Havers and Jeffrey Kozack; at the Imperial War Museum in London the Keeper of Documents, Anthony Richards; and at the National World War II Museum the president emeritus, Dr. Nick Mueller, and the new president, Stephen Watson, and his staff—especially Jeremy Collins—for enabling me to meet in person so many fellow WWII scholars and history devotees at the annual WWII and Churchill Society conferences. The members of the New York Military Affairs Symposium have been unfailingly encouraging. My especial gratitude also to my colleagues in the Boston Biographers Group, the New Orleans Non-Fiction Writers Group, and the Biographers International Organization (BIO).

At the University of Massachusetts Boston I'd like to thank the dean of the McCormack Graduate School of Policy and Global Studies, Dr. David Cash, as well as Robert Turner and my colleagues there, including the university library staff — as also the staff of the Widener Library at Harvard and Boston College. I was fortunate to have been able to interview the late Lieutenant Commander George Elsey, of FDR's wartime Map Room, and FDR's grandchildren, Mrs. Ellie Seagraves and the late Curtis Seagraves. My fellow members of the Tavern Club, Boston, have been supportive throughout — and I miss the late Tom Halsted there, who shared his memories of his stepmother, Anna Roosevelt Halsted. Most especially I'd like to thank once again my agent Ike Williams, and his colleagues Hope Denekamp and Katherine Flynn at Kneerim & Williams.

Without a publisher an author cuts a sorry figure. At Houghton Mifflin Harcourt I want to mark my great gratitude to my ever-patient and supportive editor and publisher, Bruce Nichols, together with his staff, especially Ivy Givens, Larry Cooper, and publicist Michelle Triant. Without the dedicated, painstaking efforts, moreover, of my copyeditor, Melissa Dobson — who has performed the crucial task, including fact-checking, on all three volumes — the trilogy would have been sadly flawed. It has truly been a team effort. I can only hope *War and Peace* — indeed the FDR at War trilogy — does justice to their great contributions.

NIGEL HAMILTON
John W. McCormack Graduate School of Policy
and Global Studies, UMass Boston

Photo Credits

A Trip to Tehran. Arlington Cemetery, November 11, 1943: UPS / INS / FDR Library; on board with Admiral King, Admiral Leahy, and General Marshall: USASC / FDR Library; USS *Iowa:* Naval History and Heritage Command

    Interviewing Eisenhower. The specially fitted C-54, Sacred Cow: FDR Library; FDR and Eisenhower on the Sacred Cow: U.S. Army / Eisenhower Library; FDR in Tunis with Generals Eisenhower, Spaatz, Bedell Smith, and others, November 20, 1943: Eisenhower Library

    Cairo. FDR with Churchill in the garden of Kirk villa, Cairo: FDR Library; FDR visiting the pyramids: FDR Library; Chiang Kai-shek, FDR, Churchill, and chiefs of staff before departure to Tehran: FDR Library

    Tehran. FDR in jeep, reviewing troops, Tehran: FDR Library; FDR with Stalin at birthday dinner for Churchill, British Legation, November 30, 1943: FDR Library

    Saving D-day. FDR posing with Stalin and Churchill on the steps of the Soviet Embassy, Tehran: FDR Library; close-up photo at Soviet Embassy, with Hopkins, Molotov, and Eden behind: FDR Library

    Who Will Command Overlord? FDR in jeep with Eisenhower, Castelvetrano airfield, Sicily, December 8, 1943, en route home: FDR Library; awarding General Clark the Distinguished Service Cross: FDR Library; FDR riding in jeep with Ike, Patton standing at left: FDR Library

    Triumphant Return. Battleship USS *Iowa:* Naval History and Heritage Command; FDR greeted by members of cabinet, Congress, and others at White House, December 17, 1943: FDR Library; FDR greeted by Secretary of State Hull and Judge Byrnes: FDR Library

    Christmas 1943. Eleanor, FDR, and their family assembled at Hyde Park: FDR Library; FDR's Christmas Eve broadcast, December 24, 1943: FDR Library

    Anzio. Ike warns Churchill against hasty Anzio invasion: Imperial War Museum; Allied landings, Anzio, January 22, 1944: Getty Images; hospital ship evacuates Allied wounded in March 1944: U.S. Navy / FPG / Getty Images; bombed and overcrowded Allied military hospital at Anzio, February 1944: George Silk / *Life* / Getty Images

    The Triumph of D-day. Eisenhower and Montgomery inspect U.S. assault troops preparing for D-day: Frank Scherschel / *Life* / Getty Images; FDR's D-day prayer: FDR Library; U.S. troops landing on Omaha Beach, June 6, 1944: Robert Sargent / U.S. Coast Guard / National Archives

    The Bomb Plot. FDR attending Marine Corps amphibious assault rehearsal with son Colonel Jimmy Roosevelt and Admiral Davis, Oceanside, California, July 20, 1944: U.S. Navy / FDR Library; Hitler and Mussolini at Wolf's Lair HQ, Rastenburg, East Prussia: Heinrich Hoffmann / Ullstein / Getty Images; Hitler shows Mussolini the operations hut where he was nearly killed, July 20, 1944: Bundesarchiv, Germany; Hitler broadcasts from the Wolf's Lair, July 20, 1944: Heinrich Hoffmann / Getty Images; FDR simultaneously broadcasts from special car on *Ferdinand Magellan,* San Diego, July 20, 1944 (Dr. Bruenn in foreground): George Skadding / *Life* / Getty Images

    To Be, or Not to Be. Democratic convention, Chicago, July 1944: Keystone-France / Gamma-Keystone / Getty Images; election poster: FDR Library; the heavy cruiser USS *Baltimore* off California, 1944: Fahey Collection / Naval History and Heritage Command

Hawaii. Aboard USS *Baltimore,* FDR receives General MacArthur and Admiral Nimitz, with Admiral Leahy, July 26, 1944: U.S. Navy / FDR Library; FDR tours installations, Hawaii, with General MacArthur and Admiral Nimitz, July 27, 1944: U.S. Navy / FDR Library; Admiral Nimitz and General MacArthur present their plans to FDR and Admiral Leahy, Holmes mansion, Waikiki, July 28, 1944: U.S. Navy / FDR Library

The Fall of '44. FDR has minor heart attack while giving speech aboard USS *Cummings,* Puget Sound Navy Yard, August 10, 1944: FDR Library; FDR campaigning with Senator Truman: Corbis / Getty Images; Inauguration Day, White House, January 20, 1945: Library of Congress

Yalta. FDR aboard USS *Quincy* arriving in Malta, saluted by Winston Churchill (foreground), February 2, 1945: UPI (Acme) / FDR Library; FDR on arrival at Saki airfield, Crimea, with Churchill and Molotov: U.S. Army Signal Corps (USASC) / FDR Library; FDR and Churchill in ballroom, Livadia Palace, Yalta, February 4, 1945, USASC / FDR Library; FDR and Stalin in FDR's study, Livadia Palace, February 4, 1945: USASC / FDR Library; the Big Three at Livadia Palace, February 9, 1945: USASC / National Archives, courtesy Naval History and Heritage Command

Warm Springs. FDR reports to Congress, March 1, 1945: FDR Library; FDR at his work table, Little White House, Warm Springs, April 1945: Margaret Suckley / FDR Library; the widow Lucy Rutherfurd at the Little White House, April 11, 1945: Nicholas Robbins / FDR Library; FDR posing for Elizabeth Shoumatoff portrait, April 11, 1945: FDR Library; "FDR Dies," front page, *San Francisco Chronicle,* April 13, 1945: *San Francisco Chronicle* / Polaris Images.

Notes

PROLOGUE

1. Second of Churchill's three major speeches to the House of Commons during the Battle of France, given on June 4, 1940: "A Colossal Military Disaster," in Winston Churchill, *The War Speeches of the Rt. Hon. Winston S. Churchill,* comp. Charles Eade, vol. 1 (London: Cassell, 1951).
2. "Evening Situation Report, probably December 20, 1943," section titled "The West, danger of invasion," in Helmut Heiber, ed., *Hitler and His Generals: Military Conferences 1942–1945* (New York: Enigma Books, 2003), 314 and 313.
3. Evan Thomas, "War Comes to America" (review of Nigel Hamilton, *The Mantle of Command: FDR at War, 1941–1942*), *New York Times,* August 1, 2014.
4. Lieutenant Commander George Elsey, interview with the author, September 12, 2011.
5. Entry of September 14, 1944, Diaries of William Lyon Mackenzie King, Library and Archives Canada, Ottawa.
6. Entry of September 20, 1944, in Geoffrey C. Ward, ed., *Closest Companion: The Unknown Story of the Intimate Friendship Between Franklin Roosevelt and Margaret Suckley* (Boston: Houghton Mifflin, 1995), 328.
7. Elsey, interview with the author.
8. See David Reynolds, *Summits: Six Meetings That Shaped the Twentieth Century* (New York: Basic Books, 2007), 161.

1. A TRIP TO THE MEDITERRANEAN

1. John McCrea, "'Iowa' — President and Joint Chiefs of Staff to Africa and Return," manuscript memoir, John L. McCrea Papers, FDR Presidential Library, Hyde Park, NY.
2. Argentia had made history in August 1941, when President Franklin Roosevelt and Prime Minister Winston Churchill had drawn up the famous Atlantic Charter aboard their respective warships. "Tiny villages cluster in the shoulders of her hills," the *Iowa's* chronicler described, "and mists that shroud the valleys lend an ethereal quality to this corner of Newfoundland. The population is mostly Irish and the

climate is wind-swept, foggy and crisply sombre." Twin peaks on the horizon were likened by the crew to the legendary bosom of Mae West — who, when informed of this, was said to have replied: "Thanks, boys. I hope they are standing up." The ocean ranged "from rolling, roughish grey to lake-water calms of sapphire brilliance. It is a quiet place, a place to drill, to study and prepare": "Iowa" (no author), unpublished TS, John L. McCrea Papers, 1898–1984, Library of Congress, Washington, DC.

3. The mishap took place on July 16, 1943, and led to a court of inquiry. President Roosevelt sent McCrea a box of good Cuban cigars in sympathy, as the fault was entirely McCrea's: John L. McCrea, *Captain McCrea's War: The World War II Memoir of Franklin D. Roosevelt's Naval Aide and USS* Iowa's *First Commanding Officer*, ed. Julia C. Tobey (New York: Skyhorse, 2016), 171.

4. McCrea, "'Iowa' — President and Joint Chiefs of Staff to Africa and Return."

5. Nigel Hamilton, *Commander in Chief: FDR's Battle with Churchill, 1943* (Boston: Houghton Mifflin Harcourt, 2016), 4–9 and 63–129.

6. Ibid., 55–60.

7. Ibid., 35–38.

8. McCrea, "'Iowa' — President and Joint Chiefs of Staff to Africa and Return."

2. THE MEETING IS ON

1. Hamilton, *Commander in Chief*, 228–34.

2. Ibid., 265–66.

3. Ibid., 360–66.

4. Ibid., 19–23 et seq.

5. Elizabeth Maclean, *Joseph E. Davies: Envoy to the Soviets* (Westport, CT: Praeger, 1992), 108.

6. Entries of October 30, 1943, and November 6, 1943, Ward, *Closest Companion*, 250 and 253.

3. MAXIMUM SECRECY

1. McCrea, "'Iowa' — President and Joint Chiefs of Staff to Africa and Return." See also McCrea, *Captain McCrea's War*, 77 et seq.

2. Ibid.

3. Ibid.

4. Ibid.

5. Ibid.

6. "An Historic Voyage," chapter in "Iowa" (no author), McCrea Papers, Library of Congress.

7. Ibid.

8. See Hamilton, *The Mantle of Command: FDR at War, 1941–1942* (Boston: Houghton Mifflin Harcourt, 2014), 3–18.

9. Cable 146, Stalin to Roosevelt, November 10, 1944, in Susan Butler, ed., *My Dear Mr. Stalin: The Complete Correspondence Between Franklin D. Roosevelt and Joseph V. Stalin* (New Haven, CT: Yale University Press, 2005), 182.
10. "Iowa" (no author), McCrea Papers, Library of Congress.
11. See Hamilton, *Commander in Chief*, 179–91.
12. Foreword to "Log of the President's Trip to Africa and the Middle East, November-December 1943," Franklin D. Roosevelt, Papers as President: Map Room Papers, 1941–1945, Box 24, FDR Presidential Library, Hyde Park, NY.
13. Ibid.
14. Entry of November 5, 1943, Ward, *Closest Companion,* 252.

4. SETTING SAIL

1. Entry of October 30, 1943, Ward, *Closest Companion,* 250.
2. Ibid., entry of November 8, 1943, 254.
3. Entry of November 12, 1943, Leahy Diary, William D. Leahy Papers, Library of Congress, Washington, DC.
4. McCrea, "'Iowa' — President and Joint Chiefs of Staff to Africa and Return."
5. Ibid.
6. Typed FDR Diary, in "War Conference in Cairo, Teheran, Malta, etc., November 11–December 17, 1943," Franklin D. Roosevelt, Papers as President: The President's Official File, Part 1, 1933–1945, 200-3-N, Box 64, FDR Presidential Library, Hyde Park, NY. (This is a typed version of FDR's handwritten original diary, also in file, bearing note: "This typed copy is the one corrected by F.D.R."; it contains FDR's additions, such as extracts from his letters, as dictated to his secretary, Grace Tully, upon his return.)
7. William M. Rigdon, with James Derieux, *White House Sailor* (Garden City, NY: Doubleday, 1962), 61.
8. Entry of November 13, 1943, Typed FDR Diary, "War Conference in Cairo, Teheran, Malta."

5. SHEER MADNESS

1. Entry of November 13, 1943, Typed FDR Diary, "War Conference in Cairo, Teheran, Malta."
2. Entry of November, 4, 1943, Stimson Diary, Henry L. Stimson Papers, Yale University Library, New Haven, CT.
3. Field Marshal Bernard Montgomery to author, multiple occasions, 1963–66.
4. Carlo D'Este, *Warlord: A Life of Winston Churchill at War, 1874–1945* (New York: HarperCollins, 2008), 230–34.
5. Ibid., 251–57.
6. "Prime Minister's Personal Minute, D. 178/3, Most Secret," October 19, 1943, in Martin Gilbert, *Winston S. Churchill,* vol. 7, *Road to Victory* (Toronto: Stoddart, 1986), 533.

7. C-441, October 8, 1943, in Warren F. Kimball, ed., *Churchill and Roosevelt: The Complete Correspondence,* vol. 2, *Alliance Forged, November 1942–February 1944* (Princeton, NJ: Princeton University Press, 1984), 503.
8. Max Hastings, *Winston's War: Churchill, 1940–1945* (New York: Knopf, 2009), 323–40.
9. Kimball, *Churchill and Roosevelt,* 498.
10. Ibid., R-379, October 7, 1943, 379.
11. Ibid., C-441, October 8, 1943, 503.
12. Ibid.
13. Ibid.
14. Ibid.
15. David Reynolds, *In Command of History: Churchill Fighting and Writing the Second World War* (New York: Random House, 2005), 376.
16. Entry of October 8, 1943, in Arthur Bryant, *Triumph in the West* (London: Collins, 1959), 51.
17. Ibid.
18. Ibid.
19. Ibid.
20. Entry of October 19, 1943, Bryant, *Triumph in the West,* 55, and Alan Brooke, *War Diaries, 1939–1945: Field Marshal Lord Alanbrooke,* eds. Alex Danchev and Daniel Todman (Berkeley: University of California Press, 2001), 461.
21. Entry of October 19, 1943, in Brooke, *War Diaries,* 461.
22. C-471, October 23, 1943, Kimball, *Churchill and Roosevelt,* 555.
23. Ibid.
24. Elsey, interview with the author.
25. C-475, October 26, 1943, Kimball, *Churchill and Roosevelt,* 562.
26. Ibid., C-471, October 23, 1943, 556.
27. Ibid.
28. Ibid., 555, and C-472, 558.

6. CHURCHILL'S IMPROPER ACT

1. See Hamilton, *Commander in Chief,* 235–42.
2. Entry of October 24, 1943, in the diaries kept by Sir Charles Wilson, Lord Moran: Moran, *Churchill: The Struggle for Survival, 1940–1965* (Boston: Houghton Mifflin, 1966), 122.
3. Cable W 3325/#1806, October 25, 1943, in Dwight D. Eisenhower, *The Papers of Dwight David Eisenhower: The War Years,* ed. Alfred Chandler, vol. 3 (Baltimore, MD: Johns Hopkins Press, 1970), 1529. To Eden, the Prime Minister cabled that the British "would do our very best for 'Overlord' but it is no use planning for defeat in the field in order to give temporary political satisfaction." Overlord was, in Churchill's view, however, still a nonstarter. Any assurances Eden had given "about May 'Overlord'" had now to be "modified by the exigencies of the battle in Italy." Nothing would "alter my determination not to throw away the battle in Italy at this

juncture," the Prime Minister stated emphatically; "Eisenhower and Alexander must have what they need to win the battle, no matter what effect is produced on subsequent operations. This may certainly affect the date of 'Overlord,'" he cabled (CHAR 20/122/43, Papers of Sir Winston Churchill, Churchill Archives Centre, Cambridge, UK).

4. "A radiogram came from General Deane, our military man with Mr. Hull, and this radiogram said that Churchill had sent to Moscow a copy of Alexander's rather pessimistic summary of the situation in Italy and had directed Eden to read it aloud to Stalin," together with "comments I think by Churchill that this would mean that the Second Front would be delayed or abandoned": Entry of October 28, 1943, Stimson Diary.

5. Ibid.

6. Ibid.

7. "Proposed Draft of Cable, From: The President, To: The Prime Minister," October 27, 1943, Pentagon Office, 1938–1951, Correspondence, Box 81, Papers of George Catlett Marshall, George C. Marshall Foundation Library, Lexington, VA.

8. Entry of October 31, 1943, Stimson Diary.

9. Ibid., entry of November 4, 1943.

10. Sent November 4, received November 6, 1943: *Foreign Relations of the United States: The Conferences at Cairo and Tehran, 1943* (hereinafter *FRUS I*) (Washington, DC: U.S. Government Printing Office, 1961), 65.

7. TORPEDO!

1. McCrea, "'Iowa' — President and Joint Chiefs of Staff to Africa and Return."

2. Ibid.

3. Ibid.

4. Rigdon, *White House Sailor*, 64.

5. Entry of November 14, 1943, in Henry H. Arnold, *American Airpower Comes of Age: General Henry H. "Hap" Arnold's World War II Diaries,* ed. John W. Huston, vol. 2 (Maxwell Air Force Base, AL: Air University Press, 2002), 76.

6. McCrea, "'Iowa' — President and Joint Chiefs of Staff to Africa and Return," and similar in McCrea, *Captain McCrea's War*, 186.

7. Ibid. Harry Hopkins's friend Robert Sherwood expressed his skepticism with this wording later, when writing Hopkins's biography. As an accomplished playwright Sherwood thought the shout would far more likely have been: "This ain't no drill!": Robert E. Sherwood, *Roosevelt and Hopkins: An Intimate History* (New York: Harper, 1948), 768.

8. McCrea, "'Iowa' — President and Joint Chiefs of Staff to Africa and Return."

9. Ibid.

10. Ibid.

11. Ibid.

12. Ibid.

13. Ibid.

14. Sherwood, *Roosevelt and Hopkins,* 768.

15. H. H. Arnold, *Global Mission* (New York: Harper, 1949), 455.

16. Rigdon, *White House Sailor,* 64.

17. Ibid.

18. In his memoirs King wrote that "many people thought the ship had been hit": Ernest J. King and Walter M. Whitehill, *Fleet Admiral King: A Naval Record* (New York: Norton, 1952), 501.

19. McCrea, "'Iowa' — President and Joint Chiefs of Staff to Africa and Return."

20. Entry of November 14, 1943 (Atlantic Ocean), Arnold, *American Air Power Comes of Age,* 76.

21. Arnold, *Global Mission,* 455.

22. McCrea, "'Iowa' — President and Joint Chiefs of Staff to Africa and Return."

23. Entry of November 14, 1943 (Atlantic Ocean), Arnold, *American Air Power Comes of Age,* 76.

24. Arnold, *Global Mission,* 455.

25. "Nov 18. From Letter," in Typed FDR Diary, "War Conference in Cairo, Teheran, Malta."

26. Ibid., entry of November 19, 1943.

27. McCrea, "'Iowa' — President and Joint chiefs of Staff to Africa and Return."

28. Sherwood, *Roosevelt and Hopkins,* 768.

29. Entry of November 14, 1943 (Atlantic Ocean), in Arnold, *American Air Power Comes of Age,* 76.

30. Quoted in Arnold, *Global Mission,* 455.

31. Rigdon, *White House Sailor,* 64. The captain of the USS *William D. Porter* swiftly signaled to explain what had happened. The torpedo was not meant to be actually fired; he had merely been trying to rehearse the procedure, in time-honored rules of such exercises, where a friendly vessel is used as the putative target. Salt spray had, he claimed, "bridged an open electric switch on one of the destroyer's torpedo tubes, thus setting off the ejection mechanism and sending the armed torpedo on its way": ibid. As McCrea later noted, this did not sound at all convincing. In truth the *Porter*'s chief petty officer, after testing "to see if it would fit" properly, had failed — as the President correctly noted afterwards — to remove the firing primer before the voyage began. Once the captain decided to rehearse the firing of a torpedo — but without having been told of the dignitaries aboard the *Iowa* — the aiming mechanism, directed from the bridge, made it almost certain the torpedo would not only be fired but would hit the innocent target. Had the seas been still heavier that day, the lookout on the *Iowa* might not have seen the torpedo racing toward the battleship, twenty feet beneath the waves, and "it no doubt would have hit us," McCrea later reflected soberly. Fate had been kind — though not, McCrea recorded sadly, to the USS *Porter* — which was subsequently posted to the Pacific, only to be hit and sunk there in a Japanese kamikaze plane assault, with the loss of all hands, the following year.

8. A PRETTY SERIOUS SET-TO

1. Entry of November 9, 1943, in Brooke, *War Diaries,* 468.

2. Ibid., entry of November 10, 1943, 468.

3. Entry of November 11, 1943, Bryant, *Triumph in the West,* 67. See also Brooke, *War Diaries,* 469.

4. Recommendation on strategy by the British chiefs of staff, November 11, 1943, in Bryant, *Triumph in the West,* 65.

5. Max Domarus, ed., *Hitler, Speeches and Proclamations 1932–1945: The Chronicle of a Dictatorship,* vol. 4, *The Years 1941 to 1945* (Wauconda, IL: Bolchazy-Carducci, 1977), 2843.

6. Ibid.

7. Ibid., 2837.

8. Ibid., 2838.

9. Ibid.

10. Ibid.

11. Ibid.

12. Ibid., 2840

13. Ibid.

14. Ibid., 2842.

15. Ibid., 2843.

16. Entry of 14.11.1943, in Joseph Goebbels, *Die Tagebücher von Joseph Goebbels* [The Diaries of Joseph Goebbbels], ed. Elke Froehlich (Munich: K. G. Saur, 1993), Band 10 (hereinafter *Tagebücher 10*), 290. Quotes from this source have been translated by the author.

9. MARSHALL: COMMANDER IN CHIEF AGAINST GERMANY

1. "Minutes of Meeting, Between the President and the Chiefs of Staff, held on board ship in The President's Cabin, 15 November 1943, at 1400," 4, Franklin D. Roosevelt, Papers as President: Map Room Papers, 1941–1945, Box 29, FDR Presidential Library, Hyde Park, NY.

2. Reynolds, *In Command of History,* 383.

3. Ibid.

4. Ibid., 381.

5. Ibid., 385.

6. Entry of October 27, 1943, in Alexander Cadogan, *The Diaries of Sir Alexander Cadogan, O.M., 1938–1945,* ed. David Dilks (London: Cassell, 1971), 571.

7. See entry of November 16, 1943, Moran, *Churchill,* 126–27.

8. Reynolds, *In Command of History,* 389.

9. "Minutes of Meeting, Between the President and the Chiefs of Staff, held on board ship in The President's Cabin, 15 November 1943."

10. Ibid. (Author's italics.)

11. Ibid. The word "all" would be important.

10. A WITCHES' BREW

1. Entry of November 16, 1943, in Harold Macmillan, *War Diaries: Politics and War in the Mediterranean, January 1943–May 1945* (London: Macmillan, 1984), 294. (Italics in original.)
2. Ibid.
3. Martin Gilbert, *Churchill and America* (New York: Free Press, 2005), xxiii–xxiv. "No lover ever studied every whim of his mistress as I did those of President Roosevelt," Churchill also reflected: ibid., 386.
4. Entry of November 16, 1943, Macmillan, *War Diaries*, 294.
5. Ibid., 295.
6. CHAR 20/122/43, Churchill Archives.
7. Ibid.
8. Quoted in Churchill, *The Second World War*, vol. 5, *Closing the Ring* (London: Cassell, 1952), 259.
9. CHAR 20/122/80–83, October 29, 1943, Churchill Archives.
10. Entry of November 25, 1943, Macmillan, *War Diaries*, 303.
11. Entry of November 18, 1943, Bryant, *Triumph in the West*, 7.
12. Entry of November 18, 1943, Brooke, *War Diaries*, 472.
13. Ibid.
14. Ibid., 472–73.
15. Entry of November 17, 1943, in Harry Butcher, *My Three Years with Eisenhower: The Personal Diary of Captain Harry C. Butcher, USNR, Naval Aide to General Eisenhower, 1942 to 1945* (New York: Simon & Schuster, 1946), 442.

11. FULLEST GUIDANCE

1. Letter of December 2, 1943, Papers of Sir John Martin, Churchill Archives Centre, Cambridge, UK.
2. "Former Naval Person to Admiral Queen," C-505/1, November 18, 1943, Kimball, *Churchill and Roosevelt*, 602.
3. Maurice Matloff, *Strategic Planning for Coalition Warfare, 1943–1944* (Washington, DC: Office of Chief of Military History, U.S. Government Printing Office, 1959), 338.
4. Forrest Pogue, *George C. Marshall*, vol. 3, *Organizer of Victory, 1943–1949* (New York: Viking, 1973), 301, quoting John Kennedy, *The Business of War*, 305.

12. ON BOARD THE *IOWA*

1. "Minutes of Meeting, Between the President and the Chiefs of Staff, held on board ship in The Admiral's Cabin, on Friday, 19 November 1943, at 1500," Franklin D. Roosevelt, Papers as President: Map Room Papers, 1941–1945, Box 29, FDR Presidential Library.
2. Ibid.
3. Ibid.
4. Ibid.

5. Ibid.
6. Ibid.
7. Ibid.
8. Ibid.
9. Ibid.
10. Entry of November 18, 1943, Bryant, *Triumph in the West,* 70.
11. "Minutes of Meeting, Between the President and the Chiefs of Staff, held on board ship in The Admiral's Cabin, on Friday, 19 November 1943."
12. Ibid.

13. IN THE FOOTSTEPS OF SCIPIO AND HANNIBAL

1. Entry of November 20, 1943, Typed FDR Diary, "War Conference in Cairo, Teheran, Malta."
2. Elliott Roosevelt, *As He Saw It* (New York: Duell, Sloan and Pearce, 1946), 132.
3. Ibid.
4. Entry of November 20, 1943, Typed FDR Diary, "War Conference in Cairo, Teheran, Malta."
5. Roosevelt, *As He Saw It,* 136.
6. Elliott Roosevelt, quoting his brother Franklin Jr., in ibid., 136–38.
7. Dwight D. Eisenhower, *Crusade in Europe* (New York: Doubleday, 1948), 195.
8. "Log of the President's Trip to Africa and the Middle East."
9. Eisenhower, *Crusade in Europe,* 195.
10. Kay Summersby, *Eisenhower Was My Boss* (London: Werner Laurie, 1949), 88.
11. Ibid., 86–87.
12. Entry of November 16, 1943, Moran, *Churchill,* 126–27.

14. TWO PIECES IN A CHESS GAME

1. Eisenhower, *Crusade in Europe,* 194.
2. "Mr. Churchill told me, confidentially, that it had been most embarrassing to him to have to tell Brooke" — to whom the supreme command had hitherto been promised — "of the change because he appreciated and sympathized with the anguished disappointment that Brooke was thus compelled to suffer": Dwight. D. Eisenhower, TS of handwritten draft chapter, unpublished memoirs, 11/17/66, "Churchill-Marshall (1)," 43, Kevin McCann Papers, in Papers, Post-Presidential, 1961–1969, Eisenhower Presidential Library, Abilene, KS.
3. Ibid., 44.
4. Eisenhower, *Crusade in Europe,* 195.
5. "Minutes of Meeting, Between the President and the Chiefs of Staff, on board ship in The Admiral's Cabin, on Friday, 19 November 1943."
6. Ibid.
7. Eisenhower, *Crusade in Europe,* 197.
8. Eisenhower, draft memoir TS, 45.

9. Ibid.

10. Ibid., 47.

11. Ibid., 46.

12. Eisenhower, *Crusade in Europe,* 197.

13. Ibid.

14. "He (admiral Leahy) did not feel we should accept this until we have fought out the matter of a Supreme Allied Commander" for all Europe: "Minutes of Meeting, Between the President and the Chiefs of Staff, on board ship in The Admiral's Cabin, on Friday, 19 November 1943."

15. Eisenhower, draft memoir TS, 46–47.

16. Entry of November 21, 1943, Typed FDR Diary, "War Conference in Cairo, Teheran, Malta."

17. Roosevelt, *As He Saw It,* 137.

18. Ibid.

19. Summersby, *Eisenhower Was My Boss,* 86.

20. The route flown, according to the President's log, was 1,851 miles: Entry of November 22, 1943, "Log of the President's Trip to Africa and the Middle East."

21. Roosevelt, *As He Saw It,* 138.

22. Entry of November 22, 1943, Leahy Diary.

15. AIRY VISIONS

1. Speech at the Lord Mayor's Day Luncheon at Mansion House, London, November 9, 1943: "No Time to Relax," in Winston Churchill, *The War Speeches of the Rt. Hon. Winston S. Churchill,* comp. Charles Eade, vol. 3 (London: Cassell, 1951).

2. Ibid., 65–68.

3. "A Decade of American Foreign Policy 1941–1949: Connally Resolution November 5, 1943," Avalon Project: Documents in Law, History and Diplomacy, http://avalon.law. yale.edu/20th_century/decade10.asp.

4. Entry of 7.11.1943, in Joseph Goebbels, *Die Tagebücher von Joseph Goebbels* [The Diaries of Joseph Goebbels], ed. Elke Froehlich (Munich: K. G. Saur, 1993), Band 10 (hereinafter *Tagebücher 10*), 244. Quotes from this source have been translated by the author.

5. Ibid., entry of 10.11.1943, 267.

6. Ibid., entry of 20.11.1943, 322.

7. Ibid., entry of 25.11.1943, 356.

16. THE AMERICAN SPHINX

1. Entry of November 22, 1943, Typed FDR Diary, in "War Conference in Cairo, Teheran, Malta, etc., November 11–December 17, 1943," Franklin D. Roosevelt, Papers as President: The President's Official File, Part 1, 1933–1945, 200-3-N, Box 64, FDR Presidential Library, Hyde Park, NY.

2. Michael F. Reilly, as told to William J. Slocum, *Reilly of the White House* (New York: Simon & Schuster, 1947), 170.

3. Entry of November 22, 1943, "Log of the President's Trip to Africa and the Middle East, November–December 1943," Franklin D. Roosevelt, Papers as President: Map Room Papers, 1941–1945, Box 24, FDR Presidential Library, Hyde Park, NY.

4. Entry of November 22, 1943, Typed FDR Diary, "War Conference in Cairo, Teheran, Malta."

5. Entry of November 25, 1943, in Harold Macmillan, *War Diaries: Politics and War in the Mediterranean, January 1943–May 1945* (London: Macmillan, 1984), 203.

6. Entry of November 22, 1943, "Log of the President's Trip to Africa and the Middle East."

7. See ibid., entry of November 25, 1943, on Bryan's and Reilly's return from Tehran.

8. See Nigel Hamilton, *Commander in Chief: FDR's Battle With Churchill, 1943* (Boston: Houghton Mifflin Harcourt, 2016), 204–58.

9. Entry of November 22, 1943, Typed FDR Diary, "War Conference in Cairo, Teheran, Malta." Churchill was heard to say, of their outing: "The two most talkative people in the world meeting the most silent": Letter of December 2, 1943, Papers of Sir John Martin, Churchill Archives Centre, Cambridge, UK.

17. CHURCHILL'S "INDICTMENT"

1. Entry of November 18, 1943, Lord Moran, *Churchill: The Struggle for Survival, 1940–1965* (Boston: Houghton Mifflin, 1966), 129; also Winston Churchill, *The Second World War*, vol. 5, *Closing the Ring* (London: Cassell, 1952), 291.

2. Winston Churchill, quoting his "indictment of our mismanagement of operations in the Mediterranean," given to the British chiefs of staff, quoted in Churchill, *Closing the Ring*, 293.

3. Churchill Minute, "Future Operations in the European and Mediterranean Theatre," November 20, 1943, in Martin Gilbert, *Winston S. Churchill*, vol. 7, *Road to Victory: 1941–1945* (Toronto: Stoddart, 1986), 558–59.

4. Ibid., 558.

5. Ibid.

6. Entry of November 20, 1943, in Arthur Bryant, *Triumph in the West* (London: Collins, 1959), 74.

7. Ibid., entry of November 21, 1943, 74–75.

8. Ibid., entry of November 22, 1943, 75.

9. Ibid., annotation to entry of November 21, 1943, 75.

10. Hastings Lionel Ismay, *The Memoirs of General Lord Ismay* (London: Heinemann, 1960), 337.

11. Annotation to entry of November 21, 1943, in Bryant, *Triumph in the West*, 75.

12. Churchill, *Closing the Ring*, 289–90.

13. Elliott Roosevelt, *As He Saw It* (New York: Duell, Sloan and Pearce, 1946), 144.

14. Ibid.

15. Ibid.

16. Ibid., 142.

17. November 22, 1943, *Foreign Relations of the United States: The Conferences at Cairo and Tehran, 1943* (hereinafter *FRUS I*) (Washington, DC: U.S. Government Printing Office, 1961), 303.

18. Entry of November 23, 1943, in H. H. Arnold, *American Air Power Comes of Age: General "Hap" Arnold's World War II Diaries*, ed. John W. Huston (Maxwell Air Force Base, AL: Air University Press, 2002), 85.

19. Joseph W. Stilwell, *The Stilwell Papers* (New York: Sloane, 1948), 245; Barbara W. Tuchman, *Stilwell and the American Experience in China, 1911–1945* (New York: Macmillan, 1971), 403.

18. SHOWDOWN

1. "Meeting of the Combined Chiefs of Staff with Roosevelt and Churchill, November 24, 1943, 11 a.m., President's Villa," *FRUS I*, 334.

2. Ibid.

3. Entry of November 24, 1943, Bryant, *Triumph in the West*, 82.

4. Entry of November 24, 1943, Leahy Diary, William D. Leahy Papers, Library of Congress, Washington, DC.

5. "Meeting of the Combined Chiefs of Staff with Roosevelt and Churchill," *FRUS I*, 334.

6. Entry of November 24, 1943, in Arnold, *American Air Power Comes of Age*, 86.

7. The President's Log at Cairo, *FRUS I*, 298–99.

8. Entry of November 25, 1943, Leahy Diary.

9. In his written rebuttal, Churchill strenuously objected to the notion of a single supreme commander "to command all United Nations operations against Germany" — especially if it were to be an American officer who could then pronounce "in favour of concentrating on Overlord irrespective of the injury done to our affairs in the Mediterranean": "Memorandum by Prime Minister Churchill," Cairo, November 25, 1943 (Roosevelt Papers), in *FRUS I*, 407.

10. "Note by the British Chiefs of Staff," CCS 409, "Overlord and the Mediterranean," Cairo, November 25, 1943, *FRUS I*, 409.

11. Entry of November 26, 1943, Bryant, *Triumph in the West*, 84.

12. Entry of November 26, 1943, Leahy Diary.

13. Entry of November 26, 1943, Typed FDR Diary, "War Conference in Cairo, Teheran, Malta."

19. A VISION OF THE POSTWAR WORLD

1. See Nigel Hamilton, *Commander in Chief: FDR's Battle with Churchill, 1943* (Boston: Houghton Mifflin Harcourt, 2014), 22–23.

2. Memorandum by the Assistant Secretary of War (McCloy), Attachment 1, November 25, 1943, *Foreign Relations of the United States: The Conferences at Cairo and Tehran, 1943* (hereinafter *FRUS I*) (Washington, DC: U.S. Government Printing Office, 1961), 418.

3. Ibid.
4. See Hamilton, *Commander in Chief*, 370–72.
5. Memorandum by the Assistant Secretary of War (McCloy), *FRUS I*, 418.
6. Ibid.
7. See Hamilton, *Commander in Chief*, 69.
8. Entry of November 27, 1943, "Log of the President's Trip to Africa and the Middle East, November–December 1943," Franklin D. Roosevelt, Papers as President: Map Room Papers, 1941–1945, Box 24, FDR Presidential Library, Hyde Park, NY.

20. IN THE RUSSIAN COMPOUND

1. Susan Butler, *Roosevelt and Stalin: Portrait of a Partnership* (New York: Knopf, 2015), 42.
2. Hastings Lionel Ismay, *The Memoirs of General Lord Ismay* (London: Heinemann, 1960), 337.
3. Martin Gilbert, *Winston S. Churchill*, vol. 7, *Road to Victory: 1941–1945* (Toronto: Stoddart, 1986), quoting J. H. Colegrave, a British staff officer at Tehran, 568.
4. Letter of December 4, 1943, in Sarah Churchill, *Keep On Dancing: An Autobiography* (London: Coward, McCann & Geoghegan, 1981), 70.
5. Entry of November 6, 1943, in Geoffrey C. Ward, ed., *Closest Companion: The Unknown Story of the Intimate Friendship Between Franklin Roosevelt and Margaret Suckley* (Boston: Houghton Mifflin, 1995), 253.
6. Entry of November 28, 1943, "Log of the President's Trip to Africa and the Middle East."
7. Averell Harriman and Elie Abel, *Special Envoy to Churchill and Stalin, 1941–1946* (London: Hutchinson, 1976), 264.
8. "Minutes of Meeting, Between the President and the Joint Chiefs of Staff held in the American Legation, Tehran, Iran, on Sunday, 28 November 1943, at 11:30," 1, Franklin D. Roosevelt, Papers as President: Map Room Papers, Box 29, FDR Presidential Library.
9. Ibid.
10. Ibid., 3.
11. Ibid., 2.
12. Ibid., 3.
13. Ibid., 4.
14. Ibid.
15. Ibid., 3.
16. Ibid., 5.
17. Ibid., 4.

21. THE GRAND DEBATE

1. Keith Eubank, *Summit at Teheran: The Untold Story* (New York: William Morrow, 1985), 190.
2. Charles Bohlen, *Witness to History, 1929–1969* (New York: Norton, 1973), 135–36.

3. Ibid., 136–37.
4. Ibid., 137.
5. Ibid., 139.
6. Ibid.
7. Ibid.
8. Ibid.
9. "Roosevelt-Stalin Meeting, November 28, 1943, 3 p.m., Roosevelt's Quarters, Soviet Embassy," Bohlen Minutes, *FRUS I*, 483.
10. Ibid., 484.
11. Ibid., 484–85.
12. Ibid.
13. H. H. Arnold, *American Airpower Comes of Age: General Henry H. "Hap" Arnold's World War II Diaries*, vol. 2, ed. John W. Huston (Maxwell Air Force Base, AL: Air University Press), 89.
14. Harriman and Abel, *Special Envoy*, 265.
15. Ibid.
16. A. H. Birse, *Memoirs of an Interpreter* (London: Michael Joseph, 1967), 155.
17. Bohlen, *Witness to History*, 142.
18. "First Plenary Meeting, November 28, 1943, 4 p.m., Conference Room, Soviet Embassy," Bohlen Minutes, *FRUS I*, 487.
19. Ibid.
20. Birse, *Memoirs of an Interpreter*, 155.
21. "First Plenary Meeting," Bohlen Minutes, *FRUS I*, 488–89.
22. Ibid., 489.
23. Ibid.
24. Ibid.
25. Ibid., 489–90.
26. Ibid., 490–91.
27. Ibid., 491.
28. Entry of November 28, 1943, in Arthur Bryant, *Triumph in the West* (London: Collins, 1959), 89.
29. Ibid.
30. Entry of November 28, 1943, in Lord Moran, *Churchill: The Struggle for Survival, 1940–1965* (Boston: Houghton Mifflin, 1966), 135.
31. "First Plenary Meeting," Bohlen Minutes, *FRUS I*, 491.
32. Ibid., 495.
33. Ibid.
34. Ibid.
35. Ibid.
36. Ibid., 496.
37. Ibid.
38. Ibid., 497.
39. Annotation to entry of November 28, 1943, Bryant, *Triumph in the West*, 90.
40. Ibid.

41. Ismay, *Memoirs,* 338.
42. Entry of November 28, 1943, Moran, *Churchill,* 134.
43. Ismay, *Memoirs,* 338.
44. Ibid., 339.
45. "Discussion following 'Lecture on Some Aspects of the High Command in World War II by Fleet Admiral Ernest J. King,'" National War College, Washington, DC, April 29, 1947, in Papers of Ernest J. King, 1908–1966, Box 29, Library of Congress.
46. Ibid.
47. "First Plenary Meeting," Bohlen Minutes, *FRUS I,* 497–508.
48. Raymond Clapper, "Confidential" — TS notes on "sixth off-the-record seminar with Admiral King," Alexandria, VA, July 26, 1945, Raymond Clapper Papers, 1908–1962, Library of Congress, Washington, DC.
49. Entry of November 29, 1943, Moran, *Churchill,* 135.

22. A REAL SCARE

1. Bohlen, *Witness to History,* 143.
2. Ibid.
3. "Tripartite Dinner Meeting, November 28, 1943, 8:30 p.m., Roosevelt's Quarters, Soviet Embassy," *FRUS I,* 509.
4. Ibid., 510.
5. Ibid.
6. Bohlen, *Witness to History,* 143–44.
7. Robert E. Sherwood, *Roosevelt and Hopkins: An Intimate History* (New York: Harper, 1948), 781.
8. Birse, *Memoirs of an Interpreter,* 156.
9. Entry of November 28, 1943, Leahy Diary, William D. Leahy Papers, Library of Congress, Washington, DC.
10. William M. Rigdon, with James Derieux, *White House Sailor* (Garden City, NY: Doubleday, 1962), 84.
11. Ibid.
12. Steven Lomazow and Eric Fettmann, *FDR's Deadly Secret* (New York: PublicAffairs, 2009), 11; also Robert H. Ferrell, *The Dying President: Franklin D. Roosevelt, 1944–1945* (Columbia: University of Missouri Press, 1998), 23.
13. Ferrell, *The Dying President,* 17, 23.
14. Harry Goldsmith, *A Conspiracy of Silence: The Health and Death of Franklin D. Roosevelt* (New York: iUniverse, 2007), 172.

23. IMPASSE

1. Entry of November 29, 1943, Leahy Diary.
2. Rigdon, *White House Sailor,* 84.
3. Bohlen, *Witness to History,* 145.
4. Entry of November 29, 1943, Leahy Diary.

5. "Tripartite Military Meeting, November 29, 1943, 10:30 a.m., Conference Room, Soviet Embassy," *FRUS I*, 515–27.

6. Ibid.

7. Ibid., 520.

8. Ibid., 524.

24. PRICKING CHURCHILL'S BUBBLE

1. Ward, *Closest Companion*, 299.

2. Entry of November 29, 1943, Moran, *Churchill*, 136.

3. Ibid.

4. Elliott Roosevelt, *As He Saw It* (New York: Duell, Sloan and Pearce, 1946), 179.

5. "Roosevelt-Stalin Meeting, November 29, 2:45 p.m., Roosevelt's Quarters, Soviet Embassy," Bohlen Minutes, *FRUS I*, 530. The sketch, reproduced in Sherwood, *Roosevelt and Hopkins*, 789, showed three separate bubbles for the three parts of the proposed organization — with forty members of the main "U.N." body.

6. "Roosevelt-Stalin Meeting," Bohlen Minutes, *FRUS I*, 530. Roosevelt's annotation on his sketch read: "ILO — Health, Agric, Food": Sherwood, *Roosevelt and Hopkins*, 789.

7. "Roosevelt-Stalin Meeting," Bohlen Minutes, *FRUS I*, 530.

8. Bohlen, *Witness to History*, 145.

9. "Roosevelt-Stalin Meeting," Bohlen Minutes, *FRUS I*, 531.

10. Ibid., 532.

11. Roosevelt, *As He Saw It*, 180.

12. Entry of November 29, 1943, Moran, *Churchill*, 136.

13. "Roosevelt-Stalin Meeting," Bohlen Minutes, *FRUS I*, 535; entry of November 29, 1943, Moran, *Churchill*, 137.

14. Bohlen, *Witness to History*, 145.

15. Entry of November 29, 1943, Moran, *Churchill*, 137.

16. "Second Plenary Meeting, November 29, 1943, 4 p.m., Conference Room, Soviet Embassy," *FRUS I*, 535.

17. Ibid.

18. Ibid.

19. Entry of November 29, 1943, Bryant, *Triumph in the West*, 92.

20. Ibid.

21. "Second Plenary Meeting," *FRUS I*, 535.

22. Ibid., 536.

23. Ibid., 538.

24. Bryant, *Triumph in the West*, 93. Also further entry in Alan Brooke, *War Diaries, 1939–1945: Field Marshal Lord Alanbrooke*, eds. Alex Danchev and Daniel Todman (Berkeley: University of California Press, 2001), 485.

25. Entry of November 29, 1943, Leahy Diary.

26. "Second Plenary Meeting," *FRUS I*, 546.
27. Ibid.
28. Ibid., 545.
29. Ibid., 546.
30. Ibid., 547.
31. Ibid.
32. Ibid.
33. Ibid.
34. Ibid., 548.
35. Ibid., 549–50.
36. Ibid., 550–51.
37. November 18, 1943, Nigel Hamilton, *Master of the Battlefield: Monty's War Years, 1942–1944* (New York: McGraw Hill, 1984), 455.
38. Ibid.
39. Sherwood, *Roosevelt and Hopkins*, 788–89.

25. WAR AND PEACE

1. Entry of November 29, 1943, Leahy Diary.
2. Entry of November 29, 1943, Moran, *Churchill*, 138.
3. Ibid.
4. Entry of November 30, 1943, "Log of the President's Trip to Africa and the Middle East." See also "Tripartite Dinner Meeting, November 30, 1943, 8:30 p.m., British Legation," Bohlen Minutes, *FRUS I*, 584.
5. "Tripartite Dinner Meeting," Bohlen Minutes, *FRUS I*, 585.
6. Entry of November 29, 1943, Brooke, *War Diaries*, 485.

26. A COMMANDER FOR OVERLORD

1. Appendix D, "Log of the President's Trip to Africa and the Middle East, November–December 1943," Franklin D. Roosevelt, Papers as President: Map Room Papers, 1941–1945, Box 24, FDR Presidential Library, Hyde Park, NY.
2. William D. Leahy, *I Was There* (New York: McGraw-Hill, 1950), 207.
3. Appendix D, "Log of the President's Trip to Africa and the Middle East."
4. Ibid.
5. Entry of 1.12.1943, Joseph Goebbels, *Die Tagebücher von Joseph Goebbels* [The Diaries of Joseph Goebbbels], ed. Elke Froehlich (Munich: K. G. Saur, 1993) Band 10 (hereinafter *Tagebücher 10*), 399. Quotes from this source have been translated by the author.
6. Joseph Lelyveld, *His Final Battle: The Last Months of Franklin Roosevelt* (New York: Knopf, 2016), 40.
7. Entry of December 2, 1943, Leahy Diary, William D. Leahy Papers, Library of Congress, Washington, DC.

27. A MOMENTOUS DECISION

1. Joseph Persico, *Roosevelt's Centurions: FDR and the Commanders He Led to Victory in World War II* (New York: Random House, 2013), 340.
2. Stimson to Hopkins, for the President, November 10, 1943, Stimson Diary, Henry L. Stimson Papers, Yale University Library, New Haven, CT.
3. General Pershing to the President, September 16, 1943, in Forrest Pogue, *George C. Marshall,* vol. 3, *Organizer of Victory, 1943–1949* (New York: Viking, 1973), 272.
4. Roosevelt to Pershing, September 20, 1943, *The Papers of George Catlett Marshall,* vol. 4, 129.
5. Ibid.
6. Ibid., 343.
7. See Nigel Hamilton, *The Mantle of Command: FDR at War, 1941–1942* (Boston: Houghton Mifflin Harcourt, 2014), 330–42, and Hamilton, *Commander in Chief: FDR's Battle with Churchill, 1943* (Boston: Houghton Mifflin Harcourt, 2016), 55–60 and 97–99.
8. George C. Marshall, *Interviews and Reminiscences for Forrest C. Pogue* (Lexington, VA: George C. Marshall Foundation, 1996), 343.
9. Later still General Marshall even wondered whether the President had been pressed to make such an urgent decision because the matter had been "stirred around politically over here in this country (the U.S.A.)," or "in the press, rather": ibid., 343. This was, however, a speculation Marshall made more than a decade after the events, when attempting to recall the exact circumstances, and is not indicated by any contemporary documents.
10. Robert E. Sherwood, *Roosevelt and Hopkins: An Intimate History* (New York: Harper, 1948), 803.
11. Winston Churchill, *The Second World War,* vol. 5, *Closing the Ring* (London: Cassell, 1952), 340 and 370.
12. "Meeting of the Combined Chiefs of Staff with Roosevelt and Churchill, December 4, 1943, 11 a.m., Roosevelt's Villa," *Foreign Relations of the United States: The Conferences at Cairo and Tehran, 1943* (hereinafter *FRUS I*), 675. Also Churchill, *Closing the Ring,* 362.
13. Sherwood, *Roosevelt and Hopkins,* 803.
14. Ibid.
15. Ibid., 802.
16. See Churchill, *Closing the Ring,* 370 inter alia.
17. Sherwood, *Roosevelt and Hopkins,* 803.

28. A BAD TELEGRAM

1. Entry of December 8, 1943, Stimson Diary.
2. Ibid., entry of December 11, 1943.
3. Ibid., Weekly Survey, December 9, 1943.

4. Entry of December 4, 1943, H. H. Arnold, *American Air Power Comes of Age: General "Hap" Arnold's World War II Diaries,* ed. John W. Huston (Maxwell Air Force Base, AL: Air University Press, 2002), 95.

5. Entry of December 4, 1943, in Arthur Bryant, *Triumph in the West* (London: Collins, 1959), 105.

6. Churchill, *Closing the Ring,* 370.

29. PERFIDIOUS ALBION REDUX

1. Entry of December 3, 1943, Arnold, *American Air Power Comes of Age,* 94.

2. Ibid., entry of December 4, 1943, 95.

3. Entry of December 3, 1943, Bryant, *Triumph in the West,* 104.

4. Churchill, *Closing the Ring,* 800–801.

5. Entry of December 4, 1943, Leahy Diary.

6. Ibid., entry of December 5, 1943.

7. See draft FDR cable to Chiang Kai-shek of December 5, 1943, in Sherwood, *Roosevelt and Hopkins,* 801.

8. William D. Leahy, *I Was There* (New York: McGraw-Hill, 1950), 213–14.

9. Ibid.

10. Marshall, *Interviews and Reminiscences,* 622. Concerning Churchill's obsession with Rhodes and the Aegean, as well as his deliberate failure to consult the U.S. Joint Chiefs when ordering the unilateral invasion of the islands in September 1943, see Marshall interview of November 15, 1956 (ibid., 321).

11. Ernest J. King and Walter M. Whitehill, *Fleet Admiral King: A Naval Record* (New York: Norton, 1952), 525.

12. Joseph W. Stilwell, *The Stilwell Papers* (New York: Sloane, 1948), 251–54.

13. King and Whitehill, *Fleet Admiral King,* 525.

14. Facsimile of original in Dwight D. Eisenhower, *Crusade in Europe* (New York: Doubleday, 1948), 208. According to the Map Room files at the White House, declassified three decades later, the historic cable was received in Washington that night "as Black 79 from the President" for "transmittal to Marshal Stalin." It had been rephrased as: "The decision had been made to appoint General Eisenhower immediately to command of cross-Channel operations," and was signed "Roosevelt." It was then released to be dispatched onward to Moscow by the Navy Code Room at 9:15 p.m., December 6, 1943, Eastern Standard Time, or 4:15 a.m. in Cairo, December 7, 1943. A note, in hand, confirms it was received in Moscow at 10:20 a.m.: Franklin D. Roosevelt, Papers as President: Map Room Papers, 1941–1945, Box 8, FDR Presidential Library.

30. IN THE FIELD WITH EISENHOWER

1. Transcript of part of a letter (undoubtedly December 8, 1944) to Daisy Suckley, in Typed FDR Diary, in "War Conference in Cairo, Teheran, Malta, etc., November 11–December 17, 1943," Franklin D. Roosevelt, Papers as President: The

President's Official File, Part 1, 1933–1945, 200-3-N, Box 64, FDR Presidential Library.

2. Entry of December 11, 1944, in Geoffrey C. Ward, ed., *Closest Companion: The Unknown Story of the Intimate Friendship Between Franklin Roosevelt and Margaret Suckley* (Boston: Houghton Mifflin, 1995), 261.

3. Entry of December 7, 1943, Typed FDR Diary, "War Conference in Cairo, Teheran, Malta."

4. Ross T. McIntire, *White House Physician* (New York: Putnam's, 1946), 177.

5. Eisenhower, *Crusade in Europe*, 207.

6. Ibid., 204.

7. Letter of November 20, 1943, Typed FDR Diary, "War Conference in Cairo, Teheran, Malta."

31. A FLAP AT MALTA

1. McIntire, *White House Physician*, 178.

2. Ibid.

3. Ibid.

4. William M. Rigdon, with James Derieux, *White House Sailor* (Garden City, NY: Doubleday, 1962), 93. See also entry of December 8, 1943, in "Log of the President's Trip to Africa and the Middle East."

5. Lord Gort had won the Victoria Cross for gallantry as a battalion commander in World War I, and had then commanded the British Expeditionary Force in the ill-fated advance into Belgium, then retreat to Dunkirk in 1940.

6. Entry of December 8, 1943, "Log of the President's Trip to Africa and the Middle East."

7. Entry of December 8, 1943, Leahy Diary.

8. Entry of December 8, 1943, "Log of the President's Trip to Africa and the Middle East."

9. Ibid.

10. Entry of December 8, 1943, Leahy Diary.

11. Sherwood, *Roosevelt and Hopkins*, 803.

12. Ibid.

13. Keith Eubank, *Summit at Tehran: The Untold Story* (New York: William Morrow, 1985), 287.

14. Eisenhower, *Crusade in Europe*, 194.

15. Eisenhower, draft memoir, tss 45, Eisenhower Library.

32. HOMEWARD BOUND!

1. Entry of December 8, 1943, Typed FDR Diary, "War Conference in Cairo, Teheran, Malta."

2. Entry of December 8, 1943, "Log of the President's Trip to Africa and the Middle East."

3. Leahy, *I Was There*, 215.

4. Rick Atkinson, *The Day of Battle: The War in Sicily and Italy, 1943–1944* (New York: Henry Holt, 2007), 297.

5. Michael F. Reilly, as told to William J. Slocum, *Reilly of the White House* (New York: Simon & Schuster, 1947), 188.

6. Eisenhower, *Crusade in Europe*, 207.

7. Kay Summersby, *Eisenhower Was My Boss* (London: Werner Laurie, 1949), 101.

8. Extract from letter, December 9, 1943, Typed FDR Diary, "War Conference in Cairo, Teheran, Malta."

9. John McCrea, "'Iowa' — President and Joint Chiefs of Staff to Africa and Return," manuscript memoir, John L. McCrea Papers, FDR Presidential Library.

10. Entry of December 10, 1943, in Typed FDR Diary, "War Conference in Cairo, Teheran, Malta."

33. THE ODYSSEY IS OVER

1. Entry of December 16, 1943, Typed FDR Diary, "War Conference in Cairo, Teheran, Malta."

2. Entries of December 9, 11, and 16, 1943, Leahy Diary.

3. Entry of December 16, 1943, Typed FDR Diary, "War Conference in Cairo, Teheran, Malta."

4. Entry of December 15, 1943, "Log of the President's Trip to Africa and the Middle East."

5. Entry of December 16, 1943, Typed FDR Diary, "War Conference in Cairo, Teheran, Malta."

6. Entry of December 16, 1943, Leahy Diary.

7. Appendix K, "The President's Remarks on Leaving the USS *Iowa*, 16 December 1943," in "Log of the President's Trip to Africa and the Middle East."

8. Ibid.

9. Ibid.

10. McCrea, "'Iowa' — President and Joint Chiefs of Staff to Africa and Return."

11. Ibid.

12. Entry of December 16, 1943, Leahy Diary.

13. Entry of December 17, 1943, Stimson Diary.

14. Entry of December 5, 1943, Ickes Diary, Ickes Papers, Library of Congress.

15. Entry of December 17, 1943, Ickes Diary.

16. Ibid.

17. Entry of December 17, 1943, Ickes Diary.

18. Entry of December 17, 1943, Stimson Diary.

19. John H. Crider, Special to the *New York Times*, December 17, 1943.

20. Press and Radio Conference #927, December 17, 1943, 4:17 p.m., Press Conferences of President Franklin D. Roosevelt, 1933–1945, Series 1: Press Conference Transcripts, FDR Presidential Library.

21. Ibid.

22. "Senators Hold Up Patton Promotion," UP Report, *New York Times,* December 16, 1943.

23. Press and Radio Conference #927.

24. Eisenhower, *Crusade in Europe,* 208.

25. Admiral King was a great deal less cautious, or simply more trusting: at a private meeting with five chosen press correspondents, including the Associated Press reporter Lyle Wilson, King shared with them an account of what had happened, including the choice of Eisenhower to command Overlord, though asking them to hold back publication until after the President's Christmas Eve broadcast: "Admiral King, Saturday night, December 18, 1943," in Raymond Clapper Papers, Library of Congress.

34. CHURCHILL'S RESURRECTION

1. Entry of December 17, 1943, in "Secret Diary" of Lord Halifax, Papers of Lord Halifax, Hickleton Papers, Borthwick Institute of Historical Research, University of York, Yorkshire, England.

2. Ibid.

3. Ibid.

4. Letter of December 16, 1943, Martin Gilbert, *Winston S. Churchill,* vol. 7, *Road to Victory: 1941–1945* (Toronto: Stoddart, 1986), 609.

5. Entry of December 18, 1943, Stimson Diary, Henry L. Stimson Papers, Yale University Library, New Haven, CT.

6. Ibid.

7. Ibid.

8. Ibid.

9. Ibid.

10. Ibid., entry of December 10, 1943.

11. Ibid., entry of December 18, 1943.

12. "Evening Situation Report, probably December 20, 1943," section titled "The West, danger of invasion," in Helmut Heiber, ed., *Hitler and His Generals: Military Conferences 1942–1945* (New York: Enigma Books, 2003), 311.

35. IN THE PINK AT HYDE PARK

1. Entry of December 23, 1943, in William D. Hassett, *Off the Record with F.D.R.: 1942–1945* (New Brunswick, NJ: Rutgers University Press, 1958), 222.

2. Ibid.

3. Ross T. McIntire, *White House Physician* (New York: Putnam's, 1946), 180.

4. Entry of December 24, 1943, Hassett, *Off the Record,* 223.

5. Russell D. Buhite and David W. Levy, eds., *FDR's Fireside Chats* (Norman: University of Oklahoma Press, 1992), 272–81.

6. Press and Radio Conference #929, December 28, 1943, 4:07 p.m., EWT, Press

Conferences of President Franklin D. Roosevelt, 1933–1945, Series 1: Press Conference Transcripts, FDR Presidential Library, Hyde Park, NY.

7. Ibid.

8. Entry of December 28, 1943, in Geoffrey C. Ward, ed., *Closest Companion: The Unknown Story of the Intimate Friendship Between Franklin Roosevelt and Margaret Suckley* (Boston: Houghton Mifflin, 1995), 264.

9. Ibid., entry of December 30, 1943, 266.

10. Ibid.

36. SICK

1. McIntire, *White House Physician*, 183.

2. Ibid., 182.

3. Entry of December 19, 1943, Diaries of William Lyon Mackenzie King, Library and Archives Canada, Ottawa (hereinafter Mackenzie King Diary).

4. Washington, DC, Radio Address to Nation, State of the Union Message to Congress, January 11, 1944 (speech file 1501), Franklin D. Roosevelt: Master Speech File, 1898–1945, Box 76, FDR Presidential Library.

5. Samuel L. Rosenman, *Working with Roosevelt* (New York: Harper, 1952), 422.

6. Ibid, 421.

7. Annual Message to Congress — State of the Union (speech file 1501), January 11, 1944, Franklin D. Roosevelt, Master Speech File, 1898–1945, Box 76, FDR Presidential Library, Hyde Park; also in Buhite and Levy, *FDR's Fireside Chats*, 283–93.

8. Ibid.

9. Ibid.

10. Ibid.

11. Rosenman, *Working with Roosevelt*, 427.

12. Ibid.

37. ANZIO

1. Lord Moran, *Churchill: The Struggle for Survival, 1940–1965* (Boston: Houghton Mifflin, 1966), 152.

2. Winston Churchill, *The Second World War*, vol. 5, *Closing the Ring* (London: Cassell, 1952), 292.

3. Ibid., 378.

4. Grand #736, December 22, 1943, in Gilbert, *Road to Victory*, 618.

5. Mark Clark, *Calculated Risk: His Personal Story of the War in North Africa and Italy* (London: Harrap, 1951), 243–45.

6. Entry of December 13, 1943, in Arthur Bryant, *Triumph in the West* (London: Collins, 1959), 120.

7. For Montgomery's predictions regarding Anzio, see Nigel Hamilton, *Master of the Battlefield: Monty's War Years* (New York: McGraw-Hill, 1983), 441 et seq.

8. Dwight D. Eisenhower, *Crusade in Europe* (New York: Doubleday, 1948), 212.
9. "Record of the Conference of 25 December 1943 (General Hollis to War Cabinet Offices)," in Gilbert, *Road to Victory*, 620.
10. Ibid.
11. C-521, Prime Minister to President Roosevelt, December 26, 1943, Warren F. Kimball, ed., *Churchill and Roosevelt: The Complete Correspondence*, vol. 2, *Alliance Forged, November 1942–February 1945* (Princeton, NJ: Princeton University Press, 1984), 633.
12. Ibid., R-427 cable, "Personal and Secret for the Former Naval Person," December 27, 1943, 636.
13. Entry of December 27, 1943, Leahy Diary, William D. Leahy Papers, Library of Congress, Washington, DC.
14. Gilbert, *Road to Victory*, 606.

38. THE PRESIDENT'S UNPLEASANT ATTITUDE

1. Entry of 26.12.1943, in Joseph Goebbels, *Die Tagebücher von Joseph Goebbels* [The Diaries of Joseph Goebbbels], ed. Elke Froehlich (Munich: K. G. Saur, 1993), Band 10 (hereinafter *Tagebücher 10*), 550. Quotes from this source have been translated by the author.
2. Cable 6513 to Bedell Smith, January 5, 1943, in Dwight D. Eisenhower, *The Papers of Dwight David Eisenhower: The War Years*, ed. Alfred Chandler, vol. 3 (Baltimore, MD: Johns Hopkins Press, 1970), 1652.
3. Ibid., note 3, 1651, and note 4, 1653.
4. Entry of January 12, 1944, Stimson Diary.
5. Ibid.
6. Ibid.
7. Ibid.
8. Entry of January 7, 1944, Harold D. Smith Diary, quoted in Robert H. Ferrell, *The Dying President: Franklin D. Roosevelt, 1944–1945* (Columbia: University of Missouri Press, 1998), 30.
9. Francis Bacon, first Viscount St. Alban, Aphorism 46, *Novum Organum*, 1620.
10. Entry of January 19, 1944, in Alan Brooke, *War Diaries, 1939–1945: Field Marshal Lord Alanbrooke*, eds. Alex Danchev and Daniel Todman (Berkeley: University of California Press, 2001), 515.
11. Ibid., entry of January 22, 1944, 515.
12. Entry of January 31, 1944, Bryant, *Triumph in the West*, 142.
13. Ibid., entry of February 3, 1944, 143.
14. Addendum to entry of September 23, 1944, Moran, *Churchill*, 188.
15. Entry of February 29, 1944, Bryant, *Triumph in the West*, 160.
16. Ibid., entry of February 25, 1944, 154.
17. Entry of February 25, 1944, Brooke, *War Diaries*, 525.

18. Ibid., entry of February 28, 1944, 527.
19. Ibid., annotation to entry of February 25, 1944, 525.
20. Ibid., entry of March 3, 1944, 528.
21. Ibid., entries of March 8, 13, and 14, 530–31.

39. CRIMES AGAINST HUMANITY

1. McIntire, *White House Physician,* 182.
2. Entry of March 13, 1944, Stimson Diary.
3. R-506, March 20, 1944, Warren F. Kimball, ed., *Churchill and Roosevelt: The Complete Correspondence,* vol. 3, *Alliance Declining, February 1944–April 1945* (Princeton, NJ: Princeton University Press, 1984), 59.
4. Entry of March 23, 1944, Ward, *Closest Companion,* 286.
5. Entry of March 24, 1944, Hassett, *Off the Record,* 239.
6. Press and Radio Conference #944, March 24, 1944, 11:09 a.m., Press Conferences of President Franklin D. Roosevelt, 1933–1945, Series 1: Press Conference Transcripts, FDR Presidential Library, Hyde Park, NY.
7. Ibid. Italics added.
8. Ibid.
9. Ibid.
10. Ibid.
11. Ibid.
12. Adam Hochschild, *King Leopold's Ghost: A Story of Greed, Terror and Heroism in Colonial Africa* (Boston: Houghton Mifflin, 1999), 96.
13. Press and Radio Conference #944.
14. Ibid.

40. LATE LOVE

1. Jean Edward Smith, *FDR* (New York: Random House, 2007), 156.
2. Elliott Roosevelt, *An Untold Story: The Roosevelts of Hyde Park* (New York: Putnam, 1973), 81.
3. Jonathan Daniels, *Washington Quadrille* (New York: Doubleday, 1968), 145.
4. Resa Willis, *Franklin and Lucy: Lovers and Friends* (New York: Routledge, 2004), 38–40; Smith, *FDR,* 156–57.
5. Joseph P. Lash, *Eleanor and Franklin: The Story of Their Relationship* (New York: Norton, 1971), 220.
6. Willis, *Franklin and Lucy,* 30.
7. James Roosevelt with Bill Libby, *My Parents: A Differing View* (Chicago: Playboy, 1976), 101.
8. Willis, *Franklin and Lucy,* 33.
9. Smith, *FDR,* 214.
10. Eleanor Roosevelt, "If You Ask Me," *McCalls,* January 1952.

11. Willis, *Franklin and Lucy*, 61.
12. Elizabeth Shoumatoff, *FDR's Unfinished Portrait: A Memoir* (Pittsburgh: University of Pittsburgh Press, 1990), 72.

41. IN THE LAST STAGES OF CONSUMPTION

1. Entry of March 25, 1944, Ward, *Closest Companion,* 287.
2. Entry of March 24, 1944, Hassett, *Off the Record,* 240.
3. Entry of March 27, 1944, Ward, *Closest Companion,* 288.
4. Ferrell, *The Dying President,* 37.
5. Howard Bruenn, "Clinical Notes on the Illness and Death of President Franklin D. Roosevelt," *Annals of Internal Medicine* 72, no. 4 (1970): 579–80.
6. Doris Kearns Goodwin, *No Ordinary Time: Franklin and Eleanor Roosevelt: The Home Front in World War II* (New York: Simon & Schuster, 1994), 494.
7. Howard Bruenn, typewritten notes, undated, Harold Bruenn Papers, 1944–1946, FDR Presidential Library.
8. See Ward, *Closest Companion,* 289, and Steven Lomazow and Eric Fettmann, *FDR's Deadly Secret* (New York: PublicAffairs, 2009), 98.
9. Bruenn, typewritten notes, Bruenn Papers.
10. Bruenn, "Clinical Notes on the Illness and Death of President Franklin D. Roosevelt."
11. Jan Herman, Historian, "Oral History with LCDR (ret) Howard Bruenn," January 31, 1990, Office of Medical History, Bureau of Medicine and Surgery, Washington, DC, 3.
12. Ibid.
13. Bruenn, "Clinical Notes on the Illness and Death of President Franklin D. Roosevelt."
14. Lomazow and Fettmann, *FDR's Deadly Secret,* 103.
15. Howard Bruenn, typewritten notes, Bruenn Papers.
16. Ibid.
17. Ibid.
18. Bruenn, "Clinical Notes on the Illness and Death of President Franklin D. Roosevelt."
19. Bruenn, typewritten notes, Bruenn Papers.
20. Entry of March 28, 1944, Ward, *Closest Companion,* 289.
21. Ibid.
22. Bruenn, typewritten notes, Bruenn Papers.
23. Ibid.
24. Bruenn, "Clinical Notes on the Illness and Death of President Franklin D. Roosevelt."
25. Ibid.
26. Lomazov and Fettmann, *FDR's Deadly Secret,* 104.
27. Herman, "Oral History with LCDR (ret) Howard Bruenn," 4.
28. Bruenn, "Clinical Notes on the Illness and Death of President Franklin D. Roosevelt."
29. Quoted in Joseph Lelyveld, *His Final Battle: The Last Months of Franklin Roosevelt* (New York: Knopf, 2016), 104.
30. Herman, "Oral History with LCDR (ret) Howard Bruenn," 3.
31. Bruenn, typewritten notes, Bruenn Papers.

32. Bruenn, "Clinical Notes on the Illness and Death of President Franklin D. Roosevelt."

33. McIntire, *White House Physician,* 187.

34. Quoted in editor's annotation, Ward, *Closest Companion,* 289.

35. Ibid., entry of May 5, 1944, 296.

36. McIntire, *White House Physician,* 185.

42. "THIS ATTACK WILL DECIDE THE WAR"

1. "The West, danger of invasion"; "Evening Situation Report, probably December 20, 1943," in Helmut Heiber, ed., *Hitler and His Generals: Military Conferences 1942–1945* (New York: Enigma Books, 2003), 311.

2. Hitler Rede from the Wolfschanze, or Wolf's Lair, January 30, 1944, Deutsches Nachrichtenbüro, Max Domarus, ed., *Hitler, Speeches and Proclamations 1932–1945: The Chronicle of a Dictatorship,* vol. 4, *The Years 1941 to 1945* (Wauconda, IL: Bolchazy-Carducci, 1977), 2872.

3. Ibid., 2875–76.

4. Statistisches Reichsamt (Hrsg.): *Statistisches Jahrbuch für das Deutsche Reich,* 1919–1941/42.

5. See, among others, Ian Kershaw, *The End: The Defiance and Destruction of Hitler's Germany, 1944–1945* (New York: Penguin, 2011).

6. Entry of 25.2.1944, Joseph Goebbels, *Die Tagebücher von Joseph Goebbels* [The Diaries of Joseph Goebbbels], ed. Elke Froehlich (Munich: K. G. Saur, 1993), Band 11 (hereinafter *Tagebücher 11*), 347–48.

7. Entry of 4.3.1944, Goebbels, *Tagebücher 11,* 399–40.

8. Ibid., 340.

9. Entry of 18.4.1944, Goebbels, *Tagebücher 11,* 131.

10. Detlef Vogel, "German and Allied Conduct of the War in the West," Part 2 of Horst Boog, Gerhard Krebs, and Detlef Vogel, *Germany and the Second World War,* vol. 7 (Oxford: Oxford University Press, 2006), 509.

11. Ian Kershaw, *Hitler, 1936–1945: Nemesis* (London: Allen Lane, 2000), 631.

12. Santi Corvaja, *Hitler and Mussolini: The Secret Meetings* (New York: Enigma Books, 2008), 282.

13. Ibid., 283.

43. SIMPLICITY OF PURPOSE

1. Entry of May 5, 1944, in Geoffrey C. Ward, ed., *Closest Companion: The Unknown Story of the Intimate Friendship Between Franklin Roosevelt and Margaret Suckley* (Boston: Houghton Mifflin, 1995), 296.

2. C-624, Prime Minister to President, March 18, 1944, Warren F. Kimball, *Churchill and Roosevelt: The Complete Correspondence,* vol. 3, *Alliance Declining, February 1944– April 1945* (Princeton, NJ: Princeton University Press, 1984), 54.

3. Ibid., R-506, "From the President to the Former Naval Person," March 24, 1944, 60.

4. Entry of March 16, 1944, Stimson Diary, Henry L. Stimson Papers, Yale University Library, New Haven, CT.

5. Ibid., entry of March 22, 1944.

6. The statistical figure was later recorded as 75 percent: Mark Wells, *Courage and Air Warfare: The Allied Aircrew Experience in the Second World War* (London: Frank Cass, 1995), 46.

7. C-643, Prime Minister to President, April 12, 1944, in Kimball, *Churchill and Roosevelt*, vol. 2, 87.

8. Memorandum for the Secretary of State, April 1, 1944, in Franklin D. Roosevelt, *FDR: His Personal Letters, 1928–1945*, ed. Elliott Roosevelt, vol. 2 (New York: Duell, Sloan and Pearce, 1950), 1504.

9. Ibid., Memorandum for the Secretary of State, April 5, 1944, 1505.

10. Eleanor Roosevelt, letters of March 30 and April 2, 1944, to Joseph Lash, in Joseph P. Lash, *Eleanor and Franklin: The Story of Their Relationship* (New York: Norton, 1971), 697.

11. Ibid.

12. Footnote, quoting Eleanor Roosevelt and Anna, her daughter, in Lash, *Eleanor and Franklin*, 697.

13. Quoted in Joseph Lelyveld, *His Final Battle: The Last Months of Franklin Roosevelt* (New York: Knopf, 2016), 103.

14. Lieutenant Commander George Elsey, interview with the author, September 12, 2011.

15. Quoted in Lelyveld, *His Final Battle*, 103.

16. Jan Herman, Historian, "Oral History with LCDR (ret) Howard Bruenn," January 31, 1990, Office of Medical History, Bureau of Medicine and Surgery, Washington, DC.

17. Ibid.

44. THE HOBCAW BARONY

1. Bernard Baruch, *My Own Story* (New York: Holt, Rinehart, and Winston, 1957), 268.

2. Ibid., 271.

3. Entry of April 4, 1944, Ward, *Closest Companion*, 291.

4. Herman, "Oral History with LCDR (ret) Howard Bruenn," 5.

5. Undated draft letter, 1944, Ward, *Closest Companion*, 295.

6. Herman, "Oral History with LCDR (ret) Howard Bruenn," 8.

7. Ibid., 4.

8. Ross T. McIntire, *White House Physician* (New York: Putnam's, 1946), 188.

9. Entry of April 28, 1944, in "Secret Diary" of Lord Halifax, Papers of Lord Halifax, Hickleton Papers, Borthwick Institute of Historical Research, University of York, Yorkshire, England. No suspected cancer was found.

10. William M. Rigdon with James Derieux, *White House Sailor* (Garden City, NY: Doubleday, 1962), 98.

11. Entry of April 18, 1944, Leahy Diary, William D. Leahy Papers, Library of Congress, Washington, DC.

12. Rigdon, *White House Sailor*, 99.

13. McIntire, *White House Physician*, 187.

14. Howard Bruenn, "Clinical Notes on the Illness and Death of President Franklin D. Roosevelt," *Annals of Internal Medicine* 72, no. 4 (1970): 579–80.

15. Entry of April 18, 1944, Leahy Diary.

16. Clark, Mark Clark, *Calculated Risk: His Personal Story of the War in North Africa and Italy* (London: Harrap, 1951), 318.

17. Entry of April 22, 1944, Leahy Diary.

18. Ibid.

19. Joseph Persico, *Franklin and Lucy,: President Roosevelt, Mrs. Rutherfurd, and the Other Remarkable Women in His Life* (New York: Random House, 2008), 299.

20. Bruenn, "Clinical Notes on the Illness and Death of President Franklin D. Roosevelt."

21. Press and Radio Conference #947, April 28, 1944, at 8:55 p.m., EWT, Press Conferences of President Franklin D. Roosevelt, 1933–1945, Series 1: Press Conference Transcripts, FDR Presidential Library, Hyde Park, NY.

22. Persico, *Franklin and Lucy*, 300; A. Merriman Smith, *Thank You, Mr. President: A White House Notebook* (New York: Harper, 1946), 140–141.

23. Entry of May 4, 1944, Ward, *Closest Companion*, 294.

45. A DUAL-PURPOSE PLAN

1. Entry of May 6, 1944, Leahy Diary.

2. Herman, "Oral History with LCDR (ret) Howard Bruenn," 6.

3. Ibid., 7.

4. Ibid.

5. Ibid., 5.

6. Ibid.

7. Ibid.

8. Lash, *Eleanor and Franklin*, 698, quoting letter to Maude Gray, May 1, 1944.

9. Nigel Hamilton, *Master of the Battlefield: Monty's War Years, 1942–1944* (New York: McGraw-Hill, 1983), 591.

10. Entry of May 15, 1944, in Arthur Bryant, *Triumph in the West* (London: Collins, 1959), 189–90.

11. See Hamilton, *Master of the Battlefield*, 495.

12. Entry of May 15, 1944, Leahy Diary.

13. Ibid.

14. Ibid.

46. D-DAY

1. Entry of May 19, 1944, Ward, *Closest Companion*, 300.

2. Ibid., 301, 305, 308.

3. Ibid., entry of June 4, 1944, 308.

4. Ibid., entry of May 22, 1944, 301.

5. Ibid., 302.

6.   Ibid., entry of June 6, 1944, 309.

7.   Elizabeth Shoumatoff, *FDR's Unfinished Portrait: A Memoir* (Pittsburgh: University of Pittsburgh Press, 1990), 72.

8.   Resa Willis, *FDR and Lucy: Lovers and Friends* (New York: Routledge, 2004), 95; Anna Roosevelt Halsted Papers, 1886–1976, Box 70, FDR Presidential Library.

9.   Ibid.

10. Radio Address re "Fall of Rome" (speech file 1518), June 5, 1944, in Franklin D. Roosevelt, Master Speech File, 1898–1945, Box 78, FDR Presidential Library; also "Report on the Capture of Rome," in Russell D. Buhite and David W. Levy, eds., *FDR's Fireside Chats* (Norman: University of Oklahoma Press, 1992), 294–98.

11. Ibid.

12. Entry of June 5, 1944, Ward, *Closest Companion*, 309.

13. Ibid., entry of June 6, 1944, 309.

14. "Communiqué No. One," quoted by John Snagge, BBC Radio, Special Bulletin, 12 Midday, June 6, 1944, BBC Archive, British Library, London.

15. Carlo D'Este, *Eisenhower: A Soldier's Life* (New York: Henry Holt, 2002), 500.

16. Winston Churchill, C-643 to President Roosevelt, April 12, 1944, Kimball, *Churchill and Roosevelt*, vol. 3, 87, and (after Presentation of Plans at Montgomery's headquarters) in Dwight D. Eisenhower, *Crusade in Europe* (New York: Doubleday, 1948), 245.

17. Press and Radio Conference #954, June 6, 1944, 4:10 p.m., Press Conferences of President Franklin D. Roosevelt, 1933–1945, Series 1: Press Conference Transcripts, FDR Presidential Library.

18. Ibid.

19. Ibid.

20. Ibid.

21. Ibid.

22. Ibid.

23. Ibid.

24. Samuel L. Rosenman, *Working with Roosevelt* (New York: Harper, 1952), 433.

25. Address to the Delegates of the American Youth Congress (speech file 1273), February 10, 1940, Master Speech File, Box 50, FDR Presidential Library.

26. Franklin D. Roosevelt, "Letter on Religion in Democracy," December 16, 1940, American Presidency Project, http://www.presidency.ucsb.edu/ws/?pid=15911.

27. Entry of June 4, 1944, in Ward, *Closest Companion*, 308.

28. FDR-61: D-Day Prayer, Original Reading Copy, June 6, 1944, Significant Documents Collection, Box 1, FDR Presidential Library.

29. Ibid.

47. THE DECIDING DICE OF WAR

1.   Entry of 6.6.1944, in Joseph Goebbels, *Die Tagebücher von Joseph Goebbels* [The Diaries of Joseph Goebbbels], ed. Elke Froehlich (Munich: K. G. Saur, 1993), Band 12

(hereinafter *Tagebücher 12*), 406. Quotes from this source have been translated by the author.

2. Ibid.
3. Ibid., 405.
4. Ibid.
5. Ibid., 415.
6. Ibid., entry of 7.6.1944, 416.
7. Ibid.
8. According to infantry general Günther Blumentritt, one advanced Kampfgruppe from each of the two armored divisions, Panzer Lehr and Twelfth Panzer, had been ordered to Normandy before dawn on D-day, following reports of Allied paratroop landings: "OB West on D-Day," in David C. Isby, ed., *Fighting the Invasion: The German Army at D-Day* (Barnsley, UK: Frontline Books, 2016), 173. The two divisions were formally committed at 4:00 p.m. — ibid.
9. Entry of 7.6.1944, Goebbels, *Tagebücher 12,* 418.
10. Ibid., 421.
11. Ibid.
12. Ibid.
13. Ibid.
14. Ibid., entry of 8.6.1944, 424.
15. Typed radio message to the President, June 14, 1944, in *The Papers of George Catlett Marshall,* eds. Larry I. Bland and Sharon Ritenour Stevens, vol. 4 (Baltimore, MD: Johns Hopkins University Press, 1996), 479–80.
16. Press and Radio Conference #957, June 13, 1944, 4:19 p.m., Press Conferences of President Franklin D. Roosevelt, 1933–1945, Series 1: Press Conference Transcripts, FDR Presidential Library.
17. Ibid.

48. ARCHITECT OF VICTORY

1. Entry of June 22, 1944, Stimson Diary.
2. Ibid.
3. Nigel Hamilton, *The Mantle of Command: FDR at War, 1941–1942* (Boston: Houghton Mifflin Harcourt, 2014), 295–98.
4. Nigel Hamilton, *Commander in Chief: FDR's Battle with Churchill, 1943* (Boston: Houghton Mifflin Harcourt, 2016), 49–50.
5. Ibid., 343–45.
6. Entry of June 22, 1944, Stimson Diary.
7. Ibid.
8. "From the President for the Former Naval Person," R-541, May 18, 1944, in Kimball, *Churchill and Roosevelt,* vol. 3, 134–35.
9. Ibid., C-680, May 25, 1944, 142–43.
10. Ibid., 149.

11.   From the President for the Former Naval Person, R-551, June 6, 1944, in Kimball, *Churchill and Roosevelt*, vol. 3, 167.

49. TO BE, OR NOT TO BE

1.   Walter Warlimont, *Inside Hitler's Headquarters* (London: Weidenfeld and Nicolson, 1964), 434.
2.   Ibid.
3.   See Ian W. Toll, *The Conquering Tide: War in the Pacific Islands, 1942–1944* (New York: Norton, 2015), 477–97. Also, James Hornfisher, *The Fleet at Flood Tide: America at Total War in the Pacific, 1944–1945* (New York: Bantam, 2016), 178–211.
4.   C-712, June 23, 1944, in Kimball, *Churchill and Roosevelt*, vol. 3, 203.
5.   Entry of June 20, 1944, in Ward, *Closest Companion*, 311.
6.   Ibid.

50. A SOLDIER OF MANKIND

1.   Entry of July 5, 1944, in Geoffrey C. Ward, ed., *Closest Companion: The Unknown Story of the Intimate Friendship Between Franklin Roosevelt and Margaret Suckley* (Boston: Houghton Mifflin, 1995), 316.
2.   Ibid., 317.
3.   Harry Goldsmith, *A Conspiracy of Silence: The Health and Death of Franklin D. Roosevelt* (New York: iUniverse, 2007), 171–72.
4.   Ibid.
5.   Entry of June 28, 1944, in Ward, *Closest Companion*, 301.
6.   Joseph Persico, *Franklin and Lucy: President Roosevelt, Mrs. Rutherfurd, and the Other Remarkable Women in His Life* (New York: Random House, 2008), 303.
7.   Jim Bishop, *FDR's Last Year: April 1944–April 1945* (New York: William Morrow, 1974), 71. See also Joseph Lelyveld, *His Final Battle: The Last Months of Franklin Roosevelt* (New York: Knopf, 2016), 94–95 and 148–50.
8.   Press and Radio Conference #961, July 11, 1944, 11:07 a.m., Press Conferences of President Franklin D. Roosevelt, 1933–1945, Series 1: Press Conference Transcripts, FDR Presidential Library, Hyde Park, NY.
9.   Ibid.
10.   Ibid.
11.   Entry of July 11, 1944, Ward, *Closest Companion*, 318.

51. MISSOURI COMPROMISE

1.   Entry of July 11, 1944, Ward, *Closest Companion*, 318.
2.   Ibid.
3.   David McCullough, *Truman* (New York: Simon & Schuster, 1992), 308.
4.   Ibid., 317–18.

5. Samuel L. Rosenman, *Working with Roosevelt,* (New York: Harper, 1952), 439.

6. Ibid., 445.

7. McCullough, *Truman,* 302.

8. Entry of July 18, 1944, Leahy Diary, William D. Leahy Papers, Library of Congress, Washington, DC.

9. Merle Miller, *Plain Speaking: An Oral Biography of Harry S. Truman* (New York: Berkley, 1974), 181.

10. Ibid., 182; Rosenman, *Working with Roosevelt,* 451.

11. Miller, *Plain Speaking,* 182. In fact Roosevelt's train had left Chicago on July 15, 1944, the day before Senator Truman arrived in Chicago. All accounts testify to Truman's surprise, however: McCullough, *Truman,* 314, and Rosenman, *Working with Roosevelt,* 451.

52. THE JULY PLOT

1. James Roosevelt and Sidney Shalett, *Affectionately, F.D.R.: A Son's Story of a Lonely Man* (New York: Harcourt, Brace, 1959), 351.

2. Ibid.

3. Ibid.

4. Ibid., 352.

5. David Irving, *The Trail of the Fox: Field Marshal Erwin Rommel* (New York: Morrow, 1977), 566–67. At an earlier meeting at Hitler's Wolf's Canyon (*Wolfsschlucht 2*) Western Front headquarters in Margival, near Soissons, on June 17, 1944, Rommel had similarly argued that the "struggle was hopeless," but had been assured that the revenge weapons — V-1s — which had finally been launched en masse against London on June 15, would change the tide: see ibid., 549–52, and Robert M. Citino, *The Wehrmacht's Last Stand: The German Campaigns of 1944–1945* (Lawrence: University Press of Kansas, 2017), 247.

6. Ian Kershaw, *Hitler, 1936–1945: Nemesis* (London: Allen Lane, 2000), 674.

7. Max Domarus ed., *Hitler, Speeches and Proclamations 1932–1945: The Chronicle of a Dictatorship,* vol. 4, *The Years 1941 to 1945* (Wauconda, IL: Bolchazy-Carducci, 1977), 2922.

8. Ibid., 2925.

9. Ibid., 2926.

10. Kershaw, *Hitler: Nemesis,* 688.

11. Roosevelt, *Affectionately, F.D.R.,* 352.

12. Ibid.

13. Trip Log: President's Pacific Inspection Trip, July–August 1944, Franklin D. Roosevelt, Papers as President: Map Room Papers, 1941–1945, Box 24, FDR Presidential Library.

14. Text of the President's Acceptance Speech, *New York Times,* July 21, 1944.

15. Rosenman, *Working with Roosevelt,* 453.

16. Entry of August 6, 1944, Ickes Diary, Harold L. Ickes Papers, 1815–1969, Library of Congress, Washington, DC.

17. Lelyveld, *His Final Battle,* 176.
18. Rosenman, *Working with Roosevelt,* 453.
19. David Irving, *The Secret Diaries of Hitler's Doctor* (New York: Macmillan, 1983), 171.
20. Ibid., 175.
21. Erwin Rommel, *The Rommel Papers,* ed. B. H. Liddell Hart (London: Collins, 1953), 487.

53. WAR IN THE PACIFIC

1. Christopher Thorne, *Allies of a Kind: The United States, Britain and the War Against Japan, 1941–1945* (London: Hamish Hamilton, 1978), 337.
2. E. B. Potter, *Nimitz* (Annapolis, MD: Naval Institute Press, 1976), 280.
3. Ibid.
4. Ian Toll, *The Conquering Tide: War in the Pacific Islands, 1942–1944* (New York: Norton, 2015), 444.
5. Potter, *Nimitz,* 288.
6. Ibid., 289.
7. Arthur Vandenberg, *The Private Papers of Senator Vandenberg* (Boston: Houghton Mifflin, 1952), 85.
8. Ibid., entry of April 30, 1944. See also Hendrik Meijer, *Arthur Vandenberg: The Man in the Middle of the American Century* (Chicago: University of Chicago Press, 2017), 217–21.
9. Vandenberg, *Private Papers,* 86.
10. Ibid., 84.
11. Ibid., letter of March 18, 1944, 82–83.
12. George C. Marshall, *Interviews and Reminiscences for Forrest C. Pogue* (Lexington, VA: George C. Marshall Foundation, 1996), 626.
13. Ibid., quoting Henry Stimson.
14. Ibid., 365.

54. DEUS EX MACHINA

1. Entry of July 26, Trip Log: President's Pacific Inspection Trip, July–August 1944, Franklin D. Roosevelt, Papers as President: Map Room Papers, 1941–1945, Box 24, FDR Presidential Library, Hyde Park, NY.
2. Jan Herman, Historian, "Oral History with LCDR (ret) Howard Bruenn," January 31, 1990, Office of Medical History, Bureau of Medicine and Surgery, Washington, DC, 8.
3. Samuel L. Rosenman, *Working with Roosevelt* (New York: Harper, 1952), 456.
4. Trip Log: President's Pacific Inspection Trip, July–August 1944.
5. Herman, "Oral History with LCDR (ret) Howard Bruenn."
6. Ibid.
7. Rosenman, *Working with Roosevelt,* 457.
8. Potter, *Nimitz,* 316.

55. SLOW TORTURE

1.   Entry of July 26, Trip Log: President's Pacific Inspection Trip, July–August 1944.
2.   William Manchester, *American Caesar: Douglas MacArthur 1880–1964* (Boston: Little, Brown, 1978), 368.
3.   Douglas MacArthur, *Reminiscences* (New York: McGraw-Hill, 1964), 199.
4.   Frazier Hunt, *The Untold Story of Douglas MacArthur* (New York: Devin-Adair, 1954), 332.
5.   Ibid.
6.   Trip Log: President's Pacific Inspection Trip, July–August 1944.
7.   Ibid.
8.   Ibid.
9.   Ibid.
10. D. Clayton James, *The Years of MacArthur*, vol. 2, *1941–1945* (Boston: Houghton Mifflin, 1975), 528.
11. Trip Log: President's Pacific Inspection Trip, July–August 1944.
12. MacArthur, *Reminiscences*, 197.
13. James, *The Years of MacArthur*, vol. 2, 530.

56. IN THE EXAMINATION ROOM

1.   Manchester, *American Caesar*, 368.
2.   MacArthur, *Reminiscences*, 197.
3.   Entry of July 27, 1944, Leahy Diary, William D. Leahy Papers, Library of Congress, Washington, DC.
4.   Potter, *Nimitz*, 318.
5.   William D. Leahy, *I Was There* (New York: McGraw-Hill, 1950), 251.
6.   Ibid.
7.   See Nigel Hamilton, *The Mantle of Command: FDR at War, 1941–1942* (Boston: Houghton Mifflin Harcourt, 2014), 177–90.
8.   MacArthur, *Reminiscences*, 198.
9.   Ibid.
10. James, *The Years of MacArthur*, vol. 2, 533.
11. MacArthur's usual plane, *Bataan I*, was a converted B-17E, but according to the pilot, Weldon "Dusty" Rhoads, a Pan American Airways C-54 was commandeered for the trip, with three rows of seats removed, while *Bataan II*, a C-54 Skymaster, like the President's Sacred Cow, was being readied for MacArthur: Walter R. Borneman, *MacArthur at War* (New York: Little, Brown, 2016), 396
12. Entry of July 28, 1944, Leahy Diary.
13. Press and Radio Conference #962, at Waikiki, Honolulu, July 29, 1944, 4:45 p.m., Press Conferences of President Franklin D. Roosevelt, 1933–1945, Series 1: Press Conference Transcripts, FDR Presidential Library.
14. William M. Rigdon with James Derieux, *White House Sailor* (Garden City, NY: Doubleday, 1962), 118.

15. Rosenman, *Working with Roosevelt*, 458–59.
16. Press and Radio Conference #963, held on the train en route to Washington, DC, August 15, 1944, Press Conferences of President Franklin D. Roosevelt, 1933–1945, Series 1: Press Conference Transcripts, FDR Presidential Library.
17. Franklin D. Roosevelt, *FDR: His Personal Letters, 1928–1945*, ed. Elliott Roosevelt, vol. 2 (New York: Duell, Sloan and Pearce, 1950), 1527.

57. A TERRIBLE MISTAKE

1. Martin Sheridan, "FDR Confers in Hawaii to Speed War on Japs," August 11, 1944, *Boston Globe*.
2. Howard Bruenn, "Clinical Notes on the Illness and Death of President Franklin D. Roosevelt," *Annals of Internal Medicine* 72, no. 4 (1970), 586.
3. Herman, "Oral History with LCDR (ret) Howard Bruenn," 6–7.
4. Leahy, *I Was There*, 254.
5. Rosenman, *Working with Roosevelt*, 461.
6. Ibid., 462.

58. A REDUNDANT CONFERENCE

1. Entry of September 10, 1944, Diaries of William Lyon Mackenzie King, Library and Archives Canada, Ottawa (hereinafter Mackenzie King Diary).
2. Entry of August 29, 1944, in Henry Wallace, *The Price of Vision: The Diaries of Henry A. Wallace, 1942–1946* (Boston: Houghton Mifflin, 1973), 384.

59. THE COMPLETE SETTING FOR A NOVEL

1. Merle Miller, *Plain Speaking: An Oral Biography of Harry S. Truman* (New York: Berkley, 1974), 183.
2. Ibid.
3. Entry of August 22, 1944 (misdated), in Geoffrey C. Ward., ed., *Closest Companion: The Unknown Story of the Intimate Friendship Between Franklin Roosevelt and Margaret Suckley* (Boston: Houghton Mifflin, 1995), 321.
4. Entry of August 16, 1944, in Wallace, *The Price of Vision*, 379–80.
5. Robert E. Sherwood, *Roosevelt and Hopkins: An Intimate History* (New York: Harper, 1948), 820.
6. Ibid.
7. Entry of August 19, 1944, in "Secret Diary" of Lord Halifax, Papers of Lord Halifax, Hickleton Papers, Borthwick Institute of Historical Research, University of York, Yorkshire, England.
8. Resa Willis, *FDR and Lucy: Lovers and Friends* (New York: Routledge, 2004), 131.
9. Two of the death sentences on the eight saboteurs were commuted to thirty years' imprisonment by the President for having betrayed the plot — see John L. McCrea, *Captain McCrea's War: The World War II Memoir of Franklin D. Roosevelt's Naval*

Aide and USS Iowa's *First Commanding Officer,* ed. Julia C. Tobey (New York: Skyhorse, 2016). In 1948 the two men were returned to Germany.

10. Entry of August 29, 1944, Ward, *Closest Companion,* 322.
11. Entry of August 22, 1944, in William D. Hassett, *Off the Record with FDR: 1942–1945* (New Brunswick, NJ: Rutgers University Press, 1958), 267.
12. Entry of September 1, 1944, Ward, *Closest Companion,* 323.
13. Ibid.
14. Ibid., 324.
15. Ibid.
16. Ibid.

60. TWO SICK MEN

1. Annotations, Alan Brooke, *War Diaries, 1939–1945: Field Marshal Lord Alanbrooke,* eds. Alex Danchev and Daniel Todman (Berkeley: University of California Press, 2001), 588.
2. Ibid.
3. Quoted in Andrew Roberts, *Masters and Commanders: How Four Titans Won the War in the West, 1941–1945* (New York: Harper, 2009), 512.
4. Entry of September 8, 1944, Brooke, *War Diaries,* 589.
5. Ibid., entry of September 9, 1944, 590.
6. Ibid., entry of September 10, 1944.
7. Ibid.
8. Ibid.
9. Ibid.
10. Entry of September 11, 1944, Mackenzie King Diary.
11. Ibid.
12. Ibid.
13. Ibid.
14. Hastings Lionel Ismay, *The Memoirs of General Lord Ismay* (London: Heinemann, 1960), 373.

61. CHURCHILL'S IMPERIAL WARS

1. Martin Gilbert, *Winston S. Churchill,* vol. 7, *Road to Victory: 1941–1945* (Toronto: Stoddart, 1986), 971, quoting diary of Sir Andrew Cunningham.
2. Entry of September 11, 1944, Mackenzie King Diary.
3. Entry of September 12, 1944, in John Colville, *The Fringes of Power: 10 Downing Street Diaries, 1939–1955* (London: Hodder & Stoughton, 1985), 513.
4. Annotation, Colville, *The Fringes of Power,* 514.
5. Entry of September 11, 1944, Mackenzie King Diary.
6. Ibid.
7. Ibid.
8. Ibid.

9. Ibid.
10. Gilbert, *Road to Victory,* 969.
11. Entry of September 12, 1944, Mackenzie King Diary.
12. Ibid., entry of September 13, 1944.
13. Ibid.

62. A STAB IN THE ARMPIT

1. Entry of September 13, 1944, Brooke, *War Diaries,* 591.
2. "Meeting of the Combined Chiefs of Staff with Roosevelt and Churchill, September 13, 1944, 11:45 a.m., the Citadel," in *Foreign Relations of the United States: Conference at Quebec, 1944* (hereinafter *FRUS II*) (Washington, DC: Government Printing Office, 1972), 314.
3. "Meeting of the Combined Chiefs of Staff, September 12, 1944, Noon, Main Conference Room, Chateau Frontenac," in *FRUS II,* 303.
4. Michael Howard, *The Mediterranean Strategy in the Second World War* (London: Weidenfeld and Nicolson, 1968), 66.
5. Entry of September 13, 1944, Brooke, *War Diaries,* 591–92.
6. "Meeting of the Combined Chiefs of Staff, September 12, 1944, Noon, Main Conference Room, Chateau Frontenac," *FRUS II,* 303.
7. Ibid.
8. Ibid.
9. Entry of September 13, 1944, Brooke, *War Diaries,* 591–92.
10. Ibid., annotation, 593.
11. "Prime Minister to President Roosevelt, C-772, August 29, 1944, in Warren F. Kimball, ed., *Churchill and Roosevelt: The Complete Correspondence,* vol. 3, *Alliance Declining, February 1944–April 1945* (Princeton, NJ: Princeton University Press 1984), 300.
12. "Meeting of the Combined Chiefs of Staff with Roosevelt and Churchill, September 13, 1944, 11:45 a.m., the Citadel," in *FRUS II,* 316.
13. Ibid.
14. Ibid.
15. Ibid.
16. Ibid.
17. Ibid.
18. Ibid.
19. Entry of September 14, 1944, Brooke, *War Diaries,* 593.
20. Gilbert, *Road to Victory,* 960.
21. Entry of September 15, 1944, Brooke, *War Diaries,* 593.

63. THE MORGENTHAU PLAN

1. Memorandum of August 25, 1944, in Carolyn Eisenberg, *Drawing the Line: The American Decision to Divide Germany, 1944–1949* (Cambridge: Cambridge University Press, 1996), 36.

2. Memo of September 6, 1944, in Stimson Diary, Henry L. Stimson Papers, Yale University Library, New Haven, CT.
3. Ibid., entry of September 11, 1944.
4. Ibid., entry of September 13, 1944.
5. Entry of September 13, Mackenzie King Diary.
6. Ibid.
7. Entry of September 13, 1944, Leahy Diary, William D. Leahy Papers, Library of Congress, Washington, DC.
8. Harry Dexter White Memorandum dated 9/25/44, in *FRUS II*, 326.
9. Entry of September 20, 1944, Stimson Diary.
10. Harry Dexter White Memorandum, in *FRUS II*, 327.
11. Ibid., 325.
12. Ibid., 327. Also Henry Morgenthau Jr., "Our Policy Toward Germany: Morgenthau's Inside Story," *New York Post*, November 28, 1947, 18, in ibid., 326.
13. Entry of September 13, 1944, in Lord Moran, *Churchill: The Struggle for Survival, 1940–1965* (Boston: Houghton Mifflin, 1966), 177.
14. Ibid.

64. BEYOND THE DREAMS OF AVARICE

1. Treasury Files, in *FRUS II*, 348.
2. "He dictated the memorandum, which finally stood just the way he dictated it. He dictates extremely well," Morgenthau noted in his presidential diary, "because he is accustomed to doing it when he is writing his books": *FRUS II*, 361.
3. Ibid.
4. Morgenthau Presidential Diary, *FRUS II*, 362.
5. Entry of September 15, 1944, Stimson Diary.
6. Michael Beschloss, *The Conquerors: Roosevelt, Truman and the Destruction of Hitler's Germany, 1941–1945* (New York: Simon & Schuster, 2002), 118.
7. "Memorandum for the President," included with entry of September 15, 1944, Stimson Diary.
8. Ibid.
9. Ibid.

65. THE PRESIDENT IS GAGA

1. Entry of September 20, 1944, Ward, *Closest Companion*, 328.
2. Beschloss, *The Conquerors*, 139.
3. Ibid., 142.
4. Richard Norton Smith, *Thomas E. Dewey and His Times* (New York: Simon & Schuster, 1982), 432.
5. Eisenberg, *Drawing the Line*, 45.
6. Beschloss, *The Conquerors*, 145.
7. Calls to bomb railway lines to Auschwitz had prompted War Department and U.S.

Army Air Forces feasibility studies, but with the Germans able to repair tracks within days, if not hours, and no way in which the gas chambers could be effectively destroyed without killing large numbers of inmates, they had been turned down as impracticable — see Robert Beir, *Roosevelt and the Holocaust* (Fort Lee, NJ: BarricadeBooks, 2006), 249–52. On November 26, 1944, Himmler, recognizing ultimate defeat was inevitable, "stopped the carnage" at Auschwitz. "He turned his attention to destroying the evidence" — ibid., 252. Auschwitz was only one of many extermination and killing programs, however. It is believed another quarter of a million Jews were deliberately murdered between the cessation at Auschwitz and German surrender — see Richard Breitman and Allan J. Lichtman, *FDR and the Jews* (Cambridge, MA: Harvard University Press, 2013), 287–88.

8. E.g., in the *New York Times* and *Tribune*, as well as the Washington press and syndicated Associated Press: Entry of September 24, 1944, Stimson Diary.

9. Ibid., entry of September 27, 1944.

10. Ibid., entry of October 3, 1944.

11. Ibid.

12. Beschloss, *The Conquerors*, 149.

13. Entry of October 3, 1944, Stimson Diary.

14. Ibid.

15. Entry of November 8, 1944, in Alan Lascelles, *King's Counsellor: Abdication and War; The Diaries of Sir Alan Lascelles* (London: Orion, 2006), 268.

66. OUTWARD BOUND

1. Richard Norton Smith, *Thomas E. Dewey and His Times* (New York: Simon & Schuster, 1982), 444.

2. James Reston, quoted in Classic Senate Speeches, Arthur H. Vandenberg, January 10, 1945, www.senate.gov/artandhistory/history/common/generic/Speeches_Vandenberg.htm.

3. Samuel L. Rosenman, *Working with Roosevelt* (New York: Harper, 1952), 510.

4. See Nigel Hamilton, *Commander in Chief: FDR's Battle with Churchill, 1943* (Boston: Houghton Mifflin Harcourt, 2016), 90–92.

67. LIGHT OF THE PRESIDENT'S FADING LIFE

1. S. M. Plokhy, *Yalta: The Price of Peace* (New York: Viking, 2012), 26.

2. Entry of June 12, 1944, "Secret Diary" of Lord Halifax, Papers of Lord Halifax, Hickleton Papers, Borthwick Institute of Historical Research, University of York, Yorkshire, England, referring to a conversation with Reston "a day or two ago," i.e., circa June 10, 1944.

3. Not even Setaro — nicknamed Lenny — really believed this. "He's all excited. I say, 'Prez, what are you tryin' to do? Kid me?'": Robert H. Ferrell, *The Dying President: Franklin D. Roosevelt, 1944–1945* (Columbia: University of Missouri Press, 1998), 100.

4. James Roosevelt and Sidney Shalett, *Affectionately, F.D.R.: A Son's Story of a Lonely Man* (New York: Harcourt, Brace, 1959), 354.

5. Ibid., 355.

6. Ibid., 347.

7. Ibid., 355.

8. Bert Edward Park, *The Impact of Illness on World Leaders* (Philadelphia: University of Pennsylvania Press, 1986), 258.

9. Frances Perkins, *The Roosevelt I Knew* (New York: Viking, 1946), 391–94, and Ferrell, *The Dying President*, 103.

10. Letter of February 9, 1945, in Geoffrey C. Ward, *Closest Companion: The Unknown Story of the Intimate Friendship Between Franklin Roosevelt and Margaret Suckley* (Boston: Houghton Mifflin, 1995), 394.

11. Ibid.

12. Ibid., entry of November 29, 1944, 348.

13. Ibid., entry of December 1, 1944, 352.

14. Ibid., entry of December 2, 1944, 353.

15. Ibid., entry of December 3, 1944, 353.

16. Ibid.

17. Ibid., entry of December 17, 1944, 365.

18. Ibid., entry of January 12, 1945, 380.

19. Ibid., entry of January 22, 1945, 390.

68. ABOARD THE USS *QUINCY*

1. Joseph P. Lash, *Eleanor and Franklin: The Story of Their Relationship* (New York: Norton, 1971), 918.

2. Ibid., letter of December 4, 1944, 919.

3. Ibid.

4. Ibid., 922.

5. John R. Boettiger, *A Love in the Shadow* (New York: Norton, 1978), 256.

6. Entry of January 23, 1945, in Anna Roosevelt Boettiger, Yalta Diary, Anna Roosevelt Halsted Papers, Notes Folder, Box 84, FDR Presidential Library, Hyde Park, NY.

7. Ibid., entry of November 24.

8. Ibid., entry of February 1, 1945.

9. Entry of February 1, 1945, Leahy Diary, William D. Leahy Papers, Library of Congress, Washington, DC.

10. Entry of February 2, 1945, Anna Roosevelt Boettiger, Yalta Diary, FDR Presidential Library.

11. Ibid.

12. "Log of the Trip," in *Foreign Relations of the United States: Conferences at Malta and Yalta, 1945* (Washington, DC: U.S. Government Printing Office, 1945) (hereinafter *FRUS III*), 459.

13. Plokhy, *Yalta,* 19.
14. Anthony Eden, *The Reckoning* (Boston: Houghton Mifflin, 1965), 511–12.
15. Ibid.

69. HARDLY IN THIS WORLD

1. C-894 of January 24, 1944, in Warren F. Kimball, ed., *Churchill and Roosevelt: The Complete Correspondence,* vol. 3, *Alliance Declining, February 1944–April 1945* (Princeton, NJ: Princeton University Press, 1984), 518.
2. "Log of the Trip," *FRUS III,* 460.
3. George Marshall, *George C. Marshall: Interviews and Reminiscences for Forrest C. Pogue* (Lexington, VA: George C. Marshall Foundation, 1966), 406.
4. William D. Leahy, *I Was There* (New York: McGraw-Hill, 1950), 294.
5. Martin Gilbert, *Winston S. Churchill,* vol. 7, *Road to Victory: 1941–1945,* (Toronto: Stoddart, 1986), 1167.
6. Anthony Eden, Diary, February 2, 1945, in David B. Woolner, *The Last 100 Days: FDR at War and at Peace* (New York: Basic Books, 2017), 60.
7. David Roll, *The Hopkins Touch: Harry Hopkins and the Forging of the Alliance to Defeat Hitler* (Oxford: Oxford University Press, 2013), 361.
8. Charles Bohlen, *Witness to History, 1929–1969* (New York: Norton, 1973), 171.
9. Entry of February 2, 1945, Anna Roosevelt Boettiger, Yalta Diary, FDR Presidential Library.
10. Leahy, *I Was There,* 295.
11. Hastings Lionel Ismay, *The Memoirs of General Lord Ismay* (London: Heinemann, 1960), 385.
12. Eden, *The Reckoning,* 512.
13. Entry of February 3, 1945, Anna Roosevelt Boettiger, Yalta Diary, FDR Presidential Library.
14. Ibid.
15. Howard Bruenn, "Clinical Notes on the Illness and Death of President Franklin D. Roosevelt," *Annals of Internal Medicine* 72, no. 4 (1970), 588.

70. "A PRETTY EXTRAORDINARY ACHIEVEMENT"

1. Entry of 16.1.1945, in Joseph Goebbels, *Die Tagebücher von Joseph Goebbels* [The Diaries of Joseph Goebbbels], ed. Elke Froehlich (Munich: K. G. Saur, 1993), Band 15 (hereinafter *Tagebücher 15*), 135. Quotes from this source have been translated by the author. See also Ian Kershaw, *Hitler, 1936–1945: Nemesis* (London: Allen Lane, 2000), 757; and Robert M. Citino, *The Wehrmacht's Last Stand: The German Campaigns of 1944–1945* (Lawrence: Kansas University Press, 2017), 417–19.
2. Entry of 23.1.1945, Goebbels, *Tagebücher 15,* 193.
3. Kershaw, *Hitler: Nemesis,* 753.
4. Entry of 18.1.1945, Goebbels, *Tagebücher 15,* 144.
5. Ibid., entry of 23.1.1945, 192.

6.   Ibid., 196–97.
7.   Ibid., 192.
8.   Ibid., entry of 25.1.1945, 220.
9.   Ibid., 217.
10. Ibid., entry of 18.1.1945, 146.
11. Ibid., entry of 29.1.1945, 262.
12. Ibid., entry of 31.1.1945, 285.
13. Entry of January 31, 1945, in John Colville, *The Fringes of Power: 10 Downing Street Diaries, 1939–1955* (London: Hodder & Stoughton, 1985), 557.
14. Adolf Hitler, last radio address, January 30, 1945,' Internet Archive, https://archive.org/stream/AdolfHitlerLastRadioSpeechJan301945/ AdolfHitlerLastRadioSpeechJan301945_djvu.txt.
15. Ibid.
16. Ibid.
17. Ibid.
18. Ian Kershaw, *The End: The Defiance and Destruction of Hitler's Germany, 1944– 1945* (New York: Penguin, 2011), 211.
19. Kershaw, *Hitler: Nemesis*, 762.
20. Ibid., 767.
21. Ibid., 762.
22. Ibid., 763–64.
23. Hitler, last radio address.
24. Entry of 26.1.1945, Goebbels, *Tagebücher 15*, 232.
25. Kershaw, *Hitler: Nemesis*, 771.
26. Ibid., 780.
27. Ibid., 773.
28. Hitler, last radio address.
29. Entry of 30.1.1945, Goebbels, *Tagebücher 15*, 273.
30. Kershaw, *Hitler: Nemesis*, 771.

71. ONE ULTIMATE GOAL

1.   Bohlen, *Witness to History*, 172.
2.   Ibid., 171–72.
3.   Martin Gilbert, *Winston S. Churchill*, vol. 7, *Road to Victory: 1941–1945* (Toronto: Stoddart, 1986), 1166.
4.   Entry of February 3, 1945, Leahy Diary.
5.   Bruenn, Clinical Notes.
6.   Ibid.

72. IN THE LAND OF THE CZARS

1.   Entry of Febrary 3, 1945 in Anna Roosevelt Boettiger, Yalta Diary, Anna Roosevelt Halsted Papers, Notes Folder, Box 84, FDR Presidential Library.

2. Ibid.

3. Entry of February 3, 1945, Lord Moran, *Churchill: The Struggle for Survival, 1940–1965* (London: Constable, 1966), 218.

4. Ibid.

5. Ibid.

6. Entry of February 3, 1945, in Anna Roosevelt Boettiger, Yalta Diary, FDR Presidential Library.

7. Ibid., and Michael F. Reilly, *Reilly of the White House* (New York: Simon & Schuster, 1947), 210–11.

8. Entry of February 3, 1945, in Anna Roosevelt Boettiger, Yalta Diary, FDR Presidential Library.

9. Ibid.

10. E.g., General Deane Memorandum for General Marshall of December 2, 1944, shown by Secretary Stimson to President Roosevelt, January 3, 1945, in *FRUS III*, 447–49.

11. Citino, *The Wehrmacht's Last Stand*, 424.

12. "Commanding General, U.S. Military Mission in the Soviet Union (Deane) to the Chief of Staff, U.S. Army (Marshall), Moscow, December 2, 1944," forwarded by the Secretary of War, Henry Stimson, to the President, January 3, 1945, *FRUS III*, 447–48.

73. THE ATOM BOMB

1. Entry of February 3, 1945, in Anna Roosevelt Boettiger, Yalta Diary, FDR Presidential Library.

2. Ibid.

3. See Hamilton, *Commander in Chief*, 360–66.

4. Accused by his private secretary of "bowing down in the House of Rimmon" by expressing support for Russia on the eve of Hitler's Operation Barbarossa in 1941, Churchill had responded that "he had only one single purpose — the destruction of Hitler," and making the quoted remark: Diary entry of June 21, 1941, in Colville, *The Fringes of Power*, 404.

5. Richard Rhodes, *The Making of the Atomic Bomb* (New York: Simon & Schuster, 1986), 314.

6. Ibid., 533.

7. Ibid., 537.

8. Ibid., 606–7.

9. Lavrenti Beria, head of Soviet state security, had informed Stalin of the Manhattan Project already in March 1942: see Simon Sebag Montefiore, *Stalin: The Court of the Red Tsar* (New York: Random House, 2003), 497.

10. Rhodes, *The Making of the Atomic Bomb*, 500–502.

11. Ibid., 605.

12. Ibid., 500.

13. Entry of December 31, 1944, Stimson Diary, Henry L. Stimson Papers, Yale University Library, New Haven, CT.

14. "General Groves to the Chiefs of Staff, Subject Fission Bombs, December 30, 1944," *FRUS III*, 383.
15. Letter to Lady Theodosia Cadogan, February 2, 1945, in Alexander Cadogan, *The Diaries of Sir Alexander Cadogan, O.M., 1938–1945*, ed. David Dilks (London: Cassell, 1971) (hereinafter *Cadogan Diaries*), 701.

74. RIVIERA OF HADES

1. Plokhy, *Yalta*, 53.
2. Martin Gilbert: *Churchill: A Life* (New York: Henry Holt, 1991), 809.
3. Gilbert, *The Road to Victory*, 1173.
4. Brian Lavery, *Churchill Goes to War: Winston's Wartime Journeys* (London: Conway, 2007), 331–32.
5. Bohlen, *Witness to History*, 174.

75. RUSSIAN MILITARY COOPERATION

1. Bohlen, *Witness to History*, 180.
2. Roosevelt-Stalin Meeting, February 4, 1945, 4 p.m., Livadia Palace, Bohlen Minutes, *FRUS III*, 570.
3. Entry of 24.1.1945, Goebbels, *Tagebücher 15*, 208.
4. See James Scott, *Rampage: MacArthur, Yamashita, and the Battle of Manila* (New York: Norton, 2018).
5. Roosevelt-Stalin Meeting, February 4, 1945, 4 p.m., Livadia Palace, Bohlen Minutes, *FRUS III*, 571.

76. MAKING HISTORY

1. Leahy Diary.
2. Robert Hopkins, "'How Would You Like to Be Attached to the Red Army?'" *American Heritage*, June/July 2005.
3. See Citino, *The Wehrmacht's Last Stand*, 430, and Plokhy, *Yalta*, 84, inter alia.
4. Bohlen Minutes, *FRUS III*, 579.
5. Bohlen, *Witness to History*, 180.
6. Roosevelt-Stalin Meeting, February 4, 1945, 4 p.m., Livadia Palace, Bohlen Minutes, *FRUS III*, 579.
7. Ibid., 580.

77. A SILENT PRESIDENT

1. "Tripartite Dinner Meeting, February 4, 1945, 8:30 p.m., Livadia Palace," Bohlen Minutes, *FRUS III*, 590.
2. Bohlen, *Witness to History*, 181.
3. Entry of February 4, 1945, Moran, *Churchill*, 223.

4. Ibid.
5. Gilbert, *Road to Victory*, 1175.
6. Letter of February 11, 1945, *Cadogan Diaries*, 709.
7. Entry of February 4, 1945, Anna Roosevelt Boettiger, Yalta Diary, FDR Presidential Library.
8. "Tripartite Dinner Meeting, February 4, 1945, 8:30 p.m., Livadia Palace," Bohlen Minutes, *FRUS III*, 590.

78. KENNAN'S WARNING

1. Bohlen, *Witness to History*, 175.
2. Ibid.
3. Ibid.
4. Ibid., 176.
5. Ibid., 177.
6. Bruenn, "Clinical Notes," 589.

79. A WORLD SECURITY ORGANIZATION

1. Bohlen, *Witness to History*, 179.
2. Letter of February 6, 1945, *Cadogan Diaries*, 704.
3. Ibid., letter of February 7, 1945, 705.
4. "Fifth Plenary Meeting, February 8, 1945, 4 p.m., Livadia Palace," *FRUS III*, 773.

80. POLAND

1. Ibid., Matthews Minutes, *FRUS III*, 788.
2. Ibid., 789.
3. Ibid., 779–80.

81. *PULSUS ALTERNANS*

1. "Tripartite Dinner Meeting, February 8, 1945, 9 p.m., Yusupov Palace," Bohlen Minutes, *FRUS III*, 798.
2. Ibid.
3. Ibid.
4. Entry of February 8, Leahy Diary.

82. THE PRIME MINISTER GOES BALLISTIC

1. Ross T. McIntire, *White House Physician* (New York: Putnam's, 1946), 217.
2. Ibid., 216.
3. "Sixth Plenary Meeting, February 9, 1945, 4 p.m., Livadia Palace," *FRUS III*, 842.

4. Ibid.
5. Ibid., 843.
6. Ibid., 844.
7. Ibid.
8. Entry of February 9, 1945, Leahy Diary.
9. "Sixth Plenary Meeting, February 9, 1945, 4 p.m., Livadia Palace," Hiss Notes, *FRUS III*, 856.
10. Ibid., 847.
11. Ibid., 848.
12. "United States Draft of a Declaration on Liberated Europe," Yalta, February 5, 1945, Hiss Collection, *FRUS III*, 860.
13. "Sixth Plenary Meeting, February 9, 1945, 4 p.m., Livadia Palace," Bohlen Minutes, *FRUS III*, 848.
14. Ibid., Hiss Notes, 856.
15. "Sixth Plenary Meeting, February 9, 1945, 4 p.m., Livadia Palace," *FRUS III*, 848.
16. Ibid., Hiss Notes, 856.
17. Richard Toye, *Churchill's Empire: The World That Made Him and the World He Made* (London: Macmillan, 2010), 255.
18. See Stanley Wolpert, *Shameful Flight: The Last Years of the British Empire in India* (Oxford: Oxford University Press, 2009), 69–72 inter alia.
19. "Sixth Plenary Meeting, February 9, 1945, 4 p.m., Livadia Palace," Bohlen Minutes, *FRUS III*, 849. Willkie had died on October 8, 1944.
20. Entry of July 4, 1944, referring to telegram from Churchill, in *Wavell: The Viceroy's Journal*, ed. Penderel Moon (Delhi, India: Oxford University Press, 1973), 78.
21. "Tripartite Dinner Meeting, February 10, 1945, 9 p.m., Vorontsov Villa," Bohlen Minutes, *FRUS III*, 921–22.
22. Ibid., 923.

83. THE YALTA COMMUNIQUÉ

1. Bohlen, *Witness to History*, 185.
2. Ibid., 172.
3. Entry of February 11, 1945, Leahy Diary.
4. Ibid.
5. Ibid.
6. Entry of February 9, 1945, in Alan Brooke, *War Diaries, 1939–1945: Field Marshal Lord Alanbrooke*, eds. Alex Danchev and Daniel Todman (Berkeley: University of California Press, 2001), 661.
7. Bruenn, "Clinical Notes."
8. Jan Herman, Historian, "Oral History with LCDR (ret) Howard Bruenn," January 31, 1990, office of Medical History, Bureau of Medicine and Surgery, 16.
9. Letter of February 12, 1945, Ward, *Closest Companion*, 395.
10. Trilateral Documents: Communiqué Issued at the End of the Conference, Report of the Crimea Conference, *FRUS III*, 968–75.

11. Sarah Churchill, *Keep On Dancing* (London: Coward, McCann & Geoghegan, 1981), 77–78.
12. Ibid.
13. Franklin D. Roosevelt, *FDR: His Personal Letters, 1928–1945*, ed. Elliott Roosevelt, vol. 2 (New York: Duell, Sloan and Pearce, 1950).
14. Roll, *The Hopkins Touch*, 374.
15. Herman, "Oral History with LCDR (ret) Howard Bruenn," 16.
16. Andrew Roberts, *Masters and Commanders: How Four Titans Won the War in the West, 1941–1945* (New York: Harper, 2009), 549.
17. Woolner, *The Last 100 Days*, 175.
18. "The President's Trip to the Crimea Conference and Great Bitter Lake, Egypt, Janaury 22 to February 28, 1945" in "Logs of the President's Trips," Grace Tully Papers, Box 7, FDR Presidential Library, Hyde Park, NY.
19. Winston Churchill, *The Second World War*, vol. 6, *Triumph and Tragedy* (Boston: Houghton Mifflin, 1953), 397.
20. Woolner, *The Last 100 Days*, 175.
21. Churchill, *Triumph and Tragedy*, 397.

84. THE END OF HITLER'S DREAMS

1. Entry of 12.2.1945, Goebbels, *Tagebücher 15*, 368.
2. Ibid.
3. Ibid., 369.
4. Ibid., entry of 13.2.1945.
5. Ibid., 382.

85. KING ODYSSEUS

1. Entry of April 6, 1945, in Geoffrey C. Ward, ed., *Closest Companion: The Unknown Story of the Intimate Friendship Between Franklin Roosevelt and Margaret Suckley* (Boston: Houghton Mifflin, 1995), 411.
2. Ibid., noted in entry of April 4, 1945, 409.
3. Ibid., entry of March 25, 1945, 401.
4. Ibid., entry of April 6, 1945, 411.
5. Entry of March 30, 1945, in William D. Hassett, *Off the Record with FDR: 1942–1945* (New Brunswick, NJ: Rutgers University Press, 1958), 327.
6. Ibid, 327–28.
7. Ibid., 328.
8. Ibid., entry of March 31, 1945, 329.

86. IN THE WELL OF CONGRESS

1. Lieutenant William Rigdon, accompanying the President, noted later the "surprise of those of us who considered a Presidential invitation the same as a command":

William M. Rigdon with James Derieux, *White House Sailor* (Garden City, NY: Doubleday, 1962), 174.

2. Samuel L. Rosenman, *Working with Roosevelt* (New York: Harper, 1952), 522.
3. Ibid.
4. Ibid.
5. Ibid., 523.
6. Jan Herman, Historian, "Oral History with LCDR (ret) Howard Bruenn," January 31, 1990, Office of Medical History, Bureau of Medicine and Surgery, Washington, DC.
7. Rosenman, *Working with Roosevelt*, 524.
8. Ibid., 527.
9. Howard Bruenn, "Clinical Notes on the Illness and Death of President Franklin D. Roosevelt," *Annals of Internal Medicine* 72, no. 4 (1970), 591.
10. Ibid.
11. Entry of March 1, 1945, in "Secret Diary" of Lord Halifax, Papers of Lord Halifax, Hickleton Papers, Borthwick Institute of Historical Research, University of York, Yorkshire, England.

87. APPEASERS BECOME WARMONGERS

1. Martin Gilbert, *Winston S. Churchill*, vol. 7, *Road to Victory: 1941–1945* (Toronto: Stoddart, 1986), 1234.
2. Entry of February 27, 1945, in Harold Nicolson, *Diaries and Letters, 1939-1945*, ed. Nigel Nicolson (London: Collins, 1967), 437.
3. David Reynolds, *Summits: Six Meetings That Shaped the Twentieth Century* (New York: Basic Books, 2007), 161.
4. Entry of March 3, 1945, Ward, *Closest Companion*, 397.
5. Entry of March 9, 1945, Diaries of William Lyon Mackenzie King, Library and Archives Canada, Ottawa (hereinafter Mackenzie King Diary).

88. MACKENZIE KING'S LAST VISIT

1. Entry of March 9, 1945, Mackenzie King Diary.
2. See Nigel Hamilton, *Commander in Chief: FDR's Battle with Churchill, 1943* (Boston: Houghton Mifflin Harcourt, 2016), 35–38.
3. Robert E. Sherwood, *Roosevelt and Hopkins: An Intimate History* (New York: Harper, 1948), 873.
4. Richard Breitman and Allan J. Lichtman, *FDR and the Jews* (Cambridge, MA: Harvard University Press, 2013), 304; David B. Woolner, *The Last 100 Days: FDR at War and at Peace* (New York: Basic Books, 2017), 155–65; Joseph Lelyveld, *His Final Battle: The Last Months of Franklin Roosevelt* (New York: Knopf, 2016), 291–92.
5. Entry of March 9, 1945, Mackenzie King Diary.
6. Ibid.
7. Ibid.
8. Ibid.

9. Ibid.
10. Ibid.
11. Ibid.
12. Ibid.
13. Ibid.
14. Ibid.
15. Ibid., entry of March 10, 1945.
16. Charles Bohlen, *Witness to History, 1929–1969* (New York: Norton, 1973), 206.
17. Entry of March 10, 1945, Mackenzie King Diary.
18. Ibid.
19. Ibid.

89. OPERATION SUNRISE

1. "It is noteworthy that all the German participants in Sunrise negotiations — Zimmer, Wolff's adjutant Wenner, and Wolff himself — survived relatively unscathed in the immediate postwar period," despite their known crimes against humanity: Professor Richard Breitman, Interagency Working Group (IWG) Director of Historical Research, "RG 263 Detailed Report, Guido Zimmer," National Archives, Washington, DC.
2. Entry of March 11, 1945, Stimson Diary, Henry L. Stimson Papers, Yale University Library, New Haven, CT.
3. S. M. Plokhy, *Yalta: The Price of Peace* (New York: Viking, 2012), 361.
4. Kerstin von Lingen, *Allen Dulles, the OSS, and Nazi War Criminals: The Dynamics of Selective Prosecution* (Cambridge: Cambridge University Press, 2013); Kerstin von Lingen, "Conspiracy of Silence: How the 'Old Boys' of American Intelligence Shielded SS General Karl Wolff from Prosecution," *Holocaust and Genocide Studies* 22, no. 1 (2008): 74–109.
5. Entry of March 13, 1945, Stimson Diary.
6. Ibid.
7. Entry of March 13, 1945, Mackenzie King Diary.
8. Plokhy, *Yalta*, 360, and Woolner, *The Last 100 Days*, 252.

90. NO MORE BARBAROSSAS!

1. Robert Ferrell, *The Dying President: Franklin D. Roosevelt, 1944-1945* (Columbia: University of Missouri Press, 1998), 114.
2. Ibid.
3. Joseph Persico, *Franklin and Lucy* (New York: Random House, 2008), 325.
4. Letter of April 1, 1945, in Joseph P. Lash, *Eleanor and Franklin: The Story of Their Relationship* (New York: Norton, 1971), 925.
5. Ibid.
6. Ibid.
7. Entry of March 13, 1945, Mackenzie King Diary.

8. Ibid.
9. Ibid.
10. Ibid.
11. See Nigel Hamilton, *Monty: Final Years of the Field Marshal, 1944–1976* (New York: McGraw-Hill, 1987), 445–60. Also Churchill cables to Roosevelt, C-931, C-933, C-934, in Warren F. Kimball, ed., *Churchill and Roosevelt: The Complete Correspondence*, vol. 3, *Alliance Declining, February 1944–April 1945* (Princeton, NJ: Princeton University Press, 1984), 602–5, and 612–13.
12. Rick Atkinson, *The Guns at Last Light: The War in Western Europe, 1944–1945* (New York: Henry Holt, 2013), 578.
13. Woolner, *The Last 100 Days*, 234.
14. Entry of March 28, 1945, Halifax Diary.
15. Grace Tully, *F.D.R., My Boss* (Chicago: People's Book Club, 1949), 357.
16. Lelyveld, *His Final Battle*, 310.
17. Jim Bishop, *FDR'S Last Year: April 1944–April 1945* (New York: William Morrow, 1974), 750.
18. Elizabeth Shoumatoff, *FDR's Unfinished Portrait: A Memoir* (Pittsburgh: University of Pittsburgh Press, 1990), 98.
19. Ibid.

91. THE END

1. Entry of March 29, 1945, Ward, *Closest Companion*, 401.
2. Bishop, *FDR's Last Year*, 711.
3. Ibid., 723.
4. Personal and Secret from Marshal J. V. Stalin to President F. D. Roosevelt, April 3, 1945, Cable 300, *My Dear Mr. Stalin*, ed. Susan Butler (New Haven, CT: Yale University Press, 2005), 312–13.
5. Entry of April 4, 1945, Leahy Diary, William D. Leahy Papers, Library of Congress, Washington, DC.
6. Ibid.
7. Ibid., Personal from the President for Marshal Stalin, April 4, 1945, Cable 301, 314–15.
8. Ibid., Personal and Secret from Marshal J. V. Stalin to President F. D. Roosevelt, April 7, 1945, Cable 302, 315.
9. Ibid., 445.
10. Entry of April 6, 1945, Leahy Diary.
11. Personal from the President for the Prime Minister, March 11, 1945, Cable R-714, in Kimball, *Churchill and Roosevelt*, vol. 3, 562.
12. Prime Minister to President Roosevelt, April 5, 1945, Cable C-933, in Kimball, *Churchill and Roosevelt*, vol. 3, 612.
13. Woolner, *The Last 100 Days*, 260.
14. Entry of April 5, 1945, Ward, *Closest Companion*, 410.
15. Ibid., entry of April 6, 1945, 411–12.
16. Ibid.

17. Ibid., entry of April 8, 1945, 412.
18. Ibid., entry of April 9, 1945, 413.
19. Bishop, *FDR's Last Year*, 749.
20. Entry of April 9, 1945, Ward, *Closest Companion*, 413.
21. Shoumatoff, *FDR's Unfinished Portrait*, 101.
22. Ibid.
23. Entry of April 9, 1945, Ward, *Closest Companion*, 413.
24. Ibid., entry of April 11, 1945, 415–16.
25. Ibid., 416.
26. Entries of April 10 and 11, 1945, Leahy Diary.
27. Ibid.
28. Entry of April 11, 1945, in Henry Morgenthau Diary, Morgenthau Papers, FDR Presidential Library, Hyde Park, NY.
29. Entry of April 12, 1945, Ward, *Closest Companion*, 417.
30. Shoumatoff, *FDR's Unfinished Portrait*, 116.
31. Ibid., 117.
32. Entry of April 12, 1945, Ward, *Closest Companion*, 418.
33. Shoumatoff, *FDR's Unfinished Portrait*, 118.
34. Entry of March 31, 1945, Ward, *Closest Companion*, 418.

Index